GW00363737

THE STORY OF THE
HAURAKI
GULF

THE STORY OF THE
HAURAKI GULF

Discovery | Transformation | Restoration

Raewyn Peart

Bateman

 EDS
ENVIRONMENTAL DEFENCE SOCIETY

To the Hauraki Gulf:
A place that has greatly enriched my life

Text © Raewyn Peart and Environmental Defence Society, 2016
Typographical design © David Bateman Ltd, 2016

Published in 2016 by David Bateman Ltd
30 Tarndale Grove, Albany, Auckland, New Zealand
www.batemanpublishing.co.nz

Reprinted 2016, 2017

ISBN 978-1-86953-940-5

This book is copyright. Except for the purpose of fair review, no part may be stored or transmitted in any form or by any means, electronic or mechanical, including recording or storage in any information retrieval systems, without permission in writing from the publisher. No reproduction may be made, whether by photocopying or by any other means, unless a licence has been obtained from the publisher or its agent.

No responsibility for loss caused to any individual or organisation acting on or refraining from action as a result of the material in this publication can be accepted by David Bateman Ltd or the author.

Front cover images: (top) Wharf at Tiritiri Matangi Island; (bottom left) Bean Rock Lighthouse; (bottom right) Classic yachts *Ngatira* (B2) and *Waitangi* (A6) sailing in the Waitematā Harbour.
Spine: Great Mercury Island.
Back cover: Channel Island Colville Channel.
Page 1: Mansion House Bay, Kawau Island
Pages 2–3: Hobbs Beach, Tiritiri Matangi Island
Photographs: all Raewyn Peart unless credited otherwise
Book design: Nick Turzynski, redinc Book Design
Printed in China through Colorcraft Ltd, Hong Kong

Acknowledgements

I would like firstly to thank the Auckland Council, Hauraki Gulf Forum, Tindall Foundation, Ports of Auckland Limited, Watercare Services Limited and Foundation North, which provided the financial support and assistance in kind that made this book possible.

I would also like to thank the many people who agreed to be interviewed for and/or provided assistance in compiling the material in the book. They include Don Armitage, Doug Armstrong, Russell Ashworth, Bill Ballantine, Laurie Beamish, Charlie Blackwell, Barrie Brown, Bill Burrill, Dave Clark, Adam Clow, Phil Clow, Tipa Compain, Isobel Conning, Rochelle Constantine, Bill Cook, Joe Davis, Jim Dollimore, Leith Duncan, Tony Enderby, Michael Fay, Rob Fenwick, Christine Fletcher, Louise Furey, Ross Garrett, Chris Gaskin, John Gaukrodger, Kaaren Goodall, Bruce and Marion Goodfellow, Roger Grace, David Gray, Alison Henry, Daniel Hicks, Tim Higham, Arthur Hinds, Mook Hohneck, Marjorie Holmes, George Hudson, Richelle Kahui-McConnell, Dave Kellian, Harold Kidd, John Laurence, Mike Lee, Tony and Carol Litherland, Callum McCallum, John McCallum, Dave McIntosh, Bruce Marler, Ronnie Martin, Paul Monin, Toby Morcom, David Moore, Dave Moran, Margaret Morley, Mark Morrison, Sue Neureuter, Wayne Parkes, Darren Parsons, Lindsay Peart, Ed Pridham, Doug Pulford, Brenda Sewell, Darren Shields, Richard Simpson, Elaine Stark, John Street, Merv Strongman, Tamaiti Tamaariki, Moana Tamaariki-Pohe, Chad Thompson, Simon Thrush, Barry Torkington, Gray Townshend, Peter Vitasovich, Ray Walters, Bob Whitmore, Keith Woodley and John Zeldis.

I would like to acknowledge those who supported the book by providing images at no or very reduced cost. These include Archives New Zealand, Doug Armstrong, Auckland Art Gallery, Alan Ashworth, Auckland Council Library, Auckland War Memorial Museum, Auckland Whale and Dolphin Safari, Stephanie Behrens, Abe Borker, VC Browne & Son, Bill Burrill, Dave Clark, Clough and Associates Limited, Phil Clow, Tipa Compain, Isobel Conning, Rochelle Constantine, David Rumsey Map Collection, Department of Conservation, Devonport Historical and Museum Society, Jim Dollimore, Nick Eagles, Tony Enderby, Neil Fitzgerald, Christine Fletcher, Bruce Foster, Fullers Group, Louise Furey, Ross Garrett, Chris Gaskin, GNS Science, Tim Higham, Marjorie Holmes, Richelle Kahui-McConnell, Julie Kidd, John Laurence, Mike Lee, Shaun Lee, Tony and Carol Litherland, Mercury Bay Museum, Marler family, Janice Molloy, John Montgomery, Dave Moran, Toby Morcom, Margaret Morley, Mark Morrison, New Zealand Electronic Text Collection, New Zealand Hartley Association, New Zealand Maritime Museum, New Zealand Royal Society, New Zealand Underwater Association, Darren Parsons, Larry Paul, Tanya Peart, Dianne Peart, Ports of Auckland, Craig Potton, Revive Our Gulf, Rotoroa Island Trust, Salvation Army Heritage Centre and Archives, Darren Shields, Richard Simpson, Glen and Merv Strongman, Richard Taylor, Simon Thrush, Tino Rawa Trust, United Kingdom Hydrographic Office, Jane Ussher, Warkworth District Museum, Watercare Services, Bob Whitmore, Keith Woodley and John Zeldis. Images were also provided by David Wall, the Alexander Turnbull Library and the Hocken Library, University of Otago. Peter Bawden kindly took me out in his boat to take various images of the Hauraki Gulf islands. Unfortunately, due to space constraints, not all stories or images provided were able to be used.

There are many others who supported the project. At the EDS, I would like to warmly thank my colleague Gary Taylor who was pivotal in helping to raise the funds to commence the project, and providing me the time to complete it. Gary has been a strong support for my many ambitious projects over the years. Fiona Driver was a great help in providing sailing contacts and images, and in helping with administration.

My family has also been a great support. My mother Margaret Peart edited and proof read several versions of the text, helping to improve the flow and correct my grammar. My husband Charles Crothers read the entire manuscript and made many helpful comments. My daughter Tanya helped to keep my spirits up with her infectious humour through the long grind of writing and rewriting the text. My father Lindsay Peart engendered in me a strong passion for the Hauraki Gulf through our many adventurous family cruises and provided the inspiration for the book. He maintained a close interest in progress throughout the project.

Finally I would like to thank Tracey Borgfeldt and Caroline List at David Bateman Limited for taking on the project and turning the manuscript into a beautiful book.

All errors and omissions remain the responsibility of the author. I have endeavoured to check the accuracy of the content and to obtain permissions to reproduce all the images used, but please advise of any issues, and we will endeavor to remedy these in any subsequent editions.

Contents

Preface   8
Introduction   10
Maps: Hauraki Gulf Marine Park   14

PART ONE: EARLY SETTLEMENT   16

1   Discovery and first settlement   18
2   Abundance of kaimoana   34
3   Rediscovery and exploration   46

PART TWO: DEVELOPING THE SHORES   64

4   Establishment of Auckland   66
5   Growing metropolis   80
6   Transforming the land   100

PART THREE: BLUE PATHWAYS   118

7   Connecting the gulf   120
8   Racing the gulf   144

Port Jackson, Coromandel Peninsula.

PART FOUR: ENJOYING THE GULF 160

9 Enjoying the islands 162
10 Enjoying the sea 188

PART FIVE: COMMERCIAL HARVEST 212

11 Early commercial fishing 214
12 From plunder to precision 236

PART SIX: UNDERSTANDING THE GULF 258

13 The gulf's treasures 260
14 Scientific understanding 282

PART SEVEN: NEW BEGINNINGS 302

15 Restoring the land 304
16 Restoring the sea 326

Epilogue 346
Notes 347
References 354
Index 360

Preface

It's hard to imagine an Auckland without a gulf, a Hauraki without Tīkapa Moana, a Pākiri without Te Moananui ā Toi. The waters that surround us provide identity. The ebb and flow of the tides give meaning and rhythm to our lives.

I grew up on the shores of the gulf, mucking around in boats, taking home feeds of fish to the family bach at Scandrett Beach. In the '60s there were islands a short sail away; some farmed, with sparse native vegetation and with a menagerie of introduced animals. It's easy to take these surroundings for granted. They seem immutable.

In 2000 I was appointed to the Hauraki Gulf Forum to promote the newly minted Hauraki Gulf Marine Park Act. Since 2007 I have chaired its deliberations. What I've learned is that we take the gulf for granted at our peril, that change for the worse, and for the better, is just a turn of the political dial away. The snapper and kahawai that once seemed plentiful were much harder to catch by the '80s, reduced in fisheries-management-speak to 10 per cent of their unfished biomass. Estuaries and reefs that play vital parts in their life histories had become muddier and more barren.

We adjust — as do the populations of animals that rely on these places — in a process known as 'shifting baselines'. We come to accept as normal a new, diminished environmental state. But other actions can release ecological potential. The first island eradication of rats happened in the '60s, on Maria Island in the Noises group, and in the '80s a 'spade brigade' brought forests back to Tiritiri Matangi — encouraged by the Hauraki Gulf Maritime Park Board of the day. One of the world's first no-take marine reserves was created at Leigh in 1975. These have gone on to create global success stories.

Charting these broad changes in ecological fortune and understanding the consequences of them for society is an essential part of the work of the Hauraki Gulf Forum. Every three years we are required to publish a state-of-the-environment report which serves as a measure of our collective ability to do the right things by and for the gulf.

In 2011 we drew attention to the incredible transformation wrought on the gulf in just two human life spans, and to the majority of environmental indicators that either showed negative trends or were stuck at levels which equate to poor environmental condition. We warned that further loss was inevitable unless bold, sustained and innovative steps were taken. Since then we have looked for ways to turn the tide.

We celebrated with the Department of Conservation the success of its operation to remove ten introduced pests from Rangitoto and Motutapu, paving the way for an ambitious programme of restoration and species introductions. These and other motu of the gulf have since been returned to mana whenua as part of historic Treaty of Waitangi settlements, their future now enshrined in co-governance arrangements.

On one, Te Hauturu-o-Toi/Little Barrier Island, the New Zealand storm petrel, which just ten years ago was considered to have been extinct for over a century, was found breeding deep in its forested valleys. I like to think its back is covered now by two complementary traditions: the kaitiakitanga of Māori and the nature preservation ethics of Western culture.

The 2011 *State of our Gulf* report also drew attention to the potential loss of two of the gulf's most iconic species. Resident Bryde's whales, which number a couple of hundred at most, were being struck and killed by large vessels at an average rate of two per year.

Majestic black petrels, which breed only on the gulf's Barrier islands, were identified as New Zealand's most vulnerable seabird to commercial fisheries, potentially being caught on long-line hooks fourteen times faster than its population could sustain. We responded by initiating and supporting collaborative groups, to see if we could find urgent and innovative solutions to these issues. Today speeds of large vessels through the gulf have dropped markedly, encouraged by a transit protocol developed by Ports of Auckland and supported by all shipping industry groups.

All 50-odd snapper and bluenose long-lining boats operating around the gulf now employ seabird-smart fishing techniques, undergo crew training, regularly volunteer to assist researchers in petrel colonies and have successfully trialed monitoring cameras on their boats.

To celebrate such successes we initiated annual Holdaway Awards, named after conservation pioneer and former chair of the Hauraki Gulf Maritime Park Board Jim Holdaway, and have recognised emerging leaders working on behalf of seabirds, whales, shorebirds, islands, marine reserves and land owned by iwi and hapū.

In 2012 the gulf's first marine habitat restoration project was catalyzed by the Hauraki Gulf Marine Park seminar we host annually with Auckland Museum. It was themed *Charting the Enhancement Pathway.*

Borrowing from the successes of the gulf's many island community trusts, the *Revive our Gulf* project has since 'planted' 3.5 million green-lipped mussels to recreate and research sub-tidal mussel reefs. Until the first half of last century the reefs carpeted extensive parts of the Firth of Thames and Tāmaki Strait, naturally filtering water and providing habitat for ten times the number of fish and other species than the muds that replaced them after extensive dredging. An important, in fact vital, dimension of the project is the contribution of business to the task. Mussel growers have donated the seed stock for the enterprise and its previous waste stream of undersize and reject mussels is tagged to fuel the project's expansion. A restoration purpose could be built into the mussel industry's business model.

The gulf's inshore areas are shared fisheries where significant economic and social value is derived from cultural, recreational and nature-based tourism use. This has been recognised in the Government's proposals on marine protected areas and recreational fishing parks. Shifting ecological baselines to support an abundance-driven economy is an exciting opportunity that will demand more of the successful collaborative approaches we are learning to practice in the gulf. Innovative farmers and forestry companies are moving in this same direction, to align land-use practice and products with changing public expectations for environmental quality and the Government's limit-setting agenda.

Education and engagement are essential if we are to bring the pieces of the management jigsaw together as intended by the Hauraki Gulf Marine Park Act. The Forum has invested heavily in this, showcasing leading thinking and practice in the annual seminars and reminding residents of the essential wonders of the gulf in a popular poster series in partnership with the *New Zealand Herald* over six years.

By 2013, influenced and encouraged by the Forum's recommendations, publications and events, management agencies and mana whenua committed to the first marine spatial planning exercise in New Zealand; one to be drafted by representatives of the stakeholders of the gulf, mandated through a series of selection meetings. A remarkable consensus emerged early in deliberations: a desire to protect and improve the abundance, the productivity and the mauri of the waters of the gulf. The spatial plan promises to resolve the conflicts between environmental and development concerns that often polarise and stall decision-making processes, making them costly and ineffective. It is based on the premise that good knowledge from science and mātauranga can be deployed to enable two complementary dynamics: economic activity in well-suited places and regenerative processes in ecologically significant parts of the gulf.

Raewyn's book is a timely contribution to this discussion because, to be successful, the context for the Sea Change Tai Timu Tai Pari spatial plan, due for completion this year, must be apparent to all. By providing an ecological and social history Raewyn unmasks the shifting baseline trajectory and the necessity of new awareness, commitments and investment that gears resource use to ecological health. Her story-telling ability illuminates the deep bonds that tie us to the gulf and drive our senses of place and well being. We are richer for her endeavour and for the collective efforts of gulf stewardship and kaitiakitanga that will be invoked with careful reading.

This is a timely book and one that I hope will build on the Forum's work and help set the stage for strong, shared governance of the remarkable Hauraki Gulf Marine Park.

Mayor John Tregidga, MNZM, JP; Chair Hauraki Gulf Forum, 2007-2016

Introduction

Like many of us, I grew up enjoying the wonders of the Hauraki Gulf. Although my family was based in land-locked Hamilton, some years before I was born my father and grandfather had bought a rough, sloping coastal section on the south-eastern fringe of Auckland. It had few services, but glorious views overlooking Tāmaki Strait and out towards Waiheke Island. During weekends and holidays, the two men gradually built the simple fibrolite-clad structure which was to become a cherished part of our family history.

Accommodation in the bach was spartan. We four kids were crammed into creaky bunks in one small bedroom while my parents tried to sleep on a saggy mattress next door. Rusty-coloured water trickled from the small corrugated iron tank which drained the roof. The sanitary arrangements consisted of a smelly long drop dug out the back, a place that filled me with dread after dark.

There were many magical moments. I can remember getting up at dawn and rowing out over the tranquil sea to catch fresh snapper for breakfast. I can remember feasting on the rich-red summer plums which dripped from trees sprouting through the cracked clay soil. And I can remember hours spent lazily on the beach, exposing salty skin to the warm summer sun, blissfully unaware of the dangers of skin cancer.

Then the arrival of boys prompted a change to our summer holiday plans. My three older sisters had reached their teenage years and were attracting what my father considered to be 'undesirable types'. Rather than spending the summer worrying that his daughters were being led astray, he decided to take up boating. A family holiday at sea had one key advantage in his view: if my sisters attracted undesirable attention, the anchor could simply be raised and the family relocated to a more isolated spot.

So began the glorious summers during the 1970s when our family cruised the Hauraki Gulf and beyond. We took to sea in a small, and then a slightly larger, plywood trimaran, both of which my father had rebuilt in the garage of our Hamilton home. The accommodation on these flimsy craft was never really adequate. Many nights were spent ashore,

cuddled up in sleeping bags next to the dying embers of our cooking fire.

A strong camaraderie built up between the crews of the relatively small number of boats which ventured out in those days. Many of these crews consisted of young men enjoying themselves in rudimentary mullet boats. New Year's Eve was the highlight. I remember big bonfires at Smokehouse Bay on Great Barrier Island, where all the yachties gathered to collectively see in the coming year. There were the parties in Mansion House Bay on Kawau Island, where the yachts rafted up together and the crews drank to excess in the bar behind the beach and then later on board.

We roamed the gulf's islands exploring rock pools, caves and abandoned huts. But there some were places where we couldn't go. By that time Pakatoa had been turned into a resort and it was festooned with private property signs. This felt like a gross infringement of what we saw as our unalienable right as New Zealanders to access the islands. Rotoroa was also off limits. We used to anchor in Home Bay and watch the former alcoholics go about their daily lives. I remember the clear water and seeing all the grog bottles littering the seabed. At the time I thought they had come from the recovering alcoholics having a drink on the sly, but I now realise that they would have been tossed overboard from the numerous boats that moored in the sheltered bay, because that's what we did with rubbish in those days: we simply tossed it overboard.

Many days were spent trying to sail to our destination in fickle winds, our only auxiliary being a small, unreliable Seagull outboard. As we lazily drifted around the gulf, we were not alone. There were dolphins, which to our delight would race towards our boat and joyfully play in the bow waves. There were sunfish, with their enormous fins and stubby tails, ignoring us as they slowly swam along. There were evil-looking sharks, with their triangular fins cutting through the water, and enormous flocks of seabirds.

It was not long before we acquired snorkelling gear and started exploring under the surface. The kelp-festooned reefs were full of life. I remember rows of crayfish, sitting in crevices hidden amongst the rocks, bristling with feelers. But I could never pluck up enough courage to grab one. There were young snapper with their iridescent blue spots. There were the large, dark-striped red moki hiding amongst the kelp. There were clouds of brightly coloured blue maomao. Schools of torpedo-shaped kahawai and mullet would scoot by. There were the extraordinary-looking leatherjackets, sitting almost motionless in the water, their fins quivering.

The leatherjacket is the only fish I ever successfully speared. My father had given me a small fibreglass Hawaiian sling for Christmas. I was determined to show my mettle as a hunter, but on the rare occasions that I managed to hit a fish, the barbs of the multi-pronged spear just bounced off. Not so for the leatherjacket that I lined up. It just sat there and looked at me as I closed in. Next thing it was stuck on the end of my spear, weakly flapping. I was immediately mortified. I had killed this beautiful fish that had seemingly trusted me. I never went spearfishing again.

Time moved on, my sisters and I left home, and the era of family sailing holidays came to an end. I eventually married Charles and we moved overseas.

It was our daughter Tanya who drew me back and reconnected me with the Hauraki Gulf. We were living in South Africa when she was born and I felt a strong sense that I wanted her to grow up experiencing the richness of the New Zealand coast, as I had. So in 2001 we returned to live in Auckland. By this time my father had acquired a much more substantial vessel, a 36-foot keeler. We joined him for a cruise each summer. But things had changed. The sea was now eerily quiet. On the long sail to Great Barrier Island, it was not unusual to see nothing above the surface: no seabirds, no dolphins, no sharks, no schooling fish, no marine life of any kind.

When I took Tanya snorkelling to experience the marvels of life under the water, the change was even more stark. In some places much of the kelp had disappeared and bare rocks were festooned with sea urchins. Even in places where the kelp was intact, there were almost no fish, just the occasional small spottie which darted away as soon as we approached. I was shocked.

Much of the professional work I have undertaken over the past decade has been in an endeavour to understand what had happened to the place I loved. I knew that species such as snapper had been fished down and therefore were understandably scarce. But many of the small reef fish, which were not explicitly targeted by fishers, had also disappeared. It seemed that something more fundamental must have gone wrong. In writing this book, I have sought to provide some answers.

The direct impetus for my endeavours came from the groundbreaking work undertaken by the Hauraki Gulf Forum, led by Executive Officer Tim Higham and Chair John Tregidga. Their production of the *State of our Gulf* report in 2011 shifted many people's thinking, including my own. By placing the current state of the gulf's natural environment within the context of what it was most probably like before human arrival, the enormity of the change became apparent. The gulf was once an extraordinarily productive place, abundant with marine life. It was full of enormous schools of fish, flocks of seabirds, and pods of dolphins and whales. Although still remarkable, it is now only a shadow of what it once was.

This book is not a natural history of the Hauraki Gulf; it is an environmental, social and cultural history of our association with this extraordinary place. It describes the impact that the Hauraki Gulf has had on us and the impact that we have had on it.

The culture and knowledge base of the numerous Māori groupings who lived around the Hauraki Gulf's shores developed as a result of their long association with the place. They learnt to treat the gulf with care and it sustained them for centuries. Europeans brought with them a very different world view, honed through their association with northern hemisphere environments. While Māori saw themselves as an integral part of their onshore and marine environments, Pākehā saw the gulf largely as a place from which to exploit resources: kauri, flax, minerals, sand and fish. It was also seen as a convenient place to dispose of unwanted things: sewage, household and industrial waste, vessels which had reached the end of their working lives and harbour dredgings. The abundance of the Hauraki Gulf was such that, initially, the resources seemed inexhaustible, but it turned out that they weren't. It took a long time for attitudes and management

approaches to adjust to this reality and we still have a way to go in this respect.

The shores of the Hauraki Gulf were the preferred place to settle in New Zealand for both Māori and Pākehā. When Hobson was searching for a site for the new capital of New Zealand in 1840, land adjacent to the Waitematā was in the end the obvious choice. It provided a sheltered harbour, fertile soils and excellent access, via a myriad of waterways, to other parts of the country. There was also a welcoming landowner, Ngāti Whātua Ōrākei, who invited Hobson to move to the area.

Until relatively recent times, the gulf was the highway, the primary way that people travelled from place to place. From the very first settlement, the islands of the gulf were stopping-off places for canoes (waka) travelling up and down the coast. When European vessels were adopted, the coast became festooned with cutters, schooners, mullet boats and scows. The Hauraki Gulf became the maritime hub of the country, the centre of the boatbuilding industry and the cradle of sailing innovation.

But the gulf wasn't only a place of work; it was a place to relax and to enjoy the natural world. Generations of people have visited the many wonderful islands, bays and waters of the Hauraki Gulf for picnicking, shell collecting, swimming, surfing, sailing, diving and fishing. It is often

The author's passion for the Hauraki Gulf stems back to early family sailing holidays in the area. Shown here, in 1971, is the Peart family off Maraetai Beach, readying their home-built 24-foot Piver trimaran for a summer cruise. The author, at twelve years of age, is standing on the cabin top preparing to attach the mainsail. (Dianne Wells)

such experiences of the gulf that people have had as young children that have engendered in them a strong connection with the place as adults.

The full impacts of all our various activities on the Hauraki Gulf have only come to light very recently as scientists have started to understand more completely the various pieces that make up the gulf as a functioning alive system. What this has shown is that there have been some fundamental changes and they are not positive.

There has been the gradual but insidious loss of species from our inshore areas: the myriad of interesting shells that used to be picked up off the beaches are no longer found; many of the rich cockle, pipi and scallop beds which were regularly harvested have now disappeared.

Perhaps one of the most notable absences is crayfish. Crayfish used to be so numerous around the fringes of the gulf's coast that they could be picked up out of the shallow seaweed by their feelers. Fishermen harvested them by the sackful, but could hardly find a market for them, as they were so abundant and easily caught. Now, it would be a very lucky diver who could find even one in the inner gulf.

There has been a noticeable reduction in the quantity of schooling fish and the occurrence of huge 'boil-ups' which were a feature of the gulf in the past. They were so impressive that they were specifically commented on by visitors, such as American author and game fisherman Zane Grey. Circumstantial evidence suggests that this diminution in aggregations of fish may be impacting on seabirds and also, potentially, on marine mammals, which are reliant on them as a food source. Some seabirds are now foraging much further afield and, consequently, their chick survival rate has reduced.

The rich habitats of seagrass beds, and green-lipped and horse mussels, that covered much of the sea floor of the gulf have largely gone. We now know that they played a critical role in providing food and refuge for juvenile fish, which are otherwise preyed on and thus fail to reach adulthood. They also supported diverse and highly productive marine communities. The ability of the Hauraki Gulf to support life and regenerate fish stocks has therefore been significantly impaired.

It is only in the past couple of years that perhaps an even greater threat to the life-supporting abilities of the Hauraki Gulf has come to light. Now, during autumn every year, at the head of the Firth of Thames where the water is deep enough to stratify over the calmer summer months, oxygen is being sucked out of the bottom waters due to heavy nutrient loads and an excess of algal growth.

So it looks like the Hauraki Gulf may be heading towards a tipping point and, if we don't take action soon, it may be too late.

But it's not all bad news. There have been some wonderful achievements in regenerating and restoring parts of the Hauraki Gulf. The most impressive progress has been made on the gulf islands. Armies of volunteers and workers, spurred on by visionary leaders and philanthropists, have transformed Tiritiri Matangi, Motutapu, Motuihe and Rotoroa islands from degraded, pest-ridden pasturelands to lush indigenous forest areas where endangered birds and other species are now flourishing, right on the doorstep of Auckland City. It is something that, even a decade or two ago, would have been thought impossible.

Unfortunately, progress in the marine space has been less transformational. Although the marine reserve near Leigh has been a stunning success and has inspired further marine protection projects in the gulf and elsewhere, efforts to set aside more of the marine area to allow its recovery have come to a halt. We now have six marine reserves in the Hauraki Gulf, which is a great start, but they cover less than 0.3 per cent of the total marine space. The last reserve to be established, at Te Matuku Bay, was created over a decade ago.

It is the leadership being increasingly shown by the original settlers of the Hauraki Gulf, the numerous tribes (iwi) and clan (hapū) groups that have dwelt on its shores, that may help illuminate the way forward. Their holistic view of the environment and strong relationship with it, and the obligations of stewardship and care (kaitiakitanga) that inextricably flow from that, provide an approach that seeks to sustain both the welfare of the people and the environment on which they depend. It is this interdependence that all of us need to better understand and recognise.

This book tells the story of the Hauraki Gulf through three layers. The first is the underlying narrative that is largely based on published sources. In writing this part of the book, I am heavily indebted to the many people who, through their detailed research and writings, have brought to light the Hauraki Gulf's fascinating history.

The second layer is told through people's reminiscences, based on their memories of the gulf over their lifetimes. These stories are designed to bring the narrative to life. For these, I interviewed over 60 people whose lives have intersected with the Hauraki Gulf in various ways. It has been a great privilege to hear their fascinating stories and learn of their experiences. I am indebted to them for their kindness and generosity in making the time available to meet with me.

The third layer of the story is told through images. There is a very rich visual history of the Hauraki Gulf encapsulated in the numerous historical photographs and drawings held by museums and libraries. I have complemented these with contemporary photographs. This book is strongly about place and the images serve to show that place, as it was in the past and as it is now.

I hope that the stories in this book will prompt readers to recall their own special stories of the Hauraki Gulf and of other treasured locations. Because it is only if we remember our stories, if we tell our stories and if we act on them that we can ensure that our special places will endure.

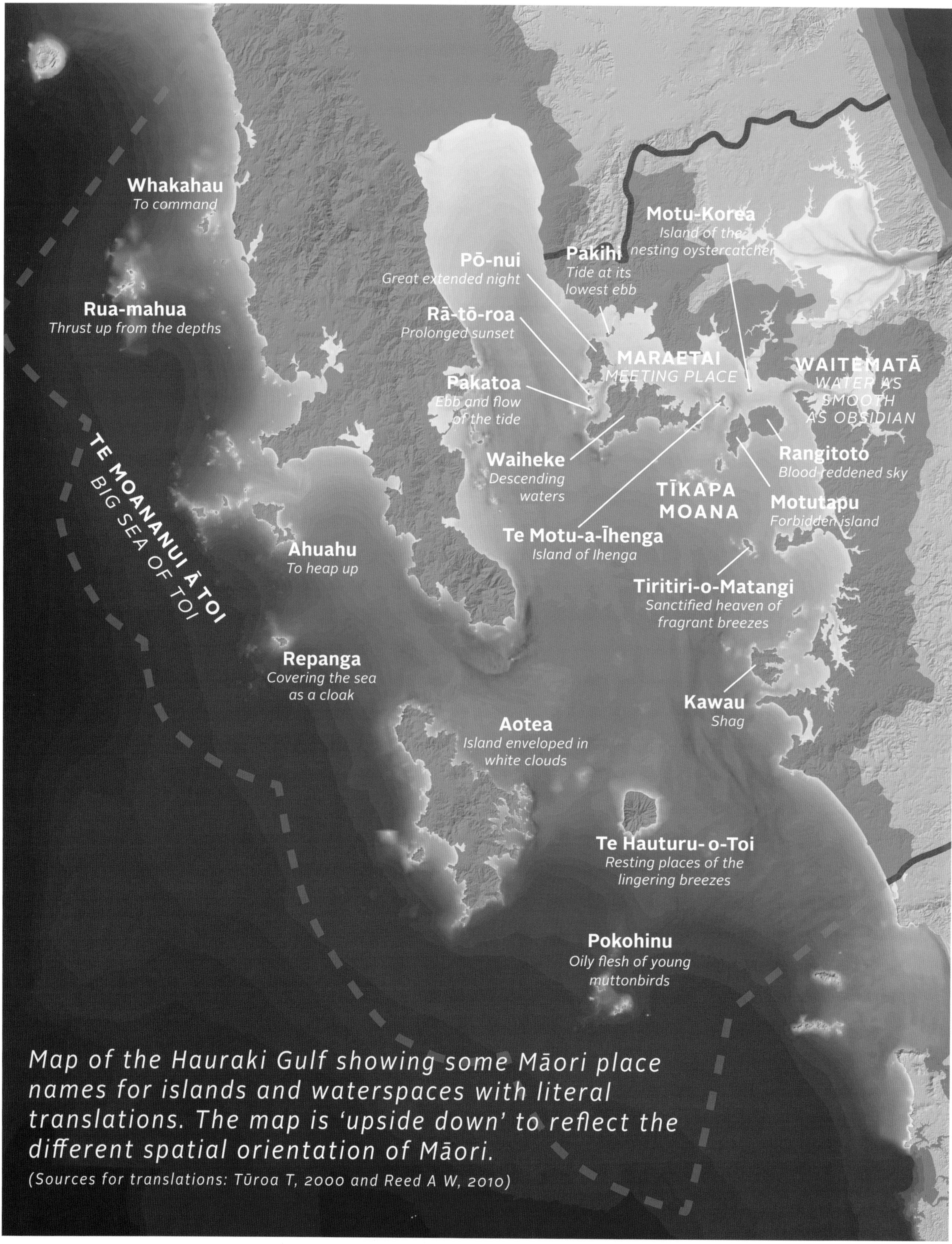

Whakahau
To command

Motu-Korea
Island of the nesting oystercatcher

Pō-nui
Great extended night

Pakihi
Tide at its lowest ebb

Rua-mahua
Thrust up from the depths

Rā-tō-roa
Prolonged sunset

MARAETAI
MEETING PLACE

WAITEMATĀ
WATER AS SMOOTH AS OBSIDIAN

Pakatoa
Ebb and flow of the tide

TE MOANANUI Ā TOI
BIG SEA OF TOI

Waiheke
Descending waters

Rangitoto
Blood reddened sky

TĪKAPA MOANA

Motutapu
Forbidden island

Te Motu-a-Īhenga
Island of Ihenga

Ahuahu
To heap up

Tiritiri-o-Matangi
Sanctified heaven of fragrant breezes

Repanga
Covering the sea as a cloak

Kawau
Shag

Aotea
Island enveloped in white clouds

Te Hauturu-o-Toi
Resting places of the lingering breezes

Pokohinu
Oily flesh of young muttonbirds

Map of the Hauraki Gulf showing some Māori place names for islands and waterspaces with literal translations. The map is 'upside down' to reflect the different spatial orientation of Māori.

(Sources for translations: Tūroa T, 2000 and Reed A W, 2010)

HAURAKI GULF MARINE PARK

PACIFIC OCEAN

0 10 20
km

N

Mokohinau

CRADOCK CHANNEL

Rakitu

JELLICOE CHANNEL

Little Barrier

Great Barrier

CAPE RODNEY–ŌKAKARI MARINE RESERVE

TĀWHARANUI MARINE RESERVE

Kawau

COLVILLE CHANNEL

Cuvier

Moturekareka

Motuora

Tiritiri Matangi

WHANGAPARĀOA PENINSULA

Great Mercury

Colville

Red Mercury

LONG BAY -OKURA MARINE RESERVE

The Noises

Rākino

Waiheke

Coromandel

Motutapu

Whitianga

Rangitoto

Pakatoa

Auckland

Motuihe

Rotoroa

TĀMAKI STRAIT

Pōnui

TE WHANGANUI-A-HEI MARINE RESERVE

POLLEN ISLAND MARINE RESERVE

TE MATUKU MARINE RESERVE

Aldermen

Tairua

FIRTH OF THAMES

COROMANDEL PENINSULA

Kaiaua

Slipper

AUCKLAND

Thames

Whangamatā

HAURAKI PLAINS

Mayor

WAIKATO

Nᵒ 2.
Rangitoto 9ᵇ

Part One:
EARLY SETTLEMENT

Chapter 1
**Discovery and
first settlement**

The first humans to encounter the Hauraki Gulf would have sailed into its waters long before the next wave of explorers, Europeans, arrived. They were from one of the greatest seafaring peoples of all time. Long before the European Age of Discovery, these ancient explorers were navigating the largest ocean on earth, the mighty Pacific, with confidence.

Discovery

Originating in island south-east Asia around 3500 years ago, these seaborne explorers began settling the small island groups scattered across the face of the Pacific, from west to east.[1] At first the sailing technology required was fairly rudimentary, with short island hops taking the new settlers through the Solomon Island group, down to Vanuatu and then on to New Caledonia. But land in the eastern Pacific was much more sparse and the distances between islands were much greater. Traversing wide expanses of ocean required larger, more seaworthy craft and sophisticated navigational techniques.

Large ocean-going double-hulled waka were probably first developed in Fiji and neighbouring islands. They were powered by Oceanic spritsails which, unlike the modern Bermuda rig, had the apex of the sail near the deck. One long side of the sail was attached to a fixed mast, with the other side attached to a moving spar controlled by a rope, more akin to a boom.[2]

But it was not Fiji that became the centre of the most adventurous voyaging that the world had ever seen; it was a small grouping of islands in east Polynesia: the Society Islands and Cook Islands, which were settled after AD 1000. Seafarers from this smattering of islands made it, via the Marquesas, to Hawai'i, a distance of over 1400 nautical miles.

Pages 16–17: Fishing camp on Rangitoto Island, c. 1850s. (Charles Heaphy, Ref: C-025002, Alexander Turnbull Library, Wellington, New Zealand)
Opposite: Harataonga Beach, Great Barrier Island.

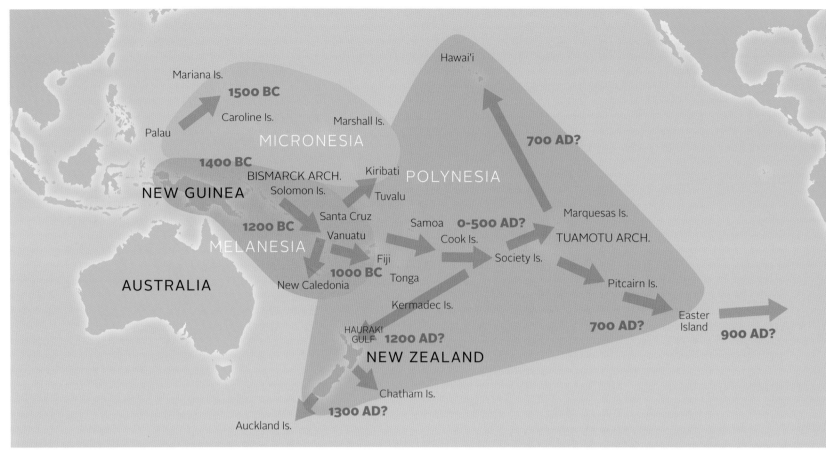

Mariana Is.
1500 BC
Caroline Is.   Marshall Is.
Palau   Hawai'i
          MICRONESIA
1400 BC
          Kiribati   POLYNESIA
BISMARCK ARCH.
NEW GUINEA   **700 AD?**
Solomon Is.   Tuvalu
Santa Cruz
1200 BC   Samoa   **0-500 AD?**   Marquesas Is.
Vanuatu   Cook Is.   TUAMOTU ARCH.
MELANESIA
                    Fiji   Society Is.
AUSTRALIA   New Caledonia   Tonga   Pitcairn Is.
          Kermadec Is.
                                        700 AD?   Easter   **900 AD?**
HAURAKI   Island
GULF   **1200 AD?**
          NEW ZEALAND
                    Chatham Is.
          1300 AD?
Auckland Is.

Even more astonishing, these audacious sailors pushed further east, to Pitcairn and Easter islands, and then eventually right across the Pacific Ocean to Chile. They brought back with them the bottle gourd (hue), as well as a sweet potato (kūmara), a valuable food crop which had been domesticated in South America some 7000 years earlier.[3]

Why these intrepid explorers eventually decided to sail south is less clear. Their exploration and settlement had, up until then, been largely confined to the tropical Pacific, an area characterised by warm temperatures and gentle trade winds. Going south was more risky, with the weather being much colder and stormier. But as the available tropical islands became settled and populations on the small islands grew, land ownership and control became stratified. To have opportunity, younger siblings needed to look elsewhere.[4] Inspiration to head into unknown waters may have come from watching the long-tailed cuckoo (koekoeā), flying south each spring. It was a land-based bird, so there must be land to the south they may have reasoned.[5]

So south they eventually went, following the path of the koekoeā. The explorers probably left at about the same time as the birds, in late spring or early summer, heading west with the trade winds behind them, and then south through the variable and often stormy transition zone, before picking up an easterly on top of a high-pressure system, or a northerly on its western side, to finally reach New Zealand's shores.

Their double-hulled waka were probably between 50 and 70 feet long, twin-masted and capable of averaging something like 8 knots. They were carefully constructed vessels: long planks of wood were lashed together with coconut-fibre rope to form two V-shaped hulls, and these were attached to a set of ribs and a shallow keel. The seams were caulked with fine coconut fibre and then breadfruit sap applied to waterproof them. The hulls were joined with a series of crossbeams, and on these a large platform was constructed to carry shelter, people and stores.[6]

Opposite top: Polynesians, who first discovered and settled the Hauraki Gulf, were the greatest seafarers of all time. By the time they sailed south to New Zealand, probably during the mid-thirteenth century, they had explored the vast Pacific Ocean all the way to Chile.

Opposite: Polynesians developed ocean-going double-hulled canoes (waka) that were capable of sailing large distances across the Pacific and south through colder and stormier seas to the Hauraki Gulf in Aotearoa.

Navigation was by dead reckoning, using the angle of stars at night and the direction of ocean swells during the day to steer by. The navigator, a very highly trained and skilled professional, maintained a mental running fix of the vessel's position, taking into account the course steered, speed travelled, time elapsed and likely impact of ocean currents.[7]

The voyage to New Zealand probably took between two and five weeks, depending on the wind. The explorers would have detected the presence of land well before they sighted it. First, there may have been an obvious calming of the seas, as the waka travelled sufficiently south, to obtain shelter from North Cape. Then there would have been billowing white clouds piling over distant mountains, a distinct change in ocean swells as they reflected off the land, clumps of seaweed floating in the water and seabirds, huge noisy clouds of them, returning to land each night.[8]

For explorers headed towards the Hauraki Gulf, the first glimpse of land may have been the white rhyolite cliffs of Great Mercury Island (Ahuahu) or the rugged silhouette of Great Barrier Island (Aotea) — Aotea translates as 'the island enveloped in white clouds'.[9] The craggy, bush-covered volcanic peaks of Mount Hobson (Hirakimata) would have been visible for more than 40 miles out to sea, if the day was clear. As they sailed closer, the mighty peak of Moehau, perched on the end of the Coromandel Peninsula, would have come into view, serving to impress on the intrepid voyagers the great size and richness of this new place.

These first people to encounter the Hauraki Gulf may have been the very first humans to reach New Zealand, but of this we can never be sure. The initial landing was almost certainly on the north-east coast of the North Island, that part of the country closest to eastern Polynesia.

The vessel which made that landing may have been captained by the great legendary explorer Kupe. Hauraki tradition tells of Kupe making landfall at Whitianga on the eastern shores of the Coromandel Peninsula, recorded in the full name Te Whitianga-o-Kupe which means 'the arrival place of Kupe after having crossed over from Hawaiki'.[10]

On approaching the coastal edge, these first gulf explorers would most likely have seen, in the clear shallows, numerous snapper (tāmure), large shoals of yellow-eyed mullet (aua), extensive tracts of thin green-bladed seagrass and enormous shellfish beds. On shore would have been luxuriant forest spilling down to the coast, clear-running streams, oyster-encrusted rocks and beaches piled high with white sand. Pōhutukawa fringing the coastal edge were likely to be in bloom, sporting a profusion of spiky crimson flowers, dripping with nectar. In a place which had never seen humans before, there would have been a multitude of land and seabirds.

For the small group of people who had managed to survive a long, perilous ocean crossing, the Hauraki Gulf might have seemed like heaven on earth.

As they explored further into the gulf, the first arrivals may have been astonished by the sheer quantity of marine life present in its sheltered waters. If they arrived in spring, they would have seen the gulf at its most productive time. During the previous winter, strong westerly winds would have blown seawater away from the coast, causing an upwelling of deep nitrogen-rich water into the embayment. In the spring, the increased intensity of sunlight radiating into the enriched seawater would have generated massive blooms of phytoplankton, the microscopic organisms that underpin the gulf's food chain and support its prolific marine life.[11]

On their travels around the gulf, the explorers would almost certainly have encountered an enormous melee of fish, seabirds, dolphins and whales. These massive boil-ups would have developed when large schools of pilchard (mohimohi) and anchovy (kokowhāwhā) congregated to feed on the rich spring plankton. The numerous small fish would have attracted larger carnivores, such as kahawai and kingfish (warehenga), as well as sharks. Pods of common dolphins (aihe) would have been working in concert to herd the fish into a tight ball and drive them to the surface. Here they would have attracted the attention of the Australasian gannets which would then repeatedly dive bomb the fish ball to catch a meal. Bryde's whales would also likely have been in attendance, scooping up large quantities of the schooling fish in their massive mouths and straining them out from the seawater through their large baleen plates.

After exploring his new discovery, Kupe almost certainly sailed back home to report the news of the bountiful southern land. Some of his crew may have stayed behind as the first settlers. One of the few eastern Polynesia artefacts found in New Zealand, which has been dated to be from earliest settlement times, is a small Marquesan pearl-fishing lure found at Tairua, on the eastern shores of the Coromandel Peninsula. If it wasn't the first, the east coast of the Coromandel Peninsula was probably one of the earliest places in the country to be settled.

Kupe would have brought back to East Polynesia exciting and intriguing stories of a very large, highly productive and uninhabited land to the south — a very

attractive-sounding place to people living on small resource-limited islands. He provided navigational directions for future voyagers wanting to find this new land: 'Keep the sun, moon or Venus just to the right of the bow of the vessel and steer nearly south-west.'[12]

Exploration

The first explorer to follow Kupe's directions may have been Toi-te-huatahi (Toi the only child). Legend tells of Toi first heading out to sea in search of his grandson, who had failed to return after a waka race. Unable to find the lost sailor, Toi decided to sail south following Kupe's route. He made landfall in the Hauraki Gulf and initially decided to stay. He lived for a time on Great Barrier Island and Little Barrier Island (Te Hauturu-o-Toi) before moving on to Whakatāne where he finally settled.[13]

Toi is remembered in one of the traditional names for the Hauraki Gulf islands which is Ngā Pōito-o-Te Kupenga-o-Toi-te-huatahi or 'the floats of the fishing net of Toi-te-huatahi'. One of the names for the waters south of Rangitoto Island is Whanganui-o-Toi or 'the great harbour of Toi'.[14] The sea of the large bight between the Coromandel

In their travels around the gulf, the first explorers would almost certainly have encountered massive 'boil-ups' of fish, seabirds, dolphins and the Bryde's whale, shown here. (Auckland Whale and Dolphin Safari)

Peninsula and East Cape, encompassing the Bay of Plenty, is known by some iwi as Te-Moana-Nui-o-Toi-te-huatahi or 'the big sea of Toi'.[15]

These early Hauraki Gulf explorers were eventually followed by others, including those on *Te Arawa* and *Tainui* waka. These two notable vessels may have arrived in the gulf at about the same time. It has even been suggested that they were two halves of a double canoe that sailed as a united vessel to New Zealand and then separated into two single-hulled waka after arrival.[16]

Te Arawa, commanded by Tama-te-kapua and navigated by Ngātoro-i-rangi, is said to have made landfall at Whangaparāoa on Cape Runaway, near the northern tip of East Cape. The vessel subsequently sailed north to the Hauraki Gulf, and stopped on the north-east coast of the Coromandel Peninsula just north of Port Charles, at Sandy Bay (Ō-kahu-tai). Tama-te-kapua named the highest peak of the Coromandel Peninsula Te Moengahau-o-Tamatekapua or 'the windy sleeping place of Tama-te-kapua'. The shortened form, Mount Moehau, is used today. Tama-te-kapua was so impressed by this peak that when he neared the end of his life he travelled back to the mountain to be buried on its summit.[17]

The crew of *Te Arawa* went on to explore and name many other places in the gulf. In order for a claim to be staked over the new lands, the waka may have stopped at a small island off the northern point of Waiheke Island, Gannet Rock (Tīkapa), to perform the ceremony of uruuru-whenua. This ancient rite includes reciting prayers (karakia) and placing sacred objects (mauri) on the rocks which then became sacred or forbidden (tapu). Many years later, a Tainui descendant called Marutūahu placed mauri on Tīkapa to claim possession of land won by conquest. Marutūahu is the ancestor of Ngāti Roungoū, Ngāti Tamaterā, Ngāti Whanaunga, Ngāti Maru and Ngāti Paoa. Today, Hauraki iwi still refer to the Hauraki Gulf as Tīkapa Moana.

Before heading south again to reach its final resting place at Maketū, in the Bay of Plenty, *Te Arawa* stopped at the tip of the Coromandel Peninsula. The commander's son, Tūhoromatakakā, and a chief, Hei, disembarked with a group of followers and settled in

Top: On its departure from the Hauraki Gulf, *Te Arawa* visited Cuvier Island (Repanga) and released two birds to act as kaitiaki (guardians) for future voyagers. (Lloyd Homer GNS Science)

Left: Tama-te-kapua, the commander of *Te Arawa*, is depicted here in a carving inside the Tamatekapua meeting house at Ōhinemutu, Rotorua. (Burton Bros. Ref: PA7-05-36, Alexander Turnbull Library, Wellington, New Zealand)

the region. Their descendants formed the Ngāti Huarere and Ngāti Hei peoples.[18] The commander's other son, Kahumatamoemoe, later returned to live on Waiheke Island and also at Ōrākei in Auckland.[19]

As the remaining crew were leaving the gulf, *Te Arawa* visited Cuvier Island (Repanga) where two birds were released. The birds were thought to be guardians that would help future voyagers by forecasting and subduing stormy weather. Still today, cloud patterns around the island serve to herald the forthcoming arrival of an easterly storm.[20]

The *Tainui* waka, which arrived at a similar time, was commanded by Hoturoa and navigated by Riu-ki-uta. Tradition suggests that the original navigator was Ngatoro-i-rangi, but that he and his wife were kidnapped by Te Arawa crew during a stopover at Rarotonga and sailed on that waka instead. Many of the stories of *Te Arawa* are shared with *Tainui*.

Tradition tells of *Tainui* being accompanied on her voyage by a water spirit (taniwha) called Paneiraira, who appeared in the form of a sperm whale. Paneiraira kept the waka safe during its voyage, smoothing the waters in front of the vessel and helping it to avoid sea monsters. When *Tainui* approached the Hauraki Gulf, the water became too shallow for the whale, so Paneiraira called on the assistance of a taniwha called Ureia. Ureia assumed the shape of a dolphin and escorted the *Tainui* safely into the gulf.

It was not all plain sailing, however. It is said that the *Tainui* became marooned on one of the sandbanks at the mouth of the Piako River. While the crew attempted to refloat the vessel, one of its paddles became stuck in the mud. Later the paddle floated free and was carried upstream by the tide. It eventually came to rest close to Tahuna, with the mountain to the west being named Te Hoe-o-Tainui meaning 'the paddle of the *Tainui* canoe'.[21]

After the crew had extensively explored the gulf and named many places, the *Tainui* was transported over the Ōtāhuhu portage to the Manukau Harbour and finally came to rest at Kawhia.

Accurately dating material from early archaeological sites is enormously difficult. Radiocarbon dating has proved problematic and archaeologists have looked to geological events to provide more reliable markers of time. The large Kaharoa volcanic eruption in the vicinity of Mount Tarawera, which has been dated at around 1314,[22] provides a useful marker, as it spread ash right over the Coromandel Peninsula and Great Barrier Island. A core sample from the Te Rerenga swamp in Whangapoua Harbour on Great Barrier Island has revealed the presence of rat-gnawed berries immediately below the volcanic tephra, indicating the presence of people just prior to the eruption.[23]

There is also evidence that a site near Ōpito Bay on the Coromandel Peninsula, known as Cross Creek, was first occupied close to the time of the Kaharoa eruption. Those present at that time were probably members of a small hunting and fishing party.[24]

Excavations under way at Cross Creek, Coromandel Peninsula during the early 1980s. (Brenda Sewell)

Settlement

What kind of people first settled the gulf? They were agriculturalists, fishermen, shellfish gatherers and bird hunters. They came from small tropical islands where life was lived very close to nature, particularly close to the sea. They brought with them a spiritual understanding of the natural world founded on a pantheon of gods: for example, Tane brought forth life, Tangaroa oversaw the sea, Rongo was in charge of cultivated foods and Tū was the god of war.[25]

The early settlers did not come alone. They brought with them a wealth of tropical plant species: kūmara, taro, yam (uwhi) and Pacific cabbage tree (tī pore) for food; the bottle gourd (hue) to provide containers for food and water; and the paper mulberry (aute) as a source of fibre to make tapa cloth. They also brought domesticated dogs for companionship and food and a small Pacific rat (kiore), which may have been carried for food or may have stowed away.

The new land was very different from the old. The climate was much colder and more stormy and tropical crops did not grow well, if at all. The indigenous species of fish, shellfish, birds and plants were not the same and the settlers had to learn about these new resources. Establishing a new life in this foreign place would not have been easy.

But the Hauraki Gulf provided a better place to settle in New Zealand than most. There were extensive forests, seas abounding with food and rich volcanic soils. These, coupled with a mild climate, enabled the population to thrive. The name Hauraki literally translates to mean 'the arid north wind'[26] and indicates the warm northerly winds that can blow on the back of slow-moving high-pressure systems during summer.

There is still considerable debate about when exactly the first peoples settled in the Hauraki Gulf, but archaeological information suggests that it was sometime around 700 to 800 years ago. The earliest settlements may have been on the eastern shores of the Coromandel Peninsula and on

Story of the Gulf | **Dr Louise Furey**

ARCHAEOLOGIST, AUCKLAND[27]

Louise comes from a family of Coromandel and Waihi gold miners and she has spent much of her life immersed in the Hauraki Gulf's past.

'Being an archaeologist is like being a detective. You scrape away layers of soil, uncover things and then try to reconstruct what people did there, such as how they made things, how they arranged settlements and from where they obtained stone. You build up a picture of the past, trying to make a credible story from the evidence placed in front of you.'

Louise started her research career in the early 1980s, working on the Coromandel Peninsula. She has a long-standing association with archaeological investigations on Great Mercury Island which began in 1982 and continue today. She has also analysed the 3000 or so artefacts extracted from the Oruarangi site located on the Waihou River in the Hauraki Plains.

'What many people don't realise is that middens are repositories of a wealth of information. They can tell you not only the species of shellfish that people were eating at any given time, but also about what the environment was like then and how it has changed. For example, the early sites have provided valuable information about the distribution of moa. One or two sites on the Coromandel Peninsula have kākāpō, a bird that is now solely confined to Fiordland. So we know that the bird was much more widely distributed in the past. Middens are not just piles of shells, they are records of people living in these places and carrying out their daily activities.

'The sad thing is that we are losing many of these sites to coastal erosion. For example, at Sarah's Gully near Ōpito Bay on the Coromandel Peninsula, a big storm hit two years ago and washed away a lot of material. If we don't protect these areas, in 20 or 30 years many of our important sites will be gone, and there is so much more we could learn from them.'

Dr Louise Furey (left) working at an archaeological site on Great Mercury Island. (Tim Mackrell, University of Auckland)

Great Mercury and Great Barrier islands. These areas were particularly rich in the natural resources that would help support humans seeking to establish a new way of life.

Early settlement sites on the Coromandel Peninsula were primarily located on coastal dune lands, near river mouths and the coastal edge. Many have since been lost through coastal erosion, so our knowledge of them is patchy. The nearby dense broad-leafed coastal forest provided ample wood, leaves and fibre for housing construction and waka-building purposes. Unexpectedly, it also provided a major food source. The settlers soon discovered that enormous flightless birds, the like of which they had never seen, lived within the forest and along its fringes.

During the late 1840s, English explorer William Cormack was the first European to find moa bones on the Coromandel Peninsula. The sea had eroded the frontal dune at Ōpito Bay and this exposed the edge of an ancient midden. Within it, Cormack found a femur and a tibia of one of the great birds.[28] Moa remains have been subsequently unearthed at a number of locations on the peninsula, including Port Jackson, Sarahs Gully (west of Ōpito Bay), Hot Water Beach, Tairua, Whangamatā and Wheritoa.[29]

It is now thought that four species of moa probably lived around the Hauraki Gulf. They included the enormous North Island giant moa (*Dinornis novaezealandiae*) which could stretch up to over 3 metres tall. Its powerful sharp

Bones of a Mantell's moa found at Amodeo Bay, Coromandel Peninsula, 1926. (Auckland War Memorial Museum Tāmaki Paenga Hira)

beak and strong neck enabled the bird to eat a wide range of plants and even the branches of some trees. There were also the shorter and stockier Mantell's moa (*Pachyornis geranoides*) which dwelt in swamps and along the forest margins, the North Island broad-billed moa (*Euryapteryx curtus*) which specialised in eating leaves and fruit, and the much smaller bush moa (*Anomalopteryx didiformis*) which lived deep within the forest.[30]

It is not known how the massive birds were captured, but it is thought likely that snares were used, or that in some cases dogs were deployed to run down the large game.[31] Moa did not last long in the Hauraki Gulf once hunting began and were probably extinct within a hundred years of first settlement.

Moa provided a substantial food source for the early settlers, but it was the much more fatty New Zealand fur seal (*Arctocephalus forsteri*) which formed the mainstay of their diet. On their arrival, the new settlers would have been astonished to see large colonies of fur seals dotted along the rocky shores. There had been no similar animals in their tropical Pacific homeland and they would have known little about these novel creatures, which they named kekeno or 'look abouts'.[32]

Although seals are now only infrequent visitors to the gulf, we know that they once bred along the outer eastern coastline. Mothers and pups do not travel far from breeding sites and their bones have been found in early settlements scattered along the eastern Coromandel coast. Sea lion and

sea elephant bones have also been found but there is no evidence that they were breeding in the area.

The marine mammals had no innate fear of humans and were easily approached on land. A blow to the head with a heavy club would have quickly killed them, a single animal providing a large quantity of rich and nourishing food.[33] The archaeological record indicates that only a few animals were taken at a time, and likely for immediate consumption rather than preservation, but the regular harvesting gradually took its toll.[34]

Tradition tells of the inner Hauraki Gulf islands being settled by the ancestors of the Te Wai-o-Hua and Ngāi Tai peoples. One of the early settlements in the inner gulf was located on Motutapu Island. Known as the Sunde site, it is a small flat area located behind the beach and near the stream mouth at West Point. People were living here shortly before the large Rangitoto eruption which probably occurred, at the earliest, around 1400. Another settlement site of a similar age has been located just to the north at Pig Bay.[35]

Prior to the eruption, Motutapu was largely covered in coastal lowland forest.[36] The early settlers eked out an existence on the narrow margin between the forest and the sea. They harvested a variety of birds, including tūī, kākā, kākāriki and kererū from the forest and shags and oystercatchers from the coastal edge. From the sea came snapper, mullet and shellfish. An occasional seal, sea lion or elephant seal, which ventured into the gulf, supplemented

New Zealand fur seal. (Auckland Whale and Dolphin Safari)

New Zealand fur seals and sea lions in the Hauraki Gulf

New Zealand fur seals and sea lions were prolific in the Hauraki Gulf when humans first arrived, but were gone before AD 1500. The national fur seal population is now recovering, with numerous mainland breeding sites found in the South Island and colonies re-establishing on the west coast of the North Island.[37] More recently, seals have started returning to the gulf and they are likely to become more frequent visitors in the future. Conceivably, breeding sites could eventually re-establish on the eastern coast of the Coromandel Peninsula and Great Barrier Island.

It is a different story with sea lions. A recent comparison of the DNA taken from sea lion bones found in ancient middens in the Hauraki Gulf and elsewhere on the mainland with that of sea lions from remnant populations in the Sub-Antarctic Islands, has established that they are different species, with the mainland sea lion now extinct. This means that sea lions are unlikely to come back to the gulf.

their diet. Adzes were hewn from greywacke on the island and used to clear some of the forest. Crops may have been grown in the newly cleared areas, but the soil was heavy with clay and difficult to work.

When people returned to Motutapu after the major eruption, they would have found much of the forest on the western side of the island destroyed. The ground was covered in a layer of rich ash, in places up to a metre deep. The newly cleared and enriched soils created ideal conditions for agriculture.

A 1981 excavation of the Sunde site revealed human and dog footprints which had been etched into the ash layer and then preserved. These may have been made by someone returning to the island with their dog to check on the damage or to re-establish the settlement there. There is evidence of human activity during the later lighter ash showers, as gardens were reconstructed. Eventually most of the forest on the island was cleared and extensive gardens created. A sizeable population had a presence on the island for several hundred years. Then, during the 1820s, the Musket Wars caused Motutapu to be evacuated.

We know much less about the first settlement of the Tāmaki isthmus, because the development of Auckland City has destroyed much of the archaeological evidence there. The first arrivals, possibly the ancestors of Ngāti Huarere and Te Wai-o-Hua, would have encountered an area largely covered with broad-leafed coastal forest, but interspersed with over 50 volcanic cones and large open volcanic boulder fields. There would have been many small lakes and wetlands which were created when lava flows blocked natural drainage patterns.[38]

The isthmus proved strategically important and occupation there became hotly contested, reflected in the name Tāmaki which means battle. Settlers had access to both the prolific marine resources within the gulf and those in the extensive Manukau Harbour to the west. The isthmus was also the hub of important waka portage routes. These enabled travel between coasts without the need to make the very long, and at times dangerous, trip around North Cape.

Tāmaki may have been one of the earliest areas in the country to be extensively cultivated. The volcanic cones provided excellent sites for both gardening and settlement and were probably the first areas on the isthmus to be settled. The rich, friable ash-laden soils were easily contoured and cultivated. The slopes of the cones were terraced to provide living spaces, with soil dug out from the inside of the slope and packed down on the outside. This was supplemented with the disposal of huge quantities of shells along the edges of the terraces, derived mainly from cockles harvested from the highly productive Waitematā and Manukau harbours.[39]

As the population on the isthmus increased, activity spread out from the cones, most of the forest was cleared and much larger gardened and settled areas were established. Evidence of most of these lowland activities has since been destroyed by urban development, but remnants are still visible at some places, such as the ancient Ōtuataua stonefields near Māngere.

Rangitoto eruption

The Rangitoto eruption would have been a stupendous event for the early settlers. Although it was long believed that the majestic volcanic cone rose from the sea in one major event shortly after AD 1400, this has recently been questioned by scientists. A more detailed study of core samples from underneath Lake Pupuke at Takapuna has indicated that the volcano may have initially erupted as early as AD 500, long before humans arrived in the country.[40]

But the eruptions which occurred after people first settled on Motutapu would have been spectacular and frightening. The volcano produced a series of ash showers: four major ones followed by ten to twenty lighter showers.[41] The settlers almost certainly evacuated the island once the eruptions started and there is no evidence that anyone was killed.[42]

Looking towards Rangitoto from the Sunde site, Motutapu Island, where human and dog footprints were found etched in the ash layer from the Rangitoto eruption.

The early Hauraki Gulf settlers probably lived in small family-based groups and they would have frequently moved about to exploit available food resources as they came into season. With the growing importance of agriculture, people started to live more permanently in larger settlements. University of Otago archaeologist Dr Ian Smith has estimated that, by 1400, possibly 2000 people were living in the Hauraki Gulf and surrounding area. But by 1550, this had likely increased five-fold to more than 10,000.[43]

The impacts of this population increase on the natural environment, and the lifestyle of those who were reliant on it for survival, were profound. Many species vanished, most significantly those large and easily caught prey which provided a major food source for the early settlers. The first to disappear may have been the moa, followed by sea lions and seals. Other bird species which were harvested during early settlement times quickly disappeared from the archaeological record and have long been extinct. They included the giant harrier, a large predatory bird second only to the enormous South Island Haast's eagle, and a fish-eating duck.[44]

The overall quantity of birds diminished significantly, due to the cumulative impact of loss of forest habitat, predation by kiore and human harvesting. Some species, such as the kākāpō, little spotted kiwi and New Zealand king shag, became locally extinct.

The main source of protein for the Hauraki Gulf peoples, after the seals and moa were gone, was seafood: primarily snapper and shark as well as shellfish, such as pipi, cockle and tuatua. Māori living around the gulf became very much a marine-dependent people, with their well-being inextricably linked to the productivity of the gulf. Fishing and shellfish gathering become major seasonal occupations and the gulf communities became highly skilled in these pursuits.

Story of the Gulf | **Laurie Beamish**
KAUMĀTUA, NGĀI TAI, UMUPUIA[45]

Laurie was born in Auckland but spent some of his early years on Great Barrier Island, where his parents helped run a rehabilitation centre at Karaka Bay, Port Abercrombie. After leaving school and working for some years in the clothing industry, in 1974 Laurie decided to go commercial fishing. He was following in the footsteps of his great-grandfather and other family members (whānau) who had been involved in the commercial fishing industry.

In the early 1990s Laurie's great-aunt, Rachel Ngeungeu Te Irirangi Zister, called him back to Umupuia to help look after Ngāi Tai's fisheries settlement entitlements. By that time Rachel was in her late 90s. She was an influential tribal elder (kuia), having been brought up for a time with Te Puea Hērangi, the future Kīngitanga leader. In 1982 Rachel had given part of her land at Umupuia for the re-establishment of a Ngāi Tai meeting place (marae). She proceeded to raise funds to support its development through renting out paddocks behind Umupuia Beach to campers and operating a small beachfront shop. The marae was officially dedicated in November 1990. Rachel died six years later in May 1997, aged 103. Laurie now oversees the marae's operation.

The name Umupuia shows ancient links back to the Pacific islands where the word umu (rather than the Māori word hangi) refers to an earth oven. Puia translates to spring and may refer to the hot-water springs in the area. Unlike most early tribal groups associated with the Hauraki Gulf, Ngāi Tai maintained uninterrupted occupation of their tribal heartland prior to European settlement. The 400 hectares of remaining tribal land at Umupuia has 'never been out of our possession. It's never been bought, sold or leased. The significance of this is that Ngāi Tai have retained their mana [prestige and spiritual power] from time immemorial. We continue to assert our mana from this place to the rest of our areas where we have acknowledged interests and involvement.

'Ngāi Tai are a maritime people. We travelled widely by sea, frequently as far afield as the Far North and East Cape, trading obsidian, Tahanga basalt and other items. The sea was our highway. The old sayings of our people refer to fleets of canoes being so numerous as to appear like shoals of herrings.

'We are located at a maritime crossroads. The name Maraetai [now attached to the coastal settlement to the north of Umupuia] means a meeting place of, or on, the sea. It refers to the sheltered waters of the Tāmaki Strait, a place where you could gather waka in calm water after a rough sea passage. An ancient name for Waiheke Island was Te Motu-arai-roa or the long sheltering island, referring to the sheltered waters that the island provides off its southern coast.

'We extensively gardened the islands in the gulf to enjoy the frost free areas and to enable year-round cultivation. On Motuihe we solely grew the hue [gourd] to keep its integrity as a single crop. On other islands we grew kūmara and taro in the different favourable microclimates. My great-aunt's tupuna [ancestor] Tara-te-irirangi was one of the last chiefs living on Motutapu and Rangitoto. His home was located close to where the causeway between the two islands has since been built, which was where we had our kāinga [homes] and fishing camps. Motutapu had fertile gardens and was a very important place to us. Our oral history says that the footprints found in the ash at the Sunde site were made by our ancestor and this is supported by the fact that no one else claims them.

'When Auckland was established, we frequently travelled there with supplies for the early settlers. But during the time of the Waikato wars the Crown troops came through and smashed up all of our canoes. This meant that our transport and provision lines were crippled. We lost our economic base and never recovered.

'The Wairoa [long river] was located within the inner sanctum of Ngāi Tai and is very sacred. There was a portage from the river to the Papakura Stream providing easy waka access between the Hauraki Gulf and the Manukau Harbour. The whole river itself is wāhi tapu [a sacred place] with many burial sites situated on its banks and around the river mouth. An old whakataukī [proverb] says that 'we are the river and the river is us'. Sheer population pressure and the increase in numbers have affected our near-shore harvesting capabilities. On our beach here at Umupuia, when my great-aunt was alive during the 1940s, she could get a sack of scallops without getting her knees wet. There are no scallops or pipi here now. There is a place near Pōnui that we call Tara's Rock after our chief Tara-te-irirangi. That was always a place where we could get crayfish, kina [sea urchins] and mussels. But it's now been stripped.

'We've had a rāhui [harvest closure] on the beach for the past eight years to grow the cockles back. They're increasing well now in number and size. But we have to ask ourselves, how are we going to manage them when the closure is lifted? We have witnessed other places where, once the restrictions are removed, the harvesting effort is intense. We want to build on what we have achieved with our rāhui, rather than watch it get stripped away again by uncontrolled harvesting. Recent surveys suggest that this beach and one or two others are now the last strongholds of the large cockle populations. We need to be cognisant of the fact that Umupuia might end up being the last bastion for them.

'In terms of customary gathering, we are now forced to obtain our kaimoana [seafood] from the islands where access is more difficult. With the recent advent of a large number of recreational boats and cheap, easily available technology, even these places are coming under severe harvest pressure.

'Ngāi Tai had an advantageous relationship with the Pākehā from early on when our chief's daughter Ngeungeu married Thomas Maxwell in the 1820s. We tried to remain neutral during the Waikato wars, but despite this the Crown confiscated much of our land in Hunua and on the south side of the Wairoa River. Other Ngāi Tai land on the gulf islands, at Clevedon and elsewhere, was acquired through 'shonky' practices and the Crown has now acknowledged this.

'Our iwi is currently going through a Treaty settlement ratification process and I see this as a turning point. We are moving out of the grievance mode and hope to grow our asset base as a result of the settlement. We've established a tourist venture, Te Haerenga, which will provide an authentic guided cultural tourism experience based around the names and stories of Rangitoto and Motutapu. We want to re-build our economy around the islands, based on manaakitanga [our hosting of people] and our ability to educate them.

'Once our deed is ratified it will free up our thinking. We can draw our visionary threads together to create a picture of what our maritime future will look like. We were sailors

Ngāi Tai kaumātua Laurie Beamish oversees the operation of the Umupuia marae which was re-established by his great-aunt Rachel Ngeungeu Te Irirangi Zister during the 1980s.

and had the best vessels around. That historic mastery of the ocean will take a lot of recreating. But we won't be hide-bound by totara and kauri log vessels that were paddled. We aspire to acquire a new fleet based on modern technology: fast efficient sailing vessels like catamarans, that are future-proofed and move away from dependence on fossil fuels. Māori have never been slow to adapt to new technologies and ideas. We want to combine the best of the modern world with all the valuable lessons from the past.'

Story of the Gulf | **Sir Michael Fay**

RESIDENT, GREAT MERCURY ISLAND (AHUAHU)[46]

Sir Michael Fay first visited Great Mercury Island in 1975 when he was 26 years old. From a young age he had always been interested in picking up objects and on this trip he picked up something special, an ancient adze lying on the ground. This helped to cement his feeling that there was something extraordinary, almost spiritual, about the island.

Two years later Michael bought the island with his business partner David Richwhite. Their tenure of the island, which has now spanned 40 years, has been one of custodianship, getting to know the land well and carefully managing it. One of their key concerns was to preserve the very rich archaeological landscape. Much of the land is grazed to preserve the historic features, but only light stock is used and fences are positioned away from important features.

A big storm in 2008, which eroded the dunes on Whites Beach exposing a midden site, highlighted the dangers of losing the rich archaeological information before it had even been explored. This motivated Michael to set up the Great Mercury Island Archaeological Project to investigate the settlement history of the island. The project, which commenced in 2012, is a collaboration between Michael (representing the landowners), Ngāti Hei, The University of Auckland and the Auckland War Memorial Museum.

The island was once heavily settled, with archaeological evidence of extensive garden areas and 23 defended villages (pā) — a very large number for a land area only 10 kilometres in length and 5 kilometres at its widest part. Stone was brought to the island from surrounding areas to be worked into tools: basalt from Ōpito and obsidian from Cook's Beach, Hāhei, Whangamatā and Mayor Island. Bones from moa, seals, whales, birds and fish have also been recovered.

One of the earliest settlement sites to have been identified is at Te Mataku on the north side of Coralie Bay. Archaeologists have found evidence of cooking and stone working. A moa leg bone was also found, as well as a one-piece moa-bone fish hook. The site is located right on the coastal edge and has been eroding for over 40 years.[47]

Pat Mizen, a farmer who lived on Great Mercury Island for 47 years and who wrote Māori and Pākehā histories of the place, noted that the island was located directly on the navigational course covering the shortest distance between the eastern Pacific Islands and Aotearoa. The white rhyolite cliffs of Pari Nui te Rā, which reflect the sunlight, may have been the first land to appear over the horizon as waka approached.[48] The island has a subtropical climate, fertile soils and rich marine life. It is strategically located at the centre of a network of lands accessible via short waka journeys — Great Barrier Island, Cuvier Island, Ōpito and the north-east coast of the Coromandel Peninsula. It has been postulated by Mizen and others that Great Mercury Island may in fact have been the place referred to in Māori legend as Pari Nui te Ra, Ahuahu which was said to be located in Hawaiiki. This was a place where kūmara survived the winter in the ground and therefore from where stocks could be replenished.[49]

Mizen estimates that the population of the island reached a maximum of 8000 people somewhere between AD 1200 and 1400.[50] By 1832, due to warfare, there were no inhabitants remaining. From 1858 to 1865, the Crown bought up all the parcels of land from the various Māori owners. According to historian Paul Monin, the principal rights-holders in the Mercury Islands were Ngāti Whanaunga and a hapū of that tribe, Ngāti Karaua.[51]

The government leased Great Mercury Island to a Mr J Buchanan who started farming it. The island went through several owners and was eventually transformed into a successful sheep and cattle station. Edward Mizen bought the island in 1929. Eventually his son Pat took over the running of the farm, but it was hard to make a living, particularly with the added cost of having to transport stock and goods to and from the mainland.[52]

When Pat was heading towards retirement he started investigating other options for the island. In 1975 he approached the Hauraki Gulf Maritime Park Board to see if he could sell part of the island to add to the maritime park. But agreement on the terms of purchase could not be reached mainly because, for stock to survive during the summer drought period, Pat needed access to the whole island, particularly the cool bush valleys and grass areas of the back country, which were the very areas that the board was most interested in purchasing.[53]

Shortly thereafter, in August 1975, the government announced a plan to lease coastal properties for the use of the public. Pat contacted Darcy O'Brien, the then Commissioner of Crown Lands for Auckland. But negotiations again failed, this time due to disagreement on the amount payable for the lease. Instead the island was leased to Michael Fay and David Richwhite and two years later the pair bought the island outright.

The numerous bays of Great Mercury Island are frequently utilised by boaties and, since Michael took over the running of the island, visitors have always been welcomed, so long as a few basic rules are adhered to. During 2014 feral cats and rats were eradicated from the island through a partnership with the Department of Conservation and the landowners. This has resulted in a markedly improved breeding success of seabirds. Just prior to the eradication, only one grey-faced petrel chick survived the breeding season and the year afterwards there were 20 survivors.

The island will soon once again support a wide variety of indigenous birds and other species. But it is the rich human history of the island, spanning over 700 years of occupation, that makes it extraordinary. As he reaches his later years, Michael is considering how the island might be managed in the future to ensure that its special qualities are preserved for future generations.

Top: Te Mataku, located on the northern end of Coralie Bay (the calm, semicircular sandy bay near the top right of the image), is one of the earliest settlement sites investigated by archaeologists on Great Mercury Island.

Bottom: Sir Michael Fay has been joint owner of Great Mercury Island for the past 40 years and is currently exploring how the island's special qualities can be preserved for future generations. (Jane Ussher)

Chapter 2
Abundance of kaimoana

The Hauraki Gulf's early settlers became some of the most skilled fishers in the world. Certainly their fishing technology was way ahead of that used in Europe at the time. Their careful management of the resource also ensured that there was a notable abundance of fish and shellfish when Europeans first arrived over 500 years later.

Approach to kaimoana harvesting

The early fishermen deployed their fishing equipment with great skill, being closely attuned to the life cycles, movements and behaviours of the marine species they were seeking. 'The indiscriminate dropping of a baited line in the hope of hooking anything that came along is rightly regarded by the Māori as the action of a kūware — a person devoid of practical sense.'[1] Fishing was a serious business, the community relied on its success and it was not something to be taken lightly.

A fishing trip was a well-planned expedition, with the appropriate day and time, the fishing grounds to be visited and the species to be targeted identified well in advance. Snapper was a commonly targeted fish in the Hauraki Gulf. It would be particularly selected when known to be seasonally abundant or in prime condition.[2]

Fishing gear was often kept in special storehouses, and it was sorted and organised on the day prior to the trip. The right-sized hooks for the species being sought were selected and the lines were carefully measured

Pearl shell trolling lure shank found in 1964 at Tairua, Coromandel Peninsula, in an occupation layer dated to the early-mid 1300s. The shell is from a species of oyster only found in the tropics, so must have been brought to the Hauraki Gulf by the early settlers. (Ref: AU1785, Auckland War Memorial Museum Tāmaki Paenga Hira)

This Charles Heaphy sketch shows a Māori fishing camp at Pakihi Island. Portrayed are two fishing waka, a temporary shelter and a fish drying rack. (Ref: PD56(85), Auckland War Memorial Museum Tāmaki Paenga Hira)

to ensure that the hooks lay at the appropriate depth, taking into account the nature of the fishing grounds and the targeted species.[3]

No food was permitted on a fishing expedition, signalling the seriousness of the endeavour. Bait, such as shrimp, was caught in baskets deployed from the shore. Before departure, the bait would be apportioned to ensure that each member of the fishing party had sufficient and that none was wasted.[4]

The fishing ground, which would have its own distinctive name, would be identified by rocks and islands in the vicinity or by visual transects with prominent landmarks on shore.[5] Some areas of the Hauraki Gulf were given names indicating the abundance of a particular species. For example, Wai-mangō, on the west side of the Firth of Thames some 12 kilometres north of Kaiaua, means 'waters of the dogfish'.[6] Kōherurahi Point to the west of Kawakawa Bay refers to the once abundant horse mackerel (kōheru) in the area.

The first fish caught, known as te ika tuatahi, was returned to the sea as an offering to the deity Tangaroa. Through thus paying their respects, the fishermen could be assured of a good catch and a safe return home.[7] They knew that it was important to maintain the delicate balance of the marine environment, otherwise the fish might not remain in the area. It was forbidden to throw any waste into the sea, including fish waste, undersized fish or excess bait. For this

reason, fish were not gutted at sea, but were landed whole.[8]

Only men were permitted to fish and when they returned home, they were greeted from the shore by their womenfolk who eagerly received the catch, cleaned the fish and prepared it for immediate consumption or preservation. The women would have been very happy to see their menfolk return safely. Fishing in canoes, sometimes many miles out to sea, could be a risky operation if the weather turned inclement.

A warning of what can happen if things go wrong is contained in the name given to Tukituki Bay, just south of Colville. It means 'dash to pieces'. This refers to the misfortune that befell a fishing party that was headed to the Motukawao Islands. On the day of the trip there were strong westerly winds blowing across the Firth of Thames and the wind had whipped up large waves which were breaking on the shore. The canoe made its way carefully north, hugging the shoreline, but was unexpectedly struck by a huge wave. This capsized the canoe and dashed it onto the shore where it was pounded to pieces on the rocks.[9]

Seasonal fishing calendar

Fishing and shellfish gathering were seasonal occupations and, throughout the fishing calendar, fishing parties would temporarily camp at the various favoured locations. Māori had developed a detailed lunar calendar (maramataka), running from new moon to the next new moon, to provide guidance on the right time to fish.

Spring and early summer were a time of great abundance. In the Firth of Thames it heralded the arrival of juvenile kahawai, mullet and flounder (pātiki), which moved into the estuarine and seagrass nursery areas. Female sharks would also arrive to give birth to their young. The tiny glass eels, juvenile whitebait (predominantly inanga) and common smelt would move up into the estuaries and lower reaches of the Waihou and Piako rivers. Adult flounder, snapper and kahawai would also be found in abundance as they moved into the firth to feed amongst the rich mussel beds. In addition, this was the time when the shellfish spawned and settled.[10]

To support the community through the less productive

The naming of Kōherurahi Point to the west of Kawakawa Bay refers to the abundance of kōheru (horse mackerel) which was found in the area. The point is the site of an historic pā and is currently contained within the Waitawa Regional Park.

winter months, large quantities of seafood would be harvested and preserved during spring and summer. Galatea Bay on Pōnui Island is an example of a seasonal fishing site where large quantities of snapper were caught, dried and then taken away from the island.[11]

Harbours and estuaries were the source of enormous quantities of shellfish, particularly cockle and pipi, and these were harvested over the spring and summer months each year. The shellfish were either initially cooked in a steam oven or placed under a brush fire on the ground. Once the shells had opened, the meat was extracted, threaded on to flax strings and hung up to dry.[12]

From the Matarangi spit, bordering the Whangapoua Harbour on the Coromandel Peninsula, the dominant species collected was cockle.[13] Pipi were gathered from the Ōmaha spit bordering the Whangateau Harbour in

Traditional Hauraki Gulf shark fishery

Smaller shark species were highly prized by Māori because the meat kept well when dried, with dried shark meat being a staple for travellers. In addition, oil from the shark livers was mixed with red ochre (kōkōwai) to make distinctive paint used to decorate buildings and waka. Small sharks were caught with nets, in the early morning or evening, as the light changed.[14] Large sharks were caught with hooks to avoid damage to nets.

The Firth of Thames was well known as an important shark pupping and nursery area. In spring, spotted dogfish (pioke) would move into the inner reaches of the firth. They would be followed during late spring and summer by school shark (tupere) and other species.[15] J S Polack, who visited in the 1830s, wrote that 'In the river Thames, during the season for catching sharks, the banks are occupied by numerous fishers. Fishing employs much of the time of these people, and large hoards are preserved for winter provision by desiccation.'[16]

Mahurangi was another area where large fishing parties, from as far away as the Thames-Coromandel coast, gathered each summer season to catch large quantities of shark.

During this time Kawau Bay 'swarmed with sharks'.[17] Other areas were also important to the shark fishery. For example, there are reports in May 1867 of Ngāti Paoa fishermen catching and drying nearly 3000 sharks near Waiheke Island over a six-week period. They were for a large funeral (tangi) to be held in Taupō.[18] There was also a well-known shark-fishing ground at the entrance to the Wairoa River near Clevedon. Each summer, Ngāi Tai fishing parties would travel to Whakakaiwhara Point to catch large quantities of pioke which schooled around the mouth of the river. Once landed, the sharks were cut into strips and dried in the branches of a large pōhutukawa tree.[19]

Once caught in small nets, dogfish (kapetā) were gutted and hung up to dry on poles. This shark-drying process is shown here at Tokohiwai, Whangārei Harbour, in 1914. It is similar to what would have taken place in the Hauraki Gulf. (Ref: 7-A14507, Sir George Grey Special Collections, Auckland Libraries)

Early hooks were fashioned in one piece out of materials such as cetacean tooth (top centre) and moa bone (top left and top right). When moa became scarce, two-piece hooks were manufactured from other materials such as dog jaw bone (used in the shank on bottom left) and Cooks turban shell (bottom right). (Auckland War Memorial Museum Tāmaki Paenga Hira)

north Auckland. The fact that over 300 middens have been identified on this spit, with most consisting entirely of shell, indicates the extent of this activity. Most of the middens have now been lost as a result of the area being developed for housing.[20]

Many other places had an abundance of shellfish and were the focus of seasonal activities. Large pipi beds extended along the southern and eastern shores of the Firth of Thames. This is indicated by the place name Pipiroa on the Piako River, which means the 'long pipi', and most probably refers to the abundant pipi beds in the area. Cockle beds were found at Te Mātā and Colville Bay and mud snails (tītiko) were found between the Kauaeranga River mouth and Thames.[21] The name of the settlement of Te Mātā on the Thames coast means 'the heaped layer of shells'. This refers to the effect of the prevailing westerly winds, which generate large waves, and which in turn sweep up and deposit large mounds of shellfish on the shore.[22]

Hook-and-line equipment

Māori developed very effective hook-and-line fishing equipment, to the extent that their traditional hook design has been used by some New Zealand commercial longline fishermen. The Māori C-shaped circle fishing hook has a very dissimilar shape to the European sharply pointed J-shaped one and it operates in quite a different manner. The European hook is relatively small and is often swallowed by the fish. It has a wide opening, a sharp point which is designed to pierce the flesh of the fish like a gaff and on which the bait is attached, and a barb to help prevent the hook disengaging once the fish is caught.

The traditional Māori hook was much larger, as it was designed not to be swallowed. It was more circular in shape and only had a small opening between the point and the shank. The bait was not attached to the point but was tied on to the bottom loop of the hook with a small piece of flax. The purpose of the point was not to pierce the fish, but to guide its jaw through the small opening in the hook. Internal barbs were used on some hooks to narrow the opening. Once the hook was in place around the jaw, when the fish tried to escape by pulling away, the hook rotated and the jaw was trapped.[23]

When Europeans first sighted these different-looking hooks, they were highly dismissive. The hooks looked exceedingly clumsy in comparison to the European ones and they did not believe that the large circular contraptions, which lacked a barb, could actually catch fish.[24] But the Europeans were wrong. For hundreds of years, Māori very effectively caught large numbers of fish with these hooks.

Since the 1960s, some commercial longline fishers have started using circle hooks in preference to J-shaped ones. They found that their catch rates improved with the traditional-styled hooks and also that the fish were in better condition when retrieved and easier to remove from the hooks. Although circle hooks are not as efficient as J-shaped hooks in initially catching fish, once they are caught, fewer manage to escape.[25]

In the Hauraki Gulf, early hooks were fashioned in one piece out of moa bone. The bones of these enormous birds were large, dense and strong, making them ideal for the task. The outside form of the hook was first shaped from the bone with chisels, and then material drilled from the inside to form the thin circular shape. The rough surface was then smoothed with a stone rasp.[26]

An early fish hook manufacturing site was located on the sand dunes in Ōpito Bay, with 230 moa-bone fish hooks and fragments being found in just one midden.[27] Moa bones appear to have been taken to Great Barrier Island for such manufacturing purposes. It is still uncertain whether the great birds actually ever lived on the island.[28]

With the demise of the moa after a century or so, hooks started to be manufactured from other materials. Because these weren't as strong as moa bone, the larger hooks were made in two pieces, which were lashed together with fine flax-fibre cord (muka). Wood or stone was commonly used for the shank and a sharper material used to fashion the point. These points were variously made out of the jawbones and teeth of dog, human and sea-mammal bone, and Cook's turban shell.

Large wooden hooks for catching sharks were obtained through training young plants to grow in coils. As the plant matured, the wood hardened and then the curved parts of the wood were cut out of the tree. The wood was then toughened by heating it in hot earth beneath a fire. The preferred woods were tauhini root and mangemange.[29]

The hooks were attached to a line (aho) made from flax fibre which was rolled on a person's thigh to form a two- or three-ply twisted cord, with the thickness of the cord depending on the size of the fish being targeted.[30] These flax lines were stronger than those used by Europeans at the time. Stone sinkers were used to weigh the hooks down.

Kahawai were caught with specially designed unbaited lures (pā kahawai) which were trolled through the water from canoes paddled at speed. The lures were inlaid with pāua shell and had bunches of feathers from kiwi, kingfisher or blue penguin secured to the end to partially obscure the hook. The lures were slightly curved so that when they were trolled, they would spin and reflect light from the shell to attract the fish.[31]

Kahawai were caught with specially-designed unbaited lures inlaid with pāua shell and decorated with feathers. Their slightly curved shape ensured that they spun and reflected the light whilst being towed through the water. (Auckland War Memorial Museum Tāmaki Paenga Hira)

Fishing equipment at Oruarangi pā

One of the largest collections of Māori fishing equipment, obtained from one locality in New Zealand, was that found at the Oruarangi pā in the Hauraki Plains. This extensive settlement, which was located on the banks of the Waihou River near the confluence of the Matatoki Stream, was occupied by Ngāti Whanaunga peoples.

The pā was vacated after the Ngā Puhi attacks on Hauraki tribes in 1821 and the surrounding land was subsequently alienated from Māori ownership, drained and turned into farmland. The pā site itself was retained in customary ownership as a burial ground (urupā) but was effectively incorporated into the adjacent farm.[32]

In 1932 curio hunters started to target the ancient pā site to dig for artefacts. These early diggers included Toss (Bill) Hammond, Dr Jim Liggins, Selwyn (Sonny) Te Moananui Hovell and Reginald Bell. They were rewarded with numerous finds. But as their interest was mainly in obtaining interesting objects, rather than in understanding the rich history of the area, little information about the positioning and location of the artefacts was recorded.[33]

Items collected from the site, now largely held by the Auckland War Memorial Museum, include 790 individual pieces of fishing gear. The large majority of these (558) are the bone points of two-piece fish hooks. Other types of fishing gear collected included hook points made from shell, bone and teeth, the shanks of trolling lures, and a large number of fishing sinkers (87).[34] This impressive quantity of fishing gear indicates the great importance of fishing to the people of the area.

Fishing nets and traps

Although fishing with a hook and line was very effective, far greater quantities of fish could be landed through the use of large seine nets (taharoa). These were particularly effective at catching inshore schooling fish, such as yellow-eyed mullet and mackerel.

Making the large nets was a major endeavour, something that involved the whole community. The nets were made in smaller sections which were then assembled and joined together. Every net was carefully designed and each part had a different name. The mesh was smaller in the middle part of the net and larger at the ends.

The net makers (kaita) carefully chose the most suitable flax leaves for each net. These needed to be of the right thickness and consistency. The selected leaves, which were about 3 to 4 feet long, were cut and then hung up in a sheltered location for several days to partially dry. This helped to ensure that the flax remained flexible enough to be worked, but was dry enough to ensure that the knots would not slip.[35]

When they were ready, the flax leaves would be split into long thin strips of between 3 and 6 millimetres wide. Then the netting could begin. The net maker would take the first strip and knot one end. It would then be looped over a supporting strong plaited cord at the top, knotted to form a loop, looped over again and knotted. This rhythm was repeated until the end of the length of the section was reached. A second row would then be knotted along the first and so on until the section was completed. A special net gauge made out of wood or whale bone was often used to ensure the correct gauge. Some kaita used their fingers instead.[36]

Netted bags were attached to the bottom of the net to provide for sinkers of smooth worn stone to be inserted to weigh the net down. Pieces of a very light wood from the whau tree were attached to the top, to act as floats.

Some nets were of very large proportions with reports of seines being over 900 metres long. These large nets could only be set by using two canoes tied together, with a platform lashed across the two hulls providing a place to pile the enormous net. A crew of around 30 men would be required to manage the vessel and net.[37]

Similar to the deployment of hooks and lines, nets were not set in a haphazard manner in the hope of catching something. The most experienced fisherman in the community would have the role of determining when the net should be cast. He would carefully watch the approaching shoals of fish and give the signal to deploy the net when he judged the time to be right.

Crayfishing at Great Mercury Island (Ahuahu)

Although Māori had a wide range of sophisticated fishing equipment at their disposal, some species in the Hauraki Gulf were so prolific that they could simply be grasped by hand. Cameron Buchanan describes a crayfishing party which arrived at Great Mercury Island in about 1872:

When I was about fourteen I saw a wonderful display of skill in catching the elusive crayfish which abounded in the seaweed that fringed the beaches and reefs around the island. On this afternoon two large canoe loads of Māori arrived and landed to camp for the night near our house [in Huruhi Harbour]. They had pigs, dogs and even domestic fowl on board which they turned loose, but the livestock did not wander far from camp it being near feeding time. Some of the women collected firewood and soon had the umu heating up, while others after divesting themselves of nearly all their clothes and being barefooted, waded into the seaweed. They felt the crayfish with their feet then reached down and caught them by their long feelers bringing them up and throwing them onto the beach where they were soon captured by the men . . . In, I should say, twenty minutes they got twelve or fifteen. Very few escaped once the ladies got hold of them. In a very short time they had a good meal ready consisting of potatoes, mussels, fish, oysters and the succulent crayfish which was greatly relished by all.[38]

Archaeological investigations on Great Mercury Island have identified a midden containing a large number of mouth parts of crayfish, although at a different location from that described by Buchanan.[39]

Huruhi Harbour, Great Mercury Island.

Several place names around the gulf indicate the prolific nature of the shoal fish which could be caught in these large seine nets. Kaiaua, on the western side of the Firth of Thames, means 'the abundant food resource of aua', the yellow-eyed mullet.[40] These fish were also prolific in Coromandel Harbour, known by some as Wai-au 'swirling current' or Wai-aua 'waters containing aua'. Iwi historian Taimoana Tūroa tells a story associated with this name:

When Kahumatamomoe, the son of Tamatekapua of Te Arawa descent, descended from the Toka-tea Mountain, he and his followers reached Wai-au. While

traversing the shoreline, he saw an enormous school of
yellow-eyed mullet (aua) being herded on the full tide
by other larger fish. When the larger fish struck, the
panicking herring le[a]pt out of the water to escape
and stranded themselves on the shore in droves. Kahu
and his followers were thus able to eat their fill before
continuing their journey south.[41]

There is an 1889 account of a seine net being set across the Waihou River, near the Warahoe Stream. Two posts were fixed into the riverbed and the mouth of a large seine net, over 6 metres long, was affixed to them. The net tapered off into a pocket. When the fish came up the river on the incoming tide, they were trapped in the pocket and then emptied into a waiting canoe. The catch was diverse, including herrings, sprats, kahawai, snapper, mullet, gurnard, flounder and eels.[42]

To catch fish in the gulf, Māori also used a range of smaller nets and traps, such as drag and scoop nets. After the nets were used, they were hung up to dry and then carefully folded and stored in a sheltered location. These nets were not very durable and were constantly in need of repair or replacement. This meant that net making was a constant activity in the gulf's coastal communities.

Stone fishing traps (poraka) were also used from time to time. They were constructed using rocks to prevent fish from escaping as the tide receded. Remains of fishing traps built by Ngāti Tamaterā can still be seen in Colville Harbour and on Browns Island.

Fisheries management

Kaimoana harvesting was carefully managed to ensure the ongoing health and productivity of the stock. This management was informed by mātauranga Māori, described by the Waitangi Tribunal as 'the unique Māori way of viewing themselves and the world, which encompasses (among other things) Māori traditional knowledge and culture'.[43] In the Māori world view everything is connected and interdependent, with mauri being the life force that gives things being and form. Management was focused on 'sustaining the mauri to ensure that the balance was maintained between people and the natural and spiritual worlds'.[44] This was achieved through the laws of tapu, which were used to preserve and restore mauri. 'Tapu involved imposing a prohibition or ban on anything when it was evident that the mauri was devitalised. Tapu gave time for that force to be restored, revitalised, or preserved.'[45]

When a tapu had been implemented it was referred to as rāhui tapu. When protecting an area, such as a fishing ground, the prohibited area was often indicated by the placement of a post. This practice allowed depleted fisheries to restore themselves.[46] Rāhui is still used today to protect depleted stocks, especially shellfish.

Customary rights applied to the marine space in a similar way as on land. Rights could be derived from ancestry (whakapapa), conquest (raupatu) or gift (tuku).

Deployment of traditional seine nets

Although there are no detailed written accounts of enormous seine nets being deployed in the Hauraki Gulf, Elsdon Best reports on a net, almost 2 kilometres long, being set at Maketū in 1885. The methodology would have been similar in the gulf:

An old expert, from a point of vantage, was to give the signal for operations to commence. He allowed shoal after shoal of fish to pass, to the disappointment of many observers; when an apparently small shoal appeared he gave the word, 'Haukotia mai' [Intercept it]. The waka taurua *swung out across the front of the advancing shoal as the seine-tenders payed out the huge net, which, however, was not wholly expended. The spectators, not less than a thousand persons, were unable to haul the net. The spare ends of the seine had to be doubled back to reinforce the centre, and twice the net had to be lifted to allow a large part of the catch to escape. At full tide the great net was hauled in as far as possible and secured to stout posts until the receding tide left it and the multitudes of Tangaroa out of water . . . some 37,000 fish were tallied, not including many small-fry and a number of sharks.*[47]

Access to productive fishing grounds was highly sought after. This was most evident in the rich flounder grounds in the Firth of Thames. 'By about 1750, a complex settlement had been reached, interests in the fishery being delineated by stakes planted close to the shore. The one-and-a-half mile [2.4 kilometre] stretch of foreshore between Tararu Point and the mouth of the Kauaeranga River was divided into forty-five such interests.'[48]

By the time of European rediscovery of the Hauraki Gulf in 1769, the long-standing residents had developed a lifestyle closely associated with the sea, with the abundant marine life of the gulf sustaining them for generations. This was achieved through the development of a deep understanding of the marine environment (mātauranga Māori) and the careful exercise of guardianship (kaitiakitanga) over it. However, things were soon to change radically.

Mātauranga Māori

Mātauranga Māori (traditional knowledge and culture) is the platform that enables Māori to manage the marine space and life within it.

Underpinning it are two core values — whanaungatanga and kaitiakitanga. Whanaungatanga (kinship) describes relationships including those amongst people and between people and the environment. These relationships are based on whakapapa (genealogy). 'The first step in understanding the Māori relationship with the landscape (for example) is to understand that descent from it is an essential Māori belief.' Kaitiakitanga is a product of whanaungatanga, 'an intergenerational obligation that arises by virtue of the kin relationship'. It is similar to the concept of guardianship or stewardship but also has a core spiritual element.[49]

'The idea of a kin relationship with taonga [treasures], and the kaitiakitanga obligation that kinship creates, explains why iwi refer to iconic mountains, rivers, lakes and harbours in the same way that they refer to close human relations. It explains why elders feel comfortable speaking directly to those elements and features, and why those elements and features are viewed as embodying distinct spiritual, as well as physical, qualities. It also explains why relationships with the environment are so important . . . It is through those relationships that Māori culture evolved, and through those relationships that it has a future.'[50]

Piritahi marae, Blackpool, Waiheke Island.

Story of the Gulf | **Tamaiti Tamaariki**
KAUMĀTUA, NGĀTI WHĀTUA ŌRĀKEI[51]

As Tamaiti Tamaariki sat on the beach at Ōkahu Bay, he recalled his long association with the surrounding marine area. 'I look at the fish jumping around out there and I immediately see the harbour as it was 70 years ago. How plentiful it was then.'

Tamaiti grew up in the village (kāinga) located on the flats behind Ōkahu Bay. He was born just after the sewerage pipe was first constructed around the edge of the bay and shortly before Tāmaki Drive was built. The village was razed to the ground in 1951 by the government and the residents were moved to state housing built on the overlooking hill at Kitemoana Street.

'Uncle Bob [Hawke] would call out to my dad when it was time to fish. He knew we were all going to be fed with the fish as they were so plentiful. We would cross the road with our nets and drag them in the water. Pipi and mussel were always plentiful, stretching right across the bay. There were tuangi (cockle) in the eastern corner. There were also horse mussels out past where the boats are currently moored.

'One of my greatest memories is of all the kuia going down to the wharf to fish for pātiki. They are such sweet fish. We would all have our favourite possies along the wharf. You would never catch one there today.

'We always had boats and when things got hard here we would go across to Devonport. It wasn't developed over there then and there were good currents running through. We took pāua (abalone) and octopus. Minnehaha, a little bay north of Takapuna, was always good.'

Tamaiti developed a deep understanding of the marine environment based on mātauranga Māori passed on by his father. 'I was the fifth child out of a family of ten. I was the sickly one so that brought me closer to Mum and Dad.' Tamaiti would frequently go on fishing trips with his father. 'I would get into the boat with Dad. I would never look in his basket of kai [food]. We might go over to Rangitoto and be staying there for four days. I remember this quite clearly. There was only one onion in the basket. I never questioned him on this. We built our kai around that one onion for four days. I really treasure those moments. Dad had total faith in the abundance of the sea. He just knew it was there.

'Dad was so clever he could make his own dive goggles out of the bottoms of glass milk bottles. He would cut the tempered glass with scissors and then make goggle surrounds so they would seal. He didn't need a wetsuit. He would ferment chillies and then take a chilli bottle out with him on dive trips. He would take a huge swig of chilli to raise his body temperature, go diving, and come back with what was needed.

Diving came with risk. 'There's a place on the lighthouse side of Rangitoto Island where I dived down and the next thing I felt was someone grabbing my leg and pulling me up. Dad knew that there was a hole there and if he let me go down it I would drown. In later years I did dive down into the hole and it was so beautiful. The kina were enormous. But if you dive at the wrong time, the current takes you straight in, and locks you in there under the water.

'We knew all the places on the coast where you could catch decent-sized snapper. This was based on understanding the currents and knowing where the shellfish beds were. For example, I was sitting at the club one day and Jackson said he wanted to go fishing tomorrow. So I said "okay" and looked at the sun, wind and tide. I said, "What time Jackson?" He said, "About 11 o'clock." I replied, "See those pylons, you go over there halfway between the second pylon and the boats." He said, "But there's no water there." I responded, "But tomorrow at 11 am there will be water there." So the next day he went there, put his line down and caught fourteen snapper.

'Knowing how to anchor your boat is also important. The current moves the boat, and if you anchor it right, it will sit in the right place and you will catch fish.

'My grandfather and grandmother had close connections with Kaiaua, so when a storm hit here at Ōkahu we would go down in our waka and pick kaimoana off the beach at Kaiaua. Mostly green-lipped mussels would wash up onto the beach in the storm, but also a lot of kina and scallops. They were so plentiful that we weren't taking from anyone. They would have just rotted otherwise.

Top: Tamaiti Tamaariki grew up in the village (kāinga) located on the flats behind Ōkahu Bay, shown here.

Bottom left: As a child, Tamaiti dived with his father on the reef next to the Rangitoto light.

Bottom right: Tamaiti is passing down the in-depth knowledge of the marine environment (mātauranga Māori), which he learnt from his father, to his children and grandchildren. He is shown here, on the left, laying mussels in Ōkahu Bay. (Charlotte Graham)

'Up until the 1980s, kaimoana was still plentiful along the coast from the Tāmaki Yacht Club right around to Point England [in the Tāmaki River]. Things are different now. Although the flounder still spawn in the bay there are fewer to target. Other marine species have also declined. We very rarely see sharks in here now. It was about 30 years ago now when someone dived in to save a guy who panicked because of a shark.'

Tamaiti is passing his knowledge on to the following generations. 'My youngest grandchild Logan just wants to talk. He calls out to me to sit down, he turns the TV off, and we sit in the darkness and talk. I really treasure that. Logan and my other grandson Jackson talk about going out with Tangaroa. He's a person, somebody they know, trust and respect. It comes through in their conversations. If you didn't know what they were talking about you would think that Tangaroa was one of their mates.'

S. Parkinson del.

View of an Arched Rock, on the Coast of New Zealand; with an Hippa, o

Plate XXIV.

J. Newton sculp
lace of Retreat, on the Top of it.

Chapter 3
Rediscovery and exploration

Cook's arrival

It was a stormy spring morning on 3 November 1769 when a group of seafarers from the other side of the globe rediscovered the Hauraki Gulf. Battling the elements as it was close-hauled into the teeth of a north-easterly gale, the barque HMS *Endeavour*, captained by Yorkshireman James Cook, slowly edged northwards along the eastern coast of the Coromandel Peninsula. By breakfast time a cluster of small islands and rocks, known by Hauraki Māori as Rua-mahua (thrust up from the depths), came into view on the starboard side of the vessel.

Cook was particularly impressed by the way the narrow perpendicular rocks pointed skywards like needles. 'The most of them are barren rocks, and of these there is a very great Variety, some of them are of as small a Compass as the Monument of London, and Spire up to a much greater height.'[1] He whimsically named the island group the Court of Aldermen, referring to elected councillors in England. He had named the large island to the south, where the *Endeavour* had sheltered the previous night, the Mayor.[2]

As they sailed past the rocks, botanist Joseph Banks, who had accompanied Cook on the voyage, entertained himself and his companions 'with giving names to each of them from their resemblance, thick and squat or lank and tall, to someone or other of those respectable citizens'.[3]

Around 1 pm, the *Endeavour* neared the southern end of Te Whanganui-o-Hei, which Cook later called Mercury Bay on account of the observations of the planet Mercury he made from there. It was here that the explorers made their first contact with the Hauraki Gulf peoples, probably members of Ngāti Hei. It was not a very positive start, as Banks describes in his journal:

About dinner time 3 Canoes came alongside of much the most simple construction of any we have seen, being no more than the trunks of trees hollowed out by fire without the least carving or even the addition of a washboard on their gunnels; the people in them were almost naked and blacker than any we had seen only 21 in all, yet these few despicable gentry sang their song of defiance and promisd us as heartily as the most

Engraving of an arched rock near Whitianga supporting a small pā, 1784. The *Endeavour* can be seen on the far right. The arch was later lost to erosion. (Sydney Parkinson, Ref: PUBL-0037-24, Alexander Turnbull Library, Wellington, New Zealand)

Captain James Cook's voyage to New Zealand

Captain James Cook was just 40 years old when he took command of the *Endeavour*. He had come from humble beginnings, his father being a farm labourer, but had quickly risen through the ranks by sheer talent. He proved to be one of the most skilled navigators and cartographers of all time.

The *Endeavour* was a former coal carrier from Whitby, a maritime town on the north-east coast of England. Being 32 metres long and close to 9 metres wide, she was strongly built with a square stern, deep hold and flat long keel. Barque-rigged with three masts, square sails hoisted on the front two and a mizzen sail set on the sternmost mast, her maximum speed was around 8 knots, slower than the double-hulled waka which had preceded her. The ship was crewed by 85 men and boys, mostly in their twenties. In addition, wealthy botanist John Banks, who was 25 years of age, joined the vessel, as did Swedish botanist Daniel Solander. The scientists brought with them an entourage of assistants and servants, so that when the ship left port there were 94 people on board.[4]

Cook's instructions from the Admiralty were to sail to Tahiti, an island only just rediscovered by a British ship, the *Dolphin*, in 1767, to observe the transit of Venus. He was ordered to then sail secretly to the south, in order to chart the coastline of the great 'Unknown Southern Continent' which was thought to exist at that time. If he failed to find it, Cook was directed to explore the eastern side of the southern land discovered by Tasman 127 years earlier, which had been identified on Dutch charts as Nieuw Zeeland.[5]

During his voyage to New Zealand, Cook had on board a highly skilled Polynesian navigator, Tupaia, who had joined the ship in Ra'iātea, one of the Society Islands. On 9 August 1769 the *Endeavour* left Ra'iātea and headed south into unknown waters.

After almost two months at sea, the explorers knew that land must be close. They started to encounter fresh clumps of seaweed and barnacle-encrusted branches floating in the sea. They also sighted seals, which they knew did not travel far from land, and then land birds in the sky.[6] On 6 October land was finally sighted — a promontory close to Gisborne which local Māori called Te Ūpotio -o-te-kurī-a-Pāoa and Cook named Young Nicks

Head, after the young boy on the ship who first sighted it. After exploring the Poverty Bay and East Cape area, the *Endeavour* sailed up the east coast of the North Island towards the Hauraki Gulf, looking for a safe harbour from which to observe the transit of Mercury.

Left: Portrait of Captain James Cook, 1728–1779. (Ref: 4-1348, Sir George Grey Special Collections, Auckland Libraries)

Bottom: Dimensional sketch of HMS *Endeavour*, 1923. (Francis Bayldon, Ref B-011-022, Alexander Turnbull Library, Wellington, New Zealand)

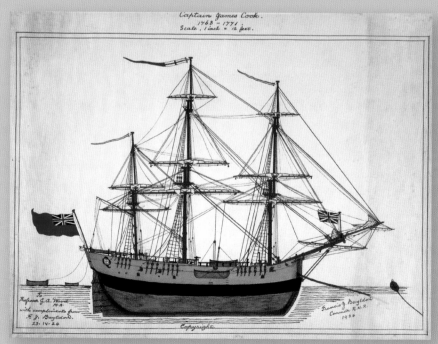

*respectable of their countrymen that they would kill us
all. They remain some time out of stone's throw but at
last ventured close to the ship; one of our people gave them
a rope from the side to save them the trouble of Padling,
this they accepted and rewarded the man who gave it
by thrusting at him with a pike which however took
no effect; they then went a few yards from the ship and
threw a lance into her which struck nobody; a musket was
fird over them on which they all went off.*[7]

At 7.30 pm the *Endeavour* anchored near the entrance of
Whitianga Harbour for the night. As the large ship entered
the bay, it was watched with amazement by members of
a Ngāti Whanaunga group, who were visiting the area to
harvest seafood.

Cook was keen to find a safe anchorage, close to a suitable
place on land from which to observe the transit of Mercury,
due to occur on 9 November. So next morning he took out
one of the ship's tenders to take depth soundings and explore
the bay. He found what he was looking for off what is now
called Cooks Beach. Here the ship could tuck in behind
a hilly bluff, which would provide some shelter from the
north-easterly winds that blew straight into Mercury Bay.
The anchorage was directly in front of a beautiful white sandy
beach which would provide an easy place to land and was
close to the Pūrangi River, which would enable replenishment
of the ship's freshwater stores.

During the transit, Cook knew that Mercury would
be visible as a small black dot moving across the face of
the sun. By recording the times that the planet touched
the sun's outside edges during its passage, Cook hoped
that it would be possible to calculate the longitude of his
position and consequently determine the precise location of
New Zealand.

Once safely anchored off Cooks Beach, Cook was keen
to supplement the ship's hard rations with fresh food. So
next morning a small party rowed to the mouth of the
Pūrangi River and deployed a small seine net, but they
managed to catch only a few mullet. They had more success
shooting birds 'of which there were great numbers to land
on the other side'. Banks described them as being black,
with red bills and feet, so they were almost certainly variable
oystercatchers, although the birds actually have pink feet.[8]
Fortunately, Cook had by now managed to establish friendly
relations with the local residents. He was assisted by his
onboard guide Tupaia, who was able to communicate with

them in Tahitian, a language similar to Māori. The locals
were far more proficient at harvesting seafood than Cook's
men and provided enough small cockles, clams and mussels
for all on board the *Endeavour*, indicating that the shellfish
were 'found in great plenty upon the Sand Banks of the
[Pūrangi] River'. When walking on shore, Banks observed
'vast heaps of shells often many wagon loads together, some
appearing to be very old',[9] which suggested that the area had
been used for prolific shellfish gathering for many years.

Dr Solander observed the local harvesting of crayfish
where 'they walkd among the rocks at low water about
middle deep in water and still felt about with their feet till
they felt one, on which they dived down and constantly
brought him up'. According to Banks, they were 'the largest
and best I have ever eat'.[10] As Cook was readying for the
crucial observation of the transit of Mercury on 9 November,
local fishermen were supplying the ship with large quantities
of mackerel, probably caught in one of their enormous seine
nets. The volume of fish was so great that 'by 8 O'clock the
ship had more fish on board than all hands could eat in 2 or
3 days, and before night so many that every mess who could
raise salt corned as many as will last them this month or
more'.[11] When the day of the 9th finally dawned, Cook was
relieved to see that the sky was clear with no clouds to impede
their view of the sun. Cook headed ashore, with astronomer
Charles Green and his assistant Zachary Hicks, to undertake
the crucial celestial observations. But although Green
managed to record the transit, their efforts ultimately proved
in vain. The observations were not accurate enough to be of
practical use and Cook did not record any longitude derived
from them.[12]

Cook's party later explored the head of the Whitianga
Harbour in their small boats and found it prolific with
mangroves, shellfish, birds and fish:

*'It here branched into several Channels, and form'd a
Number of very low flat Islands, all cover'd with a sort
of Mangrove Trees, and several places of the Shores of
both sides of the River were Cover'd with the same sort of
wood. The sand banks were well stored with Cockles and
Clams, and in many places were Rock Oysters. Here is
likewise pretty plenty of Wild Fowl, such as Shags, Ducks,
Curlews, and a Black bird, about as big as a Crow, with
a long, sharp bill of a Colour between Red and Yellow
[variable oystercatcher]; we also saw fish in the River, but
of what sort I know not.*'[13]

Cook found a secure anchorage for the *Endeavour* at the southern end of Cooks Beach, where a steep bluff provided shelter and fresh water was available from the Pūrangi River, shown here. His crew found copious amounts of dredge oysters in the river and thus Cook named it 'Oyster River'. (davidwallphoto.com)

The Aldermen Islands were the first part of the Hauraki Gulf region rediscovered by Europeans in November 1769. Captain James Cook named them after elected councillors in England. (Lloyd Homer, GNS Science)

Cook named the harbour River of Mangroves 'because of the great quantity of these Trees that are found in it'.[14] He saw small lumps of kauri gum on the beach and then sticking to the mangroves themselves, leading him to erroneously conclude that the gum was exuded directly from the plants.[15]

Although Cook's men had not experienced great success at fishing, they did eventually manage to harvest significant quantities of oysters, probably of the Bluff oyster species (*Ostrea chilensis*) which grow unattached on soft sediment, which they found on a sandbank in the Pūrangi River. Cook remarked on the 'immense quantity of Oysters and other small Shell fish' there, with the long boat returning from the estuary 'loaded as deep as she could swim with Oysters'. For this reason Cook named the waterway Oyster River.[16]

On first arriving in Mercury Bay, Cook had observed Whare-taewa, a large fortified Ngāti Hei village on the north side of the bay south of Simpsons Beach (Wharekaho). The residents eventually showed Cook's party through the area and they saw 'vast heaps of Dryd fish' and piles of fern root within the palisades. There were also numerous houses outside the pā defences and large fishing nets. Other small hamlets were located on a series of rocky islets extending out from the peninsula. One was on the top of a spectacular natural rocky archway, which was reproduced by the ship's artist Sydney Parkinson. Unfortunately this impressive landmark has since been lost to erosion.[17] Before leaving the bay, Cook carved

the ship's name and date on a tree. After displaying the English Colours, he took formal possession of the place in the name of His Majesty the King of England. Cook also left behind, as a gift, two handfuls of seed potatoes which local Māori planted. They found the potato (also originating from South America like the kūmara) to be an easily grown and nutritious crop which stored well, being much superior to the kūmara in these respects. After three years, the potato harvest had increased sufficiently to enable the wide distribution of seed potatoes throughout the Waikato and Hauraki tribes.[18]

After a stay of twelve days, the *Endeavour* sailed out of Mercury Bay under a light westerly breeze. As night fell, the ship tacked out to the eastern coast of Great Barrier Island which Cook named the Barrier Isles, then back across to Waikawau Bay. By Saturday morning the wind had dropped and backed to a gentle southerly, allowing the *Endeavour* to head directly for the tip of the Coromandel Peninsula. At around 6.00 am the vessel passed a large open bay, which Cook named Port Charles, and an hour later it was abreast Moehau. As Cook neared the northernmost point of the Coromandel Peninsula, he obtained his first glimpse of the large embayment on the other side, forming the heart of the Hauraki Gulf:

From this point [Cape Colville] the Land trends W. ½ S. near one league [3 nautical miles], then S.S.E. as far

Te Horetā Te Taniwha

Ngāti Whanaunga leader Te Horetā was a key figure in early Māori–Pākehā interactions in the Hauraki Gulf. He was a 12-year-old boy when Cook first arrived in Mercury Bay in 1769 and later recalled his elders referring to the ship as an atua (god) and the people on board as tupua (strange people or goblins). He and his family watched in awe as the boat anchored and the crew lowered a small boat into the water and started to row ashore. Because the rowers faced backwards to the direction they were heading, Te Taniwha's people thought that they must be some strange kind of goblin that had eyes in the back of their heads.[19]

Te Taniwha later went on board the strange ship with some trepidation, but was surprised by the captain's kindness. Cook had smiled at him, had patted him on the head and had given him an iron nail as a present. He kept the nail for years and it became one of his most prized possessions.[20]

As an adult, Te Taniwha was on board Captain Downie's ship the *Coromandel* in 1820 when it headed from the Bay of Islands to the Firth of Thames in search of spars. He helped Downie locate a good stand of accessible kauri near his main settlement at Waiau (Coromandel Harbour).

During the late 1830s, Te Taniwha was a patron of American trader William Webster, allowing him to set up a trading station on Whanganui Island on the outskirts of the Coromandel Harbour. Te Taniwha signed the Treaty of Waitangi on 4 May 1840.

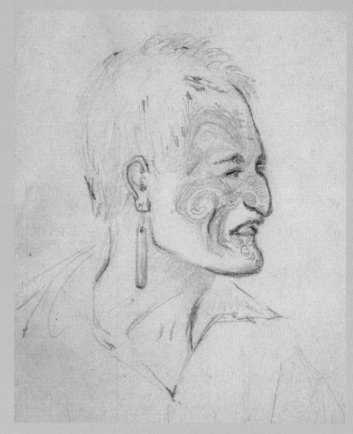

Portrait of Te Horetā Te Taniwha, c. 1850. (Charles Heaphy, Ref: A-147-001, Alexander Turnbull Library, Wellington, New Zealand)

It was on Te Taniwha's land at Coromandel that gold was discovered in 1852, the first to be found in New Zealand. An old man by this time, he agreed to allow the miners onto his land. He died a year later, on 21 November 1853, at Coromandel.[21]

---

as we could see. Besides the Islands laying without us we could see land round by the S.W. as far as N.W., but whether this was the Main or Islands was not possible for us at this Time to determine, the fear of loosing the Main land determin'd me to follow its direction. With this view we hauld round the point [Cape Colville] and Steer'd to the Southward . . .[22]

By this time the wind had all but disappeared and the *Endeavour* lay becalmed off the tip of the peninsula, inside Channel Island. Cook later decided to call the promontory Cape Colville in honour of Rear Admiral Lord Colville whom Cook had served under in Newfoundland. The channel to the north now also bears Colville's name.[23] By early afternoon an easterly breeze had developed and the

Endeavour sailed down the western coast of the Coromandel Peninsula, eventually anchoring in the vicinity of Te Puru. The next day at first daylight, Cook set out with Banks, Solander and Tupaia in two small boats to explore the coast. They rowed south for about 9 nautical miles, until they reached the head of the firth. The flood of the incoming tide then helped carry them up the Waihou River (the newly formed waters).[24] Cook renamed the river Thames 'on account of its bearing some resemblance to that River in England'. The riverbanks were heavily populated and Cook's party visited the large Ngāti Whanaunga settlement of Oruarangi at the mouth of the Matatoki Stream.[25] The inhabitants warmly welcomed the explorers, having already heard of the *Endeavour*'s arrival in the area from their kinfolk who had returned from visiting Mercury Bay.

After travelling almost to the mouth of the Hikutaia Stream, around 19 kilometres upriver, the explorers turned back to catch the ebbing tide.[26] Cook was particularly impressed by the rich kahikatea forest which bordered the river and also noted the numerous fishing poles:

About the Entrance of the narrow part of the River the land is mostly cover'd with Mangroves and other Shrubs, but farther in are immense woods of as stout lofty timber as is to be found perhaps in any other part of the world. In many places the woods grow close upon the very banks of the River, but where it does not the land is Marshey such as we find about the Thames in England. We saw poles stuck up in many places in the River to set nets for Catching of fish; from this we imagin'd that there must be plenty of fish, but of what sort we know not for we saw none.[27]

Cook planned to leave the next day on an outgoing tide, but the wind was too strong and he could not raise the anchor. For the next few days the wind blew into the firth, and as the *Endeavour* was unable to sail into the wind, the only way progress could be made was to use the tidal flow to gradually carry the boat out into open water. So when the tide ebbed, the anchors were hauled up to allow the ship to float with the tide, and when the tide turned, the anchors were dropped again. Whilst stranded in the firth, Cook decided to explore land to the west 'but found there neither inhabitants or anything else worthy of Note'.[28]

Cook explored much of the coast of the Hauraki Gulf in small boats, which could be rowed or sailed, possibly similar to the one shown here near Waiheke Island in 1849. (Charles Heaphy, Ref: PD56(87), Auckland War Memorial Museum Tāmaki Paenga Hira)

It was not until Thursday, 23 November that Cook finally got under way. The wind was now blowing strongly from the south-west, which enabled the *Endeavour* to sail north. Strong squalls were coming off the mainland, so Cook could not sail close inshore and as a result he did not venture into the Tāmaki Strait. He 'had but a slight and distant View of the Coast and was not able to distinguish wether the points we saw were parts of the Main or Islands laying before it, for we never once lost sight of the Main Land.'[29] Cook noted the likelihood of good harbours in the vicinity of Coromandel and amongst the islands on the west side of the firth (Pōnui and Waiheke), although he was not able to see them for himself.

The *Endeavour* sailed past Little Barrier Island to the east, which Cook noted as 'a very high Island', and a rocky headland to the west which he named Point Rodney after Admiral Sir George Bridges Rodney who was a celebrated British mariner at that time.[30] He could now see several small islands to the north, which he named the Hen and Chicken Islands. The *Endeavour* anchored close to the islands, in a place Cook named Bream Bay, on account of catching between 90 and 100 snapper (which looked

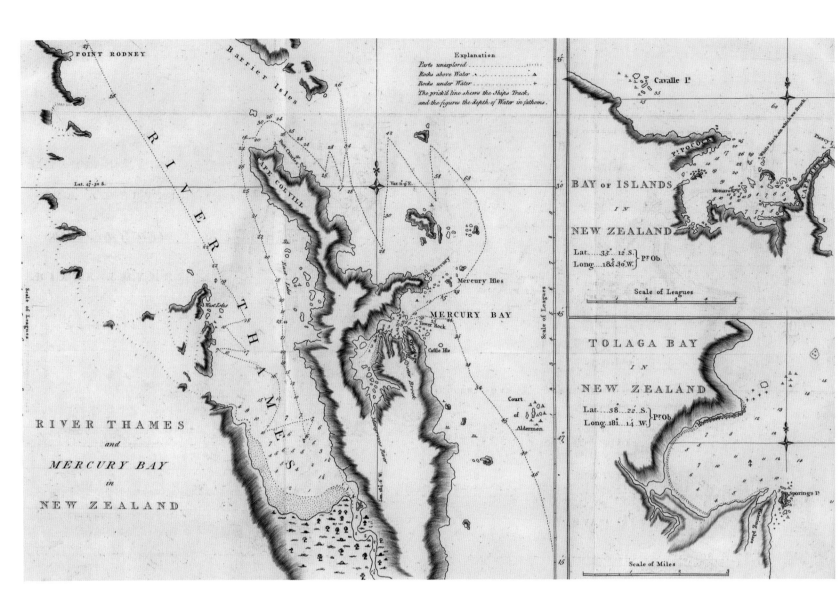

This chart of the Coromandel Peninsula and Firth of Thames, drawn by Cook in 1769–70, shows the course followed by the *Endeavour* and the names that Cook assigned to various places. Due to the adverse wind direction, Cook did not manage to reach the inner Hauraki Gulf. (David Rumsey Map Collection)

similar to the English bream) soon after anchoring.

Although Cook revisited New Zealand on two subsequent voyages, he never did return to the Hauraki Gulf. But his reports of rich kahikatea forests surrounding the Waihou River eventually attracted other European vessels to the area. They were initially traders, in search of marketable trees which could be sold for a profit as ships' spars.

Spar ships

The *Fancy*, commanded by Captain Edgar Dell, reached the Firth of Thames on 12 December 1794. It was likely to have been the first European arrival after Cook. The ship quickly headed up the Waihou River, seeking out the trees which Cook had so enthusiastically described. But before long the vessel had grounded in mud off the north end of Tuitahi Island. The crew eventually managed to refloat the ship and then slowly kedged it up the river, repeatedly rowing out its anchor, dropping it, and then pulling the ship forward on the anchor rope.

Finally the *Fancy* anchored upstream of the Matatoki River, in a place where the large kahikatea trees crowded around the water. The area was still heavily populated, with Dell sighting a large number of canoes and up to 2000 people on shore.[31]

With help from local Māori, the crew set about cutting down the enormous trees. After spending three months up the river, they had managed to cut 213 spars. They also

Captain James Downie's 1820–21 chart of the Hauraki Gulf shows the coast he explored in HMS *Coromandel*. He charted for the first time details of the Coromandel Harbour, Tāmaki Strait and the inner Hauraki Gulf islands. (Ref: MapColl-832.15aj/ [1820]/Acc.1159, Alexander Turnbull Library, Wellington, New Zealand)

replaced most of the *Fancy*'s rigging with flax-fibre rope, as there were 'some thousand acres of the flax plant growing in a very luxuriant manner'. Dell was impressed by the prolific life within the river, writing that it 'abounds in salmon, flounders, bream, soles, and many other fish; also great quantities of crabs, clams, etc'.[32]

Five years later, in 1799, the trading ship *Hunter* arrived in the Waihou River, also looking for kahikatea spars. The vessel was owned by an Australian ex-convict entrepreneur and had earlier been a Spanish war prize. While stationed in the river, four crewmen deserted ship. One of them, named Taylor, was still living in the area when another trading ship, the *Royal Admiral* captained by William Wilson, visited in 1801.[33] Taylor is the first recorded European settler in the Hauraki Gulf.

It soon became apparent that kahikatea was totally unsuitable for ships' spars, as the wood readily rotted. So

trading interest turned to the much more durable kauri. As a result, the geographical focus of European interest in the Hauraki Gulf shifted away from the kahikatea wetlands of the Waihou River and towards the kauri forests of the Coromandel Ranges and western coast.

The superior qualities of kauri soon engaged the interest of the British Royal Navy, which was actively searching for suitable spars with which to rig its warships. In 1819 the HMS *Coromandel*, under the command of Captain James Downie, sailed from England to New South Wales transporting convicts. After discharging her human cargo, the vessel was refitted in order to carry timber. Downie then sailed to New Zealand with the purpose of collecting spars in the Firth of Thames. The *Coromandel* first called in at the Bay of Islands where the captain made the acquaintance of Anglican cleric Samuel Marsden. Marsden had briefly visited the Firth of Thames five years earlier and therefore had some

In 1820, Ngāti Whātua chief Āpihai Te Kawau gave the British sailors from the *Coromandel* permission to take kauri trees from around the Waitematā Harbour. He is shown here in an 1842 portrait. (Joseph Merrett, Ref: PUBL-0076-174, Alexander Turnbull Library, Wellington, New Zealand)

and immediately encountered strong headwinds. After beating down the coast for several days, the ship finally arrived off Cape Colville on 12 June. When Marsden subsequently went ashore in search of large kauri trees, he was shocked by what he found. The houses in the area had all been burnt or destroyed and there was no one to be seen. Marsden recorded in his journal that Tuhi, a Māori who was on board, pointed out a beach which 'he said was covered in dead bodies like a butcher's shop only a few months before'. An entire tribe had been cut off and killed with only two or three people managing to escape.[34] Marsden found no suitable trees, so they returned back on board.

Early the next morning the *Coromandel* sailed south through heavy seas and eventually anchored at the head of the Firth of Thames, off Tararu. But the area provided little shelter and the ship pitched and tossed about in the short, sharp waves. When the weather finally moderated, Marsden set out in search of local residents who could advise on where suitable spar timber might be located.[35] Instead of the flourishing settlements of only a few years earlier, Marsden found a people under siege. Their houses and crops had been destroyed by Ngāti Paoa warriors, who had obtained guns from their Northland Ngā Puhi allies.[36]

knowledge of the area. He was also well respected among Māori. So Downie invited him to join the expedition. Ngāti Whanaunga leader Te Horetā was also on board.

The *Coromandel* left the Bay of Islands on 7 June 1820

Te Horetā advised that fine timber called kauri grew further north, on the east side of the saltwater river. So Downie weighed anchor and headed back up the firth, looking

Origin of the place name Coromandel

Coromandel Harbour was named after the visit of the HMS *Coromandel* to the harbour in June 1820. The entire peninsula now also bears the vessel's name. The name itself originates from India, where the *Coromandel* was originally built, and refers to the Indian south-eastern coast.

Coromandel Harbour c. 1852. (Charles Heaphy, Ref: B-043-023, Alexander Turnbull Library, Wellington, New Zealand)

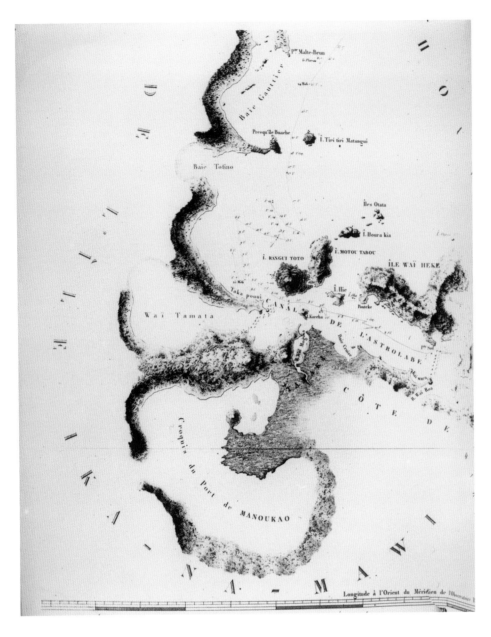

Frenchman Captain Dumont D'Urville produced the first nautical chart of the Waitematā Harbour in 1827, but only a smattering of the place names that he used have survived until today. (Ref: 4-179D, Sir George Grey Special Collections, Auckland Libraries)

for a more secure anchorage close to where good timber might be found. He located 'a most excellent harbour . . . behind two small islands on the east side of the Thames', a place long known by Hauraki Māori as Wai-au or 'swirling current' and nowadays called Coromandel Harbour after Downie's ship. Finally the ship had a secure and sheltered anchorage, providing protection from the gulf's stormy winter weather.

Now safely anchored, the ship's crew managed to locate a good stand of kauri about 17 miles south and they established a camp there as a base for the tree-cutting work.[37]

While the ship's crew were cutting spars, Marsden spent his time exploring the surrounding region. On 25 July he entered the Waiheke Channel on the ship's small sailing launch, anchoring off one of the islands overnight. A Māori companion who was on board indicated that there

were some fine spars to be had up the Waitematā. So the following day they sailed along the Tāmaki Strait, under a 'strong fair breeze', and into the Waitematā Harbour which Marsden described as 'a large river, in some places five or six miles wide, with a sufficient depth of water for large ships'. Although they found 'some very fine spars' they were 'not long enough for first-rate men-of-war'.[38]

Early the next morning, Marsden's party heard musket shots and were then met by a canoe full of warriors, including Ngāti Paoa chief Te Hinaki from Mokoia (Panmure) and Ngāti Whatua chief Āpihai Te Kawau from Kaipara. Te Kawau advised that the land around the Waitematā Harbour belonged to him but that he was willing to allow the British to take the trees.[39]

Marsden later visited Mokoia and observed that it was

Captain Dumont D'Urville

In 1827, 58 years after Cook's visit, Captain Dumont D'Urville led the second exploration voyage to the Hauraki Gulf in the *Astrolabe*. D'Urville had visited New Zealand three years earlier, as second in command of the same vessel, but had only stopped at the Bay of Islands. One of the main purposes of D'Urville's second voyage to New Zealand was to complete Cook's charting of the coast.

D'Urville came from a French aristocratic family and he was somewhat dismissive of the working-class Englishman's cartographic efforts. In addition, unlike Cook, he was a scientist of some note with expertise in botany and linguistics.[40]

Top: Prior to reaching the Hauraki Gulf, D'Urville was caught in a furious storm off the Bay of Plenty, depicted here in this 1833 lithograph. This may partly explain why he was so enamoured of the Tāmaki Strait where his ship was sheltered by land extending in all directions. (Joseph Lemercier, Louis Auguste de Sainson and Fèlix-Achille Saint-Aulaire, Ref: 2009/3/6, Auckland Art Gallery Toi o Tāmaki)

D'Urville was the second European explorer to visit the Gulf and he extensively charted the region. (A Maurin, Ref: 4-1349, Sir George Grey Special Collections, Auckland Libraries) 'a very populous settlement, and contains the finest race of people I have seen in New Zealand, and very healthy. Their houses are superior to most I have met with. Their stores were full of potatoes, containing some thousands of baskets, and they have some very fine hogs. The soil is uncommonly rich and easily cultivated.'[41]

Ships looking for spars continued to visit the Hauraki Gulf. These included, in December 1825, the *St Patrick* captained by Peter Dillon. Dillon's extensive trips up the Firth of Thames and Tāmaki Strait impressed on him the rich resources of the area, including the fertile volcanic soils, and he became one of the earliest advocates for the establishment of a European settlement in the Tāmaki area.[42]

D'Urville's visit

Charting of the western side of the Hauraki Gulf was only progressed in 1827, when Captain Dumont D'Urville visited the area in his 29-metre-long corvette *Astrolabe*. By this time the gulf had been significantly depopulated due to warfare.

D'Urville first visited Golden Bay and he charted that area, leaving names such as D'Urville Island and French Pass. After sailing through Cook Strait, D'Urville headed northwards up the coast. He eventually sighted Great Barrier Island on 20 February, and on passing its northern tip observed that 'the island is terminated by a peninsula, without vegetation, of a brownish colour, and the flanks of which, battered by the sea, have something of a lugubrious though imposing appearance. It is also accompanied by some pointed rocks of singular shape, some of which are very slender on top'.[43] He named the area Pointe des Aiguilles; *aiguille* is French for needle. Today, it is still called Aiguilles Island.

When the *Astrolabe* sailed past Great Barrier Island, the inner Hauraki Gulf came into view for the first time and D'Urville was impressed by what he saw:

As soon as we had passed the Pointe Aiguilles, we discovered successively the numerous islands dispersed at the entrance to the Bay of Shouraki [Hauraki], a view which produced a most picturesque and animated scene. Here the work of Cook was again found to be very unexact, and a new exploration became indispensable.[44]

Although D'Urville was keen to explore the gulf, the weather was against him. The wind was blowing from the north-west and initially he flattened his sails, hoping to tack into the embayment. But then a large squall hit from the south-west and he was forced to sail away from the coast. He carried on to the north and eventually reached Whangarei Heads.

As a linguist, D'Urville had not been enamoured of Cook's approach to naming places on his charts, which often ignored the local Māori names and replaced them with English ones. With some delight, D'Urville relates his experience of discussing place names with Ngā Puhi chief Te Rangui, whilst anchored at Whangarei:

At my request he [Te Rangui] gave me, with intelligence and complaisance, the names, in the language of the country, of the adjacent lands and islands, which I have, as usual, substituted for those of Cook.

On these coasts, occupied by a people endowed with so much sagacity, and who have left not an islet, a rock, a corner of the land without a name, it seems odd to a navigator to see no one but English names, often applied without taste . . . Without doubt it is a sacred duty on the part of the navigator to respect the names given by the first discoverer of uninhabited places; but everywhere else, I think that those of the indigenous people should prevail so soon as they are known. A time will come when these names will be the only vestiges of the language spoken by the primitive inhabitants.

The *Astrolabe* left Whangarei Heads on 23 February under a brisk northerly breeze. When darkness fell, the ship hove to in calm waters, between Little Barrier Island and Cape Rodney. As daylight broke, D'Urville discovered that a current had carried the ship towards Cape Colville, so he headed back towards the western coastline 'for my intention was to enter amongst the islands to the west that Cook had only noticed hastily and in a very vague manner, so much was I desirous to complete the work of that great navigator'.[45]

During that morning the *Astrolabe* sailed past the Tāwharanui Peninsula, and then 'a deep bay, which contains many islets, bays and channels' (Kawau Bay) which D'Urville named Baie Gautier on his expedition's new chart of the area. At around 2.00 pm the ship passed between Tiritiri Matangi Island on the port and the Whangaparāoa Peninsula on the starboard, bringing the inner Hauraki Gulf into view. D'Urville described what he saw:

The first place D'Urville anchored in the Hauraki Gulf was off Gull Point (Toroa), to the south of Long Bay, Auckland. Within minutes, his crew was able to catch large quantities of snapper for dinner.

This splendid basin extends from ten to twelve miles in every direction. It has a chain of well wooded islands of moderate height along its S.E. shore; on the W. stretches an unbroken coastline of perpendicular cliffs, mournful and sterile; on the N.N.W. a wide channel [Weiti River] seemed to run up into the land; but I preferred to direct my researches towards another opening in the south [Waitematā Harbour], which according to my calculations, should bring me nearer to the opposite coast of New Zealand and reduce the width of Ika-na-Mawi [North Island] to a very short distance at this point. I was even almost inclined to think that there might be a channel here, dividing the land into two islands.[46]

He did not see any trace of inhabitants and only noticed one or two fires a long way off in the interior. The wind faded as evening came on and the *Astrolabe* dropped anchor off Gull Point (Toroa) to the south of Long Bay. D'Urville reported that 'within minutes the crew caught with their lines an enormous number of splendid fish which were most delicious to eat'. These were almost certainly snapper.[47]

The ship was under way again by 5.00 am the next day, but light headwinds saw the crew tacking in order to reach the Waitematā Harbour. Eager to see the harbour for himself as soon as possible, D'Urville leapt into a whaleboat to begin exploring, leaving the other officers to undertake the painstaking process of tacking the *Astrolabe* into the bay.

As D'Urville looked out from the Rangitoto Channel, he could see 'a magnificent inner basin that showed a regular depth of six to eight fathoms of water and soon branched off into two channels; one stretched away towards the east and we were not able to see the farther end of it [Tāmaki Strait]; the other, which ran to the west, seemed to be bounded by land two or three leagues farther on [Waitematā Harbour]'.

The party landed on the shores of what is now Devonport and walked up Mount Victoria. D'Urville wrote of the surrounding landscape: 'Although it was well covered with plenty of herbaceous plants, there were no trees growing here, only bushes.' There were also very few birds and they were barely able to shoot a couple of shore species. They crossed to Ōrākei, on the other side of the harbour, but found only a deserted village.

Meanwhile, the crew had successfully tacked the *Astrolabe* down towards the Rangitoto Channel, helped by an incoming tide, and the ship now lay off Takapuna. Rejoining the ship, D'Urville decided to sail towards the Tāmaki Strait. He became concerned when the depth suddenly dropped to less than seven metres and the ship became surrounded by reefs on the southern coast (the Bastion Reefs), but he then relaxed as the depth steadily increased again. The ship was encircled by land on every side and the view was stunning. D'Urville

slowly along the coast of Waiheke Island and then up through the Waiheke Channel and past Shag Island (Tarakihi) where swarms of cormorants sat on the rocks. D'Urville was captivated by what he saw:

> ... *the wind grew stronger in the west and we sailed rapidly through unknown channels, whose shores were adorned with smiling vegetation and where we enjoyed charming views every moment. So we sailed among islands for about two hours; some were lofty and mountainous, covered with magnificent forests, others lower and only covered with more ordinary vegetation ... I regretted leaving these beautiful spots without being able to explore them more carefully and without taking a further selection of all their natural products. But time urged me on and other tasks called us away from these shores.*[49]

D'Urville was so taken by the beauty of the place that he decided to bestow the name of his ship 'on the lovely channel that we had just sailed through from one end to the other and had explored so successfully'. He called the Tāmaki Strait 'Canal de L'Astrolabe' and thought it 'one of the finest anchorages in the world to ships of any size'.[50]

Although D'Urville was keen to explore the southern Firth of Thames area, this proved not to be achievable when the wind veered to the south. At times the wind disappeared altogether and the crew filled in their time fishing, while the ship lay becalmed. D'Urville was particularly impressed by the abundance of fish:

> *Whenever we are becalmed, the crew immediately catch with their lines an amazing quantity of splendid fish, belonging to the dorado group, which are delicious food. It is the fish that Cook called seabream [snapper]; it seems to be extraordinarily abundant in these waters. While we were anchored in the mouth of the river Magoia [Tāmaki River], the Tāmaki natives filled their canoes in a few hours. Today the crew had soon caught hundreds of them and they had enough for each mess to be able to salt down a good stock.*[51]

On 3 March, after a visit of nine days, the *Astrolabe* sailed out of the Hauraki Gulf. D'Urville's legacy in the gulf includes a smattering of place names that have survived and the first nautical chart of the Waitematā Harbour.

decided to anchor in sheltered waters between the islands of Motukorea (island of the oystercatcher or tōrea) and Motuihe where 'it was delightfully calm and I could at last enjoy a perfect night's rest'.[48]

The next day D'Urville was keen to continue his explorations of the area, but the weather would not cooperate. It was a beautiful day and at daybreak there was a light south-westerly wind. But soon the wind failed altogether. As the *Astrolabe* sat becalmed in the Tāmaki Strait, three canoes approached from the southern shore. Chief Rangi-hua and his brother Tawhiti came on board. They explained that their people were being ravaged by the northern tribes who came each year with firearms to raid their territory.

As they sat gently drifting in the sun, D'Urville asked the two men about the names of the places they could see around them. They identified Rangitoto, Takapuna, Waitematā, Wai Makoia [Tāmaki River] and the Wairoa River. D'Urville put these names on his chart. The Māori men made it clear that the Waitematā did not reach the western coast as D'Urville had thought, but that by following the Tāmaki River, a place could be reached which was only a short distance from the banks of the Manukau Harbour. D'Urville's men went to check this out. Later in the day, other canoes came alongside and delivered an enormous quantity of fish, most likely snapper.

At daybreak the *Astrolabe* was under way again, sailing

Story of the Gulf | **Joe Davis**

KAUMĀTUA, NGĀTI HEI, WHAREKAHO[52]

In 1998, Joe Davies returned to his tribal land at Wharekaho with his partner and three children. 'This was to maintain my ahi kā [rights to the land], to keep my fire burning. I returned under the mana of my grandfather who was a tuakana [surviving oldest born] and whose responsibilities passed on to my father and then on to me.'

Raised in Auckland and the Bay of Islands and a mechanical engineer by trade, Joe has dedicated the past seventeen years of his life to rebuilding the resource base, mana and kaitiaki role of Ngāti Hei. 'Some of us have turned our backs on flash city lives and jobs that we were trained to do. We have gone home to take up the burden of kaitiaki in our respective rohe [territory].'

Ngāti Hei is one of the ancient tribes of Hauraki. Its founding goes back to Hei, who is said to have been the uncle of Tama-te-kapua, commander of *Te Arawa* canoe. The tribe established itself along the east coast of the Coromandel Peninsula, from Whangapoua in the north to Whangamatā in the south, living for centuries in relative harmony and peace. Ngāti Hei was there to greet Cook and his men when they arrived at Whitianga and they helped to provision the *Endeavour*.

'Thousands of people were living here when Cook came. He was amazed at all the structures over the rocks. They were all claimed. Imagine the impact of the *Endeavour* coming into the bay. It would have been like seeing a UFO landing. They would have thought — is this real or is it some kind of fantastic dream?'

Unlike many of the Hauraki tribes, who retreated in the face of the Ngā Puhi assaults of the 1820s, Ngāti Hei held their ground and as a result were almost totally wiped out. A population of several thousand was reduced to as little as 25 people. Their abandoned lands were subsequently acquired by the Crown through various legislative instruments. The tribal holdings now consist of a property at Wharekaho, where Cook visited in 1769, and Ohinau Island in Mercury Bay which was returned to Ngāti Hei in 1995.

'The sea was very much part of our blood. It was our food basket and the way we travelled. We would gather food seasonally: pāua, crayfish, tītī [muttonbird] and other species of bird. We not only had to maintain the sustainability of those food sources but we guarded them to the point of war. If you went into another rohe or stepped over the mark in terms of where you could gather food you were in serious trouble. So the rohe moana and its sustainability were very important to us.

'We were very in tune with nature. The arrival of the whales would mark the beginning of a new season. Before the establishment of the whaling industry, the whales would have been everywhere. The timing of the calls of certain birds would provide an omen as to whether it would be a good season or would indicate whether it was too dangerous to go out fishing.

'The real pressure on our resources came after Cook visited and after he went back to England and put New Zealand on the map. Then the whalers and shipwrights came down here looking for whales, timber and kauri gum. Māori showed them how to extract kai [food] and that put more pressure on food resources. We started to see depletions about the turn of the century. Markets started to develop and our kaimoana was turned into a commodity.

'The days of picking up crayfish by their feelers, and of harvesting large pāua and kina, are gone. Dad used to catch huge sharks off the wharf and eels from the creek. There are no eels in our creek any more. You don't even see little elvers migrating upstream. We don't go harvesting any more, not even for tītī. I love my muttonbirds but there's not enough for the harvest to be sustainable. We might get the odd feed of pāua, but the pāua are small and are becoming badly depleted. We now have a ban on the customary allocation of pāua and crayfish, as there's not enough out there.

'The pressure is increasing. Whitianga is one of the few towns on the coast that has been growing. People come here, go fishing and stock up huge freezers with fish, crayfish and pāua. It sits in their freezer all year and then next season they dump what's left and start fishing again. I get rung up by the boys at the rubbish dump who say, "Joe, this is shocking — all the seafood being dumped."

'We are now looking to open up Ohinau Island to the public in a commercially sustainable way. We want the island

Top: Joe Davis has observed increasing pressure on marine life due to the growth of Whitianga, including the development of the Whitianga Waterways, shown here.

to be an educational centre and for people to be able to visit in a controlled manner. We want to strengthen the ecology of the island and to share our culture. There are many species of bird which used to be here and could be here. But we are taking our time. When we introduce a certain species we seek to introduce its whole food chain.

'I would love to see lots of restoration projects around here. The forest used to be right down to the shoreline with birds flying from island to island. I would love to see the seabirds coming back to the mainland and to hear the dawn chorus. My dad said that you could hear the snapping of the branches in the forest as the birds all perched on a branch. Then you would hear the thunder of their wings as they flew off in different directions.

'I would love to see our food stores back to sustainable levels and kai everywhere. We need to get back to feeding our people and our people need to come home.'

Joe has returned to his tribal heartland at Wharekaho to rebuild the kaitiaki role of Ngāti Hei. He is shown here in front of the Whare-taewa pā site visited by Captain Cook in 1769.

Part Two:
DEVELOPING THE SHORES

Auckland, looking north-west in 1843–44. (Edward Ashworth, Ref: A-275-008, Alexander Turnbull Library, Wellington, New Zealand)

Chapter 4
Establishment of Auckland

Hobson's arrival

The identification of the site for the first capital of New Zealand, and its naming, was left in the hands of a doughty Irish sailor, Captain William Hobson. On 29 January 1840, Hobson arrived in the Bay of Islands as Lieutenant Governor aboard the HMS *Herald*. Travelling on the ship with him was Londoner Felton Mathew who had been appointed Acting Surveyor-General of New Zealand. Mathew had joined Hobson in Port Jackson, having previously worked as the town surveyor for Sydney.

After reaching New Zealand, Hobson lost no time in executing his orders and, by 6 February, he had successfully obtained the signatures of over 40 Ngā Puhi chiefs to the Treaty of Waitangi. He now faced the challenge of obtaining further signatures from iwi in other areas, as well as identifying the location for the seat of government and consequently the new capital of the colony.

The day after reaching the Bay of Islands, Hobson met the Reverend Henry Williams, a forceful man who had led the Church Missionary Society in New Zealand since 1823. Being a fluent Māori speaker, Williams had taken on the task of translating the Treaty into Māori and of explaining its import to the chiefs who had gathered at Waitangi. He was well respected amongst both Māori and Pākehā.

Williams had travelled widely within New Zealand and so Hobson asked his advice on where the future seat of government should be located. Williams dismissed the Bay of Islands as being too confined, too populated and too far towards one extremity of the country. But he knew of another place which he thought would be ideal. It was currently unoccupied, was strategically located at

Pages 64–65: Auckland port today, from the east. (Courtesy of Ports of Auckland Limited)

Right: Reverend Henry Williams recommended the Tāmaki isthmus on the Waitematā Harbour as an ideal location for the new capital of the colony. (Ref: 4-1352, Sir George Grey Special Collections, Auckland Libraries)

the centre of a network of waterways which provided access to the interior of the country, and provided safe anchorages for vessels of all sizes. In his view, the Tāmaki isthmus and the Waitematā Harbour would provide an ideal location for the new capital.[1]

Ngāti Whatua invitation

Hobson was soon aware that British settlement in the area would be welcomed by the owners of the land, Ngāti Whatua o Tāmaki. After being driven from the isthmus during the early 1820s as a result of conflict with Ngā Puhi, Āpihai Te Kawau had started re-establishing his people on their former Tāmaki lands. But they did not feel entirely secure. Their old enemies Ngāti Paoa lived as close as Maraetai and Waiheke, and Ngā Puhi were still active just to the north at Whangārei.[2]

Soon after the news of Hobson's arrival in the Bay of Islands reached the Waitematā, Te Whatarangi (Te Kawau's cousin) convened a meeting (hui) of tribal leaders at Ōrākei, in order to discuss how the tribe could best secure peace in the future. There was lengthy discussion of the issue but no clear strategy emerged.[3] Then Titai, a respected prophet (matakite), rose to speak. The solution to their collective problem had come to him during a dream the previous night. Titai used metaphor to convey his insight, embodied in the words of a song he proceeded to intone.[4]

He aha te hau e wawara mai
He tiu, he raaki
Nāna i ā mai te pūpūtarakihi ki uta
E tikina atu e au ki te kōtiu
Kukume mai ai?
Koia te pou whakairo ka tū ki Waitematā
I aku wairangi e

What is that murmuring sound
Upon the north wind
That cast my paper nautilus ashore
Which I plucked from the north wind
And thus claimed?
It is the carved pillar that stands in the Waitematā Harbour
That I see in my distressed state

Āpihai Te Kawau

Ngāti Whātua leader Āpihai Te Kawau played a key role in the decision to establish Auckland in the Waitematā, encouraging Hobson to locate the new capital city on his Tāmaki lands. He led his people's return to Ōkahu and signed the Treaty of Waitangi on 29 March 1840. After initially being willing to sell land, by the early 1850s he spoke out publicly against sales. But he was unable to stem the loss of land. In 1868 he obtained a Native Land Court title to the remaining 700 acres of land at Ōrākei. He died the following year and was buried at Kaipara.[5]

Āpihai Te Kawau (seated) with his nephew Wiremu Te Rewiti at Ōrākei, 1847. (George Angas, Ref: 7-C70, Sir George Grey Special Collections, Auckland Libraries)

The meaning was clear and the message was a compelling one. The nautilus was a Pākehā ship and the carved pillar the British flag. Enduring peace would only come to the Waitematā if Hobson was invited to establish the seat of government there. It was a vision that was to help change the future trajectory of the Hauraki Gulf.

Captain William Hobson

Hobson had joined the Royal Navy in 1803 at just nine years of age. For over a quarter of a century he rode the seas, sailing in the Napoleonic Wars, engaging in battles against the French and the Americans, and pitting himself against pirates in the West Indies. He had been captured twice and managed to escape both times. But then, at 36 years of age, his career suddenly came to a halt. He was left ashore without a command for six long years.[6]

At that time, the Royal Navy operated through a powerful patronage system, where commands were often allocated on the basis of personal connections rather than on merit. Not being part of the aristocracy (his father was a barrister), Hobson lacked the crucial patron that he needed to get reassigned to a ship. But then his luck changed. Lord Auckland was appointed the First Lord of the Admiralty and he gave Hobson command of the frigate HMS *Rattlesnake*. Hobson was extremely grateful and did not forget Auckland's support.[7]

One of the *Rattlesnake*'s missions was to provide support to British subjects living in the Bay of Islands at a time when they felt imperilled by tribal warfare. So Hobson first visited New Zealand in 1837 and he became interested in seeking an official posting there. On his return to England he wrote a report on the New Zealand situation. It was well received, and when the British government decided to establish a colony on the small island group on the other side of the world, Hobson was chosen as the man to head it.[8]

Portrait of William Hobson. (James McDonald, Ref: G-826-1, Alexander Turnbull Library, Wellington, New Zealand)

A delegation of seven chiefs, headed by Te Reweti Tāmaki (Te Kawau's nephew), was quickly despatched to the Bay of Islands to persuade Hobson to establish the capital at Tāmaki. As an inducement, they offered to gift Hobson land for the new settlement.[9]

Hobson's Waitematā visit

Not everyone was so enamoured by the Tāmaki option. The New Zealand Company, led by the Wakefield brothers, had recently established a settlement at Port Nicholson (Wellington Harbour), with the first 148 settlers having arrived on 22 January 1840. These settlers considered that the capital would be much better located at the southern end of the North Island, which now had the largest European population. They were keen for Hobson to visit and to view the advantages of Port Nicholson for himself.

So, on 21 February, less than a month after his arrival in the country, Hobson set out on a voyage that was designed to secure additional signatures to the Treaty and also to inspect potential sites for the new capital. On board the HMS *Herald*, for their return trip home, were members of the Ngāti Whātua delegation who were eager to personally show Hobson the benefits of the Waitematā. Whilst his tribal delegation had been away, Te Kawau shifted his headquarters back to Ōkahu and he was ready to receive the British dignitaries.[10]

During Hobson's first visit to the Waitematā in March 1840, seventeen Ngāti Paoa and Ngāti Maru chiefs signed the Treaty of Waitangi, most probably at Karaka Bay, shown here. (W Jordan, Ref: PD75, Auckland War Memorial Museum Tāmaki Paenga Hira)

The *Herald* arrived in the Waitematā the next morning and Hobson's party spent several days exploring the area. Hobson seemed particularly taken with a potential site in the upper harbour, probably near present-day Hobsonville. But Felton Mathew, who accompanied Hobson on the trip, was more impressed by Tāmaki Strait which 'gradually opened into a magnificent Bay of some fifteen Miles diameter, one side of which was formed by the Mainland, and the other by the Island of "waihekeh", which is a most lovely spot, broken into gently swelling hills and delicious valleys, and about 18 miles in length.' Like explorer D'Urville, Mathew was enchanted by the beauty of the wide, sheltered strait which he thought far surpassed that of the Waitematā Harbour.[11]

But on 1 March, before the party could take their explorations further, Hobson suffered a crippling stroke. They impatiently awaited the return of Henry Williams, who had been sent off to recruit Māori support for the Treaty of Waitangi, so that they could take Hobson back to the Bay of Islands to recover. Williams eventually arrived and brought with him a party of seventeen Ngāti Paoa and Ngāti Maru chiefs who had agreed to sign the Treaty. The signing took place on 4 March at a location which is still uncertain but was likely to be in the vicinity of Karaka Bay.[12] More signatures for the Treaty had been successfully obtained, but the decision on the site of the future capital was left hanging.

Felton Mathew's site investigations

With Hobson incapacitated and the need to establish the new capital becoming more urgent, Mathew was sent back south in the cutter *Ranger* to find an eligible site as speedily as possible. There were a number of requirements that any suitable site needed to fulfil. There should be 'a good anchorage close to shore, sufficient level land for the Town close to the shore, facility of communication with the interior, and an adequate supply of timber, water, building-stone, etc., in the vicinity'.[13]

Mathew, who was accompanied by his wife Sarah, was away for two months. During that time he carefully examined the harbours at Whangārei, Mahurangi, Waitematā and Tāmaki, and the coastline in between. Whangārei was quickly dismissed as having too little level land for settlement and lacking sufficient water depth in the upper harbour. It was in the Mahurangi Harbour that the Mathews first saw the famed 'Koudi' tree which dominated the forests cloaking the hillsides. These forests were full of pigeons and there were also large numbers of wild ducks in the harbour.[14] But although the area provided good shelter for vessels, the surrounding land was too steep for a large settlement to be established and the hills impeded travel further inland.

Surveyor-General Felton Mathew was convinced that the Panmure Basin (depicted here during the 1850s) would make an ideal location for the first capital of New Zealand. (Patrick Hogan, Ref: 7-A5881, Sir George Grey Special Collections, Auckland Libraries)

The *Ranger* then headed down to the Waitematā and the Mathews spent considerable time exploring the upper reaches of the harbour in a small boat. In the main river, which extends up to Riverhead, they found 'a beautiful creek thickly wooded on both banks. Numbers of wild ducks rose from amongst the mangroves, which everywhere fringed the edge of the water, in many places extending far out, forming extensive banks of sand at low water.' They also saw innumerable pigeons and shot several for a meal. The party filled their water casks 'at a beautiful natural basin of rock into which fell a stream of pure water'.[15]

While later exploring a lower branch of the harbour, probably the Whau River, the Mathews encountered extensive mudflats on which the boat grounded several times. 'Fully two-thirds of the river's bed was nothing but banks of mud covered with oysters and mangroves, the former literally growing to the branches of the latter.'[16] The party then headed over to Point Chevalier Beach where they 'found it nothing but shells, principally cockleshells, almost triturated to sand; these shells seem thrown up continually, forming large beds which each tide rolls backwards and forwards, always breaking, always accumulating'.[17] The large number of cockle shells was evidence of the rich

shellfish beds thriving in the inner harbour.

Having fully explored the Waitematā, the Mathews proceeded to the Tāmaki River and 'found it a wide and beautiful stream, the entrance only encumbered by shoals, the channel of deep water being narrow and intricate'. But by noon they reached 'a very curious basin surrounded by high ground thickly covered with fern and brush' (the Panmure Basin).[18] They later explored upriver and were impressed with what they saw. As Mrs Mathew wrote in her diary, 'The country is very beautiful here; the outline of the hills on the horizon is bold, varied and picturesque; the sea gates on the Eastern and Western coasts are distinctly visible, the low land between is undulating and, judging by the lank luxuriance of the fern and underwood, must be of the greatest fertility.'[19]

The Mathews' party also tried to ascend the peak of Rangitoto, but failed due to the impenetrable vegetation. Around the island's rugged shores, scattered with scoria boulders, they saw 'masses of oysters which seem to grow in clusters on anything that is partly covered by salt water' including intertidal rocks and the branches of mangroves.

The *Ranger* then headed down to the Firth of Thames and the Mathews explored the Piako River, seeing 'mud flats all covered with innumerable seabirds'. As they headed further upstream, the party encountered regular weirs which had been placed across the river by local Māori in order to catch fish. 'Innumerable ducks covered the stream and arose in flocks from the marshy banks and lagoons on each side of the river.'[20]

On returning to the Bay of Islands, Mathew provided Hobson with a comprehensive report on what he had found. He considered the Hobsonville location, which Hobson had initially favoured, as impracticable because of the very shallow water adjacent to the shore and the infertile land which consisted of red and white clay, only supporting stunted ferns. In addition, there was no obvious wood, stone or water supply and the land was not free-draining.[21]

He wrote a much more glowing report of the Tāmaki River and a potential site on the northern shores of the Panmure Basin, at the base of Mount Wellington. He quickly noted the major drawback of this location as being the sandbank which extended across the mouth of the river. But he suggested that a port could be established on the Waitematā, with small boats ferrying cargo and people up the river to a town located at Mokoia (Panmure). The land there was low lying and undulating, the volcanic soil fertile, and drainage from nearby Maungarei (Mount Wellington) provided an abundance of fresh water. The area was close to the Manukau Harbour portage and to the extensive Waikato and Hauraki plains which with some prescience he thought 'must become the great agricultural district of the Island'. Although the area had few trees, Mathew thought that wood for firewood and building materials could be easily provided from Waiheke Island, which at that stage was still covered in luxuriant forest.[22]

Hobson's second visit to the Waitematā

On receiving Mathew's report, Hobson remained unconvinced. Now partially recovered from his stroke but still weak, he decided to revisit the Waitematā to resolve the issue of the site of the capital once and for all. So just over two weeks later, in early July, Hobson embarked on the *Ranger* accompanied by his physician Dr Johnson, Felton Mathew and Captain David Rough who was later to become the first harbour master of Auckland.

On 6 July, after anchoring off Waiheke and observing the Sabbath, the *Ranger* headed to the Tāmaki to view

Captain David Rough, shown here in the 1880s, helped survey the Waitematā Harbour in the vicinity of Herne Bay, to establish its suitability for a major port. He later became the first harbour master of Auckland. (William Reed, Ref: 661-61, Sir George Grey Special Collections, Auckland Libraries)

Mathew's preferred location for the new settlement. Although they managed to get the boat up to the Panmure lagoon, Rough records that 'the channel appeared to be so intricate that the Governor gave up all idea of selecting that part as the site of an important settlement'. So within the first days of the voyage, the prospect of Mathew's Panmure metropolis was at an end.

Hobson obtained the signatures of seven more chiefs to the Treaty before sailing north-west to the Waitematā. He was keen to explore the upper harbour site that he had been so enamoured with during his earlier trip. It was late when they reached the inner harbour and the *Ranger* anchored for the night off the Sentinel or Watchman Island (Te Kākāwhakaara), in the vicinity of what is now Herne Bay. As the sun starting sinking in the sky, Johnson (who was an artist as well as a medical doctor) took in the surrounding landscape and commented on the inviting appearance of land on the southern shore. So Rough offered to stay back the next day to explore the area and to take soundings of the depth close to land, especially at low water.[23]

At daybreak, Hobson eagerly headed up the harbour on *Ranger*, to inspect the Hobsonville site. But it was soon evident that in this case Mathew had been right. The channel narrowed markedly near the point and the land looked unpromising. Hobson was almost certainly despairing by this stage, with the only two candidate sites having been rejected.

Whilst Hobson had been exploring the upper harbour, Rough had been investigating the area near Herne Bay. As he later recalled, 'Just as the sun rose I climbed up the cliffs to where Ponsonby now is, and beheld a vast expanse of undulating country, mostly covered with fern and manuka scrub; several volcanic hills in sight, and near the shore, valleys and ravines in which many species of native trees are growing, whilst the projecting cliffs and headlands were crowned with pohutukawa trees [*Metrosideros excelsa*] whose

rich scarlet flowers form in summer so gorgeous a feature of New Zealand coast scenery in the North Island.'

When the *Ranger* returned to its anchorage near Te Kākāwhakaara, Hobson went ashore with his party to examine the area that had so impressed Johnson and which Rough had further explored. Of all the sites he had viewed, this looked the most promising. Although he didn't make a decision right then, after returning to the Bay of Islands, Hobson determined that the site of the new settlement would be on the Waitematā, on the south shore, close to the harbour entrance.[24] He decided to call the new settlement Auckland, in honour of his benefactor Lord Auckland.

Establishing the new settlement

Preparations were put in train to construct a brand new town amongst the fern and scrub and to transport the seat of government south. As his health was still poor, Hobson decided to stay in Russell whilst the new town was being built. He sent a party led by Captain William Cornwallis Symonds (the newly appointed Chief Magistrate) to accomplish the task. Symonds was charged with taking

The British flag was first raised on the shore of the Waitematā on 18 September 1840. The ceremony took place on Britomart Point, a promontory which has long since disappeared, initially through excavation to facilitate access around the shoreline and then through reclamation. (Elizabeth Hocken, Ref: Hocken Pictorial Collections 12,954 a42, Hocken Collections, Uare Taoka o Hākena, University of Otago)

possession of the area 'in the name of her Most Gracious Majesty', hoisting the British flag and negotiating occupation rights with Ngāti Whātua.[25]

As Surveyor-General, Mathew was tasked with selecting the most suitable location for the settlement, within the general vicinity chosen by Hobson. He needed to decide where stores should be landed and where Government House should be erected. William Mason, who was appointed Superintendent of Works, was tasked with identifying the best places 'for felling timber, forming a brick-yard, lime-burning, and collecting sand'.[26]

On 13 September 1840, the barque *Anna Watson* set sail from the Bay of Islands, with the people and goods on board required to establish the new capital. The passengers included seven government officials and 32 workmen and their families. These were to be the first Auckland settlers,

Hobson describing the advantages of Auckland to the UK Secretary of State

[F]rom the documents now in your Lordship's possession showing the site of Auckland to be on the shores of a harbour, safe and commodious, and easy of access, and within five miles of Manukau, certainly the best harbour on the whole of the western coast of New Zealand — within fifteen miles of the harbour of Kaipara, into which four considerable rivers discharge themselves — at no great distance from the Waikato, which waters the fertile and extensive plains of the Waipa, on the western side of the island — and the fertile valley of the Thames on the east; having, too, in its immediate neighbourhood, some hundreds of thousands of acres of level, open, fertile land, possessing abundant means of water-communication, and being in the centre of the bulk of a native population, now British subjects, rapidly assuming European habits, and acquiring a taste for our manufactures — your Lordship will be satisfied that this neighbourhood has been well chosen for the site of the seat of Government of New Zealand, and that it combines advantages for a large and prosperous agricultural and commercial settlement not found elsewhere in the colony... I do not hesitate to state my opinion that the neighbourhood of Auckland combines advantages for a very extensive and prosperous settlement not to be found in any other part of this colony.[27]

but they were soon joined by many others. As they sailed up the Waitematā Harbour, the passengers could see the New Zealand Company ship *Platina* resting at anchor. She had brought with her the prefabricated parts of Government House, which the company promoters had thought would be erected at Port Nicholson but which, to their severe disappointment, was now to be located further north. Several dissatisfied settlers from Port Nicholson were also on board and were keen to be part of the new northern town.

The pressure was now on Mathew. He had to decide where exactly the new port and town would be built. The squally, unsettled spring weather did not make the task any easier. Rough carefully sounded the depths along the coastline and established that the deepest water along the southern shores was in a small bay just to the west of a promontory known by Māori as Te Rerenga-ora-iti and later named Point Britomart after the troopship HMS *Britomart* which visited the area. The *Anna Watson* was moved east and re-anchored in the deeper water.

Mathew went ashore to have a good look around. He climbed Point Britomart and this gave him a commanding view of the surrounding countryside and harbour area. But the location of the new capital was ultimately decided by water depth. The deep water bay where the *Anna Watson* was now anchored would make the best port, he reasoned, so it was here that he decided to locate the Government Stores (close to the site of the current Ferry Building). The bay

called Oneoneroa (the long sandspits) by Māori took on the name Store Bay and later became Commercial Bay, before disappearing beneath reclamation works.

The officials' residences were to be located in a 'beautiful wooded bay'[28] on the eastern side of Point Britomart, known by Māori as Waiariki (noble waters) and dubbed Official Bay (now Beach Road) and the workers' housing was to be sited further to the south-east in a sharply indented bay known by Māori as Te Taongaroa (the long hauling) and called Mechanics Bay (where Beach Road and the Strand now intersect).

With the location of the settlement decided, Symonds had the job of negotiating its sale with Ngāti Whātua. The *Anna Watson* had not long been in her new anchorage when a canoe carrying a Ngāti Whātua contingent, probably led by Te Reweti Tāmaki, arrived. The bargaining over the sale of the site was vigorous and ran over two days. Provisional agreement was finally reached on the sale of a wedged-shaped piece of land of around 1200 hectares, with boundaries extending on the west from Opou (Coxs Creek) to the summit of Mangawhau (renamed Mount Eden after Lord Auckland's family name) and then back down to the western side of Waitaramoa (renamed Hobson Bay).[29]

Friday, 18 September, the day after the agreement was reached, was when the new settlement of Auckland was to be formally established. It dawned a beautiful fine spring day. Just after noon, the officials and others on board the two

The first European building to be constructed in Auckland was the Government Store, shown here in the foreground. It was located just behind the shore of what was then named Commercial Bay. (Ref: 4-504, Sir George Grey Special Collections, Auckland Libraries)

British vessels clambered ashore and made their way up to the top of Point Britomart to meet the Ngāti Whātua contingent. Symonds read out the terms of the purchase which had been agreed the day before, with Williams translating into Māori.

Then something unexpected happened. One of the Ngāti Whātua chiefs stepped forward and strongly objected to the agreement. He stated that he had been advised that if the Pākehā settled amongst them, the Queen of England would take all of their land. This did turn out to be largely the case. But at that stage, Ngāti Whātua were keen to have the British living in the area, for security and also to provide access to British manufactured goods. At the same time, the chiefs wanted to send a warning signal to Symonds' party — the British must keep within the limits agreed. After some vigorous toing and froing and slight renegotiation of boundaries, the agreement was finally signed by both sides.[30]

This was the signal for Rough to raise the flag on a kauri pole which had been erected on the point for this purpose. As Sarah Mathew related: 'Then the Flag was run up, and the whole assembly gave three cheers, the ship's colours were also instantly hoisted and a Salute of 21 guns fired, Her Majesty's health was then most rapturously drunk with cheers long and loud repeated from the ships; to the evident delight of the Natives of whom nearly 100 had assembled round us.'[31]

To further celebrate the establishment of Auckland, a series of boat races was soon under way. There was a rowing race between the surveyor-general's and the captain's gigs (small oared boats) manned by civilians. Then the sailors raced each other in two whaleboats. Finally Ngāti Whātua raced their impressive canoes. The harbour master's whaleboat won the regatta and a purse of £5.[32]

Work then got under way to build the new settlement. The ships were unloaded and the land cleared of fern and shrubs. The settlers moved ashore and erected tents. The first building to be constructed was the Government Store in Commercial Bay and this immediately housed the prefabricated structure and furniture for Government House. Nearby ran the Horotiu, 'a stream of clear water overhung by native trees'[33] which had several tributaries in the Upper Queen Street area that merged into a wetland near today's Aotea Square, and then flowed in one stream down the western side of Queen Street into a marshy area near the harbour. Other government buildings were to follow in the vicinity of lower Princes Street. Barracks to house government forces were later built on Point Britomart which became known as Fort Britomart.

The workers initially settled further to the east of Official Bay, on the flats behind what became known as Mechanics Bay, shown here in 1843. (Edward Ashworth, Ref 1915/6/3, Auckland Art Gallery Toi o Tāmaki)

The officials settled in the bay to the east. As Rough later described, 'Our tents were pitched amongst the rich green evergreen trees then growing on the slopes, and at that spring season adorned with beautiful white clematis. A terrace, now Jermyn-street [subsequently Anzac Avenue], was formed in front of the tents, commanding a charming view of the harbour and picturesque islands beyond.' Sarah Mathew was also very impressed with the locality, writing: 'There is a beautiful stream running through the centre of the little amphitheatre or valley, and the landscape is really a gem.'[34] The area, which had become known as Official Bay, was also dubbed Exclusion Bay by some, because settlers were not permitted to erect their tents there without permission. The workers settled in Mechanics Bay to the east.

First town plan

Mathew quickly set about undertaking a survey of the land, which was a prerequisite for creating and selling lots to private purchasers. This necessitated burning off the thick scrubby growth which covered the area and made walking difficult. An early scrub fire quickly got out of control and swept down from the hills into Commercial Bay destroying settlers' goods, including 'a newly-invented Machine for dressing the New Zealand flax'. It was only with great difficulty that the Government Store itself was saved.[35]

In less than a month's time, Mathew's initial survey of the entire extent of the land acquired from Ngāti Whātua was completed and he had developed a proposed plan for the new capital. The plan was approved by Hobson and then sent on to Sydney for final sign-off. By this time Hobson had briefly visited Auckland, had approved the location of the settlement and key sites chosen by Mathew, and had finalised the land purchase agreement.

Mathew's plan included 'Trafalgar Circus' at the peak of the summit where the University of Auckland currently sits. Other crescents were to gracefully circle around the peak. Queen Street was to run to the west of the crescents, bordering on the lower ground in Commercial Bay, which was divided into a grid pattern. But Mathew proposed to break the grid up with two grand squares provisionally named Hobson Square and Wellington Square. Mathew had considered the difficulty of the shallow water close to the shore, where the seabed was exposed at low tide, making it impossible for ships to lie to and offload. As a solution he proposed a large reclamation extending out into deep water from Point Britomart, running south to the western side of the headland named Point Stanley.

Much of the plan was subsequently implemented, with the exception of the flourishes of squares and circles which were considered too extravagant — only four crescents were actually built. This meant that the Auckland central business district ended up largely being divided into a grid pattern. The reclamation of the harbour eventually extended far further than Mathew could have imagined.

The next task Mathew faced was to precisely survey allotments of land which could then be offered up for

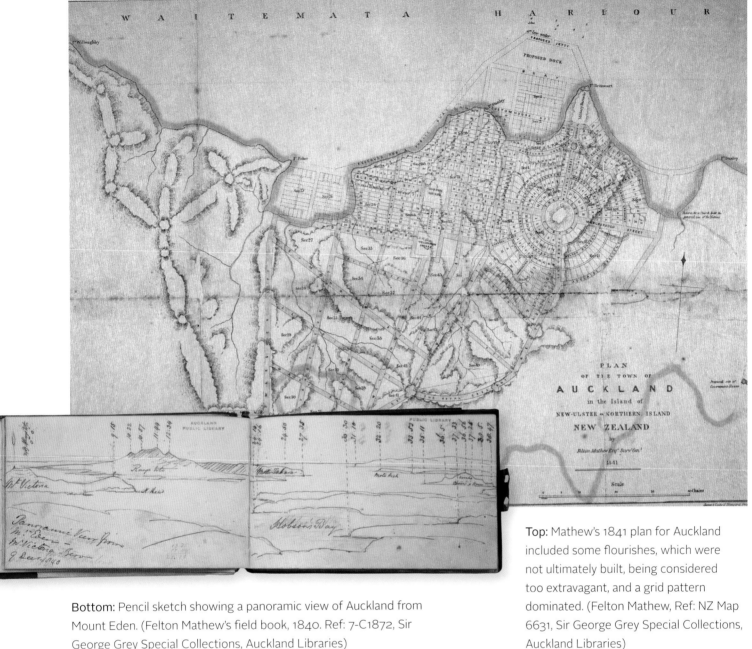

Top: Mathew's 1841 plan for Auckland included some flourishes, which were not ultimately built, being considered too extravagant, and a grid pattern dominated. (Felton Mathew, Ref: NZ Map 6631, Sir George Grey Special Collections, Auckland Libraries)

Bottom: Pencil sketch showing a panoramic view of Auckland from Mount Eden. (Felton Mathew's field book, 1840. Ref: 7-C1872, Sir George Grey Special Collections, Auckland Libraries)

sale. Whilst he was busy with this work, tents started mushrooming amongst the scrub. Many speculators were arriving hoping to buy land at a cheap price and to onsell at a profit. They were forced to squat in tents in Commercial Bay while they waited for the survey to be completed.

Amongst the speculators were Scottish medical doctor John Logan Campbell, and his business associate, Dundee lawyer William Brown, who had arrived in Auckland during December 1840. In May that year, the partners had managed to purchase Motu-Koreka (later named Browns Island) from its Ngāti Tamaterā owners after an abortive attempt to purchase land on the isthmus from Ngāti Whātua. Campbell was to become a hugely successful Auckland businessman, prominent politician and generous philanthropist.

Hobson took up official residence in Auckland on 14 March 1841 and thus the settlement officially became the capital of New Zealand. The first sale of 119 allotments took place just over a month later, on 19 April 1841. The sale had been delayed and interest had grown to the effect that the sections sold for an average of £555 per acre, more than five times the reserve price. To everyone's amazement the prices were so high that they were comparable to those for land in London at the time.

Hobson was delighted, as now the government's coffers were replenished by the large profits from the sale. But most sections were bought by speculators rather than genuine settlers and much of the capital which could have gone into establishing the new town was expended in meeting the inflated land prices.[36]

Growth of town

Notwithstanding these high land prices, the new town started to flourish. The large sections were soon subdivided into smaller allotments which were onsold at a profit. By the end of the year there were 1835 Europeans living in Auckland.[37] The fern-covered hills dotted with tents soon transformed into a bustling metropolis of wooden cottages and commercial premises. On 9 October 1842 two Scottish immigrant ships, the *Jane Gifford* and the *Duchess of Argyle*, arrived in Auckland bringing over 500 planned immigrants to the city. Further immigrant ships were to follow.

The establishment of the new town was strongly supported by Ngāti Whātua and eventually other neighbouring tribes. They provided much needed labour, food and firewood for the new settlers. They also built them thatched whare. In 1853 William Swainson, who was Attorney-General of New Zealand, wrote of nearly 2000 canoes arriving in port each year.

The fish caught near Auckland, although of but moderate quality, is plentiful and cheap. Vegetables are also abundant; during the summer of 1852, there were brought into market by the natives, in canoes alone, upwards of 1,100 kits of onions [about 20 tons]; upwards of 4,000 kits of potatoes [more than 100 tons]; besides corn, cabbages and kumeras. Peaches grown by the natives, and sufficiently good for culinary purposes, are very abundant and cheap: during the present summer upwards of 1,200 kits were brought into Auckland by canoes alone.[38]

Taurarua (Judges Bay), shown here with Attorney-General William Swainson's house located behind the bay, became a favourite camping place for Māori who had travelled to Auckland to trade and were unable to return home the same day. (Thomas Hutton, Ref: 1939/17/15, Auckland Art Gallery Toi o Tāmaki)

The value of the produce brought into the settlement by canoe was significant, increasing from £3564 in 1852 to £12,417 just two years later.[39]

In 1842 Mary Ann Martin, the wife of the first chief justice who lived in Judges Bay (Taurarua), recalled that the area was a favourite camping place for Māori who had travelled to Auckland to trade and were unable to return home the same day. 'In a short time, the canoes were drawn up high and dry, their triangular sails set up as tents. The men would be busy cutting fern from the hill for their beds, while the women and girls scraped potatoes for that evening meal, or waded with bare legs into the mud at low water to find their favourite shellfish.'[40]

Mechanics Bay became the centre of Māori trading in Auckland. A hostel was built there for the use of visiting traders but was never used, due to the lack of hygiene and heating, and the absence of partitions to separate the different tribal groups.[41]

As Auckland's population and economy mushroomed, the infrastructure needs of the burgeoning settlement started to overwhelm the beautiful natural setting, which had so impressed Hobson's exploratory party on the *Ranger* and the earliest European settlers.

Top: The first two immigrant ships to arrive in Auckland, in 1842, were the *Duchess of Argyle* and the *Jane Gifford* (shown here), both originating from Scotland. They brought with them 500 planned immigrants, many of whom became prominent in the life of the new settlement. (Matthew Clayton, Ref 7-C4, Sir George Grey Special Collections, Auckland Libraries)

Bottom: Auckland grew quickly in its first decade of existence and before long it was a bustling settlement. Depicted here in 1852, Commercial Bay can be seen on the right, Point Britomart in the centre and Officials Bay to the left. (Patrick Hogan, Ref: 4-619, Sir George Grey Special Collections, Auckland Libraries)

Chapter 5
Growing metropolis

Despite its abundant natural attributes, it was not certain that Auckland would flourish. From the very first, labour was scarce and, to make matters worse, the 1848 California gold rush sucked able-bodied men away, as did the 1851 rush in Australia. There were also problems with vessel access.

Development of the port

The Waitematā port was the lifeblood of the new settlement but, due to the tidal nature of the shoreline, larger vessels had to anchor well offshore and smaller 'lighters' were used to transport goods and people to the beaches. Smaller vessels would ground at high tide and offload cargo before waiting for the next tide in order to float off. But this situation was hardly satisfactory for New Zealand's capital city. So, in 1851, work started on the construction of the first public wharf in Auckland, located in Official Bay.

The long, narrow wooden wharf snaked its way over the mudflats and into deeper water. A water supply was subsequently provided on the wharf to enable ships to reprovision whilst tied up alongside. The new structure was named Wynyard Wharf after Lieutenant Colonel Robert Wynyard, who was at that time commander of the military forces in New Zealand.[1] The name has survived to the present, but at a different location, with Wynyard Wharf and Wynyard Quarter now being located on reclaimed land to the west of the Viaduct Basin.

Auckland waterfront, 1852. (Charles Heaphy, Ref: 1937/14, Auckland Art Gallery Toi o Tāmaki)

Top: Construction of the Queen Street wharf started in 1852 and it soon became the main shipping pier for local and overseas vessels. Shown here in 1866, the wharf eventually extended almost half a kilometre from the shore, in order to provide sufficient deep berthage for increasing volumes of shipping. (Ref: 4-1005, Sir George Grey Special Collections, Auckland Libraries)

Left: The Auckland waterfront is shown here in 1864, with coastal traders grounded in the tidal mud against the seawall along Custom House Street (now Customs Street). The excavations for Point Britomart can be seen in the background. (New Zealand Maritime Museum)

In 1852, work started on constructing a second wharf in Commercial Bay. This was named the Queen Street Wharf, as it formed a natural extension of Queen Street, which ran down the steep Horotiu valley. Being located in the heart of Auckland's commercial district, the wharf rapidly became the main shipping pier for local and overseas vessels.

A smaller quay along Customs House Street was eventually built to provide berths for lighter coastal vessels. Over the years, the Queen Street Wharf was extended in length and it eventually became almost half a kilometre (470 metres) long with three smaller extensions being built at right angles along the main arm to provide additional wharfage.[2]

The New Zealand Wars of the 1860s brought additional British troops into Auckland, buoying up the economy for a while. But in 1865 the seat of government moved to Wellington, taking with it the substantial cadre of public servants, and by 1870 the external troops had departed. Auckland was saved by the discovery of rich gold deposits at Thames and Waihi, as well as by a booming kauri timber trade. The footprint of the settlement expanded onto the hills and valleys backing the harbour, with Fencible outposts of mainly retired Irish soldiers and their families appearing to the south, at Howick, Onehunga, Panmure and Ōtāhuhu.[3]

The shallow tidal waters in Commercial Bay were an ongoing problem for shipping and in 1859 work started on reclaiming the bay. Land was extended out from Fort Street (which was originally called Fore Street because it ran along the foreshore) to a new Customs House Street (now called Customs Street), which extended along the waterfront from Smales Point to Point Britomart.

Despite the new shoreline, shipping into Auckland faced considerable risks. When there was a gale, boats anchored in the harbour would regularly come adrift and the resulting damage could be considerable. In late March 1871, a north-east gale caused a trading schooner to break free from her anchor. She was then blown onto three cutters, with the four boats jointly crashing onto the end of the Queen Street Wharf. At least seven vessels were lost as a result of the storm and 30 others were badly damaged.[4] Three years later, when another storm hit the harbour, chaos again ensued. A paddle steamer that was moored up against the wharf, and had two anchors down, became a total loss when another boat ran into her and dragged her from her moorings.[5]

As well as being dangerous, the harbour was becoming crowded and there were few facilities. Maritime historian Clifford Hawkins reports that during one day in 1883 there were 73 local sailing vessels either berthed at or moored off Auckland.[6] These vessels required safer moorings and adequate wharf space to load and unload cargo. It was clear that something needed to be done.

So, in 1871, the Auckland Harbour Board was established to sort things out and the government endowed

The programme of extending the port into the Waitematā brushed aside any consideration of the rights of Ngāti Whātua, who had never sold the foreshore and who regularly harvested shellfish there. The harbour works, along with the discharge of sewage from the Queen Street sewer, destroyed these traditional fishing grounds.[7]

Throughout the 1880s, Ngāti Whātua continued to strongly protest against the port reclamations. They were concerned about the 'taking by the Harbours Board of the foreshore in front of Māori lands' and the interference with Māori fishing grounds. They petitioned Parliament, 'stating that their shellfish and fisheries, which were secured to them by the Treaty of Waitangi, had been buried by reclamations'. But there was no substantive response and the reclamations and harbour works only intensified.[8]

Reclamation of Commercial Bay, Auckland, 1859. (Ref: 4-511, Sir George Grey Special Collections, Auckland Libraries)

it with over 2000 hectares of seabed. The board was chaired by Captain William Daldy, a publicly minded seaman turned politician, and he energetically set about developing the port. A decision was quickly made to demolish Point Britomart, a promontory which obstructed access around the waterfront, and to use the substrate to fill in harbour reclamation works. Old sailing vessels and rubbish were also used to reclaim the foreshore. This was the beginning of a process of extensive reclamation, which was to fundamentally change Auckland's coastline and which is still ongoing more than 160 years later.

In 1886, the Auckland Harbour Board's then engineer, J McGregor, came up with an ambitious plan for the future development of the port. This didn't rely on reclamation, but proposed creating a whole series of tidal basins, extending along the coast from Point Erin to Ōkahu Point. Wharves were to be located on the breakwaters which protected the basins, with the line of the inner coastline remaining much as it was. But the plan was seen as expensive and it was not adopted.

In 1903, the board acquired a new engineer, W H Hamer, who had come directly from working for the London Dock Company. Hamer came up with quite a different plan for the development of the port, one that involved extensive reclamation to push the land out into deeper water. As well as providing deeper berths, reclamation had the added financial benefit of creating valuable waterfront land.

The plan also sought to make use of the uneven gullies that were present in the seabed as a result of historic river valleys running out from the land. Hamer located the port infrastructure so that larger vessels could use the deeper gullies, with the jetties being located over shallower areas. This, he hoped, would help to avoid the need for costly blasting and rock excavation. Two large solid tide deflectors were designed to minimise the effect of currents around the wharves.[9] The Hamer plan was largely implemented and it created much of the footprint of Auckland's waterfront today.

During the early 1950s, the then General Manager of the Auckland Harbour Board, A C Clarke, conceived an innovative plan for reducing the turnaround time for ships visiting the increasingly congested port and therefore also reducing the need for more wharf space. A group of barges called lighters would be used to ferry cargo ashore from anchored ships. A lighter basin was constructed by excavating sandstone back to Gaunt Street, and twelve

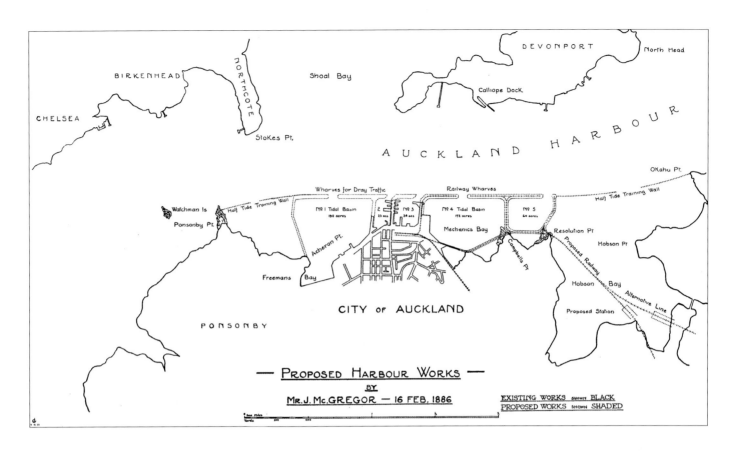

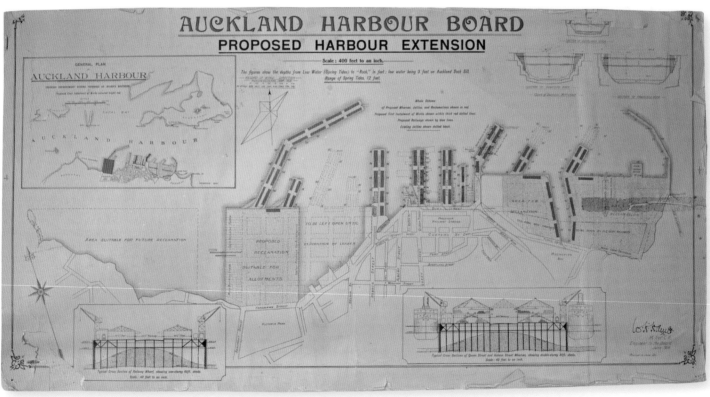

Top: McGregor's 1886 plan for Auckland Harbour involved creating a series of tidal basins protected by wharves. (New Zealand Maritime Museum)

Bottom: Hamer's plan (1904–1911) for harbour works involved extensive reclamation to push land out into deeper water. (New Zealand Maritime Museum)

An archaeological investigation of the reclamation that had been constructed between Customs and Quay streets from 1879 to 1885 was commenced in 2002. The reclamation works had enclosed parts of various wharves and jetties as well as the Customs Street sea wall.

The excavations confirmed that the reclamation had initially been filled with spoil from the demolition of Point Britomart. But later the area was used as a rubbish dump, with large quantities of bottles, as well as cloth, leather and metal offcuts being found. A small clinker-built boat was also uncovered. 'One of the most dramatic finds' was the remains of the original Gore Street Jetty within the main reclamation area.[10]

Remains of a small clinker boat excavated at Britomart, 2002. (Barry Baquié, Clough and Associates Limited)

lighters were built. But the new arrangement proved to be very unpopular due to the high amount of manpower and lengthy time required to transship cargo between the ships, the barges and the shore. It was quickly abandoned. Instead, the development of reclamations and wharves continued to provide for increasing shipping.[11]

Disposal of dredgings

As well as reclamation, the development of the port resulted in the dredging of berths and shipping channels. Initially, this was to deepen the areas and later to regularly remove sediment to maintain the required depth. Much of the dredged sediment was disposed of in the inner Hauraki Gulf. A report prepared for the Department of Conservation in 1991 estimated that over 6 million cubic metres of dredgings had been dumped in the gulf over the past 100 years.[12]

The main disposal site was on the north-west side of Rangitoto Island, with another site being occasionally used on the north-west side of Browns Island. The practice didn't raise public controversy until 1987. By then marinas had started to appear around the coast, initially at Westhaven, then at Half Moon Bay and Pine Harbour.

The 1987 controversy arose when the Auckland Harbour Board dropped a large quantity of dredged sediment, totalling 147,000 cubic metres, in shallow water of around 5 to 7 metres deep off Browns Island. The impact on the marine environment was soon apparent and it raised the ire

of the fishing, boating and diving communities. The practice was only halted after the Environmental Defence Society threatened legal action.

The Auckland Harbour Board then commissioned marine ecologist Dr Roger Grace to carry out an ecological survey of the site. He recorded an almost total (97 per cent) loss of marine life within the disposal site. He also found that the dredgings had dispersed over an area of 150 hectares, considerably larger than the disposal site itself, which was only 21 hectares in size.

With dumping at Browns Island halted, a new site was urgently sought. By 1989 the Auckland Harbour Board's role in operating the port had been taken over by the newly established Ports of Auckland Limited. A new site was identified 3 kilometres to the north of the Noises Islands, which at 30 metres, was much deeper than the Browns Island location. But there was strong opposition to this option also. Nevertheless, consent was granted for maintenance dredgings to be disposed of there and dumping commenced in August 1992.

Tony Enderby remembers diving off the Noises after the dumping occurred. 'There was a huge scallop bed that we used to go to between Motutapu and Rākino. That was completely destroyed when they dumped sediment from the Pine Harbour marina at the Noises. We decided to dive the area and about 1 metre from the bottom we dropped into this black ooze. There was nothing there. I was completely horrified. The club wrote to the Minister and said: "If we are going to be dragged through the court system if we are two or three scallops over the limit, how was it that someone could wipe out three million?'"

As a result of all the controversy, dumping was moved to a site over the edge of the continental shelf, in an area which had been used by the Navy as an explosives dump site. This is the area that is currently used for the disposal of material at sea. It is possible, however, not to dump dredgings at all, and the port company has been achieving this recently through producing 'mudcrete' from dredged material and placing it within its newly built reclamations.

As late as 2013, dredgings were still being disposed of in the Hauraki Gulf, but this practice has now stopped. The last tranche came from maintenance dredging at the Pine Harbour marina. The dredgings had been deposited on the intertidal flats adjacent to the navigation channel, but consent to continue the dumping was declined.

Sewage

Another challenge raised by the burgeoning settlement of Auckland, which directly impacted on the Waitematā, was the disposal of waste, particularly sewage. From early on, the Waitematā Harbour was used as a convenient and cheap recipient of the settlement's liquid waste. The first settlers,

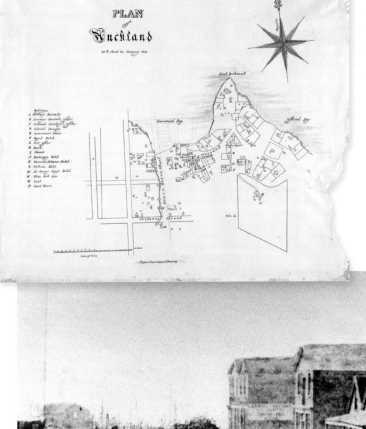

Left: Plan of Auckland showing the Ligar canal running along Lower Queen Street, and discharging into Commercial Bay in 1842. (Ref: NZ Map 4601, Sir George Grey Special Collections, Auckland Libraries)

Bottom: By the time this photograph was taken, during the 1860s, the Ligar canal had become a major public nuisance. The image shows the canal partially collapsed after heavy rain. (Ref: 4-400, Sir George Grey Special Collections, Auckland Libraries)

Story of the Gulf | **Mike Lee**

REGIONAL POLITICIAN, WAIHEKE ISLAND[13]

Born and bred in Wellington, Mike developed a strong affinity for the Hauraki Gulf during his career as a ship's officer transiting to and from Auckland.

During the 1970s he moved to Waiheke Island to live at Rocky Bay. 'The idea of Waiheke captured my imagination. I first read about the island in the *8 O'Clock* and then a sailor I met had a property there and invited me over. There were a lot of seafarers on Waiheke in those days. It was very difficult to commute. Only the most hardened commuters would get on the *Glen Rosa* at 6.15 in the morning. It would take over an hour to get to town. Commuting right through the winter, in the dark for trips both ways, discouraged a lot of shore-side workers from living there. But if you had a job at sea, you could have a cheap bach on Waiheke and then go away to sea for weeks and months on end.'

From 1972 Mike started regularly transiting the gulf on ships heading to the Cook Islands and other places, and he became very familiar with all the island landmarks in the inner and outer gulf. 'When submissions were called for on Denis Marshall's proposed Hauraki Gulf Marine Park, I took a different position from that expressed by the Auckland Regional Council at that time, which argued for a smaller "recreational park". My time at sea was probably one of the reasons why I argued that Cuvier Island should be included in a more extensive marine park, as it was a mariners' signpost into and out of Auckland when sailing to and from the Pacific. After passing Cuvier light, we would watch the land slip away over the horizon and only then we felt we were out of the Hauraki Gulf and at sea.'

Mike was elected to the Auckland Regional Council in 1992 and was chairman from 2004 until its disestablishment in 2010. He has since been the Waitematā and Gulf ward councillor on the Auckland Council. One of the issues that propelled Mike into politics was the dumping of dredgings on fishing grounds off the Noises Islands. 'I took to the dumping issue very emotionally I guess. I saw it as some sort of violation. I was also intellectually opposed to dumping in such an ecologically sensitive and relatively shallow site. It seemed totally wrong that a publicly owned port company, and a regional authority which should be protecting the gulf, were doing the opposite. I found that wrong and offensive.

Mike Lee releasing a common gecko on Crusoe Island (Pāpākōhatu), a small island located between Motuihe and Waiheke Islands. (Courtesy of Mike Lee)

So I worked hard to stop it, and with the help of many Aucklanders, especially Waiheke and Great Barrier people, we eventually succeeded. I took inspiration from the campaign Dove-Myer Robinson undertook to stop the Browns Island sewerage scheme. It was virtually mission impossible, but Robinson stopped it. I was always mindful of that during the darker days when I was fighting the sludge dumping.

'Marine dumping first became a public issue when a whole lot of dredgings from the Pine Harbour marina were dumped off Browns Island. A great big muddy plume was seen everywhere and people started asking what was going on. The *Auckland Star* got involved and it set off a public uproar. It was not long afterwards that the Ports of Auckland wanted to dump dredgings. So the powers that be thought they had better move from Browns Island further out to the Noises. This was apparently based on the same mentality that the gulf ended somewhere inshore of the islands and that they would be far enough away.

'The public fallout from the Noises dumping, in which myself and Greenpeace members Rob Morton and Hanne Sorensen were arrested, led to my successfully putting a notice of motion into the Auckland Regional Council which recommended making dumping a prohibited activity in the new regional policy statement and regional coastal plan. This led

on to a multi-party Dumping Options Advisory Group chaired by Judge Augusta Wallace, which finally persuaded the port company to desist from further dumping inside the gulf.

'The port company decided to move the dumping site much further out, past the continental shelf, and to use the Waitematā sediments to create mudcrete to expand reclamation around the container terminal. This was the last reclamation that the environmental and yachting groups agreed to and of course reclamation is now a major environmental issue with the public signalling that this must come to an end also. Other marina owners realised that it would be easier to go to the offshore site. I was chairman when the council publicly notified the Pine Harbour dumping application in 2010 and I gave an almost two-hour long submission opposing it.'

Although the dumping fight has now been won, Mike sees that there are still challenges to overcome in the future. 'We're achieving a lot on regional parks and especially on islands in terms of restoration of ecosystems. We need to replicate that in the coastal marine areas. For some mysterious reason there is a political and cultural roadblock about protecting the sea, as opposed to the land. People love to live next to reserves and parks. But from recent experience on Waiheke Island, some people object to having a marine reserve next to their coastal frontage. It's not

Top: The disposal of sediment off the Noises Islands (shown here) during the 1990s sparked public protest.
Bottom: Mike Lee was staunchly opposed to dumping in the gulf. He is shown here participating in a Greenpeace anti-dumping protest in 1992. (Courtesy of Mike Lee)

particularly logical, but it's a deeply held view. It took me fifteen years to get the Tāwharanui Marine Park turned into a fully fledged marine reserve in 2010, but there has been little else happening. The present generation will not look well in history because of our reluctance to do anything meaningful about marine protection.'

who lived in tents, then raupō whares and finally wooden houses, dug shallow wells to provide a water supply on site and disposed of sewage into cesspools, similarly dug into the soil. Not surprisingly, the water supply soon became polluted. Rubbish and sewage were also being channelled into the Horotiu Stream, now renamed the Ligar Canal after Charles Ligar who had taken over as surveyor-general from Mathew in 1841. The polluted stream then discharged into the harbour at the foot of Queen Street.[14]

In 1854, to help address this problem, the council decided to construct a main sewer down Queen Street alongside the canal. This helped to reduce the amount of sewage entering the canal itself, but the infrastructure was rudimentary and consisted of channelling raw sewage directly into the harbour.

As the population continued to grow, the Ligar Canal became a stinking open sewer. In 1870, by which time the population of Auckland had increased to just under 13,000, the *Daily Southern Cross* reported:

A great deal has been said and written about the Ligar Canal, but as yet nothing has been done to remedy the nuisance which it creates. Along the whole length of the canal, between Wellesley-street and Victoria-street, there

is an open canal full of stagnant water, which forms the receptacle of all the rubbish and garbage of the market and the dwelling-houses in the vicinity. In the summer time fetid odours are emitted from the canal, destructive to the health of the community and offensive to the nostrils of those who happen to approach the place. We sincerely hope that ere long something will be done to get rid of this abominable nuisance and standing disgrace to the sanitary authorities of the city.[15]

As the sewage issue continued to ferment in the public mind, the Auckland Harbour Board also became concerned. The raw sewage being discharged off the end of the Queen Street wharf was polluting the harbour and silting it up.[16] As a result of public protest, the council did eventually cover over the Ligar Canal. But it also continued a programme of connecting more properties to the sewerage system, thereby funnelling greater quantities of raw sewage into the harbour. By 1906, sewage was being discharged from five points along the coastline from Coxs Creek to Mechanics Bay. Due to the high level of siltation, only constant dredging kept the mouths of the pipes open.[17]

Around 1904, the idea emerged of discharging screened sewage into the harbour at Takaparawha Point, Ōrākei, on the outgoing tide. This was the narrowest part of the harbour entrance and therefore where the tidal flow was maximised. The scheme would of necessity accommodate stormwater as well as sewage, because both were channelled down the city's pipes, thereby requiring large storage tanks to be constructed. Not separating out stormwater was the norm at

Extensive works were required at Takaparawha Point to build storage tanks (shown here in 1911), a screening building and a discharge outlet. Part of these tanks now house Kelly Tarlton's Underwater World. (Watercare Services Limited)

Sewage discharge into the Hauraki Gulf, 1930s[18]

In 1933, W K Hounsell described the arrangements for sewage disposal in Auckland. 'The Auckland system discharges at a point 875 feet north-east of the Ōrākei Jetty. Sewage is discharged during each tidal period of 6½ hours commencing 2½ hours before high water. Provision is made, however, for automatic discharge during excessive rain storms occurring during the remaining period of the tide. On Saturdays, Sundays and public holidays the discharge is confined to night tides. Before being discharged all sewage passes through a screening apparatus of ¼ inch mesh.'

At that time there were separate outfalls for the North Shore. As Hounsell explains, 'the Devonport system has two outfalls. Both discharge crude sewage continuously. One outfall is situated at North Head and discharges at a depth of about six feet below L.W.S.T [Low Water Standard Tide]. The other outfall is off the southern end of Narrow Neck Beach and discharges into the Rangitoto Channel at a point about 9 feet below L.W.S.T.

'The Takapuna system has two outfalls. Both discharge crude sewage from storage tanks. The northern outfall discharges into the Rangitoto Channel at Black Rock near Milford Beach . . . The southern outfall also discharges into the Rangitoto Channel at a point off St. Leonards Road to the south of Takapuna Beach.' Northcote Point also had an outfall discharging untreated effluent at Stokes Point and there were two outfalls in the Tāmaki River discharging effluent continuously.

At that time, Hounsell estimated that on average 69 million litres of untreated sewage were being pumped into the Hauraki Gulf from Auckland each day.

the time because of the need to flush away horse droppings on the roadway surfaces and household yards.[19]

There was strong opposition to the proposal from Ngāti Whātua, as well as some other sections of the public. A Clean Harbour League was formed to protest. But the council assured the public that the screened sewage would disappear within a few yards of the outlet and that the seawater would naturally oxidise and cleanse any suspended organic matter. The harbour board withdrew its opposition in 1908, on the basis that there would be only one properly dredged outfall and that no contamination of the shores would occur. The concerns of Ngāti Whātua were brushed aside.

The Ōrākei works duly went ahead and were opened with great ceremony on 25 March 1914 by the Mayor of Auckland, James Parr. He asserted that the new works would serve Auckland, which at that stage had a population of just under 90,000, until it reached half a million. As far as the council was concerned, the sewage problem was fixed for at least another generation.[20] But it was not to be.

The council confidently expanded sewerage reticulation across the isthmus. But the growing volumes of sewage did not magically disappear into the sea as promised. When the wind and tides were adverse, the smelly discharge cycled back into the harbour and contaminated the beaches. The Ōrākei plant was becoming not only a public nuisance, but a potential health hazard.

By the late 1920s, various investigations into the sewage issue were being undertaken. The council's engineer, H H Watkins, travelled overseas to investigate alternatives. In December 1931 he released a report which proposed to abandon the Ōrākei outfall and replace it with a submarine sewer connecting to treatment works to be constructed on Browns Island, with a discharge point in the nearby Motukorea channel. The 'treatment' was to consist of screening and settling the sewage before discharge. The sludge was to be dumped in the outer gulf.[21]

As the debate over the future of Auckland's sewage raged, Aucklander Dove-Myer Robinson was concentrating on managing his thriving children's clothing manufacturing business. Robinson owned a palatial home in Glendowie, which overlooked the entrance to the Tāmaki River and had its own private beach. It was at this beach that his infant son swallowed seawater and contracted meningitis, taking over three months in hospital to recover. Robinson became convinced that the cause of his son's illness was pollution from the Ōrākei works.[22]

Robinson's interest was piqued, and in 1944 he attended an initial meeting of the Auckland and Suburban Drainage League, which had been established to challenge the Browns Island scheme. If Robinson's son had not fallen ill, thereby drawing his attention to the issue, Auckland's sewage would likely still be discharging into the inner Hauraki Gulf today.

This 1937 montage of photographs shows the Browns Island scheme (top), the existing treatment building on Tāmaki Drive (bottom right), the location of the Ōrākei discharge pipe (bottom left) and H H Watkins, who conceived of the Browns Island scheme (centre left). (*Auckland Weekly News*, Ref 7-A12173, Sir George Grey Special Collections, Auckland Libraries)

By the mid-1940s, the Ōrākei outfall had become a burning issue. It was now common practice for yachtsmen entering or leaving the harbour to wear a handkerchief over their mouths, so as not to inhale spray laden with germs.[23]

Then, in the early spring of 1947, just after the swimming season had opened, the first cases of poliomyelitis (infantile paralysis) were recorded in Auckland. By the end of November, a child had died from the disease. The public was cautioned against bathing in the polluted harbour waters, where the virus could survive for many days. When the new school term arrived in February, the schools were kept closed. By the time they opened a month later, in March 1948, 113 children had been admitted to local hospitals with the disease and the epidemic had resulted in eight deaths.[24]

This health crisis provided the incentive to accelerate the Browns Island scheme. In March 1949, the government appointed a commission of inquiry to look into the feasibility of the project. Meanwhile the drainage league, now under the leadership of Robinson, had developed quite a different and audacious concept. Robinson had studied sewerage systems overseas and was impressed by an approach adopted by some small-scale plants in the USA, which used oxidation ponds for treatment. Oxidation ponds were unheard of in New Zealand and had only been deployed on a small scale overseas. Nevertheless, Robinson proposed that the system be adopted in Auckland, with the ponds being constructed in the Manukau Harbour.[25]

The idea was too revolutionary for the establishment, and when the commission of inquiry reported in August 1949, it supported the Browns Island scheme. The Auckland Metropolitan Drainage Board, a joint councils' representative body, duly set about designing the infrastructure. In 1951, legislation to enable the scheme was before Parliament. Robinson and the league mounted strong opposition to its passing. One of the main planks of their argument was that the float tests undertaken by the scheme's proponents, in order to determine the direction in which the sewage would flow, had been inadequate. No tests had been undertaken in easterly wind conditions, when the sewage was likely to be driven into the Waitematā Harbour. Despite the vigorous challenge, Parliament passed legislation enabling the scheme.[26] It now looked very much like a fait accompli.

This portrait of Sir Dove-Myer Robinson was taken during the 1940s when he was actively opposing the Browns Island scheme. (Clifton Firth, Ref: 34-R259, Sir George Grey Special Collections, Auckland Libraries)

Then in March 1952, a vacancy occurred on the Auckland City Council, due to a councillor being disqualified from office. Robinson was asked to consider standing for election. He campaigned on the sewage issue and won, being the first independent candidate to be elected to the council since 1935. Robinson then managed to get himself elected on to the drainage board as a council representative.[27]

By this stage, controversy over sewage was reaching a boiling point in Glendowie. The suburb was largely serviced by septic tanks, and there were reports that 'sewage was seeping onto streets, oozing from banks, fouling lawns'. It was increasingly apparent that the residents were living on the top of an enormous cesspit.[28]

Urgent action was required, but the drainage board did not want to connect the suburb to the soon to be defunct Ōrākei works. So it hatched a plan to connect it to the main sewer of the Browns Island scheme, which would temporarily discharge untreated sewerage north of West Tāmaki Head, prior to its connection to the Browns Island works.

In August 1952 the drainage board announced that Karaka Bay, which was the most popular Glendowie beach, would be out of bounds for swimming once the outfall started working. This prompted public outrage. The St Heliers Bay-Glendowie Progressive Association held a public meeting in response and more than 600 people attended.[29] When the temporary outfall came into operation in 1953, Karaka Bay was closed, reigniting local opposition.

Undeterred, the drainage board continued to implement the scheme. In May 1953 it let the contract for the construction of the project to Etude et Enterprises. It was the biggest local government contract at the time. Work started in June, with an official commencement ceremony being held in August.[30] At this stage, Robinson might have been expected to admit defeat. He had fought the scheme strongly for eight years with every resource he could muster, but he had failed to stop it and now a legal contract had been entered into and construction was under way.

The local body elections were scheduled for October 1953 and Robinson decided to have one last shot at derailing the sewerage scheme. With 50 friends he formed a party called the United Independents to fight the elections. They did not win a majority of seats, but with five councillors they held the balance of power on a council split between the Citizens and Ratepayers group and Labour.[31]

Fortuitously, for most of October and November, the Etude et Enterprises contract had been plagued with labour disputes. It also transpired that the contract had started without the required consent from the Marine Department. As result, the first major stage of the project was still uncompleted when the newly appointed drainage board first met in February 1954. Labour and the United Independents agreed to elect Robinson as chairman of the board and to split the council seats on the board between the two parties. By this stage over £100,000 had been spent on the project.[32]

The drainage board took a month to undertake a review of the options, after which they decided to slow down the Browns Island contract, pending a full-scale investigation by overseas experts. Work came to a halt, the international review concluded that the project would not be able to comply with official discharge standards and the scheme was scrapped. Robinson's innovative oxidation ponds were constructed on the Manukau Harbour instead.[33] Work began on the Manukau scheme in November 1955 and it was commissioned in September 1960, significantly reducing sewage inflows into the Waitematā. At that

Sewerage and Ngāti Whātua Ōrākei

Prior to 1911, the land behind Ōkahu Bay housed a vibrant Ngāti Whātua village (papakāinga or ancestral home base). It was supplied by its surrounding farms and provisioned by the productive harbour on its waterfront. Then the Ōrākei sewerage works started snaking around the waterfront to the bay.

The large concrete sewer pipe, 2.6 metres high and 1.7 metres wide, eventually ran around the edge of the entire bay, cutting off the papakāinga from the foreshore and leading to the outfall that was built on the north-eastern headland (Takaparawha Point). As a result of the pipe and the accompanying retaining wall, the view of the sea from the papakāinga was lost, as was access for people and vessels. In addition, the concrete structure obstructed drainage of the land and so, when it rained, the settlement flooded and turned into a swampy marsh.[34]

After the works became operational, raw sewage started discharging into the marine area adjacent to the bay, contaminating the rich shellfish beds which had sustained the community for generations. 'There could have been no greater insult to a Māori tribe even if one were intended. The disposal of human waste to water, especially in such great volumes offends all sensibilities of Māori people, particularly in proximity to the main habitation place, profaning that which is sacred. It would have indicated to Ngāti Whātua what Auckland thought of them even without the spiritual connotations of Māoridom. It may also have indicated that Auckland expected they would soon no longer be there.'[35]

When a road was built along the beachfront over the sewer pipeline in 1921, the flooding of the papakāinga became worse. Three years later, most people had left the settlement and the government was keenly acquiring land parcels there. In 1936, the original tidal creek stopped flowing naturally into the eastern end of the bay. It was directed through a pipe and discharged via a culvert onto the beach.

In 1951, Auckland City Council compulsorily acquired the remaining Māori-owned land in the bay, apart from a small urupa site. The residents were evicted and their buildings demolished. One reason for the removal was that the village was considered 'a dreadful eyesore and potential disease centre' on the route that the Queen planned to take on her 1953 official visit to Auckland.[36]

Tamaiti Tamaariki grew up in the papakāinga after the sewage pipe was built around the bay. He lived with his uncle who had the job of operating the sewage outfall. 'An hour after full tide he would open the gates and let all the sewage out.' Even though the sewage was discharged on the outgoing tide, 'in a north-east wind it would push everything right back into the bay. In the morning it would be all around the beaches. The backwash would go up the creek. It was filthy.' The children still swam in the bay, enjoying the warmth of the sewage-laden water and being unaware of the disease risk.[37]

Looking south-west from Takaparawha Point across Ōkahu Bay, showing the sewer running along the foreshore, 1921. (Ref: 4-4429, Sir George Grey Special Collections, Auckland Libraries)

time, the oxidation ponds were the largest in the world in full-time service.[38] The ponds themselves have since been removed, being replaced with more modern technology, but the Māngere scheme is still processing the bulk of Auckland's sewage over 50 years later.

Dove-Myer Robinson (known affectionately as Robbie) later became Auckland's longest-serving mayor and he was knighted in 1970. He pushed for the establishment of a regional body in Auckland, the Auckland Regional Authority, and was its founding chair. He also advocated for rapid rail as a far-sighted, long-term solution to Auckland's transportation needs but the government reneged on a pledge to pay for the scheme.[39]

Solid waste disposal

As well as being the recipient of Auckland's sewage for many years, the Waitematā Harbour was also targeted for the disposal of household and industrial waste. In the early days of Auckland, individuals managed their own waste, disposing of it where they could. Some went into the harbour reclamations. The council started a collection service in the early 1900s and, until the 1930s, most refuse was burnt in an incinerator. Then a system of controlled tipping was instituted, with estuaries and low-lying areas on the fringes of the gulf particularly targeted. Tipping was seen as a convenient way of disposing of waste and, at the same time, of reclaiming tidal inlets and turning what were considered to be muddy wastelands into valuable waterfront land.

As the city grew and living standards rose, so did the amount of rubbish produced. The establishment of formal tipping sites was intended to reduce the large amount of illegal tipping that was occurring. But such sites were quickly filled and councils looked around the waterfront for new dumps.

By 1964, the Devonport Borough Council had run out of capacity for refuse. There was a tip at Narrow Neck Beach on Seabreeze Road (at that time called Malvern Road) but this was now full, to the relief of nearby residents. 'No more rats as big as cats, no more billowing smoke filling up their homes, no more weekend scavengers raking about among muck and rubbish which others have cast off.'[40] There had been a proposal to tip rubbish at the end of Kawerau Avenue (at that time called Princes Street), but this had been dropped due to objections from local residents. So attention turned to Ngataringa Bay, at a location adjacent to the war memorial on Lake Road. This was a proposal that

Motions Creek and the landward end of Meola Reef, shown here in 1953, were transformed by Auckland's largest harbour landfill. (Whites Aviation, Ref: WA-33142-F, Alexander Turnbull Library, Wellington, New Zealand)

received support from the editor of the *North Shore Times* who (reflecting the prevalent thinking of the time about tidal inlets) wrote in an editorial on 11 March 1964:

Ngataringa Bay foreshore with its mangroves is a vast area of emptiness just asking for something to be done to it. The obvious way is to start with a rubbish dump . . . There may be some inconvenience to nearby residents, but if the council keeps meticulous watch on the proposed dump's nuisance value, Ngataringa Bay could grow and grow, without detriment to health, and truly become an asset to Devonport. It is a long-term scheme but filling in the bay — with rubbish and what-have-you — should not be delayed.[41]

The proposal went ahead. By the early 1970s, there were some 14 tips on the edge of the Hauraki Gulf, extending north to Whangateau and south to Kaiaua. The largest of these was at Meola Reef, near Motions Creek. The tip extended from Motions Road to the reef and during the 1970s, before its closure, was taking around 34,600 tons of refuse a year.[42]

Local residents have vivid memories of the Meola landfill during their youth. Tony Goodwin recalls, as a child, building canoes out of corrugated iron to 'invade' the tip by sea and rummage for treasure. By the time he was a teenager, Meola Road had been built through the tip and access was easier. He used to go there with friends to hunt for rats that 'lived here in their tens of thousands'.[43] Denis Reidy recalls the stench from the tip drifting over his home in summer, the rats, and finding useful bits for his trolleys, radios and bicycles.[44]

Although new sites had been located around the harbour edge, they too were becoming overwhelmed. A rubbish crisis was developing. As described by *New Zealand Herald* staff reporter Alan Hill in 1971: 'The simple fact is that Aucklanders are producing more and more rubbish from more and more people and [they are] rapidly running out of places to put it.'[45] Councils started looking inland for sites that were away from residential areas and could be better managed. The old harbour edge sites were all gradually closed and capped. Many were turned into parks. But pollutants still continue to leach from these old sites into the sea.

Quarrying sand and shingle

The fast-growing settlement of Auckland required sand, shingle and shell for use in the construction of roads, bridges and buildings. The most readily available sources were the numerous beaches and bays dotted around the Hauraki Gulf. In the early days, material was freely sourced from beaches close to Auckland. Small ketches and cutters would be grounded on the sand and would lie over on their sides when the tide went out. Sand would then be scooped into their holds with long-handled shovels before the vessels floated off on the next tide.[46]

The Marine Department endeavoured to bring the practice under control and, for a small royalty, started issuing permits to allow the removal of shell and shingle from designated beaches. Material was initially sourced from the beaches closest to Auckland, but as those sources were exhausted, scow owners and aggregate merchants looked further afield.

At first, the department seemed more concerned with collecting royalties for the extraction activities, rather than with managing any impacts on the affected beaches. But gradually, as land started eroding and property owners complained, issues of sediment supply were given greater consideration. At this time, knowledge of sediment dynamics was rudimentary at best and assessment of whether or not a beach could sustain

quarrying was based on a simple physical examination.

Early on, sediment sources in the Hauraki Gulf were considered to be unlimited. It was not understood at the time, that the seemingly vast sand and gravel resources in the gulf had arrived largely as a result of the Waikato River historically discharging into the Firth of Thames, and bringing with it large quantities of material from the rapidly eroding central plateau. About 20,000 years ago, when the course of the river changed to discharge at Port Waikato, the main sediment supply to the gulf was cut off. This meant that beaches that were quarried were unlikely to be naturally replenished.

Concerned about the removal of sediment from their beaches, the Chamberlin family who owned Pōnui Island, went to court to uphold their rights. They obtained a ruling to the effect that material could not be removed from the foreshore (above mean high water) without the landowner's consent. As a result, some landowners kept their beaches off limits. But many others saw the aggregate trade as a way of generating additional income during hard times and they 'sold' their beaches in exchange for a royalty payment. Many of these quarrying contracts were picked up by the major shingle merchants at that time, including Winstone, James Craig, the Bryants and the McCallum brothers.[47]

The two most productive beaches for the provision of shingle were Hooks Bay (Te Patu) on the far eastern end of Waiheke Island and Waikawau on the Thames coast.

James Craig became a substantial shingle merchant in Auckland. As well as removing large volumes of shingle from Te Patu, he took significant amounts off Owhanake Bay at Waiheke Island and off the Pōnui Island beaches. Closer to Auckland, Craig purchased the Couldrey farm at Maraetai in 1911 and took shell and gravel from the beach. The mining of Maraetai Beach took place for the next 30 years, despite attempts by the Marine Department, from 1910 onwards, to stop it. The scows would work at night and were therefore hard to catch.[48]

Len Pollard, who holidayed at Maraetai during the early 1920s, can remember the excitement when the scows came to load up on the beach and he would go aboard to have a look around. 'The men worked at low tide filling the wheelbarrows which had three foot high plank sides. They were very heavy when filled with sand and the men were exceptionally strong. They used oil-soaked rags for lights when working at night.'[49]

As early as 1910 erosion was affecting the Maraetai

For years scowmen were a common sight around the Hauraki Gulf, scooping shingle and sand up off the beaches. Shown here is the *Waiti* taking on a load of shingle at Kawakawa Bay during the 1920s. (Kawakawa Bay Historical Society, Auckland Libraries Footprints number 00790)

coastal road and a seawall had to be built to protect it. Somewhat ironically, the stone to build the wall was taken from the beach.

The North Shore was another readily accessible location where sand, shell and rocks were extracted. By January 1910, residents at Milford Beach were strongly objecting to the wholesale removal of sand and shell from the beach by scows and the beach was finally closed to extraction in 1912, as it was by then 'showing rapid signs of depletion by the removal of sand'. But illegal quarrying still occurred and residents complained of scows taking away many loads. In addition, it was revealed that the foreman of works for the Waitemata City Council often sent his men to the beach to get sand for road-building purposes.[50]

Interest then moved to Campbells Bay (Waipapa), which was further to the north and considered to be far enough away from the residential settlements at Takapuna and Milford to be out of the public eye. But the owners of land nearby became concerned that the loss of sand was destroying the recreational values of the beach and its future prospect as a holiday-home subdivision. This was in spite of the fact that the Marine Department, after an inspection in March 1912, reported that they could 'see no trace whatever of the alleged spoilation of this beach, as the supply of sand is simply unlimited. In several places we dug deep holes, but were unable to reach bottom, which fact I think proves that the removal of material from below high water

mark has so far not affected this beach.' But the property owners prevailed and the beach was closed for two years. It was reopened for quarrying in 1914 when Motuihe Island, which at that time was being used for sand extraction, was closed for use as a war detention centre.

Meanwhile the beach at Campbells Bay was subdivided and the properties sold on the basis that they were located on a 'private beach'. Owners camped on their sites or built baches there. Scows started arriving on the beach and large loads of sand were shovelled up. The owners protested vigorously, expressing concerns that the quarrying was depreciating the value of their property and that it was making bathing on the beach dangerous. In addition they complained that the privacy of the beach was gone with the arrival of the scows and that it was certainly no longer 'suitable for ladies and children to be bathing when scows are there loading, as most of the crews work in clothes that can only be fittingly described as "scant"'.

The Campbells Bay operations were finally closed for good and the search was on for other suitable quarrying sites. So in 1914 the inspector of beaches and the superintendent of marine conducted a survey and identified a range of beaches where 'the material found thereon is of the highest quality, and in most cases of unlimited quantity'. In addition the men were 'both satisfied that if these beaches are opened, no damage is likely to occur to the adjacent land, and that they are never likely to be

Removal of shingle at Hooks Bay (Te Patu), Waiheke Island

The Hook family started farming the remote land at Te Patu during the 1860s. By the turn of the century, demand for shingle was strong and scowmen were poaching gravel from the beach.

In 1913, John Hook sold sole extraction rights to J J Craig Limited for £50. Shingle scows became frequent visitors to the bay during the day and night. John's son Alf recalls coming home from school, during the dark in mid-winter, and seeing 'the lights flickering all along our bay, the wicks in bowls on stands driven into the shingle. It was such a pretty sight. Five or six boats were working the shingle at our own beach.'[51]

Alf's brother Jimmy was employed to wheelbarrow the shingle down the beach to the mid-tide level before the scows arrived. Here it was deposited to allow the tide to wash it clean. The scows would then arrive two hours after high water. Narrow planks would be set up between the beach and the hold of the scow, and the scowmen would race up and down from the beach, along the narrow gangway, with their heavy loads. It was a highly skilled operation, as one mistake and the wheelbarrow and shingle would tumble to the beach. The skipper was always keeping an eye on the tide and weather, to make sure that they were loaded and away on the next tide. To be caught grounded on an exposed beach during a storm could mean disaster and several scows were wrecked on the beach.[52]

The Te Patu shingle helped to build much of Auckland, including Grafton Bridge. But there was a cost. The removal of such large quantities of material affected the dynamics of the beach and the sea started moving inland, eventually flooding 8 hectares of foreshore. Sheep yards, vegetables and flower gardens were submerged and the farmhouse had to be moved inland to avoid the floods. The Hooks cut the house in half, put it on runners and towed it to higher ground. In 1981 Arthur Hook sold the farm to the late John Spencer.[53]

required as a Public resort'. In hindsight, they couldn't have been more wrong on the second point. The beaches identified included Long Bay, now a very popular regional park, Tawhitokino, another regional park, and Oneroa Bay, now one of the most popular beaches on Waiheke Island.

By the 1920s, during the post-war boom and at a time when supplies of indigenous timber started to run out, prices for sand and shingle had soared. As the 'open' beaches became worked out and the cost of accessing them rose, there was a growing incentive to poach off the 'closed' beaches that had a more generous supply of sand and gravel. Ted Ashby, in his book *Phantom Fleet*, describes how as a scowman during the 1920s and '30s he was involved in regular poaching. In an example of a double standard, Ashby vowed never to take a pebble off his home beach at Ōrere, but he stole shingle from a closed beach on the Thames coast, claiming that the source was Ōrere where he held a permit. As he recounted:

> There are two good shingle beaches just north of
> Coromandel and they had been closed for years as the
> property was controlled by some Māori trust. The shingle
> had really built up there and was nearly perfect aggregate.
> We picked the weather and tide right, dirty nor'easterly,
> high tide around 1 am, punched across the gulf, pushed
> the barges shoulder-in on the beach at 11 pm, and were
> away loaded before high tide. This was exceptionally good
> shingle and soon I had an order for another load.[54]

Ashby also relates how another scowman illegally took a load of shell-derived sand off the end of St Heliers Bay beach. It was during the day this time and, in the process of loading the sand, the scow became stranded. He could easily have been caught red-handed, but the tide soon washed away the incriminating evidence of sand removal. In addition, it was not unusual for scows to be seen on beaches in those days, moving cargo around the gulf. He was able to refloat during the evening's high tide and finally make his escape. Motuihe Island was another location for poached shell sand.[55]

The extensive shell banks in the Hauraki Gulf were also exploited for a variety of purposes. Shell was burnt to make lime, an important component of brick making, and later fertiliser. A number of limeworks were established

In 1912, the Marine Department concluded that the supply of sand at Campbells Bay was 'simply unlimited'. This proved not to be the case and significant erosion has now occurred, baring the bedrock.

around the gulf. For example, from about 1870 to 1920, John Granger operated limeworks at his farm bordering Eastern Beach. The raw material was the large cockle shells which had deposited in mounds up to several metres thick on the flats. Railway lines were built to carry the shell on small trucks from the beach to the kilns. The burnt lime was loaded onto scows. After the operation had ceased the area was subdivided and built on.[56]

During the early 1930s, in order to provide cheap fertiliser for farms that were lime deficient, Herbie Tait and Charlie Hodge established the Miranda Lime Works, based on the extensive shell banks in the area. The resultant lime was used on nearby farms, barged to Thames and carted to the railway at Pokeno for wider distribution. The works burnt down twice and were rebuilt. They finally closed for good in the early 1950s. Shell from Miranda was also processed as fowl grit. During the 1930s, scows would go up to the Miranda shell banks on king tides, shovel up the shell and sell it in Auckland.[57]

The quarrying of sand and shingle from beaches in the gulf has left its mark. There are few records of the quantities of sand taken in the early days, but extraction continued for many years. Many of the beaches only replenish sediment slowly, if at all, so its removal has often resulted in coastal erosion and loss of sandy beaches.

A 1982 study undertaken by Applied Geology Associates assessed the extent of historical mining. It documented over 750,000 cubic metres being extracted from Ōmaha spit from the 1940s to the 1980s. Resultant erosion of the end of the spit imperilled a subdivision there. Significant amounts were also extracted from Hydes Beach on the Tāwharanui Peninsula, but magnitudes were considerably less, at just over 74,000 cubic metres. As early as the 1940s, erosion was reported at this beach. Sand was also removed from Kawakawa Bay during the late 1960s and early 1970s, with levels exceeding over 5000 cubic metres a year for seven years. There is now little sand left on this beach.[58]

The Auckland City Council recently spent millions of dollars reversing some of the impacts of sand mining by replenishing sand on inner city beaches, such as St Heliers, Kohimaramara and Point Chevalier, so that Aucklanders can better enjoy them.

The development of the urban fabric of Auckland has left a large footprint on the Hauraki Gulf. In the early days of settlement, the gulf was largely seen as a place from which to extract resources and to wrest dry land from the sea, as well as being a convenient location to dispose of waste. In more recent times, waste disposal has largely been moved away from the gulf marine area and sand is no longer quarried off its beaches. Reclamation has slowed but still continues. A legacy of a highly modified environment remains.

Chapter 6
Transforming the land

In addition to the abundant resources in the sea, it was the rich natural wealth of the shores of the Hauraki Gulf that supported its communities. Early European economies in the region were very much based on exploiting those resources, both for use by the new settlers and for sale to export markets.

Port Jackson, Coromandel Peninsula.

the like. Auckland itself was fuelling a strong demand for timber, with an 1861 survey revealing that 5236 of the 6036 buildings recorded in the settlement were constructed from kauri.[1] But much of the timber was exported to places such as Sydney and California.

Coromandel Peninsula

The Coromandel Peninsula was one of the early locations for kauri logging in the Hauraki Gulf. Sydney merchant Gordon Browne built the first water-powered timber mill in Mercury Bay around 1837. Browne had purchased 1500 hectares of land from Ngāti Hei: one block in the upper catchment of the Whitianga River and the other extending west from the Pūrangi River at the eastern end of Cooks Beach to Ferry Landing on the eastern shores of the mouth of Whitianga Harbour. He built a stone wharf at Ferry Landing for vessels to tie up to and load timber and this is still in use as a ferry wharf today.[2]

The mill itself was built in the Ounuroa Valley, in an area that became known as Mill Creek. Ngāti Hei did most of the work to fell the trees and the timber was sent to Sydney. It was here that one of the largest living forest giants was recorded. The tree had a girth of more than 22 metres and was over 20 metres high to the first branch. It was sighted during the 1840s, but a decade later had been killed by fire.[3] Despite the abundance of large kauri in the area, Browne struggled to make the operation pay, and the stress of mounting debt affected his mental health. He died in 1842.[4]

By the 1860s, kauri logging had extended to the rugged hills behind Whitianga. Unlike other native timbers, kauri floated and could therefore be transported via water. Numerous kauri dams were built across creeks to trap water and stockpile the logs. Once a sufficient head of water had accumulated, it could be released in one massive burst, driving the logs downstream at great speed. Prior to undertaking log drives, obstacles in the water-courses were removed, often through blasting. Booms constructed in the lower reaches of the rivers would contain the logs once they had hurtled down the hillsides. They were then either milled locally and shipped out or connected into rafts and towed to the Auckland mills situated in Freemans Bay.[5]

As the volumes of timber coming out of the hinterland increased, further mills were built, the largest being constructed at Whitianga in 1883. Waste slabs of wood and sawdust were burnt on Buffalo Beach, in a fire that was kept

The rich kauri forests were logged, minerals extracted, wetlands drained, scrub crushed and burnt, and farms established. Kauri logging was one of the early activities. The trees grow to an enormous size, with some living for 3000 years, several times longer than the entire span of human settlement in the gulf. Early cutting of these forest giants, which grew abundantly in the lush catchments of the Hauraki Gulf, was largely to supply ships' spars. But it was not long before accessible trees that were suitable for this purpose had been largely cut out. The focus then moved to pit-sawn timber for construction of boats, houses and

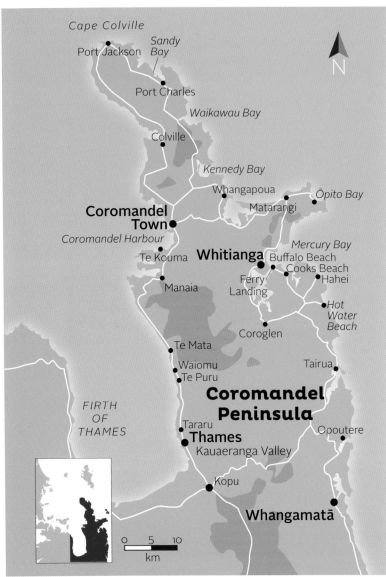

continuously going for 40 years. In 1922, the large mill was finally closed and the equipment shipped to Great Barrier Island; the kauri that had fuelled the local economy for over 80 years had been finally exhausted.[6]

One of the last areas to be logged there was at No Gum, so called because there was no kauri gum to be found in the ground. Tenders were called for in 1918 and the last timber came out during the early 1920s.[7] The destruction of this area was described by one commentator as a tragedy because it was 'comparable in beauty and interest with Waipoua Forest and Trounson Park'. Even the loggers had some misgivings about felling the exceptional forest giants found in the block.[8]

At the head of the valley was a group of around 40 majestic kauri trees, averaging 12 metres high to the first branch. Amongst them was one of the most perfect trees that logger and bush photographer Tudor Collins had ever seen. He and his co-worker nicknamed it the 'Umbrella Tree, for its crown of perfectly balanced branches spread out over 30 feet, giving sufficient shelter for a hundred head of wild cattle'. But they were contracted to fell the tree and so they did.[9]

Kauri was milled at Whitianga over a period of 85 years. This 1886 image shows the first timber mill that was built on the Whitianga flats by the Mercury Bay Timber Company. (Ref: 535, Mercury Bay Museum)

William Webster: King of the Waiau

USA-born William Webster arrived in New Zealand in 1835. He initially worked for Gordon Browne at Mercury Bay but soon set up a timber and trading post at Herekino Bay on Whanganui Island at the mouth of the Coromandel Harbour.

He married Ngāti Whanaunga chief Te Horeta's daughter. Webster was involved in several of the gulf's early resource-based industries — timber, mining and farming. By the late 1830s he had established a virtual monopoly over trading between Pākehā and Māori in the Hauraki Gulf.[10]

John Logan Campbell wrote about Webster, whom he called 'The King of Waiau', in his autobiography *Poenamo*. Campbell described the setting of Webster's trading station when he visited in 1840:

> *We are in a beautiful little land-locked circular harbour, but with hardly deep-water anchorage for more than half-a-dozen large ships to swing clear, though room enough for a large fleet of small craft. The shore shoals suddenly all round, where it meets the flat land at the base of the high range of hills forming the background; a steep range more than a thousand feet high, timber-covered to the very summit with evergreen foliage. Snow never falls on these hills. Between the spurs sloping down towards the shore are tiny, beautiful valleys, in which native villages can be seen nestling picturesquely. We are lying off a small island which forms part of the small harbour; we can see not far off a narrow passage between the island and the mainland, so narrow that I was often afterwards navigated across on the back of a Māori wahine when none of the male sex were at hand. Abreast of us there is quite a pretty little bay and fine beach. We can see an incongruous collection of buildings, some weather-boarded, some evidently of native construction; then again there are quite a number of log huts, and there is the frame of a small craft on the stocks with all her ribs nearly completed. This little bay rejoiced in the name of Herekino when I knew it in the days of yore. And here lived and reigned the King of Waiau . . .*[11]

Entrance of Coromandel Heads, East. (Charles Heaphy, Ref: PD-1952-2-2-18, Auckland War Memorial Museum Tāmaki Paenga Hira)

Further down the coast, Aucklander Richard Seccombe obtained rights from Ngāti Hei to cut timber on a large block of land surrounding Tairua. The agreement permitted him to build a mill on the edge of the harbour, which he did in 1864. Like Browne in Whitianga, Seccombe struggled to make the mill pay, but he developed a very successful brewery business which eventually became the Lion Brewery.[12] The sawdust and waste slabs from the mill were dumped on the foreshore, reclaiming an area of 3 hectares, which provided a place for stacking sawn timber. The mill closed in 1906 and the last rafts of timber logs were hauled out of the small township in 1917. Most of the population then left as their timber-based jobs disappeared.[13]

Sawmills were constructed in many other bays dotted around the Coromandel Peninsula during the kauri logging era, including Colville, Coromandel Harbour, Port Charles, Waikawau Bay, Kennedys Bay and Whangapoua.[14]

The Thames gold rush, which began in the late 1860s, generated an enormous demand for timber from the hinterland — to build the flourishing town, for supports inside the mines and to fuel the numerous stamper batteries used to crush the hard quartz rock. The hillsides around Thames were soon stripped bare and interest turned to timber stands further inland. In 1871, seizing the financial opportunity created by the strong demand, Auckland businessman C J Stone managed to secure from the Māori landowners 99-year cutting rights over large areas of the Kauaeranga Valley. With his brother Robert, he constructed a sawmill at the mouth of the river and a huge chain boom at Parawai to hold the logs that came down the valley.[15] On one day, in November 1873, 2000 logs were released from behind a dam, hurtling at speed down the streambed to the booms below.[16] By the early twentieth century, accessible kauri in the valley had been worked out and the lower flats developed into farms. The last timber was extracted from high up in the hills after the First World War.

As a result of kauri logging, many hills around the Coromandel Peninsula were shorn of their indigenous forest. But another legacy of the kauri era was the scoured-out rivers where the logs had been driven down the valleys. As Tairua resident Phyllis Cory-Wright reminisced in 1988, 'Fifty years ago, the history of the River Waiwawa at Coroglen could be clearly seen: the banks and bush growth had been swept away by the passage of thousands of great kauri trunks in the drives to the sea. All soil and sand had gone, and the once deep bed of the river had been filled with friction-smoothed boulders which had rolled down its steep course.'[17]

During the mid-1920s, work started on replanting

The demands of the gold-mining industry in Thames initially fuelled the exploitation of kauri in the Kauaeranga Valley. This 1922 image shows an enormous kauri, 35.5 metres in girth, which was felled in the area. (Tudor Collins, Ref: 191, Mercury Bay Museum)

Story of the Gulf | **Toby Morcom**

RETIRED FARMER, COOKS BEACH[18]

Toby grew up on his family's dairy farm in Tokoroa. One day his father saw an advertisement for 400 acres [160 hectares] of cheap land near the 309 Road in Coromandel. So he and his father went up to take a look.

'When we got there the land agent said, "Frankly I wouldn't like to sell this land to you. But," he said, "I've got a place on my books that's only just come on the market. It's 2500 acres [1000 hectares] just across the river behind Cooks Beach." Dad says, "Do I look like a millionaire?" And the bloke said, "This is what they want for it and I would be surprised if 100 acres of dairy in Tokoroa wouldn't get that kind of money, anyway." So that changed the whole situation as far as we were concerned.

'We went to have a look at the property. The previous owners were Englishmen, who knew nothing about farming, but had bought the land to get Cook's Beach subdivided. Now they wanted to get rid of the balance of the land. There was a little cottage in Flaxmill Bay that was only twelve months old. It was an absolutely gorgeous spot. There were a couple of blocks of grass in the valleys and it was milking 70 cows, the same as we were doing in Tokoroa, so the income would have been about the same. Dad and I talked about the property on the five-hour drive south and, by the time we got home, Mum didn't have a chance.

'We all moved here in August 1953. We just loved the place. I had never really been boating before, but after two months we bought a 25-foot launch. You didn't have any trouble catching fish then, they were everywhere.

'After a couple of years, Dad sold me 1200 acres [500 hectares] on the eastern end of the farm. I borrowed the purchase money from the Marginal Lands Board which had very easy terms, only 5 per cent interest, and they compounded it on the capital as you went. I borrowed an old Fordson for the first year or so. It had steel wheels and I ran it around crushing scrub. Then I got a loan, bought a second-hand crawler tractor and got stuck into the rest. I did a lot of fencing and built a wool shed and cattle yards. I gradually developed the place until we had about 800 acres [320 hectares] in grass and we grazed 2000 sheep and 200 beef cattle.

'Infrastructure was rudimentary at the beginning. We got power in 1962 and before that had generators. Initially we would row across the harbour to Whitianga to get supplies. Eventually we got an outboard so we could motor across.'

There are other differences since Toby first arrived in the area. Looking over the Pūrangi River, he observes: 'the mangroves weren't there. There was a thin line on the edge of the hill and all the rest was rushes covered at high tide. Now a very vast expanse of mangroves has grown up. They get a fair bit of nutrition, as I was not the only person breaking in country in the headwaters of the Pūrangi. All the guys at Hāhei were busy breaking land in. When you get an easterly deluge, then the creek runs yellow with silt and it all ends up in the estuary and feeds the mangroves. Nobody's doing much clearing anymore, but there's still erosion during heavy rain.'

Right: Cooks Beach farmer Toby Morcom has seen many changes over his 60 years living in the area.
Bottom: Morcom family picnic on land at Cooks Beach. (Courtesy of Toby Morcom)

Huge kauri driving dams, such as the one shown here in the Kauaeranga Valley, were used to drive the logs down the rivers to the sea. This image illustrates the damage done to the rivers by this practice, with the beds scoured out by the logs. (Ref: 0059, Mercury Bay Museum)

forests to replenish those that had been removed. Kauri was replaced with much faster-growing exotic pine species. The first afforestation project was established in the hills behind the Tairua and Whangamatā harbours, and became known as the Tairua State Forest. During the 1940s, further planting took place in the Kauaeranga Valley and at Whangapoua.[19] These forests are now clear-fell harvested on an approximately 30-year cycle.

After the Second World War, the government pursued a programme of settling returned servicemen onto rural land and, by the 1950s, a 'marginal lands' policy was in place. This encouraged farmers to convert steeper marginal land, which was reverting to bush, into pasture. Farming expanded into the Coromandel Ranges and former mill towns, such as

Tairua and Whitianga, became small rural service centres. They eventually took on new life as popular holiday-home settlements after roading improved during the 1960s.

Great Barrier Island

Great Barrier Island became the focus of a large timber-focused commercial operation during the early twentieth century. As a result of the 1880s depression, demand for kauri plummeted and the mills struggled to make ends meet. Taking advantage of the depressed market, a syndicate of Melbourne businessmen formed the Kauri Timber Company with the intent of acquiring a major stake in the New Zealand kauri industry. The company acquired 24 mills, freehold title over 60,000 hectares of land and timber leases over a further 100,000 hectares. This comprised virtually all the interests in the kauri industry, aside from those held by the Crown.[20]

The company's Auckland mill in Freemans Bay could not keep up with the large number of logs coming out of the Pukete Bush in the Bay of Islands. Instead of building a mill at Pukete, which would need to be removed when the kauri there ran out, the company looked for a more central location where kauri logs coming from a range of sources could be processed over a longer period of time. It also sought to close down smaller, less economical mills, such as the one at Tairua, to centralise processing on fewer larger operations.

The company identified Whangaparapara Harbour, located on the western coast of Great Barrier Island, as being an excellent location for a large new mill. This was particularly due to its deep sheltered harbour, which would enable vessels to tie up close to the shore to load sawn timber, avoiding the need to ferry the wood out in small rowboats. The harbour was close to the Coromandel Peninsula, where there were significant kauri stands, and was also on a direct route from the Bay of Islands, which at that time was the other main logging area. The remote location may also have enabled the company to avoid the customs duty which was payable on goods entering Auckland Harbour. Timber could be exported directly overseas from the island.[21]

A timber mill was constructed at the head of Whangaparapara Harbour in 1909. At that time the mill was reputed to be the largest in the southern hemisphere, employing 50 men. A township of 200 people grew up around it, including a shop, post office, school, hall and library. A large wharf, 275 metres long, was built out into the bay to enable ships to tie up alongside. The harbour became a busy international port, with ships loaded for destinations as far afield as Norway and Italy, as well as for Australia and other parts of New Zealand. Up to eight vessels were in the harbour at a time, waiting to take on loads. The mill operated until the outbreak of the First Word War. It closed in 1914, due to a lack of labour and a decreasing demand for timber, and was never reopened.[22]

Remains of the mill can still be seen. These include wharf piles, railway tracks, a chimney stack and machinery. Also evident along the shoreline are reclaimed areas where sawdust and waste wood were dumped into the harbour.[23]

With the mill closed, attention turned to logging the inaccessible stands of relatively small kauri left on the island. They were located on steep and rugged terrain and required the extensive use of dams and blasting to get the logs down the hills and into the sea. During the mid-1920s, seven kauri dams were built on the Kaiarāra Stream

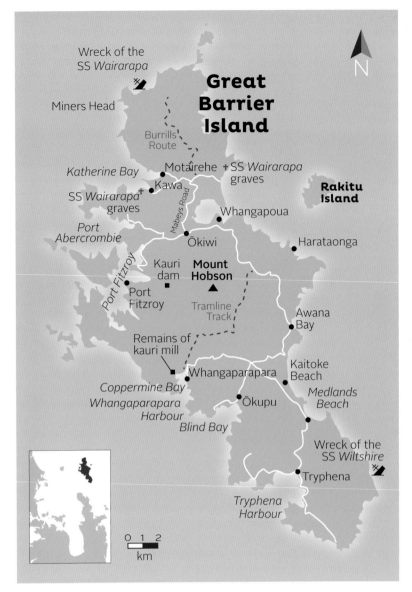

on the western slopes of Mount Hobson (Hirakimata). They were some of the last built anywhere in New Zealand. When he visited during the 1930s, John Mowbray described the carnage wreaked on the Kaiarāra Stream by the log drives:

The banks of the stream had been torn and mutilated. Its bed was four or five times its former width. The trim little shingle bars of two years previously had been lacerated or swept out of existence. In their place lay enormous yellow boulders. It gradually dawned on me that this is what happened when the timber men carried out their flooding operations to get the kauri to the sea. The defacement of the valley was complete. One realised that it was inevitable. But never again will the Kaiarāra be what it was. The clumps of kauri that I remembered were gone. There were dead branches and leaves among the undergrowth, and here and there a young or withered tree. But the plumes that had decked the skyline were no longer there.[24]

Story of the Gulf | **Bill Burrill**

RETIRED FARMER AND LOCAL GOVERNMENT POLITICIAN, AUCKLAND[25]

Bill Burrill's father Max purchased the 4826-hectare Ōkiwi Station (formerly the Arundel Estate) on the northern end of Great Barrier Island in 1964. The property included the old copper mine workings at Miners Head.

Max bought the land from Great Barrier Farms Limited, an enterprise of three partners who a decade earlier had hoped to start a farming and timber-milling operation on the block. But they failed. When the Burrills took over, there was just over a hectare of cleared land and a couple of dilapidated Lockwood houses.

Max had already established a solid reputation as a prosperous farmer. Wellington born, he started off his farming career driving stock on his family's Ōtara farm. At 25 years of age, he became a dairy farmer in his own right on a property in Wiri. He did well and eventually owned three profitable farms in South Auckland. Max made the decision to buy the Great Barrier block after reading a soil survey map which indicated that the island was covered in karaka soil, similar to that found at East Tāmaki and Māngere, which was extremely productive when converted to pasture. In addition, there were government incentives available for developing marginal land.

Bill remembers the first expedition to establish themselves on the land. Bert Subritzky took them over on a barge with around 70 tons of goods, including a power generator, a truck, drums of diesel and a contractor with a bulldozer and tractor. The barge landed at Motairehe in Katherine Bay and the gear had to be carted some distance over the hill to Ōkiwi. The first area they cleared was 60 hectares on the seaward side of the road adjoining the Whangapoua estuary. It had reverted from early pasture and was covered in manuka up to 20 feet high.

They built a scrub-crushing roller from an old boiler filled with sand. This was towed behind the bulldozer, crushing the trees, which were then left to dry for several weeks before being burnt. The soil was then harrowed with a disc, fertilised, seeded and fenced. A flock of ewes was sent over that winter after the grass had established. For the first year they used a contractor, but then Max bought a bulldozer and the Burrills did the clearing work themselves. By year five they were clearing land on both sides of Mabeys Road which curved around the Whangapoua wetland and estuary.

Bill recalls 'the burn aspect of it was bloody scary. There was three to four hundred acres [120–160 hectares] of

Farmer Max Burrill at the entrance to Ōkiwi Station. Max eventually gifted much of the land to the people of New Zealand. (Courtesy of Bill Burrill)

crushed manuka, kanuka and akeake lit up and back burnt so it was burning into the centre all at once. The only tool I had was a length of milking machine pipe with wadded rag in one end and a cork in the top. I had a box of matches to light it. The pipe was full of diesel and I dobbed the burning end on the ground every stride. I kept walking briskly as the fire was coming right behind me.'

The success of the farm development was such that, in 1970, the government brought the British Common Market negotiator Geoffrey Rippon to the Ōkiwi property to see the land development process first-hand. Of the visit, The *New Zealand Herald* reporter wrote: 'On Mr Burrill's property at Ōkiwi, which was bought in a derelict state only six years ago, he saw how good green acres are still being won from virgin scrubland.' By that stage 400 hectares had been cleared and grassed and there were 3500 sheep and 375 cattle on the property.

After about eight years of relying on the vagaries of shipping companies to move stock and equipment off and on the island, the Burrills decided to buy their own barge landing craft, the *Ngapuhi*. Bill became the skipper: 'I had a watch, a compass and

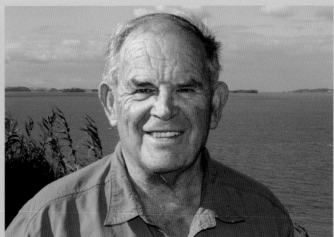

a chart and I could find my way around the gulf. I did every trip at night as livestock travel better then as it's cooler.'

It was around this time that the Burrills were approached by the Rākino Residents and Ratepayers Association. 'They realised that Rākino Island was a firebomb and that the thick layer of dead buffalo grass and kikuyu was hazardous to baches. So we obtained a licence to graze the island and did so for the following eleven years. It operated like a little ranch, with only one paddock surrounding the stockyard.

This started a period when Bill was busy moving stock around the Hauraki Gulf, as well as running his own dairy farm in South Auckland. 'I would hop on *Ngapuhi* with a mate and set sail from the Tāmaki River near Highbrook on an outgoing tide. It was a ten-hour trip to Port Fitzroy. We would arrive at some ungodly time in the morning. There were no lights, so I would have to find my way up to the Fitzroy wharf in the dark. We would tie up 'til daylight and sleep until Gordon and the other staff from the farm arrived to start unloading.

'Then it was seven hours from Port Fitzroy to Rākino. We would run the barge into the bay, let down the landing ramp, open the gates and chase the animals out. We would then pull out and go back to Fitzroy, another six to seven hours' trip. Later that day, to coincide with the high tide in the Tāmaki Estuary, we would load either sheep or mature cattle and head back to the mainland. Arriving on high tide we would put into the dock, drop the ramp and let the animals run ashore.

'During these trips it was two hours on, two hours off. However, on occasions when I discovered that the deckhand couldn't read a compass, I would end up steering all night.'

By the 1980s, farming marginal land was becoming less profitable, with Britain in the European Union and farming subsidies being wound back. It became increasingly difficult to

Left: The Burrills used a roller, made from an old boiler filled with sand, to crush the scrub before burning the vegetation off and planting the soil with pasture seed. (Courtesy of Bill Burrill)

Right: Bill Burrill spent much of his early life clearing land in the Hauraki Gulf, but he has spent much of the last two decades seeking to reverse the process.

sustain the Great Barrier farming operation. In 1983, when Max was 69 years old, he had a serious accident on his East Tāmaki farm and ended up in hospital for a period. While he was there he did some thinking about the future. From his hospital bed, he negotiated the sale of the operating farm to the Department of Lands and Survey and insisted that the rest of the land, about 3600 hectares, would be a gift from the Burrill family to the people of New Zealand. His decision to gift the land came as a total surprise to his family.

The land was transferred on 1 April 1984. Max died suddenly less than four months later. Initially, the operating farm was owned by Landcorp, and the gifted portion of the land by the Department of Conservation. Eventually the department purchased the farmland as well, so that the entire property is now part of the department's conservation estate.

After his father's death, Bill kept farming but then, in 1992, decided to run for the Auckland Regional Council serving six terms. Bill sat on the Gulf Islands Committee of Auckland City Council and then the Hauraki Gulf Forum. For nine years he chaired the Regional Council Parks Committee and sat on the Auckland Conservation Board for seven years.

Reflecting back on his past, Bill observes: 'I spent 20 years of my life turning tea tree into pasture and then more than another 20 turning pasture into tea tree.'

After the Melbourne-owned Kauri Timber Company bought up most of the kauri industry during the depression of the 1880s, it centralised much of its timber-milling operations at Whangaparapara Harbour on Great Barrier Island. The mill, wharf and waiting ships are shown here in 1910. (William Price, Ref: PAColl-5521-05, Alexander Turnbull Library, Wellington, New Zealand)

Sediment impacts of land clearance

Sediment cores can identify changes over time in the rate of sediment coming off the land and being deposited in the Hauraki Gulf. In general, the amount of sediment entering the marine area has increased by around five times since European settlement and the wholesale removal of indigenous forest cover. The greatest levels of sedimentation have occurred on the intertidal flats in the southern Firth of Thames. These have been accreting at a rate of around 25 millimetres per year for the past 90 years or so.[26]

In the Firth of Thames, and in many estuaries around the gulf, the increase in sediment has been accompanied by an expansion of mangroves. For example, scientists have calculated that between 1971 and 1995 mangrove coverage increased by 215 per cent in Tairua harbour.[27]

The findings of scientists on the high levels of sedimentation are supported by anecdotal accounts from local residents. Phil Clow commercially fishes out of Whitianga and has spent the best part of 40 years out on the water. During that time he's observed changes in water quality and the presence of shellfish beds. 'After a storm, I've seen the water going past the Whitianga wharf yellow with clay from what appeared to be forestry run-off. The land is steep and fragile and we have cleared and farmed unsuitable country. One farm cleared marginal land and now there is a

layer of mud over the old bed. Cockles don't do mud.'

Cooks Beach resident Alison Henry has also noticed some disturbing changes over the 20 years she has lived in the area. 'Every time we have a Coromandel downpour, if you stand up on Shakespeare Cliff, you see an enormous brown plume coming down the Pūrangi and Whitianga rivers and flowing right out into the bay. There are now virtually no crabs on the rocks around Shakespeare Cliff and I know it would have been a real haven for crabs 20 years ago. When we first came here, there would always be horse mussel shells and sand dollars washing up. That doesn't happen now. These changes have all happened over a very short time period.'

High levels of sedimentation can fundamentally change the marine environment. Sediment reduces water clarity and can result in the loss of species reliant on photosynthesis, such as seagrass and seaweeds. Murky water can make it harder for juvenile fish, such as snapper, to find prey and reduce their ability to survive. The sediment can also cause their gills to deform.[28] Particles of soil in the water column make it difficult for filter feeders, such as cockles, pipi and scallops, to feed efficiently and it reduces the survival chances of larvae and juvenile shellfish. Overall, high levels of sedimentation reduce the abundance and diversity of species and the ability of the marine system to support productive fisheries.[29]

As well as dams, tramways were built and bullocks and engines were used to haul the logs out. Many of the tramways are now used as tramping tracks.[30] The only kauri trees not logged on the island were those around Mount Hobson and this was because they were too inaccessible.

Hauraki Plains

The Hauraki Plains are a rift valley that, historically, was a very extensive wetland area. The plains acted as a giant sponge, absorbing water that poured off the Coromandel and Kaimai ranges and flooded the low-lying land. The wetlands supported enormous kahikatea stands, as well as areas of flax, raupō, rushes and sedges. In the spring, large amounts of plankton would bloom in the swampy areas, supporting insects and algae that, in turn, provided food for great flocks of waterfowl. In the rivers of the plains, as well as a wide variety of fish, there were numerous eels (tuna) which could live for over 100 years, before swimming to the tropics to spawn.[31]

To the Māori who lived there, the wetlands provided abundant resources. This was attested by the large settlement established on the banks of the Waihou River, at Oruarangi, which was occupied for around 400 years.[32] But to Pākehā the wetlands were wastelands, something that needed to be improved, drained and turned into more productive pasture.

One of the early European industries established on the Hauraki Plains was based on the abundant quantities of flax. As early as 1832, a trader had established a house and store near the mouth of the Piako River, with the flax being collected and prepared by local Māori.[33] Several flax mills were built during the early 1900s, but most were short-lived. Only the Kerepehi Flaxmilling Company survived for any length of time, eventually closing down in the 1960s. Rawiri Wharengo recalled cutting flax for

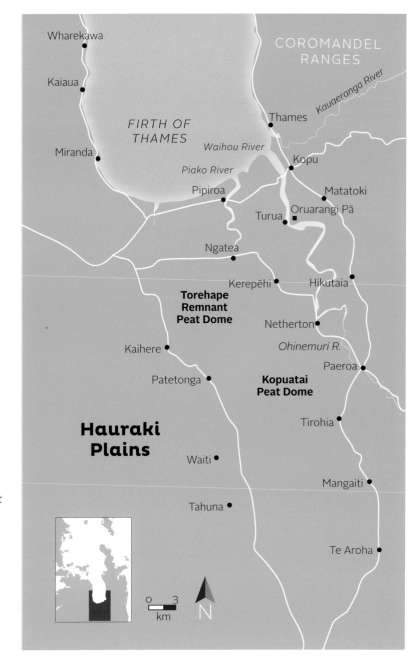

Bottom: A flax industry was established on the Hauraki Plains in 1902. This 1907 image shows bundles of flax and boats waiting to take them down the Piako River. (*Auckland Weekly News*, Ref: AWNS-19070822-8-3, Sir George Grey Special Collections, Auckland Libraries)

Waikino, shown here in 1906, became a processing centre for gold-bearing quartz, which was crushed in enormous stamper batteries. Large cyanide vats were used to extract the gold from the rock fragments. The sludge was poured into the Ōhinemuri River, significantly degrading it and causing extensive flooding. (*Auckland Weekly News*, Ref: AWNS-19061025-15-2, Sir George Grey Special Collections, Auckland Libraries)

the mill at nine shillings a ton, with five tons being a good day's cutting. They would float the bundles of flax down the drains to the Kerepehi mill.[34]

In 1865, the Hauraki Sawmill Company obtained logging rights to an area of rich kahikatea forests near Turua and established a mill there. The wood was destined for butter boxes and much was exported to Canterbury. The company later leased its forestry interests to the Bagnall Brothers, who subsequently acquired rights to the land. When they had exhausted the stands of trees, they subdivided the forestry block and small farms were established on the fertile mineral soils.[35]

The biggest discovery of gold in the region was at Waihi and this was to have significant implications for the plains. The mining company built a battery to crush the ore at Waikino, on the junction of the Waitawheta Stream and

the Ōhinemuri River. The Ōhinemuri River was dammed to provide hydro-electricity to drive the stampers. The operation quickly grew. By 1905 there were 330 stamp heads in operation, crushing 330,000 tons of ore a year.[36]

In 1885, the government declared the Ōhinemuri River and the Waihou River into which it discharged to be sludge channels under the Mining Act. This was to enable miners to discharge the talcum-like residue, left over after the silver and gold minerals were extracted from the quartz ore, into the waterway. Over 25,000 tons per annum were to be disposed of in this manner.[37]

It did not take long for the large quantity of waste to have an effect. In the late 1880s, the Tarariki wharf on the Ōhinemuri River was closed due to silting and the main wharf at Paeroa was moved downstream. As the silting became worse, vessels struggled to navigate up the clogged river.[38] Although undocumented, the discharge of large quantities of cyanide-contaminated silt would almost certainly have impacted on the once abundant life in the rivers, that had sustained Hauraki Māori for generations and had so impressed the early European explorers to the region.

Then, in 1885, the flooding started. By the first decade of the twentieth century, there were two or three floods a year. Property, roads, railway lines and stock were damaged. The floodwaters raced through the towns of Paeroa and Thames. It deposited a layer of fine tailings over farmland that, if not washed off immediately, would leave a hard crust smothering the pasture. The biggest flood occurred on 1 April 1910,

The choking up of the Hauraki Plains rivers with mining sludge resulted in the flooding of settlements and land downstream. This image shows the flooding of Paeroa in 1898. (*Auckland Weekly News*, Ref: AWNS-18980702-1-2, Sir George Grey Special Collections, Auckland Libraries)

when one eye-witness reported seeing the Ōhinemuri River rising by 3 metres per hour.[39]

Although it was clear that the dumping of mining sludge into the river was contributing to the flooding, the government was reluctant to act for fear of having to compensate the mining companies. Flooding was also exacerbated by the removal of vegetation from the steep hills bordering the plains, primarily to provide wood for the mines. Instead of addressing the causes of the problem, it was decided to channel the raging floodwaters further downstream by constructing stopbanks. These were initially placed along the banks of the Ōhinemuri and Waihou rivers downstream of Te Aroha and Mangaiti.[40]

During the 1890s, the government adopted a policy of encouraging 'close settlement' of rural land. As part of this policy, it set out to purchase large tracts of Māori land in the Hauraki Plains, where it had developed a plan for a comprehensive drainage scheme.[41] The Hauraki Plains Act 1908 enabled the drainage scheme to proceed with a view to settling the area with small farmers. Its provisions included the ability to compulsorily acquire the remaining Māori land for inclusion in the scheme and around

Story of the Gulf | **Elsie McDonald**

RESIDENT, WESTERN HAURAKI PLAINS[42]

Elsie McDonald went with her family to live on a farm between Kaihere and Patetonga when she was around three years old. In 1929 she wrote a history of the area.[43] In this, she described the process to transform the western Hauraki Plains into farms.

First drains were cut through the land and then, in 1914, came the big burn-off. 'For miles around there was nothing but flames, effectively ridding the land of much of the unwanted growth, and often threatening some little home in the midst of it'. During the following spring, after the farm had dried out due to the drainage, 'the first cattle were introduced, for cattle are necessary to tramp the land solid. In the ashes grew the most luxurious grass, a very tempting sight for those cattle. But under that grass, green and fresh, was very soft ground. The cattle sank at every step and it took a whole day to get them to cross 100 yards.

'Soon, however, with draining, the ground hardened and then a new trouble presented itself, timber. Where before had been level ground, stumps appeared, first as lumps, then a whole buried forest came to the surface, whole tree trunks

and stumps, fallen giants of long ago. As this unexpected timber was cleared away, another layer presented itself and now the third and, it is hoped, the last layer being cleared, leaving a layer of giant tea tree.

'In 1915 the ground was solid enough for a house to be built and so, after roughing it for a year, comparative comfort came. The stumps were a difficulty to contend with here too, as they had an uncomfortable habit of coming up underneath and giving the house a tilt, or jamming all the doors, and causing endless trouble to the men trying to get them out.

'With the solid ground it was now possible to start milking and Patetonga, which had become the centre, began to progress. A cream depot was built at Patetonga, with the cream sent down the tramline to the river and taken by launch to Kopu near Thames, a journey of four hours.'

Hauraki Plains settlers near drainage channel, 1910. (*Auckland Weekly News*, Ref: 7-A9540, Sir George Grey Special Collections, Auckland Libraries)

In 1908, the government passed legislation to facilitate the large-scale drainage of the Hauraki Plains. Shown here in October 1908 is part of the early drainage works on the Piako wetland. (*Auckland Weekly News*, Ref: AWNS-19081022-10-1, Sir George Grey Special Collections, Auckland Libraries)

800 hectares were obtained in this manner. As a result 'Māori communities on the plains lost almost all of their remaining lands along the floodplain between the Piako and Waihou Rivers, and the swamps which had been a source of food and materials for generations.'[44]

By 1910, the government had balloted 104 sections for which there were 1300 applicants. But many of them had not seen the sections and were unaware of the difficulties of converting the swampy ground to productive farmland. First they would have to dig a network of drains on their property. These frequently collapsed and would have to be dug again and again. It took a long time before the peat could carry the weight of cattle. In addition, many of the grass seed varieties that were sown failed.

By 1911, over 2000 hectares of the plains had been drained and burned. The subsequent Hauraki Plains Act

1926 made provision for the drainage and development of a further 50,000 hectares of wetland.

Returned soldiers from the First World War were settled on farms near Waiti and Patetonga, but they struggled to break in the land. As Hauraki Plains farmer Gray Townshend explains, 'the peat was 7 feet deep. They all virtually went broke and, around 1930, they were resettled in Kerepehi where there was shallower peat. Peat is just unrotted plant material. When it gets wet there is an acid reaction and it doesn't rot. But when you dry it out, it will burn. Peat is very drought prone and acid. You have to get lime on it and get the pH up to a certain level until the grass will grow well.'[45]

While farmers started transforming the landscape of the Hauraki Plains, engineers were busy 'improving' the rivers. As land in the upper catchment was being cleared for farms, more water was running at a faster rate into lower-lying areas. The drainage of the huge wetland in the plains meant that the rivers were flooding again, as there was no longer a natural mechanism in place to absorb the floodwaters. Flood control work started on the Waihou River in 1912 and on the Ōhinemuri River a year later. A suction dredge was used to suck up silt from the bottom of the rivers. This was used to build stopbanks which were then capped with clay. Willows were cleared from the banks and cuts made to reduce river bends. By 1920, the Waihou River had been shortened by 7 kilometres.[46]

But despite the extensive works, increasing clearance of the surrounding hills helped to generate further floods. 'Hundreds of cubic yards of gravel and soil were washed off the steep western slopes of the Kaimai Range, covering the lower farmland and filling the river channel.'[47] Much of it eventually ended up in the Firth of Thames. A notable flood occurred in 1924, when farmland in the Netherton area was under water for seven weeks. A similar flood happened in 1936. Then in 1954, two farmers were killed trying to move their stock to higher ground to avoid rising waters. In a 1960 flood there was another death. The Hauraki Plains Catchment Board then took over the rivers 'improvement' scheme.

When the board assumed control, 93 kilometres of stopbanks had been constructed along with 100 floodgates and culverts, but this had not been enough to stop the flooding. In 1965 a revised scheme was designed and implemented, at an estimated cost of $12 million. Central government agreed to subsidise the works at $3 to $1 paid locally, so the general taxpayer funded three-quarters of the cost.[48]

By 1977–78 the estimated cost of the scheme had risen to $38 million, with much of the rise blamed on rampant inflation that was increasing the cost of acquiring land. By mid-1979, the board ran out of money to complete the scheme and it was not keeping ahead of growing flooding pressures from land clearances.[49]

In February 1985 a severe storm hit, streams flooded and in Te Aroha three members of a family were swept to their deaths when water smashed into their house, completely wrecking it. In Thames, the foundations of a two-storeyed house were ripped away, throwing a 77-year-old woman out of the building. She was swept to her death. Debris was spread far and wide with an estimated $7 million worth of damage.[50]

River works continued and were finally completed in

Health of the Waihou and Piako rivers

The two largest rivers flowing into the Hauraki Gulf are the Waihou and Piako and they are not in good health. Results of river water-quality monitoring of the Piako concluded that its condition was 'generally poor, being somewhat oxygen-depleted and murky, and with particularly high concentrations of total N [nitrogen] and total P [phosphorus] (5–7 times higher than guideline values). Concentrations of E. coli were also high (6 times higher than guideline values).' In contrast water quality of the much larger Waihou 'was intermediate: at the most downstream site on the main-stem the water was often well-oxygenated, but was murky and concentrations of total N, total P and E. Coli were 2 to 3 times higher than guideline values.'[51]

1995, at which stage they were described as the 'Rolls-Royce' of all flood protection schemes.[52] All tall vegetation from the Waihou River floodway had been removed and the river was transformed from a meandering, tree-lined waterway to something resembling a large open drain. This allowed water to travel down the river at speed during floods, but it also significantly reduced the amenity of the river and removed the shading and spawning areas required by eels and freshwater fish.

Most of the other catchments feeding into the Hauraki Gulf were transformed from forest to farms. But, of these, the Hauraki Plains was by far the largest and it became one of the most productive dairy farming areas in the country. At the same time, the engineering drainage works served to channel large amounts of sediment and other nutrients from dairy farming directly into the Firth of Thames, one of the most productive fisheries nursery grounds in the gulf.

As well as fuelling local economies, and providing jobs and livelihoods for settlers, the activities that took place within the catchments of the Hauraki Gulf had significant flow-on effects for the marine area. Much soil, which had developed under dense forest cover, washed off the land, filling up estuaries and smothering the wider seabed, in a process that continues today.

Story of the Gulf | **Gray Townshend**
RETIRED HAURAKI PLAINS FARMER, NGATEA[53]

'During the 1920s my dad, who was 22 years old at the time, and his parents came up from the King Country to get some of the flat, fertile land in the plains.' In Gray's view the settlement of the Hauraki Plains was really a 'major con job. The plains had two distinct soil types: the eastern half, where kahikatea forest grew on mineral soils which were quite fertile, and the western half where areas were all peat morass.' The early farms were established on the fertile soils and so, during the 1920s, the plains 'got the reputation that it was so fertile it didn't need topdressing'.

His family bought a block at Netherton and moved onto it in March 1924. They had only been on the land for two months when the whole place flooded after the Waihou River broke its banks. 'The land was under water above your knees.' They had to take their cattle to graze up on the hills at Te Aroha and lost a few in the process. But it was good land and they never looked back. 'Initially it was all cream supply. We separated out the skim milk and fed it to the pigs. The cream, which went to the nearest butter factory, provided the cash income.' Initially transport was via the river, but that ended by about 1930. Then, until 1948, there was a twice-weekly steamer service from Paeroa to Auckland.

During the 1940s, they ran about 60–70 cows on 40 hectares, but now with topdressing and more productive strains of ryegrass, the norm is 100 cows per 40 hectares, so the carrying capacity has increased significantly. 'Mechanisation has also meant a lot more storage of pasture in silage or hay, so you can store more to carry the stock through the winter.'

Gray went farming on his own account after meeting and marrying Marie in 1952. They bought a 22-hectare farm and milked 45 cows. In the summertime, Marie would milk the cows in the afternoon while Gray did contracting work for extra income, initially spraying weeds and then sowing pastures. Later, Marie's father retired and offered the couple his farm at Ngatea. So they went from 45 to 130 cows and had to employ labour.

The price of feed determines the stocking rates of the farms now. 'When palm kernels became available at an economic price, almost without exception farmers increased stocking rates. When the price of butterfat went up to $8.60, farmers didn't hesitate to put more cows on their land and when they ran out of feed they bought palm kernels. So dairying intensified. The first year on our farm we had 130 cows. We now milk 900 on our original property and the adjoining five farms which we have successively bought. There are lots of

Gray and Marie Townshend have spent their lives farming the Hauraki Plains.

500-plus herds now. Milking 60 to 80 cows is long gone.

'The whole plains were set up on a one-family-per-farm basis. Netherton, for example, was cut up into 60 to 70-acre [24-28 hectare] blocks. One of the characteristics of the plains, in the early days, was the multiplicity of small settlements. Each had its own school, dairy factory, church, post office and exchange. They were like separate countries. That has long gone now. The farms have amalgamated and you now put in one big rotary milking shed. The labour requirements reduce and the population decreases, although not as much as you might think, as the farm houses are rented out.'

But there has been rural depopulation. There used to be five townships on the plains, but now, apart from Ngatea and Turua which has partly become a dormitory town for Thames, the rest have gone. Currently, Ngatea is the only town of any size. It has become a thriving rural centre with a highly successful secondary school and good sporting facilities. The community is close and pulls together to undertake joint projects. On reflection, Gray considers that 'the plains are tracking in the right direction'.

Part Three:
BLUE PATHWAYS

Chapter 7
Connecting the gulf

Prior to the expansion of North Island roading networks after the First World War, it was the waters, not the land, that connected the people of the Hauraki Gulf. Many places were only practicably accessible by sea, due to the rugged topography of the interior, and waterborne travel was the norm. People's lives were closely intertwined with the sea and many regularly faced the considerable dangers of negotiating rock-strewn and often stormy waters, in paddling, sailing and then motor-driven craft.

The first vessels to provide transport around the gulf were waka, laboriously crafted vessels which were mainly paddled but also sailed downwind. War canoes (waka taua) were large, at around 18–21 metres long and 1.5–1.8 metres wide, and heavily decorated. The hull was fashioned out of large kauri or tōtara logs. Washstrakes were lashed along the top edge to increase the freeboard. These, along with bow and stern pieces, were ornately carved. Simpler, smaller vessels (waka tētē) were primarily used for fishing and

Pages 118–119: The scow *Jane Gifford* sailing out of Auckland.
Left: Bean Rock lighthouse.

Hauraki Gulf, the busiest pre-European waterway

Gulf historian Paul Monin describes the use of the Hauraki Gulf by waka: 'The Gulf islands lay alongside surely the busiest waterways of pre-European Aotearoa, those connecting Northland with the Waitematā, the Waikato and Bay of Plenty (and beyond to East Cape). All canoe traffic between the Bay of Islands and the Bay of Plenty passed close by Great Barrier, Little Barrier and the Mercury and Aldermen Islands. Meanwhile, all canoe traffic utilising the portages of the Tāmaki River, which granted straightforward passage across the Tāmaki isthmus between the Waitematā and Manukau harbours and between northern Aotearoa and the Waikato River system, passed close by the inner Gulf islands: Waiheke, Pōnui etc. . . .

'It is possible, over certain periods, that some islands may even have served as "Grand Central Stations", in the sense that they functioned as concourses for intertribal water traffic, claimed resolutely by no particular kin-group. Travellers could break journey there for rest and resupply without necessarily receiving the usual challenge from the tangata whenua.'[1]

Top: Waka taua (war canoes), such as Paora Tuhaere's here at Ōrākei c. 1875, were very impressive, heavily decorated vessels which could rapidly transport large groups of people around the Hauraki Gulf and further afield. (Ref: 4-1597, Sir George Grey Special Collections, Auckland Libraries)

Bottom: Waka taua have intricately carved figureheads (tauihu), as shown here on the Ngāti Paoa waka taua *Kōtuiti II*. The tauihu also acts as a breakwater, reducing the amount of water coming over the bow.

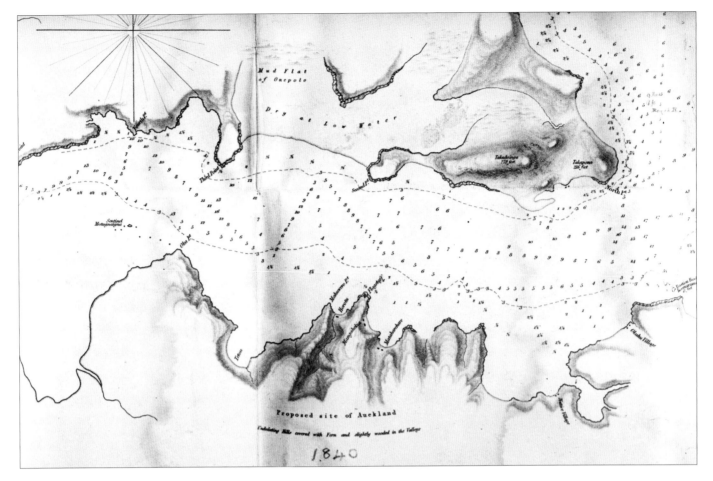

Captain Owen Stanley, commander of HM Brig *Britomart*, prepared a chart of the Waitematā Harbour in 1840, providing detail on the depths and topography. (Ref 4-163, Sir George Grey Special Collections, Auckland Libraries)

later extensively used for trading.[2] During the early days of Auckland settlement, numerous waka were used to bring food and other goods to the Auckland market.

The early European-style vessels negotiating the gulf were initially large ocean-going ships which had travelled from the northern hemisphere, often via Sydney. They were traders, British, French and Spanish navy ships and vessels designed to carry immigrants. Auckland became a centre of Pacific trade and also an important stop-off point between Australia and the western coast of North America. During the 1840s, as Auckland expanded and other settlements became established around the gulf, commerce flourished and the number of vessels carrying goods and people rose exponentially. Many of these were coastal traders, specifically designed and built within the gulf for local conditions. They were owned and operated by both Māori and European traders.

The growing fleet increasingly demanded maritime infrastructure: charts and pilot notes to assist with safe navigation, beacons and lights to identify marine hazards, wharves, and boatbuilding and repair yards.

Charting

When Governor Hobson visited the Waitematā during February 1840, looking for a settlement site for the capital, Captain Nias and the crew of the *Herald* busied themselves undertaking the first comprehensive survey of the harbour. Such nautical surveys were critical to the safety of visiting ships, as they identified places suitable for anchorages and hazards, such as submerged rocks.

As a small boat sailed slowly backwards and forwards across the harbour, the 'leadsman' positioned himself at the bow with a carefully prepared line (leadline), which had a piece of triangular-shaped lead (called a plummet) attached to the end. This wide base enabled the lead weight to sit neatly, in an upright position, on the seabed. The line itself was marked with thin strips of various kinds of materials which were threaded through the strands of fibre at carefully measured intervals. Each marker strip was designed to look and feel different, so that the correct depth could be easily determined, even at night.

The leadsman repeatedly swung the line up high and cast it forward into the sea. The line went slack when the lead reached the seabed and then pulled up tightly when the ship moved forwards and came directly overhead. The depth could then be measured from the markers in the line, taking into account the distance between the height of the leadsman on

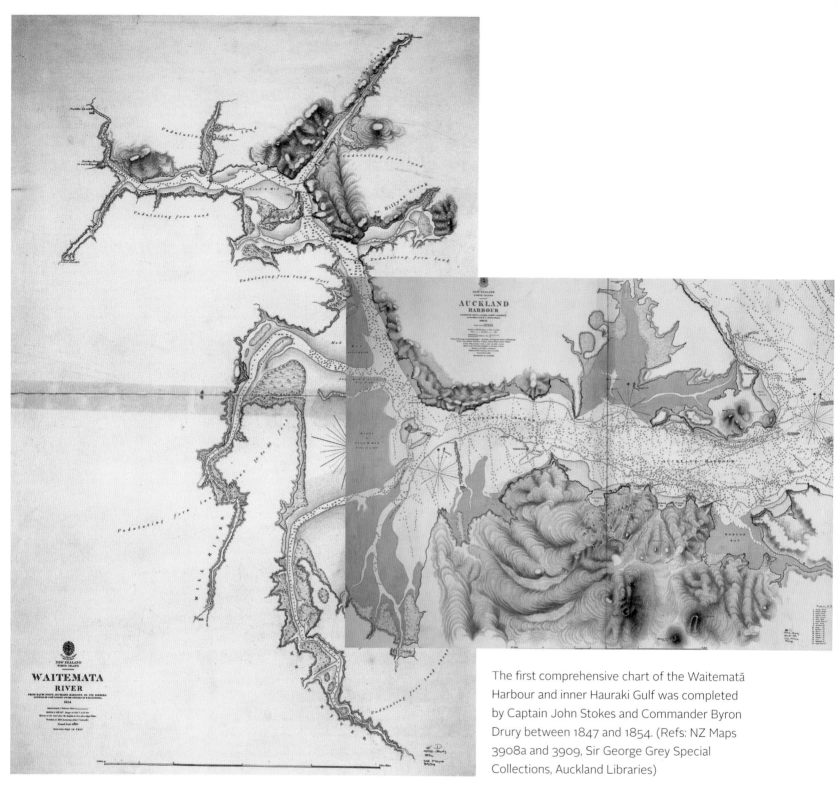

The first comprehensive chart of the Waitematā Harbour and inner Hauraki Gulf was completed by Captain John Stokes and Commander Byron Drury between 1847 and 1854. (Refs: NZ Maps 3908a and 3909, Sir George Grey Special Collections, Auckland Libraries)

the bow of the boat and the surface of the sea. When the lead was retrieved, materials adhering to tallow inserted into its hollowed-out base provided information on the nature of the seabed and whether it was mud, sand or rock. This helped indicate whether an anchor was likely to hold fast.

The *Herald* crew worked their way across the harbour and up the main river as far as a small island, which they named Herald's Island on the resulting chart. This chart, dated 28 February 1840, drew the outline of the coastline,

indicated water depths and noted that the bottom was a mixture of blue mud and clay. A 'Native Village' was shown in the location of the current Auckland CBD and a short way to the east was a 'Watering Place', at the location of the former Horotiu Stream.

Once the site of Auckland was proclaimed in September 1840, Harbour Master Captain David Rough quickly set about identifying potential hazards to shipping. He soon placed a beacon on Bean Rocks, named after the master of

the *Herald*, Mr P Bean,[3] and he also marked a submerged rock off Bastion Point.

Rough was instrumental in noting other dangers on admiralty charts. When he was advised of breakers in otherwise deep water off the south-eastern coast of Tiritiri Matangi, Rough named the obstruction Shearer Rock after the master of a small cutter who had sighted it. He named a rock situated in the channel between Little and Great Barrier islands the Horn after the vessel from which it was observed.[4] The rocky promontory on the North Shore known to Ngāi Tai as Te Onewa was called Rough Point in honour of the harbour master and his efforts to make the gulf safer for shipping.

Only weeks after the first Auckland settlers started erecting their tents ashore, the HM Brig *Britomart*, under the command of Captain Owen Stanley, arrived in the Waitematā Harbour. Stanley was soon busily undertaking a second survey of the harbour. Auckland's most prominent headland was labelled Flagstaff, but Surveyor-General Felton Mathew later

This trig station in Windsor Reserve, Devonport formed the starting point for the survey of the Waitematā Harbour undertaken by Captain Stokes in 1847.

renamed it Point Britomart after Stanley's vessel. Mathew also renamed Observation Point after the captain himself and it stills bears the name Stanley Point today.

As vessel traffic increased within the gulf and around the wider New Zealand coast, the British Navy realised that there was an urgent need for a systematic survey. Up until then, charts had been prepared on an ad hoc basis, and their extent and accuracy depended on the interest and skill of the crews on passing vessels. The first official survey started in 1847 and was headed by Welshman Captain John Lort Stokes. Stokes had joined the Navy at the tender age of thirteen and had served under Captain Fitzroy on the HMS *Beagle* when it had undertaken Charles Darwin's scientifically ground-breaking trip around the world in the 1830s.

Stokes' vessel for the survey was the HMS *Acheron*, a sailing

Story of the Gulf | **Tipa Compain**

PARE HAURAKI, AUCKLAND[5]

Tipa grew up in Kelston, Auckland, close to the Whau River. Through his mother he is related to several tribes in the Hauraki Gulf, including Ngāti Whanaunga, Ngāti Maru, Ngāti Tamaterā, Ngāti Paoa and Ngāi Tai. He is also related to Waikato tribes. Tipa has studied law and Māori at university and is currently Iwi Liaison Manager at Auckland Transport.

Māori was not promoted in the suburb where Tipa lived as a child. It was only through spending time with his maternal grandparents that Tipa developed a keen interest in Māoritanga. 'I was lucky enough to be raised for a short time by my grandparents. When I went to gatherings at my grandmother's Whatapaka marae at Karaka-Papakura some of my aunties and uncles noticed my interest and they would foster it. They realised that I had a really good ear for genealogy; I can remember names, a skill that not everyone has. So they would give me whakapapa [genealogy].'

From an early age Tipa developed a close affinity with the sea. 'I played around with canoes as a kid not knowing that my people were a canoe-faring people, using both sail and hoe [paddles]. I got involved with *Te Kōtuiti Tuarua*, the Ngāti Paoa waka taua that was built to celebrate the 150th anniversary of the signing of the Treaty of Waitangi in 1990. I've been on many waka since and have come to love our histories and stories of the sea.

'Tīkapa Moana [Hauraki Gulf] was our highway, the way we got around. There's plenty of evidence that smaller waka used to frequently move one or two families, around 15–20 people, between the islands and the mainland. The sea was also our kāpata kai [food cupboard]. It's a place where you can go, relax and be yourself. It can also be a dangerous place and you have to respect Tangaroa [spirit of the sea].

'My generation wants to regenerate the knowledge of sailing waka — not the larger sea-going ones, but the inner harbour ones. It's knowledge that's retained by a few in the tribe: understanding the waka, the water, and when to sail and not to sail. It's knowledge that still has practical application today. For example, the council approached us and said they

Tipa Compain has been working hard to regenerate traditional knowledge of sailing waka. He is shown here in charge of the steering paddle on the Ngāti Paoa waka taua *Kōtuiti II*. See detail on p. 122. (Courtesy of Tipa Compain)

wanted to put in a kayak trail. We said, "Great, it's good to get people out on the water." The council asked us, "Where should we put the stop-off points?" I said, "Put them at the tauranga waka [traditional canoe landing places]. Our people used them for many generations. They are places where waka can come in safely, in all weathers and tides, and have easy access to the land."

'Some of us have started the journey of learning how to navigate in the traditional ways. We are also learning how to build waka, using traditional methods, but looking at modern materials as well. As coastal people of Hauraki, Tīkapa Moana means so much to us. We have a passion for the sea. It's in our blood.'

The 'Tiri' light became a prominent landmark for the rapidly increasing vessel traffic coming into the Waitematā Harbour, as shown by this 1883 watercolour: *Grey day off Tiri*. (Alfred Sharpe, Ref: 1975/26, Auckland Art Gallery Toi o Tāmaki)

ship also equipped as a paddle steamer. Its 280-horsepower steam engines could drive the boat at up to 10 knots and they enabled the vessel to safely venture close into the coast, something which took greater skill in a solely sail-driven vessel.

The *Acheron* arrived in Auckland on 7 November 1847 and Stokes immediately commenced a preliminary survey of the Waitematā Harbour. He established a trig station at the then naval base in Devonport, now the Windsor Reserve adjacent to Devonport Beach. This provided a known point to which surveyed areas in the harbour could be related. The survey of the main harbour was completed the following year. Stokes then busied himself charting the entrances to the harbour, the Great Barrier Island coast and Kawau Bay.

After surveying other parts of the New Zealand coast, Stokes left in 1851.[6] Rough Point was renamed Stokes Point in his honour. Commander Byron Drury, in the smaller sailing ship *Pandora*, was tasked with completing the survey during the early 1850s and this included charting the remaining parts of the Hauraki Gulf.[7]

The completion of the 'Great Survey' in 1855 resulted in the production of the first *New Zealand Pilot* the following year. It contained detailed descriptions of the various approaches to Auckland, anchorages and hazards for vessels. In the *Pilot*, the Admiralty Hydrographic Office confidently asserted that ' . . . there is no doubt that the intelligent seaman, if in possession of the Admiralty Charts, may visit every part of the [New Zealand] group [of islands] in safety and security'.[8] The joint efforts of the crews on these survey ships made the gulf immensely safer for shipping, but there were still many dangers and numerous ships and lives were still lost.

Lighthouses

Vessels arriving at night had no navigational assistance in finding a safe passage into Auckland and there was soon strong pressure for the establishment of a light. By 1854, Tiritiri Matangi Island had been identified as a possible site due to its prominent position on the outer edge of the northern approach to Auckland. But it was not until 1863 that the light was approved. The tower itself was built out of cast iron, with sections constructed in London, shipped out to Auckland and then finally out to the island. All the material for the lighthouse and the keepers' houses was laboriously sledded up from the beach onto the building platform on the southern end of the island — a back-breaking job. On 1 January 1865 the Tiritiri light, the first to operate within the gulf, was turned on. It sported a fixed white light which could be seen from up to 23 miles away.[9]

Left: The first lighthouse in the Hauraki Gulf was constructed on Tiritiri Matangi Island, being lit on 1 January 1865. Shown here c. 1911 are lighthouse keepers and their families on the island. (Ref 1/2-0326540-F, Alexander Turnbull Library, Wellington, New Zealand)

Right: In the early years, lighthouse keepers on Burgess Island in the Mokohinau group were largely left to their own devices. Stores arrived only every four months or so. Due to the lack of a jetty, they had to be winched onto the shore and manually carried up to the houses and lighthouse, as shown here in 1902. (Henry Winkelmann, Ref: PH-NEG-2009, Auckland War Memorial Museum Tāmaki Paenga Hira)

The light was initially powered by three wicks burning colza (canola) oil. There were two lighthouse keepers in residence and they would keep six-hourly watches each night. The first shift would involve lighting the wicks at dusk and staying on watch until midnight when the second shift would start. At dawn, the keeper on the second shift would turn off the light, clean the lenses and then milk the family cow. The keepers were also kept busy gardening, as the families grew all their own vegetables as well as raising hens and sheep. In the early days, a lighthouse service ship would call only once every three months.[10]

A lighthouse on Burgess Island, in the Mokohinau Group, followed in 1883. This was to provide a landfall sign for seafarers transiting to and from the Pacific. The lighthouse was manned for almost 100 years until the light was automated in 1980. Unlike the Tiritiri

Matangi lighthouse which was close to the mainland, the Mokohinau lighthouse was very remote. In the early days there was little outside communication and mail and stores only arrived every four months, deliveries which could be delayed if there was bad weather.

In 1908 the keepers on Burgess Island were desperate for stores. With no supply ship in sight, they used their ingenuity to send for help. From an old tin can, they fashioned a little sailing vessel that was powered by tin sails. Inside the hull, they placed three letters: the first addressed to the Marine Department, the second to the nearest general store and the third to a friend. On the deck of the tiny boat the keepers painted a notice asking the finder to send the letters on. When the wind direction was favourable, they launched the boat. The ploy worked and within nine days a stores ship arrived at the island.[11]

Peter Taylor was stationed at the lighthouse in 1958. He found his new island home to be a fisherman's paradise, surrounded by enormous shoals of fish. 'They were sometimes acres in extent, vast areas of seething water churned up by trevalli, underneath them kahawai, beneath them kingfish and beneath them again snapper — great pyramids of fish whose thrashings we could hear from the houses if the day was calm.' The keepers caught large hāpuku off the shallow reefs. From their kitchen window, they would also occasionally see whales swimming past, 'rising and falling as they spouted their way past us to the north'. One day a group of whales with their calves cavorted in the bay. During the early 1960s, the keepers had been instructed to advise the whaling station on Great

Man O' War Bay, Waiheke Island

During the 1840s and '50s, the western end of Waiheke Island became a popular stopping-off place for outgoing ships wanting to take on water, supplies and kauri spars.[12] As well as having an accessible freshwater stream, there were plentiful fish that could be caught in nets. The bay was described in the 1856 *New Zealand Pilot* as 'a favourite watering place; a vessel may anchor as near as convenient to the stream'.[13] The frequency of navy ships visiting the area resulted in the adoption of the current name, Man O' War Bay, that now applies to the smaller bay Māori knew as Huruhe, but which initially referred to the entire north end of the Waiheke Channel.[14]

Man O' War Bay, Waiheke Island, 2015. On the right-hand side of the bay is shown the much-reduced flow of the river, which used to provide copious amounts of fresh water for large ships.

Barrier Island if they saw any whales, but they could not bring themselves to do so.[15]

The third manned lighthouse in the Hauraki Gulf was lit in 1889, also to provide guidance for vessels transiting to the Pacific. It was located on the island known as Repanga by Māori, but renamed Cuvier Island by D'Urville in 1827 (after French naturalist Baron Georges Cuvier). Cuvier was one of the least-favoured lighthouse postings due to its isolation and propensity to be surrounded by heavy fog. The houses of the three keepers were located in a valley close to sea level so each night the keepers had to climb a steep slope to reach the light. Communications were so poor in the early days that carrier pigeons were utilised to carry messages, although with little success.[16]

Other lights followed, including the Rangitoto Channel light, which was the first to be built out of Wilson's Portland cement. Although constructed in 1882, it didn't operate until 1905 due to disagreements between the Auckland Harbour Board and the Marine Department. A light at Flat Rock, to the east of Kawau Island, only became operational in 1918. Earlier attempted unmanned beacons were swept away in 1867, 1870 and 1872.[17]

Early boatbuilding

Scottish trader Thomas Maxwell probably built the first ship in the Hauraki Gulf. He took up residence at Opopo (north of Man O' War Bay) on the eastern end of Waiheke Island

Story of the Gulf | **Ray Walter**

RETIRED LIGHTHOUSE KEEPER, AUCKLAND[18]

Ray Walter spent much of his working life as a professional lighthouse keeper, serving over a decade in the Hauraki Gulf. He was sent to the Burgess Island station on the Mokohinau Islands in 1972 and spent seven and a half years there. The island was small, only 60 hectares in extent, and it was very steep and exposed.

Initially there were three keepers and their families on the island. The keepers turned the light on and off each day and maintained the buildings and equipment. They also sent in weather reports every three hours, a total of eight each day. They grew their own vegetables and ran cattle for meat. A supply ship would arrive every two weeks with stores. But other than that, the keepers were pretty much left on their own, to sort out any problems the best they could.

Ray found it 'an absolutely beautiful place to live, very isolated'. The thing that really impressed him was the fishing. 'You could always go to the wharf, toss in a line, catch a fish and go home.' But while he was stationed on the island, Ray observed some disturbing changes. Two particular events still stand out in his mind.

'The Mokohinaus had a very large red-billed gull population, occupying maybe two hectares opposite the houses. The red-bills used to arrive during September and October, set up their nesting sites and raise their chicks. This went on for about four years while we were there. They were a nuisance as they would crap in our water supply, but that was part of living on the island, so we got used to it.

'At that time you could stand on the top of the Mokohinaus and see huge schools of trevally, acres in size. Maybe on a good day you might see seven to eight upwellings of these fish, huge numbers of them. All of a sudden some purse seiners came from Pago Pago, America Samoa, supposedly fishing for tuna to take back to Samoa for processing. These boats were fitted with helicopters and they would fly around spotting fish. I was doing the weather report one night and I heard two purse seiners talking on the radio. One said, "Could you help me out? I'm just inside the Poor Knights and we are trailing a net with 700 tons of fish."

'I don't know how long this went on for, probably a couple of years. All of a sudden we noticed that the red-billed gulls were not raising their chicks to maturity and were abandoning the nests. When I left in 1980, for about the three previous

Ray and Barbara Walter have a long association with Tiritiri Matangi Island, stemming from Ray's sojourn there as a lighthouse keeper during the early 1980s.

years the colony had been completely abandoned. We also noticed that the number of upwellings of trevally seemed to disappear overnight.

'The other change we noticed was that, all of a sudden, there seemed to be a lot more sports fishing boats turning up there, particularly from Marsden Point. There were a couple of very fast boats that used to come out and lay set nets around the island. One day we saw a boat run a net through the Edith passage, off the wharf, and towards Little Barrier. The net was the better part of a mile long. Then the weather blew up and the boat disappeared. About a week later we went out to find that the net was still there. It was full of numerous dead crayfish and all sorts of reef fish, just a terrible mess. We couldn't do anything, so we left it there. About a week later the boat turned up, overhauled the net and took it away. The damage they did to reef fish was colossal.'

In 1980, when the Mokohinau light was automated, Ray and his family were posted to the Tiritiri Matangi lighthouse station. Living on this inner gulf island was an entirely different experience. There was mains power, good gardens and sheep and cattle. It was relatively easy to get into town. But the fishing was not the same. 'We still caught a few fish when we first went there but our main source of fish was the local trawlers that tied up at the wharf at night. We used to take milk and cream down to the boats and exchange them for a few fish.'

Ray got to know the trawlermen well and he liked them. He wasn't worried about their fishing per se, but he did become concerned about the slap-happy approach that some applied to their activities. He saw boats fishing in prohibited areas. There was the dumping of little snapper. One day a boat tied up to the wharf and the crew tipped six to seven tonnes of stingrays out of the cod end of their net. 'There were dead sting and eagle rays everywhere.'

The worst thing Ray saw at Tiritiri Matangi, which happened shortly after he arrived, was the set netting. 'There was a boat that used to come out from the Wade River. He would set two set nets, starting at the wharf, coming out to the lighthouse off Shearer Rock, then extending out to Shag Rock at the top end of the island and then back to the wharf. Two nets right around the island. He would lay them in the morning and pick them up in the afternoon. That kind of activity just destroys inshore reef fishing.'

Ray also observed the scallop bed being destroyed. 'There were scallop beds off the wharf. The pleasure boats would come in, drop a scallop dredge on the ground, steam out and drag it along the bottom. As soon as the scallop season opened they would rape and pillage. There are no scallops there now.'

Ray is not sure, but he thinks the reduction in fish that he has observed around the island may have affected the survival of juvenile little blue penguins. Large numbers of the penguins nest on Tiritiri Matangi. Initially the parents feed the young ones, but when they are ready to go to sea, the adults move offshore and call the juveniles into the water. There

The automation of the Tiritiri Matangi light in 1984 saw the end of lighthouse keeping as a profession in the Hauraki Gulf.

they are left to feed on their own. 'Unless there are lots of small fish that are easy to catch they do suffer.'

When the Tiritiri Matangi lighthouse was automated in 1984, Ray and his wife Barbara stayed on to help with the restoration programme which at that time was just being established on the island. Ray retrained as a nursery worker and Barbara took on the role of volunteer coordinator. They moved off the island in 2006, but still return from time to time to work there as volunteers themselves.

in 1838. Prior to this, Maxwell had spent time in the Bay of Islands and whilst there he married Ngeungeu, daughter of Ngāi Tai chief Tara Te Irirangi. Maxwell subsequently returned to his wife's people at Umupuia and then established a kauri timber operation on Waiheke.[19]

Using Waiheke kauri, Maxwell built a 13.3-metre, 42-tonne, two-masted schooner, which he named *Sarah Maxwell* after his wife whom he called Sarah. In December 1841 he sailed the vessel to Auckland and put her up for sale. A month later he joined her for a voyage to Port Nicholson, but the vessel encountered a strong north-east gale soon after leaving Auckland and nothing was heard of the *Sarah Maxwell* or its crew again.[20]

A couple of years after Maxwell launched his vessel, boatbuilders Henry Niccol (originally spelt Nichol) and

Nagel Cove, Great Barrier Island became a centre of boat building due to the rich kauri forests located there. The largest sailing vessel (by tonnage) to be constructed in the Hauraki Gulf was built there during the 1840s. It is shown here on the stocks in 1847. (William Bainbridge, REF: A-090-018, Alexander Turnbull Library, Wellington, New Zealand)

Archibald Sharp came to Waiheke Island. Just prior, in 1842, they had arrived in Auckland on one of the first immigrant ships, the *Jane Gifford*. The Scotsmen were using the island's then excellent kauri and pōhutukawa timbers to build a 10.4-metre-long schooner. The *Thistle*, which they named in memory of their homeland, was launched in 1844 and sold for £60. Four years later it disappeared whilst sailing to Tahiti.[22]

With money in hand from the sale of their first vessel, Niccol and Sharp moved to Auckland and initially established a boatbuilding yard amongst the scrub and fern on the northern corner of what are now Queen Street and Vulcan Lane. It was from here that they built three small pleasure craft for Auckland's then sheriff — probably the first boats built in Auckland itself. The boatbuilders subsequently obtained an order from Governor Fitzroy for a topsail schooner. To build it, they moved to a more suitable site in Mechanics Bay. It was still a difficult existence and, each time a vessel was completed, Niccol would send her down to Waiheke to obtain a load of sawn timber for his next project, prior to handing her over to the new owners.[23]

As their business flourished, Niccol and Sharp were commissioned to construct a 100-foot, 106-ton brig which they called *Maukin*. It was the first large ship to be built in Auckland. She was destined for the trans-Tasman trade

Te Hēmara Tauhia's trading enterprise

Māori were multiskilled and highly entrepreneurial when it came to trading with the new settlers. For example, Ngāti Rongo chief Te Hēmara Tauhia paid Pākehā to saw his timber at Mahurangi and then 'commissioned the building of the 20-ton *Duke of Wellington* to transport it to Auckland. Like many other chiefs, Te Hēmara not only superintended sales and kept accounts himself but also captained the vessel.' The cost of the vessel was £370, but this was likely covered by the proceeds of one or two trading trips to Auckland, which during the 1850s were highly profitable.[21]

Ōruawharu to Islington Bay, Rangitoto Island

Author Angela Woolnough describes various names given to the bay between Rangitoto and Motutapu islands. 'The original name of Islington Bay was Ōruawharu ("the place of the extended gap"). However, in the old sailing ship days, it became known as Drunken Bay. This was because the outward bound ships often called at the bay in order to sober up their crews. They had been picked up in various stages of intoxication from hostelries, such as the old "Ambassador", in Auckland. Sometimes the crew were in such poor condition that the ships had to be towed across to Rangitoto! . . . In later years Drunken Bay was officially named Islington Bay after Lord Islington, Governor of New Zealand.'[33] It is still a popular anchorage.

and in January 1846 set sail for Sydney on her maiden voyage. During her short life she carried timber, flax, wool and copper ore to Australia and she ran gold miners to California. In early 1852 she was back in Auckland being refitted to undertake a whaling cruise. But she came to grief soon after, near North Cape, when the vessel was caught in a gale on a lee shore. The captain was forced to drive her onto the beach, where she was smashed to pieces by enormous waves.[24]

Niccol soon became widely recognised as one of the foremost boatbuilders in Australasia. The launching of each completed vessel became a major social event, with dignitaries officiating and crowds of people gathering. One of his most famous vessels was the 236-ton brig *Moa* which operated on the trans-Tasman run and was kept in service for 77 years, until being finally broken up in 1926.[25]

Niccol later moved his business to Devonport and he died there in 1887. During his lifetime he built over 180 boats, including brigs, schooners, cutters and smaller yachts. He had also trained numerous boatbuilders who went on to establish their own businesses. His yard came to be referred to as 'the nursery of Auckland shipbuilding'.[26] After his death, Niccol's sons Thomas and George carried on the business.

Māori were quick to recognise the advantages of European-style sailing craft, which were more stable than waka, could be sailed in a wider range of conditions and could carry larger loads. Open sailing whaleboats, around 9 metres long, were adopted initially and became known as peach boats because they brought vegetables and fruit, including peaches, from the gulf islands to the port of Auckland. One of the strongholds of the peach trade was the Ngāti Paoa settlement at Te Huruhi, a protuberance of fertile land on the western end of Waiheke Island. Here extensive cultivations of peaches and melons flourished and produce was ferried across the Tāmaki Strait in Ngāti Paoa sailing boats.[27] But then larger, more sophisticated vessels were procured, some in payment for land purchases and others funded from the proceeds of trade.

As early as 1847, Hauraki tribes were the registered owners of 15 cutters and schooners. As Hauraki historian Paul Monin observed, 'A schooner was a potent display of hapū wealth, as well as a useful means of transportation. No large hapū or high-ranking chief could afford to be without one.'[28] The larger, faster and safer craft enabled tribes from further afield to also supply the Auckland market and this created a demand for even more vessels.

One of Niccol's fellow immigrant passengers on the *Jane Gifford* was Scotsman boatbuilder George Darroch. Whereas Niccol specialised in large ocean-going ships, Darroch mainly built smaller coastal traders, designed to bring produce to the Auckland markets. His key clients were Bay of Plenty Māori. Darroch initially set up a boatbuilding business in Victoria Street, where completed boats could be slipped into the Horotiu River and floated out on the tide. He later moved his operations to the Auckland waterfront and then to the Mahurangi Harbour, where there were good kauri timber supplies.[29]

Great Barrier Island, having rich kauri forests, also became an early centre for boatbuilding activity. In 1841, on the shores of Nagle Cove, a deep sheltered bay in Port Abercrombie, work started on the largest sailing vessel (by tonnage) yet to be constructed in the Hauraki Gulf. Shipbuilder Robert Menzies, and from 1846 John Gillies, took charge of constructing the 106-foot, 409-ton barque *Stirlingshire*. With two decks and a large square stern, her enormous hull gradually took shape as hand-sawn kauri and tōtara planks were secured and strengthened with pōhutukawa 'knees'. Construction was finally completed in early 1849. Once launched, the vessel headed over to Australia to engage in coastal trading and then on to London.[30] Boatbuilding continued on Great Barrier and in 1856 the *New Zealand Pilot* said of Nagel Cove, 'here is the ship-building establishment; fresh water and fuel may be obtained without difficulty, and also numerous wild goats in the neighbourhood'.[31]

Boatbuilding quickly became an important local industry in the Hauraki Gulf and, as early as 1848, *The New Zealander* newspaper was extolling its virtues:

It is a matter of much gratulation to the colony — especially to the Northern Province, which has distanced all Southern competition — that ship building is being carried on with so much spirit, and so much acknowledged excellence of workmanship and material. Van Diemen's Land has acquired a high and well merited reputation for the beauty and stability of her vessels, and we rejoice to think that from the shores of the Barrier and the Waitematā, specimens of naval architecture equally substantial and equally graceful are gradually launching on the Pacific Wave.[32]

The scows

As Auckland grew, the demand for timber increased. Much of this was sourced from the kauri forests around the Hauraki Gulf and further north. Many of the locations for timber operations were adjacent to narrow creeks and estuaries, which were difficult for cargo ships to access. In addition, outside of the port of Auckland there were few jetties. Most cargo had to be hauled out in small dinghies or lighters to coastal traders which were anchored in deep water. If the vessels came in too close, they would ground at low tide and heel over markedly on their rounded bilges. There was a pressing need for a new type of vessel — the scow.

The first New Zealand scow was built by the Scottish Mieklejohn family at Ōmaha in the Whangateau Harbour. Inspired by the timber scows which operated on the Great Lakes in North America, Yankee Captain George Spence commissioned Septimus Mieklejohn to build a similar craft for the timber and firewood trade in the gulf. This resulted in the construction of *Lake Erie*. Completed in 1873, she was an ugly, square, clumsy boat of just over 18.3 metres, rigged as a schooner. She proved to be inordinately slow, but drew just over 1 metre and sat squarely on the beach at low tide. Also, unlike the other trading vessels, she carried all her cargo on deck, making loading and offloading considerably easier.[33]

Other boatbuilders became interested in the new style of vessel, and within three years another three scows had been built with improved design. Eventually a uniquely New Zealand design was developed with a clipper bow, sheer lines and convex stern. These wide, flat-bottomed, square-sterned boats quickly became ubiquitous throughout the gulf. George Darroch's son David (known as Davey) went on to become one of the most notable scow builders.

Davey Darroch started work at the Mieklejohn Ōmaha boatyard in the early 1880s, but soon set up his own operation. In 1883 he launched his first scow *Una*, a vessel which was just under 22.3 metres long. Overall, Davey Darroch built 32 scows at Ōmaha, the largest being the 31.4-metre three-masted topsail schooner named *Eunice*, which was launched in 1902.

The early scows were designed primarily to carry timber, but later they were utilised to transport shingle, sand and livestock as well as general cargo. Over 130 scows were built in New Zealand during a period of 50 years. George Niccol, who carried on his father's boatbuilding business in Auckland, was also prolific at producing scows, building 35 in all. The last scow to be built was *Alwyn G*, launched by Davey Darroch in 1925.[34]

The men who manned the scows were a tough breed. Safely negotiating these awkward vessels on and off beaches in all kinds of weather conditions was a highly skilled task, as was sailing them to windward and avoiding being blown onto the shore and wrecked. Although generally safe vessels, scows did sink and lives were lost. The continual beating that the hulls endured from regular groundings meant that

Although generally safe, scows came to harm from time to time. The scow *Flora* sank on her anchorage in the Waitematā Harbour in 1905. The men survived by climbing up the rigging and awaiting rescue. The crew member who attempted to swim ashore to raise the alarm unfortunately drowned. (*Auckland Weekly News*, Ref: AWNS-19050810-4-2, Sir George Grey Special Collections, Auckland Libraries)

most scows leaked. Their heavy cargos created considerable hazards if they shifted and caused the vessel to list to one side. There were no Plimsoll lines in those days and scows were often overloaded.

In July 1909 the scow *Flora*, which was heavily laden with shingle from Waiheke Island, sank off her anchorage in Auckland when the wind rose. The men aboard survived by climbing up the vessel's rigging, but one crew member who attempted to swim ashore to raise the alarm drowned. The subsequent inquiry concluded that the vessel was leaking, overloaded and unseaworthy.[35]

In another incident during July 1928 the crew of the *Herald*, whilst heading to Coromandel Harbour from Whangārei, found themselves on a lee shore near

Scows were once a common sight around the Hauraki Gulf. The heavily laden scow *Kauri* can be seen here in Auckland Harbour transporting a load of timber in 1904. (Henry Winkelmann, Ref: 1-W1147, Sir George Grey Special Collections, Auckland Libraries)

Kawau Island. 'The vessel was tacking in a southerly direction against a strong wind when, in going about, missed stays [got caught in irons] and was driven by squalls on to the rock.' The four crew members abandoned ship and huddled on Flat Rock through the stormy night, fearing for their lives. The *Herald* eventually blew free and drifted off, stranding the crew. Luckily, the next afternoon, they were rescued from the rock by a passing boat.[36]

When internal combustion engines became more readily available from the 1920s onwards, the sailing scows started to disappear from the gulf. Some lost their sails and were used as motorised barges. Others were left to rot away.

The steamers

Engines ultimately took over from sail on the Hauraki Gulf, and the hundreds of small cutters, schooners and scows started to diminish in numbers. The first steamer to be built in New Zealand was the *Governor Wynyard*, constructed at Freemans Bay by Robert Stone in 1851. She was designed to transport people around the Hauraki Gulf in comfort. Her first commercial trip, in mid-January 1852, involved transporting 30 passengers on a return trip from Auckland

to Panmure. The trip took a lengthy three and a quarter hours one way. She then started regular trips from Auckland, up the Tāmaki River to Ōtāhuhu, with stops along the way. But the venture was not commercially successful and later in the year she headed to Melbourne where she was sold.[37]

As settlement on the North Shore of Auckland grew, there were increasing demands for a regular ferry service across the Waitematā Harbour into central Auckland. Many residents had to use their own boats to make the passage and those who didn't own boats had to cadge a ride off those who did.

The first ferry service, which was subsidised by the government, started on 1 February 1854. It took the form of an open sailing boat crewed by two men and accommodating up to 20 passengers. When the wind was light, passengers took turns at manning the oars. The service operated from Stokes Point once a day on Monday, Wednesday, Thursday and Saturday, leaving at 9.00 am and

The scow *Jane Gifford*

The *Jane Gifford* was built in 1908 by Davey Darroch at his Ōmaha boatyard. She was named after the Scottish immigrant ship which had brought Darroch and his family to Auckland in 1842. She was just over 21 metres long, had a beam of 5.7 metres and was rigged as a ketch with two masts. She was powered purely by sail for the first thirteen years of her life and then an engine was installed.

The *Jane Gifford* had a varied life during her 77 years of service in the Hauraki Gulf. Initially she was used to cart granite from Paritu Bay north of Colville to Auckland. Between 1916 and 1937 she was based mainly in Warkworth, mostly carrying shell from Miranda to the Wilsons cement works on the banks of the Mahurangi River until they closed in the late 1920s. For a time she carried road-building metal from Motutara Island in Kawau Bay to Warkworth. She also transported stock to and from Great Barrier Island.

In the mid-1930s, the *Jane Gifford* was moved to the Tāmaki River to seek more work. For the last 23 years of her working life she was operated as a power barge by the Subritzky Shipping Line, carting general cargo to Waiheke and Great Barrier islands. Her final commercial job was maintaining boat moorings in the Waitematā Harbour.

In 1985 Captain Subritzky donated the old scow to the Waiuku Museum Society for restoration and use on the Manukau Harbour. The restoration saw her sailing again, but the repairs were ultimately not successful and she deteriorated further. The vessel was in need of major restoration. Then, in 2005, two Warkworth residents came to her rescue: Peter Thompson and Hugh Gladwell. They were keen to bring the old vessel home to the harbour. In 2005 they set up the Jane Gifford Restoration Trust and purchased the old hulk for $10. They trucked her back to Warkworth and set about raising the funds, and mobilising the volunteer labour, that were required for an almost total rebuild. The final cost was in the vicinity of $700,000 and it was mainly covered by donations.[38]

The restored vessel was launched with fanfare on 16 May 2009. The *Jane Gifford* can now be seen tied up to the wharf at Warkworth. She operates a full schedule of sailings for schools and members of the public.

The first steamer to be constructed in New Zealand was the *Governor Wynyard*, built at Freemans Bay in 1851. She is shown in the foreground of this 1852 painting of Auckland. Not being commercially successful, she was sold to Melbourne within a year of being launched. (Patrick Hogan, Ref: C-010-018, Alexander Turnbull Library, Wellington, New Zealand)

returning at 3.00 pm. Shoal Bay was serviced once a week on a Tuesday with the time of departure scheduled to be one hour before high tide. The Sandspit (now Devonport Wharf) and Flagstaff (now Torpedo Bay) were serviced on a Friday, which was market day in Auckland.[39]

The trip across the harbour was often slow and therefore it was to the delight of North Shore residents that in 1860 a small paddle steamer arrived in Auckland and was subsequently contracted by the government to provide a ferry service. The run commenced on 1 May. The 24.4-metre *Emu*, owned and captained by Ferdinand Kreft, was equipped with 20 horsepower engines and she was able to make the trip across the harbour from Northcote in ten minutes.[40] She also took on other charters and one trip was to Motutapu Island.

Robert Graham was a *Jane Gifford* settler who bought the island off the Crown in 1857. He introduced exotic animals, including wallabies, ostriches and deer.[41] By 1860,

Graham was a member of Parliament and he had invited his fellow parliamentarians to join him for a picnic on the island. He hired the steamer *Emu* for the day to transport the party to and from the island. Fifty-five people turned out for the event on 20 October 1860, which started well. In the morning, the excursionists were dropped off on the south of the island, and they walked across to Home Bay. There, under the spreading trees next to his farm buildings, Graham had set out an elaborate feast. There was turkey, chicken, duck, ham, tongues, beef, tarts and pies. Sherry, port, brandy and champagne were also in abundance.[42] After the meal, the parliamentarians played games, including throwing stones at bottles, running races and leapfrog.

At 5.00 pm the revellers reboarded the *Emu* in Home Bay and then motored around to the south bay in order to pick up the other passengers who had walked back over the island. But as they neared land, a squall hit the boat and it came to a juddering halt. Water rushed into the bilges and it became evident that the *Emu* had hit a rock. The passengers were ferried ashore to safety in the vessel's dinghy, but the steamer was a complete wreck. Luckily there were no casualties. The complement of passengers on the steamer that day comprised 80 per cent of New Zealand's members of Parliament, so the disaster, if it had been worse, could have removed a large portion of New Zealand's governing elite in one stroke.[43]

The incident left Auckland without a steam ferry and it was back to open sailing boats, a move that did not impress North Shore residents. The rock which the steamer hit, the bay where the disaster occurred and the nearby point have all been named in memory of Auckland's first steamer ferry — Emu Rock, Emu Bay and Emu Point respectively.

In 1864 the construction of a new steamer was commissioned by the recently established Waitemata Steam Ferry Company. The 21.3-metre double-ended *Waitemata* was built by Holmes Bros in Devonport and was propelled by steam-driven paddle wheels.[44] So began the steam era of the Waitematā ferries. By the early 1900s, the paddle steamers were replaced by propeller-driven craft. These graceful double-ended vessels regularly plied the Waitematā for 50 years, until the opening of the Harbour Bridge in 1959 saw their demise. Ferry travel became a special part of life for North Shore residents. In his book *Steam on the Waitemata*, W W Stewart describes the experience of travelling on the North Shore steam ferries:

Here on the ferries was ship life on a small scale; the smoking cabin, with businessmen discussing the share market or taxation, footballers playing the match over again, political groups with their arguments, racing men picking winners . . . Then there was the ladies' cabin. Here

The North Shore steam ferry service operated from 1864 until its demise when the harbour bridge was opened in 1959. Shown here is the ferry *Peregrine* berthing at Auckland in 1915. (Frederick Radcliffe, Ref: 35-R48, Sir George Grey Special Collections, Auckland Libraries)

were the knitters, the gossips giggling over a choice piece of Devonport scandal, or noting the unfortunate girl in the corner who had worn the same dress for three weeks.

Up on the deck cabins reclined the readers, or those who were just relaxing, while around the funnels stood those who wanted to get off first or who felt the cold. The fresh air fiends were up forward on the hurricane deck, and the small boys raced down below to look at the engines. The lovers stayed at the bow or stern, depending on the wind, and the outside seats were claimed by the nature lovers admiring the beauty of the harbour. All these people enjoyed the amenities of that convivial club during the fifteen-minute journey. And when they disembarked, the ferry returned to the city for a repeat performance.[45]

Steamer services expanded to other parts of the gulf where land was being settled and farmed. Often these vessels provided the only means of bringing in essential goods to the settlers and of exporting their produce. There were

Story of the Gulf | **George Hudson**

RETIRED FERRY OPERATOR, TAURANGA[46]

George started his first bus company in the King Country when he was only 22 years old. He went on to establish a successful career in passenger road transport, before buying up North Shore Ferries from Leo Dromgoole in 1981. 'I decided to take over the ferries in a moment of weakness. I saw the potential of the Hauraki Gulf as a tourist attraction, something which wasn't being exploited at the time. At that stage the ferry business mainly provided a commuter service. It was very run down and wasn't being promoted.

'When we bought the business, it owned three ex-Second World War Fairmiles, as well as the *Kestrel* and the *Baroona*. They were all wooden boats. We then looked at how to raise capital to upgrade the fleet. Part of the business we bought from Leo Dromgoole included a substantial land holding on Rākino Island. Leo had subdivided the property before we took over and we then sold the sections. The proceeds from the sales, along with an urban transport subsidy, enabled us to commission the construction of the *Quickcat*. It came into service in 1987 and halved the commuting time for Waiheke Islanders from one hour to 30 minutes.'

The quicker service to the island encouraged more people to live there, which in turn supported more frequent trips. There were three sailings a day to Waiheke Island when George took over the business and around 3500 people living on the island. The population has now increased to over 8000 and there are more than 20 ferry trips a day. George lived on Waiheke Island for ten years. 'I think Waiheke Island has one of the best ferry services in the Southern Hemisphere, but many people don't appreciate that. They are very quick to complain when something goes wrong, but when you are dealing with mechanical equipment, it will fail sometimes.'

One of the challenges George encountered when building up the business was obtaining suitable land-based facilities to support the ferry services. To operate a regular service they needed berthing facilities that could handle all weathers, tides and conditions. 'People were standing out in the rain in the early days. But as a ferry operator we had no control over what happened on shore as this was controlled by public agencies.'

The business was rebranded 'Fullers Group' in the late 1980s after George and fellow shareholders bought the

George Hudson took over the North Shore ferries in 1981 and built the business up to be the successful Fullers Group today. He is shown in this image with, in the foreground, one of the Quick Cat ferries that he introduced to the Waitematā Harbour. (Jim Auckland)

Auckland assets of Fullers Corporation when it went into receivership. There have been several subsequent changes in ownership. George stepped down from his role as chairman of the company in 2007, but his son Douglas continues the family involvement in the company.

In the worst shipping disaster in the Hauraki Gulf, and the third worst in the country, the SS *Wairarapa* ploughed full speed into rocky cliffs near Miners Head on the north-west coast of Great Barrier Island on 29 October 1894. It is thought that around 130 people drowned. (Ref 4-1023, Sir George Grey Special Collections, Auckland Libraries)

regular services up the Wairoa River to Clevedon and also up the Waihou River. It is thought that the first powered vessel to enter the Waihou was the small steam launch *Gemini* which, in 1867, went as far as the junction with the Ōhinemuri River near current-day Paeroa. In 1874 the small steamer *Fairy* made it right up to Te Aroha.[47]

Long-time Kawau Island resident Bob Edwards recalls the steamer service to the island. 'The trip from Auckland was quite interesting, calling first at Emptage Island (Motuora), Mr Emptage coming out in a big punt with his cream, which was taken aboard and stores put into the punt. The next stop was Scandretts at Mullet Point. Same thing there, out in a punt with wool and picking up their stores and mail. Next were Goldsworthys and Algies, then across to Mansion House and from there to Sandspit, unloading mail, etc. The farmers came on horseback and sledge as there was no road and they had to cross the creek where the Motor Camp is now. Also the steamer loaded shark fins and shark oil from the shark factory opposite

the wharf, the fins bound for China.'[48]

During the twentieth century, steamers started to give way to kerosene, petrol and then eventually diesel vessels.

Shipwrecks

Despite efforts to make the Hauraki Gulf safer for shipping, numerous boats have been wrecked. One of the early recorded shipwrecks in the Hauraki Gulf was at Whitianga. The HMS *Buffalo*, under the command of James Wood, had transported rebels from the 1837 rebellion of Upper Canada to Tasmania and Sydney, and then troops and the governor's wife, Mrs Hobson, from Sydney to the Bay of Islands, before heading to Te Karo Bay just north of Tairua to take on a cargo of kauri spars.

On 25 July 1840, while some of the crew were onshore preparing spars with local Māori, the vessel struck bad weather and was forced to head into Mercury Bay and anchor, to wait for better conditions. But the weather worsened and by the next day a strong easterly gale was whipping into the bay. The short-handed crew managed to keep the vessel fast for two days in the teeth of the storm but, on 28 July, the last of her anchors gave way. Unable to save her, Wood drove the vessel onto the sandy beach. His efforts saved the lives of most of the 93 men who were on board, with only two drowning. The *Buffalo* was a total loss.[49]

Moturekareka Island, located in Kawau Bay close to Kawau Island on the north-western edge of the Hauraki Gulf, has long been treasured by Hauraki Gulf peoples.

The island was ostensibly purchased from Ngāti Paoa by timber sawyer John Hayden in 1845, along with Motuketekete and Motutara. Ownership of the islands subsequently passed to the Crown.[50]

In 1920, Charles (Charlie) Hansen bought Moturekareka and the neighbouring islands of Motutara, Kohatutara and Motuketekete. Hansen hailed from Scotland and had travelled out to New Zealand as a young man. He fought in the Anglo-Boer War and the First World War before becoming a sheep farmer. But he struggled financially and in the late 1920s he moved onto Moturekareka to live.

In 1930 Hansen bought the rusting hulk of a steel 3000-tonne, four-masted barque named *Rewa*. Formerly called *Alice A. Leigh*, the *Rewa* had been an ocean trader, carrying goods, such as jute, grain and wool, from the United States, India and Australia to London. But for some years before Hansen bought her, the old ship had been left moored near the Chelsea Sugar Works on the northern shores of the Waitematā Harbour.

On 28 June 1930, the *Rewa* was towed to Moturekareka by an Auckland Harbour Board tug — a trip that took seven hours. The ship was then run ashore in the front of the bay where Hansen lived. Reports indicate that the prime purpose Hansen had in mind, when he bought the hulk, was to provide a breakwater for his beach. But he may also have intended to use the vessel for accommodation and for a cabaret.

A Mr G Bennett was installed as caretaker of the vessel and he slept on board. On 2 July at 'about 2 o'clock in the morning, the barque started to list slightly and there were mysterious rumblings and the sound of falling materials almost continually throughout the night. At about 5 o'clock there was a crash. The bow-line parted with a loud report, and the barque heeled over to her port'. Bennett scrambled ashore under torchlight and the stranded vessel was left with a 45 degree list.[51]

Hansen used material from the ship's superstructure to build a shack on the top of the hill. He also let visiting yachties, such as Johnny Wray, take pieces. Wray describes his visit to Moturekareka in his book *South Sea Vagabonds*:

To anyone nautically minded his house was a perfect delight. It was built largely from gear salvaged from the ship 'in his front garden', as he called it. Lifebelts, binnacles, wheels, flags, shrouds, ropes, rails; in fact everything dear to the heart of a sailor was built into that little home. There was a library there that must have contained every nautical book ever published, a library that would be the heart's desire of any true sea-lover. A perfect home for an old sailor.[52]

It is said that Hansen had a telescope and would enjoy watching the ladies skinny-dip at Ladys Bay on Kawau Island.[53] During the 1940s, Hansen sold the islands and moved to Auckland where he died in 1944.

In 1962, Snow Harris moved into Hansen's shack on the island. Harris had built dinghies and was also a keen yachtie. But later in life he turned to drink and lived as a hermit on Moturekareka. Harris would row all the way to Kawau Island each month to collect his pension and pick up booze.

Kawau Island resident Marjorie Holmes got to know Harris well. She ran the island's post office and would pay out his pension. She recalls, 'if you went to visit him, the first thing he would ask you when you were rowing ashore was "have you got any booze?" If you didn't have any he didn't want to know you.' Harris used to spend most of his pension on alcohol, but Marjorie started putting a bit aside each month to buy him other things. 'I got him new shoes and new socks to wear. I got him a radio that he could listen to with a battery supply. He had awful trouble with mice so I got him two airtight containers and a new mattress.'

Harris died on the island in June 1978. He was 73 years old. Marjorie was asked to identify the body and was able to use all of his money that she had saved towards the funeral. Near the end, Marjorie 'knew from the way he was talking that he was having regrets about hermitising himself. His only consolation was his drink. I would see him rowing over. He had cut his hair and done himself up to come ashore. He was a very nice person and I was sad to see someone do that with his life.'[54]

DOC purchased Moturekareka as a recreation reserve in October 1993. The *Rewa* is still marooned in the bay, but she is a shadow of her former majestic form. Her rusting hull continues to provide interest for swimmers and snorkellers.

Opposite top: When the barque *Rewa* was beached off Moturekareka Island in 1930, she was fully rigged and made an impressive sight. (Ref: PH-NEG-C13473, Auckland War Memorial Museum Tāmaki Paenga Hira)

Opposite bottom: Snow Harris moved onto Moturekareka Island in 1962 to live as a hermit. He died on the island in 1978 and it was subsequently purchased by DOC and is now managed as a scenic reserve. (Ref: PH-RES-2617, Auckland War Memorial Museum Tāmaki Paenga Hira)

Buffalo Beach was named after the shipwreck and from time to time relics are discovered in its sands. In March 1947, a pair of leg irons were recovered, a relic from the *Buffalo*'s convict-carrying days. After a tsunami scoured out the beach in May 1960, the wreckage was exposed for a while and various artefacts collected.[55]

During the late 1800s, steamers took over the Sydney to Auckland run and, although they were generally safer than sailing vessels, there were still notable disasters. In the early morning of 29 October 1894, the 87-metre steamer SS *Wairarapa* ploughed full speed into cliffs on the north-western coast of Great Barrier Island, near Miners Head. It was a stormy, foggy night and the ship's officers had unwittingly steered the boat off course through failing to take into account the effects of current on the ship's passage. When the ship hit the rocks the captain, who had been drinking, had no idea where they actually were.

The ship quickly filled with water and then listed over to port, allowing large waves to sweep passengers off the deck. In all, it is thought that around 130 people drowned, making it the third worst disaster in New Zealand's history. Those that made it to shore huddled on the rocks for 30 hours before a party of Ngāti Rehua from Katherine Bay rescued them.[56]

The large number of vessels operating within the gulf created a disposal problem when they reached the end of their useful lives. Many vessels were scuttled at sea, but eventually this became a hazard for trawlers and the laying of undersea cables, so was discouraged.[57]

Many other ships were dumped on the foreshore in places such as Rangitoto Island, Browns Island and Herald Island and left to rot or rust away.[58] During the depression of the 1930s, gulf fisherman and writer Bill Owen recalled seeing the old steamers laid up at Shoal Bay rotting away. There were so many of them that the area between Bayswater and Northcote Point became known as Rotten Row.[59]

The remnants of dumped vessels can still be viewed at low tide off Wreck Bay on the western shore of Rangitoto Island. They provide a watery memorial to the days when Auckland's harbour was filled with a great variety of sailing and steam-driven trading vessels.

For centuries, the Hauraki Gulf has been a maritime hub and it continues to play that important role today. The rich maritime history of the area serves to underscore how closely intertwined the marine area and the lives of people living around its shores have become.

Chapter 8
Racing the gulf

The Hauraki Gulf has produced some of the most skilled sailors and fastest sailing boats in the world. These revolutionary vessels emerged from the boatbuilding hub which rapidly developed around both shores of the Waitematā. The high level of competition, especially between two Auckland yacht designing and building dynasties, drove innovation.

Auckland Anniversary Regatta

The Auckland Anniversary Regatta became established as a competitive boating event as early as the 1850s. Prior to that, the day commemorating the settlement's founding had been celebrated with horse racing at Epsom. But after the anniversary celebration embraced the sea, it never looked back. The 1851 regatta was celebrated in grand style. It included races for all kinds of vessels, including traders, whaleboats and dinghies. One of the key attractions was the waka taua race which attracted five entries. After a vigorous paddle over several kilometres, the prize of £8 was won by Waikato chief Te Wherowhero in *Wharepunga*. Coming in a close second was Ngāti Paoa's *Tamahu*.[1]

By the 1860s, the peach boats were ascendant as a regatta highlight. These open vessels were used during the year by Māori to transport produce around the gulf. On regatta day, these and similar vessels were pressed into service as race boats, some hired by Europeans and others sailed by their Māori skippers and crew.[2] Decked trading vessels and scows were a major feature at later regattas. Maritime historian P A Eaddy describes the festivities in these early days:

> *Imagine a great land-locked stretch of water like the Auckland Harbour alive with sailing craft of every description, and in the centre of all this activity a beautiful full-rigged clipper ship, gay with vividly coloured bunting, lying peacefully at anchor.*
>
> *She would be thrown open to the public, her decks would be crowded with sightseers from the young city. Old-fashioned paddle-wheel ferry boats would be plying to and fro between the flagship and the wharves and, as the morning advanced and the wind freshened in strength to a good sailing breeze from the south-west, the earliest starters would be seen congregating round the stately flagship.*[3]

In 1884, the scows raced around Tiritiri Matangi for the first time and made a spectacular showing, although one of the contestants struck a rock off the island and partially sank. The crew had to cling onto the upturned hull while she was towed back to safety.[4]

As the scows and other trading vessels were normally fully engaged carrying cargo around the coast, their skippers had to make a special effort to get into Auckland in time

The Auckland Anniversary Regatta embraced the sea in 1851 and never looked back. Depicted here in 1862, it held races for all kinds of vessels, including traders, scows, whale boats, waka taua (war canoes) and dinghies. (Frederick Stack, Auckland Art Gallery Toi o Tāmaki)

As most Aucklanders lived close to the sea, clustered around the many shallow bays and inlets of the harbour, boating was an affordable and accessible recreational activity for men of all classes and walks of life. The thrill of competitive racing attracted the interest of many. Spurred on by substantial prize money and lively public interest, sailors honed their skills at regular regattas held in the gulf.

The racing scows in the Auckland Anniversary Regatta made a spectacular show. Pictured here are the scows *Seagull* and *Gannet* racing past the Rangitoto light during the 1906 regatta. (Ref: 4-5543, Sir George Grey Special Collections, Auckland Libraries)

for the regatta. Eaddy described what sometimes took place. During the early hours of regatta day a heavily loaded scow would berth in Auckland. Spare sails and gear would be brought aboard whilst the timber cargo was quickly hauled ashore. A heavy 25-gallon keg would be rolled onto the wharf, onto the deck, and then stowed in the cabin. Great loads of bread and cheese would be passed aboard as extra crew embarked. The scow would often carry 20 or 30 men as racing crew, rather than the handful that manned her normally. Then they were off, sometimes with part of the timber cargo still aboard, due to lack of time to offload it before the start.[5] The racing scows, carrying their full complement of sails, made a wonderful sight on the harbour.

An annual regatta was also held in the Mahurangi Harbour from the 1850s and continued up until the Second World War, when it ceased. The event, which features classic yachts, was revived in 1977 by the Friends of the Mahurangi and, like the Auckland Anniversary Regatta, is still going strong today.

Arrival of Bailey and Logan

The 1870s saw a major increase in Auckland's population to around 25,000. The economy was prospering and many men (but not women) started spending their leisure time mucking about in small boats. There arose a demand, not just for working boats which transported people and goods around the Hauraki Gulf's inaccessible coastline, but for racing boats — vessels which could sail fast in the often windy and choppy conditions present in the gulf.

The scene was set for one of the strongest rivalries in

New Zealand's boatbuilding history — a competition between two families which would last for the best part of 60 years and which would bring Waitematā boats and sailors to the attention of the world.

Charles Bailey was born in Auckland in 1843. After a series of jobs, including as a house painter and a photographer's assistant, he eventually signed up for a boatbuilding apprenticeship at the Niccol's yard in Devonport. Bailey had found his calling at last. Despite having no training in draughting, he proved to be a genius at yacht design. In 1871, Bailey left Henry Niccol to become foreman at George Beddoes' boatbuilding yard, which was located at the foot of Church Street in Devonport. He subsequently took over the business when Beddoes shifted to Fiji.[6]

In 1874, Scotsman Robert Logan arrived in Auckland with his wife and six children, following his brother James who had become established in Auckland and was running a harbour steamer service. Logan took a job nearby at Henry Niccol's yard, now on the Devonport foreshore. Unlike Bailey, who had fully learnt his trade in Auckland, Logan had had the benefit of working at the epicentre of innovative European design and shipbuilding, which at that time was located in the Clyde region of Scotland. Of particular significance to the approach he subsequently took to yacht construction in Auckland was Logan's involvement in building lifeboats for the numerous large ships being produced in the area. Instead of using horizontal planking fixed around a series of ribs, which was the traditional construction method, the lifeboats were constructed using diagonal strips of wood, moulded into shape as two layers. This resulted in very light, robust and strong boats.[7]

By the early 1870s the work began to dry up. The firm Logan worked for on the mouth of the Clyde had specialised in constructing clippers for the Chinese tea trade, and these were now being overtaken by steamers. Logan realised he would need to look for work opportunities elsewhere. By 1880, he had set up his own yard in Devonport, at the foot of Anne Street. Bailey's son, Charles Junior, who had inherited his father's design genius, had joined the Bailey business nearby.[8]

Scotsman Robert Logan arrived in Auckland in 1874 and revolutionised yacht design and construction. Many of his yachts are still sailing the Hauraki Gulf today. He is shown here in 1902. (Ref: The Cyclopedia of New Zealand [Auckland Provincial District], New Zealand Electronic Text Collection)

Building boats in the early days was a back-breaking business. There was no electricity and therefore no power tools. Initially, each kauri log had to be first squared and then sawn into planks, using a massive hand saw operated vertically in a pit with one man on each end. Then the wood needed to be dressed, to square the edges and smooth the surfaces using adzes and planes.[9] By the 1880s, sophisticated steam-powered sawmills were in operation. Bailey and Logan turned out beautiful-looking boats, many of which have survived until today. A large number were working boats, but these early boatbuilders' real masterpieces were their racing yachts.

Logan was the first boatbuilder in New Zealand to consistently use a three-skin construction method for his yachts. The inner two skins were laid in opposing diagonals, with the outer layer consisting of horizontal planking. Kauri was the preferred timber for the hull and most was sourced from Whakapirau on the Kaipara.[10]

Developments in yacht design

Yacht design developed rapidly during the early 1880s. Robert Logan launched the *Jessie Logan* which adopted a new experimental design. Two years later, Bailey launched the first modern keel boat built in New Zealand, a 13.7-metre cutter named *Rita*. Unlike earlier yachts, the lead ballast was placed outside her hull. Sailed by Rākino fisherman Albert Sanford, *Rita* went on to win the 1882 Anniversary Regatta. Significantly, she beat the new Logan 12.5-metre yacht *Toroa*. Not one to take defeat easily, Logan responded with a new boat, the *Arawa*, specifically designed to beat his rival. She proved up to the task and the two boats engaged in close competition for the next decade.

The *Jessie Logan*

During the 1880s New Zealand plunged into an economic depression, yachting became less affordable and the North Shore boatbuilders struggled to obtain commissions. By this time Logan had eight children to support and he was looking to raise additional income.

In 1880 he built a yacht on spec, an 8.5-metre centreboard cutter named *Jessie Logan* after his nine-year-old daughter. The design was experimental, with the shape of the hull narrower and more wedge-shaped than the norm. He launched the yacht in January 1880 and raced it in the Anniversary Regatta, winning convincingly. But despite the yacht's evident sailing abilities he was unable to find a buyer. So he conceived the idea of raffling her.[11]

At that time, the only legal raffles in New Zealand were known as the Art Unions. They were supervised by the police and designed as a mechanism to enable charities to raise funds through raffling works of art. Logan managed to persuade the authorities to raffle *Jessie Logan* as an artwork with the charity to benefit from the proceeds being his boatbuilding firm. Two hundred tickets were sold at £1 each and the raffle was drawn amongst an excited crowd at the Waitemata Hotel. The raffle was won by warehouseman and chandler James Ansenne, who decided to keep the boat.[12]

Jessie Logan dominated her class in Auckland yacht racing for a decade and helped to cement Logan's reputation for building fine fast yachts. She passed through several owners and was raced for some years by Ponsonby-based Walter Jones, who was recognised as one of the greatest yachtsmen in New Zealand at the time. Then in 1889, to the relief of her Auckland competitors, the yacht was sold to a buyer in Wellington where she also dominated the fleet for some years.[13] She was eventually converted to a launch and fishing boat and worked out of the top of the South Island for close on 70 years.

Lawyer, sailor, author and classic-yacht enthusiast Harold Kidd was the one who eventually rescued her. Growing up in Devonport, Harold had heard stories from his neighbours about sailing with the Logans on the *Jessie Logan*. Years later, while on holiday with his family in Nelson, Harold spotted an old launch moored off the foreshore. With some excitement, he was just able to make out the name *Jessie Logan* on the transom. Heading back to Auckland, Harold kept thinking about the old yacht. Subsequently, *Jessie Logan* was washed ashore by a storm and wrecked. Her remains were sold to a Nelson couple, who installed them in their yard as

The 28-foot centre-boarder *Jessie Logan*, built by Robert Logan in 1879, represented a breakthrough in yacht design. (Ref: PH-ALB-245, Auckland War Memorial Museum Tāmaki Paenga Hira)

a playground for their children. This fortunately enabled the yacht to be preserved for posterity.[14]

Kidd was keen to do something, but it was some years before he was in a position to act. Finally, in February 1988, he extracted *Jessie Logan* from the Nelson garden and trailered her back to Auckland. The restoration process proved tricky, but eventually she was returned to her original specifications.[15] Now, more than 130 years after her first launching, the *Jessie Logan* can be seen sailing again on the Hauraki Gulf sporting her beautiful lines and enormous gaff rig.

As well as running his legal practice and restoring the *Jessie Logan*, Kidd has written widely on the Hauraki Gulf's yachting history. Books he has co-authored with Robin Elliot include histories of the Ponsonby, Richmond and Devonport yachting clubs, a New Zealand history of yachting called *Southern Breeze*, and a book on the legendary Logan boatbuilding family. 'What really prompted the histories was that there were a few books written, but they were full of mistakes and also had vast omissions. We got fed up with that and decided to fill in the blanks. We found that the past history of yachting was much more varied and interesting than the publications portrayed.'

Near the end of the nineteenth century there was a revolution in Auckland yacht design, with boats becoming lighter, beamier and having rounded 'spoon' bows. This change is shown in this image of *Waitangi* (A6), which was built by Robert Logan Snr in 1894 (a relatively large heavy boat with a schooner bow), and the lighter, sleeker *Ngatira* (B2) built by Chas Bailey Jnr in 1904.

The 1890s brought about another revolution in yacht design, with boats becoming lighter and beamier and having rounded spoon bows rather than straight stems or S-shaped schooner bows. In 1892, two of Logan's sons set up business on the city side of the harbour trading as R & A Logan. A third brother eventually joined and the trading name morphed into Logan Bros. Robert Logan senior closed his Devonport yard in 1894 and moved next door to his sons, but specialised in building steamers. The Baileys also moved city-side in 1879 and the sons took over the firm in 1894. The brothers eventually split, with Charles Bailey Junior operating under his own name and his brother Walter establishing a firm called Bailey and Lowe.

Boatbuilding businesses boomed. Between 1891 and 1899, the Logans built no less than 45 sailing boats.[16] Arch Logan was the most talented designer of the brothers and he was largely responsible for their most successful designs.

These included *Ariki*, a 16.5-metre keeler with gaff cutter rig, built for Charles Horton of the Horton publishing dynasty and launched in 1904. *Ariki* was big and powerful and dominated racing in Auckland for 35 years. No one could beat her. When *Ariki*'s reign of glory ended in the 1930s, she continued to have an eventful life racing and cruising out of Auckland.[17]

Early yacht clubs

The beautiful Logan and Bailey yachts were largely sailed by more affluent Aucklanders who had built their houses on the north-facing slopes of Herne Bay, further to the east in Parnell and on the North Shore. Racing was under the auspices of the Auckland Yacht Club which was originally established around 1887. It assumed its current name, the Royal New Zealand Yacht Squadron, in 1902.[18]

A very different kind of yacht racing developed around Ponsonby, a suburb which had grown up during the 1870s when Auckland started to spread up the harbour. This was where many men who worked in the local maritime industries lived. Ponsonby was a working-class suburb and the sporting men who lived there developed a tradition of playing hard rugby in the winter and seriously racing sailing boats over the summer.[19]

RETIRED BUSINESSMAN, AUCKLAND[20]

Bruce Marler was eighteen years old when he first set eyes on _Rawhiti_, the 16.5-metre Logan designed and built cutter, which had been first launched in 1905. It was now 1946 and, after finishing school, Bruce had travelled up to Russell to meet his father Hec who had sailed the yacht over from Sydney.

Hec ran the successful Marler shoe company and regularly travelled to Australia on business. While there, he had spotted _Rawhiti_ in a shed on the edge of Sydney Harbour. She had been under wraps since the start of the Second World War, during which time yacht racing had been put on hold. Hec approached the vessel's owner, Frank Albert, to enquire about purchasing the yacht. Frank was not too keen as he hoped to sell the yacht to another Australian. But Hec persisted and eventually prevailed. The yacht was refurbished and he sailed her across the Tasman with four crew.

As Bruce travelled over from Paihia on the car ferry, 'the first thing I saw was this lovely yacht bobbing and curtsying off the Russell wharf. It was just a fantastic sight.' His father disembarked and travelled the rest of the way by land while Bruce joined the crew for a ten-day cruise down the Northland coast to Auckland. As Bruce recalls, 'It was the beginning of a love affair with a magnificent yacht.'

The family raced the yacht during summer weekends and also cruised her. 'In those days we didn't have an engine in _Rawhiti_ so we went everywhere under sail. But there were times after a long weekend when it was difficult to get home. On a couple of occasions we left Te Kouma at midday on Sunday to get home before dark and the wind would fall away. We finished up lashing the dinghy with our little 10-horsepower Seagull outboard alongside and doing about one knot against an ebb tide. We would finally get into Ōkahu Bay at 2 am on Monday morning and try to report into the office at 8 am.'

Unfortunately Hec did not get much pleasure from the yacht. His business activities kept him in Australia much of the time and in 1954 he died from cancer. Bruce bought the yacht from his father's estate. Each winter he would haul the boat out of the water and the crew would spend Saturday afternoons and Sundays readying it for the racing season the next spring. 'In those days the paint preparation and varnish finishes were not as sophisticated as today and it was necessary to haul the boats out and keep them on dry land over the winter, covered up.'

Bruce continued to race the boat with a close-knit crew through until the late 1960s. 'We had a lot of fun and laughter. Sometimes we went on cruising races, and after the finish, all the yachts would anchor in the bay near the finishing line. Whatever yacht had won the race would entertain us all with a few beers (only beer in those days, no hard liquor) and we often used to engage in sing-songs. My father used to play the ukulele on such trips and I continued. We had a little group called the "Rawhiti Rhythm Rascals".' During this time Bruce served as Commodore of the Royal New Zealand Yacht Squadron and he was a key supporter behind Chris Bouzaid's campaign to win the One Ton Cup in Germany in 1969.

Then Bruce became much busier with his business and he also wanted to spend more time with his family. Racing and maintaining the boat had taken up all his weekends. The crew had also started to split up. So in 1969 he reluctantly sold _Rawhiti_ to the Brookes, a well-known and respected yachting family. Jack Brooke owned the 'K' Class yacht _Kiariki_ and allowed his son Don to take charge of _Rawhiti_. 'Don's family enjoyed cruising, but the headroom below deck on _Rawhiti_ was only 5 foot 2 inches [1.57 metres], making it uncomfortable for some of his family. So he had a cabin top built above the deck and he also shortened the length of the yacht's counter stern. Her beautiful sheer lines were gone.'

Rawhiti was eventually sold to lawyer Greg Lee, who couldn't resist the lure of the old Logan yacht, and he embarked on a major restoration. 'He virtually gave away his practice and spent a couple of years at Peter Brooke's yard in Waimauku. She was stripped right out and they returned her outline to the way she was originally built with a flush deck and long beautiful counter. They rigged her as she had been when my father brought her over from Sydney.' But when she was finally launched around five years later she didn't

Top: Bruce is shown here at the helm of *Rawhiti* with his wife Sonia and two sons Rod and Chris in the foreground. (Brian Brake)

Left: Bruce Marler's father, Hec, brought the 54-foot 1905 Logan yacht *Rawhiti* back to Auckland from Sydney in 1946. (Courtesy of the Marler family)

perform as well in races as Greg was expecting. 'She did very well in the light weather but not in the heavy. The average wind strength in Sydney is 12 knots but in Auckland it's 18 to 22 knots, which is almost twice as much. So they had over-canvased her.'

Greg sadly decided to sell his beloved yacht. The cost of restoring and maintaining these classic yachts is now so high that it is often beyond the resources of a single owner. They also require a large crew and finding people who can take time off to sail regularly is becoming more of a challenge. 'The good news is that *Rawhiti* was recently purchased by

Ian Cook, Rear Commodore of the Royal New Zealand Yacht Squadron, and Mike Malcolm, who have put together a crew to compete in the 2016 racing season. Ian is also the owner of *Ranger*, the champion classic yacht, and I am sure that with his knowledge of sailing in the gulf he will restore *Rawhiti*'s fame as one of the best of the Logan classics.'

One of Bruce's most exhilarating memories of sailing *Rawhiti* was 'running downwind with a spinnaker drawing but almost dead astern, being careful not to jibe over in a big following sea.'

The Richmond Cruising Club was established in 1903 and, at Sloanes Beach in Herne Bay, members subsequently built clubrooms, shown here in 1937. Yachts drawn up onto the hard over the winter were a typical sight around Auckland beaches at that time. (Ref: 7-A15860, Sir George Grey Special Collections, Auckland Libraries)

The sailing was largely in open boats and matches were organised in the local pubs. There was heavy betting on the highly competitive contests, with bookmakers setting up tents on the foreshore and excited spectators crowding the edge of the water. In 1879, a Ponsonby Regatta Committee was established to run an Easter regatta for the small boats. This became a very popular festive event with spectators being transported out to the steamer flagship in order to obtain a close view of the racing. As well as yacht racing, the regatta included a range of fun competitions, such as a greasy pole contest and a cigar and umbrella race.[21]

The idea of forming the Ponsonby Cruising Club was hatched in 1900 at Ponsonby's Gluepot Tavern, a favoured haunt for sailors living in the area. By the end of the week the club had 60 members and their first event attracted 75 boats. A year later, members numbered 300. The club's emphasis on cruising soon gave way to harbour racing and mullet boats dominated. The Ponsonby Cruising Club and the mullet boat soon became synonymous.[22]

The Ponsonby Cruising Club established premises on the shores of St Marys Bay, which at that time was a yachting hub. Then in 1903, a breakaway group formed, calling themselves the Victoria Cruising Club. In the same year, the Richmond Cruising Club was established by several Herne Bay yachting families and in 1913 it established a clubhouse at Herne Bay's Sloanes Beach.[23] The clubs ended up cooperating with each other and many boat owners belonged to all three in order to participate in a wide variety of races.

By the turn of the century, boating had become very popular amongst Auckland's fast-growing population. Boat sheds and haul-out areas started appearing throughout the numerous small bays and estuaries where people lived. Men would spend their winter weekends working on the high-maintenance wooden boats and readying them for summer racing and cruising.

The Auckland Yacht and Motor Boat Association was formed in 1913 and a year later, after the outbreak of war, it implemented a registration system for sailing vessels where each was given a sail number. In addition, the association managed the racing programme on the Waitematā, allocating each club two days per year on which to run their club regattas. This meant that the entire harbour fleet would move from club to club to race over the season, thereby ensuring sufficient boats to race at each event and a thrilling spectacle for onlookers.[24]

The years of 1917 and 1918 saw the Waitematā hammered by cyclonic storms and many boats were destroyed. This heightened demands for the construction of a safe yacht harbour in Auckland. In response, a solid breakwater was

constructed along the western end of St Marys Bay during the late 1930s, and this provided better shelter. Several inner-city yacht clubs moved to the breakwater and conducted centreboard yacht racing in the adjacent deep water, an area later spanned by the Harbour Bridge.[25]

Oil launches

During the early twentieth century, technological advances had resulted in the development of oil launches, small boats that were propelled by internal combustion engines, initially fuelled by benzene. The motors had little power, were unreliable and were prone to cause fires. But the ability to motor to one's destination in a small craft, rather than having to rely on the vagaries of the wind, was revolutionary. An oil launch boom was quickly under way and Auckland boatbuilders could not turn them out quickly enough. They collectively produced launches which were used all over New Zealand. Launches became so popular that some speculated that it would result in the end of keel yachts. But this underestimated the enthusiasm that people retained for sailing.[26]

Launches initially looked like yachts, without the large rigging, and the mullet-boat-type design was popular. Smaller masts were retained for a time, so that sails could be used in the event that the motor failed. Then hulls eventually became longer, thinner and sleeker, in an attempt to obtain speed, prior to the development of wide, flat planing hulls.

Early motor launches racing in the Ponsonby Regatta in 1904. (*Auckland Weekly News*, Ref: AWNS-1904-12222-6-3, Sir George Grey Special Collections, Auckland Libraries)

Launch racing became popular as did cruising. For the first time, women and children were brought along and this fundamentally changed the boating scene in the Hauraki Gulf. Prior to this development, boating had been very much a male-only sport. In popular anchorages men were used to swimming naked, but the arrival of families on the water put a stop to this practice.[27]

Sailing dinghies

Two new designs for small sailing boats were developed in 1920, and these enabled numerous youngsters to learn to sail on the Hauraki Gulf, amongst them some of New Zealand's most successful sailors. The first new design was a 2.1-metre dinghy that Whangārei-based Ministry of Works engineer Harry Highet designed for a friend's young son. Highet subsequently moved to Tauranga, where the local boating club promoted the small yacht for beginner sailors, with the yachts becoming known as the Tauranga Class. But it was not until the Ponsonby Cruising Club adopted the small craft in 1941, sailing them under the shelter of the Westhaven breakwater, that the class became popular in the Hauraki Gulf. Ponsonby club members used the letter 'P' on their sails, and their yachts so dominated the class that it

Mullet boats

From the early days of Auckland's establishment, a unique style of sailing vessel evolved, one which was particularly suited to netting the abundant fish schooling in the shallow bays and estuaries of the Waitematā Harbour and Tāmaki Strait. Initially known as smacks along with other fishing boats, by the 1890s these small, light and beamy centreboarders, which were around 7.3 metres in length, were referred to as mullet boats.

Mullet boats, originally designed for netting schools of fish in the shallow embayments of the Hauraki Gulf, soon became very popular for cruising and harbour racing. Shown here racing in 1915 are *Omatere* in the centre and *Foam* on the right. (Henry Winkelmann, Ref: PH-NEG-8891, Auckland War Memorial Museum Tāmaki Paenga Hira)

Somewhat ironically, by this stage, the shoals of mullet that fishermen had targeted from these small boats had long since disappeared and their utility for fishing was soon overshadowed by the oil launches that became available during the early twentieth century. But, by then, the mullet boats had become hugely popular for recreational use, harbour racing and cruising around the gulf. They were fast, exhilarating to sail, roomy, relatively cheap and particularly suited for the local conditions.[28]

To retain the key features of this unique type of boat, the Ponsonby Regatta Committee put in place restrictions to govern design, thus encouraging mullet boats as a racing class. Boatbuilders started constructing mullet boats specifically for racing, and sailing clubs on the western shores of the Waitematā fostered their use.[29]

The mullet-boat class was given a boost by the establishment in 1922 of the annual Lipton Cup competition. The impressive silver cup which the boats competed for was provided by Sir Thomas Lipton, who in 1905 had been appointed Vice-President of the Ponsonby Cruising Club. Lipton was a successful Scottish entrepreneur, having launched the Lipton tea brand, and he was also a passionate yachtsman. He had presented a silver cup to the Royal Prince Alfred Yacht Club of Sydney and was keen to do something similar for New Zealand 'to prove a stimulant and encouragement to yacht racing in New Zealand water'.[30] The cup is still raced for today and its status has helped to keep the mullet-boat fleet alive in Auckland.

The 'Z' Class yachts, affectionately known as 'Zeddies', were a very popular class of boat from the 1920s. A fleet of Zeddies is shown here in 1940. (Ref: PH-NEG-C44854, Auckland War Memorial Museum Tāmaki Paenga Hira)

became known nationwide as the P Class.[31]

The P-Class yachts became the most numerous of any class of boat in New Zealand. They were difficult boats to sail, particularly in the heavy winds that are common in the Hauraki Gulf, having a tendency to nosedive going downwind. This encouraged young sailors to hone their skills. Many notable sailors trained in the tiny boats, including Sir Peter Blake, Dean Barker, Sir Russell Coutts, Chris Dickson and Leslie Egnot. Although diminished in numbers, P Class boats are still raced by young sailors in the gulf today.

Also in 1920, the Takapuna Boating Club was formed with the purpose of promoting small craft which were particularly suitable for sailing in Shoal Bay, the large shallow inlet on Auckland's North Shore. To help achieve this, club members asked Northcote resident Bob Brown to design a boat that would be simple and cheap to build and easy to sail.[32]

After trialling several prototypes, Brown settled on a 3.8-metre boat with a hard chine. The club made full-size patterns available for a small fee and several more boats were soon built. It proved to be a fun boat to sail and the class rapidly grew in popularity. Originally known as the Takapuna Class due to their origins, the boats were affectionately known as Zeddies, after the Z Class identifier which was shown on their sails. Youngsters would often learn to sail in a P Class and then move on to a Zeddie. The class survived until the 1950s, when it was overtaken by new lighter designs, such as the Cherubs.

Just two years after the first P and Z class boats were built, Arch Logan received an order from brothers Fred and Willie Wilson to build two identical 5.5-metre yachts which could be used for cruising and racing by their sons. Willie Wilson, who at that stage owned *Ariki*, was a close friend of Logan. The brief was to develop a boat which was suited for

the Waitematā and inner Hauraki Gulf. The result was two identical clinker-built kauri boats which were three-quarters decked and designed to be sailed by a crew of between three and five. They were named *Mawhiti* and *Matarere*. The boys raced the boats, and they were allocated the letter M for their class. Further boats of the same design were built and these engaged in close racing.[33]

When Arch Logan died in 1940, many sailors wanted to memorialise his great achievements in yacht design. George Dennes, who led the Herne Bay Junior Yacht Club, set about raising funds for a trophy. As a result, the Arch Logan Memorial Trophy was created, which took the shape of a miniature M-Class yacht. The trophy is still raced for each year by M-Class boats, which now comprise one of the few pre-Second World War centreboard classes to survive to the present.

Lou Tercel and *Ranger*

During the 1930s Auckland, along with the rest of the country, was in the grip of a depression and many people were out of work. One of these was Lou Tercel, a man of Slovenian and Irish roots who had grown up on the Kaipara Harbour, in Whangārei and then in Auckland. In 1931 he was made redundant from his job as a wharf crane operator for the Auckland Harbour Board. Tercel was a keen sailor and had been the commodore of the Victoria Cruising Club. In the mid-1930s, Tercel and his brothers kept food on the table by building boats on commission. Their 'boatyard' was located in a shelter on the side of their family's Ponsonby Terrace property.[34]

Then, when the economy improved and Tercel got his job back at the Auckland Harbour Board, he decided he wanted

The revolutionary yacht *Ranger* was designed and built by wharf crane operator Lou Tercel and launched in 1938. *Ranger* was virtually unbeaten for the next 28 years. She is shown here fully restored.

to build something for himself, something that would beat *Ariki*, the Arch Logan-designed boat which had been at the front of the Auckland fleet now for over 30 years. Tercel had spent considerable time studying the latest in American yacht design, especially the America's Cup boats, through subscribing to American yachting magazines. He was confident that he could come up with something which would sail very fast in the Waitematā's variable conditions.[35]

Once Tercel had come up with a concept, he made several small wooden models and tested them in Coxs Creek. The hull shape that showed the least resistance to the fast flowing water was the one he chose. Tercel and his brothers began building the new yacht in 1937, working in the evenings and during the weekends. After a year, the 18.3-metre kauri hull had been completed and in October 1938 she was transported to St Marys Bay for launching. One of the most innovative aspects of the new boat was her

rig. Many of the older boats had gaff rigs with long booms, but Tercel decided to put his sail area up high, where there was more wind. He built an enormous 21.6-metre-high mast and used a relatively short boom. In addition, he made provision for three headsails — a genoa, a staysail and a flying jib. This enabled the sail area to be easily changed in response to different wind conditions.[36]

Tercel named the revolutionary yacht after the cutter *Ranger* which, back in 1840, had taken Hobson, Mathew and Rough to the Waitematā to find a location for the new capital. *Ranger*'s first racing outing was in January 1939 and she romped across the line ahead of all the other boats. She then got the gun again in that year's Auckland Anniversary Regatta.[37] *Ranger* was pretty much unbeaten for the next 28 years until *Infidel*, a radically new boat designed by John Spencer, managed to take her on in 1967.

Those who crewed on *Ranger* were totally committed. Over the summer, they would race her most weekends. In addition, one night every week they would tie her up to the old wharf at St Marys Bay. Once the tide was out, often in the middle of the night, they would clean her hull to remove any growths that might reduce her speed. Early the next morning, the crew members would float the vessel on the incoming tide and return *Ranger* to her moorings, before heading off to work. *Ranger* would be fully hauled out over the winter. The crew would play rugby on a Saturday and then work on the boat each Sunday to ensure she was in top condition for the next racing season.[38] When the boat came up for sale in 1996 after Tercel's death, Auckland boatbuilder Ian Cook bought her. He could remember watching the beautiful boat sailing up the harbour when he was a boy and couldn't resist the challenge of restoring her to her former glory. She can still be seen racing out in the Waitematā.[39]

Post–Second World War

Yachting was pretty much put on hold during the Second World War: many sailors were away fighting, there were booms across the harbour entrance for security, and materials were scarce. But once the war was over there was an explosion in boating activity on the gulf: a proliferation of new boats, new designers and designs, and new sailing clubs.

Viv Blows recalls her involvement with the Devonport Yacht Club in the late 1940s and the recommissioning of her family's boat, which had been laid up during the war. As materials were still scarce, her husband ripped out the kauri

Jack Brooke and sailing dinghies

North Shore resident John Brooke (known as Jack) trained as an engineer and he used his engineering understanding to develop innovative yacht designs.[40] These included the Wakatere he designed in 1932 for use on Devonport's Narrow Neck Beach by members of the Wakatere Canoe Club (later renamed the Wakatere Boating Club) which he established in 1926.

In particular, the boats were designed to be light enough to be lifted out of the water after racing and carried through the large waves, which often built up on the exposed beach. Although they quickly proved popular, the design was not robust and most of the boats were destroyed in a cyclone during the mid-1930s. This led Jack in 1938 to design a stronger clinker-built boat, which became the very popular Frostbite. Within three years, a hundred Frostbites had been constructed.[41]

In 1957 Jack designed the Sabot and then, in 1964, the hugely successful Sunburst. By 1978, this 3.6-metre two-person dinghy was the third most popular centreboarder in the country, with 1000 boats on the water. By the 1990s over 5000 had been built.[42]

Jack passed away on 6 August 1992. During his lifetime he had designed 250 yachts, including the *Spirit of Adventure* which was built as a training ship for young sailers.[43]

---

match lining from their house and used it to build the boat's cabin top. This was despite having no replacement wall covering. She explains: 'Members were good friends and when we visited them there was no need to apologise for the state of the walls — we all understood.'[44]

People started to build their own boats in great numbers. New materials, such as marine plywood and resin glues, were now available, making building cheaper and easier. During the six years from 1944 to 1950, the Auckland Yacht and Motor Boat Association registered more than 1000 new pleasure boats in the Auckland area.[45] New designs rapidly emerged.

The construction of the Auckland Harbour Bridge, which opened in 1959, fundamentally changed the yacht-racing scene in Auckland. The bridge was located directly across the main centreboard racing grounds operated by the Ponsonby, Richmond and Victoria clubs. It also opened up the North Shore of Auckland to massive suburban growth. Centreboard racing moved out of the inner Waitematā Harbour to the periphery, with youth training strongholds today in places such as the Murrays Bay Boating Club and the Kohimarama Yacht Club.

More than a century of competitive yacht racing on the Hauraki Gulf set the stage for New Zealand yacht designers and sailors to take on the world. In 1969, Aucklander Chris Bouzaid went on to win the One Ton Cup in Germany in his boat *Rainbow II*, winning the final race on the day that man first stepped on the moon. Bouzaid named his yacht after *Rainbow*, the 1898 Logan yacht which his father Leo had owned for many years and which had beaten most of the other yachts on Auckland Harbour during her prime.

Other successes followed the One Ton Cup victory, with New Zealand winning the Whitbread Round the World Race and the America's Cup.[46]

Talented Aucklanders became internationally competitive yacht designers. They included the likes of Laurie Davidson, Ron Holland, Jim Young, Greg Elliot, Murray Ross and Paul Whiting. But Bruce Farr was the most successful. Farr started his career designing and building dinghies and then apprenticed to Jim Young. His designs quickly dominated racing fleets and in 1973 he gave up boatbuilding to establish a design office at Kohimarama, Auckland, with his sailing partner Russell Bowler. Within the decade, the pair had moved to the USA and Farr designs were dominating international racing. Farr designed *Ceramco*, Sir Peter Blake's first yacht to enter the 1981–82 Whitbread Round the World Race. Of the 32-boat fleet entering the 1989–90 Round the World Race, eight were Farr designs, including *Steinlager 2* which won all legs.[47]

The last all-kauri yacht was built in Auckland in 1974. The 74-foot ketch *Victoria*, which was based on an American Herreshoff design, was launched from the Percy Vos yard on Hamer Street, Auckland. It signalled the end of an era.

Yacht racing has long been an important feature of activities on the Hauraki Gulf. The gulf's excellent sailing grounds, coupled with ample supplies of suitable wood to build yachts (in the form of kauri), helped to spur the development of world-leading yacht designers, builders and sailors. Yacht racing continues around the shores of the gulf today. It underpins an important maritime industry and enriches the lives of many.

Story of the Gulf | **John Street**

CHAIRMAN, CLASSIC YACHT CHARITABLE TRUST, AUCKLAND

Former owner of the A. Foster & Co chandlery, John Street has been a driving force behind the Classic Yacht Charitable Trust which was established in 2003.

John grew up in Auckland near the Ōrākei basin and learnt to sail in an old P Class yacht. When he joined his father's chandlery business in 1959, after working as an accountant, John started to rub shoulders with the boatbuilders that were clustered around Beaumont Street, supplying them with chandlery. Although not a woodworker himself, John became fascinated by the trade. 'I always admired the skills of the wooden boatbuilder. Nothing was square. Everything had to be custom made. Their skills with hand tools were fascinating to me.'[48]

Prior to the establishment of the trust, the idea of setting up an organisation that would preserve New Zealand's classic yachts had been circulating amongst the yachting fraternity for some years. But it was finally taken forward when broadcaster Bill McCarthy, who was researching a series on classic yachts, approached John to discuss the concept. John came up with the idea of establishing a charitable trust to rescue boats that might disappear overseas or were rotting away in creeks. The Classic Yacht Charitable Trust was soon born.[49]

The first yacht that was acquired by the then yet to be incorporated trust was *Gloriana*, a 10.4-metre cutter built by Robert Logan's sons in 1892. John and Bill rescued her from the Bay of Islands in 2002 and a delivery crew sailed her back to Auckland. She then underwent a major restoration.

In the same year, *Waitangi*, an 1894 Robert Logan classic yacht which was at that stage based in Melbourne, was put up for international tender. There was strong interest from American buyers, generating concern amongst the Auckland yachting fraternity that she would be lost from the region. When he got wind of the sale, John quickly headed to Melbourne to negotiate the purchase of the yacht, providing the funds himself. The trust now owned two yachts.

In 2004, the Cato family donated the 13.4-metre 1906 Logan yacht *Frances* to the trust. This was followed in 2006 by the purchase of *Thelma*, a 22.6-metre 1897 Logan classic, the largest racing yacht built by the Logan brothers. The yacht was in France and John had to negotiate her release by the French authorities, something which took considerable time and finesse.

Top: John Street, a former owner of the A. Foster & Co chandlery, has been one of the prime movers behind restoring Auckland's maritime heritage.

Opposite: *Waitangi* (A6) was returned to Auckland in 2002 and now regularly sails on the harbour.

The trust now has seven classic vessels under its care: six yachts and an ex-harbour board tug. They are maintained and crewed by volunteers. But keeping the old wooden boats in good repair requires a high level of wooden boatbuilding skill, something that is being lost in the modern age. John is part of an initiative to bring wooden boatbuilding back to the Auckland waterfront, through restoring and utilising the former Vos boatbuilding yard in Hamer Street. The Percy Vos Charitable Trust was established in 2011 to progress this vision. John was also a prime mover behind the establishment of the New Zealand Maritime Museum, which first opened on the Auckland waterfront in 1993.

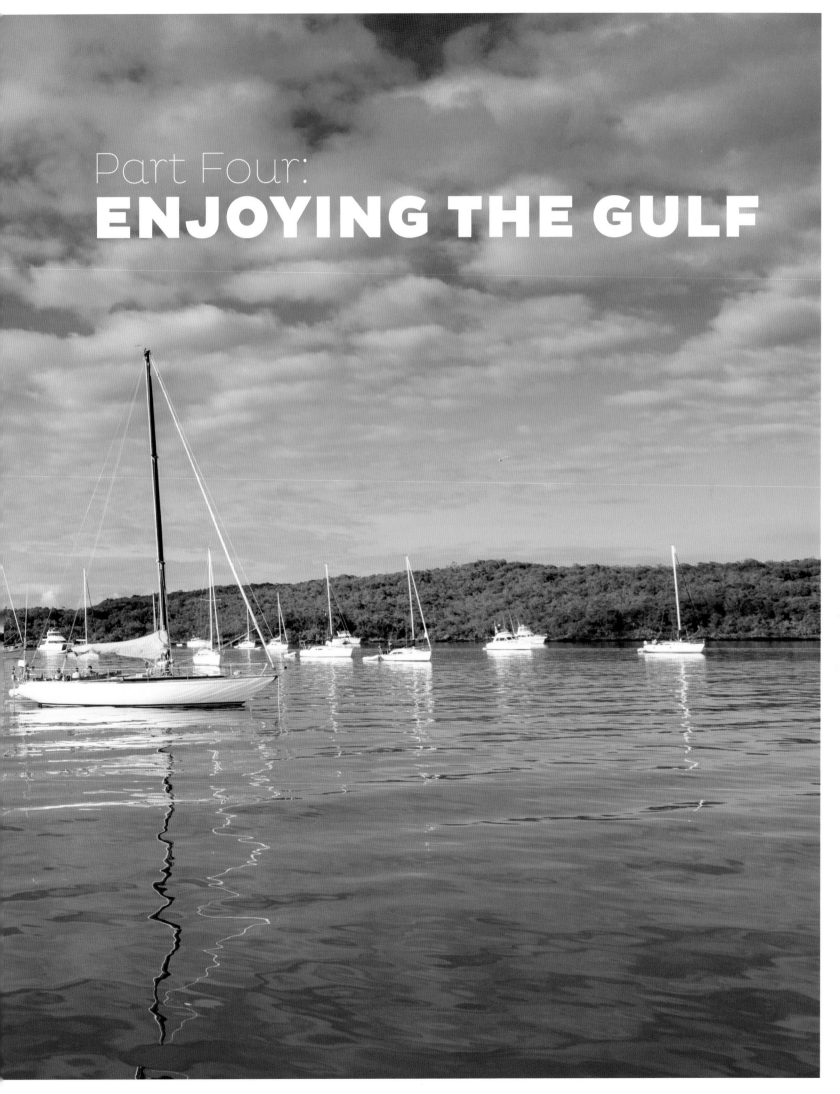

Part Four:
ENJOYING THE GULF

Chapter 9
Enjoying the islands

As well as being a place of work, a means of transportation and somewhere to compete, the Hauraki Gulf has long been a place that people enjoy. For generations, the gulf's charming islands have attracted holidaymakers to their shores for rest and relaxation. Many older people have vivid childhood memories of summer holidays spent on these islands and, as the years have passed, they have sought to introduce their own children and grandchildren to similar delights. However, over the years, the islands and the seas around their shores have significantly changed. Some have become public reserves, others bach settlements and yet others are now more like urban suburbs.

Motutapu Island

By the turn of the twentieth century, picnicking on the shores of the gulf islands had become a very popular pastime, as well as the focus for company staff events. One of the largest regular picnics was the Manchester Unity of Oddfellows Premier Picnic that took place at Home Bay, Motutapu during February each year. The picnic was hosted by the hospitable Reid brothers, Scottish farmers who had bought the island off Robert Graham in 1869.

The picnic was first held in 1892 in order to celebrate the anniversary of the Auckland District Manchester Unity of Oddfellows, a local branch of the friendly society which originated in Manchester, England. The precise day that the picnic was held each year was chosen with care, to ensure that the tide was high during the early morning and late evening hours, enabling ferries to navigate tidal rivers to pick up excursionists.[1]

Thousands attended the picnic, from right around the region, with some travelling from as far away as Taumarunui.

On the day of the event, special ferry trips ran from Coromandel, Thames, Paeroa and Warkworth, as well as other places. There was also a special excursion train running from Cambridge to deliver picnickers to the ferries.[2]

An enthusiastic attendee at the 1893 picnic later wrote glowingly of the event in the *Observer*. He described the running races, where the prize for the married ladies' race was a baby's pram. There was the tug of war in which the Thames Oddfellows, being in 'fine form', beat the Auckland contingent. Someone shot a deer with impressive antlers. 'But fun?' he questioned. 'There was heaps of it! The hills all round were dotted with spoony couples and the air was full of yummy-yumminess.' Even the trip home proved an adventure:

The home trip would have been much pleasanter had there been fewer aboard. Rather a tight fit. But as most of the

Pages 160–161: Islington Bay, Rangitoto Island.
Above: Ōtata Island, the Noises.

Top: One of the largest regular picnics ever held in the Hauraki Gulf was the Manchester Unity of Oddfellows Premier Picnic at Home Bay, Motutapu Island. Picnickers and yachties are shown here c. 1910, with a paddle steamer berthed at the wharf in the background. (William Price, Ref: 1/2-001101-G, Alexander Turnbull Library, Wellington, New Zealand)

Bottom: Home Bay is still a popular anchorage for pleasure craft, and campers now enjoy the large flat area behind the beach where thousands of picnickers frolicked during the turn of the twentieth century.

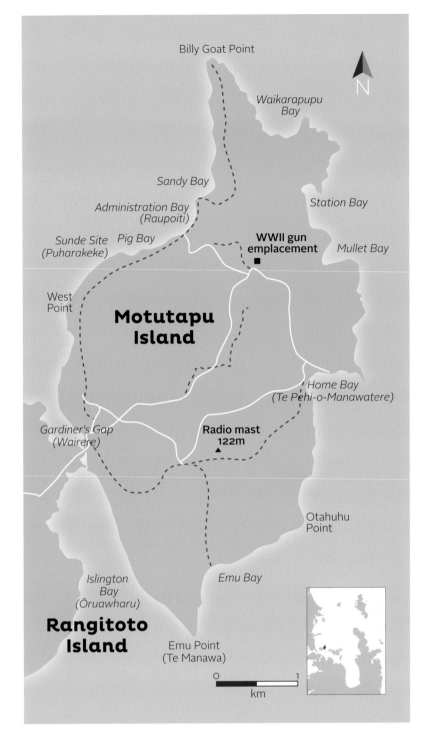

marquees were erected behind the beach. There were brass and pipe bands, running races, tug of war contests and donkey rides for the children.[4]

The island is now part of the Hauraki Gulf Marine Park and is managed by the Department of Conservation. The Reid homestead in Home Bay has been restored. The bay remains a popular destination for pleasure craft, and campers now occupy the flats behind the beach, where the enormous Oddfellows picnics were once held.

Rangitoto Island

Some of the earliest baches in the Hauraki Gulf were constructed on the lava-strewn shores of Rangitoto Island. The government had purchased the island from Ngāti Paoa in 1854, primarily as a source of stone for construction in the fast-growing Auckland settlement. A number of quarries were subsequently established on the island.[5]

Being unsuitable for farming, due to the lack of soil, the island was declared a recreational reserve in 1890. The Devonport Borough became the governing body and the Rangitoto Island Domain Board was established to undertake day-to-day administration. The domain board quickly pursued a policy of opening up the island for public enjoyment. The first projects involved the construction of a wharf (Rangitoto Wharf) on the southern side and the development of a track from the wharf to the summit, both of which were opened with great fanfare in 1897.[6]

In 1911, as they were struggling to raise sufficient money to cover the costs of administering the island, the domain board decided to lease out sites to campers. These were located in three areas: adjacent to Rangitoto Wharf, in the sheltered Islington Bay to the east and to the west in McKenzie Bay near the Rangitoto beacon.[7]

The first campers to take up a site were a group of men from a workingmen's club, who called themselves the Rangitoto Recreation Club. They rowed the 2½ nautical miles from St Heliers to the island in their 4.3-metre boat, then pitched their tent amongst the pōhutukawa on the small beach near Rangitoto Wharf. There the men would spend the weekend walking, fishing and playing cards. Eventually, they built a shed on the island to store their camping equipment.[8]

A group from Devonport established baches near the Rangitoto beacon and the area become known as McKenzie Bay, after one of the early bach owners, Captain

girls sat on the young men's laps it didn't make so very much difference. The boys didn't seem to mind it anyhow — or the girls either. The journey was enlivened by the sweet strains of Hunter's band which, by the way, rendered good service throughout the day. Ah, and that double-Irish jig coming home by the two old officials. It was a tough contract for such old hands, but they got through all right and were rewarded with rounds of applause.[3]

By 1903, the picnic was firmly established as one of the major events in the gulf, with ten steamers ferrying more than 12,000 people to Motutapu Island for the day. Large

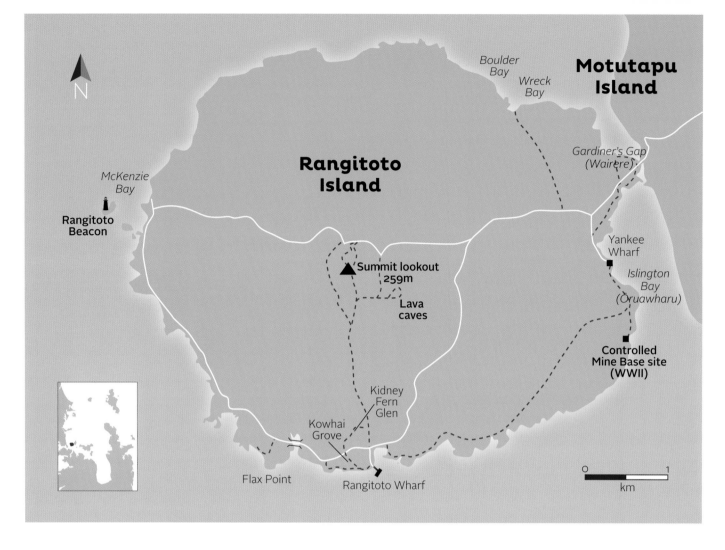

George McKenzie. These Aucklanders would row their dinghies across to the island from Cheltenham Beach, carting all their provisions, in one case including a coal range. The trip could be hazardous. One early bach owner drowned with his companion whilst making the trip.[9]

As more people started visiting the island, William Pooley, who eventually became a resident caretaker on the island, built a kiosk near the Rangitoto Wharf. With his family, he started selling refreshments, including his wife's freshly baked cakes and scones, to the weekend visitors.[10]

By 1918 the domain board had decided to clamp down on camping, which was considered to be unsanitary, and only permanent building sites were subsequently approved. The bach settlements started to flourish. This was, however, only through the tenacity of those who sought to build on the island. All building materials had to be brought over by boat and then manhandled over rocky terrain to the building site, where rocks had to be levelled using a pickaxe. In addition, a long-drop toilet had to be excavated through the rock.[11]

The early baches were constructed largely out of old car packing cases and corrugated iron. Some building materials were scavenged from the vessels dumped at Wreck and

Boulder bays. But, as time went on, the buildings were improved and some were professionally built. Prison labour was used during the 1920s to construct roads linking the three settlements. Then, this labour was used to construct a hall and the beginnings of a tennis court at Islington Bay, and a swimming pool and public toilets at Rangitoto Wharf. By 1927 there were 59 baches on the island. A decade later this had increased to 140.[12]

There was no electricity or refrigeration on the island and fishing was a key part of island life. Fathers would frequently take their children out to fish in small dinghies. Some would go floundering. Others would gather pipi and cockles. Fish were abundant and the catches were often enormous. It was not unusual to catch 40 snapper over a weekend. Some bach owners remember, as children, the excitement of going down to Rangitoto Wharf to see kingfish swimming around.[13]

One Islington Bay bach owner, Jock Loch, was noted for his unusual fishing methods. Wanting to fish from the comfort of his verandah, he rigged up a line around a couple of pulleys, with one end attached to the outside of his house and the other anchored in the sea. After baiting up his hooks, he would wind them down into the tide, tying a bell

onto the rope so that he would be alerted if there was a bite. He would then wind the line back up to his house, with the fish attached.[14]

Another innovative bach owner at Rangitoto Wharf, Reg Noble, decided to create a beach in an area where there was little sand. Seeking to achieve this, he transplanted thousands of live pipi from other areas of the island. His rationale was that the pipi would encourage the retention of sand, through sieving it out of the seawater and depositing it on the seabed. In addition, he hoped that the shells of dead animals would break up and accumulate on the shoreline. Apparently he was successful and a small beach, named Reg's Beach, built up for children to play on.[15]

As early as the 1920s, officials started expressing disquiet over the baches on the island, seeing the development of infrastructure and gardens as destroying the island's ecology. In 1937, a policy of gradually removing the buildings was adopted, with owners being given 20 years to vacate the island and remove their structures. In 1957, after the 20 years' time limit had been reached, the remaining owners fought to retain their baches. They were successful in obtaining a reprieve, being granted a new lease which lasted 33 years or the lifetime of the current owner, whichever was reached soonest. Over the next few decades, the baches started disappearing from the landscape, as the owners gradually died.[16]

Top: This charming old bach at Islington Bay, shown here in 2005, was for years owned by Mrs Myra Crooks. She was known locally as the 'wallaby lady', as she encouraged children to feed the wallabies that frequented her bach at dusk.

Bottom: This photograph shows a group of baches along the shores of Gardiner's Gap, at the head of Islington Bay, in 1936. (Whites Aviation, Ref: WA-55955-G, Alexander Turnbull Library, Wellington, New Zealand)

BACH OWNER, RANGITOTO ISLAND[17]

Isobel was three years old when she first set eyes on Rangitoto Island in 1925. Her family who were living in Sandringham, Auckland, had been given permission to camp on the Reid farm at Motutapu. Her father, a railway guard, was so taken with the place that he sought permission from the Rangitoto Island Domain Board to build a bach at Islington Bay.

Permission was obtained in February 1927, and a one-roomed bach was constructed. It has been expanded over the years. Every December, on the day after school ended for the year, the Simmons family would pack their personal belongings and provisions sufficient for the six-week holiday, and head by launch to Islington Bay. The family stayed on the island until Anniversary Day when they would head back home for the start of the school term the next day.

Conditions in the bach were basic. Sometimes up to fourteen people would sleep there, in bunks, hammocks, stretchers and the few available beds. Cooking was on an outdoor open fire and candles and kerosene lamps were used for lighting. Every morning, before breakfast, the children would go out collecting firewood. Fresh water was always scarce. For the first few years, all fresh water had to be collected from springs on Motutapu Island. The children would row across to Emu Point with billies to fill up or walk over to a spring near the farmhouse. Sometimes vegetables were cooked in salt water which was also used to scrub out the bach. Eventually water tanks were installed and occasionally, during drought periods, residents from Waiheke Island would come over and steal their water.

The family very much lived off the sea. There were fat mussels on Mossy Rock inside Islington Bay and at Emu Point. Rich pipi beds were located where the water flowed briskly through Gardners Gap, the passage between the two islands. The rocks were thick with oysters, but it was illegal to take them. A longline set near Emu Point would catch plenty of fish for breakfast, as well as unwanted sharks.

After carrying out their daily tasks, the children were left to roam freely. They swam, sunbathed, walked and fossicked. There was a lovely white sandy beach to play on just across the gap, on Motutapu Island. On wet days they would play board games and cards and every night they played the card game 500 with their mother.

Isobel remembers wonderful times before the Second

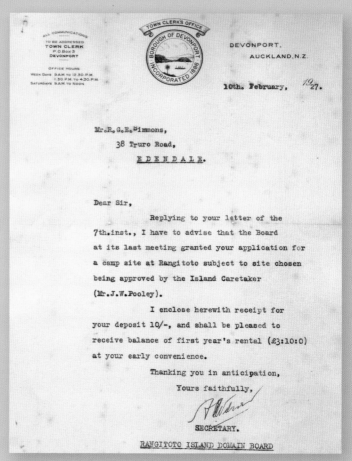

In February 1927, Isobel Conning's father was given permission by the Rangitoto Island Domain Board to build a bach at Islington Bay, on payment of a first year's rental of three pounds 10 shillings. (Courtesy of Isobel Conning)

World War. 'At night the bay would be full of yachts and launches. They were so numerous that you could almost walk across the bay on boats. Then someone, on one of the boats, would start up with a mouth organ. Someone else, on another boat, would follow. The crews would start singing and then people on the shore would join in.' When the hall was opened in 1934, there was a dance every Saturday night. A particular highlight was the New Year's Day celebrations.

Things changed after the war. A causeway had been built between the two islands and this impeded the flow of

tidal water. The head of the bay started to silt up. The sandy swimming beach disappeared. Boats could no longer travel through the gap. The once-rich pipi beds dwindled.

When her father died, the lease for the bach was passed on to Isobel's older sister. When her sister also passed away in 1999, the family was required to leave the island within two years and either shift or destroy the bach.

This was a very distressing time for Isobel's family, as it was for other Rangitoto bach owners. Their long-treasured shelters were being demolished, often by the authorities, with the remains left lying in ruins or simply burnt to the ground. For people who had a lifetime association with their family bach, seeing it destroyed like that simply 'broke their hearts'. There were originally 42 baches in Islington Bay and now only around 10 remain.

Isobel's family was one of the luckier ones. Just as they were getting ready to vacate their bach, a successful High Court action resulted in a stay of execution. What the future holds is still unclear but, meanwhile, the family has been able to retain the bach and they continue to enjoy it.

Isobel's daughter Bunny is now the custodian of the family's heritage. For her, Islington Bay is a paradise where

Isobel Conning has enjoyed the family bach at Rangitoto for over 80 years and Islington Bay will always be a place of special memories for her. She is shown here (on the far right) in front of the bach with her husband Des and friend Judy Somerfield. (Courtesy of Isobel Conning)

she wants for nothing. It is also a place of deep friendships between members of the families that have grown up there together. The Islington Bay bach has become a touchstone for the whole family. Whenever family members have undergone difficult times in their lives, they have been sent a special photograph of the Rangitoto bach. The treasured photograph has gone to family members all over the world.

Bunny would like to keep the bach as a place that her children and their children can continue to enjoy. In her view, the remaining bach-holders are caretakers of the island, treating it with care and respect. One of the big challenges now is actually getting there. Fullers discontinued its ferry service into Islington Bay more than a decade ago, so family members need access to a private boat.

Isobel is now 93 years old and is not able to travel to the family bach very often. But for her Islington Bay will always be a place of very special memories.

Cultural connections with Rangitoto Island[18]

Moana Tamaariki-Pohe is linked to Ngāti Whātua Ōrākei and she recalls 'our grandfather often used to go over to Rangitoto with my dad. It was where they always used to fish. They went so often, that they eventually dug a big hole and buried all their cooking utensils, so they wouldn't have to load up the canoe every time. When they went back, they knew where to dig to retrieve their gear.

'One of my favourite activities as a kid was to head out to Rangitoto in an overloaded boat to go camping. I had no idea that what we were doing was illegal. Eventually the Department of Conservation told us to move and as a ten-year old I thought, "why do we have to move?" It was my first lesson in that kind of thing.

'In my father's generation the island was your rohe and you just went wherever you wanted to. It was our pātaka kai [food cupboard] and we knew where to go to get what we wanted. Then in the 1970s we were told "don't do it". It didn't stop us from going back, but it stopped us from staying there. I have photos of our whanau sitting around the campfire with sleeping bags. Our kids won't experience that.'

As the baches retreated, efforts increased to restore the island's unique ecology. Alison Henry joined the Department of Conservation Auckland office in 1990 as part of the department's public awareness group. One of the first projects she was involved in was the eradication of the possums and wallabies on Rangitoto and Motutapu islands.

'From an island point of view, it was an extraordinary education on how devastating these introduced animals are on our native flora. The pōhutukawa forest grows directly on the rock and the trees get water, not from soil, but from the freshwater lens which lies under the island and percolates up through the black lava. The forest is unique in New Zealand and probably its only counterpart is in Hawai'i.

'Before we did the pest eradication, the forest was actually dying. It didn't flower because the possums were eating the new growth every year. The trees were starving. Once the animals disappeared it was extraordinary to see how the trees regenerated and started to grow again. With the growth came back the flowers. And with the flowers came back the honey. Botanists had a wonderful time watching many plants, thought to be gone from the island, reappearing after all the years of being repressed.'[19] In 2011, the other pest species on the island were removed, including rats, cats and stoats. This is enabling the bird population to recover.

In 2016 some 34 baches remained. But rather than being seen as a blot on the landscape, their historical and cultural value has now been recognised. This was only after a group of bach owners took the Minister of Conservation to the High Court, successfully challenging their eviction notices.

The Rangitoto Island Conservation Trust is in the process of restoring some of the baches, so that they can be used by the public. Others are being retained for private use and their future is still uncertain.

Kawau Island

Kawau Island (meaning cormorant or shag) was owned by Ngāi Tai and Ngāti Wai at the time of European settlement.[20] Pākehā interest in the island was initially focused on copper mining. The North British Australian Loan and Investment Company first discovered manganese, while grazing cattle and sheep on the island for the Australian market, and then copper. The company's agent, James Forbes Beatie, formed the Kawau Company which brought out miners from Cornwall to start mining in 1844. They settled in a small village established at Momona Bay (subsequently renamed Mansion House Bay). Captain James Ninnis, the mine's superintendent, built the original house on the foreshore. Another settlement was established in what became known as Miners Bay, to the south-east of the old copper mine engine house and chimney which are still visible.[21]

The initial intention was to ship the ore to Wales for smelting, but it was found to be high in sulphides and therefore subject to spontaneous combustion. So in 1848 a party of smelterers came out from Swansea to operate a smelting house in what became known as Smelting House Bay. The landward end of the Mansion House Bay wharf is built of slag blocks from the old smelting house.[22]

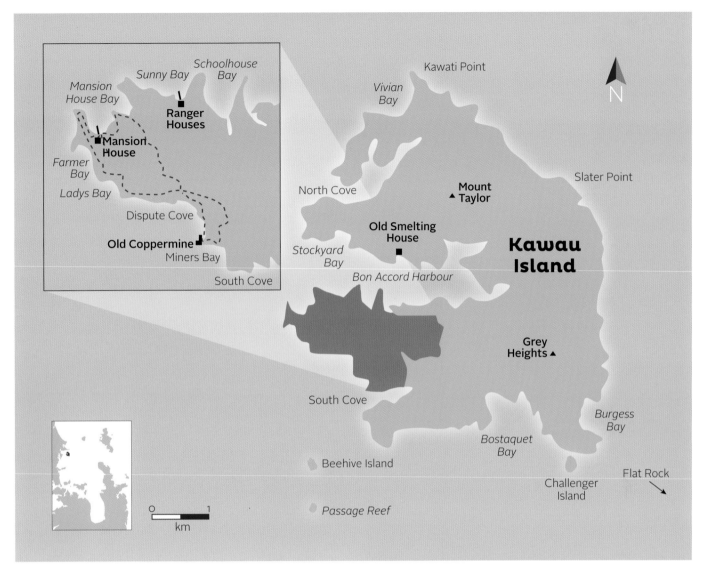

Kawati Point

Vivian
Bay

North Cove

Stockyard
Bay

Old Smelting
House

Mount
▲ Taylor

Slater Point

**Kawau
Island**

Bon Accord Harbour

Grey
Heights ▲

South Cove

Bostaquet
Bay

Burgess
Bay

Beehive Island

Challenger
Island

Flat Rock

Passage Reef

*Schoolhouse
Bay*

Sunny Bay

*Mansion
House Bay*

**Ranger
Houses**

**Mansion
House**

*Farmer
Bay*

Ladys Bay

Dispute Cove

Old Coppermine

Miners Bay

South Cove

O   1
km

Right: The remains of the old copper-mine engine house on Kawau Island are still an iconic feature of the island.

Bottom: Copper mining started on Kawau Island in 1844. This image shows the copper-mine engine house, buildings and pier in 1900. (Henry Winkelmann, Ref: PH-NEG-2364, Auckland War Memorial Museum Tāmaki Paenga Hira)

Top: Mansion House Bay, Kawau Island has long been a popular place for excursionists. Two steamships which have brought visitors to the bay are shown berthed at the wharf in this image from c. 1914. (Frederick Radclifffe, Ref: 35-R260, Sir George Grey Special Collections, Auckland Libraries)

Left: Sir George Grey developed Mansion House during the 1860s. It was subsequently turned into a hotel and then, in 1977, work began on restoring the building to its original form. It is now open to the public as a museum.

By the early 1850s there were 300 Cornish miners and Welsh smelterers, and their families, on the island along with 200 Māori. But then disaster befell the operation. A competing consortium formed by Frederick Whitaker and Theophilus Heale obtained a grant over the area below high water, adjacent to the copper workings. They were not allowed to land on Kawau Island, so their workers lived on neighbouring Motuketekete Island. They also built their smelting house there. But the grant gave Whitaker and Heale control over the Kawau Company's wharf and the reclamation built to stockpile ore, as these were located below high water.

The pair drilled into the copper ore from below sea level and this allowed seawater to flood the workings. In 1855, mining had stopped after efforts to pump out the seawater failed.[23] By then, around 2500 tonnes of ore had been extracted.[24] There were attempts to restart the mine around the turn of the century, but these failed.

After the demise of copper mining, the island became a popular destination for people seeking to escape the rigours of urban life. Steamers started to regularly stop by at Mansion House Bay. On the foreshore, Sir George Grey had built onto the original miner's house to establish a majestic two-storeyed home, surrounded by extensive gardens. Purchasing the island in 1862, after the demise of mining operations, Grey had set about pursuing his interest as a collector of exotic plants and animals. He planted hundreds of different plants on the island and introduced a range of exotic creatures including wallabies, kookaburras, peacocks, zebras and monkeys.[25]

Story of the Gulf | **Marjorie Holmes**

FORMER RESIDENT, KAWAU ISLAND[26]

Marjorie Holmes first moved to Kawau Island in 1971 when she was 40 years old. By that time her children had left home and her husband was working as a crayfisherman. The family had emigrated from England in 1947, in order to work for the fishing company Sanford, which was recommissioning its fishing boats after the war. On a visit to Kawau Island on their fishing boat in 1970, the couple spotted their dream home, a house on the waterfront in North Cove. They moved to the island at the end of 1971.

Whilst her husband was fishing out of Kawau Island, Marjorie decided to keep busy and she established a small coffee lounge on their waterside property. This provided somewhere for crews from visiting boats to come ashore, relax and chat. She enjoyed the wide range of people who would drop by, many of whom became regulars. One was a 'sailing doctor' who cruised around the gulf over the summer season providing medical services.

Eventually Marjorie expanded the coffee lounge to include a store and, in 1975, she took over the island post office, operating it until it was closed in 1980. Other island residents engaged in innovative business enterprises at that time, including wallaby farming and the production of charcoal from manuka. After closing the store, Marjorie researched the history of Kawau Island and wrote it up in a series called *The Life and Times of Kawau Island*.

Marjorie considers the 30 years she spent on Kawau Island to be the most interesting in her life. She had her animals, her interests and a wonderful freedom. 'Every morning I would get up, I would go out and I would take deep breaths of the beautiful clear air of Kawau. I would see people going past, putting up their sails and going out for the day. It was just an absolute pleasure for me. I've never ever since or before lived in a place where I was so happy with my way of life. It was very, very special.'

Top: At North Cove, Kawau Island, Marjorie Holmes found her dream home, with the front door opening onto the jetty where she and her husband berthed their fishing boat. She established tearooms, a store and post office adjacent to the house. (Courtesy of Marjorie Holmes)

Right: Marjorie Holmes considers the 30 years she spent on Kawau Island, between 1971 and 2001, to be the most interesting of her long and varied life.

Memories of Kawau Island

Kawau Island resident Arthur Grey recalls his first visit to the island in 1920 as crew on a 26-foot keeler. They anchored in Mansion House Bay and then looked for somewhere to replenish their water supply. The crew of an adjacent boat helpfully advised them to head over to 'Watering Bay' (Stockyards Bay) where there was a good creek. So they sailed over to the bay and collected water from a small creek where 'water cascaded over a rocky face, making miniature waterfalls'. Grey recalls that they 'were surprised to see how clear the water was. When looking over the side, we could clearly see the bottom, so over we went for a swim.' They spent the night in the bay and left early the next morning to sail to Coromandel. Stockyards Bay left a strong impression on Grey and he later returned to make his home there.[27]

Island resident Bunty Palmer remembers that, before the war, 'it was a common occurrence to pick up a hāpuku or two' at flat rock. During one fishing trip to the rock, on her family's launch *Adelaide V*, she remembers the crew hauling in 24 hāpuku and several huge snapper within 45 minutes.[28]

Grey sold the island in 1888 and the house was subsequently turned into a hotel. At that stage the verandahs were added. For years, steamers ran very popular day trips to the island, even though it was four hours' steaming each way from Auckland and many passengers became seasick en route. Nora Wilson, whose family bought the hotel in 1924, recalls a day in January 1929 when the steamers brought 1100 day trippers to the island. The bay was packed with yachts and launches and the Royal New Zealand Navy was also visiting with families and girlfriends.[29]

Yachts and launches regularly headed to the island during summer weekends. Their crews would attend dances held in Mansion House or congregate on board the boats to drink beer and feast on the island's copious supply of oysters and cockles.[30] By the 1970s, they could also have a sly drink around the back of the hotel in the 'snake pit'. When the owner subsequently obtained a liquor licence, he set up a bar behind the guesthouse; it became known as the Elephant House. A camping ground was set up behind Mansion House. The bay attracted numerous yachts and, along with the campers, there could be up to 400 people staying on the island over the summer.[31]

Auckland boat designer Alan Wright fondly remembers cruising the gulf where 'a favourite way of beer bottle disposal, there being no cans in those days, was to sink them by holding a bottle in each hand and breaking one against the other . . . the bottom of Mansion House Bay was so covered with sunken bottles that it could be difficult to anchor.'[32] After the Hauraki Gulf Maritime Park Board took over management of the area in 1967, it dredged the bay to remove the large number of compacted cans and bottles.[33]

In 1907, a former mayor of Te Aroha, Andrew Farmer, made one of the early attempts to subdivide his Kawau Island land for a small township. The site was on the north-sloping hills near Mansion House, but the plan never came to anything. Farmer also had aspirations to develop the island into a major resort. He built a 2-storey 30-bedroom guesthouse, installed a generator to provide electricity and commissioned the building of a 33.8-metre steamer, the *Daphne*, to bring guests to the island. But the venture was not successful and in 1909 the guesthouse burnt down.[34]

After the failure of his first attempt to sell off sections and the demise of his guesthouse, Farmer started subdividing and selling off small blocks of land around the foreshore in Bon Accord Harbour, North Cove and Vivian Bay. He also sold off a larger 1200-hectare block. But this was not enough to stave off financial ruin and, in 1922, he was declared bankrupt. Subsequently, subdivision of the island accelerated and houses and jetties started to appear around the shoreline.[35] Much of the island is still in private ownership, with the Department of Conservation managing a historic reserve centred around Mansion House Bay. About 45 people live permanently on the island.

Pakatoa Island

Pakatoa Island, a small lump of land comprising only 24 hectares, sits on the north-eastern fringes of the Waiheke Channel just to the north of Rotoroa Island. The name Pakatoa refers to the flow of the tide, possibly reflecting the rocky, tidal waters surrounding the island. At the time of the

Pakatoa Island was turned into an island holiday resort during the 1960s. The resort has since fallen into disrepair and the future of the privately owned island is uncertain.

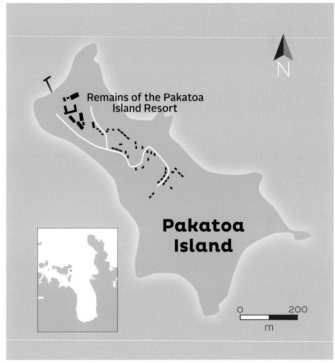

Remains of the Pakatoa Island Resort

Pakatoa Island

0 ___ 200
m

establishment of Auckland, Ngāti Paoa and Ngāi Tai had interests in the island. In 1844, Charles McIntosh purchased the island from Ngāti Paoa chiefs, under a waiver of the Crown pre-emption on Māori land sales.[36] Fisherman Albert Sanford based himself on the island in 1870, building a fish-curing plant there. But he found the snapper to be in poor condition so, after a couple of years, he moved on.[37] During the gold boom of the 1880s, Pakatoa was possibly used as a holiday resort for Coromandel and Thames residents.

In the early twentieth century, the island was bought by the Salvation Army and used for the rehabilitation of alcoholics. This was in response to the Habitual Drunkards Act of 1906, which enabled persons to be declared habitual drunkards and to be committed to an institution. At that time, there were no suitable places to accommodate alcoholics, so the government invited the Salvation Army (known as the Sallies) to provide one. The islands of the gulf seemed to provide an ideal location for such a facility, where alcoholics could be kept away from the temptations of drink and be brought back to health through 'fresh air, healthy employment, careful diet and moral and religious influence'.[38]

The Sallies opened their first facility on Pakatoa Island in 1907. One early inmate reported a favourable impression of

his stay there: 'Each man, young or old, was expected to take a share of the daily duties of the establishment. There was much gardening to do, and there were cows to milk, and work of that sort to be performed. The men were also supposed to bring in a daily supply of fresh fish, of which abundance might be caught about the coast of the little island.'[39]

Numbers at Pakatoa soon grew to as many as 50 inmates and it was clear that the island was not large enough to cater

Pakatoa was, for 35 years, used as a retreat for alcoholics. This 1951 photograph shows the island two years after it was sold by the Salvation Army and shortly before it was developed into a resort. (Whites Aviation, Ref: WA-26866-F, Alexander Turnbull Library, Wellington, New Zealand)

for the growing demand. So, in 1910, the Sallies negotiated the purchase of the neighbouring larger Rotoroa Island, with a view to relocating male alcoholics there and retaining Pakatoa for the women. The island continued to be run as a female alcoholic facility until 1942. It was then reconfigured as an aged men's retreat before being sold by the Sallies in 1949.[40]

In 1964 the island was purchased by Kerridge Odeon Tourist Services and developed into the Pakatoa Island Tourist and Holiday Resort. Thirty-three chalets, ten cabana units and a central administration building were initially constructed on the island. The facilities advertised included a shopping centre, restaurant, coffee lounge, bar, outdoor dining area, heated swimming pool, children's play area and fishing opportunities.

In its marketing material, the promoters claimed 'Pakatoa — the gem of the Pacific. Indeed it surpasses any other world-renowned tourist resort. A discovery as thrilling as an oil or gold strike.'[41] The resort ran successfully for some years, but then lost popularity, as competing overseas holiday destinations became more affordable. The owner was caught up in the 1987 share-market crash and encountered financial difficulties. The buildings were later damaged by fire.

In 1994, businessman John Ramsey bought the island for $4.2 million. For a while he ran the complex as a hotel and corporate function centre. It now receives little use. The island has recently been listed for sale at an asking price of some $30 million. Ramsey has also indicated that he has development plans for the island that include an upmarket housing estate.[42] Meanwhile the island remains off-limits to the public.

Rākino Island

Rākino Island was 'purchased' from Ngāi Tai, Ngāti Paoa and others in January 1840 by Scottish trader and boat-builder Thomas Maxwell.[43] Sir George Grey later purchased the island in 1862 and began building a mansion on it. However, he subsequently became more enamoured with Kawau Island and moved his residence there, never actually living on Rākino. Grey onsold the island in 1872.

Rākino Island has had various owners over the decades. Fisherman Albert Sanford and his wife Ann based themselves there for many years and their son Gilbert farmed the island until 1946, running mainly sheep.

According to island historian Ivan Whyle, the island was bought by the United People's Organisation in 1963 for the equivalent of $75,000. The organisation was run by Dr Maxwell Rickard, a clinical psychologist who was also a hypnotherapist performing under the name The Great Ricardo. Rickard had philanthropic purposes in mind and initially planned to develop the island as 'a retreat from the rush of modern life'. There were plans to develop homes for unmarried mothers, orphans and the aged. However, soon running short of money, Rickard decided to sell the land. He first offered the entire island to the Auckland City Council for little more than he bought it for, but both the council and the newly formed Auckland Regional Authority sadly declined. A second offer was made to the regional authority in 1965 to sell 40 hectares, but this was also turned down. So Rickard decided to subdivide.[44]

The island was divided into 4-hectare lots, with two residential suburbs being created: one on the peninsula between Sandy and Orange bays (called Marine Park) and another on the hills overlooking Māori Garden Bay (called Ocean View). Two of the purchasers of the larger lots applied to subdivide and created urban developments on

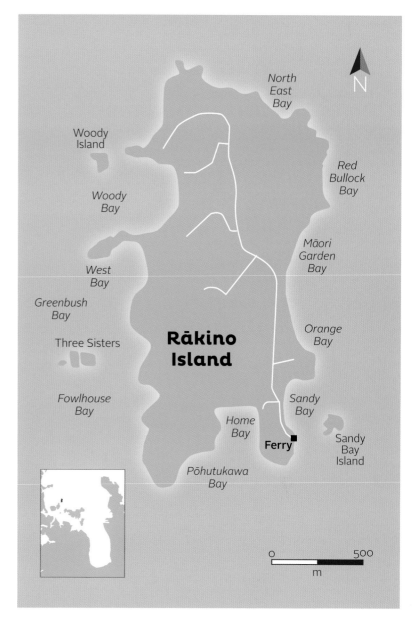

the northern and southern side of Woody Bay.[45]

Even with the sale of the lots, Rickard did not raise sufficient funds to develop the roads that had been required by council before title could be issued. So the purchasers of the larger sections were asked to make a substantial voluntary donation towards the cost of the roading.

Māori Garden Bay, Rākino Island

During the Waikato Wars, Īhaka Takanini, his family and a small group of followers sought to retain neutrality, but were arrested by government troops. In November 1863, when the government concluded that there were no legal grounds on which to hold them, the group was interned on Rākino Island at a place that, as a result, came to be called Māori Garden Bay. The specific location of the settlement was chosen due to the soil being suitable for gardening. The group was given a weatherboard house, a whaleboat, a pair of horses, a plough and some seeds. Some of the group died in custody before reaching the island and Īhaka survived only three months after arriving there. Others remained until 1866, when they were resettled on land near Papakura.[46]

Story of the Gulf | **Doug Armstrong**

RETIRED PROFESSIONAL ENGINEER, KARAKA BAY, AUCKLAND[47]

While at university during the late 1950s, Doug Armstrong used to go waterskiing and skin diving around Rākino Island and he got to know the island quite well.

He subsequently worked as an engineer and then went into business with his friend John. 'We were idealists then. We did a bit of skin diving in the Far North and loved the coastline. One day, in around 1973, I was looking in the paper and I saw a property for sale on Rākino Island. So we hopped into John's boat and headed out to the island to have a look.

'We wandered over the site and thought we could buy a bit of land that looked like Northland, right here in the gulf. We bought a property for what seems like a small sum these days, the equivalent of $16,000 or so, but it was quite a lot in those days and we borrowed most of it off the bank. We subsequently built a little bach.

'You fall in love with Rākino Island. The attraction for me is owning an acreage (we run some sheep on it) and the solitude and beauty of the island. You really feel you've

Right: Doug Armstrong has owned a property on Rākino Island for over 40 years. During that time he has fallen in love with the island and has passed that love down to his children and grandchildren.

Bottom: The building known as 'Sno's shed' on Doug Armstrong's Rākino property was built in 1960 and is one of the earliest baches constructed on the island. (Doug Armstrong)

visited somewhere when you visit Rākino. My two daughters have grown up spending time on the island and experiencing island life. They've now got kids of their own who are doing the same thing. The kids have a great loyalty to the island and love for it. I expect that my property will remain in the family and pass down through the generations.

'The pest eradication on the island has been an amazing story. There were always rats on the island when we first went there. They were in plague proportions. They chewed through the walls of houses to get at any food that was there. Then the Department of Conservation decided to have a go at getting rid of the rats. A land-based poisoning campaign took place, over about a year, which resulted in the rats being

totally eradicated in 2002. The bird life on the island is now terrific. One of my friends on the island, who compiles a list of the species of birds he's seen, has recorded up to 40 or so. People also like to plant on the island. I've planted hundreds of pōhutukawa on my place. But some people worry that trees will block their views.'

Many of the sections on Rākino are still not built on, and the property boundaries bear little relationship to the actual contours of the island. 'I would like to see the planners do something different on the island, to help create a place that is interesting, a Mecca for interesting people, interesting crafts and so on. You could allow subdivision in a way where the public benefited from greater access to the coast, where you got improved section configuration and where there was better care taken of the island. It could be a win-win situation.

'When we first went to Rākino in the late 1950s we would dive off the far north end of the island and see large red moki, the odd crayfish and the odd blue moki. You could see the sort of fish you saw up north. But nowadays it's become quite barren from a diving point of view. So have the Noises Islands. There was a surge in the popularity of skin diving around the 1970s and I think that resulted in a huge fall-off in the variety of fish there. It's hardly worth having a snorkel these days. Occasionally I snorkel off Rākino with the kids and barely see a fish.

'I wouldn't mind if there was a marine reserve around parts of Rākino. I've always thought a marine reserve around the Noises would be fantastic, as you could then get people going out from the city, visitors and locals, who could snorkel around a Goat Island-type of environment relatively close to the city.'

Doug Armstrong uses a tugboat to travel out to Rākino Island from his Karaka Bay home. (Doug Armstrong)

The Auckland City Council was given the opportunity to purchase Rākino Island in the early 1960s, but sadly declined. As a result, the island was subdivided and developed. This 2008 image shows the 'Ocean View' settlement in Māori Garden Bay in the centre foreground, the old homestead in Home Bay to the bottom left and the sprawling development behind Woody Bay in the background. (Craig Potton)

The organisation went into liquidation in 1969.

Leo Dromgool, who owned North Shore Ferries, bought about two-thirds of the island at auction, with ideas of turning it into a resort-type place that he could service with his ferries. He also got into financial difficulties and, as a result, subdivided. The sections were onsold to the public by George Hudson who bought Dromgool's ferry business in 1981.[48] This opened the island up to further development. There were no building controls at the time, as the island did not come under the jurisdiction of any council. Property owners barged across building materials, and even entire buildings, and the settlements slowly developed.[49]

Today, the island is largely privately owned and there are around 76 dwellings. About fifteen people live full-time on the island.[50]

Waiheke Island

Both Ngāti Paoa and Ngāti Maru laid claim to lands on Waiheke Island at the time of the establishment of Auckland. From 1838 onwards, various parcels of land on the island were sold. By the late 1860s, the only Māori-owned land remaining was at Te Huruhi on the western end of the island. The rich kauri forests on the island were logged and much land converted to pasture.

Around the turn of the twentieth century, Waiheke Island became a popular destination for excursionists and holidaymakers. One event that served to bring thousands of visitors to the island was the New Year Waiheke Regatta. The first event was held at Man O' War Bay in 1882 but, by the 1890s it was centred further south around Cowes Bay (Pikau), with sailing races starting in the adjacent Arran Bay.

As the regatta became more popular, it brought enormous crowds to the area. Paul Monin, in his history of Waiheke Island, describes the festivities:

After alighting from trams at the foot of Queen Street, excursionists filed up to tiny ticket booths, paid the fare and boarded the two or more steamers laid on for the

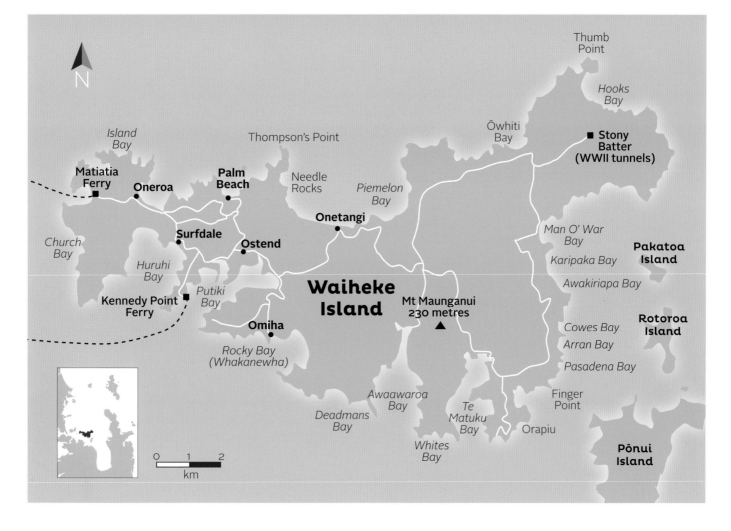

Bottom: The New Year Regatta held at Waiheke Island became a very popular event during the early 1900s. Shown here is an assemblage of pleasure craft and steamers in Cowes Bay in 1906. (Ref: 7-A4633, Sir George Grey Special Collections, Auckland Libraries)

Pre-Second World War memories of Cowes Bay

From 1936 to 1942, George Rose worked as a launch man for the Insley Guesthouse in Cowes Bay. He took guests out on fishing trips and for excursions around the coast. Once a week he would take guests for an all-day picnic, usually to Pōnui Island. After dropping the guests off at the beach, Rose would go out and catch fish for their lunch. 'The guests would have a couple of kerosene tins — one with fresh water for the tea and one with salt water. We'd toss the fish in the salt water with the potatoes and a dob of butter, and that was lunch.'[51]

occasion by the Northern Steamship Co. The paddle steamer Wakatere, *with a gross weight of 440 tons and a carrying capacity of 1200 passengers, was queen of the fleet. Lucky ones got seats, but late-comers had to settle for standing room only, an uncomfortable prospect with the two-hour journey ahead. Dressed with colourful streamers of bunting and flags, the steamers pushed down the harbour into the gulf jockeying for position and billowing plumes of smoke. Invariably the first to arrive at Cowes Bay,* Wakatere *took up position at the end of the wharf and on arrival the slower steamers stacked up alongside her. The slowest of them had to disembark her passengers across the beams of all the others. In all, between 2000 and 4000 passengers were landed, depending on the popularity of the regatta in a particular year. There would already have been an average of 60 yachts in the bay and a multitude of dinghies.*[52]

Cowes was also a popular location for company picnics, with Auckland firms, such as Milne and Choyce, Courts and Sanford, holding events there. At the Sanford picnics there were competitions for singing and dancing, with Scottish pipers joining the festivities.[53]

It was around the time the regatta moved to Cowes Bay that Portuguese sailor Innes Parris established a guesthouse there. He felled several trees to provide timber and built five additional rooms onto his house. The rooms were simply furnished, with just a bed and boxes covered with fabric.[54]

In 1904 the establishment was taken over by the Insley family, who turned it into an upmarket private hotel. Henry Insley had been a shipboard chief steward and he understood what it took to provide first-class service. The Insleys enlarged the hotel buildings, eventually catering for 100 guests. They provided sumptuous food, with much fresh produce provided by the farm. There was a dance hall, a band and hot saltwater baths. Guests could also play tennis, golf and croquet or go fishing in boats provided for their use.

In 1905, the Northern Steam Ship Company built a wharf in the bay, making access much easier. Prior to that, guests and supplies from passing steamers had to be ferried ashore by dinghy. The guesthouse ran until the early 1950s, when it was closed and subsequently destroyed by fire.[55] The property has since been turned into a private luxury residence.[56]

In 1915, a firm of gum merchants purchased a large piece of land extending across the island from Onetangi to Pūtiki Bay. They built a wharf in the bay and then, in February 1916, auctioned off sections, with about 30 being sold for prices ranging between £10 and £21.[57] Over the next few years hundreds of sections were sold. The new subdivision, called Ostend, was named after a town in Belgium that was the scene of battles during the First World War.

Advertising material described Ostend as giving 'ample opportunity for the pleasures of the seaside. The pretty Putiki Bay, so nicely sheltered, affords ample facilities for bathing and boating while there is no finer spot in New Zealand for surf-bathing than on Onetangi Beach with its one-and-a-quarter miles of beautiful hard sand.'[58] A boarding house was quickly built on one of the sections, followed by a dance hall. Dances were held every Saturday night and people would come to them from all over the island, as well as from visiting yachts.[59]

During the early 1920s, the subdivision at Ostend was quickly followed by those in Surfdale (Huruhi Bay), Rocky Bay (Ōmiha) and Palm Beach. At that time, subdivision was largely unrestricted and there were no building controls.

The name Surfdale came from a competition run by the developers, with the winning entry receiving a free section in the subdivision. It was a curious choice, given that the subdivision was located on the shores of a sheltered bay with no surf. Prospective purchasers were enticed with the offer of 'One shilling a day. No interest. No rates'. There was no electricity and only muddy tracks for access. Most purchasers lived in tents on their sections over the first summer and then baches started springing up. Many were built from packing cases. One enterprising bach builder, who

Top: Extensive subdivision took place on the western end of Waiheke Island during the 1920s. This 1946 image shows subdivision at Blackpool in the foreground and Surfdale to the rear. (Whites Aviation, Ref: WA-04060-G, Alexander Turnbull Library, Wellington, New Zealand)

Bottom: The first bach sections on Waiheke Island were sold at Ostend in 1916 for as little as £10 each. A promotional sign is shown here on the Ostend wharf during the 1920s. (Catalogue No 8, File 'Ostend', Waiheke Island Historical Society)

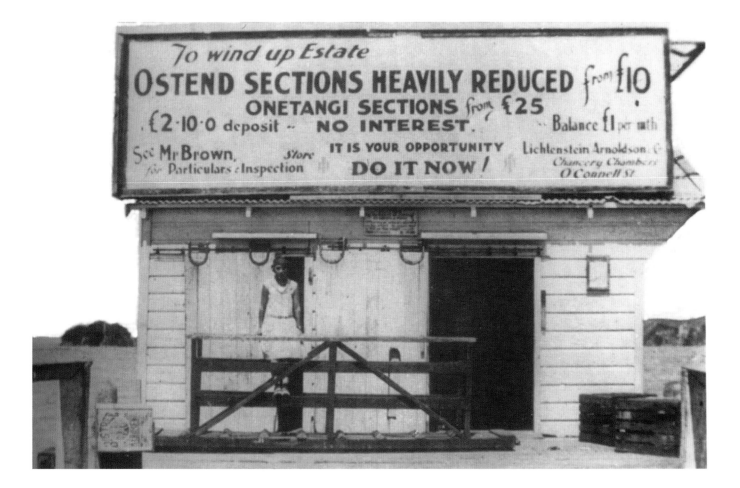

Memories of Surfdale

Long-time Waiheke resident Bill Mack recalls that, during the weekends, numerous yachts would arrive in the bay. 'There would be 15 or 20 camped on Surfdale beach. They would just pull up their centreboards, come right up on the beach and live there like a gypsy encampment.' Everyone had a lot of fun together and helped each other out when needed.[60]

Barry Ormerod holidayed at the beach for 58 years. He remembers the amazing fishing in the early days. He would row out into the channel and hook 30 or 40 snapper. There was no need to buy bait, as they would catch it on the way out or stop to collect some mussels from the rocks.[61]

worked at the city markets, built his bach out of banana cases. He cut them into shingles, dipped each piece in creosote, and assembled them over a wooden frame.[62]

The popularity of Waiheke Island received a boost during the Second World War. Worried about the risk of seaborne attack, the government closed off all the islands in the inner gulf to the public, except for Waiheke. People started to come to Waiheke for their holidays. They ended up buying sections there and erected dwellings.[63] The bach settlements flourished and many more people started to live on the island.

Torbay resident Dr Ross Garrett remembers, as a child, spending many summers at his family bach at Oneroa beach. In 1925 Ross's father, who was a keen yachtsman, built the bach on half an acre of land. There were about half a dozen other baches at the time, scattered along the beach, and virtually no roads. Ross remembers travelling to the bach on the steam ferry *Duchess*, which took an hour to get to Matiatia from Auckland. 'Although there were buses that went part-way to our bach, we sometimes chose to walk across country, all the way from Matiatia to the northern end of Oneroa carrying our bags. This was possible because the whole area was grassland; there were no trees, just a few sheep.' Even getting to the shops at the other end of the beach required a 20-minute walk. When he was fifteen years old, Ross's mother died and the bach was sold for £150. On returning to Oneroa, more than half a century later, it was the great number of trees that impressed Ross the most.[64]

Today, Waiheke Island has become largely a commuter suburb of Auckland, with a resident population of over 8000. However, it is still a popular recreational destination. There are around 4000 holiday homes on the island and it receives more than 30,000 visitors each year.[65]

The islands have played an enormous role in building our relationships with the Hauraki Gulf. Whether it be day-tripping and picnicking, anchoring in secluded bays or spending long summer holidays in island baches, multitudes of people have long enjoyed the gulf islands' special charms.

Story of the Gulf | Sue Neureuter

LANDSCAPE GARDENER, COOKS BEACH[66]

Sue Neureuter has been going to the Noises Islands, a wide scattering of tiny pieces of land and rock to the north-east of Rākino Island, since she was only a few months old. The island group's current name may stem back to French explorer D'Urville who called the islands Noisettes, being French for hazelnuts. Ngāi Tai were the customary owners. The islands were sold in 1874 to a Mr Aitken for £28 and passed through various owners over the years, including quarryman J J Craig.[67]

Although the islands have never been purposefully cleared or farmed, an accidental fire on Ōtata during the late 1920s burnt most of the vegetation to the ground. Sue's great-uncle, Captain Frederick Wainhouse, bought the islands in 1933 for £200. Shortly thereafter he married Sue's great-aunt Marta Neureuter. Wainhouse was a retired master mariner who had worked for the Auckland Harbour Board. The current small bach on the island dates from the late 1920s and the couple lived there permanently after the Second World War. They established fruit trees and large vegetable gardens on the island and kept chickens. The abundant sea around them provided much of their protein. There was no power, refrigeration or telecommunication system.

Sue's father, Brian Neureuter, ran a boat on the Auckland Harbour and regularly took supplies out to his uncle and aunt on Ōtata. His uncle eventually died on the island and, being so isolated, his aunt was only able to summon help by lighting a big fire on the beach.

The ownership of the islands passed to Sue's father, who had a deep love for them and succeeded in instilling a similar affection for the place in his children. The family lived in Auckland, at Te Atatū North near the Henderson Creek, and they would go out to the island for three to four weeks each summer.

A boat would drop them off on the island for the duration of their stay. Due to the lack of a sheltered anchorage, it was not possible to keep a large boat on the island and the family only had a small dinghy that could be pulled up the beach out of harm's way when a storm approached. Getting gear ashore onto the steep beach could be difficult and, during rough weather, it was sometimes not possible to get on or off the island.

The Neureuter family had little contact with the outside world while staying on the island. They took provisions with them and had a small vegetable garden, but they largely lived off the sea — scallops from the bay, mussels from the rocks, fish

Sue Neureuter has been visiting the Noises Islands with her family since she was only a few months old. She is shown here on the beach of her beloved Ōtata Island.

from the abundant waters and numerous crayfish from the reef.

Some of Sue's earliest memories of the island are of playing in the rock pools, mucking about in a dinghy and going fishing with her father. 'We would go fishing with Dad at night and you never knew what you would catch. Sometimes it would be blue cod, something I haven't seen out there for years. There would be the odd octopus and all sorts of weird things on your line. We would pull little hand nets out from the beach and catch piper, sprats and trevally. My father would talk about huge schools of kingfish frequenting the bay in the past and catching them while towing a piece of orange peel on a hook from his dinghy. He also remembered big schools of trevally.'

As she got older Sue started collecting shells off the beach. 'Back then you could collect fantastic shells out there. I now have Mum's shell collection and it's alarming to see the things I had forgotten about and which are not on the island any more.'

At around seven years of age, Sue put on a mask and snorkel for the first time. 'I remember sticking my head under the water and only seeing pebbles and then tiny fish, and thinking "wow!". That opened up a whole new realm.' Sue would go off exploring all day with her younger brother Rod and sister Zoe. 'We would dive under the ecklonia [kelp] forests, into a channel, and come up the other side holding our breath. It was a bit scary, but there were urchins, fish and crabs. There was just so much life.'

Other vivid memories include the sounds of the seabirds. There were not may bush birds back then, as the forest was recovering from the fire. But there were huge colonies of red-billed and black-backed gulls and white-fronted terns, as well as spotted shags. 'The beach was so covered in birds you could hardly see the pebbles. There were huge work-ups, with gannets diving and the sea boiling with life. When you were little you thought it would always be there.'

But then things changed. 'We really noticed a difference by the late 1970s. Suddenly the ecklonia was gone. The kina arrived and wiped out the whole layer of life that relied on the kelp. It just happened so fast, within about three to four years.'

Sue eventually left home and went overseas for a number of years. When she returned in the mid-1990s, she noticed a marked deterioration in the marine life at the Noises. 'There was a huge depletion of reef fish. There used to be huge schools of parore, blue maomao, red moki, hiwihiwi, kelp fish, marblefish, pataki and leatherjackets. I'm not saying they've gone, but they are only a shadow of what they once were.'

In 1995, the islands were put into a family trust with her brother Rod as trustee. Sue's parents both passed away in the mid-2000s. The remaining family members still go out to the island regularly and are heavily involved in weed and pest-control efforts there. The smaller Maria Island (Ruapuke) was

Ownership of the Noises Islands has passed down through three generations of the Neureuter family. Rod Neureuter (shown here catching dinner in the vicinity of the islands) is the trustee of the family trust which owns the island and he hopes to eventually pass its care onto the next generation.

the first offshore island in New Zealand to have a successful rat eradication programme. It became rat free in 1960, as a result of efforts by Don Merton, who was alarmed by the rats' killing spree on the white-faced storm petrels. But the establishment of a light on the island, during the 1950s, allowed the introduction of weed species which are very hard to control.

The other islands have been rat free, on and off, since the 1980s but with several reinvasions occurring. The problem was only sorted in 2002, when rats were also eradicated from Rākino Island. The neighbouring island had been a stepping stone for the rodents which are able to swim significant distances.

Sue observes, 'as the bush has recovered and regenerated, more birds have come and more bird species. But the seas have gone completely the opposite way. The maomao have

gone and this summer the sprats, the yellow-eyed mullet and the piper have gone. Trevally is now only a rarity.

'Commercial fishers would come into the bay with huge nets and scoop large schools of piper out of the bay. Recently, gill nets have been used to catch kahawai at night. We used to see such big schools of them. There has been a huge increase in the number of recreational fishermen, plus advances in technology. On fine days you see divers swarming over the reefs, at times almost outnumbering the fish.'

'A lot of people are now coming for the scallops and some of them are dredging, even though it's not necessary, as the shellfish are only in 5–6 metres of water. When I first dived on the scallop bed there were lots of sponges and horse mussels. These have now been crushed, with huge furrows dredged through the bed. When I see the damage I feel like crying.

'The ecklonia has started to come back a little bit, but not nearly to the depth it used to be. There may now be too much sediment in the water and therefore not enough light for the

Life on Ōtata Island is kept simple by the Neureuter family, with only a small two-roomed bach for accommodation and an outdoor kitchen for cooking. There is no electricity or refrigeration and the family very much provision from the sea.

seaweed to survive at lower depths. When you swim around Ōtata you can often see a cloud of sediment in the current. I don't recall the sediment being so marked when I was young.'

Although the Neureuters are keen fishers and largely live off the sea when they are on the island, they are willing to consider establishing a marine reserve around part of the islands. 'Fishing is a huge part of our life. But do you stand by and keep trying to catch fish or do you do something now that will put back what you had as a kid, the things you held dear?'

The three Neureuter siblings are jointly considering the future of the islands. Their preference is to pass ownership down through the family. If the next generation displays the same love for the islands as they do, they believe that the islands will flourish in private care.

Chapter 10
Enjoying the sea

For generations, the waters of the Hauraki Gulf have been a hugely important recreational resource for people living around its shores and further afield. Popular water activities have included swimming, surfing, boating, underwater diving and fishing.

Swimming

It was not until later in the nineteenth century that swimming in the gulf became a popular pastime for European settlers. Prior to this, entering the sea was seen as a dangerous activity. Most people couldn't swim, there were many drownings and there was also the risk of shark attack.

As well as being dangerous, swimming was considered to be morally suspect, due to the need to wear relatively skimpy clothing and the opportunity it provided for members of both sexes to mix unsupervised. Around 1890, Takapuna Beach became a popular location for swimming. Men were used to entering the water nude from boats, which were a male-only preserve, and started doing the same from the beach. At that stage, Takapuna was outside the jurisdiction of any local council, so the activity was unregulated. But the nearby Devonport Borough Council was not amused. Its official history records:

> *In 1891 public opinion was against the encouragement of swimming by ladies and even went so far as to limit the hours of bathing by males on beaches to before 8 a.m. and*

Recreational vessel leaving the Motuihe Island wharf headed towards Browns Island in the distance.

LAKE BEACH. TAKAPUNA. 2640.

after 6 p.m. Mixed bathing on the beaches is forbidden so far as local bodies could do so. It was found practically impossible to compel men swimmers to use the then accepted form of bathing suit or, in fact, any suit at all. The councillors were also shocked by the fact that city visitors persisted in coming over to the Shore and swimming during church hours on Sundays.[1]

Swimming gradually became more acceptable and, in 1909, the proprietor of the Mon Desir Hotel was given permission by the Waitematā County Council to hire out six bathing

Before the twentieth century, swimming was considered by European settlers to be morally suspect and even dangerous. The nearest most people got to the water was paddling in the shallows, as shown in this 1909 photograph of promenaders on Takapuna Beach. (William Price, Ref: 1/2-000424-G, Alexander Turnbull Library, Wellington, New Zealand)

houses on Takapuna Beach. They consisted of small wooden enclosures that were mounted on large wheels. Once the female bather had climbed aboard, the shed was wheeled down the beach to the water's edge and the occupant could

Waitematā Harbour shark attacks

During the early decades of Auckland's settlement, there was a series of gruesome encounters with sharks in the Waitematā Harbour. One of the most horrific attacks occurred in Official Bay. A soldier was swimming just off the wharf, when he was attacked by a shark and bitten in two. Another incident occurred in St Georges Bay, when a man accidentally stepped on a shark whilst exiting the water after a swim. The shark attacked and the man bled to death on the beach. Yet another encounter occurred

at the foot of Hobson Street, when a man's leg was seized by a shark as he was coming ashore. Although the swimmer initially managed to free himself, the shark attacked again, mutilating his leg. He finally managed to reach the shore alive, but his leg had to be amputated.[2] As late as 1912, a man was pursued by a shark off Takapuna Beach, but managed to reach the shore with only a slightly lacerated leg.[3]

Sunbathing banned in Auckland, 1913

During the early twentieth century, 'loitering' on the beach, and displaying one's body to soak up the sun, was frowned upon. It was even illegal for a time. In 1913 the Auckland City Council passed by-laws stating that 'No person shall be or remain dressed in bathing costume upon any beach or on any street or public place adjoining any beach, for a longer time than is reasonably necessary for enabling him to pass from the dressing place to the water, or from the water to the dressing place, as the case may be . . .'.[4]

Although initially frowned upon, by the 1920s exposing the body to the sun was seen as providing health benefits, and the culture of sunbathing developed. Sunbathers are shown here at Cheltenham Beach in 1910. (*Auckland Weekly News*, Ref: AWNS-19100127-16-3, Sir George Grey Special Collections, Auckland Libraries)

make a dash for the water without revealing any naked flesh. But the enterprise did not ultimately prove successful. The heavy wheels sank into the soft, wet sand and the bathing sheds became stuck.[5]

When swimming itself became acceptable, the council tried to enforce a strict dress code. Bathing costumes were to extend 'from neck to knee' and men were not permitted to expose bare torsos. In 1914, the newly established Borough of Takapuna quickly passed a set of bathing by-laws. These prescribed that 'No person, male or female, shall use the foreshore of or abutting the borough for the purposes of bathing, unless such person shall be attired in proper and suitable costume, extending at least from the neck to the knees, so as to secure the due observance of decency.' Anyone caught with a non-complying bathing costume would be ordered to 'at once resume his or her ordinary dress'.[6]

By the 1920s, things had radically changed. Medical doctors started extolling the health benefits of exposing the body to the sun. Sunlight was seen as the cure for weakness and illness. Bathing costumes shrank in response to the desire to let more sun reach the skin. In 1927, daylight saving was introduced and this enabled people to enjoy longer evenings and more sun during the summer months.

During the late 1920s, Milford Beach became *the* place to hang out. The Devonport Ferry Company was keen to increase demand for ferry trips across the harbour, so had

The Devonport Ferry Company constructed a large dance hall and restaurant, called 'Ye Olde Pirate Shippe', on the foreshore at Milford Beach, to increase demand for ferry services across the harbour. The popular attraction is shown here during the 1930s. (Ref: T0359, Sir George Grey Special Collections, Auckland Libraries)

built on the foreshore a large dance hall and restaurant called 'Ye Olde Pirate Shippe'. Big bands regularly played at the venue and large crowds made the trip to the North Shore to dance the night away. Then in 1936, to increase the attraction of the area, the company built a seawater swimming pool at the mouth of the Wairau Estuary. The pool was eventually closed after the Second World War and the Olde Pirate Shippe was demolished in 1957.[7]

Milford was also the location of the first life-saving club established in Auckland. The club got going around 1925. It originally had mixed membership, but the Milford Girls' Lifesaving Club was eventually set up in 1932, being the first

women-only club in the country. The members stored their gear in a small room at the base of the Olde Pirate Shippe and learnt rescue and resuscitation on the ballroom floor.[8]

The second life-saving club was established at Takapuna Beach in 1927. Its 20–30 members, all men, would regularly patrol the beach and entertain the beachgoers with wrestling and gymnastic displays.[9] Other clubs followed in quick succession, initially based at the beaches close to Auckland, but eventually extending to popular beaches further afield. The development of the lifesaving movement helped to make the coast safer for swimming, as well as later on for surfing, and this encouraged more people to enjoy the beaches. Swimming and relaxing on the beach remain hugely popular recreational activities around the Hauraki Gulf today.

Surfing

It was the 1960s that saw the real flowering of beach culture in the gulf. It was a time of post-war affluence and the government's extensive road-building programme was opening up beaches further afield, particularly on the Coromandel Peninsula. Surfing began to grow in popularity.

Takapuna Beach was the location of some of the earliest surfing in the region. Rodney Davidson was one of the first surfers there, beginning the sport in 1963 when he was nineteen years old. He initially borrowed boards to ride on and then built his own in a shed at the back of his parents' Bayswater house. This was the beginning of a business which saw him personally build over 1000 surfboards.[10]

As surfing became more popular at Takapuna Beach, there

In 1925 Milford Beach was the location of the first lifesaving club established in the Hauraki Gulf. Lifesaving activities are shown in this postcard-like image of the beach during the 1920s, with lifesaving reels on the beach and a line of lifesavers taking a rope out into the water. (Ref: T0342, Sir George Grey Special Collections, Auckland Libraries)

were conflicts with swimmers, who were in danger of being hit by errant boards. There were no leg ropes in the early days and, when a surfer fell off, the board could become a loose missile. The Takapuna Borough Council became concerned and looked at ways of controlling the situation. Discovering it had no jurisdiction to create surf lanes in the water, the council tried to ban surfing altogether, through the use of a by-law. Only one surfer was ever fined for surfing at the beach before the by-law was struck down as being illegal.[11]

In any event, there were much better and more regular waves to be found elsewhere, with particularly good surf at Whangamatā. One of the early surfers there was Cindy Webb, who first tried surfing in 1961 on a board she had borrowed from a member of the Whangamatā Surf Life Saving Club. She wasn't sure what she was supposed to do, but she eventually mastered standing up on the board and riding into the beach on white water. It wasn't until a couple of other surfers appeared that she discovered that surfing involved catching the wave before it broke. Cindy went on to win the women's section of the national surfing championships in 1964 and '65.[12]

Keen Auckland surfers often headed down to Whangamatā and slept overnight on the beach, which became known as the Sands Hotel. As surfer Wayne Parkes

Story of the Gulf | **Wayne Parkes**
SURFER AND SURFBOARD SHAPER, AUCKLAND[13]

Wayne was born in Whangārei, but he moved with his family to Takapuna Beach in 1957. 'The first time I walked on Takapuna Beach, when I was seven years old, I knew this was something. It was fantastic.

In the early days we just swam and body-surfed. We had little ply boards and then any little piece of foam that we could find.' In the early 1960s, surfboards started to show up in New Zealand and, when he was just twelve years old, Wayne saved up enough money from selling old bottles and scrap metal to buy his own surfboard.

'We surfed Takapuna and then, when we could get a lift, we went to Ōrewa, then Pākiri and Mangawhai, all along the north-east coast. It was beautiful up there. Some days you would paddle out and the whole bottom of the sea would move, being covered in stingrays. Occasionally, killer whales would come right in close. You could walk out to them and they would show you their calves. The beaches in those days were just amazing. There was no traffic going up to them and you would have the entire place all to yourself.'

Wayne established a successful business at Takapuna shaping surfboards. He would surf most days and work at night. He was the national surfing men's division champion from 1966 to 1970 and went on to compete internationally.

'In those days surfers were rebels. It was something you did on your own, not a team thing like rugby. If I hadn't surfed, I would probably have got a bike or something and have become a "rebel without a cause".

'Surfing's the same as life really — you're learning all the time. It's just brilliant. There are times when you can be in control and other times when you've got to be part of the ocean. I've had a few close calls, mainly being held underwater by powerful waves and not being able to get to the surface.

'Surfers wake up in the morning and the first thing they know is which way the wind is blowing. The waves provide a dynamic energy source, a life force. Without thinking about it, we had a really healthy lifestyle with the ocean all around us. Everyone feels a lot better after a surf.

'Fire was a big thing with surfing. Any place where we were surfing in winter there was always a fire on the shore. That brought people together around the fire and broke the ice, so to speak. Surfers would start to talk to each other and we ended up becoming one big family.

Wayne Parkes started out surfing at Takapuna Beach in 1962 when he was just twelve years old. Since that time, he has seen many changes to the beaches around the Hauraki Gulf. He is shown here at his Takapuna surfboard-shaping shop. (Alan Ashworth)

'During the 1960s, the coast wasn't a big thing. People didn't really want to go there for the Christmas holidays. They went waterskiing at Taupo or to the uncle's farm. At places like Whangamatā there were no local surfers, just farmers, orchardists and retirees. You could have the whole beach to yourself.

'The coast has changed big time since then. During the 1950s and '60s the surf was more regular at Takapuna and we surfed there a lot more. Now the dense housing funnels the wind down the road onto the beach and this changes the sand bars, currents and all kinds of things.

'Ōmaha and Mangawhai are now built up. There are huge numbers of people surfing compared to the early days. There are too many people on each wave and too many people on each break. There's also a lot more rubbish, a lot more traffic and attitudes are different.

'In my view, there needs to be a five-year moratorium on coastal development in New Zealand. Just leave the coast alone. In the words of John Lennon, just *Let It Be*.'

Surfing grew in popularity around the Hauraki Gulf during the 1960s and it is still a popular activity today. Shown here are two surfers off the Long Bay reef in 2004. (Alan Ashworth)

observed, 'We were so at home there that one morning, when the surf life-saving patrol came along the beach in their Land Rover and told us to clean up the mess on the sand dunes, one of the boys replied, "Get your f***ing Land Rover out of my kitchen!"'[14]

It wasn't until the mid-1960s that the first surfers ventured to Great Barrier Island to explore its surfing possibilities. Mike Gardiner organised the initial trip with some mates. They lived on the beach for eight months, eating fresh fish and crayfish and spending the days out on the waves.[15] Surfing continues to be a very popular activity around the Hauraki Gulf today and there is now a resident surfing community at Whangamatā.

Home-built cruising

After the Second World War, many more people started cruising in their own home-built boats, rather than taking steamer trips and the like. The idea of building one's own cruising vessel had been popularised a couple of decades previously by Auckland adventurer Johnny Wray. In 1932, during the depths of the depression, Wray was made redundant from his job as a draughtsman. Instead of looking for another job, he decided to pursue his dream of cruising offshore. But first he needed a boat. Having almost no money, he decided to build a boat in the backyard of his parents' Remuera home. He set about teaching himself the basics of boat design and construction, whilst scrounging for the various materials required.

The wood for the hull of his 10.7-metre yacht *Ngataki* came from kauri logs that he found washed up around the gulf's shores, possibly ones that had come adrift from the early log rafts. The rigging came from the *Rewa*, the large sailing ship which Charles Hansen had grounded off Moturekareka Island as a breakwater. Wray scraped tar off the road and melted it. After dipping pieces of fencing wire into the liquid tar, he used them to staple the planks of wood together. Old clothes and pyjamas were used to caulk the seams. The keel came from the stem of an old steamer that was buried on a beach. Wray also found an ancient engine in a paddock and revived it.[16]

Less than two years later, Wray was ready to launch his new vessel. He spent six months cruising around the Hauraki Gulf before heading offshore. He sailed to the Kermadec Islands, Norfolk Island, Tonga, Niue, Australia and Tahiti. The book *South Sea Vagabonds*, which he wrote about his exploits and published in 1939, inspired a whole generation of would-be home boatbuilders.

Wray later returned to New Zealand with his Tongan wife, Loti, and they bought a property on Waiheke Island,

where he eked out a living as a fisherman. He died in 1986, but the *Ngataki* survived him. After 80 years, the boat is still in sound condition, even with her fencing wire fastenings. She has been restored to her original condition by the Tino Rawa Trust and is back sailing in the Hauraki Gulf.[17]

The 1960s and '70s saw an explosion in the number of pleasure boats. By 1970, there were an estimated 35,500 such boats in Auckland — a quarter of them sailing boats and just under a fifth inboard launches. A little over a third had outboard motors.[18] With the availability of marine ply and waterproof glues, and new simpler designs, thousands of people turned to building boats in their backyards. The popularity of home building was fostered by two Auckland-based designers, who made detailed plans available, accompanied by step-by-step construction advice.

Richard Hartley saw the need for a family yacht that could be cruised during the holidays, raced during the weekends, yet towed behind the family car. It also had to be something that could be built in the home garage over the winter. In response,

Johnny Wray (right), who built the 35-foot yacht *Ngataki* in the backyard of his parents' Remuera home and wrote about his experiences, helped to popularise the home-building of cruising yachts. He is shown here returning from the barque *Rewa* on Moturekareka Island, after a foraging expedition to obtain materials for his yacht. (Tino Rawa Trust)

he designed a 16-foot centreboard yacht, the Hartley TS-16. It was light and it was fast. It was also easy to launch, rig and sail. With a tent over the boom it could sleep a family of four. So it was the first real family 'trailer sailer'.[19]

Hartley set about promoting his boat: 'For the man with limited means, who wants a boat for day-sailing and fishing with the guarantee of being home on time, this is the boat. In fact she is a small motor sailer.'[20] To help the amateur builder, Hartley also produced a series of booklets that contained photographs of how the boat should look at each stage of the construction process.

He made it look so easy. As maritime writer Noel

Story of the Gulf | Alan Wright

BOATBUILDER AND DESIGNER, AUCKLAND

Aucklander Alan Wright made a career out of providing plans and moulded hulls to home boatbuilders. Initially training as a boatbuilder himself, Wright went on to teach at the Auckland Technical Institute. He also started designing his own boats. At first he specialised in twin-keeled 'bilge keelers'. These drew less water than traditional keeled yachts and were therefore ideal for anchoring in the numerous shallow estuaries and bays along the Hauraki Gulf and Northland coast.[21]

Wright sold his first set of yacht plans in 1966. He was soon selling numerous plans for a succession of highly successful home-built boats. They included the 1970 Variant 6.8-metre yacht. He offered plans for several versions of the boat, including different keels, cabin tops and layouts — hence the name Variant. By now plywood was being replaced by fibreglass, so hulls and decks could be cheaply produced off a mould in the factory and finished off by the home builder. Wright formed a company called Marine Moulders to produce the Variant hulls.[22]

Wright went on to design a Nova 8.5-metre yacht, specifically for the conditions in the Hauraki Gulf, and it was enormously successful. An owners' association was quickly formed, with 24 members attending the first meeting. They were all either in the process of building a Nova 28 or intending to do so.[23] Later designs included the Tracker 7.7 and Lotus

9.2. Then, in 1979, the Muldoon government brought in a 20 per cent sales tax on all pleasure boats. The commercial boatbuilding industry virtually collapsed overnight.

So many of Wright's designs were built that, in 1981, the Richmond Yacht Club started to hold an Alan Wright Day, when all Alan Wright-designed boats were invited to race. More than 100 boats would enter during the event's early years.[24]

Numerous Alan Wright-designed boats can still be seen around the Hauraki Gulf, including this Variant design with bilge keels beached at Waiheke Island.

Holmes observed in 1971, 'Men who had never even built a bookcase are now at sea in their own home-built boats as a result of Richard Hartley's guidance. They've absorbed general construction principles from his boatbuilding books, have bought full-size plans and have proceeded to "cut out" their boats as women cut out frocks.'[25]

Hartley's designs were not only successful in New Zealand, but also overseas. According to one estimate, over 6000 of the Hartley 16s have been built worldwide.[26] In 1976, a set of full-sized plans for the design, complete with lists of materials and detailed construction drawings, could be bought for as little as $30.

Hartley went on to design many other boats for the home builder. By 1978, he was selling plans for surf skis, kayaks, plywood dinghies, launches, trailer sailers, plywood

yachts, steel yachts, ferro-cement motor sailers, launches and small power boats. They ranged in size from a small dinghy to a 17.4-metre motor sailer. Each design came with its own detailed instructions, which made construction look achievable by the amateur.

With the explosion of pleasure boats around the gulf, the annual summer cruise became a feature of many families' lives, but those that ventured out had to rough it. In the days before marinas, getting all the people and gear on board by dinghy could be exhausting and tricky, especially in bad weather. Conditions on board were primitive. There was generally no standing headroom. Cooking was on a kerosene stove and lighting was from a kerosene lantern. There was no refrigeration. Dishes were washed in a basin and a bucket performed the role of

Story of the Gulf | **Lindsay Peart**

RETIRED TEACHERS' TRAINING LECTURER, AUCKLAND

Lindsay Peart grew up in Raglan and, as a twelve-year-old, first encountered the Hauraki Gulf in 1936 when he attended a camp on Pōnui Island.

He was a keen fisherman even at that young age and he can clearly remember the thick mussel beds that ringed the island. But his most vivid early memory of the gulf was of travelling out to Great Barrier Island, where he was stationed during the Second World War. 'I was hugely impressed on the trip out to the island on how the gulf teemed with life. There were masses of seabirds and we passed a big shark cruising on the surface.'

During the 1970s, Lindsay partially rebuilt two rotten plywood trimarans in the garage behind his Hamilton home. He moored them off Maraetai Beach, close to where he had built a family bach, and he used them to take family and students cruising around the Hauraki Gulf and Northland coast. 'In those days, if you wanted a boat you built it. I got the plans and simply got on with it. It was a great do-it-yourself age and everyone felt they had the ability to construct a boat. But I know that boatbuilding caused several marriage break-ups, as the men would work in their spare time until late at night during the week and also during the weekends, totally involved in constructing their vessel.'

Lindsay hugely enjoyed cruising around the Hauraki Gulf. 'People did not have great incomes and we lived simply and enjoyed living simply. Our boats were basic and we often used to camp ashore, cooking our meals on an open fire and sleeping under the stars. We roamed freely over the island farms and no one objected.

'There used to be a little store on Motuihe where you could buy a paper. Islington Bay had its own store and, in earlier days, a tennis court and cabaret. Mansion House Bay [on Kawau Island] was a great gathering place for yachties when the hotel was operating there. The whole atmosphere of the gulf has changed in the sense that all these facilities have disappeared. It's not quite the exciting place it used to be.

'The yachties used to raft up together and there would be terrific celebrations. In some respects it was more uninhibited than it is now and always friendly and fun. On New Year's Eve, we would let off all the out-of-date flares. You're not allowed to do that now. There was a strong bond between yachties in

Lindsay Peart is now in his 90s and he still enjoys cruising around the Hauraki Gulf, something he has done for much of his life. He is shown here relaxing on his yacht *Dreamtime* anchored off Tryphena, Great Barrier Island.

those days. The sea was always a happy place. Somehow it brings out the very nicest qualities in humans.'

One of the highlights of Lindsay's years cruising around the gulf was visiting the Radio Hauraki 30.8-metre scow *Tiri*, when it was moored in the Colville Channel during the late 1960s. It had gone there in order to broadcast from outside the 3-nautical-mile territorial limit, thereby breaking the broadcasting monopoly imposed by Muldoon's government. The radio 'pirates' were happy to receive visits from passing yachties.

'I've been fascinated by the sea all my life. It's just fantastic to get into a boat and onto the sea. It's not only about fish, but about enjoying those wonderful bays and sights of the gulf. It's a whole lifestyle, a total experience, and every moment to me was magic.'

The 16-foot trailer-sailer was one of Aucklander Richard Hartley's most successful designs, with over 6000 built world-wide. Two boats are shown here racing in the 50th Hartley 16 New Zealand Nationals in January 2016. (New Zealand Hartley Association)

Cruising is still hugely popular around the Hauraki Gulf with many anchorages filling up with boats during the popular summer holidays. The boats these days are more substantial and they offer many of the comforts missing from the early cruisers.

Big game fishing

In 1924, Whitianga resident Ernie Chadban, along with a group of local fishermen, decided to hunt the large game fish known to frequent the area. They trolled lures behind their boat and when a marlin was successfully hooked, they tied a 4-gallon tin to the line and waited for the fish to tire before hauling it in. They had sufficient success that in 1925 the Mercury Bay Swordfish and Mako Club was formed.[28]

But it was not until American fishing enthusiast Zane Grey visited Mercury Bay that the sport of game fishing really took off. Grey was a very successful American author, writing westerns. He also had a strong passion for fishing. His first fishing expedition to New Zealand in 1926 was to the Bay of Islands but, when he returned in 1929, he decided to try fishing in Mercury Bay. His interest had been piqued by stories he had heard about leaping mako sharks in the area.

When Grey reached Whitianga, waiting for him was the *Avalon*, a launch which had been built for him in Auckland, as well as the *Alma G* and *Zane Grey* owned by Mr Arlidge.[29] The next day the men headed out to sea. On arriving at Great Mercury Island, Grey was enraptured with the beauty of the place and he decided to set up camp in Whalers Bay, a beautiful small sandy cove on the east end of the island. Grey could not believe the abundance of life around the island. It was unlike anything he had seen during his other expeditions:

a toilet. But 'the joy of cruising the gulf islands, the fishing, the swimming, the exploring and the beautiful anchorages more than made up for any lack of luxury'.[27]

In those days, fish were abundant and it was possible to build an open fire and cook them on the beach. Parents often socialised on board with other boaties in the bay, whilst the children were sent ashore to collect firewood. Some went on to sleep under the stars around the fire. There was a strong camaraderie between those who ventured out in their home-built craft, so those on launches often helped out yachties in difficulties, auxiliary engines then being notoriously unreliable.

It proved to be an exceedingly beautiful place — lonely, wild and rugged. A little bay curved back between rocky capes to a white beach and a high bank between two mountain slopes. We went ashore, and I was enraptured. Even then I pronounced it the most wonderful site I had ever chosen to pitch camp . . .

Next day, December twenty-second [1929], we ran out to look over the fishing waters. I soon discovered that they consisted of the ocean dotted with islands of all sizes and fringed by white reefs and patched by schools of trevally and kahawai, over which hovered flocks of gulls and shearwater ducks. I had never before seen so much bait.[30]

Story of the Gulf | **Fred Ladd**

PILOT, AUCKLAND

Pilot Fred Ladd became a well-known figure around the Hauraki Gulf during the late 1950s and '60s. He was a pilot for Tourist Air Travel which, in 1955, commenced flights around the gulf in a Widgeon floatplane.

His plane was frequently seen delivering passengers to the various gulf islands. Ladd showed great daring and he was not one to follow the rules.

One day during the 1960s, when about 100 cruising boats were moored in North Harbour, Pōnui Island, over the Christmas break, a copy of the day's *New Zealand Herald* came hurtling down from the skies into the cockpit of a launch. When an amazed member of the crew picked up the paper, there were words pencilled on the top which read 'First pick-up will use, then pass around the news'.[31]

Whilst flying, Ladd had started dropping off papers from the air to the isolated farms which peppered the gulf. It was an unconventional thing to do, but Ladd had a keen sense of humour and he simply wanted to brighten up people's day. He gradually became more ambitious, dropping off papers to the cruising fleet at Pōnui and later on to a cargo vessel.

Ladd finally left the company in March 1967. He described his feelings, and those of his wife Mabel, after his last day flying: 'Leaving the Hauraki Gulf was the end of a wonderful era — it was like the break-up of a great love affair, and left us both in inward turmoil.'[32]

Fred Ladd was a pilot for Tourist Air Travel which commenced flights around the Gulf in 1955. Ladd was a larger-than-life figure who showed great daring and a sense of humour. He is shown here with his wife Mabel in 1965. (Whites Aviation, Ref: WA-63392-F, Alexander Turnbull Library, Wellington, New Zealand)

On his first attempt at fishing out from Great Mercury Island, Grey was not disappointed. The mako sharks were every bit as exciting as he had heard. He was keen to get a photo of the beast in the air, but the shark was too quick for him:

> I had hardly begun to fish when, crack! The water split and a mako shot into the air with my bait in his lean, sharp jaws. It was a sight to behold. He went down. I gave Peter my rod and dived for my camera. Too late! He came out again and went down before I could get the camera on him. Then he sounded, and I went back to the rod, feeling sure that as soon as I did he would leap again. And he did, twice — high, twisting somersaults that made me yell.[33]

The next day Grey was out fishing again, this time off a submerged reef several miles offshore. While waiting for a strike, Grey was again amazed by the sheer abundance of marine life in the area. 'I counted seven schools of kahawai and trevally, and not one of them was less than an acre in size.'[34] He caught two magnificent mako sharks that day, the largest being 580 pounds and 9 feet 6 inches long.[35]

On his fourth day of fishing the bay, Grey was again astounded by the sheer quantity of school fish. After losing a massive fish he wrote:

> After that bitter disappointment I hardly had the heart to keep on; but with a dozen huge schools of kahawai and trevally all around, now and then making the water white, I did not have the heart to quit. Some of the schools are three hundred yards long and half

Author and sports fisherman Zane Grey's visit to Mercury Bay in 1929 excited much local interest in game-fishing. He is shown here on his launch. (Ref: 1/2-044545-F, Alexander Turnbull Library, Wellington, New Zealand)

Bill Clark (right), shown here with Bert Chaney, caught a 420-kilogram black marlin on the first game-fishing trip out of Whitianga after the Second World War, which helped revive the game-fishing club. (Ref: 715, Mercury Bay Museum)

as wide — acres and acres of bait with big fish under them! There was, of course, too much bait to allow for good fishing. Still, the sight was splendid and thrilling. The schools would move across the water, making a sound like a rapid brook running over rocks. They would shine in the sun like silver gilt, and again like frost, and still again like gold-green shadows. The trevalli shone black at times and the kahawai gray. And under this surface commotion was always the shadowy mass of the body of the school, extending down fifty feet or more . . . millions of fish! When a mako or swordfish charged a school from underneath there was a white splash and a roar across the water. Then they were gone! This happened many times.[36]

Grey went game fishing for the thrill of the fight, rather than just to catch a fish. He was disparaging of the New Zealand attitude to fishing at the time, which appeared to him to be just aimed at the kill, with no consideration of the way it was done. So when a game fish was hooked on a line, it was not played, but left to tire on its own and then shot with a harpoon. Very thick hāpuku lines were used, which would not break under the strain, whereas Grey used light tackle. He also noted with distaste the local fishermen's practice of dynamiting schools of fish. But this practice continued. Whitianga resident Richard Simpson recalls working on crayfishing boats during the late 1940s, a time when there were schools of trevally everywhere. In order to get bait for the crayfish pots, they would throw a plug of dynamite amongst the school and there would be fish going everywhere.[37]

After eleven weeks fishing from Great Mercury Island, Grey's party had caught a total of 110 game fish, including 43 striped marlin and 63 mako sharks. The biggest fish they caught was a 660-pound black marlin, with the next best being a 606-pound mako shark.[38] After being weighed, the fish were dumped at sea.

When the excitement of Grey's visit died, and the Great Depression bit, the Whitianga game-fishing club faded away. But then in 1947, after the war was over, a group of

Story of the Gulf | **Richard Simpson**

RETIRED BUSINESSMAN, WHITIANGA[39]

Richard Simpson has a long association with the Mercury Bay area. His grandfather grew up in Kuaotunu and his father farmed in the area. Richard was a house builder for a time and then ran the local branch of Mitre 10 in Whitianga, before retiring in 1980 to become a charter-boat operator. He built his first game-fishing boat *Chilly Bin*, and then subsequently, *Chilly Bin II*.

When Richard started chartering in 1981, there were 'still hundreds of schools of fish around. But the seiners would come in and would put their nets around these huge schools of kahawai and trevally and scoop them up. I thought, "They can't do that forever or they will ruin it." But they kept doing it and making money at it. You never see a big school now, as all the bait fish have gone.

'In those days it was pretty easy to get a customer. I would guarantee them a fish. We targeted marlin and yellow-fin tuna, with mako sharks as a by-product. There were kahawai everywhere and we would pick some up for live bait while we were heading out to sea. Big schools of tuna would go through and they would be followed by dolphins, gannets and muttonbirds. When the schools came up to the surface, there was a mad frenzy. It was very exciting. I've had people say that, even if they don't catch a fish, just seeing the feeding frenzy is worth the trip.

'My favourite place to get kahawai was the "hole in the wall" rock. I would steam round that only once and catch two or three kahawai which was enough for the day. Now you can go around half a dozen times and get nothing, so you keep going. Most don't even bother, as it's a waste of time. They just go straight out to the grounds and put lures into the water.

'One day my crew caught ten yellow-fin tuna and I said to myself, "Why am I doing this? We don't need all those fish. What a waste." Towards the end of my chartering time there was more interest in releasing the fish. The first marlin I released was when my son Martin was with me as a deckie. When we let the fish go we were sure it looked at us and smiled. It gave us a sort of a grateful look. It was most moving.

'There are definitely fewer game fish now. It's got harder and harder to catch them and you have to steam for longer and longer. There's a heck of a lot of boats fishing for them and the catch is not increasing, because they are not there any more. There must be a limit to what you can take out of

Top: Retired businessman Richard Simpson was an active member of the Mercury Bay Game Fishing Club for many years and is shown here on the Whitianga wharf with his impressive catch of striped marlin. (Courtesy of Richard Simpson)

Bottom: Richard ran a game-fishing business out of Whitianga during the 1980s with his boat *Chilly Bin II*. (Courtesy of Richard Simpson)

the sea. I reckon we're getting pretty close to it and we might be past it. Something definitely needs to be done to conserve our stocks.'

Charter fishing was popular in the Waitematā Harbour during the 1950s and '60s. Shown here is a boat that has returned to the Auckland waterfront after a successful fishing trip in 1950. (Ref: PH-NEG-H66, Auckland War Memorial Museum Tāmaki Paenga Hira)

nine locals decided to try the sport again. They set out on Bert Chaney's launch *Ronomor* towards Red Mercury Island. They had with them a good set of second-hand game-fishing gear purchased in Auckland. On this first trip, Bill Clark managed to bring in a 420-kilogram black marlin. It had been a tough and exhilarating experience. The marlin had fought for more than 12 hours, pulling the launch well out to sea.[40]

The impressive catch increased enthusiasm for the sport and the club was revived, now being called the Mercury Bay Game Fishing Club. The inaugural president was Roy Dale, the local publican. The establishment of a formal club enabled the local fishermen to claim official records for their catch. A clubhouse was established on the wharf in 1963 and five years later there were over 1000 members.[41] The popularity of the sport supported the development of a local charter game-fishing industry.

More recently, there has been a move towards tagging and releasing game fish. Instead of weighing a fish in, it is measured on the boat, tagged and then released back into the sea. A formula utilising the length and girth of the fish enables its weight to be estimated. The release system enables many fish to survive and also provides a method of tracking the movement of the fish and their migratory patterns.

Fishing expeditions

After the war fish were plentiful, due to the reduced fishing effort during the conflict, and fishing clubs started springing up. Most were for men, but a group of keen women anglers decided to set up their own club, the Auckland Lady Anglers Club, which started operation in May 1963. The club met monthly at a croquet club and they chartered the *Lady Jocelyn* skippered by Harry Carey. At that time, leaving Dad and the kids at home while Mum went fishing was a novelty, but the women enjoyed the day away from domesticity.[42]

In his 1963 book *Maui and Me: A search for a fisherman's El Dorado*, Temple Sutherland describes his experiences of going charter fishing from Auckland. He ventured out with 40 or so keen fishermen on *Shenandoah*, but noted that her two other sister charter ships, the *Florence Kennedy* and *La Reta*, took 90 each. The boats were all fully booked out for the fishing that Friday, indicating the popularity of the trips.

His first impressions were not good. As the boat backed out from the pier, Sutherland observed the 'oily scum that had closed around her, agitating the sticks of boxwood, straws, cigarette packets, ice-cream cartons, two rotten oranges and a gnawed cork cricket ball.' Then they were off.[43] The vessel steamed out of the harbour and over towards the Coromandel Peninsula, stopping at a spot where the skipper indicated that the bottom was 'clean, with beds of horse mussels'. It was here that the fishers dropped their lines and it was not long before snapper started to be hauled up. Sutherland caught his first snapper within ten seconds of his line hitting the bottom. He managed a total of five fish before lunch and then another five before the boat headed back to port. Although it was illegal to sell the fish, on Sunday afternoons when all the boats came in at the same time, there was a huge crowd gathered hoping to buy cheap fish.[44]

Bob Whitmore recalls his first visit to Great Barrier Island on a fishing trip with his workmate Basil North during the mid-1950s. They were flown over to the island by Fred Ladd, arriving at Shoal Bay, Tryphena, half an hour later. John

Temple Sutherland described his experiences of going charter fishing in Auckland in a boat similar to the *Florence Kennedy*, shown here in the foreground tied up to the Auckland waterfront in 1973. (N M Dubois, Ref: 786-A023-4, Sir George Grey Special Collections, Auckland Libraries)

Delamain then took them across the harbour by launch to stay at his Puriri Bay Guesthouse. As they crossed the bay, Bob couldn't believe the abundance of bird and fish life:

The whole harbour was alive with surface fish, with hundreds of birds and gannets diving into the water among the schools of kahawai and kingfish. The birds were screeching and squawking as they flapped across the top of the water among the hundreds of gannets diving like dive-bombers into the water from about a hundred feet up in the air, with about a hundred or so birds hitting the water at any given time. It had to be seen to be believed. Certainly Basil and I had never seen anything like it before in our lives.[45]

A flourishing charter industry has now developed out of Coromandel township. It is focused on fishing around the mussel farms at Wilsons Bay in the Firth of Thames, where the snapper feed.

Later that day the men went fishing and caught big kahawai, kingfish and snapper. The next day they went out to Sunken Rock just south of the harbour. On the way they 'passed through about an acre of trevally schooling on the surface, all with their backs out of the water'. As they drifted off the rock, there were fish on their lines before they had even reached the bottom. They managed to half fill up the dinghy with snapper before calling it a day and heading home. But what could they do with the fish? Few people lived at Tryphena then and, although they gave some away, most ended up in the garden. They didn't go fishing in the launch again. There seemed little point.[46]

Great Barrier resident Charlie Blackwell remembers, during the late 1940s and early '50s, that snapper were so abundant that they could be seen swimming in the breakers off Kaitoke beach. He would head down to the beach with his cousin, shoot the fish in the waves, and bring home a sack of them. 'You could catch snapper whenever you wanted them.'[47]

Wharves have always been a popular place for fishing, enabling people to get their lines into deep water without the need of a boat. John Giacon recalls, as a boy, fishing off the wharves at the bottom of Queen Street during the 1950s. At that time there were 'hordes of other kids' and

some competition amongst them to secure a prime fishing spot. He used small sprat lines and also heavier lines at times in the hope of catching a parore or snapper. He then started fishing at night from the wharves, when their lights would attract schools of piper. Whereas sprats were fed to the cats, his family considered piper to be a delicacy.[48]

When Giacon was a few years older, 'armed with full parental permission and a ten-shilling note', he embarked on his first charter fishing trip on *La Reta*. He had an extraordinary day. Everyone caught fish. 'We saw porpoises, gannets working, a shark's dorsal fin and all manner of new sights and sounds.' He was hooked.

Giacon eventually started going out on full weekend trips which went out to hāpuku grounds. He often saw water-spouts and whales. 'There were always plenty of fish caught. Believe it or not, one trip was so successful we had to stop fishing simply because we ran out of storage space for fish and people! . . . And all this was only one and a half hour's sailing from the foot of Queen Street!'[49]

What a different story it was when Giacon revisited his early fishing haunts during the 1980s. Off the Auckland Downtown wharves he found 'the water quality has deteriorated to a dirty, uninviting conglomeration of flotsam and jetsam about a metre wide and heaven knows how deep'.

Fishing off wharves is a favoured pastime for those without boats. Shown here is a group of fishers trying their luck off the Waitawa Wharf near Kawakawa Bay, Auckland.

Even out in the gulf things were not the same. 'Just as sadly I have to report that for five consecutive years now I have participated in my firm's annual fishing trip out on the gulf and I can testify that only one small undersized snapper has been caught in that period. People just cannot believe that once we used to fill sugar bags with prime fish.'[50]

Spearfishing

Alf Dickenson grew up in Point Chevalier, Auckland, during the 1920s and '30s and became a keen yachtie. After he married and had a family, his yachting activities came to a halt and he focused on earning a living through establishing an engine-rebuilding business. In 1954 he was loaned a copy of French underwater explorer Jacques Cousteau's book *Silent World* and was intrigued. He was keen to plunge underwater to see for himself, but at that time there was no equipment available due to strict import restrictions.

In 1954 Alf finally managed to get hold of some crude masks and fins from Australia. With his business partner, Keith Coubray, he headed to Waiheke Island where they had their first glimpse of the underwater world. He later observed: 'No photographs or descriptions can do justice to the real thing.'[51]

Enthused by his experience, Alf endeavoured to get hold of some scuba equipment, but little was to be had. He managed to obtain a home-made regulator that Les Subritzky had made. It was based on German fire-fighting equipment. Les also loaned the pair a small twin tank. Keith's uncle offered to take them out for their first scuba dive in his 3.7-metre dinghy that was located at Stanmore Bay on the Whangaparāoa Peninsula. The pair dived off the reef, just outside the bay, in around 4–5 metres of water. They were 'completely spellbound'.[52]

Alf and Keith were frustrated at not being able to access scuba equipment, so they decided to make it themselves. Between 1955 and 1959 they manufactured over 3000 sets of regulators and tanks and these enabled many New Zealanders to embark on the new sport. When import restrictions loosened in 1959, and cheaper sets of scuba gear flooded into the country, Alf established Moray Industries to manufacture wetsuits.[53]

In 1954, the Auckland Underwater Club was formed with 42 members. That year a group from the club went spearfishing at Matheson Bay (near Leigh), a place known as Te Kohuroa (many mists) by Ngāti Manuhiri. They caught 50 fish 'not counting the kingfish that was nearly speared but got away'. By then some members had rudimentary scuba gear while others snorkelled. The club hired the Tepid Baths in Auckland for an evening each week to provide diving instruction and to test gear. Membership grew rapidly and at one stage reached over 400.[54]

Marine scientist Dr Roger Grace joined the club in 1960. They went out by boat to dive at Tiritiri Matangi, the Noises Islands and Waiheke. The main focus was on spearing fish, catching crays or harvesting scallops. Roger can vividly remember his first trip to Tiritiri in 1961:

We dived around the island on the northern side of Tiri. There was 70 feet visibility and kelp forest everywhere. At that stage, I had never seen a cray before. They were all over the place, sticking out of crevices. I grabbed my first ever crayfish sitting on a rock, not even in a hole. I had never touched a cray before. I snorkelled down, grabbed it on the back and plucked it off the wall. I was scared to squeeze it too hard in case I crushed the shell. I got to the surface and it wriggled free and disappeared.[55]

Enthused, Roger started to participate in spearfishing competitions. He was good at it and represented the Auckland club in national competitions. When he started, the spearfishing rules proscribed that no fish under 8 pounds [3.6 kilograms] was eligible for the competition. 'That eliminated most of the reef fish. Then they changed the rules, put the size limit of fish way down, and put emphasis on catching as many different species as you could. In my mind that was wrong for several reasons. It encouraged spear fishermen to catch fish they would not normally bother with from a sports point of view. It also put more emphasis on reef fish that were more vulnerable to fishing pressure. So I gradually moved away from spearfishing and tried to protect reef fish, tried to get them removed from fishing competitions.'[56]

Roger has noted major changes in the marine environment since his diving days of the 1960s and early '70s. The biggest shift has been in crayfish and kingfish populations. 'At Tiritiri Matangi, the crayfish were amazing. There are bugger all around compared to what there used to be. I've also noticed that kingfish have gone way down. During my early spearfishing days we used to spear kingfish that were up around 40–50 pounds [18–22 kilograms]. You never see big ones any more and it is rare to see even small ones.'[57]

Underwater diving pioneer Alf Dickensen is shown here with a competition-winning kingfish. (New Zealand Underwater Association)

Barry Torkington has observed many changes in the recreational fishing sector over the years. He is a former commercial fisherman out of Leigh and current adviser to LegaSea, a recreational fishing lobby group. 'The take-up in interest and participation in recreational fishing has really happened during the '70s and '80s. Two things have driven this change. The first has been rising affluence. As people have obtained more disposable income, fishing has become more popular and people have been able to buy equipment that enables them to access more grounds. The second element has been the more efficient fishing equipment that has come onto the market.

'Every aspect of fishing has attracted huge amounts of research and development to increase fishing success. So you now see high-tech braided nylon lines, a plethora of fishing lures and all manner of paraphernalia designed to catch different species, at different depths and with different techniques. Whereas, before, people used a simple hook, line and sinker; you'd see nothing like that now.

'As inshore stocks have diminished, the ability to find and target fish has increased many-fold. When the fish

Fishing at Great Mercury Island

On Great Mercury Island during his childhood in the early 1930s, Pat Mizen recalls spending most of his spare time fishing to help feed his family, as well as to provide food for their chickens and dogs. The head of Huruhi Harbour was covered in seagrass and this would attract many small sharks, as well as snapper that dug for cockles.

They used a cotton-fibre piper net and could nearly always catch 'an old copper full of either piper or yellow-eyed mullet or parore' which they then boiled up and fed to the chickens and dogs. They would set a line across the harbour to catch snapper, trevally, tarakihi, red gurnard, kahawai and the occasional kingfish. The excess fish would be smoked. Crayfish were easy to get, being caught in a pot set in Coralie Bay or speared there.[58]

Larger fish would be caught by line off the rocks. At that time, Mizen reports that kingfish could be caught from most headlands or isolated rocks. Hāpuku were only plentiful at two offshore rocks, the one off the north-east tip of the island being called Never Fail, as fishermen never failed to catch hāpuku there. It was a tricky spot to fish because of the steep drop off and strong tidal rip. But at slack low tide, it was possible to do well. Mizen recalls one trip where, within half an hour, they had caught six hāpuku averaging over 22 kilos each plus several large snapper.[59]

Fishing is still enormously popular in the Hauraki Gulf. This group of young men are fishing off the Red Mercury Island group.

become more difficult to catch, there is another increment in technology development. It's often said that you can't catch the last fish, and I'm sure you can't, but maybe you can catch the third to last.'

More and more people are enjoying the marine environment of the Hauraki Gulf. Over decades it has provided accessible city beaches for swimming, sunbathing and partying; remote places for escape, contemplation and surfing; beautiful cruising grounds for boaties; and abundant fish to hunt and hook. But the sheer number of people now seeking to participate in these activities is taking its toll. Beaches, bays and fishing spots are becoming crowded and marine life scarcer.

Story of the Gulf | **Dave Moran**

DIVER AND EDITOR OF *DIVE NEW ZEALAND* MAGAZINE [60]

Dave Moran grew up in Australia and learnt to dive there. When he moved to Auckland in 1970, he joined the Reefcombers, a local spearfishing club. Dave met up with diving legend Kelly Tarlton and joined him on many of his wreck dives. He also helped to establish Kelly Tarlton's aquarium. In 1989 Dave started the *Dive Log* which became the *Dive New Zealand* magazine in 1998. He also imports underwater photographic gear.

'Back in the 1970s, when I first came here, I went out to the Aldermen Islands with a friend, Jim Thornbury. We used to dive off the Sugarloaf, just as the tide would turn, and we would see these kingfish come past in their thousands. There was a wall as far as you could see of kingfish coming towards us like a freight train. There would be six or so of us diving and we would shoot around 30 kingfish. We never felt bad about shooting the fish as there were so many of them. I've never seen kingfish like that again.

'A few years later I went out and hung off the same spot. All of a sudden 100 kingfish went past and I thought, "What?" Last weekend I dived the Sugarloaf and never saw a kingfish. I dived back at the Aldermens and saw only four kingfish, all undersized. The sea was really empty.

'It was pretty much a free-for-all during the '70s. Guys used to dive for crayfish and sell them. One of my mates built his first house on the sale of crayfish. They knew these spots out in the gulf and there were always crayfish there. We used to catch a lot around Leigh Reef. Kingfish were also prolific there and we would shoot 25 kingfish in a swim, just outside Leigh.

'One of the things that have been detrimental to the gulf is GPS. It's a fantastic tool. But it's allowed fishermen and divers to get into boats and go straight to a little pinnacle that, back in the old days, we might find once a year if we were lucky. You would have to line up a church spire, a headland and a tree to find it and it would need to be a nice clear sunny day for you to see the markers. So all those pinnacles used to be mini marine reserves, because they were so difficult to find.

'Spearfishing shops are selling truckloads of spearguns. The reality is that it takes a lot of skill to shoot fish, especially

Dave Moran started diving in the Hauraki Gulf and further afield during the 1970s. He remembers seeing enormous schools of kingfish in the early days, something that is now absent. He is shown here off Great Barrier Island, in the mid-1970s, with a speared kingfish. (Courtesy of Dave Moran)

Opposite: Once people started to put their heads under the water, they were amazed at what they saw. Shown here is a range of sights within the gulf, including (from top left clockwise) sponge garden, finger sponge, leatherjacket, crayfish, blue cod, red moki and clown nudibranch. (Tony and Jenny Enderby)

snapper. They are quite cagey and very difficult to spear. So I fear that the fish getting hammered by people buying spearguns are all the reef fish that experienced spear fishermen wouldn't touch. They are probably shooting the red moki that live to 70–80 years old and the leatherjackets.

'All of our old divers have done their fair share of killing. What scares me is that in our lifetime, which is only a blink of an eye, we've done so much damage to the marine environment — in only one lifetime. It's like, "Whooahh!".'

Story of the Gulf | **Darren Shields**

SPEAR FISHERMAN, OWNER OF WETTIE SPEARFISHING, AUCKLAND[61]

Darren Shields was first introduced to spearfishing by his father Dave, who dived as a hobby. 'My first dive was at five years of age. I was blown away by the first fish I saw, a red moki, in kelp. Then a big school of kingfish came through and I was hooked.' In 1975, at ten years of age, Darren moved with his family to Whitianga and it was there that he really got into the sport.

'We dived all around the Mercury Islands. When I was thirteen, Dad let me take his boat out. It was an old aluminium Fyran with a big outboard on the back. We used to take a pot out with us, catch a few crayfish, cook them in the pot and eat them. There were crayfish everywhere.

'Cold was the norm. We had very little gear. My first wetsuit was a vest made out of old material. My first proper speargun was built out of mahogany by one of Dad's friends. I spent hours and hours and hours learning how to use it. I started to learn about all the species, where they lived, and I became quite a good hunter.' By the time Darren was fifteen years of age he was spending most weekends in the water. 'I loved putting a fish on the table. And there was the excitement of never knowing what you were going to see.'

After leaving school Darren moved back to Auckland and he was lucky to get a job at the then biggest outdoor and dive shop, run by Alan Mitchell. Darren helped expand the range of goods to include free-diving sports fishing gear. At that time in New Zealand, there was only small interest in the sport, where scuba equipment was banned and divers had to hold their breath while pursuing fish. Such an approach had benefits: 'It's a lot quieter, you can cover a lot more ground and be stealthier. The fish can't see or hear you coming. You can also swim against the current.'

The sport is now well organised through Spearfishing New Zealand. There are national championships held in New Zealand, with about 60 divers competing each year, and international championships overseas. 'Depending on the area, a set list of fish is given and the guy who can get the most off the list of fish wins. Sometimes it can be three of each, depending on the species.' Darren has won the national championships six times and has competed in around 20 overseas competitions.

To be successful, competitors need to be extremely fit, but they also need to be excellent hunters. 'It's hard to explain what being a good hunter means. You can go out with a guy and know if he's a good hunter straightaway. It's about understanding the signs, the type of bottom and the

currents. Fish will sit in a current to feed and then will want to rest and get out of the current. I know where a certain fish should be living. The other guy will just keep swimming by. As you become a good hunter you get a good understanding of the environment, you become really observant. I see stuff other people don't see.'

It's not an easy sport and there are plenty of dangers. Shallow water blackout is one of them, where a diver loses consciousness due to a lack of oxygen reaching the brain. Darren lost his best friend and diving companion, Paul Parkinson, to blackout off Little Barrier Island. Sharks can also be a problem. 'They can be very aggressive and they have no fear of you whatsoever. If you can't get out, you have to turn the tables and become the aggressor. If it's a very big shark, it's a very hard thing to do.'

For the past 20 years or so Darren has run his own business selling wetsuits and underwater gear. He has observed many changes both to the sport itself and to the marine environment. 'The number of people involved in the competitive side of the sport has stayed much the same, but the recreational side has gone berserk. There is access to better gear and it's cheaper. You can come to the store, get fully kitted out, watch videos and be out there spearing a feed of fish in no time.' The result has been much greater pressure on the resource.

'I call it the moving baseline. When I first started diving, in any given spot you would see 50 big kingfish, weighing 20 to 25 kilos each. You would shoot one and hardly mention it. If you got a kingfish over the 30 kilo mark you would tell others. Now if you get a kingfish over 20 kilos you talk about it. You still see them, but they are smaller. You never see bulk large fish any more. There were places where you would see hundreds of John dory and tarakihi in a day and now you see none.

'People tell me it's commercial pressure, but I see very few commercial boats when I'm out diving. I do see lots of lines from recreational fishers. In the past, if you found a good reef on sand, it would be clean. Now you find it covered in fishing line. Reefs that I used to dive on, and which had lots of fish, are now barren. But I'm not just blaming line fishermen, as spearfishing has done its fair share of damage to fish stocks as well.

'Places like the Hen and Chicken Islands, Great Barrier, Little Barrier and the Mokohinaus are nothing like they used to be. The numbers of big fish out there have decreased dramatically. There has been an especially big decline in kingfish at the Mokohinaus. I've seen the biggest decline over the last fifteen years.

'The first time I went out to the Mokohinaus with my father, when I was seventeen years old, it felt like we were going to the ends of the earth. The skipper of our 6.5-metre boat was very nervous about going all the way out there. We had heard stories about others venturing there, but the islands were so far offshore that they seemed like a myth. In the early days, you would find gutters there full of snapper, undisturbed hordes and hordes of them. Now you go there, the snapper are scarce, and you are with a fleet of 30 or 40 boats. It has to have some impact.'

Darren has been endeavouring to change the culture of spearfishing competitions. 'Nowadays my focus has changed away from spearing fish, as I have seen such a decline in fish numbers.' He provides an option where competitors can attempt to spear only four or five of the targeted fish. For the other 30-odd fish, 'if you see them, you take a photograph and leave them there. It's harder to take a photo of a fish than it is to spear it. This change has been much to the horror of diehard killers who have really fought it. I have had so much opposition to this approach, it's not funny. But it's the way of the future.'

Opposite: Darren Shields is one of New Zealand's top spear fishermen. He has become increasingly concerned about the reduction in abundance of reef fish, particularly over the past fifteen years. He is shown here with a large kingfish he has speared. (Courtesy of Darren Shields)

Right: Underwater divers in the Hauraki Gulf have been amazed at the numerous large schools of fish which they have seen, but numbers have been dwindling. Shown here is a school of kingfish. (Darren Shields)

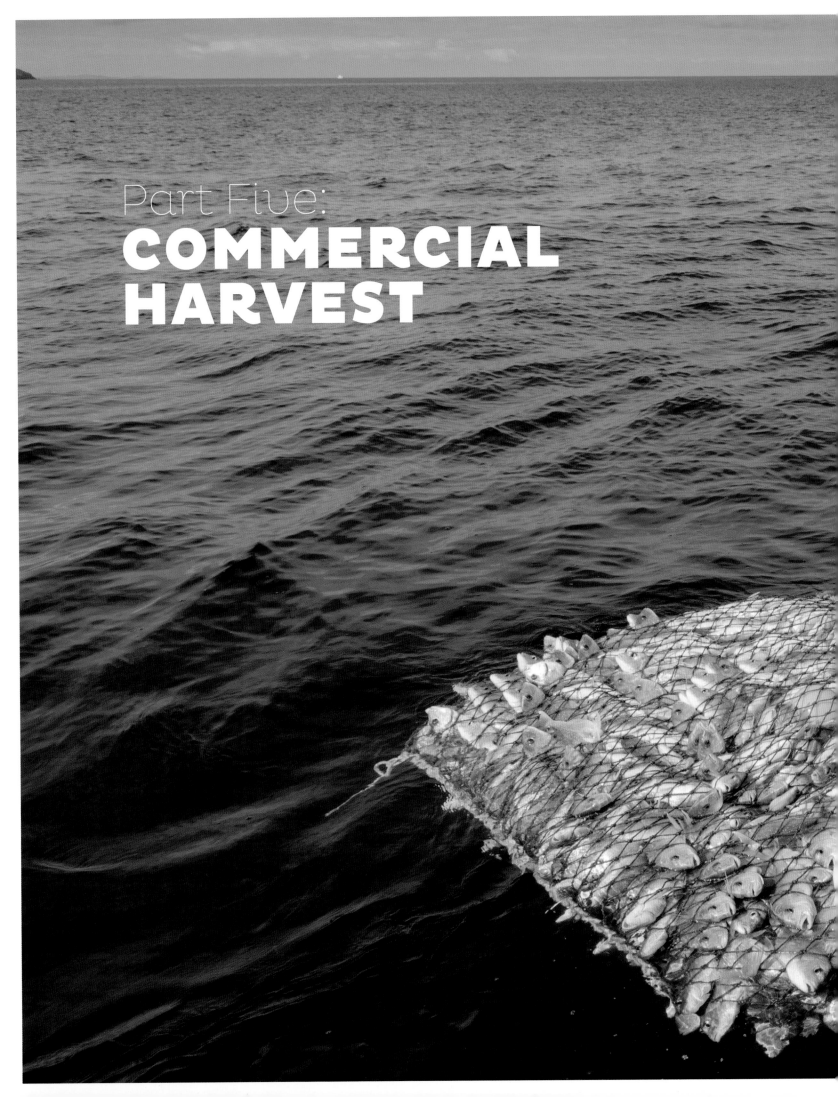

Part Five:
COMMERCIAL HARVEST

Chapter 11
Early commercial fishing

With the establishment of the European settlement in Auckland in 1840, there was a growing demand for food to feed the new settlers and one of the sources of readily obtainable protein was fish. Until the 1860s, Māori were the main commercial fishers within the gulf, using handlines and nets deployed from small sailboats. For example, Ngāti Manuhiri fisherman Tenetahi Te Riringa sailed his scow *Ida* out to the Mokohinau Islands each summer to fish for hāpuku. He and his crew 'would sail back to the Auckland markets with the huge fish cut up and hanging in the rigging to dry . . . if one passed to leeward of *Ida* at this time it was unlikely for many a day to forget the powerful fragrance of sun-drying hāpuku'.[1]

Pages 212–213: Danish seine harvest of snapper at Cape Colville, Hauraki Gulf.

Left: Fishing boat in Auckland Harbour, c. 1890. (Ref: 1991/10/4, Auckland Art Gallery Toi o Tāmaki)

One of the early Europeans to take advantage of the growing demand for fish was Albert Sanford. Born and bred in Devon, England, Sanford headed to sea on leaving school. In 1863 he crewed on the passenger ship *Victory* which docked in Auckland during the height of summer. Being impressed by the warm climate, and the considerable opportunities for advancement provided by the fast-growing new town, he deserted ship.[2]

Sanford initially obtained work in the shipbuilding yards which had sprung up at Devonport, but within a year he had accumulated sufficient funds to buy his own boat, a former pilot vessel named *Foam*. The vessel was kauri planked with half the hull decked, was rigged as a cutter with a single mast and displaced 5½ tons.[3]

Sanford started regularly heading out on *Foam* into the Hauraki Gulf to fish for snapper. He brought the catch

back to his Devonport house where he slowly cooked the fish in a backyard smokehouse. He sold the product in Auckland as 'Sanford Smoked Snapper'. But Sanford was just as interested in yacht racing as in fishing. In 1868 he entered *Foam* into the Auckland Regatta, where she won her class.[4]

In 1870 Sanford moved to Pakatoa Island with his wife Ann and young son, to be closer to the snapper fishing grounds in the Firth of Thames. He built a fish-curing plant on the island, preserved the fish by smoking it and then transported it back to the Auckland market on *Foam*. However, the venture was not successful. Although the snapper were plentiful, he found them in poor condition.[5]

The family briefly returned to Devonport, before moving to Rākino Island in 1873. Sanford found the snapper around the island to be abundant and of good quality. He smoked his catch and then sailed it back to Auckland. He would tie up *Foam* to the steps of the old Queen Street wharf and sell his fish direct from the boat. Anything that remained would be loaded up into a wheelbarrow and hawked on the busy city streets.[6]

As demand for 'Rākino Island Smoked Snapper' grew, Sanford realised that he needed premises in Auckland from which to sell his fish. In 1888 he acquired a building in Federal Street and set it up as a fish shop. When that became too small, in 1894 he opened a fish market on the corner of Customs Street West and Albert Street.[7]

Early fishing fleet

By the late 1880s, around 40 commercial fishermen were engaged in fishing in the Hauraki Gulf. They used handlines with baited hooks to catch snapper, and small set nets and beach seine nets to catch flounder and mullet. They were methods similar to those which had been used by Māori for centuries and, being on a small scale, they had little impact on the fish stocks or the environment. Fishing was largely confined to the sheltered areas close to the main settlements of Auckland and Thames.[8]

By the turn of the century, fish were still enormously abundant close to Auckland, with a wide range of species harvested. This image of a fisher in 1901 shows how many fish could be caught from a small craft, with rudimentary fishing gear, in only a few hours. (*Auckland Weekly News*, Ref: AWNS-19010503-8-3, Sir George Grey Special Collections, Auckland Libraries)

Top: In 1873 Albert Sanford moved with his wife Ann to Rākino Island, where he found snapper to be abundant and of good quality. He smoked the catch and sold it from his boat tied up to the steps of the Queen Street wharf in Auckland. The old homestead is shown here in 1926. (Tudor Collins, Ref: 7-A14510, Sir George Grey Special Collections, Auckland Libraries)

Right: As demand for 'Rākino Island Smoked Snapper' grew, Sanford acquired premises first in Federal Street and then on the corner of Customs Street West and Albert Street. By 1916 he had moved to Queen Street (shown here). (Hubert Vaile, Ref: 2-V841, Sir George Grey Special Collections, Auckland Libraries)

Their fishing boats consisted mainly of small sailing craft, although some fishermen used rowing boats. Many vessels, which became known as mullet boats, were around 7.3 metres in length, half-decked and designed to be two-handed. They were configured specifically to harvest the abundant mullet which were present in the shallow waters of the estuaries situated along the southern coast of Tāmaki Strait. Mullet boats had a centreboard which could be lifted to reduce draft in the shallow estuaries and a barn-door rudder which could be removed to enable nets to be hauled over the stern. They were rigged as gaff cutters with plenty of canvas to enable fast windward sailing back to port. A long bowsprit allowed the hoisting of two foresails and a boom that extended over the stern of the boat enabled a large mainsail to be carried.[9]

Abundance of fish in the Hauraki Gulf, 1898

In 1898, an anonymous writer described the abundance of fish in Auckland waters in *The New Zealand Herald* as follows: 'Schnapper and mullet, equally useful in their fresh, smoked or canned state, are to be had in illimitable quantities. Flounders, unexcelled for size and flavour, swarm in our estuaries and shallow bays. Hapuka, king fish, yellow-tail, John Dories, are plentiful in the deeper waters. Barracouta visit the coasts every year in vast shoals; boar fish, butter fish, mackerel, kahawai, gurnet [gurnard], cod abound nearly everywhere; while in the Firth of Thames anchovies, sardines, and herrings are almost as plentiful as in British waters.'[10]

Although fishing was good, there were problems with marketing the catch. When the weather was settled and the boats could easily get out to their fishing grounds, there would be an oversupply of fish in the Auckland markets and much would be wasted. However, when the weather was stormy, there was a shortage of fish in town. With the fish stocks being plentiful, there was also no incentive to conserve the resource.

Government officials became concerned at the wastage, particularly of small fish which were caught in nets and left to perish on the beach. They were also worried at the small size of fish, particularly flounder, which were being sold. It was said that 'almost anybody with a boat and a few lines can succeed in catching plenty of fish'.[11] Fishing provided self-employment and a healthy outdoor livelihood for those who could afford a boat.

Steam trawling

Steam trawling was first introduced to the Hauraki Gulf in April 1899. Sanford had acquired the 31-metre steamer *Minnie Casey*, which had previously been used as a ferry, and he fitted her out for beam trawling. This necessitated attaching two large beams which extended out over the water horizontally, one on each side of the ship. A large net was attached to the beams with wires.[12] The steamer was able to drag the enormous net along the seabed in the shallow reaches of the gulf, catching huge quantities of fish.

This removal of such large amounts of snapper from the inner gulf had immediate impacts on the ability of others to catch fish from their small sailing vessels. It was only a matter of months before strong opposition to trawling was expressed. By August, fishermen from Thames had presented a petition to Parliament. It sought the exclusion of trawlers from the Firth of Thames and urged Parliament to 'take some immediate action on this important question before it is too late and the schnapper in the gulf utterly annihilated'.[13]

Although trawling was new to the Hauraki Gulf, it had been a fishing method deployed in the United Kingdom and Europe for centuries. And in those places there had been similar opposition to the bulk-fishing method. This was based on concerns that the trawl nets caught large quantities of undersized fish which were then dumped, that they destroyed spawn and juvenile fish, and that they ploughed up the seabed, destroying food sources for the larger fish.[14]

The government was not keen to take action. At that time, it was endeavouring to promote the establishment of trawling as an effective fishing method in New Zealand. To this end, it had provided grants to help fishermen purchase vessels suitable for use as trawlers.[15] In 1900, it also chartered the steam trawler *Doto* to undertake experimental trawling around the New Zealand coast. *Doto* arrived in the Hauraki Gulf in early 1901 where 'good hauls of marketable fish were made on almost every occasion'. This was especially the case in the Firth of Thames 'where fish appear to be particularly plentiful and of good quality'.[16]

The trawler undertook 'extensive tests' in all parts of the gulf and found the whole bottom suitable for trawling operations. Only in the Motuihe Channel and in Whangaparapara Harbour on Great Barrier Island did the trawler experience poor catches.[17] The largest haul, caught off Kereta Bay just south of Manaia Harbour in the Firth of Thames, consisted of 593 snapper, 187 gurnard, 12 flounders, 9 lemon soles, 2 John dory, 1 shark and 6 dogfish.[18]

As well as fish, the trawler brought up material from the seabed, indicating the nature of the habitats there. When the net was hauled up after trawling along the Tāmaki Strait, they found it full of 'grass and weeds', indicating the extensive seagrass beds in the area. They found 'a lot of marine growth' to the south-west of Cape Colville on a largely sandy and shelly substrate, indicating prolific marine life.[19] Lots of large mussels were encountered along the coast between the Coromandel and Manaia harbours and off Tapu further south.[20]

The 1902 trawling ban left fishing in the inner Hauraki Gulf largely to mullet boats like these shown at the foot of Queen Street in 1902. (James Richardson, Ref 4-2519 V841, Sir George Grey Special Collections, Auckland Libraries)

The government's experimental trawls in the gulf had demonstrated that the area supported large stocks of fish, especially snapper. But tensions around the impacts of trawling were reaching boiling point. In July 1901, 40 fishermen met in the Auckland Harbour Board offices to discuss their concerns. Fish were becoming much harder to catch in the inner gulf and many believed that this was due to the trawler's activities. In particular it was thought that the trawler was catching large quantities of small fish which were then dumped. One fisherman indicated that he had worked aboard the trawler for seven weeks and on every trip they had shovelled small fish overboard.[21]

At the conclusion of the meeting, many of those attending signed a second petition which was then presented to Parliament. The petition asserted that the trawler destroyed fish eggs, larvae and juveniles, and that at least half of the fish caught in the trawl nets were undersized and therefore dumped. The impacts on the fishery extended far wider than the gulf itself, the petition asserted, as 'the gulf is the principal spawning and breeding district for most of the fish of the eastern coast of the northern part of New Zealand'.[22] There were other petitions on the trawling issue, including one from the residents of Waiheke Island who also struggled to catch fish. In addition, amateur fishermen were complaining about poor catches.

Trawling inquiry

The level of controversy about trawling in the gulf rose to such an extent that the government was forced to take action. The Inspector of Fisheries, Mr Ayson, was appointed as a commissioner to look into the fishing conflict. In December 1901, he convened a hearing in the Auckland Harbour Board offices and heard the fishermen's complaints.

Various amateur fishermen gave testimony on the scarcity of fish in the gulf. Dr James Moir, who had fished the gulf for the past thirteen years, claimed that fishing in the inner reaches had been an almost total failure over the past couple of years. The most he and three companions had been able to catch, during a day's fishing near Waiheke Island, was seven fish. He believed that continuing to allow trawling inside the Hauraki Gulf, which was a fish nursery area, would mean the total destruction of snapper fishing within a very short period.

Representatives of the Newmarket Fishing Club had experienced a decided fall-off in catches over the past

During 1901, when this catch was made in the Firth of Thames, controversy over the impacts of trawling in the gulf escalated and the government initiated an inquiry. (*Auckland Weekly News*, Ref: AWNS-19010726-8-2, Sir George Grey Special Collections, Auckland Libraries)

three years. Just the week before the hearing, 200 fishermen went out in the club's steamer for a day's fishing and had only been able to catch 30 or 40 fish. The secretary of the Auckland Fishing Club advised that 'A few years ago the members went out and caught from 800 to 1000 fish during an afternoon, with 30 lines, and always had plenty left over to send to charitable institutions. Of late years it was not worth while going out fishing.'[23]

The evidence that the abundance of fish in the inner gulf had decreased was compelling, but what was causing the scarcity? Was it the impacts of the trawler or were there other reasons?

No scientific study had been undertaken on snapper and little was known by Europeans about the fish's life cycle or behaviour. There is no evidence that Māori, who had fished snapper in the gulf for centuries and who had an intimate knowledge of the fish, were consulted. Joseph Gallagher reported that fish 'were almost extinct at the Thames'. One of the reasons for this, he thought, was that trawling was rapidly destroying the extensive mussel beds in the Hauraki Gulf which provided the principal food for snapper.[24]

Albert Sanford advanced a different theory as to why fish had become scarce around Waiheke Island. He argued that seawater was chilled on cold nights when it went up the many small tidal creeks on the island, and when it discharged on an outgoing tide it caused the fish to flee to warmer waters. He also asserted that the lack of an increase in flounder stocks was 'no doubt due to the flow of refuse and noxious drainage from factory and foundry industries in the gulf'.[25] At that time, much rubbish and contaminated water were simply being dumped into the harbour and were degrading the inshore areas.

Dr Moir had made a study of snapper behaviour and he concluded that they congregated, for the purpose of spawning, inside a line extending from the Tāwharanui Peninsula to Coromandel Harbour, but principally around Tiritiri Matangi. On becoming young fish, the snapper made their way into the shallow upper reaches of the gulf. When they had grown sufficiently, they then moved back out into deeper water to join the school fish. He also believed that the principal nursery areas for snapper along the north-east coast of the North Island were the Hauraki Gulf and the Bay of Islands.[26]

Albert Sanford junior, who captained the *Minnie Casey*, had other theories about the movement of snapper. He claimed that the gulf was not a nursery ground for the fish at all. After spawning about 7 or 8 miles east of Tiritiri, he argued that the schools of fish moved across to Cape Colville and then disappeared into deep water 'and were apparently lost'. He asserted that the schooling fish were of an entirely different kind to the snapper caught in the inner gulf. Those caught around the rocks were large and almost black (now referred to as 'kelpies'). This theory was supported by evidence given by Sanford senior.[27]

Scientists would later confirm that Moir was largely right and the Sanfords were wrong in several respects. One thing that the Sanfords did get right, though, was that the fish spawned in deep water rather than in the shallow reaches of the gulf. They had observed that, during spawning, the fish

After the trawling ban was put in place within the inner gulf in 1902, catches started to increase and there were reports of phenomenal hauls. This image shows a catch of 1500 dozen fish in Sanford's Thames fish yard in October 1905. (*Auckland Weekly News*, Ref: AWNS-19051026-12-4, Sir George Grey Special Collections, Auckland Libraries)

fed on the surface so would not be caught with a bottom trawl. They also rightly concluded that the spawn initially floated rather than sank to the bottom. Other fisherman had erroneously claimed that trawling destroyed the spawn which they had thought lay on the seabed. Scientists have also very recently confirmed that, although all the snapper in the gulf are the same species, there are two distinct types with different physical characteristics and life histories. One type is largely resident in the gulf all year round and the other, which is found within the spawning aggregations, lives in deeper water and travels much longer distances.

Ayson ultimately found that a strong case had been established against trawling. On 15 May 1902 regulations were gazetted to prohibit trawling in the inner gulf. Trawlers were to keep outside a line running from Colville Bay west across the gulf to Tiritiri Matangi Island and then north to Flat Rock. This was a serious blow to the Sanford fishing enterprise which had pioneered trawling in the gulf. The *Minnie Casey* was kept in service for a while, but she was

soon caught trawling in the prohibited area and Sanford was prosecuted and fined.[28] By 1904, *Minnie Casey* was retired from fishing, the same year that the Sanford fishing enterprise was established as a limited liability company. The old trawler was eventually broken up at Rākino Island and her timbers were used to build a jetty at Home Bay.[29]

Sanford vigorously opposed the trawling ban and within two months of the regulations being gazetted he had lodged a petition with Parliament seeking their removal. He wrote letters to the paper, arguing that instead of harming the gulf fishery, trawling would in fact increase the fish stocks. This was because, in his view, trawling would keep the number of snapper within the bounds of the available food supply. He asserted that, if numbers were allowed to increase too much, the fish became starved and weak, and were easier prey for their natural enemies, including shark. In his view 'This "want of catching" has had the effect of upsetting the "balance of power" in the sea, and natural enemies have increased and eaten the schnapper that we would have consumed, if trawling had been started years ago.'[30]

It was not long after the trawling ban was established that catches in the Hauraki Gulf started to improve. By September 1903 there were reports of 'phenomenal catches' of snapper and flounder in the gulf by fishermen based at Thames.[31] Some fishermen were now using small motor launches, powered by benzene, in place of sailing vessels,

Fishing launches powered by benzene started to dominate the Thames fishing fleet during the early 1900s. A group is shown here tied up to the Thames wharf in March 1908. (*Auckland Weekly News*, Ref: AWNS-19080312-15-4, Sir George Grey Special Collections, Auckland Libraries)

and this enabled them to travel further afield in pursuit of fish, whilst still returning to port on the same day. In October 1905, one small launch was reported to have caught 700 dozen snapper (8400 fish) in a few hours.[32] The large catches were in excess of local demand for fish and in 1906 seasonal limits on catches by individual fishermen were imposed.

Experimental trawls

The government was still keen on promoting the fishing industry and, in 1907, it chartered the steam trawler *Nora Niven* to prospect the coast. When it reached the Hauraki Gulf in October, it was required to keep outside the trawl-ban line. Trawling in the deeper water did not prove as easy as the earlier experimental trawls in shallower places. The seabed, not having been previously disturbed, was heavily encrusted with marine life.

Trawling to the west of Cape Colville and to the north of Waiheke Island (near the centre of the gulf) resulted

in the net becoming torn as it was dragged over rough ground that included horse mussel and sponge beds. When trawling halfway between Channel and Little Barrier islands, the net was badly torn due to it 'having met with foul bottom' including coral and shell. A tow off the west coast of Little Barrier also revealed a 'bottom of a dirty nature'. When the Inspector of Fisheries at the time, H Stephenson, wrote a report on the trip, he concluded: 'All the ground covered appeared to be unsuited for trawling, the bottom consisting of horse-mussel, coral and dirty mud.'[33]

If trawling was to be undertaken in the gulf, the results of this exploratory trip indicated that it needed to be in the shallow, muddier reaches of the inner Hauraki Gulf, the very place where it had been banned. The same year as the experimental trawling expedition, the government moved the trawling-line limit closer inshore in the vicinity of Kawau Island and Colville Bay, but this did not attract any trawling interest by fishermen.

Pressure to resume trawling

As the population of the greater Auckland area continued to burgeon, and to demand more fish, the industry struggled to

The *Baroona* was one of the early steam trawlers deployed in the Hauraki Gulf by Sanford Limited. Her nets caught a giant squid off Cape Colville in 1916. (Ref: 122371/2, Alexander Turnbull Library, Wellington, New Zealand)

keep up. By 1911 the settlement's population had increased by more than 50 per cent since the trawling ban came into force, and there were an additional 30,000 people to feed. This was coupled with a growing scarcity of fish, particularly in the Tāmaki Strait, as the number of fishermen grew and fishing pressure increased.

A large fleet of steam trawlers had been established in Napier, where there was no trawling ban, and this increased pressure for the boats to be allowed back into the gulf. Albert Sanford kept arguing the case for their reintroduction. He asserted that trawling would clear the bottom of the gulf of its 'old growth' and that the 'new, fresh growth which would follow would tend to attract fish in greater numbers'.[34] This thinking, which closely mirrored that of farmers who burnt indigenous tussock to promote new and more palatable growth, demonstrated a fundamental misconception of how the marine environment functioned. Removing old growth would not promote fresh growth as Sanford postulated, but would destroy complex habitats which had developed over centuries and could not recover while trawling continued.

Introduction of longlining

While trawling was effectively kept out of the Hauraki Gulf, another new method of fishing helped to increase catches once again. In 1912, some Hauraki Gulf fishermen started using longlines to catch snapper instead of single baited hooks. Longlining involved setting a lengthy main line, which had numerous branch lines or snoods connected to it, each containing a hook with bait attached. Each line could hold thousands of hooks. The method was much more efficient than single hooks and quickly became popular. Substantial motor launches had by now also largely taken over from sailing craft. These larger, faster vessels could venture further afield in pursuit of fish. They could also make quicker and more regular trips out to fishing grounds.[35] This technology change significantly increased the ability of fishermen to catch large quantities of fish and concerns about depletion faded as catches increased.

Resumption of trawling

It was only a matter of time before trawling would be resumed in the gulf. In 1914, the same year that the First World War started, the trawling ban was largely removed. Sanford Limited purchased three steam trawlers the

Story of the Gulf | **Ronnie Martin**

RETIRED LONGLINE FISHERMAN, TORBAY[36]

Ronnie Martin grew up on his family's 16-hectare farm on Dominion Road, Mount Roskill. As a youngster he had fished off the Herne Bay Wharf for flounder and sprats. He also constructed a tin canoe by folding a sheet of iron in two. He put a vegetable box in one end and used the tar from the road to seal it all up. Ronnie would row out to Watchmans Island (Te Kākāwhakaara, near Herne Bay) and fish. He loved fishing, but never dreamed that one day he would become a commercial fisherman.

After leaving school, Ronnie worked as a builder's labourer before training as a plumber. But then he decided to give up plumbing to catch fish. 'Before work I would watch guys unload fish and got to know them. I thought, "If that old guy can catch that amount of fish, I can double it."'

In 1956 Ronnie financed himself into a boat by selling a section in Kelston that his wife's parents had bought for the couple to build a house on. His new vessel *Mona* was a 7.9-metre mullet boat built by Archie Logan. It had a 10-horsepower motor which could reach a top speed of 6 knots.

Ronnie built a temporary cabin of canvas over the open hull and set up boxes of cotton lines with 150–200 hooks each. He would set the lines out over the back of the boat and then pick them up again. Initially he had to pick up the lines with a dinghy, because he couldn't control the boat well enough to retrieve them. He was targeting the lucrative snapper.

Ronnie based himself at the Viaduct Basin and at first he fished for Gus Viskovich and his son Alan. Gus ran the fish shop at Avondale. The Viskovichs were of great help to Ronnie, teaching him the ropes. 'I got the biggest shock when I tried to catch fish, because I couldn't catch enough to pay for the fuel and the boat. I would try to get 20 baskets, which was a ton of fish, each trip. When I first went out I would put the fishing lines anywhere. I didn't have a clue where to put them. On my first trip I got one and a half baskets of fish, and I had been out there for four days! If it hadn't been for the fact that all our money was tied up in the boat, I would have chucked it in.

'Then after a north-east gale blew I thought about what the District Inspector of Fisheries, Frank French, had told me. "Ron," he said, "where the oxygen is not disturbed in the water the fish will lie." "If ever he is to be proven right, this is the time," I thought. So I went up to Kawau Island and set the lines inside Goat and Rabbit islands, in shallow water and during daytime hours, rather than during the night when I

usually fished. The water was flat calm and the fish started coming. It was unbelievable the sheer size of them. In three days I got my first ton of fish. I never looked back after that.

'I had the same thing happen at Pōnui Island. After a screaming north-east gale had been blowing for four to five days, I fished in the Waiheke Channel off the point near McCallums Island [Pākihi Island]. I was so close to the rocks that I could have jumped onto them at any stage, and I was worried that the boat would hit them. I only had three lines out, which were cord at that time, but I got fifteen to sixteen baskets of fish.

'You get to know, over the years, the pattern of fish, how they move and what they do. The fish are always on the move. When things change, the fish shift and go somewhere else. In those days there were no restrictions. You could just go out there and keep catching fish by the ton. For all the bad weeks there was the incentive that you could make it up on the good weeks and get square. The money was good.'

Ronnie eventually purchased a second vessel, another mullet boat of similar length, but larger overall. He now based the boat at moorings off Torbay where he had built a house for his family. The company JBL Limited offered to finance Ronnie into a larger boat from which to use set nets. But he decided not to go ahead as he would have needed to work off the west coast to make it pay. 'People had installed big set nets with large reels coming off the back. It's absolute slaughter on the fish in some ways, mainly because of the size and make-up of the catch. I think longline is the cleanest method. Thousands of tonnes of small fish were slaughtered over the years, never used, but just wasted. With trawling, the wastage in the early days was horrendous, whereas longlining wasted very little.'

For some years, Ronnie sold his fish direct to the public from Ngāpipi Road in Ōrākei. He would row his fish around

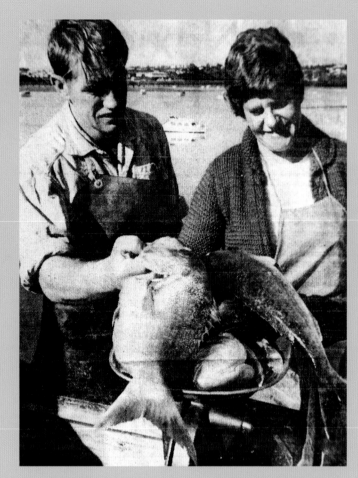

Top: Ronnie Martin used to sell his catch direct to the public at Ngāpipi Road in Ōrākei, Auckland. He is shown there in 1965 selling snapper for 1 shilling 6 pence a pound. (Courtesy of Ronnie Martin)

Right: Ronnie started longlining in the Hauraki Gulf in 1956, initially being based at the Viaduct Basin. Although he did well from fishing for a number of years, he later went into oyster farming and is now retired.

there by dinghy. He eventually poured a concrete pad and installed a steel bench for his fish 'shop'. Quite a few customers from Remuera came to buy their fish from him. Ronnie also sold fish to Fletcher Fishing and JBL.

In 1966 Ronnie sold his second boat to raise finance to enter the oyster-farming industry. Over his fishing career Ronnie estimates that he spent many hundreds of nights away from home. 'I personally believe that the fish are no worse than when I stopped fishing, due to the numbers [of fishermen] that have sold out and a lot of quota that has passed onto trawlers that can't fish in the gulf.'

However, Ronnie has noticed some disturbing changes. 'Gurnard do seem to have gone from the gulf. I used to catch a lot of gurnard. On one trip I caught nine baskets of gurnard; there was one on every second hook. But seining definitely got these fish. The rope on the seine nets used to drive the gurnard into the net, whereas the snapper swim higher up off the bottom, so they would survive a lot of shallow-water seining. The seiners caught hundreds of tons of gurnard. They used to chuck it out, as it only earned tuppence a pound in those days.'

There has also been the loss of horse-mussel beds. 'Sometimes I'd go out with the boat and set the same gear, at the same time in January, off Kawau Island and Flat Rock. I used to get huge catches there on the horse mussels. But the beds were badly damaged by seining.'

Hauraki Gulf commercial shark fishery

By the early 1900s, sharks were becoming noticeably more prolific in the Hauraki Gulf. In August 1907, the Minister of Marine, the Hon. John Millar, expressed his opinion that 'the Hauraki Gulf was swarming with sharks, which took a greater toll in fish than any trawler or fisherman could possibly do'.[37] The abundance of sharks was to change with fishing activity, but also as a result of a shark-processing industry which was established at Sandspit, near the sharks' once prolific breeding ground.

The rendering of sharks into fertiliser was encouraged by government officials as a way to reduce their competition with humans for fish. The secretary for marine wrote in his 1907 report: 'This branch of industry is an important one, and is deserving of every encouragement. It also leads to the destruction of large numbers of sharks, dog-fish, etc. which now infest some of the fishing-grounds, and which, up to recently, have been allowed to increase unmolested to the great destruction of market fish.'[38]

This view was supported by the Chief Inspector of Fisheries, L F Ayson, who, in a report presented to Parliament in 1913, stated that as a result of catching large quantities of fish 'The balance of nature has been disturbed'. The result had been large numbers of sharks and dogfish which were credited with 'taking great quantities of our market fishes'. He claimed that if these predators had been killed off in the same proportion as the fish themselves 'it is questionable whether the quantity of market fish taken by man's agency would have affected the supply to any great extent'. He suggested that fishermen should be encouraged to kill off sharks.[39] So began a largely successful effort to cull sharks from the gulf.

By this time, an industry based on turning the sharks into fertiliser had been established at Sandspit, historically a very important location for the Māori shark fishery. The sharks were caught from flat-bottomed dories that could hold up to 30 each. By around 1914, a shark-processing plant had been established by Messrs Vanderspech and Carter in an old stone store located across the river from the spit. But the venture struggled financially. The sharks could only successfully be caught in any numbers during the summer months when they came into shallow water to pup. So the Green brothers, who were local farmers, took over the industry alongside their normal farming activities.

In early February 1918, Arthur Green was interviewed by a reporter from the *Northern Advocate* and he stated that

they had started fishing in November and had already caught 500 mainly school sharks. Some days they would catch 40, 50 or even 100.[40]

All of each shark's body was ultimately used. The fins were cut off, strung up on a number-8-wire fence to dry and then sold to the Chinese market for shark-fin soup. The shark livers were placed in a bag and boiled in a big copper. The oil would seep out of the bag and float on the surface where it could be skimmed off. Shark oil was in high demand for use as a livestock supplement, being fed to calves along with skim milk. The oil was also used to reduce ticks on pigs. In addition, shark oil proved to be an excellent wood preservative and it was often painted onto farm buildings after being coloured red with ochre or lead. One shark would produce around a third of a gallon of oil. After the fins and livers had been removed, the carcasses were covered with earth and rotted down to make fertiliser, which was said to be excellent for potatoes and pumpkins.[41]

Coromandel fisherman Merv Strongman targeted sharks during the mid-1950s. He would catch mainly school sharks on longlines set with 60 hooks, but also bronze whalers. 'We used to catch sharks off Port Jackson and Watchman Island,

in October, when they were on their way into the gulf.' The sharks were exported to Australia, initially for fish and chips, 'but there was a mercury scare and the bottom fell out of that market. Then the price for the shark livers doubled to two bob a pound, so we were catching 500 a day just to take the livers out and then push them back over the side. What a waste! Synthetic cod liver oil came on the market the following year and the market for shark liver died. Fortunately the Aussies decided they liked shark again and the price went up.'

During his commercial fishing career, Merv caught a total of around 50,000 school sharks, half of those in the shallow waters of the Firth of Thames. 'All of those sharks were female and all had eggs, but I never saw one in pup. This led me to conclude that the females do not pup in the Firth of Thames.' After an encounter with a big white pointer shark, which crushed his large tin fishing-line buoy with its teeth, Merv thought, 'I will be caught one day by these jokers, so I chucked the shark fishing in.'[42]

Recent scientific modelling undertaken by NIWA scientist Dr Max Pinkerton indicates that shark populations in the Hauraki Gulf are now only around one-sixth of their original size.[43]

Opposite top: Around 1914, a shark-processing factory was established across the river from Sandspit, in an old stone store which is shown here c. 1900. (Warkworth District Museum)

Opposite bottom: David Green's father worked in the Sandspit shark factory. David is shown here displaying photographs of the shark industry in the area. (John Montgomery)

Bottom right: Thames-based commercial fisherman Merv Strongman targeted school sharks in the Hauraki Gulf during the mid-1950s. He estimated he caught about 50,000 in total.

Bottom left: During the 1950s, Merv caught this haul of school sharks using a longline. (Courtesy of the Strongman family)

An *Auckland Star* journalist described what happened when the net on a trawler fishing outside Tiritiri Matangi Island was retrieved: '... when the allotted time has elapsed the winch is started, and the great bag drawn slowly to the surface ... As the net nears the surface, startled fish imprisoned within the meshes are seen slashing through the water, and then the base of the "cod end" of the net floats to the top, sustained by the mass of fish, close packed, and struggling vainly to escape. A heavy tackle hoists the great bag of fish over the side of the vessel, and a jerk on a rope opens the "cod end" of the net to bring the mass of fish of all kinds and sizes tumbling and flapping onto the decks. Now and then some big kingfish or a fair-sized shark makes things lively for a few minutes. The great heap of fish, fresh from the sea depths, glow with all the exquisite colours and the iridescent shades which death so soon removes; but on a modern trawler bent on business there is no time lost in admiring the beauty of the catch. Sharks and dogfish, octopi and other undesirables are dispatched, and, with the under-size fish and ocean rubbish gathered by the net, tossed overboard. The remainder of the catch is quickly shovelled into the 80lb baskets and lowered below. A considerable variety of fish come up in the trawl, with schnapper, of course, predominating, but there is a good sprinkling of John dory, gurnet [gurnard], and tarakihi, besides numbers of yellow-tail, trevally, leather jackets, barracoutta, and more occasional frost fish, red cod, crayfish, and odd-looking porcupine fish.'[44]

following year. The first to be deployed within the gulf, in 1915, was the *Countess*, a former ferry boat that had been sourced from the Napier trawling fleet. She came with her former captain and mate who knew how to employ the new form of trawling, otter trawling, which had been developed in Napier. This involved the use of a large board or door attached to each warp where it connected to the net. These were towed along the seabed with the net, and the water pressure on the boards (which were angled outwards) kept the mouth of the net open. This was more efficient and avoided the need to use large beams installed on the sides of the boat to extend the mouth of the net. But it also resulted in more impact on the seabed, because it necessitated large, heavy boards being dragged through it. This method of trawling is still widely used in the gulf today, although the hydrodynamics of the nets and trawl doors have been improved.

The *Baroona* was another of Sanford's new steam trawlers. This 32.6-metre wooden vessel had been previously used as a trader and ferry, before being converted to a fishing boat. In 1916, her first outing in the gulf was to the waters around Great Barrier Island, where she caught 280 baskets of fish. Off Cape Colville that year, the ship's trawl net brought in a giant squid with tentacles over 3 metres long.[45]

Initially, it was not possible to effectively trawl much of the gulf, because the sea floor was covered in horse mussels, corals and other growths, and these would snag the nets. To address this problem, an old ship's chain was towed between two steam trawlers, out from Rangitoto Island, past the Noises Islands and into the outer gulf. This served to smash up the horse mussels and other obstructions.[46] Much of the sea floor eventually became a muddy 'paddock' which was regularly 'hoed' by trawl equipment. The term 'paddock' was how many fishermen came to refer to the gulf fishing ground.

Although it made the gulf easier to trawl, destroying the mussel and coral beds removed a major source of food and habitat for juvenile snapper, as well as for a diverse range of other species. This reduced the snapper's chances of surviving into adulthood. The result was a marine system that had less ability to produce the very thing that people wanted more of — harvestable fish.

One of the drivers behind the resumption of trawling in the Hauraki Gulf was the need to provide cheap food for New Zealanders. This was a time of austerity for the country, with the war now well under way. When the *Countess* started work in the gulf, she was able to bring in tons of fish each day, sourced from 'prolific trawling grounds which exist about two hours' steam [20 miles] from Auckland', in the vicinity of Tiritiri Matangi.[47] There was a dramatic increase in the quantity of fish landed.

The small line and net fishermen could not compete. Many had to haul up their boats and look for work elsewhere. But Sanford was upbeat, saying that the unemployed fishermen could be redeployed in the seafood-

FINE SPECIMENS OF HAPUKA

ALL HANDS HAULING IN

A BAG OF FISH COMES TO THE SURFACE

CAPTAIN J. HOLT, SKIPPER

THE CATCH, MOSTLY SCHNAPPER, RELEASED ON DECK

STRONG HANDS EFFECT NET REPAIRS

SHIP'S COOK WITH SUNDAY DINNER

THE THOMAS CURRELL RETURNING TO PORT

These images show action on the steam trawler *Humphrey* in 1946, during a trip in the Hauraki Gulf when fish stocks were abundant after the Second World War. (*Weekly News*, 5 June 1946)

Story of the Gulf | **Ed Pridham**

TRAWLER SKIPPER, AUCKLAND[48]

Ed Pridham grew up on north Auckland's Ōkura Estuary and he spent his childhood years fishing on the river with his grandfather. In 1977, after leaving school at sixteen years of age, he started working at Pearl Fisheries, a fish-processing company located on Auckland's waterfront. Part of his job involved unloading the numerous small fishing boats that came into the port to discharge their catch. Ed got to know their crews and was eventually invited to join a fishing trip to see for himself what commercial fishing was like. He was immediately hooked.

Ed put his energies into finding a job on a fishing boat and was eventually successful in securing a deckhand position on a small boat skippered by Ivan Guard, who had earlier been a part-time skipper on Radio Hauraki's pirate ship *Tiri*. Ivan was based on Great Barrier Island and Ed went to live with him there.

Wanting to advance, Ed set about getting his maritime qualifications and, by the time he was nineteen, he had gained a first level skipper's ticket. He joined Simunovich Fisheries and started skippering a boat, being the youngest to do so out of Auckland at the time. Ed has now skippered fishing boats in the Hauraki Gulf for over 35 years, first Danish seiners and then, for the past 25 years, trawlers. He currently skippers the *San Kawhia*, a 34-year-old, 18-metre trawler owned by Sanford.

When Ed got into fishing 'it was possibly the worst time for joining the industry. If I had been ten years older, I would have been ahead of the quota-management system and would have had my own boat. But as it happened, when quota for snapper was allocated in 1986, I was still driving other people's boats. Only boat owners got the quota, not the people actually catching the fish, so I missed out.

'I'm a contract harvester. Companies own the boats and I skipper them, selecting and managing my own crew. It's share fishing where I get a percentage of the value of the catch. But that share has been shrinking all the time. Whereas in the past, the boat owner would get a third, the fishermen would get a third and a third would pay for the expenses of running the boat, now I would be lucky to get 10 to 12 per cent of the value of the fish.'

Commercial fishing culture has changed over the years. 'In the early days it was a way of life and we had a lot of fun. If the weather was bad, we would tie five or six boats up together and congregate on one for a barbecue, a few beers and some laughs. There was also a pool club at Leigh and a social club on Great Barrier where we would hang out. Now you have to be more of a bookkeeper than a fisherman. Catching fish seems secondary to all the rules and regulations that you have to deal with.'

The approach to trawling has also changed during the time Ed has been at sea. 'When we first went out we tried to catch as much as we could. At times, we might catch 10 ton of snapper in a day. Now I try to catch under half a ton a shot and we do lots of shots over a day, constantly hauling the gear in and out. If you tow the net for too long you can't control the quality of the fish and it takes too long to deal with them once they've come aboard.' Most of Ed's catch is sold fresh, either at the Auckland fish market for local consumption or airfreighted to countries such as Australia.

'Fishing is in my blood. I can't help it, I like being at sea. I like working in different kinds of weather and it's rewarding to know that I can catch fish whatever the conditions. I know all the bottom structures in the Hauraki Gulf, where all the wrecks and fouls are, and where you can and can't safely put trawl gear. I've pulled up all kinds of things over the years, including a piece of a fighter jet, old boats and bits of rigging. Now, there are so many snapper around that you don't have to risk going into unknown places, scraping around rocks and reefs to get them.'

The biggest changes Ed has observed, during his time on the Hauraki Gulf, have been around the periphery. 'There used to be a reef at the entrance of the Ōkura River with weed all over it and lots of shellfish and crayfish. Now if you go there it's just sedimented over. The run-off from the city is affecting all the stuff close in.'

Ed has also seen a large increase in recreational fishers in the outer gulf. 'In the past, when we were heading out to sea, you would only have to worry about navigating through recreational boats out to Rangitoto. You would only get one

or two as far out as Tiritiri. Now they are all the way out to Great Barrier and beyond. The number of boats has grown exponentially. They are also bigger and faster and the gulf is now way more accessible.'

Reflecting on his career, Ed observes, 'I was lucky to have been able to learn from old fishermen like Ivan Guard. I now have years and years of knowledge and I'm always learning more. Every time a catch comes up I think, "How could I do it differently next time?" But I'm a dying breed. I was the youngest when I started and now I'm pretty much the oldest. Several like me will be out of the industry within the next ten years and there's no next generation coming through. There's no support for young people to get into fishing these days, no apprenticeship or incentive schemes. It will not be long before companies bring in foreigners to do these jobs.'

Top & bottom: Ed Pridham has skippered fishing vessels in the Hauraki Gulf for over 35 years and loves his life at sea. He is shown here on the Sanford trawler *San Kawhia*, berthed at the Halsey Street wharf.

packing industry that the trawlers were creating. He also confidently asserted that 'No one with any knowledge of the subject believes that it is possible to take all the fish out of the gulf', implying that the resource was limitless.[49]

Sanford Limited decided to launch a public relations exercise to generate support for the trawling enterprise. In September 1916, the company took out on its trawler an *Auckland Star* journalist and photographer, the Minister of Marine, the Hon. R McNab, the Chief Inspector of Fisheries, Mr L Y Ayson, and a member of Parliament, Mr C H Poole. The trawler headed towards Tiritiri Matangi and, once on the outer side of the island, the large net was 'shot'. Three other trawlers were seen also working the same area. The net was towed along the seabed for about two hours before being winched back on board with its catch.[50]

The lower part of the net was 'heavily protected with coconut-fibre chafing gear, to protect the ropes from the tearing action of rocks and the sharp edges of the big horse mussels which cover the bottom over the great area of the best fishing grounds.' The massive wooden otter-boards, together with the pull of the towing vessel on the cables, keeps the mouth of the net wide open 'as it creeps slowly along the bottom gathering in any fish that come in its way and do not make a smart enough escape from the danger zone'.[51]

The *Auckland Star* reporter on board the trawler was clearly impressed with what he saw and he went on to suggest that there was sea room and fish to support a hundred trawlers. In addition to an 'immense supply of the very best fish' the gulf had sheltered waters in which small trawlers could work without loss of time due to bad weather.

Trawling dwindled during the Second World War, as vessels were requisitioned for the war effort, and fish stocks recovered to some extent. Even so, an account of a 1946 fishing trip in the gulf by two 200-ton steam trawlers, the *Humphrey* and the *Thomas Currell*, referred to the difficulty the vessels had catching fish in the gulf and the need to go further afield to East Cape. There was reference to 'the hard sand of the shallower gulf with its crust of horse-mussel', which made it more difficult to trawl than the mud of deeper waters. But the heavy gear was having an impact on this. Boardman described the first shot where the net was paid out north-east of Tiritiri Matangi:

The net was paid out on 90-fathom wire cables by winches, which also dropped the three-quarter ton 'doors' or hardwood and kauri boards to furrow the ocean bed

and, planing outward kitewise, to keep the 80ft wide net open . . . Dragging along the bottom, the net cuts a swathe 80ft wide. Kept upright by numerous spherical aluminium buoys, the net is 15ft high. The two leading cables are hooked together aft the starboard side of the ship, and the net trails behind, ensnaring fish in its wings and transferring them to its bag.[52]

The trawler made a second shot off Port Charles, near the tip of the Coromandel Peninsula, and unintentionally hit a reef. Here the trawl bag, once brought back on board, delivered a varied catch indicating the wealth of species still abundant in the gulf:

The bag spilled pink schnapper, vicious blue biting barracouta, believed to be responsible for the mutilation of the many one-legged seagulls seen about Auckland, red-winged gurnard, green leatherjackets, an occasional fat-bellied hapuka, dogfish, sharks with their valuable liver oil to boost a young New Zealand industry, a few soles, electric and stingrays, a bulldog-faced Maori Chief, trevally, kahawai, kingfish and john dory in a protesting lively heap on the deck. A trawlerman pointed out the brown central marks on the sides of the john dory as the imprints of the thumbs of the Fisherman of Galilee. All were stowed below with a covering of ice. Pink fragments remaining in the net were evidence of an uncharted coral reef.[53]

Introduction of Danish seining

In 1923 a new fishing method was introduced to the gulf — Danish seining. It's advantage, when compared to trawling, was that instead of the vessel having to tow a net through the water, which required considerable power and a lot of costly fuel, the vessel remained stationary with the net being laid around a school of fish and then pulled towards the boat.[54]

Jack and Andy Andreason, who immigrated to the gulf from the Danish Faroe Islands after the First World War, introduced the new method to the region. It was a first for New Zealand. Fishermen quickly appreciated the benefits of Danish seining, a notable bonus being that seine boats could fish in the inner gulf areas which were then out of bounds to trawlers. Within a year, Auckland boasted 22 Danish seining vessels.[55]

It was not long before concerns about this new bulk-fishing method in the inner gulf were also expressed. By 1924, only a year after the method had first been introduced, it was excluded from the Firth of Thames. But by 1925 petitions had been lodged with Parliament from a diverse range of parties, including the Auckland Yacht and Motor Boat Association, the Thames Fishermen's Union, the St Heliers Road Board, the Ostend and Onetangi Ratepayers and the National Council of Women, seeking to extend the exclusion zone. It was claimed that seine nets were being worked round Waiheke within half a mile of the shore, with six nets working close to the Onetangi wharf on a single day.[56]

Others noted that the introduction of the Danish seine net 'has not been accompanied by the Danish system of fish conservation', where large areas of the coast were protected from the nets. It was alleged that 'fishermen have seen dozens of schnapper not an inch long on the deck of a seine net boat'.[57] Gradually the restrictions on the use of seine nets were tightened.

During the 1930s, the Auckland seine fleet was dominated by Dalmatians, immigrants from current-day Croatia, who came to New Zealand during the 1880s and worked the Northland kauri gum fields. As the community became established, its members diversified into orcharding, winegrowing and fishing. Investment in fishing boats was a way of ensuring supply for the many Dalmatian-owned fish shops which had become established in Auckland.[58] One of the early Dalmatian fishermen was Filip Vela, who went on to successfully establish a substantial fishing company which still operates today: Vela Fishing Limited.

Merv Strongman started fishing in the Hauraki Gulf during 1953, mainly dragnetting and then Danish seining. He recalls that 'up until about 1953 the fishing boats in Auckland were practically all seine boats and they wouldn't work the horse mussels unless they were desperate', as the sharp edges of the mussels would cut the sisal ropes on their nets. At that time he remembers there being a large solid bed of horse mussels on a deep-water shelf that covered an area from Happy Jack Island north of Coromandel Harbour, across the top of the Firth of Thames to the west of Hooks Bay on Waiheke Island and then up to just west of Port Jackson, in a triangle shape.[59]

'Tommy Williams had the scow *Lena* and he would fish over the mussel beds and catch 1 ton of fish a day with a handline. Then the trawling got going and heaps of seiners

Danish seining was a very effective means of catching schooling snapper. It required less fuel than trawling, smaller boats could be used and the harvested fish remained in better condition. A catch of snapper is shown here being hauled aboard a Danish seining vessel in October 1939. (*Auckland Weekly News*, Ref: AWNS-193910018-40-3, Sir George Grey Special Collections, Auckland Libraries)

converted to trawling. With the trawler boards and sweep wires, they knocked the top off every horse mussel and in about five years they had killed the lot. The fish caught there were large snapper with big heads and thick lips. There was always bleeding on their lips as they were chomping on the horse mussels. That breed of snapper has now gone and a different type of fish has colonised the area.'[60]

Trawling and seining were effective ways of catching large quantities of fish, but they were to take their toll on the productivity of the Hauraki Gulf. Former commercial fisherman Barry Torkington observes that 'when I was ten years old, during the 1950s, you could fish anywhere out from Leigh. It was all full of horse mussels and you knew where to go to get big fish. To me, it's inconceivable that we now have no horse mussels. The place has been dragged clear. The seaweeds and near-shore country have changed so much.

'I can't accept that the productivity of the place remains. We used to have thousands of hectares of horse mussels with crabs, worms and other creatures living in there, all the sardines coming in and all the bigger fish, the snapper, kahawai, kingies and squid coming to feed. That whole thing was bubbling away and then you tear all of that out. I just can't accept that the gulf has not been modified to the point where its productivity has collapsed.'[61]

DANISH SEINER, HOT WATER BEACH[62]

Phil Clow's father Alf was a farmer and earthmoving contractor. When he semiretired from his rural occupations, and Phil was nine years old, the family moved to Whitianga and Alf started commercial fishing. As a boy, Phil would join his father on fishing trips whenever he could. His father also introduced him to diving.

Phil was keen to go fishing when he left school, but his father said he needed to get a trade first, so he trained as a diesel mechanic. Then in 1975, Sealords was financing fishermen into the Whitianga scallop industry and Phil was able to take up the opportunity to go fishing. He had sufficient saved for a deposit on a boat. Half the proceeds of fishing were to go to Sealords, to service the debt on the boat, and half went directly to Phil.

'There weren't many suitable boats around at that time and the boat I bought turned out to be unsuitable. But I converted it to a scallop dredger and started to learn how to undertake fishing as a business, how to catch fish and how to make money doing it. But I overloaded the boat and it capsized. Luckily there were no fatalities, the boat was salvaged and we got it working again thanks to insurance.

'We caught scallops at Ōpito, Ōtama and Great Mercury Island. There were no limits and you could catch as much as you wanted. There were good years and bad years. There were also good times of the year when the scallops were nice and fat. We were paid on meat weight, so it was better to land fat scallops. Still it was very patchy. I eventually paid the boat off, sold it and then bought one that really set me up.

'Being young, I thought the grass was greener over the hill, so I started crayfishing. I was crayfishing from Mercury Bay to the back of Great Barrier. I moved the pots around, to rotate the grounds and effectively "farm" them.' Phil had a gentleman's agreement with the other crayfisherman on where they would each fish, but still there was 'a lot of friction. You might spend a lot of time breaking in new ground. You would find a nice reef in deep water and put five pots on it. One pot would have three to four crayfish in it. You would do well and then think "I'll leave it and fish it again next year." But if you are landing lots of crayfish your competitors notice. You would go back the next year and there would be 30 pots on the good spots. That led me to get out of crayfishing, as I couldn't handle not being able to fish it the way I knew it had to be fished. There was always tension and you always had to guard your patch.'

As a schoolboy, Phil Clow would join his father on fishing trips and he decided then that he wanted to become a commercial fisherman. He is shown here, in front of his father, with a large sea bass he caught during the 1960s. (Courtesy of Phil Clow)

Phil was crayfishing for nineteen years up until the early 1990s. He had built up a good catch history by the time the quota-management system came in, so he received a substantial amount of crayfish quota. He sold it and bought snapper quota. To catch the new species, Phil went down to the South Island and bought a trawler, which he converted to Danish seining. He very nearly went broke.

'Danish seining always appealed to me because of the hunting side of it. Rather than just towing a net up and down, like trawling, you are selective about where you shoot. But being a good crayfisherman doesn't mean you are good at other methods. I fished out of Whitianga, which was initially difficult, as no other seiners worked from there. It was hard to get someone to come out onto my boat to show me the ropes, but that's how I learnt. I had people like Neil Chaney, who had done some seining, and Dave Clark to help me, especially with net mending. But they were retired trawlermen, not

Left & right: Phil Clow was attracted by the hunting element of Danish seining, which required an understanding of where precisely to put the net. He is shown here (left) hauling up the ropes of the net and (right) bringing a large haul of snapper aboard.

Danish seine fishermen. At that time, trawlermen put down a net and towed it for three or four hours, so they were often not precisely sure where they had caught the fish. My biggest problem was learning where the fish were and when. Eventually it came to the crunch financially, but then I got a tremendous shot of fish and I clawed my way back up. I started to get some patterns together.

'I am now one of the lucky ones. I am out there fishing from Whitianga where there are not a lot of boats. I am able to farm my ground and it suits me fine. I love it. The ocean is a bit like a farmer's paddock. There are areas on the farm that always grow good grass and the stock go there, and there are other areas where the grass doesn't grow well and the stock avoid them. There are places in the sea which are so productive that I can go to them once a month, take a parcel of fish out and leave it while the fish fills in again.

'Without a doubt fishing is a calling. To be a good fisherman you need to be a hunter first and foremost. Being a spearfisherman helps you hugely as you learn fish behaviour underwater and how currents move to attract and hold fish. It's not a four-year apprenticeship. It takes ten to twelve years, particularly on a smaller boat where you are the skipper, a surgeon and a father figure for the younger ones. There's a

huge failure rate. About one in ten crewmen end up being a good fisherman and skipper.

'You need to be able to catch a lot of fish, so the crew get good pay. But you also need to be good at psychology and be able to handle people when you and they are tired. You need to be able to fix hydraulics, engines, electrics and fishing gear. Nowadays, you also have to attend workshops and learn about seabirds and by-catch. So catching fish is only a small part of it.

'There are also the issues with home life. You can't go to sea worrying about problems at home. If you have a wife and children, you need to manage your time, so that when you come home they're still there. There are a lot of broken marriages in fishing. I've also seen a lot of wild kids come out of fishing families, as the parents haven't put in the time required.'

Phil's son Adam is now a commercial fisherman. 'There is a difference between generations in terms of attitudes towards fishing. The younger ones are far more proactive in things like preserving the ocean. They'll go to the ends of the earth to be able to carry on doing what they're doing. It's their business and it's in their best interests to look after it. In my father's day you weren't aware of these issues. If you were aware you were looked upon as a nutter, an eccentric.'

Chapter 12
From plunder to precision

The Hauraki Gulf commercial fishing industry picked up again after the end of the Second World War. Fishing during the war had diminished, due to the requisitioning of steam trawlers for the war effort, the danger of enemy mines in the gulf and the lack of manpower. At first landings were high, due to the recovery of fish stocks during the wartime years and the redeployment of a large steam trawler and the Danish seining fleet. But then catches plummeted.

Between 1948 and 1952 reported landings into Auckland halved despite 'increased fishing effort directed towards snapper and more distant grounds being worked'. Landings didn't increase again significantly until the late 1960s, by which time the snapper stock had been strengthened by several productive years when a large number of juveniles had been produced.[1]

Despite the greater difficulty in catching fish, commercial fishing became the mainstay for many local communities

Hāpuku used to be readily caught around the Hauraki Gulf, as illustrated by this image of Mr Taylor and his haul of hāpuku after only four hours fishing near Whitianga. (Ref: 0107, Mercury Bay Museum)

around the gulf, particularly those where farming was marginal. One of those places was the remote Great Barrier Island.

Great Barrier Island

Bill Owen had taken up farming at Ōkupu Bay on Great Barrier Island in 1955. He had borrowed the money to buy the land and he planned to pay it back through the proceeds of crayfishing along the adjacent coast. This was despite warnings from locals that crayfish were becoming scarce. Undeterred, Bill built a 5-metre dory to use as his fishing vessel.[2]

Farming soon proved to be untenable. With the land stripped of its limited fertility by successive burn-offs, scrub was reinvading with a vengeance. Bill's sister Lyn and brother-in-law Ivan had joined the Owens on the island and were also crayfishing from Ōkupu. It was clear that the depleted crayfish stocks in the vicinity could not sustain two families. They considered line fishing but concluded it was not a practical option, as there was no ice on the island or any way of storing the fish before they could get it back to markets on the mainland. So Bill and Ivan decided to try crayfishing on the exposed east coast.[3]

The pair set up camp at Harataonga Beach, building a hut out of corrugated iron, timber and scrim. They used the dory to catch bait and then to lay the pots. But first, they only managed to catch a few of the smaller spiny crayfish, and they were after the much larger packhorse ones. After six weeks of concerted effort, Bill and Ivan were just about to give up.

Then suddenly, one day, they found their pots were full of packhorses. They only later discovered that the packhorse crayfish has a regular migratory pattern, arriving in the shallower waters off the coast of Great Barrier Island in August and leaving by early February the following year. Delighted with their catch, the pair transferred the crays to a holding tank they had set up in the bay and re-baited the pots.[4]

Within a few days, their holding tank was full. So they brought their working pots into the shallows and filled them up with more of their catch. They now had plenty of crayfish, but how were they going to get them to market? They had arranged for their catch to be picked up from the Tryphena Wharf by the cargo boat, the *Lady Jocelyn*, which visited the island weekly. They stuffed the crayfish into eighteen large sacks and then manhandled the sacks through the surf, up over the sandhills, and to the end of Harataonga Road. A truck was then able to pick them up and take them across the island to the wharf.

Bill and Ivan crayfished hard over the summer months, battling the sometimes strong winds and enormous surf. One day the dory was tipped up, end-over-end in the surf, throwing out its occupants and gear. On another day, sick of lugging the heavy sacks up the sandhills, the pair drove their car onto the beach. It sank into the soft sand up to its axles and became submerged by the incoming tide. This was the last straw as far as they were concerned. It was February and the packhorse crayfish were on the way out of the bay in any event. They collected their pots and drove the dory out of the bay, never, apart from one brief visit, to return.[5]

As the crayfishing industry took off at Great Barrier Island, Fred Ladd, who had started flying his amphibian aircraft there in 1955 under the banner of his company New Zealand Tourist Air Travel, saw a business opportunity. He started flying crayfish back to Auckland as return cargo and sold them to friends and colleagues. 'The crays in those days were whoppers, frequently of 10 pounds weight each, and Aucklanders just couldn't get crays like them from anywhere else.'[6]

Fred rapidly expanded his business. He started to build up a clientele of fishermen from Tryphena, Whangaparapara and Port Fitzroy. 'They'd telephone to call me in on my way back from a charter or a scheduled flight, to pick up one or two bags here, a couple of bags there. I paid them cash, flew the crays back to Mechanics Bay and handed them over to Mabel to look after . . . While I was bringing them home, Mabel would be on the phone to various restaurants and clients around Auckland . . . We used to dump them live and kicking into a back room we had, next to the office, which would be swarming with the great brutes, crawling and flapping and scratching while they awaited buyers.'[7]

Fred's black-market trade injected much-needed cash into the Barrier's community. But other fish wholesalers in Auckland were not impressed with the sudden competition. They wrote to the Marine Department in Wellington to complain. This resulted in a visit from a fisheries officer. When challenged about illegally selling the crayfish for consumption, Fred replied, 'For consumption? . . . Surely they're not doing that! Why, Mabel and I, we're selling them off as pets.' After laughing vigorously, the fisheries officer left and no further action was apparently taken.[8]

Ross Kellian also became involved in the fishing industry

The value of crayfish

It was not until crayfish became scare around the shores of the gulf that they obtained any real commercial value. Lindsay Peart, now in his nineties, recalls that, 'In the early days, crayfish were trapped in large quantities and brought to the Auckland market in sugar bags. They were not highly prized then, being so easily caught.'[9]

Barry Torkington's grandfather started crayfishing near Leigh before the Second World War and his father and brother joined the industry after the cessation of conflict. 'Initially there were sacks coming off Waiheke and North Head. Fishermen didn't need to travel to get crayfish. It was not until those stocks were depleted that people on the Coromandel and up north at Kawau and Leigh had the opportunity to supply the Auckland market. There were initial problems to overcome, like getting the crayfish to market and getting paid for them. But the problem wasn't lack of crayfish. They were everywhere. My old man started out in a dinghy and for the first two years he had only a rowboat to lift his pots.[10]

'After the war, crayfish were worth very little, something like thruppence a pound. So fishermen needed to have good catch rates to survive. As soon as an area wasn't producing, they moved on to another. They had to pull all their pots up by hand and were so inefficient that they weren't able to knock the stock down far. They took plenty but they left plenty.

'I remember when the first echo sounder came onto the market. That enabled an increase in catch, because they found all this crayfish country they didn't know was there.

So catches increased. Then improved gear, such as winches, became available. Eventually they needed a bigger boat to travel further afield, as the local stocks were fished down. But crayfish were still not worth much.

'Prices only moved up when the live export trade to Japan and China started, and that's when the pressure really came on, around 1990.' Prices have continued to increase. One New Zealand company was getting $13 a kilo in 1990 for exporting live crayfish to Japan and is now obtaining over $80 a kilo for the product in China.[11]

'Now catch rates are so poor, at only around a third of a kilo per pot, that crayfishermen are reliant on the high prices to survive. Once you denude an area of crayfish, they don't seem to return.'[12]

Scientific models suggest that, prior to human arrival, crayfish were the 'third most ecologically important benthic invertebrate group in the Hauraki Gulf'. However, the impact of fishing has been so great that they are now 'considered to be ecologically extinct'. Stocks are possibly only a quarter of their original level or less.[13]

Crayfish were once very prolific around the Hauraki Gulf and they supported a substantial commercial industry. Alf Clow is shown here with his crayfish catch out from Whitianga during the 1960s. (Courtesy of Phil Clow)

The Hauraki Gulf still supports a substantial crayfishing industry, but stocks have plummeted from the abundance of earlier times. Ian Clow is shown here crayfishing around the Mercury Islands.

Harataonga Beach was the focus of Bill Owen's early crayfishing enterprise with his brother-in-law, Ivan. They managed to catch plenty of packhorse crayfish, but the tough conditions on the exposed coast meant that they aborted the operation after just one season.

at Great Barrier Island. He had been keen to become a farmer, so when some cheap land came up for sale at Pūriri Bay, Tryphena, he leapt at the chance. But the land also proved unproductive and so, in the early 1960s, he upgraded an old guesthouse on the farm and ran it as the Tryphena Lodge. Ross procured a boat to take guests out fishing and eventually he decided to turn it into a commercial longline fishing boat.

Around 1963, island resident Bob Whitmore joined Ross for a day's fishing in the Colville Channel. 'We drifted. I had six hooks on the line and he had five hooks. They were cord lines. We were pulling in eleven fish at a time. That's how many fish there were in those days . . . We filled four washing machine bowls in the boat.'[14]

The fishing around the Barrier was excellent, but there

were problems getting fish to the mainland market in good condition. Crayfish survived for some time out of water and could be delivered to Auckland alive and fresh. But fin fish were a different story. The island had no mains power and there were no icemakers. The cost of running diesel freezers was high. So Ross Kellian got together with Bill Owen and they started smoking the fish to preserve it, setting up base at Ōkupu. In their small petrol-driven fishing boats, they regularly travelled to Auckland to deliver the smoked fish to market and to collect blocks of ice to take back to the island. The ice was stored in a large chest on the wharf before being loaded onto the boats at the start of each fishing trip.

After being caught, the fish were brought back to the Ōkupu wharf whole, to be gilled and gutted. Next, they were taken to the smokehouse for processing. There were plenty of fish, but they were only getting tuppence a pound for crayfish tails and less for the smoked snapper. It was hard to make a living and the smokehouse eventually failed.[15]

Bob Whitmore also became a commercial fisherman at Great Barrier Island, working out of Tryphena. After visiting regularly for holidays, Bob had first moved to the

Top: Ōkupu was the location of the first fish-processing plant on Great Barrier Island. It was set up by Ross Kellian and Bill Owen during the 1960s. The abandoned building can still be seen in the bay.

Right: Bob Whitmore fished out of Great Barrier Island during the 1970s and early 1980s. He is shown here with a large snapper he caught between Little and Great Barrier islands c. 1983. (Courtesy of Bob Whitmore)

island in 1963. In 1968 he built a bach on land he bought in Pūriri Bay. He took leave from his job on the Auckland wharves and decided to try his hand at fishing, as it was one of the few ways to make a living whilst being based on the island. Bob bought a 6.4-metre boat and started longlining.

A fish shop owner in Auckland had agreed to sell his fish fillets if he could get them back to town. His boat was too small to make the trip regularly, so he approached Fred Ladd who flew out the fish. 'I would go out, catch fish, fillet them on the boat and take the fillets home. I had a Lister generator and I bought an ice-cream deep freeze. I put the fillets in that. Next day I was fishing again and then up 'til midnight packing and putting them into the deep freeze. On about the third day I would send them out.' It was hard work and Bob wasn't making much money. He was paid around 30 cents a pound for snapper.

Eventually Bob sold his boat and leased a bigger vessel that enabled him to take his fish directly back to Auckland himself. It was a busy life. 'I would ice the boat up, come out to the Barrier and start fishing on Sunday, Monday, Tuesday and half of Wednesday. I would take the fish back to Auckland, unload first thing Thursday morning, wash out the boat, get more ice and bait, have a few beers at Akarana, get home Thursday night or Friday morning and back to sea on Sunday.'[16]

In the early 1970s Bob bought his own boat, an 11-metre kauri launch powered by a six-cylinder Ford engine. By then the export market to Japan had opened up and prices for snapper were skyrocketing. Instead of getting only 50 cents a kilo, fishermen were now being paid three, five and eventually seven dollars. So Bob and the other fishermen worked hard to catch as much fish as they could. Fishing facilities on Great Barrier Island had improved and they could now unload fish and pick up ice at Nagel Cove in Port Fitzroy, Whangaparapara Harbour and Ōkupu.

The high prices for fish, and the availability of government suspensory loans to purchase fishing vessels, were attracting a lot of new entrants into the industry. There were now twelve vessels fishing out of Tryphena and others based at Whangaparapara. In addition, the Ngāti Wai-linked Walker family were crayfishing from Flat Island in Port Fitzroy. The island fishermen set up a cooperative and money flowed into the local economy.

In about 1974, Bob noticed that fishing was starting to decline and the fish were becoming much harder to catch.[17] Noticeably, the schools of trevally disappeared. 'The purse-seine boats arrived on the scene in the early 1970s . . . The pair trawlers would go backwards and forwards. Single trawlers and seine boats were all having a go. They would get 60 to 70 baskets in one seine shot. I would be lying in bed at night and hear the engines going. They would be doing a shot off Palmers Beach. They had a go at everything in those days.'[18]

Fishermen started expending greater effort to maintain their catches from a dwindling stock. Nets were left out for longer periods. Echo and sonar sounders were deployed to locate shoals of fish that could be targeted. Trawler fishermen, who used to avoid foul ground, now started to

Tony and Carol Litherland live next to the old whaling station in Whangaparapara Harbour (shown here). For a number of years they were involved in purchasing catch off Great Barrier Island fishermen and sending it to market.

haul their nets across the edges of rocky outcrops, knocking them off and reducing the extent of safe havens to which fish could escape. In Bob's opinion 'Commercial fishermen have definitely destroyed all the foul ground at the back of the Barrier where exotic [reef] fish once lived. They have all gone. If these fish couldn't be sold, they were dumped.'[19]

In 1979 Tony and Carol Litherland set up a fish-receiving depot on a barge. Prior to that, Tony had worked as a boilermaker and diesel mechanic in Whangārei. A chance conversation with a director of fish company Halma Holdings led Tony and Carol, with their three children, to motor their barge down to Great Barrier Island to set up business. They saw it as a chance for an adventure. First they moored at Nagel Cove in Port Fitzroy, then off Kaikōura Island and then in Whangaparapara Harbour next to the old whaling station. They lived on board with their family in a small box on top of the barge. Much of the rest of the area was taken up with a large chiller. They paid the fishermen for their fish on behalf of Halma Holdings. The catch was then transported by boat back to the company's facilities in Tutukākā, a nine-hour trip each way. As the fishing industry on the island grew, Halma purchased the

The Litherlands set up a fish-receiving depot on a barge and also lived aboard in a small shed (in the foreground). Most of the barge was taken up with a large chiller. (Courtesy of Tony and Carol Litherland)

The Litherlands were also involved in a failed venture to export live fish to Japan. Shown here is the cage attached to the barge where the fish were kept alive before export. (Courtesy of Tony and Carol Litherland)

fish factory at Ōkupu and installed an ice plant powered by a diesel generator.[20]

There was a failed venture to export live fish and crayfish from Great Barrier Island to Japan. After being caught, the snapper and crayfish were held in floating cages in Ōkupu. When a shipment was ready, the fish were taken out of the cage and placed into a seawater-filled tank fitted with a compressor to provide oxygen. The tank was loaded onto a barge, taken back to Auckland and deposited on Wynyard Wharf ready for shipment to Japan.

If it could be make to work, prices for the live fish were a hefty $50 to $100 a kilo. But it was not to be. On the first shipment the air hose was damaged and the fish died from lack of oxygen. Then fungus started growing on the fins of the fish being held in cages. It was also soon discovered that, whilst being held in tanks, the fish changed colour from bright red (which was the preferred colour for the Japanese market) to a less favoured dark brown, typical of snapper feeding on kelp.

Snapper 'gold rush'

Records show that 1971 was the peak year for the snapper harvest in the gulf, when around 6800 tons were recorded as being landed. But only three years later this figure had plummeted to 4000 tons. The actual harvest would have been significantly larger than this, due to wastage and unreported catch; it was common practice for fishermen to under-report their catch to reduce tax liability.

The 1971 peak was driven by a Japanese market for frozen snapper opening up in 1968. By this time the Japanese wild snapper stocks had collapsed due to over-harvesting. In addition, the Japanese fleet, which had been fishing in the outer gulf since the late 1950s, was pushed outside the 12-mile limit in 1967. Prior to this, fishermen based at Coromandel could see small Japanese boats crossing the exclusion 'line' every night and poaching 'their' snapper.[21] So the Hauraki Gulf became a major supplier of 'frozen Jap packs'. These were high-quality small snapper frozen whole. The Japanese called them *tai* and used them as a ceremonial fish.

One of those who got involved in the Jap pack market was Dave Kellian who built his own boat, and went fishing on his own account, in the early 1970s. In those days it was easy to get authorisation to go fishing. Fishermen only needed to apply for a licence and register their boat. No skipper's ticket was required. They were given a book to fill in with details of the catch. 'No one took it seriously. Everyone only wrote in half of what they caught, as they sold half for cash.' Even skippers on company boats, who

Green-lipped mussels

Gus Gundlock recalled his parents and ten-year-old brother starting to hand pick mussels off the rocks at Tapu on the Thames coast, in 1909, to sell at half-a-crown a sack. They picked ten to fifteen sacks each day between the tides and then cooked them, before sale.

Eventually his father bought a dinghy and his brother constructed a small dredge net, about 0.9 by 1.2 metres in size. While his father rowed the dinghy around the rocks in shallow water, his brother dragged the net. This resulted in a doubling of the harvest each tide. The financial success enabled the purchase of a larger boat and the use of a winch for the dredge.

Gus eventually took over running the boat and the abundance of mussels encouraged the family to develop a full-time business. The mussels were now pickled in jars for sale. Eventually the family bought a substantial power-driven vessel and in 1940 they established a factory and office at the then Fishermans Wharf in Auckland.

As the business geared up, they purchased *Roa*, a 12.1-metre dredger which dragged a 2.7 by 3-metre steel net along the bottom to harvest the mussels. Once the mussels were hauled up, they were washed to remove grit and then shovelled into sacks. Back at the factory they were steamed and shelled. The discarded shells were burnt to make lime. Gus enthused at the time: 'New Zealand grows the biggest and best mussels in the world and the grounds around Auckland province are the best in New Zealand.'[22]

Even though there was soon evidence of local depletion, the Marine Department failed to bring mussel dredging under control. There was a belief that the beds were being well maintained and even that dredging would benefit the beds and make them more productive, because they were currently 'matted and congested'. In 1945 the beds around Coromandel were closed for three years thereby encouraging dredgers to work further afield.[23]

In 1949 and '50, Coromandel fisherman Merv Strongman recalls that 'all the mussels on the Coromandel side died. There were beds they couldn't dredge on hard foul and two big spits between the islands [north of Coromandel Harbour] that were smothered with green-lipped mussels. Every last one of them died and they didn't come back. I don't know what caused it. The spat was still in the water but it wasn't growing on the rocks.'[24]

By the 1950s, two types of dredge had been developed. The 'Strongman' dredge, named after the Strongman family, towed with the mouth slightly upwards and it took only a layer of mussels. The 'Gunlock' dredge had a down-facing mouth that dug deeply into the substrate and took entire mussel clusters embedded into the seabed. It may have damaged the seabed to such an extent that mussels were unable to re-establish.[25]

As concern developed about over-exploitation of the beds, the Marine Department interviewed fishers to build up a picture of their current state. They were told that the most prolific beds were along the entire Coromandel coastline from Te Puru to Colville Bay, with the densest beds being in Kikowhakarere immediately to the north of Coromandel Harbour. But by 1958 these were gone.

There were also large beds to the east and south of Pōnui Island which, by 1958, were showing signs of depletion. Extensive beds from Ōrere Point to Kaiaua provided the biggest supply during the 1950s, once the other beds were exhausted. There were also reportedly 'extensive and well-populated beds' in the Rangitoto Channel and Islington Bay contained 'good beds of limited area'.[26]

The recorded peak landings of green-lipped mussels were made in 1961, when 2800 tons of mussels were harvested, although this may underestimate actual landings through under-reporting. As late as 1963, two more vessels were licensed to dredge mussels, bringing the total to five.[27] But then the stocks collapsed. Despite more time spent searching for mussels, just five years later the landings had dropped to 100 tons, full-time dredging ceased in 1967 and the fishery closed in 1969.[28]

The rich mussel beds which had populated the gulf, and which had provided copious food and important habitat for juvenile fish and many other marine species, were gone. The sea floor had been reduced to soft mud to which little could attach.

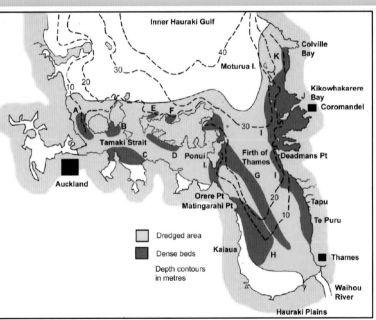

Top: Although green-lipped mussels, such as these shown at Ōtata Island, the Noises, can be found on rocky reefs around the Hauraki Gulf, the rich beds on the sea floor of the inner gulf have never returned after being dredged out.

Bottom: Most of the inner Hauraki Gulf has been dredged for mussels. This map shows the estimated extent of the original green-lipped mussel beds and the areas that were dredged. (Larry Paul)

A dredge-load of mussels is being hoisted on board the *Roa*, operating off Pōnui Island in the Firth of Thames. (*The Weekly News*, p. 31, Wednesday, August 14, 1963 Auckland: Wilson and Holton, Hocken Collections, Uare Taoka o Hākena, University of Otago)

were paid a weekly wage instead of a share, were selling fish on the side to make more money. 'They would stop and do deals before unloading the bulk of the fish on the shore.' Fish was even exchanged for fuel.[29]

Dave started longlining for Leigh Fisheries. At that time they were paying around 70 cents per kilo for snapper. Much of the fish was smoked and sold around New Zealand, but the company was also marketing the Jap packs. The Japanese preferred smaller fish, so Dave would be told to either catch the larger smokers or the smaller Jap Pack snapper. He learnt how to adjust the bait and fish in different places to get the desired size.

The new market drove an explosion in fishing effort. At the same time as the new lucrative export market opened up, the government was providing cheap finance for fishermen to purchase new vessels. It was also providing tax credits for fish exports. The number of Danish seine vessels in Auckland tripled over three years, from 13 in 1968 to 39 in 1971.[30] The race to cash in on the Japanese snapper gold mine was on.

The developing Japanese market demanded higher quality and conflict arose between the longline fishermen who were aiming for a small quantity of high-value fish and those using bulk methods. Barry Torkington described the situation in the late 1970s. 'When the market opened up for flying fish into Japan fresh, it encouraged a longline fleet to hit the water. There was always a small longline fleet, but it made longlining more profitable, so that encouraged more people. Then it became a natural conflict between those who set longlines and caught small quantities of fish and flew it out fresh and the other commercial people that were just tearing into it, fish going everywhere. You could listen to these operators on the short-wave radio discussing their catches. It was nothing for them to only be able to retain 25 per cent of what they'd caught in a particular tow and the rest would be shovelled over the side.'[31]

This snapper 'gold rush' not only attracted new fishermen into the industry but it also attracted the interest of property magnates Jim and Kevin Jeffs, who had established the company JBL Limited in 1965. They syndicated commercial property, buying up buildings, installing tenants and then selling them on to a group of investors, while JBL retained a management role. This proved enormously successful. Jim Jeffs then started investing in the fishing industry. He first targeted Sanford and mounted a takeover bid which ultimately failed. He then bought up Nelson Fisheries, a firm which was at that time based in the Viaduct Basin.

From this base in Auckland, Jeffs started syndicating fishing boats, offering higher returns than traditional investments. This was particularly attractive to older people with savings that were being eaten away by the then high inflation rates. Initially it was existing seine boats which were purchased and syndicated. But then JBL embarked on a major boatbuilding exercise that significantly increased the Auckland fleet. A total of fourteen new steel fishing vessels were ordered. Although JBL's fishing business wasn't making any money, the syndication process kept capital flowing into the company. But then, in 1972, the bubble burst and a receiver was appointed to sort out the mess. At that stage the company had a total of 3000 investors in 79 syndicates.[32]

It wasn't just snapper that were being targeted by the boats with big power nets. The big schools of kahawai and trevally that had frequented the gulf for centuries were also the focus of a concerted fishing effort. As the number and size of the schools reduced, spotter planes were employed to search for the remaining aggregations of fish. Once located, the pilot would radio back to the trawlers the position of the school and approximate tonnage. This enabled more efficient fishing effort, reducing the time spent motoring to look for the fish, but it also enabled the stocks to be rapidly depleted.[33]

Pair trawling

In 1970, the snapper boom also brought pair trawlers to the gulf for the first time. The innovation of towing one net between two boats enabled the net width to be increased by two-thirds, to more than 180 metres, and a faster towing speed could be reached. The results were spectacular, resulting in huge catches of snapper. There were also large catches of undersized and less valuable fish which were dumped over the side. Maritime historian David Johnson noted that a pair of trawlers operating out of Tauranga had dumped more than 100 tonnes of trevally, mackerel and kahawai in their first three months of operation.[34]

Box netting

The 1970s brought the introduction of box nets (also known as teiche nets) to the Hauraki Gulf. This fishing technique had been used in Japan for around 500 years. It involved the installation of a long fence, made out of netting, at right

Story of the Gulf | **Dave Clark**

RETIRED PAIR-TRAWL FISHERMAN, WHITIANGA[35]

Eighty-year-old Dave Clark was one of the early fishermen in Whitianga to shift to pair trawling. Dave had first started fishing on his own in 1963 on *La Vega*, a vessel he had built himself. He spent several years crayfishing and then longlining, before building a trawler. Subsequently, the Rural Bank offered to finance another boat if Dave agreed to go pair trawling, so he did.

'When I was single trawling I would catch snapper only about a foot [30 centimetres] long and the fishing was buggered. But when I started pair trawling with another boat, we were catching fish which were twice as large. So our catch went way up. The net we were using was much bigger and we would run the boats a quarter of a mile apart. We would do three tows a day but most of the fish were caught in the evening. We would work up as far as the Hen and Chickens and down as far as Mayor Island.'

The arrival of pair trawlers in the area was not always welcome. 'Farmers tried to stop us pairing along Whangapoua, so they dumped their stuff in the water. At one stage we got a tractor wheel and an axle in our nets. One day we did a tow along Whangapoua and looked back to see the net floating with fish. A few boats were coming out from the bay. One fella complained that he had been fishing here for a week and hadn't had a bite. Another was trying to run into the net to break it up. A third was trying to buy some fish. Different people have different ideas.'

Dave was pair trawling for nine years until the quota-management system came in and he then sold his quota and the boat. At that stage 'catches were seasonal but we were still fishing well'. In Dave's view it was the large pair trawlers that were impacting on the fishery. 'What buggered it up were the big trawlers. Sanford had three or four, 110 foot [33.5 metres] long. They had heaps of horsepower and went quite a lot faster than us. A big pair of trawlers would come over the horizon and our fishing would drop off straight away.'

It was hard work, but Dave enjoyed life as a fisherman. 'We would sail from Whitianga at about 3 pm, steam out to the Mercury Islands, throw the net, do a tow and get back here at midnight. We would ice and unload the boat and do the same every day. There was good money in fish at that time and you could make a good living.'

Being a fisherman was not the same after the quota-management system was introduced. 'Prior to the quota, you

Dave Clark started fishing for himself in 1963: crayfishing and then longlining, before moving to trawling. He pair-trawled out of Whitianga for nine years before the introduction of the quota-management system. He is shown here on his fishing boat *La Vega*, which he built himself. (Courtesy of Dave Clark)

could catch as many fish as you could. If you had a good trip, you had a good trip. Now if you catch a lot of fish you have to come in. At one stage, as long as you paid money, you could get a licence. It's too expensive to go fishing now. You've got to buy quota and your boat and the price of fuel's gone up. I think I got out at about the right time.'

From his years at sea in the Mercury Bay area Dave has noticed some significant changes. 'I used to rely on schools of fish for crayfish bait. A lot of those fish have gone. There used to be blue maomao around the rocks and they're all gone, although they were never caught. There used to be a lot of dory on the beach in Whitianga and frost fish. On the way to school I used to pick three or four dory off the beach. They're not there now.'

angles to the coast. If the fish swam towards the coast along the fence there was a passage for them to pass through. But if the fish swam towards deeper water they were channelled into an enclosed area where they were caught and held alive until release. The design was intended to catch passing school fish, which swam into deeper water, whilst avoiding the local coastal fish. It also avoided damage to the seabed which could be caused by other methods.[36]

A box net was installed at Sandy Bay just north of Whitianga in late 1972, stretching 1000 metres out into the sea. A second net was installed at Hot Water Beach in 1973. The Sandy Bay net was then removed and its netting added to the Hot Water Beach structure. This extended it 1500 metres into the sea, starting 200 metres out from the shore and running out to a depth of around 35 metres.[37]

Marine farmer Jim Dollimore recalls working on the Hot Water Beach box net, shortly after it was installed. He would dive down in order to clean the nets. 'We would radio Whitianga with what we had. They would telex Nelson and then around the world. Within ten minutes people would either buy the fish or not. They would then tell us which ones they wanted and the ones they didn't want we would push through a tunnel into a holding pen and leave them there. We would feed them on sprats which we caught. Kingfish were high in value at certain times of the year and low in value at other times, so we would keep them for some months in the holding pen, then sell them to Japan.[38]

'There would be schools of fish in the net but many more outside and nothing was damaged. The nets acted as huge fish aggregating devices. We caught schools of tuna. We would let out some of the things we caught, like orca and giant sunfish. We also saw sharks. With sharks, we had a .303 shotgun cartridge in a holder with a rod attached to it and a firing pin. We would push it into the sharks and they would blow up.' The net was eventually removed in 1980. Although it had provided high-quality fish, it was expensive to operate and the returns were not sufficient to justify the high costs.[39]

Iki jime market

In 1981, Dave Kellian and fellow Leigh fisherman Barry Torkington heard about some Japanese fishermen at Whitianga doing iki jime fish for Japan. They were spiking the fish in the brain after capture and getting high prices for the fish. Dave thought, 'If they can do it, we can do it.' So the pair decided to investigate further. They found out where the

Box nets were introduced to the Hauraki Gulf in the early 1970s and were effective in catching large quantities of high-quality fish. However, they eventually proved uneconomic. Shown here is Jim Dollimore releasing a hammerhead shark from the box net at Hot Water Beach. (Courtesy of Jim Dollimore)

Japanese company's office was in Auckland. They then jumped in Barry's Kombi van, headed to the city and stormed into the office. 'It was about 5 pm when we got there. There was a huge Japanese man with a really deep voice like gravel. He didn't want to know us, but we weren't going away. He said, "What do you want?" We told him. He said, "Go away." We sat there and said, "No, this is what we want to do . . ." He was non-committal. In the end he got out a bottle of sake and poured drinks for us. Then he threw up his hands and said, "Tell me what you want." We said: "We want to catch iki jime fish and deliver them to you at the airport. We want you to pay us what they are worth." He told us the next plane was 48 hours away. He thought we would fail.

'We drove home, iced the boat and I went out to Takatu. I knew there were beautiful red snapper there. We got the snapper and had to cut them open to find out where the brain was so we could iki jime them. So we did all that, brought the fish onshore, took them to the factory, barged in and packed the fish in poly boxes, loaded them up in the Kombi and arrived at his office at 10 the next morning. He couldn't believe his eyes. Here was a Kombi, no warrant, no registration and the rear bumper dragging on the ground, with a load of fish. He was stonkered, but he had to take the fish as it was a gentleman's agreement.

'He got rave reviews about the fish. They were better than the stuff they were catching at Whitianga. And he wanted more. We got $7 or $8 a kilo for the first load and the guy

Disappearing hāpuku

Although there is little hard data to throw light on the issue, fishermen have recently been reporting significant declines in hāpuku stocks in the Hauraki Gulf.

Commercial longliner Dave Kellian had seen photos of people filling up their dinghies with big hāpuku from Flat Rock off Kawau Island, and he had heard stories about catching tons of hāpuku off Anchorite Rock, but they had gone by the time he started commercial fishing in the early 1970s. He could still catch juveniles in these places, but there seemed to be too much fishing pressure for them to recolonise.[40]

In former commercial fisherman Barry Torkington's view, 'hāpuku are a disaster. Tiritiri was covered in hāpuku in the early days. Wellington Reef [north of Whangaparāoa Peninsula] and Shearers Rock [east of Tiritiri Matangi Island] were great hāpuku grounds. Centre Reef, Channel Island [off Cape Colville], Nor' West Reef and the Leigh Reef were all full of hāpuku.[41]

'None of the fisheries management techniques used in New Zealand are able to manage hāpuku. They are ferocious feeders. You can't avoid catching them if they're present. And generally, once you catch the fish, you can't release them as they have bladder trauma on the way up and won't survive release. They are very slow at recruiting into areas and their reproduction is poorly understood.'[42]

Danish seiner Phil Clow has observed that 'each reef structure within the range of fast recreational boats and inshore bottom longliners is being stripped of its resident hāpuku/bass.' Once the fish colonise these structures, it is thought that they live there for the rest of their lives.

Phil credits the recent decline in the fish to 'the availability of affordable, effective electronics and seaworthy boats, which have enabled the recreational fleet to access and continually target the deeper and more productive rocky structures. In addition, commercial bottom longliners have developed greater expertise in targeting the fish. Along with the availability of electronic sea-floor mapping, and a good financial return for reef fish, this has increased fishing pressure on the reef structures.'[43]

was taking a major commission. At that time the going rate for snapper was a dollar a kilo. So we said to Leigh Fisheries, "We want to fish for this Japanese firm and we want a share of it." They said, "Who do you think you are?"

'At that time fishing was tough. Fish were hard to catch as there were pair trawlers everywhere in the gulf, financed by big suspensory loans. We called a meeting of the Leigh Commercial Fishermen's Association to discuss the way forward. Leigh Fisheries had said that they would pay 10 cents a kilo more for iki jime snapper. Most fisherman were loyal and stayed with the company. But five of us said no.

'We organised for a company in Auckland to pack our fish and get them to the airport for us. We formed the Quality Fish Company. But we struggled like hell. We had to organise our own ice and pay for the iki jime bins. We set

Dave Kellian built a boat and starting fishing on his own account in the early '70s. He helped to establish the lucrative iki jime snapper during the 1980s. He is still actively commercially fishing.

Commercial fishermen Barry Torkington and Dave Kellian established a highly successful iki jime snapper business out of Leigh Harbour (shown here in 2008). Some of the longline fleet can be seen moored in the harbour.

Opposite: Iki jime fishing involves spiking the fish in the brain to kill it as soon as it is retrieved from the water. This delays the onset of rigor mortis and helps to keep the fish in top condition. The fish are then put into ice-slurry water to quickly reduce their temperature. This series of images shows the baited hooks ready to be put on the longline as it is set (top left), retrieving the line and extracting the fish from the hooks (top right) and using a spike to iki jime the fish in the brain (bottom).

a high standard and met it from the beginning. But it was hard to maintain it. Barry gave up fishing and I tried to keep it going. Barry was the believer in the quality thing. It was his baby. I focused on fishing.

'We did quite well out of it, but we were seen by Leigh Fisheries as the enemy camp, the young renegades. In the end, over half the fleet in the area, about twelve to thirteen boats, were fishing for us. We were getting $9 to $10 a kilo and the Leigh Fisheries boats were getting $1.10. The conflict split families and broke the town. It was particularly difficult for me, as my dad was fishing for Leigh Fisheries at the time and he was also on the board.'

In the end the two sides reconciled, a new manager was installed in Leigh Fisheries, and the business went from strength to strength. The fishermen negotiated an unusual deal for fishing companies at the time. Instead of the company paying fishermen a flat fee based on weight, it was to be a profit-sharing arrangement. The company would levy a packing fee and charge for packaging materials and

The fishing fleet at Tryphena wharf, Great Barrier Island, during the heyday of the industry. After the quota-management system came into force in 1986, most fishers sold out and there remains only one commercial crayfishing boat working out of the harbour. (Courtesy of Bob Whitmore)

transport at cost. It would also charge a small commission on the value of the fish; the fishermen would get the rest. So if they all did a good job, and produced high-quality fish which sold at high prices, everyone would benefit financially. And they did.

Following the lead taken at Leigh, other fishers around the gulf started iki jime fishing. For example, sole fisherman Ronnie Martin used to fish off Point Chevalier Beach in the winter, catching fish for iki jime. He would bring them back to Fletchers (at the Viaduct Basin) by 11.00 am and they were on the plane to Japan by 3.00 pm. He also fished off the rocks between Cheltenham Beach and Torbay on the North Shore, off the rocks at St Heliers Beach and off Bean Rock. 'I did very well. The highest price I ever got for snapper was $16 a kilo and that was in winter. The normal price was $10 to $12 a kilo. It was ideal for small fishermen like me.'[44]

There were a lot of boats on the water, fishing was tough and conflict rife, but everyone was making serious money. The Leigh fishermen were doing better than anyone else. They had their own label in Japan and they were able to get their fish to the Japanese auction floor within 24 hours of being caught. Their quality was the best and, if there was too much fish, the Leigh fish sold first. Then the quota-management system came in and a lot of the longline fishermen sold out. The large seine boats started doing iki jime and using ice slurries. This helped to flood the Japanese market. With an oversupplied market, the price went down. Then the Japanese started farming snapper and, by the 1990s, the Japanese market had collapsed.

Quota-management system

The golden days of fishing in the gulf were now long gone. In 1977, the government finally responded to concerns about depletion and imposed a catch quota on the Hauraki Gulf snapper fishery, although this was not strictly enforced. At the same time the government was still issuing hundreds of new fishing permits; a total of 2200 were issued in Auckland in 1978 alone. 'Every time a freezing works closed, 800 workers went and got a fishing permit.' Without new regulation there was no basis for turning permit applications down, as it was technically an open fishery.[45] In 1983 the area became a controlled fishery, to restrict new entrants into the industry. But this was 'too little, too late' and did little to deal with the existing over-investment in fishing capacity, fuelled by the government's ill-advised loan scheme. Then, in 1983, part-timer fishers were stripped of their right to commercially fish, with no compensation. This disenfranchised hundreds of fishers and created hardship for many small coastal communities and in particular for Māori. In rural settlements around the gulf, where there were few employment opportunities, hundreds of people fished part-time to provide additional income.[46] The quota-management system was finally introduced in 1986. The allocation of quota was based on the average reported catch between 1981 and 1983. This rewarded those who caught large volumes of low-quality fish through trawling, in comparison to longliners who landed fewer but higher-value fish. It also

Story of the Gulf | **Adam Clow**

LONGLINE FISHERMAN, HOT WATER BEACH

Although many fishermen sold out when the quota-management system came in, 28-year-old Adam Clow followed his father into the industry and is thriving on it. 'I enjoy hunting the fish out, finding them and developing techniques to catch them. I like seeing fish come up out of the water. I love the fact that you don't have to be that good at reading and writing, but you can use your skill at sea to benefit yourself. Every day's different. You can be frightened at sea, which will get blood rushing around your body. With fishing, there are a thousand different things — currents, moons, time of year, depth, baits, time of day, habitat, whether sharks are in the area and whether small fish are getting the bait. When you line it all up it's a good feeling, very satisfying. Then other days you can do your eighteen hours a day for $100 or a $6 an hour wage. On the calm days it's beautiful. We also get to go surfing and diving. So it's the job for me.'[47]

caught out many fishermen who regularly under-reported their catch. In order to reduce the overall take of fish, the quota allocated for snapper was around a third less than the average catch.

Most small fishers eventually sold their quota to the fishing companies, who were eager to buy quota up in order to secure control over supply. With the large companies buying up quota, many small fishermen left the industry. Those that stayed shifted from owning quota to leasing it. This fundamentally changed the nature of the fishing industry.

When Whitianga-based fisherman Phil Clow first went Danish seining, he had to mortgage himself 'to the hilt' to buy more snapper quota. Then there were reductions in allocation. The cap on the maximum commercial catch of snapper along the north-east coast of the North Island was reduced by 23 per cent 'which was a massive hit'. Luckily Phil had a bank manager who stood by him, one of the first bankers who loaned on the security of quota. After the cut, he had to buy more quota or get out. Phil bought more. This happened twice, so it made things very difficult financially.[48]

Eventually, Phil had had enough of the large mortgage and financial pressure, so he sold some of his quota. 'It hurt

me, but I think it saved my life [in terms of reducing stress]. What has happened now is that the big companies are all in the market for quota. They have bought it and now they never trade it. It's not there to buy now anything like it was in the early days and the price is through the roof. So a lot of us are now contract fishermen. We get given a tonnage of fish to catch each year and we go and catch that fish when they want it. In many cases, the income earned from fishing is inadequate to renew plant, so a lot of vessels are old. We are vulnerable and have very little control over our destiny. You could have a boat and no access to fish.'[49]

After the quota-management system came in, many of the gulf's small coastal fishing communities faded away. On Great Barrier Island, fisherman Bob Whitmore, along with most others, sold his quota, something he later regretted. 'The quota-management system came in and it was no fun any more. Before it came in, we had competitions as to who could catch the most fish. It was real war. The guys would try to pinch each other's "possie". You had to be kingpin and catch the most fish. It was real fun. But after the quota system, you didn't know when or how to catch and there was that much paperwork.

The Viaduct Basin on Auckland's waterfront still remains a fishing hub, with the Sanford seafood factory and seafood market close by.

And the government wanted to take extra fish off us.'
In 1991 fishing was the main industry on Great Barrier Island. There were about 25 boats fishing from there and they generated an estimated total income of $350,000 to $400,000 a year.[50] Now they have all gone, apart from two remaining crayfish boats, one working out of Tryphena and the other off Flat Island south of Port Fitzroy.[51]

Virtually all fishermen on Waiheke Island sold their quota and the fishing industry on the island disappeared. During the late 1970s, there had been 36 fishing vessels based there, a third of the total Auckland longline fleet.[52]

Although at least three Danish seiners and a couple of longliners held on in Coromandel, they lost their wet-fish factory and had to truck their fish to Auckland. The Whitianga fishing industry became a shadow of its former self.

There are now no commercial launches working out of Thames, a place which historically was a major fishing port, second only to Auckland. Some fishing is still undertaken with small trailer boats. One such fisherman is Doug Pulford, who managed to retain snapper quota. He sells his catch to the local Thames wholesaler and this means that fresh locally caught fish is available to restaurants and members of the public. His is the only boat that sells locally and he enjoys supporting his community in this way.[53]

The only coastal fishing community that survived relatively intact was at Leigh. Because of the high prices Leigh fishermen were getting throughout the 1980s from the iki jime market, and the support they got from Leigh

Fisheries, more fishermen held onto their quota.[54] But prices are now much lower than in the heyday of the 1980s, with fishermen getting only around $4 a kilo for snapper.[55]

Under the quota-management system catches were constrained and reduced for some species, such as snapper, allowing stocks to rebuild. Fishing is no longer about catching everything you can, but about catching the right size, number and quality of fish to meet the demands of the discerning international market. Fishing has become a precision operation that only the very skilled can successfully undertake. Catch too much at any one time, and the scarce quota is used up, resulting in lower-value fish and a reduction in overall profits. Things have moved a long way from the 'rip, shit and bust' approach of the first 170 years of commercially fishing the gulf.

Opposite: Leigh was the only small fishing community in the Hauraki Gulf that survived the introduction of the quota-management system. A substantial fishing fleet still works out of the harbour and Leigh Fisheries is flying out high-quality fish to the markets of the world. Shown here (top) is a longliner unloading its catch and (below) longline-caught fish ready for packing and export.

Story of the Gulf | **Dave Moore**

LONGLINE FISHERMAN, LEIGH[56]

Dave Moore's father Graham was a keen fisherman. He used to catch flounder in the Whau Creek in west Auckland. He was soon catching more than the family could consume, so started selling some of his catch. In 1964 he decided to go full-time fishing with a 9-foot fishing punt that he carted around on the back of his ute.

Eventually Graham built up enough capital to buy a launch with Peter Ashby, which they based in the Viaduct Basin. They started fishing for flounder on the Thames flats. Graham then commissioned a boat specially designed for floundering, being 30-foot long with a big cockpit. Dave remembers as a child 'sitting on a nail box bundling up thirteen flounders on a piece of flax'.

Graham started branching out into using drag nets and beach seines. He also did some longlining, but didn't really enjoy it. Dave joined his father on the boat for the school holidays. 'My dad's whole theory was that if you're a fisherman you should be able to catch any type of fish, not one specific fish, but whatever was going for that part of the year that paid the most. That's what we were doing. My school holidays ranged from floundering to longlining for snapper to targeting school sharks when the water warmed up. I remember setting lines for sharks between Waiheke and Maraetai. Some of the best shark fishing was in the middle of the Tāmaki Strait in January. I would always chuckle to see people swimming at Maraetai Beach and we would catch 50 to 60, sometimes up to a hundred, school sharks at night, on the hard bottom in the strait.

'Then, because we set that line overnight for the sharks, we would be sitting in a bay in Waiheke and would see a lot of yellow-eyed sprats. So we made up a net to see if we could catch them. We caught the sprats and sold them to the zoo and other places. As the waters cooled down, we would start looking for mullet. Over my winter school holidays, we would work around the coast of the Hauraki Gulf looking for mullet and trevally. We would catch a lot of snapper and trevally using the beach seine, mostly in the Tāmaki Strait.'

When Dave left school he went to work for Bert Meader, a 75-year-old Ukrainian longline fisherman. Bert could speak four or five languages and had fought in two world wars. He brought with him a range of European fishing techniques, which he taught to others fishing from the Viaduct. Dave left after a year, went to work in a bank and ended up in Maungaturoto. He joined the local rugby club and became friends with Craig

Hanna who was working on his father's dairy farm.

'Craig was back learning all this stuff off his dad about how to manage a dairy farm. I remember thinking one morning, "I wonder if my dad knows anything." So I rang him up and said I would like to come back fishing and learn from him. Dad told me to bugger off, as he had spent all this money on my education. So he wouldn't take me to start with. My cousin had an old boat that wasn't doing anything, so I leased it off him to display my enthusiasm. It was such an old dunger that after six months Dad said, "You'd better come to work for me, otherwise you'll drown yourself."'

So Dave ended up working for his father. 'It was hard, working through the middle of the night and at various odd hours. Then one day it dawned on me. We were steaming up the coast. I told myself, "Keep your head up and look around. Look where you're working, the environment you're in. How awesome it is to be working in this beautiful place and to be able to make a living out of it."'

Dave really enjoyed the mental and physical aspects of fishing. 'I like the challenge of hunting, working out how I am going to catch this fish. You're really trying to think like that fish in terms of what bait you're using and where the moon or tide is. Then there's the physical side of fishing, the whole environment you're in and the connection with nature. You hop on the boat and cast off and then everything is determined by the natural elements. You can't beat anchoring in a bay at the end of a good day's work. You're the only boat there. It's calm. You are in the most beautiful surroundings, doing the best with what you're doing.'

Dave started fishing for himself a couple of years before the quota-management system was introduced. He was longlining for snapper in the summer and catching mullet, trevally and kahawai in the winter. He then started supplying fish to Leigh Fisheries. 'That was when iki jime fishing was starting up and then the quota-management system came in. The Leigh fishermen thrived. We built new boats and invested back into the industry. We were sort of the hippies of the industry.

Top: Dave Moore's former deckhand, Darrin Fabricius, now skippers one of Dave's fishing boats, the *Coral V*. He is shown here with his crew (from left to right) Troy Ashby, Mike Hickey and Poaneki Katene back in Leigh Harbour after a longlining trip.

Right: Dave Moore has built up a small fishing business of six boats fishing out of Leigh. His vision is to operate a boutique harvesting business that provides high-quality and environmentally friendly product to consumers around the world.

I now think we are the artisans of the fishing industry, catching smaller amounts but looking after the quality.'

During the 1990s Dave bought a lifestyle block in Warkworth. While he sorted out the new property, Dave encouraged his deckhand Darrin Fabricus to get a skipper's ticket and take over the running of the boat. Dave stayed on shore, but was feeling guilty about not going out fishing. One day he was discussing his finances with his accountant and started thinking about fishing as a business. 'Most of us fishing were relatively naïve when it came to corporate thinking. Our whole enjoyment was fishing, catching fish and being out on the water.'

So Dave started to build a fishing business. He now runs six boats and employs around 20 people. All crew have been trained in-house. Fishing is a different kind of business now. 'We used to fish hard out for the two to three months which were the historical schooling season. But now it's much more market-driven. If a high-end restaurant chef accepts your produce, he wants it to be there on a continuous basis, not just seasonally. So we started ranging further away from Leigh, up and down the coast and into deeper water in the winter, to see if we could catch a similar amount of fish throughout the year. We were increasing effort in the off months and reducing our effort in the peak months, to flatten out supply.'

Dave's vision is to operate a small boutique harvesting business that provides the best quality wild fish caught in a safe, responsible and environmentally friendly manner. He believes that people both locally and overseas will pay a premium for that. 'We love fishing and are proud of the fact that what we're producing is of a global standard. I have the idea that if you take a kilo of fish out of the water, you always make sure you maximise the return for that kilo.'

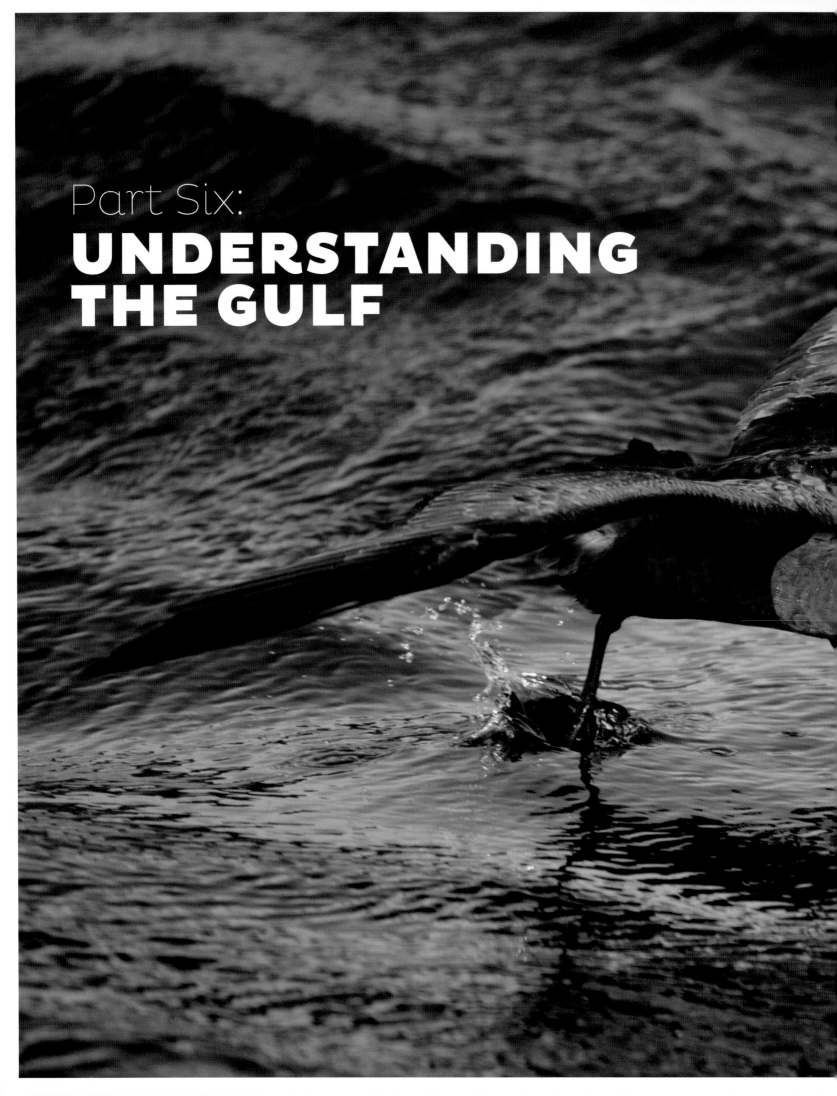

Part Six:
UNDERSTANDING THE GULF

Chapter 13
The gulf's treasures

As well as a wealth of fish and shellfish species, the highly productive waters of the Hauraki Gulf support numerous species of marine mammals and birds. These have strong cultural significance and are a source of much pleasure, wonder and delight. They also underpin several ecotourism ventures and are a critical part of the food web of the gulf.

Humpback whales

Humpback whales used to regularly pass through the Hauraki Gulf during their migrations from Antarctica to the tropics and back. During the winter months, the whales would migrate northwards through the gulf, some travelling to the west of Great Barrier Island and others to the east. Over the following spring, the whales would head south again, with some staying in the gulf for a while to feed.[1]

These large baleen whales grow to lengths of between 12 and 16 metres and typically weigh around 36,000 kilograms. Whalers named them 'humpback' because of the way the animals arch their backs before diving, which profiles the hump around their dorsal fin.[2] It is the

Pages 258–259: Black petrel. (Neil Fitzgerald)

Left: Diver and snapper at Cape Rodney-Ōkakari Point Marine Reserve. (Tony and Jenny Enderby)

remarkable abilities of the male humpbacks to produce haunting 'songs' that spearheaded the Save the Whales movement during the early 1970s. The sounds were reproduced on a 1970s album titled *Songs of the Humpback Whale* which became the best-selling natural history record of all time.[3]

There were early attempts at whaling in the Hauraki Gulf, but little is known about them. At a bay now called Whalers Cove on Great Mercury Island, a man named Cook established a small whaling enterprise and installed three large try pots against the cliff, where flues were cut up through the soft rock. The date of the activity is uncertain, but may have been around the late 1880s or 1890s. Island historian Pat Mizen was told by elderly Kuaotunu residents that no whales were ever actually caught by Cook.[4] Another whaling station was thought to have operated from the north end of Kennedy Bay on the Coromandel Peninsula.[5]

Although targeted for many decades by shore-based whalers operating elsewhere around New Zealand's coast, humpback whales were still regularly sighted in the Hauraki Gulf during the 1950s. Auckland-based fishermen had spotted whales feeding as close inshore as Kawau Bay (between Kawau Island and the mainland) and near Tiritiri Matangi Island. During a Marine Department whale survey in October 1955, five humpback whales were seen in the gulf, as well as a school of 30–40 sei whales near the northern end of Little Barrier Island.[6]

This relative abundance of whales led to the establishment of a shore whaling station in Whangaparapara Harbour, Great Barrier Island, in 1956. Hauraki Whaling Limited initiated the enterprise. Mr W A Balsillie, who had previously set up at station at Byron Bay in New South Wales, was appointed chief engineer for the project.[7]

In January 1959, Charlie Heberley and his family arrived at Whangaparapara, having travelled from the Marlborough Sounds, in an endeavour to get the station back on its feet. Hauraki Whaling had been placed in receivership in 1957, after catching only around twelve whales during each of the previous two seasons. Heberley was the fourth generation of a family who had been whalers in the Tory Channel. He had been engaged by new investors, operating under the name Barrier Whaling Co. Limited, and was to apply methods that had been successfully used in the Tory Channel.

Charlie had three months to get organised before the northward migration of whales, which was due to begin in May. He recruited two other whalers from Tory Channel — Tom Norton and Tom Gullery — as well as local men from the island who were keen to generate some additional income. In order to spot the whales, two lookout huts were built on top of hills, one on Arid Island and the other on Cape Barrier (on the south-east coast of the main island). On 3 June 1959, the first whale was spotted from Cape Barrier.

Two purpose-built petrol-engined chasers, fitted out with harpoons, were used to catch the whales. A mother ship

A whaling station operated out of Whangaparapara Harbour, Great Barrier Island, from 1956 to 1962. The station is shown here with two whales on the slip ready to be cut up and rendered down. (Ref: PH-NEG-C31362, Auckland War Memorial Museum Tāmaki Paenga Hira)

Humpback whales have long migrated through the Hauraki Gulf on their annual journey between Antarctica and the tropics. They can still be seen in the gulf today, as shown here, although in much reduced numbers. (Auckland Whale and Dolphin Safari)

Two specially built petrol-engined chasers were used to catch the whales from the Whangaparapara whaling station. Once the whale was sighted, it was shot with a high-powered harpoon, shown here on the front of the chaser. (Ref: PH-NEG-C31361, Auckland War Memorial Museum Tāmaki Paenga Hira)

then towed the carcasses back to the factory. While on the slipway, the carcasses were cut up into 0.6-metre squares. These hunks of blubber, meat and bone were put into large cookers to be boiled down. Eventually the whale's rich oil rose to the top of the liquid and was skimmed off. This was by far the most valuable product from the whale. The solids sank to the bottom and were pumped out and processed into blood-and-bone fertiliser. The baleen was dumped at sea. Some of the higher-quality whale meat was sold to restaurants in Auckland.[8]

By the end of the season, 104 whales had been caught and processed. Based on these successful results, the company invested in an upgrade of the factory and also built a house in which Charlie and his family lived.[9]

The next season proved even more profitable, with 135 whales caught. Buoyed up by two good years in a row, the shareholders invested in two more chasers. But the 1961 season proved disastrous. Only 25 whales were caught. The company was put back into receivership. Charlie wasn't so sure that the whales were disappearing. 'Perhaps they had travelled a different route that year,' he thought. So he negotiated an agreement for himself and his men to work on a profit-share basis under a new company called Gulf Whaling. But this proved to be a poor move. In 1962, only

ten humpbacks and twelve seis were sighted, of which eight humpbacks were caught. The small number of whales was not economical and the company closed its doors for good.[10]

It was many years before humpback whales were again seen around New Zealand's coast in any numbers. As well as being hunted in the gulf and elsewhere around New Zealand, their population had been decimated in Antarctica by Japanese, Russian and Norwegian factory whaling ships. Now that hunting the whales has stopped, many more of these magnificent animals are likely to frequent the gulf once again.

Bryde's whales

Another species of whale seen in the gulf is unusual in that it doesn't migrate through the area on the way to somewhere else, but lives in the vicinity all year round. Bryde's whales have chosen the Hauraki Gulf as a place to reside, most probably as

Top: Tourism businesses, focused on taking people out to see the whales and dolphins in the Hauraki Gulf, have operated since 2000. This image shows tourists viewing the magnificent Bryde's whale underwater. (Auckland Whale and Dolphin Safari)

Right: Bryde's whales occupy the same area in the Hauraki Gulf that ships transit through to reach the Port of Auckland. This has increased the risk of whales being hit by ships. (Auckland Whale and Dolphin Safari)

they can reliably get enough food and safely raise their calves.

Bryde's whales don't produce much oil, so they weren't hunted in the same way as the humpback whales were. But still, nineteen Bryde's whales were taken at the Whangaparapara whaling station. Initially Bryde's whales were thought to be sei whales, only being recognised as a distinctive species in the gulf during the late 1950s. Until recently, most of what was known about them came from observations of animals caught by the whalers. Scientist David Gaskin noted in his 1972 book *Whales, Dolphins &*

Story of the Gulf | **Dr Rochelle Constantine**

MARINE MAMMAL SCIENTIST, AUCKLAND[11]

It was around 2007 that University of Auckland marine mammal scientist Rochelle Constantine first became involved in the Bryde's whale ship-strike issue. She had been encouraged to take an interest in the whales by Professor Scott Baker, who had started the university's research on the species during the 1990s. Rochelle had spent much of her early science career researching bottlenose dolphins in the Bay of Islands and the impacts of tourism on their behaviour and welfare. Now, in the Hauraki Gulf, she was seeking to get to grips with another serious threat to the country's special marine mammals.

Initially, Rochelle tried to determine how many whale deaths there had been and what was known about the causes. 'I had a student, Steph Behrens, and I got her straight onto looking at all the archives of known dead whales from the greater Hauraki Gulf region. Records were really only kept since 1987 when DOC [the Department of Conservation] was formed.' Between 1989 and 2007, a period of eighteen years, Steph found that there had been 38 known recorded deaths. She then went through the records, photographs and any measurements, to identify the possible cause of death for those whales.

Of the 38 whales, there was sufficient information to assign possible causes of mortality for only seventeen. And of those, thirteen almost certainly died from vessel strike.[12] 'Of the other four, two were entangled in mussel spat lines, near the Firth of Thames; one other, which was dragged in near Coromandel, had marks on it consistent with entanglement in a rope of some kind. The sad thing was that, for 21 whales, we had no idea why they had died and that's just through poor record keeping.'

Then, in September 2011, a Great Barrier Air pilot spotted a dead whale floating in the Hauraki Gulf. He phoned the Department of Conservation. Departmental official Phil Brown then phoned Rochelle. As Rochelle explains, 'It was on the first day of the Rugby World Cup. Phil Brown called me up and told me about the whale sighting. I said, "We have to get that whale." He said, "There are no helicopters, there is nothing you can get hold of, because everything's busy with the World Cup opening." But he managed to find a fisherman who, thankfully, towed the whale into Port Jackson. It was a Friday. Rob Chappell from DOC went out and anchored the carcass and then the weather turned. So we left the whale for the weekend as we couldn't get a digger out until Monday.'

On Monday, the scientists, led by Stu Hunter, a pathologist from Massey University Veterinary School, undertook a necropsy to find out why the whale had died. This involved cutting open the carcass and examining the animal's internal organs and bones. 'He was a 12.1-metre male, healthy in every respect. His bottom two ribs were broken. From there to his tail, 15 vertebrae were broken. They are the size of a dinner plate and some of them were broken into four pieces. All of the ligaments and tendons that run along the spine and hold the muscle blocks under the spine were just shredded. All of his musculature along that, around a 6-metre length of his body, was just pulp, like gelatinous goo. The parts that hadn't been hit were solid muscle. It was clear he'd suffered a massive trauma. There was no doubt at all that this whale had been killed by a ship.

'The sad thing is that he was a really healthy whale. One of the things that Steph's work found was that most of the whales that are struck by ships, just over 70 per cent of them, were 11 metres long or a bit smaller. So they're not calves, but they're not full adult-sized whales. Usually Bryde's in the gulf are around 15 metres long when adults. This is consistent with global findings that sub-adult animals are more vulnerable. It may be that they are not experienced enough or that they're just not paying attention like adults would. We don't know. In recent years, though, we have found larger whales dying from ship strike. It seems all animals are vulnerable.'

The scientists started to search for ways to reduce the threat to the whales. 'We looked at the global solutions which are to re-route traffic or slow the ships down.' In order to obtain better information on where the whales were spending most of their time in the gulf, the researchers first plotted sighting data from the whale-watch boat. They also flew over 2300 nautical miles to survey the coast between Auckland and Whangarei. While in the air, they only spotted five whales, which confirmed their understanding from the

earlier Baker and Madon work that the density of whales was greatest in the inner Hauraki Gulf. They then overlaid the whale sighting data with shipping routes into the Auckland port and the 'two things overlapped perfectly. The whales are pretty much, year round, right in the path of where all the ships have to funnel into the gulf to enter the port of Auckland. It was exciting to find that out. We now knew that we couldn't re-route traffic to avoid the whales. So we needed to look at how to slow the ships down.'

At that time 'many of the ships coming and going from the Hauraki Gulf were doing around 20 knots. International research indicates that there is a 100 per cent chance of the whale dying if hit at that speed. This is consistent with what we've found. There's been no known whale in the gulf that's survived a large vessel strike. However, if a vessel is travelling at less than 10 knots and hits the whale, then it has a 75 per cent chance of surviving. For this reason we recommended slowing speeds down to 10 knots or less.'

Rochelle wanted to understand more about the behaviour of the whales and so she decided to attach D-tags to several individuals. The D-tag is a suction cup that records the depth and speed of dives, as well as the pitch and roll of the whale and any sounds that it makes. The tag stays on for up to 20 hours, then loses its suction and pops up onto the surface. The scientists retrieve the floating tag and download the information from it. That was the easy part. The biggest challenge was getting the tag on the whales in the first place.

'Whales have a really big personal space, so once you get within about 30 metres of them, they're not thrilled that

Left: This Bryde's whale was seen floating in the water near Waiheke Island on 31 January 2012. It was then towed to Calypso Bay, Motuihe Island. A necropsy confirmed that the whale had been killed by ship strike. (Rochelle Constantine)

Right: University of Auckland marine mammal scientist Dr Rochelle Constantine has spent the last few years trying to better understand the reason why so many Bryde's whales in the Hauraki Gulf are being killed by ship strike. (Paul Ensor)

you're there. We had an 8-metre-long carbon-fibre pole that's flexible. While someone was driving the boat, one of the research team would brace themselves in the front holding the pole with the tag hanging off the end, just hoping that the whale would surface and its back would come up close by, so we could pop the tag on. It has four suction feet so it just sucks onto the whale. There was some very colourful language with the many near misses we had! A lot of whales surfaced, saw the boat, decided it was too close and dived again. But we did manage to get seven deployments.'

The tags provided some critical information about the whales. 'We found that over 90 per cent of their time was spent between the surface and 12 metres down and that's the answer to why they get hit by ships. The large ships' draft is around 12.5 metres and most ships are around 8 to 10 metres. These whales are spending most of their time in that area, even though the water underneath them is 40 or 50 metres deep. They're coming even closer to the surface during the night-time, so putting an extra watch on the ships to look for the whales is not going to work. In the end, there is only one solution: the ships need to slow down and now, thankfully, they are.'

Seals that, 'It is a pity that the cessation of whaling activity in New Zealand, although affording protection to this species, also prevents us from obtaining more information on the distribution and movements of the animal.'[13]

It wasn't until 1999 that any systematic study was made of the Hauraki Gulf's special whales. Marine mammal scientist Dr Alan Baker had become interested in the species while working for the Department of Conservation. 'I'd been out on the gulf a few times and had seen these whales. I knew the history of whaling at Great Barrier and I thought it was about time that somebody looked at them. So I raked up some money and got sponsorship from various firms and spent three years doing that. We spent two years flying from Cape Colville to North Cape and back, zigzagging across the gulf.'[14]

The research confirmed that the whales were present within the gulf throughout the year, but generally in small numbers. They were often seen alone, or in small groups of up to five individuals, feeding on schools of small fish, such as pilchards, mackerel and mullet. The animals were spotted more frequently in the Hauraki Gulf than anywhere else along the coast, although there was also a clump of sightings in the Bay of Islands. Within the gulf itself, the whales preferred the inner reaches, where there was a concentration of plankton and small fish.[15]

Dr Baker reported that, whilst flying along the inside of Great Barrier Island, 'we came across six or seven whales feeding on krill there one day. It was the most beautiful sight.' From his observations, Dr Baker concluded that: 'The population wasn't that big, probably a maximum of 200 animals . . . so I think it should be managed very carefully.'[16]

The presence of the whales in the Hauraki Gulf, along with pods of common dolphins, attracted marine mammal tourism entrepreneur Steve Stembridge and his partner Louise to set up a whale- and dolphin-watching enterprise there in 2000. They had been trailblazers in the marine tourism industry, setting up the first dolphin-watching business in the Bay of Islands in 1991. But tragically, three months after the new Dolphin Explorer business got going in the gulf, Steve died from a brain haemorrhage. The business is still successfully operating under the name Auckland Whale and Dolphin Safari.

Since settling in Leigh nearly 20 years ago, in a house overlooking Ōmaha Bay, Tony Enderby started logging sightings of Bryde's whales in the bay. 'The number of whales has dropped away dramatically over the last six to eight years. With that, we are not seeing the gannet work-ups or big numbers of common dolphins in the bay. This coincides with a different sort of fishing boat in the bay collecting baitfish with a seine net. We used to see a couple of thousand gannets working out there, but the numbers have taken a plunge in the last five to six years.'[17]

It was in a report Dr Baker and Dr Bénédicte Madon produced on the Bryde's whales in 2007 that the issue of ship strike was first formally raised. Large freight and cruise ships were transiting the Hauraki Gulf and their large hulls were sailing through the very waters frequented by the whales.

A total of eighteen Bryde's whales are known to have died from ship strike in the Hauraki Gulf since 1996. The real toll is probably more, due to early poor record keeping and the likelihood that many whales sink before they are spotted. Scientists have concluded that the only practical way of reducing the risk to the whales is to reduce the speed of ships. Responding to this, in September 2013, Ports of Auckland issued a voluntary protocol that advised ships to reduce speed where possible when transiting through the Hauraki Gulf. Since then there has been one whale death, in September 2014, when a male whale was found washed up on Poutawa Beach, near Pākiri. An autopsy confirmed that it had been hit by a ship.[18]

Ships have now slowed down, with speeds almost a quarter slower, two years after the protocol was launched. Ports of Auckland is now aiming for an average speed of under 11 knots and this should significantly reduce the risk to the whales.

At times, up to 50 Bryde's whales can be found in the gulf, out of a larger population of around 150 that live along the north-east coast. The population has been identified as nationally critical by the Department of Conservation.

Bottlenose dolphins

In the Hauraki Gulf there is a small population of bottlenose dolphins that forms part of a larger group which ranges along the north-eastern coast of the North Island, comprising around 450 individuals. The dolphins live up to 50 years of age and grow to between 1.9 and 3.9 metres long.

The Hauraki Gulf was the location of probably the first and only attempt to keep bottlenose dolphins in captivity in New Zealand. This took place on Auckland's North Shore in May 1964. The project was located at the old Milford swimming pool, part of which was reconfigured

to house the dolphins, with the rest providing for water scooters and swimmers.[19]

Two dolphins were caught off Cape Colville by members of the Reefcombers Underwater Club.[20] Although reports failed to identify their species, they were almost certainly bottlenose dolphins. The pair were brought back to Milford and housed in the seawater pool. But several days later, when the water became fouled and the sluice gate was opened for flushing, one of the dolphins escaped. The animal had managed to squeeze through a rusted iron grille, down a large pipe and into the estuary.

A few days later, six more dolphins were caught off Great Barrier Island and brought back to the dolphin pool. Their arrival appeared to raise the spirits of the lone captive dolphin who 'had not eaten for six days and appeared to be listless and unsettled'.[21] But only two weeks later, the dolphin pool promoters decided to release all the animals. Dolphin trainer Mrs J Shannon explained that 'the main reason we decided to abandon the project was because the dolphins do not appear to be happy in the pool . . . Over the last two days they have been less active and have been swimming by themselves. They are still not feeding properly.'[22] Fortunately for the dolphins, they were released before they died. The failed venture was never revived.

Little is actually known about the bottlenose dolphins in the Hauraki Gulf. Research undertaken by Massey

There is a small population of bottlenose dolphins in the Hauraki Gulf that forms part of a larger group ranging along the north-eastern coast of the North Island. They appear to use the gulf as a nursery ground for their calves. (Auckland Whale and Dolphin Safari)

University marine biologist Sarah Dwyer, between 2011 and 2013, indicates that the waters off the west coast of Great Barrier Island are particularly important for around 170 bottlenose dolphins. These animals use the area all year round and are found in pods averaging 35 individuals, which is large for this species in New Zealand. Most of the pods sighted included calves and juveniles, indicating that this is an area where the dolphins bring up their young. Dwyer concluded that the area was 'a potential hotspot for bottlenose dolphins of the New Zealand North Island population'.[23] Even though this area is important, many of the dolphins swim further afield, with earlier research showing that the Bay of Islands is an important part of the range of at least some of the Hauraki Gulf population.[24]

Care may be needed to ensure that the dolphins can continue to flourish in the gulf. Potential threats include vessels that disturb or hit the dolphins and disruption to their food supply by fishing activity. As Dwyer noted, 'the location of these animals appears to be strongly linked with where their prey are found. What surprised me is the lack of information about the prey. Fisheries research tends to focus on larger and more commercially viable stocks. It's concerning that species such as pilchards are commercially fished, but yet we know hardly anything about their ecology. If these prey stocks decline, we may also lose the dolphins and whales here.'[25]

The bottlenose dolphins throughout New Zealand, including those that inhabit the Hauraki Gulf, are considered to be nationally endangered.

Common dolphins

Common dolphins are smaller than bottlenose dolphins, there are more of them and they live in larger pods. Scientists have recently estimated that there are several thousand common dolphins using the Hauraki Gulf. They are not considered to be endangered,[26] but, anecdotally, there may be fewer than there used to be. Former Whitianga-based charter-boat operator Richard Simpson observed that 'in the early days of my charter operation [the early 1980s] it was not uncommon to see huge schools of dolphins moving up the coast. I would think there could have been a thousand in some of the schools. Sadly, nowadays one can trawl all day and not see any. Occasionally you see a few.'[27]

Common dolphins were kept in captivity for a time at Ōrewa. In 1969, animal trainer Alan Horobin decided to establish a marineland on land sandwiched between the Ōrewa estuary and the nearby township. One of the highlights was to be a dolphin show. Horobin had worked

at the Napier Marineland, and then at the one established at Mount Maunganui, before deciding to open his own facility in north Auckland.

To catch dolphins for his new pool, Alan teamed up with former All Black Sid Going, whose launch *Kitty Vane* was moored at Tutukākā, two hours' drive north. They attached a large pontoon and cradle, specially designed for dolphin capture, onto the stern of the boat. Once they managed to grasp a common dolphin with a tail grab, they placed it on the lowered pontoon, which was then lifted up to the deck of the boat. The marineland was soon bustling with new inhabitants which, as well as dolphins, included California sea lions, an elephant seal and a fur seal.

In July 1975 Alan was tragically killed in a car accident. Less than a year later, a formal complaint was made to the Minister of Agriculture and Fisheries about the well-being of dolphins at the Ōrewa Marineland. It was alleged that about twelve dolphins had died there over the past twelve months.[28] In October that year Rainbow, the remaining resident captive dolphin, died. The marineland closed its doors to the public soon afterwards and that ended the last episode of marine mammals being held captive in the Hauraki Gulf.

Although they had been kept in captivity, little was known about the Hauraki Gulf common dolphins until

Common dolphins frequent the Hauraki Gulf in large pods. Little is known about population trends but, anecdotally, there appear to be fewer than in the past. (Auckland Whale and Dolphin Safari)

1998, when German marine mammal scientist Dr Dirk Neumann based himself in Mercury Bay to study the dolphin population in the area. He identified 408 individual dolphins in Mercury Bay and 500 in the inner Hauraki Gulf. His re-sighting of some of the dolphins in different locations supported a theory, held by fishermen and dolphin-tour operators in the Bay of Plenty, that the dolphins moved in an annual cycle from the East Cape, north to the Coromandel Peninsula and then offshore and back down to the East Cape. The dolphins were probably travelling with concentrations of fish that were following the movement of the plankton-rich waters.[29]

Marine mammal scientist Dr Karen Stockin, who is based at the Albany campus of Massey University, has also spent many hours out on the water observing common dolphins. She found that they were present all year round in the Hauraki Gulf and were often seen feeding on schools of fish, alongside Bryde's whales and Australasian gannets. In comparison to the common dolphins observed in Mercury Bay by Dr Neumann, the inner Hauraki Gulf population appeared to spend considerably more time foraging and resting, and less time travelling or milling about. This led Dr Stockin to conclude that the area was an important calving and nursery area for the common dolphin population. Along with the bottlenose dolphins, they may have chosen to bring up their young in the Hauraki Gulf, due to its highly productive marine environment that provides a year-round food supply and reduces the need to travel to search for food.[30]

Orca

Orca, or 'killer whales', don't live year round in the Hauraki Gulf, but they visit regularly. These enormous dolphins are part of a small national population of only several hundred. They are an apex predator and are by far the biggest member of the dolphin family, with adults reaching up to 9 metres long. Their most remarkable feature is a very large dorsal fin, proportionally larger than in any other cetacean. In male orca the dorsal fin can reach up to 1.8 metres high.[31]

Marine mammal scientist Dr Ingrid Visser has devoted her life to studying these amazing creatures. In 1992, after completing her master's thesis on commercial oyster production, she decided to focus her doctoral studies on orca. Ingrid set about establishing a photo-identification catalogue, so that individual orca could be recognised and

Dr Ingrid Visser has devoted her adult life to studying orca. She had her first encounter with the enormous dolphins in 1991, in the waters in front of the Leigh Marine Laboratory.

their behaviours and life histories tracked. Her first success was with a photograph that Bay of Islands skipper Steve Whitehouse had taken of an orca in the Waitematā Harbour in 1987. Ingrid matched his image with that of an animal she photographed off Kaikōura — a highly recognisable individual, with a bent dorsal fin and a notch along the front edge — that had been named Corkscrew by fishermen and whale-watching crew.[32] The photographic match was very significant, as it proved that orca moved between the North and South islands. A second match three weeks later confirmed that orca did indeed return to the same place over time. Having received a call about an orca sighted off Auckland, Ingrid managed to photograph it and confirmed that it was the same individual that Whitehouse had seen in 1987, in a similar location. Ingrid called this animal Nicky, because there was a large nick out of the trailing edge of its dorsal fin.[33]

In the Hauraki Gulf, as around the rest of the North Island, Ingrid found that orca most commonly hunted rays, including the eagle, long-tailed and short-tailed species that are often found in the muddy reaches of shallow inlets.

Orca regularly visit the Hauraki Gulf and can often be seen hunting stingray up shallow estuaries. (Auckland Whale and Dolphin Safari)

Ingrid saw the orca use various techniques to catch the rays, including digging up the mud with their rostrum or 'snout', doing head stands to dive to the bottom, rolling on their sides, releasing underwater bubbles and flipping the rays upside down. She also observed orca 'throwing stingrays around like frisbees', flinging them from animal to animal.[34]

Orca can still frequently be seen hunting rays in the shallow inlets of the gulf. They are considered to be nationally critically threatened.

Pilot whales

Every so often, large groups of long-finned pilot whales strand on the shores of the Hauraki Gulf. They are called pilot whales as each pod is thought to follow a pilot in the group. They are in fact dolphins, not whales. It is not known why these highly social animals strand so frequently, but it may be that, as they spend most of their time on the edge of the continental shelf, their echolocation systems are not attuned to shallow, gently sloping terrain. In addition, it has been hypothesised that, once one whale gets into difficulty, the others go to its aid and also strand.[35]

At early strandings, little was done apart from disposing of the carcasses, as there was a paucity of information on

how to rescue the animals. In 1972, 31 pilot whales stranded at Blind Bay, Great Barrier Island. When alerted to the problem, the Ministry of Transport called on the assistance of Bert Subritzky who ran vessels out to the island. Bert motored out to the island with his son-in-law, Alan Moore, battling against a 30-knot easterly, to arrive at the island in the dead of night. The next morning they were greeted with a horrendous smell from the rotting carcasses. Realising that the job of disposing of all the dead dolphins was too big for them, they called on the navy, which dispatched the naval tug *Arataki*.

The first attempt by the navy to cart a carcass out to sea was a failure. They had tied a strop over the ends of the whale's flukes in order to tow the animal. But this caused the carcass to flail wildly from side to side and it took them hours to get far enough out to sea to dispose of the animal. A more effective system was then devised. The flukes were cut off and a hole was made at the base of the tail for the strop to go through. Each carcass was then towed out past Cuvier Island, a job that took over a fortnight.[36]

Fisheries officer Martin Williscroft recalls attending a pilot whale stranding at Pūriri Bay, Tryphena, on 20 March 1984. By this time, more was known about how to rescue stranded animals and an attempt was made to save the pod. Martin was alerted to the stranding at 12.30 am and three hours later was heading out to the Barrier in the little 7.3-metre launch *Moehau*, accompanied by his colleague, Steve Whitehouse, and University of Canterbury

Pilot whales don't live year round in the Hauraki Gulf, but every so often they strand on its shores, as shown here at Cape Colville in December 2009. They are highly gregarious animals and seem reluctant to leave any members of their pod if they get into trouble. (Katrina Knill, Department of Conservation)

marine mammal scientist Steve Dawson. It was rough and waves started pouring over the top of the cabin. But they battled on and, by early morning, they had reached Pūriri Bay. There they found more than 100 pilot whales in the shallows of the beach.[37]

As Martin later recounted, 'there was a mixture of locals, fishermen and NZ Army personnel in the water doing their best to keep the whales afloat, with the local Police officer maintaining order. We were lucky in that none of the whales had actually beached, but we knew time was against us as the tide had started receding.' They managed to turn the whales towards the sea and the pod started heading out of the bay. But '[t]hen, without any apparent reason, after about 400m [metres] the pod turned sharp right, heading into the outer end of Puriri Bay and hard up on the rocky foreshore.' They did their best to head the whales back out to sea, but the animals kept circling back to shore. Things became more desperate as the tide receded. Thirty animals stranded, with the remainder swimming around in waist-deep water.

'Many of the stranded whales were packed tightly together as we were unable to separate them completely when the tide went out. As the heat of the day increased, the whales, particularly those packed tightly together, were showing signs of extreme distress. We tried to separate them by getting sheets under them to lift and drag them apart, but the weight of each whale was too much and they started to die in the heat.' Martin decided to euthanise the remaining stranded animals and 25 were shot.

The surviving whales came into the beach on the next high tide. As darkness fell, Martin pulled every one out of the water. He thought the risk to human life of carrying on the rescue effort in darkness was too high. The next morning there had been more deaths, but around 90 animals were still afloat. They had to find a better way of moving the pilot whales to open water. Overnight, the two Steves had hatched a plan. They would put a tyre inner tube around the tail of a juvenile and slowly tow it out of the bay. This, they hoped, would encourage the rest of the pod to follow, as pilot whales were known to respond to distress calls from fellow pod members. To everyone's relief the plan worked and the pod moved into deeper water. The rescuers formed a wall of boats between the animals and the shore. The pod moved out into the open sea and headed away. 'Absolutely fantastic! Then began the task of collecting the dead whales for burial.'[38]

In August the following year, Martin was able to use the lessons learned from this stranding, when around 450 pilot whales stranded at Kawa Bay on the Barrier. They were able to save around 320 of them. This was the largest recorded stranding of these whales in the gulf.[39]

Story of the Gulf | **Chris Gaskin**

RESEARCHER AND SEABIRD ADVOCATE, WHANGATEAU[40]

Chris has spent many nights with colleagues and volunteers working with seabirds below the lighthouse on Burgess Island in the Mokohinaus. The island has become a research base for studying a number of seabird species, especially their biology, physiology, foraging and migration patterns. Importantly, these seabirds include species that can provide insights into the health of the Hauraki Gulf ecosystem.

However, unlike most of his colleagues studying seabirds, who are career scientists or students, Chris's journey to seabirds has been mainly via a non-academic route. Always interested in art, Chris dropped out of university and, after stints at a variety of jobs, he worked for five years as a wildlife and landscape artist for the New Zealand Forest Service, Lands and Survey and then intermittently for the Department of Conservation. This grew into a career as an illustrator of books, mostly with natural history themes, including a number of children's books. Chris eventually set up his own company specialising in designing museum and visitor-centre exhibits. This varied background nurtured a growing passion for New Zealand's wildlife, particularly seabirds and their environment.

In 2003, with his partner Karen Baird, Chris started running seabird tours in the Hauraki Gulf and other locations around New Zealand. 'What we see in the gulf is quite different from places like Kaikōura or Stewart Island, the three accessible hotspots for New Zealand's seabirds. There is a distinctive suite of birds up here, made all the more special because you're right amongst the islands where they breed. But to see a good range of birds, you need to go out past Te Hauturu-o-Toi/Little Barrier Island and the Mokohinaus Islands to the outer gulf.

'I have spent a lot of time working with storm petrels both here in New Zealand and overseas, but the birds I really enjoy are diving petrels. They are an amazing power-packed little bundle, a bird that fits neatly into your hand. You see them out on the gulf racing about, sometimes like little skipping stones. A team of us working on Burgess Island, led by Graeme Taylor, attached tracking devices to some of them and we found that, after finishing breeding, they migrated deep to the polar front about half to two-thirds the way to Chile. Just picture them racing along — the iconic 'Buzzy Bee' toy comes to mind — little wings like a blur as they cover thousands of kilometres deep into the wild southern ocean. They depart the gulf in

Chris Gaskin has been taking people out to see seabirds in the Hauraki Gulf for over a decade and he remains fascinated by these extraordinary birds.

December and come back in April, doing it remarkably quickly. We were blown away by the results.

'I'm not an academic. Rather I prefer to see myself as an advocate. I enjoy working with others facilitating projects, in particular supporting students and other researchers, bringing talented people together to study the birds.' To this end, Chris with a group of other interested people has set up a trust to advance seabird research in northern New Zealand.

'We see many reports, but for seabirds in New Zealand one plan stands out. Prepared by Graeme Taylor and published by the Department of Conservation in 2000,[41] it set out a comprehensive plan for furthering research and conservation for New Zealand's seabirds. While we've moved on a lot in fifteen years, there's a lot in that plan still to be implemented. Some of it is basic stuff. But we are ticking the boxes.

'The birds breed at different times of the year. Because of the differences between seasons, it's hard to get a handle on changes that have occurred over the twelve years we've been observing them. But certainly there have been significant changes when you compare what we are seeing now with

what people were reporting in the 1980s. One of the biggest differences appears to be that we are losing the big schools of forage fish from the gulf — trevally, kahawai and smaller baitfish — scooped up with increasing efficiency by purse-seine fishing boats. We're swapping a vital resource, which is close to the heart of the dynamic system that is the Hauraki Gulf, for cat food and chicken feed or whatever. The spectacular work-ups that seabirds, dolphins, whales and predatory fish feed in could become a thing of the past.

'On the positive side, we do know a lot more about what's out there. The discovery of the New Zealand storm petrel, a bird thought to be extinct, in gulf waters in 2003 was in itself a staggering event. That we discovered they were breeding on Te Hauturu-o-Toi/Little Barrier Island, within sight of the night-time glow of Downtown Auckland, that was even more remarkable. The eradication of cats and rats from the island was another bonus, for without that happening we may have lost a species without our ever knowing it had been breeding there.

'Looking ahead, I would like to see us develop greater

Left: Birders from the northern hemisphere come to the Hauraki Gulf to see the area's special seabirds. Shown here are birders on a trip out to the Mokohinau Islands with Chris Gaskin.

Top right: The New Zealand storm petrel was thought to be extinct for over a hundred years, but it was recently found breeding on Little Barrier Island. (Neil Fitzgerald)

Bottom right: Chris Gaskin has become involved in supporting seabird research in the Hauraki Gulf. Shown here is a research camp on the Mokohinau Islands and flocks of birds coming back to their burrows after darkness has fallen. (Abe Borker)

understanding about our seabirds and through them the ocean environment, as well as greater respect for them as creatures that are truly remarkable. Just imagine a chick that takes months to develop and the distances its parents cover to find food for it as well as themselves. Then one day that chick will leave its burrow on its own, flying out of the forest or wherever its home was, and out to sea. It has to find its own food in an environment that it's never seen before and survive. One day it will return. Remarkable!'

Buller's shearwaters used to feed on the numerous boil-ups within the Hauraki Gulf, but more recently the birds have been found foraging as far afield as the Chatham Rise, suggesting that their food sources within the gulf have become depleted. (Neil Fitzgerald)

Seabirds

The Hauraki Gulf has an extraordinary wealth of seabirds, supported by its productive marine area, diverse habitats and numerous predator-free islands. Over 80 species have been seen in the region, around 20 per cent of the world's 360 seabird species. Of these, at least 27 species breed in the wider Hauraki Gulf region. The New Zealand fairy tern, Pycroft's petrel, black petrel and Buller's shearwater breed only in the gulf and on islands close by. The New Zealand storm petrel, thought to be extinct for over a hundred years, was recently found breeding on Little Barrier Island, its only known breeding place.[42]

Each island group in the outer Hauraki Gulf is a seabird and biodiversity hotspot. The Mokohinau Islands, north of Little Barrier, are one of those hotspots with twelve seabird species breeding there. Māori living on the islands traditionally harvested the young seabirds. The grey-faced petrel chicks, or ōi (from their call) would be pulled out of their burrows and then preserved in their own oil. Lighthouse keeper Andras Sandager was told that, in December 1888, 3000 young birds were harvested from the islands.[43]

Seabirds spend most of their lives at sea; they only come to land to breed. Although many of the birds travel enormous distances, some to the north and eastern Pacific — to waters off Japan, Hawaii, California and Ecuador — others venturing down to the Polar Front, they return each year to breed in burrows on the gulf's islands. Historically, seabirds would have also bred on New Zealand's mainland, but the destruction of habitats and predation by introduced animals have removed populations from there.

Where once seabirds brought fertility to soils, adding nutrients through the decomposition of guano and dead eggs, chicks and adults, farmers now spread fertiliser, much of it derived from seabird islands elsewhere in the Pacific.

Andras Sandager, who spent six years posted to the Mokohinau Islands lighthouse in the late 1880s, was one of the first Europeans to record detailed observations of bird life in the Hauraki Gulf. His records of seabirds are especially notable. He observed that 'numerous birds visit the islands annually for breeding or other purposes . . . for over a year after the light was first exhibited, many seabirds used to strike the lantern almost every night. This, year after year, has happened less frequently, for whereas formerly dozens of birds might be observed circling round and round the light, in a

The flesh-footed shearwater often gets caught on the hooks of longliners through diving for bait.

direction contrary to that in which the apparatus revolved, till at last they became dazzled, it rarely occurs now (after a lapse of close upon six years), if I except two species, and these only for a short time of the year.' He concluded that the birds had gradually become accustomed to the light. But two species still struck in high numbers: the Cook's petrel on its way to and from breeding sites on Little Barrier Island and the white-faced storm petrel whose last stronghold was a small island at the base of the cliffs below the light.[44]

From the early days of fishing, seabirds have been a problem for longline fishermen. The birds target their bait and get caught on the hooks. The two species most affected are the black petrel and the flesh-footed shearwater. They are thought to be at high risk from both commercial and recreational fishing in the Hauraki Gulf.[45]

Commercial fisherman Dave Kellian remembers, as a boy, fishing with his father and catching birds: 'We didn't have any awareness of ecology — it was the last thing in our thoughts. We just didn't want to hook the birds as, if you caught one, it would float up the line. The birds are only here for five months of the year. The diving petrels are the worst ones. We mostly used to fish inside the gulf and the birds weren't present there during the school season in the summer months, so we sort of avoided them in that respect. But I hate to think how many we killed in those days. We didn't care. We had no awareness.'

When Dave went surface longlining for tuna, he became much more aware of the seabird issue. There was interest from international environmental organisations, and observers were placed on the fishing boats to count how many birds were caught. The seabird issue then gained more profile in the Hauraki Gulf and observers were placed on fishing boats there. The cost of the observers was charged back to the fishing industry.

'There was a group of us who wanted to do things differently, so we started trying to make some changes, coming up with new ideas to avoid catching the birds. We were charged for the observers and we felt we were not getting value for money. So we started to come up with ways to get the numbers down. Tori lines were out there — the Japanese had them — but they didn't work for us initially. Then Janice Molloy turned up at DOC. She was young and keen and probably way out of her depth in some ways. But she changed the situation from "us and them" to working together, just with her enthusiasm and attitude. We started to take ownership of the problem.'

Dave, Janice and others within the fishing industry, government and World Wide Fund for Nature (WWF) provided the impetus behind the formation of Southern Seabird Solutions in July 2002. The organisation works with commercial and recreational fishers to reduce seabird mortality. When baited hooks are deployed, one of the ways to reduce seabird by-catch is to use tori lines. These consist of lines with streamers attached, which are strung over the setting area from a high part of the vessel, with a buoy or weight attached to the end to create drag. The streamers deter seabirds from diving onto the baits.

'It got to the stage where I was only catching two or three seabirds a year. This was through setting lines at night and using a tori line and weighted lines. But I was paying $10,000 to $12,000 a year on levies for seabird observers, so I thought that, in the long term, I needed to come up with a bolt-on solution.' Dave started experimenting while he was at sea. He discovered that birds wouldn't dive for bait if it was set 10 metres below the surface. So he approached a mate who was an engineer. Together they started constructing a device which would enable bait to be set at depth rather than from the surface. There were teething problems, and Dave nearly lost a couple of fingers, but the idea of an underwater setting capsule continues to look promising and the technology is still being developed.

Third generation fisherman, longliner Adam Clow, has also been active in addressing the seabird issue. Adam is 28 years old and has been skippering his own boat for four years. 'When you start setting hooks at dawn, the seabirds are feeding as well, so it was always part of my role to run a tori line to mitigate against catching seabirds. But as time went on there was more pressure to do the right thing around seabirds.

'Then I had the opportunity to go up Mount Hobson on Great Barrier Island. I went with a couple of other skippers, some deckhands and people from Southern Seabird Solutions. We climbed up the hill and helped tag black petrel chicks. It was personal and emotional to hold the birds. Since then I've been in contact with the Southern Seabird Solutions guys off and on every month, talking with them and discussing new ideas and techniques. I've also been engaging with other fishermen to see how they're getting on.'

There are also concerns that, in addition to being threatened by hooks, some of the birds might now be struggling to find enough food in the gulf. Research on the Buller's shearwater, a species that breeds on the Poor Knights Islands but feeds in the gulf, has indicated a significant change in breeding behaviour since the 1970s. At that time, the incubation period for eggs was four to seven days and there were huge flocks of the shearwaters feeding on shoaling fishes in the gulf. The birds are not deep divers, so they rely on the larger predatory fish to drive the baitfish to the surface. Now the incubation period for the eggs is fourteen days and the parents aren't foraging in the gulf any more, but are travelling 3860 kilometres into the Pacific Ocean and down to the Chatham Rise. This may be due to a reduction in the huge schools of trevally that used to frequent the gulf.[46]

Another bird species which has seen significant population changes in the Hauraki Gulf is the red-billed gull. In 1946 there were around 10,000 pairs nesting on Burgess Island in the Mokohinau group. In 2014 only 150 pairs were counted on the island. Scientists think that the change is also likely to be related to a reduction in the food supply in the surrounding waters.[47]

Migratory shorebirds

At one time, bar-tailed godwits were hunted (a practice known as curlew shooting), but this was stopped in 1941. In its place burgeoned the pastime of birdwatching. The new interest was led by Richard Sibson, an English classics teacher based at King's College, Auckland, who brought a passion for birds with him to New Zealand.[48]

In 1940 Sibson undertook a bicycle tour of the Firth of Thames, passing through Kawakawa Bay and down the coast to Miranda (Pūkorokoro). There he was amazed to find not only the godwits (which were migrants from the northern hemisphere), but also the wrybill with its amazing curved beak and South Island pied oystercatchers.[49]

The wrybills and oystercatchers breed in the riverbeds of the South Island and then arrive at Miranda just after Christmas. The oystercatchers leave to return south in June, the wrybills slightly later. The bar-tailed godwits and red knots arrive in September and October and leave the following March. They stop off at the Yellow Sea on the lengthy flight to the Arctic to breed.

The discovery of these fascinating birds placed Miranda on the birdwatching map. But it was an hour's drive from Auckland and there was nowhere to stay overnight. Beth Brown, a keen birder from Papakura, started to think that building a lodge near a wading bird roost would be a good idea. Miranda seemed the obvious place. Here, near the old lime works, members of the public could view the birds on the shell banks. By 1975, the Miranda Naturalists' Trust had been established, with the aim to 'establish a bird observatory and accommodation lodge on the coast at Miranda'.[50]

The trust approached the owner of the old lime-works site, Allan Lane, and members successfully negotiated a 50-year lease that allowed them to access the site and construct a building on it. Members then set about raising the funds necessary to establish an observatory and accommodation block. By 1976, they had raised $10,000 and the building had been designed. They sought permission from the Ministry of Works and Development to start construction.

Bar-tailed godwits used to be hunted, but now they are appreciated by birdwatchers. They arrive at Miranda-Pūkorokoro in September or October each year and leave the following March to head back to the Arctic. Male birds are shown here at Kaiaua with the smaller red knots. (Keith Woodley)

But then two major setbacks arose. First, the ministry would not grant permission, due to opposition from the Wildlife Service based on the potential impact of the activity on the birds. Second, most of the trust's funding was frozen due to the crash of Securitibank.[51]

This did not deter trust members, who kept on fundraising. Eventually, in 1986, alternative land was purchased at Miranda and work to establish a centre was under way. It was formally opened in 1990.

Although the trust cannot afford to do research on the birds themselves, they do offer free accommodation to students undertaking research projects. Trust members are part of an informal network around the 'international flyway', the route that the birds take every year. They have participated in surveys, counting shorebirds in New Zealand, as well as in China and Korea. These have revealed some disturbing trends, including a decline in the numbers of godwits visiting Miranda and a sharp decline in red knots. Somewhat surprisingly, given that the braided river habitat in Canterbury is under pressure, the wrybill population appears stable.[52]

Interestingly, there was a huge increase in the population of pied oystercatchers from the 1960s to the 1980s, but it then started to plateau. It is now declining sharply. This may be explained by the fact that the birds were fully protected in 1940 and had been hunted prior to that. As the population grew, they started spreading out from their natural habitat in stream beds onto pasture. As more land was brought into pasture, there were more breeding opportunities. The decline is currently unexplained and seems to be unrelated to habitat availability. One possible

explanation is the expansion and intensification of dairying, particularly in Canterbury and Southland. These regions are a stronghold for the species and cows are much more likely to trample on the nests than sheep.[53]

Although there have been marked declines in the bird populations in the Firth of Thames, this is not the case on the Manukau Harbour, another very important bird area. The difference between the two areas may be the expansion of mangroves around the southern firth, which is reducing the mudflat area available to the birds for foraging, while also impacting on high-tide roosts.[54] Another related factor may be the high levels of sedimentation in the area. The birds eat a variety of shellfish, crabs and marine worms, with bar-tailed godwits eating mainly worms, red knots eating small bivalves and oystercatchers eating various shellfish. The sediment could be reducing the abundance and diversity of these food species.[55]

The high productivity of the Hauraki Gulf's waters has attracted a wealth of marine mammal and seabird species, many breeding and bringing up their young in the area. We still know very little about many of them. Some, such as the humpback whale, are making a reappearance in the gulf, but sadly others are in decline.

Story of the Gulf | **Keith Woodley**

MANAGER, PŪKOROKORO/MIRANDA SHOREBIRD CENTRE[56]

Keith Woodley grew up about as far from the Hauraki Gulf as you can get — in Invercargill. He is an artist and developed an interest in drawing interior murals. He found animals and birds to be excellent subjects. The more he used images of birds from books as the basis for his artwork, the more he became interested in the actual birds living outside his window. 'I was born again as a birder.'

Keith was living on the Kapiti Coast when the manager's position came up at the Miranda Shorebird Centre in 1993. He was between jobs and was keen to pursue his interest in birds, so he packed his bags and moved north. He had no idea for how long he would be at Miranda, maybe a few weeks or some months. Keith started off on an unpaid basis, but then the trust managed to secure some Taskforce Green funding for his modest salary. The subsidy was for six months only, but then it was rolled over for another six months. With Keith living on-site, it was possible to open the centre seven days a week. People started dropping by. Initially it was mainly members of the trust, but then members of the general public who were driving past would stop. Miranda started to get on the birding map, a critical mass of visitors built up and the place thrived.

International visitors started to drop by. 'The wrybill is the only bird with a curved bill and you need to come to New Zealand to see it. Pūkorokoro is the only place to see a big flock. So anyone coming to New Zealand who is interested in birds, if they have done any research beforehand, will have found Pūkorokoro turning up in that research.'

The first few years were a solitary time for Keith. There were only a few visitors and he was living alone. But it gave him an opportunity to get to know the place well, the coast, where the birds were and how the birds used their environment.

Keith has noticed quite a few changes over the 22 years he has now been based at the centre. 'I guess the biggest change over the time is the decline in the numbers of birds here. This is true for most populations of birds, sadly, but is certainly true for the Arctic migrants. I've also noticed the dynamic nature of the Pūkorokoro coast and the chenier plain [shell-barrier beach] formation. The pace at which a chenier plain establishes and expands along the coast is astonishing. When I first came here, the bird hide on the coast looked out over the embayment to the outer shell bank. The embayment

Keith Woodley has spent more than 20 years running the Miranda-Pūkorokoro Shorebird Centre which has developed into a very popular visitor facility.

was a clear mudflat; inside it on a high tide were about 10,000 birds. The embayment is now full of mangroves and the shell bank has moved a kilometre down the coast. So the expansion of the chenier plain and the growth of mangroves are the standout features of change over the past 22 years.'

Currently, one of the most exciting aspects of Keith's work is engagement in the international flyway. 'The Firth of Thames is an integral link in a chain of habitats from here to the far tundra of northern Alaska and Russia.' So the welfare of the birds is dependent not only on the health of the Firth

Top: Miranda-Pūkorokoro attracts many birders who are keen to see the birds that migrate from the Arctic, as well as unusual indigenous species such as the wrybill.

Right: The wrybill has a very unusual curved beak. It breeds in the braided rivers of the South Island and migrates to Miranda-Pūkorokoro for the winter. (Keith Woodley)

of Thames, but on habitat in the other parts of the flyway. This year, Keith is on his sixth visit to China. He is also taking part in a project in South Korea to document the impact of major development on the bird populations. There is also growing engagement with North Korea and Keith visited there this year.

Keith has also continued his interest in art and he is working towards an exhibition of bird drawings. He has made many close friends through his work at Miranda, both at the centre but also around the world. His role has brought lots of special moments. 'Most days, on the turning high tide, a harrier or something puts all the birds up so you get massive formations of birds flying around overhead. It is always a stunning spectacle, even though I have witnessed it countless times every year. I love watching the wrybill flock do aerobatics, tight formation flying and twirling and twisting.'

Chapter 14
Scientific understanding

Over the centuries, Māori had developed a sophisticated understanding of the gulf's marine environment, obtained through detailed observation and experience passed down the generations. It was a systems-based understanding that recognised the integral interconnections between land and sea, and between people and the natural world.

When Europeans first arrived in the Hauraki Gulf, they brought with them an understanding of a very different marine system, in their case based on the northern latitudes. The species in the gulf were new to them, as were the conditions. They also brought with them another approach to understanding the natural world: one based on the 'scientific method' that used measurement and experimentation. Initially, scientific equipment and approaches were rudimentary. But as methods improved, so did our scientific understanding, not only of the species that live within the Hauraki Gulf, but of key linkages between fish and habitat, between the sea and the land, and between the gulf and the wider oceanic environment.

Over the years, there has been a wealth of scientific research undertaken within the Hauraki Gulf, by a large number of scientists. This chapter surveys only a small fraction of the work, focusing on some key threads, and it profiles just a few of those who have contributed to our understanding of this extraordinary place.

Early fish records

Some of the first systematic European observations of fish in the Hauraki Gulf were undertaken during the late 1880s. This was by lighthouse keepers who, on a daily basis, observed the sea and often caught fish to supplement their diet. The Marine Department attempted to collect information on fish life by distributing printed forms to all the lighthouse stations and asking the keepers to record the marine species they had seen or caught. But the quality of the information varied, depending on the interest and ability of those manning the stations.[1]

At that time, there were four manned lighthouse stations in the Hauraki Gulf, at the Mokohinau, Tiritiri Matangi, Bean Rock and

Snapper at Cape Rodney-Ōkakari Point Marine Reserve. (Tony and Jenny Enderby)

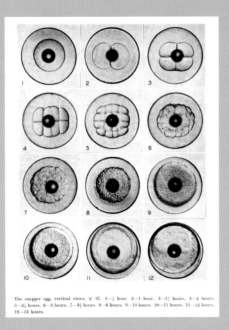
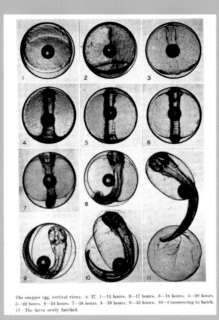
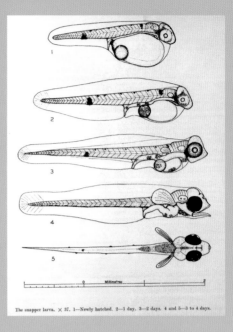

In the late 1940s, marine scientist Morrison Cassie undertook the first detailed examination of the early development stages of snapper. Shown here are his photographs of the snapper egg developing and the juvenile hatching. (R M Cassie, Royal Society of New Zealand)

Cuvier islands. Unsurprisingly, the most commonly recorded fish was snapper, which was easily recognised and found at all the stations. Examination of the stomach contents revealed that the fish ate shellfish, such as mussels and barnacles, as well as small crustaceans like crayfish, crabs and shrimps. Their ova were reported as 'ripe' from November to February, correctly indicating that this was the spawning season.[2]

The largest range of fish species was recorded at the Mokohinau Islands. This included hāpuku, kahawai, snapper, kelp fish (hiwihiwi), barracouta, trevally, maomao, rock cod, spotty, parrotfish, leatherjacket and blue drummer (korokoropounamu). Also of particular note, in the lighthouse keepers' records, was the capture of numerous sharks from the Pōnui Passage.

Snapper research

Although snapper had been an important species for commercial and recreational fishing for well over a century, it wasn't until the late 1940s that any systematic study of its life cycle was made. The work was undertaken by R Morrison Cassie, who was at that time employed as a marine biologist in the fisheries branch of the Marine Department.

Cassie was able to utilise the government fisheries research vessel *Ikatere* to catch snapper during the spawning season. He expressed eggs and milt from the fish and mixed them together in a jar of clean seawater. He then observed what happened as the fertilised eggs developed.

When the eggs first emerged from the body of the female fish, they were small colourless spheres of less than 1 millimetre in diameter, which floated to the surface. After 20 hours a distinct embryo could be seen, with a head and tail visible after 26 hours. In slightly less than two days, the embryo was ready to hatch. It achieved this by thrashing its tail to rupture the egg membrane, allowing it to escape.[3]

After first escaping from the egg, the embryo's tail remained curved and so the larva swam around in circles. Eventually, about a day later, the tail straightened out so the embryo could swim in a straight line. The newly hatched snapper initially clustered near the surface of the water, but within 24 hours the tiny fish had swum to the bottom of the container.[4]

Cassie's observations came to a halt after four days, which appeared to be the maximum length of time that the larvae could survive without ingesting food, something he was unsuccessful in providing them with under laboratory conditions.

Larry Paul, who worked in the Fisheries Research Division of the Ministry of Agriculture and Fisheries

Snapper movements in the Hauraki Gulf[5]

During the 2006–2007 summer season, Dr Darren Parsons, Dr Mark Morrison and colleagues at National Institute of Water and Atmospheric Research (NIWA) caught, tagged and released 10,000 snapper in the Hauraki Gulf. Of these, 900 were returned by fishers. An analysis of the returned fish indicated a significant difference between snapper that live around rocky reefs and those that lived further out in the gulf above the sea floor.

The snapper that live in shallow reef areas were found to be largely residential, being mainly caught only a few hundred metres from where they had been tagged. In addition, the results indicated that there were fewer snapper living in these areas and a higher percentage of them were caught, when compared to snapper living further afield. This means that snapper are more likely to be fished out of local reef areas and, if this happens, they may be slow to replenish.

In contrast, snapper living over soft sediment areas of seabed ranged further, with a median distance travelled of 19 kilometres. Most remained within the gulf, but some went further afield, including one caught off Gisborne.

These findings are consistent with more recent research, which has identified two different groups of snapper in the Hauraki Gulf, with different life histories — something that had been suggested by fishermen for years. Close examination of the physical and chemical features of the snapper identified a distinct highly mobile group of fish which travel long distances and feed at higher levels of the food chain. Fish in this group have narrower bodies and a greater number of gill rakers — small projections within the gills that increase fishing efficiency for small waterborne prey.[6]

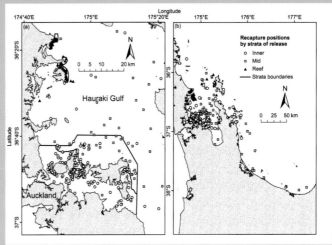

Top right: Tagging programmes help track the movements of snapper. This image shows a tag inserted into a snapper before release. (Darren Parsons)

A tagging exercise undertaken in 2006–2007 indicated that most snapper do not travel far and remain in the gulf. (Parsons D M et al, 2011, *Canadian Journal of Fisheries and Aquatic Sciences*, 68(4): 632-642)

(previously the Marine Department), undertook further investigations into snapper during the 1970s. His research indicated that the number of larval and juvenile snapper surviving to adulthood each year varied considerably and in some years there were much stronger 'year classes' than in others. This in turn affected the success of fishing, with strong year classes providing more abundant adult snapper for a time, then catch rates dropping when weaker year classes came to predominate.[7]

Paul also investigated the spatial distribution of juvenile snapper and found that one-year-old snapper were most abundant in the shallow waters of the south-western fringes of the gulf, with the young fish moving out into deeper waters to populate much of the gulf during their second year.[8]

Further work by other scientists on identifying snapper spawning and nursery grounds confirmed that they were concentrated in the inner gulf. A survey of snapper eggs, undertaken by Dr John Zeldis and his colleague Dr Chris

Francis in late 1992, found that the largest concentrations were in the outer Firth of Thames, between the eastern end of Waiheke Island and Manaia Harbour. Other dense areas of eggs were found on the western fringes of the gulf and off the south-west coast of Great Barrier Island.[9]

Dr Malcolm Francis, who was based at the Leigh Marine Laboratory, undertook further research into the life cycle of snapper. He investigated the development of juveniles and concluded that water temperature probably had 'a major influence on the growth rate of snapper'. In years where the water temperature was higher, spawning started earlier and the juvenile fish grew more quickly, resulting in bigger fish for that year class.[10]

Further research on snapper focused on better understanding their diet, movement and growth rates. Tagging experiments were undertaken to identify how far snapper ranged, but these initially proved unsuccessful because of the poor returns. Of 8000 snapper tagged between 1952 and '63, only 43 were returned by fishers. However, these did indicate that a significant portion of the snapper population was resident in the gulf and did not travel far, findings that were confirmed by later research. The greatest distance travelled by a recaptured gulf snapper was 260 nautical miles to Gisborne.[11]

Investigation of snapper gut content has revealed that the fish have a varied diet, including nearly 100 different prey species. These include crustaceans, worms, sea urchins, shellfish and small fish. The diet changes as the fish develop, with small snapper mainly feeding on soft-bodied organisms, such as worms and shrimps, and larger fish eating more hard-bodied organisms like crabs and shellfish.[12] This wide diet helps to explain why snapper have been so resilient to fishing pressure in the Hauraki Gulf, despite habitat changes. Their feeding adaptability means that they can change their diet depending on food availability. Snapper have even been found to eat large quantities of introduced species, such as Asian date mussels.[13]

Snapper are slow growing and long lived, potentially reaching up to 60 years of age and 17 kilograms in weight. In the Hauraki Gulf, they grow more slowly than elsewhere in the country, but the reason for this is not known. After four to five years, the fish reach around 30 centimetres in length, by which time they are sexually mature and have few predators other than humans.

The adult fish are extremely productive. They spawn many times over the warm summer months, with the smaller fish producing tens of thousands of eggs each season and the larger fish several million. Older fish are therefore important for their spawning potential. As well as producing many more eggs than smaller fish, their eggs are larger, which most likely improves the survival and growth of their offspring. This is important, as many snapper eggs are eaten by larger plankton, and the juveniles are preyed on by various other fish.[14]

In 2014, more than 60 years after scientists had first started researching snapper in the Hauraki Gulf, Dr Parsons and seventeen other scientists summarised what was known about the species. They started off their review acknowledging that snapper 'are one of the most widely studied fish species in New Zealand', but somewhat surprisingly, until then, 'a comprehensive review of snapper life history has not been conducted'.[15] After describing what had been discovered about the life cycle and behaviour of these fish, the scientists identified potential threats to healthy fish populations.

One of the most obvious threats was the direct effect of fishing. It is thought that, by 1988, harvesting had reduced the snapper population in the Hauraki Gulf to as little as 10 per cent of its original size. The stock increased to around 24 per cent in 2010, as a result of the government imposing reductions on commercial harvest levels through reducing the total allowable catch, and lowering the bag limit for recreational fishers. In 1986 recreational fishers had been allowed to take 30 snapper a day, but by 1997, this had reduced to just nine. A decline in snapper stocks after 2010, in the face of sharply increasing recreational fishing pressure, resulted in a further reduction of the bag limit to seven in April 2014.[16] Habitat degradation was also thought to have an impact on snapper productivity.

Seabed communities

One significant early study of the gulf's marine habitats was undertaken by Arthur Powell who was Assistant Director at the Auckland War Memorial Museum. Although trained as a commercial artist, Powell's real passion was shells and he became an avid collector. He published his first scientific paper at the age of 20 and his expertise in the area was recognised through his appointment to the museum eight years later. In 1937 he published the notable book *The Shellfish of New Zealand*,[17] followed by the more comprehensive *New Zealand Mollusca* in 1979.

Powell's interest in shells led him to undertake a study of

The use of TBT in anti-fouling paints from the late 1960s killed off a number of shellfish species in the Waitematā Harbour, including the Arabic volute (*Alcithoe arabica*). The volute is shown here in several of its life stages starting with the egg attached to another shell.

the living mollusc communities of the inner Hauraki Gulf. Over the decade between 1926 and 1936, he collected 138 samples from the seabed, using a small dredge.[18] Powell then analysed the samples, to identify what species were present and to group them into different community types. The most widely distributed community, which covered much of the inner gulf, was dominated by the common heart urchin (*Echinocardium australe*), a bivalve shellfish (*Dosinia lambata*) and the rose-coloured brittle starfish (*Amphiura rosea*).

The channels, where water was faster flowing, had developed mounds of shells and gravels and these supported a much more abundant and diverse assortment of life. On average, there were 39 species in each sample from these areas, compared with only 7.3 on the silty bottom.

Powell's work was to provide an important benchmark for later scientific research designed to identify what changes had occurred in the marine environment since the 1930s.

During the 1990s, a group of scientists headed by Dr Bruce Hayward undertook a review of the ecological changes that had occurred in the central Waitematā Harbour. They noted significant changes over the 159 years since Auckland had been established on its shores, one of the most obvious being the physical modification of the shoreline. In terms of differences in marine life, they found evidence of long-gone dense beds of large trough shells, with associated large scallops, horse mussels, cockles and the slender spindle-shaped Arabic volute shells, which once

extended right around the intertidal fringes of the central harbour. The precise reason for their demise was unclear, but it was thought likely to be due to a combination of increased mud, freshwater run-off and pollution.[19]

Ōrākei Basin, in the inner part of Hobson Bay, had undergone dramatic change, caused by the ponding of water behind the control gates installed during the 1920s. Prior to this, the floor of the basin consisted of firm shelly sand and mud populated 'with abundant cockles, wedge shells and patches of pipi, with numerous mud crabs, polychaete [bristle] worms, snails and other bivalves'. By 1996 the basin floor 'was largely covered in a thick layer (av. 30-40 cm) of soft, dark mud draped in a mat of filamentous, seasonal red and green seaweeds. Most of the original biota had disappeared or been greatly reduced in number and extent . . . 250 million introduced Asian mussels were the main animals living in the surface mud and weed, with huge introduced Pacific oysters growing out of the mud in a belt close to the shore. Shoreline rocks and other hard surfaces were covered by an introduced barnacle (*Balanus amphitrite*) and a patch of introduced cord grass grew near the boat ramp.'[20]

Other changes to the Waitematā Harbour have been caused by toxins. From the late 1960s, tributyltin (TBT) was commonly used in the antifouling of vessels. The substance leached off the hulls of vessels and washed into the sea from boat wash-down areas, accumulating in the sea-floor sediments. It was later discovered that the substance has a significant

Story of the Gulf | **Margaret Morley**

SEASHELL SCIENTIST AND COLLECTOR, AUCKLAND[21]

Margaret arrived in New Zealand from the United Kingdom in 1961 and met her husband soon thereafter. He was a keen yachtie and they spent many summer weekends and family holidays out on the waters of the gulf and along the Northland coast. They also bought a bach at Oneroa Beach, Waiheke Island. Margaret started collecting shells from the beach there, bought a book to help better identify them, and became hooked. She joined a shell club and has never looked back.

It is the wide variety of shellfish, and the ecological niches that they fill, that so fascinates Margaret. There are deposit feeders, such as the wedge shell, that digs itself deep into the sediment and puts two siphons up to the surface, one for sucking in detritus and the other for blowing out waste. 'You can see a little mark on the sand, a bit like a bird's foot, and that shows you it's there. Some grazers, such as cat's eye, eat microscopic seaweed. There are lots of seaweeds that are comprised of single cells and they reproduce between the tides. A lot of grazers eat seaweed deposits in the rock pools. Then there are the actively hunting carnivores. For example, the rock shell will sit right over something like the poor cat's eyes until it has to release and open. Then it is eaten. The scavengers hunt what's dying. These are the small darker whelks. They are the cleaners of the beach.'

Margaret has found more than 300 species of shells at Oneroa Beach. But the place has changed significantly over the past 50 years. 'When I first went down to Oneroa in the 1960s and '70s, there were just a few little baches on the beach. Now there are big houses and permanent residents. There's heaps of freshwater coming down onto the beach in drains. Even if it's not polluted, freshwater is detrimental to marine life. Marine species don't like sudden inputs of freshwater. It also carves a channel in the beach and carries sand away. People drive cars down onto the beach to launch boats now and that crushes the juvenile pipi that live higher up.'

One intertidal area, that has been less impacted, is Fletchers Bay on the northern coast of the Coromandel Peninsula. In December 2013, Margaret and colleague Dr Bruce Hayward went to Fletchers Bay and walked around to the next beach. 'The reef there was just amazing: lovely clear water, exposed beach and big "turnable" boulders and slabs. There were sponges and nudibranches [colourful sea slugs]. There was a trumpet shell, with orange and black striped tentacles, hunting for cushion stars. There were many different species of seaweeds. A lot of microscopic molluscs live on seaweeds, so I wash them off and identify them later. If you wash a small rock in a bag of seawater, things will also drop off. When you put them under the microscope, it's another world. They are as beautiful as some of the big shells. If you go to an area which is silted up, they're just not there.'

Margaret has been particularly concerned about changes at Howick Beach, close to where she lives. 'When my children were young, you could look in the rock pools at Howick and they were clean. Now they're all clogged up with flocculated [clumped up] silt. There are few microscopic species there now. Fine silt is a disaster for small marine creatures. You can sometimes see the silt coming from the Tāmaki River. When it lands it can get quite nasty, depositing half a metre of soft silt over the intertidal area. It's not surprising things don't like it. I recently took my grandson out there and he stepped into what looked to him like firm mud and he almost disappeared into the sludge.'

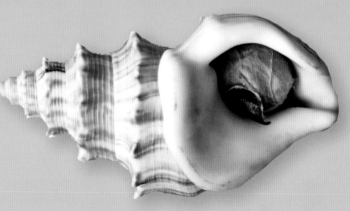

Top: Margaret Morley has been particularly concerned about the changes in marine life at Howick Beach, close to where she lives. She remembers taking her children to explore the rock pools during the late 1960s, when they were clean, but they are now clogged up with silt.

Right: The ostrich foot (*Struthiolaria papulosa*) is one of New Zealand's few endemic shellfish. It is unusual for a gastropod in that it filter feeds like a bivalve. It lies buried in the sand and puts up a siphon into the water column. This specimen was found at Oneroa Beach, Waiheke Island, in 1978, at a time when they were common there.

With Dr Bruce Hayward, Margaret undertook a survey of intertidal life on Howick Beach over the summer season of 1999 and 2000, and compared what they had found with molluscs collected by Arthur White from the same area during the 1950s. They were disturbed by the significant decreases in the abundance, diversity and size of the shellfish. Pipi and cockles, which had once been common on the beach, were now hard to find alive. Their demise was probably due to a combination of 'repeated slurries of silt and sewage overflows, in addition to heavy human harvesting'.[22]

Margaret has watched some of the nearby reefs being stripped of all shellfish life. 'I have watched people collecting between Bucklands Beach and Musick Point. They take a bucket and fill it with whelks, systematically walking along the beach and collecting everything they can see. The problem with many carnivorous shellfish, such as whelks, is that they lay eggs onto the rocks rather than into the water column, so if there are no adults laying eggs in the area then there is no next generation.'

When sand dredged from the sea floor off Pakiri Beach was used to replenish Mission Bay in 1997, Margaret and her colleagues were there taking samples, to see what animals were living in the deposited sand. They recorded 410 species. None of the animals, which had been dredged from a depth of 40 metres, could survive on the intertidal beach.

In the future, Margaret would like to see tree planting along all the waterways before they get to the sea. In her view, having a soaking area and sediment trap before freshwater comes onto the beach can make a big difference. Also, strict enforcement of 'no take' beaches can help to relieve the pressure on struggling shellfish populations.

impact on shellfish, inducing 'imposex' in several mollusc families. This is a phenomenon where female shellfish change to males and males become impotent, thereby preventing the animals from reproducing. Many species were knocked out as a result of the contaminant, including the elegant olive shell, the delicately patterned Arabic volute and the ornate octagonal murex. The use of tributyltin was finally banned in 1988, but concentrations are still present on the seabed.[23]

Heavy metals, such as copper and zinc which can be toxic to marine life, have also been accumulating in the upper Waitematā and Tāmaki estuaries. They are largely sourced from the leaching of copper-based antifouling paints which are now commonly used on vessels instead

of tributyltin, run-off from unpainted corrugated iron roofs, and stormwater from roads which carries deposits of metal particles from worn brake linings. High levels of lead have also been recorded, but are now reducing with the removal of lead from petrol. More recently, there are a number of new contaminants reaching the marine area from stormwater and sewage overflows. They including endocrine-disrupting compounds and pharmaceuticals, but little is known about their quantities or effects.[24]

Housing the busiest international container port in New Zealand, the Waitematā Harbour has been a hotspot for introduced invasive species. Most arrive attached to the hulls of vessels or through the discharge of ballast water

Loss of seagrass (*Zostera*) beds

When Powell undertook his work on the Waitematā Harbour during the 1930s, he expressed disquiet about the loss of the large seagrass beds, which had once been present there. This was of concern, because Powell thought that decaying seagrass played an important role in nourishing seabed animals. It was only later that the more crucial role that seagrass plays in providing fish nursery areas was revealed.

Powell noted that the construction of the road across Hobson Bay had resulted in an almost total loss of the seagrass that had once been abundant in the bay. He also observed that the tide-deflectors and reclamation works associated with the port had considerably reduced seagrass areas. In particular, the seagrass beds extending out to the end of Stanley Bay Wharf had disappeared.[25] Historically, seagrass beds had also covered Coxs Creek. The remaining seagrass beds were virtually wiped out during the 1940s by an outbreak of fungal slime. There has been some recovery in recent years: rich green lawn-like swards can be seen today at low tide on the beaches along the Tāmaki Drive, but they still cover only a fraction of their former area.

The extent of the degradation of the Waitematā and other gulf estuaries was emphasised by work recently undertaken by Dr Mark Morrison, who investigated seagrass beds around the country. He worked in the Parengarenga and Rangaunu ('good fishing') harbours and saw 'amazing systems' full of life. There was 'more life, more of everything, more diversity, a bigger food pyramid and species that you would normally now only see further out. They were all there. The Waitematā was probably similar to this in the old days, with extensive seagrass beds. The kelp forest probably extended right into

the Waitematā and the water would have been a lot clearer.'[26]

A major cause of seagrass loss is sediment from land clearance washing into the sea. When the health of a harbour or estuary deteriorates, seagrass is one of the first things to be lost. 'If you degrade a habitat, then you reduce the density of fish that the habitat can support. It's the subtidal seagrass [which remains submerged at low tide] that is most important to fish. If this subtidal seagrass is lost, then juvenile fish production goes with it. It has a cascade effect.'[27]

Most of the seagrass beds in the Hauraki Gulf have been lost, but those in other places, such as Rangaunu Harbour, shown here, indicate what the gulf might have been like in the past. (Mark Morrison)

The Asian date mussel (*Musculista senhousia*) arrived in the gulf during the late 1970s, probably on the hull of a ship from Asia or in ballast water discharged here. It forms dense mats in the upper Waitematā Harbour, Ōrākei Basin and Tāmaki Estuary (shown here). (Mark Morrison)

The native rock oyster (*Saccostrea cucullata*), which used to heavily encrust the rocky shores of the Hauraki Gulf, has now been outcompeted by the exotic Pacific oyster (*Crassostrea gigas*) shown here at Browns Island.

which has been taken on in another country. By 1999, at least 66 exotic species had become established in the harbour. Many are relatively benign, but a few form large populations and out-compete indigenous species.

One of the most common is the Pacific oyster (*Crassostrea gigas*) which arrived in New Zealand sometime during the early 1960s, most probably on the hull of a vessel arriving from Japan.[28] It first became evident in 1970, when it was caught on spat sticks put out in the Mahurangi Harbour to catch the young native rock oyster for cultivation.[29] The Pacific oyster is a more prolific spawner and grows more quickly than the native rock oyster. It is now the predominant oyster seen around the rocky shores of the Hauraki Gulf.

Another common invasive species in the Waitematā Harbour is the Asian date mussel (*Musculista senhousia*) that arrived during the late 1970s, most probably on the hull or in the ballast water of a vessel originating from eastern Asia. This exotic mussel forms dense mats that temporarily cover the sea floor.[30]

More recently, Auckland Council environmental report cards show that the health of the harbour is still generally poor. In 2014, the council allocated it an overall D grade on a scale from A to F.[31]

Impact of fishing gear

Despite the early concerns expressed by line and net fishers about the impacts of trawling on the marine environment and the habitat of juvenile fish, scientists were very slow to investigate this issue. One of the first studies on the topic was undertaken during the early 1990s and this related to scallop dredging. The scientific team that undertook the work, led by Dr Simon Thrush, initially struggled to secure funding. But they were eventually successful in obtaining support from the Department of Conservation, so they could get started.

The team examined areas of the seabed targeted by scallop dredges in Ōpito Bay and compared them with similar undredged areas at Hāhei. The scientists then ran a box dredge (of the type commonly used by scallop dredgers) through half of each site. After the dredge had gone through, they donned scuba gear and dived down to see what the impact had been. They found that the dredge had broken up the natural surface features of the seabed and that the teeth on the front had created deep grooves. Scavengers were actively feeding on the animals damaged by the dredge. When the scientists returned three months later, they found that the seabed community in the dredged area had still not recovered. They concluded that dredging had resulted in a loss of richness and diversity of seabed species.[32]

Dr Thrush later recalled, 'I thought the findings were important and I took them to the Ministry of Fisheries and

Dr Simon Thrush was the first scientist to investigate the impact of fishing gear on the sea floor of the Hauraki Gulf. He is shown here working out in the field. (Courtesy of Simon Thrush)

talked with colleagues there. But their argument was that, as the impacts were local and not at the scale of the fishery, they were irrelevant. I found that odd, as when you are working on the impacts of contaminants, an industry can be affected by a toxicity test in a Petri dish. But fishing didn't appear to work to the same environmental standards. So I looked at how to demonstrate the impacts at a broader scale.'[33]

In 1994, Dr Thrush and his team followed up the scallop research with an investigation into the impacts of fishing activity on the wider sea floor in the inner Hauraki Gulf. The typical trawl gear that was being dragged across the seabed at that time consisted of a pair of trawl drawers (weighing around 480 kilograms) and a ground rope strung with 140–150 millimetre-wide bobbins and steel balls. Fisheries statistics indicated that 1568 square kilometres of the gulf had been swept by bottom trawl gear during the previous year.

Other fishing methods also impact the seabed. Seine fishers drag leaded ropes over the sea floor to herd fish into the net. A much larger 8274 square kilometres of the gulf was documented as having been swept by Danish seine nets that year. Scallop dredges were thought to have affected just under 9 square kilometres.[34]

The scientific team documented the marine organisms which were present in the areas affected by different intensities of fishing activities, and compared the results with what was found in other areas of the gulf. Unsurprisingly, in the areas which had been impacted by fishing gear, they found fewer large organisms, such as sponges, starfish, scallops and horse mussels.[35]

As well as the direct and immediate impacts of seabed

disturbance by fishing, scientists became concerned about the longer-term, insidious effects of the regular disturbance of soft sediment communities. By that time the gulf had been trawled for close on 100 years. Some early fishermen had suggested that trawling might positively affect biodiversity, through opening up areas of sea floor for new colonists, similar to how a tree falling in the forest opens up opportunities for new growth. But it turned out that the marine environment is not at all like a forest, with species being more widely spaced. Where large areas of marine habitat are disturbed, faster-growing organisms are able to dominate the area and those that are slow to grow and reproduce diminish in number. As a result, with trawling, Danish seining and dredging continuing, the sea floor in the gulf has become less diverse over time.[36]

Fisheries habitat

It was not until scientists started identifying habitats of importance to fisheries that the significance of the loss of extensive seagrass meadows and mussel beds throughout the gulf was fully appreciated. Initial scientific work undertaken in Goat Island Bay, during the 1980s, found that the density of juvenile snapper differed within relatively small areas, suggesting that the small fish preferred specific habitat types.[37] Further work undertaken in Kawau Bay by Dr Simon Thrush and a team of scientists during the late 1990s linked the abundance of juvenile snapper to structures on the sea floor.[38]

Starting in 2006, Dr Mark Morrison and his scientific team sought to investigate further which habitats in the

Loss of horse-mussel (*Atrina zelandica*) beds

In Dr Simon Thrush's view 'one of the biggest changes in the gulf would be the loss of *Atrina* [horse-mussel] beds. There is no scientific documentation of this in the gulf in general. But there is anecdotal evidence that, after the Second World War, with the expansion of coastal fisheries and the increasing size and power of fishing vessels, the sea floor of much of the central and outer gulf was 'conditioned' by fishers to make it better for scallops. They dragged chains along the seabed to remove what they thought were competing species, such as horse mussels.

When Dr Thrush first started surveying the gulf in the early 1990s he would occasionally come across horse mussels. 'I would see one individual in 10 square metres of sea floor and think it was abundant. Then I was looking at sites off Ōtama Beach, diving in 16–20 metres of water, and I came across dense and extensive beds of horse mussels that had recently been disturbed by a scallop dredge. It was real classic chalk and cheese contrast. There was bare habitat with a few broken shells, and a few scavengers eating dead stuff, next to wonderfully dense *Atrina* beds. This made me start to think about what the sea floor would have looked like when it was dominated by vast beds of seashells.

'A few years later, we started to look at the Mahurangi Harbour as a region that might be undergoing future catchment development. We'd been working on the impacts of sedimentation and land run-off for a while and wanted to set up a monitoring programme. So we started work and found dense beds of *Atrina* in the seaward half of the harbour. We then started to think about the role of *Atrina* in affecting the ecology of the harbour. We conducted a number of research studies to look at their influence on the diversity of the sea floor and how they process carbon and nutrients that are both naturally in the system and result from land run-off. We found that the shellfish underpinned many of the ecosystem services that we depend on and which largely go unreported and undervalued.'[39]

Unlike the rest of the gulf, the loss of horse mussels is well documented for Mahurangi Harbour. 'When we started monitoring there in the early 1990s, there were extensive beds covering a large proportion of the harbour. They extended out to Kawau Bay and a long way along the coast. I got to know those beds very well and many of them don't exist any longer. They have become functionally extinct.' The main reason for their loss is thought to be sediment washing into the harbour from the harvesting of pine trees and the grazing of land within the steep Mahurangi catchment.

The research undertaken by a scientific team led by Dr Simon Thrush identified significant impacts of seafloor disturbance by fishing gear, as shown here in the images of a horse mussel bed before and after dredging had occurred. (Simon Thrush)

Story of the Gulf | **Dr Mark Morrison**

MARINE ECOLOGIST, AUCKLAND[40]

Mark Morrison grew up in Takapuna and he was a keen fisherman from a young age. Then he became interested in what else was under the surface, in addition to the fish he had been catching. So when he went out fishing with his father and brother, instead of targeting snapper, Mark would put down small hooks to see what other species he could catch.

On leaving school, Mark decided to study marine biology and he became a student at the University of Auckland. One thing led to another and Mark eventually enrolled for a PhD, investigating scallop ecology and the potential for enhancement of stocks in the Hauraki Gulf. At that stage, enhancement was being successfully applied in Tasman and Golden bays and a group of fishermen were interested to see if a similar approach could be applied in the gulf.

So Mark proceeded to undertake a research programme which involved collecting scallop spat on artificial collectors placed in the water column, growing them in a protected environment and then reseeding them on the sea floor when they were big enough to survive predation. At the same time, he was also studying the existing scallop beds in Ōmaha Bay.

'There were a couple of very dense scallop beds there. Then one of the scallop boats came along and ran a dredge through the whole thing and the benthos got trashed. After that, the algal blooms of 1992 came through and everything died. It wiped out Ōmaha Bay. All the scallops and surf clams died: there were dead shells everywhere. The blooms also killed all the spat and, during the second year of my spat collecting for my PhD, there was nothing; the supply had just crashed. So I had to shift the location of my research south to Kawau Bay, which hadn't been affected by the toxic bloom.' In the end, the scallop enhancement idea didn't proceed.

Mark went on to work for NIWA, initially doing trawl surveys to measure the abundance of common species in the Hauraki Gulf and elsewhere. 'It was basically counting things for stock assessment, identifying how fast they grow, their diet, etc.' But Mark was more interested in understanding the functioning of marine systems, rather than just counting things. In 1998, with colleague Dr Malcolm Francis, he secured government funding to study estuarine fish. One of the estuaries they studied was the Mahurangi Harbour. They discovered that the harbour was a big snapper nursery. Prior to this work, the significance of estuaries in the life cycle of snapper had not been fully recognised. Mark went on to study the Whangapoua Estuary in

Dr Mark Morrison's work has been valuable in providing an understanding of the importance of habitats, such as seagrass, shellfish and sponge beds, for fish recruitment. (Courtesy of Mark Morrison)

the early 2000s. 'It had nice seagrass meadows and we started catching lots of juvenile snapper and parore.' Unfortunately the subtidal elements of those beds have since disappeared and research has now had to shift to the subtidal meadows of the southern Kaipara and the Parengarenga and Rangaunu harbours in upper east Northland.

Mark has observed first-hand the impacts of humans on the Hauraki Gulf. 'People underestimate how much degradation has gone on. Snapper is a resilient species and people now go fishing in a monoculture of snapper. The less resilient fish species have gone and the snapper is the last man standing. So just because you can catch snapper, it doesn't mean that the system is healthy.'

He has seen some amazing sights during his years of researching the gulf. 'Big schools of stingrays come in at certain times of the year, dig huge pits and crush shellfish, turning the bay murky with sediments.' He's seen huge fish migrations, 'whole populations of animals coming and going. I ask myself "How do they do it? How do they know they are doing it?"' He's seen sea slugs 'form massive multiple packs of around 1000 animals or more and roar around'.

Hauraki Gulf were preferred by snapper. They identified eleven sampling areas dispersed around the inner gulf and mapped the bathymetry (depth of water) and other features of the sea floor within them. The scientists also used a video camera to observe snapper at night, whilst they were sleeping, to see where they congregated. This spatial information was overlain with statistics on how many snapper were caught in each area.[41]

After analysing the wealth of data they had compiled, Dr Morrison and his team concluded that snapper showed a preference for areas of the seabed where there was some three-dimensional structure, such as that provided by horse mussels, sponges, sea squirts, pits and burrows. Juvenile snapper were almost always observed very close to or on top of such structures. In particular, the small fish congregated in subtidal seagrass meadows and horse-mussel beds, and it was clear that these were important nursery areas that enabled the fish to survive and grow into adults.[42]

Rocky reefs

The 1962 establishment of a marine research laboratory on the rocky coastline near Leigh substantially increased our understanding of the rocky reef habitats in the gulf. The research facility came into existence largely as a result of the efforts of two influential marine scientists — Professors Valentine Chapman and John Morton.

Chapman was born and educated in England where he specialised in botany and completed a doctorate on salt marshes in East Anglia. In 1945 he was appointed as the first Professor of Botany at Auckland University College (subsequently the University of Auckland). On becoming established in Auckland, Chapman focused his research interests very much on marine plants: seaweeds, mangroves and those living in salt marshes. He harboured a dream of one day establishing a school of marine botany at Auckland.[43]

Just three years prior to Chapman taking up his chair in Auckland, John Morton had enrolled at the same institution as an undergraduate science student. As a child, Morton had

Urchin barrens

One of the significant contributions made by scientists linked with the Leigh Marine Laboratory was to enable a better understanding of the phenomena known as 'urchin barrens'.

During the 1970s, divers observed extensive strips of rocky reef that were bare of plant cover, most noticeably kelp. At the same time, they noticed large numbers of sea urchins that were known to eat kelp. This was of concern, because kelp forests significantly contribute to the productivity of the marine environment and they support a rich community of diverse species.

At first, scientists struggled to understand what was going on. But, as several marine reserves were established along the coast and the populations of snapper and crayfish recovered, the barren areas of rock also started to disappear. A 2006 survey of the rocky reef adjacent to the laboratory, which had been protected as a marine reserve since 1975, found that since that time the area of kelp forest had more than doubled from 28 to 60 per cent of the reserve area and the area of 'urchin barren' had declined from 31 to only 1 per cent of the total area.[44]

Although it is difficult to definitively prove a direct link, there is strong circumstantial evidence to indicate that the depletion of fish stocks that prey on sea urchins, including crayfish and snapper, enables sea urchin numbers to expand, and they in turn strip the kelp forests. This results in an unfortunate 'trophic cascade' which has likely contributed to the degradation of the gulf's rocky reef environments.

Story of the Gulf | **Dr Bill Ballantine**

MARINE SCIENTIST, LEIGH[45]

Dr Bill Ballantine was the first director of the Leigh Marine Laboratory. English by birth, he can remember precisely when he developed his fascination for the sea. 'It was August 1945 and the war had ended, so my father was able to take us on a summer holiday. Up until then only essential travel was allowed. So he took us to Northern Ireland where my aunt had a cottage by the seaside. On the first afternoon we were there, my mother led my sister and me down the road and saw us safely across. We then wandered across the common land to the sea. I just stood there. I was eight years old.

'I could see that behind me there were houses, roads, tennis courts and everything to do with people. But in front of me none of that occurred. It was natural. I realised that I knew a lot about life on land. But the stuff in front of me was completely different, from the seaweeds to the barnacles. I never recovered. I spent the rest of my life trying to make things more natural and diverse.'

Bill went on to university studies, first at Cambridge and then in London for a PhD on the population dynamics of limpets. It was here that he met John Morton. When Morton moved to New Zealand, Bill followed, being keen to continue working with the great scientist. He had also identified New Zealand as a promising place to continue his study of limpets. 'Marine science in New Zealand was at that time primitive and pioneering. I was always attracted to pioneering the beginning of things. Once they become polished and well organised, I tend to drift into the background and let others take over.

'I used to tell people that, at the start, there was no trouble with grants as there weren't any. We didn't think about how to make an application, as there wasn't any money. If you couldn't do it with what you had, you couldn't do it. So we became experts in how to do it without any money. For example, we surveyed the marine reserve over two summers when it was first established. It involved around 2000 dives and we didn't pay a cent for it.

'It was really quite easy. I would go down to Auckland, having offered to give a talk to a diving club, and explain that if they brought their own equipment (properly certified), sleeping gear and food and did exactly what we told them to do, we would provide the boats, the air, the dive buddies and the cooks. Instead of saying, "Come and work with us for nothing", I was saying, "Come and have a good time and we will provide the necessary". They jumped at the opportunity,

Dr Bill Ballantine devoted much of his life to running the Leigh Marine Laboratory and promoting the benefits of marine reserves in New Zealand and around the world.

because divers like diving. They came, they did what we asked, they enjoyed themselves and after a while it became self-generating.'

Unusually for a marine scientist, Bill doesn't dive himself. 'I'm the only marine biologist in the world that can't dive and I get seriously seasick. I was happy doing seashore work and I couldn't afford the gear anyway. By the time it became easy to dive, the divers at the lab wouldn't let me do it, because I was so good at getting them grants and other stuff. Students used to bring me specimens and photos to identify and I did the follow-up work. People say to me "You can't dive" and I say "You've never been to the pyramids but you know what

The marine laboratory on the coast just north of Leigh was established in 1962. During its more than 50 years of operation it has made a significant contribution to our understanding of the marine environment. (John Montogomery)

they look like." I've seen more underwater videos and photos than practically anyone.'

Reflecting on his long career, Bill observes 'most of my scientific career was spent building a marine laboratory, extending it, expanding it and chasing around trying to create marine reserves all around New Zealand and in most of the English-speaking world. To conserve habitats on land, we need to go to a lot of trouble. But to conserve them in the sea, we just have to stop buggering them up. New Zealanders will do anything in the sea except stop stuffing it about.'

In 1996 Bill was awarded the internationally prestigious Goldman Environment Prize in recognition that as 'a marine biologist and grassroots activist, Bill Ballantine successfully promoted the establishment of "no-take" marine reserves in New Zealand and internationally. These unprecedented reserves are widely considered to be a critical means of protecting marine resources which are quickly becoming depleted around the globe.'

When interviewed for this story, Bill was retired and lived close to the marine laboratory where he worked for so many years. Most days he visited the reserve and his enthusiasm for marine protection remained strong. 'My recent daydream is to say to Prime Minister John Key, "You want to do something that your children and grandchildren will remember you for? What you need to do is call an international press conference and say you will make New Zealand the first country in the world to have a representative network of marine reserves. That's Day One. On Day Two you need to invent a new Department of Marine Conservation. The Department of Conservation deals with land and freshwater and that keeps them very busy. On the Day Three news conference you should announce that you will upgrade the navy, air force and inshore marine surveillance capability because, if we're going to protect these new marine reserve areas, we have to police them. Then you need to spread the word into commerce, tourism, science and education until it's a big thing."'

Bill observes: 'Even if you want to be completely objective, the sea is more than half of everything. We treat it like the ribbon around the parcel. That's because we're lazy. Just because you can't breathe in it doesn't mean that it's not important.' Sadly, Bill passed away on 1 November 2015, only a few months after he had given an interview for this story.

Juvenile snapper 'ecological bottleneck'

Scientists have identified an 'ecological bottleneck' in the ability of juvenile snapper to survive into adulthood. Research (as described above) has shown that young snapper prefer three-dimensional habitats on the sea floor, particularly seagrass meadows, but also horse-mussel and sponge beds. It is not known why these areas are preferred, but it is thought that they provide a good source of food, protection from predators and shelter from water currents, reducing the need to expend energy swimming against them.[46]

If there is not a sufficient area of these habitats available, particularly in places close to important spawning areas, then this creates an 'ecological bottleneck' and the survival rate of juvenile snapper is likely to be lower. This has a flow-on effect for fish stocks, as it reduces the number of snapper that are recruited into the fishable adult population.

In the Hauraki Gulf, the majority of these habitats have been lost over the past 170 years, through a combination of increased levels of sediment and other pollutants entering the marine area from the land and direct damage from reclamation, harbour works, trawling and dredging. Habitat loss is still occurring in important fish nursery areas, such as the Mahurangi Harbour.

holidayed at Milford Beach and had particularly enjoyed exploring life on the seashore. He brought to his university studies a fascination for shellfish. After completing a doctorate in science at London University, Morton returned to Auckland University in 1960 to take up the newly established chair in zoology. He had a strong desire to establish a marine station, something that he had discussed with Chapman, before taking up the position.[47]

Within two years of Morton returning to Auckland, a marine laboratory was up and running. The location for the facility at Leigh was chosen for a number of reasons. It was close to Auckland, enabling students and staff to travel between the university and the new facility. It was broadly representative of the north-eastern coastal rocky reef systems and also contained a rich variety of marine habitats and species.[48] Facilities were initially rudimentary and, up until the late 1970s, scientists only had 3.7-metre dinghies to get out onto the water. Eventually a 5-metre inflatable was purchased and then even larger craft.[49]

Early research very much focused on describing what was living in the intertidal and near-shore areas, and scientists found a surprising wealth of species. By 1968 over 300 species had been identified, including 61 species of algae (seaweeds) and 122 species of molluscs (shellfish).[50] When scuba-diving equipment became available in the mid-1960s, studies extended from the intertidal area out into deeper waters and the number of species observed multiplied. By 1976, 1259 different species had been recorded in the wider Leigh area.

Research based at the laboratory spanned a wide range of fields, including the ecology of rocky-reef systems, the behaviour of marine species and the use of sensory systems by fish. Some of the more intriguing research focused on how larval fish, developing in open seawater, could locate rocky reefs in order to settle. Scientists found that the young fish were attracted by the sounds emitted by the reef system. Smell was also thought to play a role.[51]

Seawater circulation and plankton

One of the final pieces of the scientific puzzle, in terms of understanding the ecological functioning of the Hauraki Gulf, was the circulation of seawater and the development of plankton, the very basis of the food chain.

Early observations of the water circulation in the Auckland Harbour were focused on port development and sewage disposal. Then, when the potential link between snapper reproductive success and seawater temperature was observed, greater interest was shown in obtaining a wider understanding of temperature and circulation patterns. But it was not until the 1980s that any serious attempt was made to understand the relationship between the seawater in the gulf and the deeper oceanic water masses.

In 1986, the deployment of meters measuring currents indicated that there was no consistent large-scale pattern of water flow in the gulf. But under certain wind conditions, for example a persistent north to north-easterly, oceanic water would start to flow past the Mokohinau Islands and through the Jellicoe Channel (between Little Barrier Island and Cape Rodney), at times reaching Tiritiri Matangi Island and then deflecting in an easterly direction to flow out of the Colville Channel (near Cape Colville).[52]

In 1998, Dr John Zeldis (see page 300) started to regularly monitor seawater in the Firth of Thames. Remote sensing of New Zealand's oceans had shown that the Hauraki Gulf supported some of the richest phytoplankton levels in New Zealand. Dr Zeldis found a strong seasonal pattern in its water circulation and productivity. Each winter and spring there would usually be a strong upwelling of deep nitrate-rich oceanic waters, as a result of prevailing north-westerly winds blowing the surface water away from the coast, and this would fuel strong plankton growth.[53]

In summer, the warm, low-nutrient waters of the East Auckland Current would swirl into the gulf. The winds would move to the south-easterly quarter, driving surface water towards the coast and causing a downwelling pattern, thereby cutting off the oceanic nutrient supply. This seasonality of circulation and productivity causes a transition whereby, in late summer and autumn, the waters consume more organic matter by respiration than they produce by phytoplankton growth.[54]

Unexpectedly, over time, Zeldis's measurements started to show a disturbing trend. In late summer and early autumn, when the water in the Firth of Thames stopped mixing and started to stratify, he found depletion of oxygen in the deeper waters. Typically the levels of oxygen were reducing to around 70 per cent saturation — well-aerated water being 100 per cent. In one case, these low levels remained for several weeks; on another occasion, oxygen levels dropped to as low as 40 per cent.[55]

One potential cause of this depletion was an excess of nutrients driving a phytoplankton 'bloom-and-decay' cycle, where the respiration of excess amounts of phytoplankton sucks oxygen out of the water. Although this is a natural cycle, it can become enhanced through increased levels of nutrients in the water.

The process also makes seawater more acid, through the excess production of carbon dioxide. Dr Zeldis found that, in autumn, the pH level of seawater in the Firth of Thames had dropped below 7.9. This was well below its level in spring (between 8.05 and 8.1) which is the normal oceanic level.

Although the global open ocean is also acidifying (as a result of increased atmospheric levels of carbon dioxide through burning fossil fuels), the degree of acidification seen in the firth is well ahead of current global trends.[56]

Not surprisingly, the scientists were concerned by this trend and sought to better understand potential sources of nitrogen coming into the system and possible impacts on marine life. The Firth of Thames had been identified as the most important spawning ground for snapper in the gulf. It was also known that fish and crustaceans, such as crabs and crayfish, were particularly susceptible to oxygen stress. If things went seriously wrong in the Firth of Thames, it could have serious implications for fisheries elsewhere.

Measurements showed that nitrogen levels in the seawater had increased significantly over the past fifteen years[57] and this could explain the enhanced bloom-and-decay cycle. But where was the nitrogen coming from?

One obvious potential source was the water flowing out of the Hauraki Plains through the Waihou and Piako rivers. The Hauraki Plains are one of the most intensively farmed areas in the country, and dairying results in nutrient-rich run-off from fertiliser application and cow urine. The drainage works on the plains do not help, as any nutrients discharged onto the land leach directly into the rivers and are then quickly channelled out into the Firth of Thames.

Water sampling of the rivers indicates that the levels of nitrates are elevated, probably four times their natural levels, with the rivers transporting around 3360 tons of nitrates to the Firth of Thames each year. These levels are high, but have not changed much since 1989. This is probably because the benefits of improved treatment of sewage and industrial waste entering the river have been offset by increased nutrients, due to the intensification of farming during this period.[58]

One possible reason for the increase in nitrogen levels in the seawater, when there has been no concomitant increase in levels discharged by the rivers, is that the chemistry of the sea floor has changed as a result of ongoing organic enrichment. Much nitrogen entering the marine environment escapes naturally into the atmosphere as nitrogen oxide. But as the quantity of organic matter in the system increases, the ability to discharge nitrogen as a gas decreases and a greater proportion recycles from the seabed back into the water, in a negative spiral which only serves to make the problem worse.[59]

So what can be done? A report written by Dr John Zeldis and his colleague Dr Mal Green, which summarised

Story of the Gulf | **Dr John Zeldis**

MARINE SCIENTIST, CHRISTCHURCH[60]

John graduated from the University of Otago in 1983 with a PhD in marine science. His doctoral studies had concentrated on better understanding a species of plankton. A year later he was hired by the Ministry of Agriculture and Fisheries to study the early life history of snapper and to develop a better understanding of the link between climate and juvenile snapper recruitment. John spent three years undertaking field work in the Hauraki Gulf, sampling plankton and studying the oceanography of the area.

'I found that there was a relationship between productivity at the base of the food web, in terms of its abundance of phytoplankton and small zooplankton, and the quantity of larger zooplankton that survived, which in turn affected how well the larval snapper survived. I found that the food web was connected together so that the success of quite large larval snapper and small fish was closely related to production in the lower food web. Although this conclusion was not too surprising, to actually demonstrate it with real data was quite unusual.'

In 1998, John started to monitor seawater in the Hauraki Gulf. 'I would regularly go out and do the same thing over and over again. This was to start a time series, which could show how parameters varied through time and whether there were detectable ecosystem stressors developing that could be separated from natural variation. We are now up to voyage #70 in the time series, with regular sampling undertaken every three months for the past seventeen years. We've gone back to one spot in the outer Firth of Thames to sample, using a profiling set of instruments that look at the chemistry of the water and the composition of plankton. There is nothing like this happening anywhere else in New Zealand.

'The work has turned out to be very important. It is pretty clear that there are pH stressors developing and there is seasonal oxygen depletion. We do see variation through the seventeen years, with a lot of seasonal variation and lower oxygen and pH levels in autumn. We also now understand that the Firth of Thames is intimately attached to the catchment and land use, with most of the nitrogen in the system coming from the catchment and associated with agriculture. The firth has changed over the decades and there is now evidence to classify it as "mesotrophic" [having an intermediate level of productivity]. This means it has less clear water and more suspended matter in it than during the past. If such changes increase, the next step is eutrophic [where the system is dominated by algal growth].

'I rely on data to show change. If I hadn't done this work, the Waikato Regional Council wouldn't know that there were seasonally depressed oxygen and pH levels. Nobody would know that. It's getting right down to the fundamental brass tacks of how this system works and how it could be getting stressed. I think it's valuable and I feel reasonably good about having done it.'

Dr John Zeldis has spent seventeen years regularly monitoring water quality in the outer Firth of Thames and he has discovered some disturbing trends. He is shown here out in the field with his water-sampling equipment. (Courtesy of John Zeldis)

what was currently known about the issue, concluded that 'we expect that a reduction in land-side nutrient inputs will reduce the organic-matter load of the firth and consequent oxygen depletion that occurs towards the end of the phytoplankton growth season (late summer to early autumn)'.[61] Whatever the solution, it is clear that the future of the Hauraki Plains and the Firth of Thames are likely to be closely connected.

The development of scientific understanding of the gulf has enabled many of the pieces to be brought together into a better, fuller understanding of the entire system and the impacts that humans have had on it. Much is now known about snapper and this has identified a potential ecological bottleneck, with a shortage of habitat suitable for juvenile snapper. Much less is known about other fish species, but many are likely to be affected in a similar way. Research into the impacts of fishing gear on the seabed and land-sourced discharges of sediment into estuaries indicates that these have contributed to the loss of important habitats, such as

Around 70 per cent of the nitrate entering the Firth of Thames from land is sourced from agriculture on the Hauraki Plains. Nitrate levels in the Waihou River (shown here) are now several times greater than their natural levels. (Lloyd Homer, GNS Science)

seagrass and horse-mussel beds. Rocky-reef systems are also potentially suffering from a depletion of top predators. In some places, the ability of the marine environment to sustain life at all times is potentially being affected by high nutrient inflows. Bringing the system back to full health will be likely to require a holistic approach which addresses all these pressures collectively.

As well as identifying problems, scientists have also pointed us in the direction of solutions. These include the establishment of marine reserves, the adoption of less destructive fishing methods, sediment retention on land and the active restoration of sea-floor communities.

Part Seven:
NEW BEGINNINGS

Chapter 15
Restoring the land

The first century of European occupation of the Hauraki Gulf was very much focused on the extraction of its rich natural resources. In particular, most rural land (apart from very rugged areas) was stripped of its native vegetation and much was transformed to exotic pasture.

Over the past 30 years, there have been efforts to reverse this process in some places, through restoring native forest, eradicating pests and reintroducing threatened species. Restoration efforts have been focused on many of the gulf's publicly owned islands and these have heavily relied on volunteer effort. But some enlightened private island landowners have also been active in restoring their land.

Because it has proved possible to completely eradicate mammalian pest species from many of the gulf's islands, they are now providing critically important refuges for threatened bird and other species. The first refuge in the gulf was created on the remote and rugged Little Barrier Island in 1895.

Pages 302–303: Awana Beach, Great Barrier Island.

Left: Te Hauturu-o-Toi (Little Barrier Island) is the most important nature sanctuary in New Zealand and possibly the world. It is co-governed by the Ngāti Manuhiri Settlement Trust and the Department of Conservation.

Te Hauturu-o-Toi/ Little Barrier Island

According to Māori tradition, Te Hauturu-o-Toi was first inhabited by Toi's people, who later intermarried with Ngāti Wai. In later years, Ngāti Manuhiri people lived on the island and others from Great Barrier Island and Pākiri would frequently visit to harvest fish and birds. There are several pā on the island as well as kūmara pits, trenches and stone walls.[1]

From the early 1840s, the government expressed interest in buying the island. This was initially as a military asset for use during a feared Russian invasion. Later there was strong European interest in the island, due to its rich kauri forests. At that time, a small group of people linked to Ngāti Manuhiri, including Rahui Te Kiri and her husband Tenetahi Te Riringa, had been living on the island for some decades. They were growing crops and harvesting firewood for sale. Some timber-cutting rights were also granted.[2]

During the late 1880s, two naturalists based at the Auckland Museum, Thomas Cheeseman and Thomas Kirk, had become increasingly concerned that populations of native bird species were rapidly declining due to introduced predators. They thought that the creation of island reserves was possibly the only way to save them. Little Barrier Island seemed ideal, being relatively large (28 square kilometres), heavily forested and remote.

The government reinvigorated its negotiations to purchase. In 1890, Tenetahi agreed to sell the island to the Crown for £3000, conditional on all the other owners agreeing. But not all did so. Then, Tenetahi started cutting trees and transporting them back to the mills in Auckland on his scow *Irene*. This was in order to cover the high cost of several government inquiries that had been undertaken into the ownership of the land, with a related tribal group Te Kawerau also claiming rights there. But with the island being deforested, the government sought an injunction to stop the felling of the trees. It also initiated negotiations with individual shareholding owners, and purchased some shares, whilst installing a ranger on the island. But Tenetahi and his family still refused to sell.[3]

Fearing further damage to the island's habitat, the government passed the Little Barrier Island Purchase Act 1894, which enabled the island to be compulsorily acquired. A year later the island was declared a nature reserve, the first in New Zealand. The remaining residents were forcibly

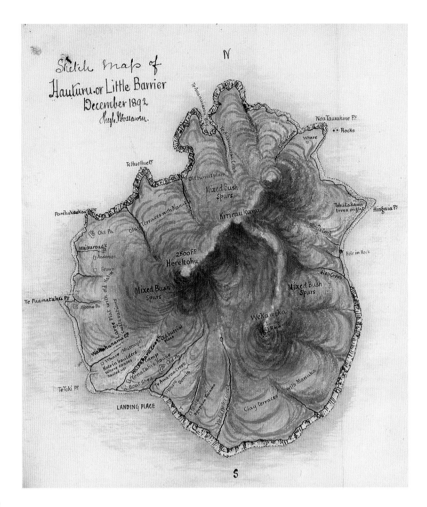

Te Hauturu-o-Toi was declared a nature reserve in 1895. This sketch map of the island shows the location of the Ngāti Manuhiri settlement prior to eviction to make way for the reserve. (Ref: NZ 2006/3174, Archives New Zealand)

evicted in January 1896.[4] By this stage about a third of the forest had been felled and the deforested land burnt.

On the creation of the nature reserve, the public was largely excluded from visiting the island and landing without a permit was prohibited. The forest was left to regenerate. Feral cats had been removed from the island by 1980 and the Polynesian rat by 2004. This enabled endangered species to rebound, including the giant wētā (wētā punga) and the stitchbird (hihi). The island is now one of the most important sanctuaries in the country and possibly in the world. It supports over 40 bird, fourteen reptile and two bat species.[5]

As a result of the Ngāti Manuhiri Treaty Settlement in 2011, Hauturu-o-Toi/Little Barrier Island was vested in Ngāti Manuhiri and then gifted back to the New Zealand people, minus a small 1.2-hectare site retained by the hapū. The Ngāti Manuhiri Settlement Trust now co-governs the island with the Department of Conservation.

Hauraki Gulf Maritime Park

For a century or so after the establishment of Auckland, recreational boat owners had been able to land on most of the islands in the Hauraki Gulf, many of which were privately owned and farmed. During the mid-1960s, the situation started to change. Pakatoa Island was developed into a resort and parts of Rākino Island were subdivided, resulting in landing rights being restricted. In addition, around this time, several islands in the Bay of Islands were purchased by overseas interests. There were fears that islands in the gulf could also be alienated from New Zealand ownership.[6] These concerns prompted calls for the government to secure public ownership of islands in the gulf.

In response, the Hauraki Gulf Maritime Park was established through special legislation in 1967.[7] The legislation also established the Hauraki Gulf Maritime Park Board to manage the new park. The board was chaired by the North Auckland Commissioner of Crown Lands, Darcy O'Brien, and included representatives from the Auckland Regional Authority, the Auckland City Council and the Devonport Borough Council.

The maritime park started modestly with just 4926 hectares of land, including Motutapu Island, Motuora Island, Little Barrier Island, two islands in the Mercury Island group (Stanley and Double islands), the Poor Knights Islands and land on Kawau and Cuvier islands. To add to the park, the government purchased the historic Mansion House and 35 hectares of adjoining land on Kawau Island, for around £80,000.[8] The park board initially received little government financial support and it had no budget for land purchase. It survived on funds derived from farming operations on Motutapu Island and from granting leases for shops and grazing on other islands. Despite this lack of funding, the board soon started to make significant progress in establishing a hugely popular maritime park.

The board's acquisition programme got off to a good start with three gifts of land. The first was by Ngāti Karau, Ngāti Whanaunga and Ngāti Hako, who gave four islands in the Mercury group. Then Mr Goodwin gifted 4 hectares

at Sharps Point on Kawau Island. In addition, Ngāti Hako and Ngāti Hei gifted the Aldermen Islands.[9]

By early 1971, an additional 3588 hectares had been added to the maritime park, including Browns Island, Motuihe Island, the Bream Islands, Casnell Island, Goat Island, the Mokohinau Islands and land on Kawau, Rākino, Rangitoto, Great Barrier and Tiritiri Matangi islands. Much of the new land, such as that used for lighthouse operations, was already owned by the Crown but had been previously managed by other public agencies.

Once all suitable land in public ownership was passed over to the board, the rate of land acquisition slowed abruptly. But accumulating 27 reserves under the mantle of a maritime park was a major achievement and an enduring legacy for future generations.

One of the ground-breaking initiatives undertaken by the park board, and something that would have wide ramifications throughout the gulf, was the restoration of Tiritiri Matangi Island.

Tiritiri Matangi open sanctuary

Tiritiri Matangi (commonly referred to as 'Tiri') is a small 220-hectare island lying to the east of the Whangaparāoa Peninsula. Its Māori name translates as 'buffeted by the wind'[10] and may refer to the exposed nature of the island. Before human contact, Tiri was densely populated by seabirds and their droppings left deposits of guano that produced very fertile soil. This supported a lush coastal broadleaf forest, which in turn provided a home for a wide variety of land birds, tuatara and other native wildlife.

Tiri has been inhabited for centuries, with Te Kawerau-a-Maki, Ngāti Paoa and Ngāti Wai having links with the island. There is evidence of occupation dating back 600 years, from before the eruption of nearby Rangitoto.[11] The island was used seasonally for fern-root gathering and fishing and, in particular, it was located close to the important shark-fishing grounds to the north.[12] The Crown bought the Mahurangi block, on the coast adjacent to Tiri, in 1841, and assumed that the sale included the island. Title was later disputed by several iwi, but the court confirmed the Crown's title in 1867.[13]

The island was farmed from the mid-1850s, with a lighthouse being established in 1865. Although some bush

Story of the Gulf | **Mook Hohneck**

KAUMĀTUA, NGĀTI MANUHIRI[14]

Mook Hohneck is a direct descendant of Rahui Te Kiri and Tenetahi Te Riringa on his mother's side. The Ngāti Manuhiri people predominantly lived in Pākiri, Whangateau, Leigh and Ōmaha. They were a coastal people who heavily utilised the northern parts of the Hauraki Gulf, including the islands of Little Barrier, Great Barrier and Kawau.

Mook grew up in Maraeroa, located in the Pureora region of the central North Island. His extended family was focused around the logging and milling of the podocarp forests in the area. Around the time of the Great Depression, a group of Ngāti Manuhiri had moved south from Pākiri to to seek work, being unable to economically survive on their small coastal farms. They settled amongst the Maniapoto-linked Ngāti Rereahu people, but strongly retained their own stories and traditions linked to their coastal homeland to the north.

Mook grew up immersed in his tribal culture, listening to the fascinating stories told by his grandmother and aunties. He enjoyed learning about his Ngāti Manuhiri whakapapa and was able to retain it. By the time he was 30 years old, Mook had successfully established his own business as a forestry contractor.

In the early 1980s, Mook's extended family decided to return to Ōmaha and Mook moved north with them. At that time, former Māori All Black Laly Haddon was living on the Pākiri land, but there were few others remaining there. The reinvigorated group set about rebuilding the marae at Ōmaha. It is currently the only marae on the east coast between Ōrakei, Tāmaki (on the Auckland isthmus) and Waipu near Whangarei. Laly had begun negotiating a Treaty settlement with the Crown. Mook was chosen to work with Laly and ultimately succeeded him as tribal leader. 'Laly was a treasure box of knowledge. He could walk in any world and he could talk and mix with anyone. He was Mister Manuhiri in my eyes. He kept things small and tight and always kept moving forward, even an inch a day.' The Treaty settlement was finalised in 2011. Laly passed away in July 2013 at 74 years of age.

'The powerful attraction to the tribe, for me, was our tupuna Te Kiri Kaiparaoa. He was born prior to the 1800s and fought in the Musket Wars. He lived until 1872, so through the signing of the Treaty of Waitangi and subsequent changes. He was renowned for his powers of fighting with traditional weapons and was able to protect our rohe against threats from other powerful tribes. Despite tribal dislocations to the north and south as a result of conflict, he managed to hold onto much of our land. This he passed down to his daughter, Rahui Te Kiri, who was also able to retain the bulk of it. Ngāti Manuhiri now hold Auckland's largest area of Māori titled land.

'In terms of our Treaty settlement, we achieved what our tupuna, Tenetahi and Rahui, wanted on Te Hauturu-o-Toi: a Crown acknowledgement that they were the rightful owners and a place to stand there. Our tribal stories tell of Rahui being evicted off the island in 1896, then swimming the 26 kilometres back there, before being evicted again. Her husband, Tenetahi, was an avid sailor who had an excellent knowledge of the sea, being a renowned tohunga in his own right, in terms of anything to do with the marine space. There are lots of stories about him and his native crew winning the gold cup in the Auckland regatta. He sailed all around the mainland and offshore islands, even up to the Pacific Islands and Australia, where he traded. Tenetahi died in 1927 at 97 years of age. Rahui died in 1930 at the age of 100, although some say she was a little older.

'When we started our Treaty negotiations, Hauturu was not up for negotiation. But we eventually got it onto the table and reached an agreement that 1.2 hectares of the island would be retained by the hapū. We will re-establish a marae there so that our people have a place to stand and a place to stay on the island.

'People ask us, "Why did you give the island back?" But we didn't give it back to the Crown, we gifted it back to the people of New Zealand. It was our way of upholding our mana. We don't own the island, only God owns it.

'Now that the treaty process has been completed, Ngāti Manuhiri can achieve more of the goals and aspirations that our old people laid down for us: to protect the environment and make sure our cultural footprint is sustained and upheld. It's about us living on our lands and maintaining our

kaitiakitanga principles that have been handed down. We need to get our people back onto the land and back out onto the water.

'One of my major concerns is the increase in Auckland's population. We have five regional parks and two marine reserves within our rohe and these provide huge recreational spaces that attract people. We've also had to put a rāhui on the taking of our traditional kaimoana in the Whāngateau, due to depleted stocks. As more people come up here from Auckland, they are taking more of our kaimoana and impacting on us as a people. It means that we have to limit our customary take and that reduces our ability to teach our kids about the gathering of kaimoana and the principles of kaitiakitanga and tikanga associated with that. As we gather less, our kids get isolated from those practices.'

Rebuilding the tribal base has been hard work. 'It's been rewarding but it comes with sacrifices. I have five children and I had to spend a lot of time away during the important part of their lives when they were growing up. But they have turned out well and I am proud of them. They're all fluent in te reo and are well connected with the marae. I have three grandsons now and they all have tupuna names, so those names have been retained down through the generations.'

had been burnt by Māori for the creation of gardens, it was the farming activities undertaken by Pākehā that had the most profound effect on Tiri's natural environment:

The 130-year farming period had a devastating effect on Tiri's environment, leaving the landscape as barren as the mainland . . . fires will have killed many ground-dwelling birds, lizards and invertebrates. Although the pōhutukawa were protected, the manuka and kanuka stands almost disappeared. Goats, in particular, will have had a major effect on the vegetation. Even where tall trees remained in the steepest gullies they were unfenced. Stock roamed, browsing out seedlings and low growing vegetation. Their hooves compressed the ground that had been previously soft and friable [and] riddled with numerous seabird burrows. Instead of soaking into the soil, heavy rain now ran off, taking with it any leaf litter and the ground became hard and bare. It has still not recovered from these changes today.[15]

In 1970 the lighthouse station on Tiri was decommissioned and the island was added to the newly created Hauraki Gulf Maritime Park. This started a very new phase in the island's history. The park board decided that farming activities should cease and that the island should be left to revert to its original native vegetation. But eight years after the cattle had been removed, very little revegetation had occurred, because bracken and grass were growing quickly and suffocating the native seedlings. The Pacific rat population had grown as well, putting further pressure on the young natives.

In 1979, University of Auckland academics Dr John Craig and Dr Neil Mitchell proposed to the park board that the island should be physically replanted and that native fauna could then be transferred to it. They also argued that the island should be created as an 'open sanctuary', a place where the public could come to see 'conservation in action'. This, they reasoned, could take some of the pressure off Little Barrier Island and the Hen and Chickens group, important wildlife reserves that were more pristine and were closed to the public. Growing interest in conservation had meant that an increasing number of people wanted to visit these remote islands. If the replanting was undertaken by public volunteers, it would save costs and also generate public support for conservation.[16]

Such an innovative plan had not been tried before in New Zealand. It met with initial resistance, as some

naturalists believed that you could only have a successful nature reserve if the public was not allowed to go there. But the park board was taken by the vision and decided to go ahead. It looked overseas for comparable models and was struck by the success of the Slimbridge Wetlands Project in Gloucestershire, England. There, a 260-hectare site which was open to the public had also very successfully served to conserve endangered duck and geese species.

The Slimbridge project was established by Sir Peter Scott in 1946 and now attracts around 200,000 visitors a year. Scott was a naturalist and artist and had also been a founding member and chair of the World Wide Fund for Nature New Zealand (WWF). The park board invited Scott to come out to New Zealand in order to provide advice and support for the Tiri project, which he did. This contact helped to secure the support of WWF, which took Tiri on as a special project in 1982, raising $40,000 for the replanting exercise. This initial funding was matched by the government on the basis of 'two for one', bringing the total available funding up to $120,000.

The university team drew up a management plan for

Tiritiri Matangi is now a hugely popular destination with over 33,000 people visiting each year. The concept of an open wildlife sanctuary, where people are welcomed, has proved highly successful. Shown here are visitors about to depart on the daily ferry.

the replanting exercise and the park board established a management subcommittee to supervise the project. It was difficult to know precisely what species should be planted, as the island was so highly modified that no one knew exactly what had been there before. In addition, such a large replanting scheme had never been attempted before in New Zealand, or anywhere else, as far as those involved knew. But trial and error gradually established what plants and planting methods were most successful on the exposed island environment.

The planting programme began in earnest in 1984. Members of the public were invited to come and help. During that first year, 43 boat trips were made to the island and 28,900 trees were planted. The numbers increased the following year.[17] The work proved extremely popular and soon there was a waiting list for groups to come and spend

Observation pillboxes can still be seen dotted around the coast of Motutapu Island, such as the one shown here at Billy Goat Point, a legacy of the role the island played in Second World War military planning.

a day planting on the island. In particular, the trips were popular amongst school groups, boy scouts and girl guides, and community and environmental groups.

The public replanting programme was completed in 1994, with quarter of a million native trees planted. In 1993 a Pacific rat eradication programme — one poison drop — was 100 per cent successful and eleven bird species have now been translocated to the island, including stitchbirds, takahē and the little spotted kiwi. Sixty per cent of the island has now been successfully reforested.

Tiri has become ecologically important, not only as a site where wildlife can thrive, but as a breeding ground for rare species that can be transferred to other islands. It has also become a popular place for visitors. A ferry calls at the island nearly every day in summer and visitor numbers have grown to over 33,000 each year. But perhaps even more importantly, the project has provided inspiration for other island restoration projects in the Hauraki Gulf and elsewhere.

Motutapu Island

Ngāi Tai maintained rights of occupation over Motutapu Island, from the time of the Rangitoto eruption, until the sale of the northern part of the island to Thomas Maxwell in 1840. Ngāti Paoa also claimed fishing rights there. The southern end of the island was sold to Williamson and Crummer in 1845.[18] The island has been farmed since the 1860s. In the lead-up to the Second World War, the island was identified as a good site for a coastal gun battery and three gun emplacements were constructed on the ridge between Administration and Sandy bays. Magazines were built underground to hold weapons and explosives. Offices, accommodation and a range of other facilities were also built on the island. In 1942, when units of the United States Navy were stationed in the Hauraki Gulf, ammunition stores for them were built on Motutapu and a base was built on Rangitoto.

Story of the Gulf | **Christine Fletcher**

COUNCILLOR, AUCKLAND COUNCIL[19]

Christine Fletcher grew up with a strong bond with the Hauraki Gulf. Her father, Ted Lees, built up the very successful Lees Industries that manufactured marine and agricultural engines and material handling equipment until the mid-1980s. Whilst fighting overseas in the Second World War, 'it was memories of the Hauraki Gulf that really inspired him to come back and make something of the country'. Ted subsequently served on the Auckland Harbour Board, the board of WWF New Zealand and the Hauraki Gulf Maritime Park Board. His view was 'that our economic prosperity was absolutely intertwined with our harbours'. Ted was passionate about the Hauraki Gulf and giving people access to it, and he passed this passion on to his three daughters.

The family spent much time on a shared coastal property at Tuturau, Kawakawa Bay. On Friday nights they would often head out on a small launch to spend the weekend exploring the gulf. As Christine recalls, 'I would be tucked up in the forward bunk, the lapping of the waves nurturing me, and then I would wake up on the Saturday morning at whatever little bay my father had decided to stop at. I would be made to dive into the water and swim ashore to explore the top of the nearest hill. I remember having to conquer my fears and head for the shoreline. The chorus of the birds, the smell of the bush, the buzz of the cicadas and the sense of adventure and possibility stay with me today. They were marvellous times and played a large part in shaping who I am.'

When Ted joined the Maritime Parks Board, Christine used to accompany him on the board's rounds of the islands and she got to know the place well, especially Motutapu where the board would frequently visit the Reid homestead and schoolhouse. Jim Holdaway was also on the board and through these trips Christine got to know Jim and his wife, Ann. They became lifelong friends.

In 1993, Christine became a member of Parliament, holding the Auckland Eden seat for the National Party. Soon after her election, Alison Henry and Graeme Campbell from the Department of Conservation, along with Jim Holdaway, approached her to assist with the establishment of the Motutapu Restoration Trust. Christine agreed, 'perhaps not fully appreciating then what a life-changing commitment this would become.' The trust was incorporated in 1994, with Christine as one of the founding trustees, and she subsequently took over as chair. She worked to partner with the Rotary Club of Newmarket, encouraging them to help

Businessman Ted Lees was an early member of the Hauraki Gulf Maritime Park Board. He inspired his daughter Christine Fletcher to become involved in restoration projects in the Hauraki Gulf. They are both shown here in Christine's parliamentary office in 2000, celebrating the announcement of the Hauraki Gulf Marine Park legislation. (Courtesy of Christine Fletcher)

with fundraising. They came on board, initially to fund the wallaby eradication programme, and have remained major sponsors of the trust ever since.

Christine was later elected mayor of Auckland City for a term and was responsible for opening up the Auckland waterfront and the Britomart Interchange.

'We took on the challenge of the restoration plan prepared for Motutapu by Graeme Campbell and endorsed by the Auckland Conservation Board. This involved not just the ecological restoration of the island, but a broad range of activities involving members of the community. The plan set out a programme to improve recreational opportunities and tourism, to restore and interpret historic features, to encourage volunteer activities and to provide an educational programme. It also envisaged a good working relationship with Ngāi Tai. My interest was not specific to Motutapu, but more in its position as a gateway to the gulf. Motutapu, along with Rangitoto, presents an unrivalled opportunity for the survival of threatened species close to our largest metropolitan city. It is important to be telling the stories about the possibilities for the gulf as a whole.

'The challenge for the trust was to inspire an army of volunteers without burdening them with the battles around the supply and funding of critical infrastructure and resources like accommodation, nurseries, roads, wharves, water supply, power supply, fuel and vessels. We made great gains on the island and then Cave Creek happened [an observation deck built by the Department of Conservation in the Paparoa National Park collapsed on 28 April 1995, killing fourteen people]. The Home Bay wharf was closed on us due to concerns over safety. Our volunteer programme was largely predicated around using the Home Bay area for access. This created enormous logistical difficulties and limitations on the number of volunteers we could use. We had to turn people away. It was heart-wrenching but we did not give up.

'We still have challenges, especially on issues like accommodation for volunteers. By the time we get them out to the island, they can work from between 11.00 am and 2.00 pm before they have to start packing up to leave again. If you want volunteers to be clamouring to be part of the project, you need to give them the privilege of overnighting on the island occasionally. This is to allow them that sense of wonder you don't get living in an urban environment. I passionately believe that we can generate a lot more volunteers across Auckland, but we need to be more generous about what we are giving them in return.

'We fought to stay true to the vision of Graeme Campbell in bringing the takahē back to Motutapu. We had a terrible battle with the subsequent conservators who said we were wasting our time and that DOC should instead be investing in the West Coast and South Island. But my approach was to follow the lessons of my father: "If you help people to fall in love with the land and the sea, they will be loyal to it." If you are really serious about conservation, you have to give people those experiences. Education takes many forms, but the most powerful education can be getting people out on the island and giving them that experience of getting their hands dirty, particularly young people. I took that very seriously.

'We've had a lot of successes. The pests have been eradicated, the wharf has been reopened and we've brought the takahē back, but we must not lose momentum.'

Top: Brother and sister Alexander and Francesca Wilson are shown here planting trees on Motutapu with their father Peter in the background. (Julie Kidd)

Bottom: Takahē were reintroduced to the island in 2011. (Courtesy of Christine Fletcher)

A project to restore Motutapu Island's indigenous forest commenced in 1992 and was spearheaded by the Motutapu Restoration Trust, which was formed in 1994. This image shows the replanting in the valley behind Home Bay.

After the conclusion of the war, the island was farmed by the Lands and Survey Department and, in 1949, a livestock quarantine station was established. After the army withdrew in 1958, the administration buildings were turned into an outdoor education centre. The island became part of the Hauraki Gulf Maritime Park in 1967 and, as already noted, the income from the farm on the island funded many of the park board's activities.[20]

During the 1990s, inspired by the success of the Tiritiri Matangi restoration project, a similar initiative was started on Motutapu Island. The vision was to create a large open sanctuary, on the very doorstep of Auckland, which could be accessed easily by members of the public. An important part of the project was to first eradicate possums and wallabies from the island. This involved a poison drop over Rangitoto and trapping, hunting and bait stations on Motutapu. It took seven years to remove the last animals.

An indigenous plant nursery was established on the island in 1992, sponsored by WWF and opened by Prince Philip. The plants were eco-sourced from the fingers of forest that remained on the island. Seeds from the remnant plants were collected, germinated and grown. Two years later, the Motutapu Restoration Trust was formed to spearhead a major restoration project.

Rick Braddock was granted a lease to operate the 1340-hectare farm on the island in 1992. He also became deputy chair of the restoration trust. Rick developed a biological approach to farming on the island that encourages deep-rooted pastures that can withstand the regular summer drought. He grazes around 3500 sheep and 1000 cattle. Much of the island will continue to be grazed, rather than be planted in indigenous forest, in order to preserve the numerous archaeological and culturally important sites on the island.[21]

Motuihe Island was operated as a navy training base from 1941 until 1963 and at one stage had accommodation for 517 people. This image of the island, taken in 1947, shows the large group of buildings which were established on the north-west headland. (Ref: Ak1-42, Auckland general, 10, FV C Browne & Son)

It was not until 2011 that all of the pests on the island, and adjacent Rangitoto, were removed. They included Norway and ship rats, mice, rabbits, hedgehogs, feral cats and stoats. This opened up the way for the return of endangered species to Auckland's doorstep, including the saddleback, takahē, brown teal (pāteke), shore plover, whitehead and the Coromandel brown kiwi. Thousands of volunteers have planted almost half a million trees and 100 hectares of forest have been restored. In addition, hundreds of pōhutukawa have been planted around the coast.[22]

Motuihe Island

Ngāi Tai and Ngāti Paoa were recognised as the owners of Motuihe Island at the time of European settlement in Auckland. The island was 'renowned for its kūmara cultivations' and there are numerous storage pits still evident.[23] There is a greywacke quarry site at the southern end of the island and evidence of adze manufacture. There

are also three documented pā, only two of which can still be seen at Mangōpare-Rua and Te Rae o Kāhu.

In 1837, the Māori owners were said to have initially sold the island to Mr Butler, and it was for a time known as Butlers Island. But then, in 1839, another sale by the Māori owners was recorded to William Fairburn. Within five months Fairburn had onsold to Mr Taylor who, five days after obtaining a Crown Grant title to the island in 1843, onsold it to John Logan Campbell and his business partner William Brown. The partners established a farming operation on the island, with the farm work mainly being undertaken by Māori. John Graham bought the island in 1858 and continued to operate it as a farm. As well as maintaining horses, cattle, sheep, pigs, turkeys and geese on the island, he introduced deer, partridges, pheasants and quail. Graham drowned while travelling out to the island in 1868. Some of the earliest olives planted in New Zealand are on the island, probably dating from the 1870s.[24]

In 1872, the island was chosen for the location of a human quarantine station and buildings were erected on the north-west headland, having been moved from the Albert Barracks in Auckland where the University of Auckland now stands. In 1874, the *Dorrette* was the first vessel to be quarantined at the island.[25]

During the First World War, the quarantine station was used to hold prisoners of war, mainly Germans and Austrians who had been living in New Zealand when war broke out, but also some Samoans. The island came into notoriety when German captive Count Felix von Luckner managed to escape from the island and get as far as the Kermadec Islands, before being recaptured.[26] After the war, the quarantine station was reopened, and a children's health camp operated from 1929 to 1931. In 1941 the navy took over the island for a training base. By this stage there were 22 buildings, with the capacity to accommodate up to 287 internees. A further fifteen buildings were constructed to increase capacity to 517. Two guns were also mounted on the island.[27]

English former nurse Eileen Slark lived on the island in the navy surgeon's cottage for two and half years during the late 1950s, with her husband Tony, who was a navy medical doctor, and their young daughter Cindy. Eileen recalls: 'Coming from England it seemed such a beautiful island. It was just such a beautiful time in our lives. Some days Tony would come back at lunchtime and say, "I've finished for the day." He got a lovely veggie garden going and the farmer brought over cream in a gin bottle during the weekends. In the summer we borrowed a tent from the navy and camp beds, and we had our friends to stay. It was magic. We quite often had all our meals outdoors: waffles for breakfast, sandwiches for lunch and a barbecue at night.

'Tony would go fishing for scallops and crayfish at a place just off Rākino Island where a big reef ran out. It became known as "Slark's larder". It was a very good place for crayfish.'[28]

In 1963, the navy moved off the island and stripped the buildings bare. They fell into disrepair and the Auckland City Council eventually demolished them. Some buildings were simply bulldozed into gullies and covered with soil. The only usable infrastructure that was left was a water tower and a Ministry of Works workshop on the headland, the former navy surgeon's cottage, the wharf shed and concrete foundations for the wharf.[29]

The island was incorporated into the Hauraki Gulf Maritime Park in 1967, but its history had left a heavy footprint. Farming operations had removed most of the indigenous vegetation and the impacts of stock and predators had damaged much of the soils. By the 1990s, the island was covered in rank grass, weeds were choking the few remnant native trees and rabbits were in plague proportions.[30]

It was the vision of Ronnie Harrison that helped to turn this situation around. Ronnie and her partner, Terry Gibbons, had a concession to farm the island and also to

During the late 1950s, former English nurse Elaine Slark lived on Motuihe Island in the navy surgeon's cottage with her husband, Tony, who was the navy medical doctor. She recalls it as being a beautiful time in their lives.

operate a canteen and manage the camping ground. In 2000, Ronnie invited Peter Whitmore and Michael Wood to form the Motuihe Island Restoration Trust, in order to spearhead the restoration of the island. Tony Slark was invited to be patron and was active in the restoration initiative until his death in 2004. Rats and mice had been eradicated in 1994, but rabbits were still on the island in force and efforts to get rid of them had so far failed. After a fire broke out on the island and destroyed the shop, the Department of Conservation decided to end Ronnie's lease, and she left the island in 2005, after living there for nearly 20 years.[31]

But this did not diminish Ronnie's enthusiasm for the island. In 2002, she had written to all the boat clubs in the Auckland area, inviting them to assist with the restoration effort. One of those who received a letter was John Laurence, who was involved with the Outboard Boating Club. The club decided to support the project and John put his considerable talents behind the initiative.

The first task was to grow the seedlings that would be needed to replant the island. Half the funding to establish a nursery on the island was sourced from WWF and the club provided the balance. The nursery was designed to produce 25,000 seedlings a year and did, all with volunteer help. But there was other expensive equipment required to actually do the replanting: a tractor, trailer, sprayer and mower. The trust applied successfully to the Sky City Community Trust for funding to cover half the cost of these items and the club covered the rest. In addition, part of the club members' subscription fees were paid over to the trust for general operating funds.[32]

Top: The establishment of a nursery on Motuihe Island to grow seedlings for use in replanting the island was funded jointly by the World Wildlife Fund and the Outboard Boating Club.

Bottom: Much of the pasture on Motuihe Island has now been planted with indigenous species. (John Laurence)

Story of the Gulf | **John Laurence**

CHAIR, MOTUIHE ISLAND RESTORATION TRUST, AUCKLAND[33]

John grew up at Kohimarama on the edge of the Hauraki Gulf. After moving away for some years, he returned to Auckland in 1984 and settled in Ōrākei. John bought a boat, joined the nearby Outboard Boating Club in Hobson Bay and was gradually drawn into the administration of the club.

'When I thought about the advantages that the OBC [Outboard Boating Club] reclamation and marina provided to a large proportion of boaties and how lucky the club was, I felt it was in the interests of the club to put something back into Auckland. I was motivated by what had been done at Tiri and I thought I could lead the OBC into doing something similar at Motuihe. The members loved the idea and got behind it big time.'

After the club decided to support the Motuihe restoration project, meetings of the trust were moved from the Department of Conservation offices to the boating club's headquarters and John took over as chairman of the trust.

'During the first couple of years we were inundated with volunteers to plant trees and we were running out of trees for them to plant. So we made a few simple additions to the nursery so that it could double production. We started planting 45,000 to 50,000 trees a year using volunteers, community groups like Rotary and thousands of school children.

'Fullers and 360 Discovery provided transport to the island, the latter offering a heavily reduced price for volunteers and running trips three times a day. That ceased three years ago when 360 Discovery was taken over by Fullers. The company now only takes volunteers out to the island once a fortnight. So this has created significant logistical problems in terms of getting volunteers out to the island.

'Our long-term vision for the island was initiated in 2003 when we and the Department of Conservation contracted John Hawley, a department landscape architect, to do a comprehensive restoration plan. This covered all aspects of the restoration, including cultural, heritage and environmental. It was circulated widely amongst iwi, universities, museums, the Historic Places Trust, boating clubs and the general public. The conservator signed it off in 2005. We have followed that plan religiously since then.

'We have now planted 400,000 trees, covering 80 per cent of the island. The island was heavily infested with weeds and we mainly removed these using volunteers on the flats and abseilers on the cliffs. But we were aware that there was a huge seed bank that would be around for the next ten to fifteen years. So we planted trees at quite a wide spacing, so that the grass would remain and hold back the germination of the seedling weeds.

'Most of the island has now been planted with primary colonisers and some final canopy species plants. We have commissioned Tonkin and Taylor to come up with a biodiversity enhancement plan. This will take into account the needs of birds, reptiles and insects. We will fill in the gaps over the next five years, with canopy species not currently growing on the island, to enhance particular areas for specific fauna. After we have finished planting, we will need to weed intensively for the next ten years and the biodiversity enhancement plan will probably take another five to ten years to roll out.

'We are working closely with Ngāti Paoa and Ngāi Tai ki Tāmaki who are involved in our annual work plans. The trust is co-funding, with the Department of Conservation, a ranger on the island. We are also looking at rebuilding the surgeon's cottage to turn it into a visitors' centre.'

John credits his inspiration for getting involved in the Motuihe project to his upbringing. 'I grew up in lucky times where I was able to run and play on the farm next door to my parents' house during the early '50s. I liked the outdoors and my parents had a lovely bach at Christian Bay near Tāwharanui. We used to holiday there every school holidays and many weekends in between. We had a 10-foot rowboat and I was able to catch fish and dive for pāua, scallops and crayfish, all around Christian Bay. It was extremely easy to do so then, with just snorkel gear. Then, over the years, it became increasingly more difficult. The bay became full of sediment. Fishing got harder and people were coming to the bay plundering the pipi beds and the oysters on the rocks, until there were no more to be collected.'

Now that the island restoration project is well under

way, John is keen to extend the restoration momentum out into the marine space. 'We applied under the department's conservation management strategy to have a marine no-take area around the island out to 10 metres water depth, but were unsuccessful.

'Motuihe is a place, within 30 minutes of Downtown Auckland, that people can travel to and see what New Zealand looked like before it was cleared for farming and urban subdivision. You can walk around the whole island in

John Laurence has been a driving force behind the restoration of Motuihe Island and he inspired members of the Outboard Boating Club to support the project. He is shown here on the island pointing towards successful dune-restoration work.

two to three hours. No matter how windy it is, you can find a lovely sheltered spot for a picnic on the beach. You can see rare and endangered birds. There is nowhere else in the gulf where you can do those things.'

In 2003, on a third attempt, the Department of Conservation finally managed to eradicate rabbits from the island and replanting work started later that year. During the first year, 6500 trees were planted by volunteers. Two years later, 25,000 trees were planted. Mobil Oil then covered the cost of the early translocations of endangered species and for the establishment of a small visitors centre.

The island is hugely popular with boaties. On some days in summer there can be up to 500 boats in the bay. It is estimated that some 40,000 people visit the island sanctuary by private boat each year.[34]

Rotoroa Island

Ngāti Paoa and Ngāi Tai have strong associations with Rotoroa Island and the remains of two defensive pā can be seen on the island.[35] The island's Māori name was originally spelt Rā-tō-roa which literally means 'the prolonged sunset'.[36] In 1841, Charles McIntosh bought the island from its Māori owners. Then retired sea captain William Ruthe purchased the land in 1886 to create a 'tourist, holiday and health resort'. It became known as Ruthes Island for a time. The narrow strip of water between Rotoroa and Pōnui islands, Ruthe Passage, still bears the sea captain's name today.

In 1908, the Salvation Army acquired the island for £400 and opened a 'Certified Inebriates Home' there in January 1911. The concept was based on removing alcoholic men from temptation on the mainland and curing them through a regime of a simple diet, hard work and sea air.

Around a hundred men were housed in the dormitories at any one time, looked after by a large retinue of Salvation Army families who undertook all the tasks needed to run the island. These included farming, cooking, cleaning, fishing, transporting goods to and from the island, providing health services and counselling. The island was virtually self-sufficient, with large vegetable gardens, orchards and a working farm. 'In fine weather, two or three men could go out daily, nine months of the year, and catch sufficient fish with a hook and line to provide one meal a day for all on the island.'[37] Eggs and wool were exported to the mainland.

The facility operated for 93 years, but by 2000 the buildings required an extensive upgrade and the provision of modern treatment services was becoming prohibitively expensive. The Salvation Army decided to close the rehabilitation centre in 2005.

Fortuitously, around this time, philanthropists Neal and Annette Plowman indicated that they wished to bequeath a special gift to the people of Auckland. Their family had a history of supporting the Salvation Army, so involvement in Rotoroa Island seemed like a good fit. Ex-merchant banker and art supporter John Gow brought the parties together.

John lives with his wife Jo in Connells Bay on Waiheke Island, facing Rotoroa Island. On hearing that the Salvation Army was pulling out of Rotoroa, John was concerned. 'Knowing the high value of the land around here, my concern was that it would be sold off to a rich American.' John was close friends with the Plowmans and they had often discussed giving a 'gift of access' to the country.[38] It took two years to negotiate an agreement. The Salvation Army didn't want to sell the island due to their long association with it. In particular, they had people buried on the island and a chapel still there. But they were not sure what to do with it, as the island was costing money to keep open. So, in 2007, an agreement was reached whereby the Salvation Army would grant, to the Rotoroa Island Trust, a 99-year lease over the island. The full cost of the lease was paid upfront by the trust and it roughly equated to the value of the island if it had been purchased outright. As Barrie Brown, chairman of the Rotoroa Island Trust noted 'this meant that the Salvation Army could take the money and do good work with it and the trust got the use of the island for close on 100 years'.[39]

The Rotoroa Island Trust was established to oversee the restoration of the island, with trustees comprising representatives of the Salvation Army, the benefactors and two independent members. Restoring the island was a major challenge. Around 20,000 pines were felled and chipped for mulch. As Barrie recalls 'we ended up with 40,000 cubic metres of mulch, the biggest pile in the southern hemisphere. The trees were not commercially viable to sell as timber and we knew we would have to put something over the island before we planted the trees, so that worked well.

'We took down most of the buildings. They were mainly built from blocks made on the island, they needed a huge amount of money spent on them and we had no practical use for them. We kept five of the old staff houses: two are used by our staff and three are available as holiday homes for the public to rent. The only historic building on the island was an old schoolhouse. We restored that and it is now used as a meeting room. We rebuilt the compound and recently constructed a room on the end of it so that school children are able to get out of the weather.' There is also a hostel

operating in the old superintendent's house. The history of the island has been captured in a modern museum and exhibition centre designed by Rick Pearson.[40]

The major part of the restoration project involved planting 450,000 indigenous trees. Mice and rats, which were in plague proportions, were also eradicated. As trust chairman, Barrie explains, 'We managed to get rid of the rats, but the mice were a real problem. Three years ago we had to close the island for three months and we did three aerial bait drops. That was the end of our mice.' Unlike the other island restoration initiatives within the Hauraki Gulf, which relied primarily on volunteers, the significant philanthropic funding of around $40 million available for the Rotoroa Island project meant that work could be undertaken by paid contractors. 'What would normally take 20 years plus to achieve in a normal restoration programme we have done in seven years.' The island was opened to the public for the first time in February 2011.

'Our initial vision was to create a park full of native trees, that the birds would eventually come back to, and a place where people could go and spend a day to picnic, walk and swim. Then about three years ago I was talking to the marketing manager from the Auckland Zoo. She asked if we could do a project together. I said, "Why don't you do a plan and I'll put it to our trustees?" and she did. We agreed on a plan to reintroduce sixteen endangered native species to the island, both birds and reptiles. We have now

By the time the Salvation Army moved off Rotoroa Island in 2005, there were extensive facilities established in Home Bay. Shown here in 1984, they included accommodation blocks, staff houses, work sheds, art and craft rooms, tennis courts and extensive vegetable gardens. (Salvation Army Heritage Centre and Archives)

introduced 40 saddlebacks and 40 whiteheads. We have just released twelve brown kiwi chicks and a pair of takahē. If the island proves suitable for takahē, and I think it will, we will probably get another two pairs.'[41] Reintroductions were not to be restricted to species that had originally inhabited the island. As Auckland Zoo director Jonathan Wilcken explained, 'we are deliberately aiming not to recreate an ecosystem, but to create an ecosystem anew. We don't frankly care very much whether those species existed on Rotoroa Island. Nor do we care very much if the species could sustain themselves if we weren't there to manage them.' The vision is to deliberately create a new managed ecosystem.[42]

This innovative zoo initiative is linked to a school education programme. Barrie explains, 'last summer 850 children visited the island for a day to learn about conservation. Around 60 per cent of the children had never been on a boat before. They have a wonderful day and the experience is highly regarded by schools.'

With the land restoration programme successfully under way, Barrie started thinking about possibilities for the adjacent

Top: Forty whiteheads have been released on Rotoroa Island along with forty saddleback, twelve brown kiwi chicks and a pair of takahē. A whitehead is shown here flying towards the bush after release. (Nick Eagles)

Left: Barrie Brown is the Chair of the Rotoroa Island Trust which is overseeing the restoration of the island, the reintroduction of endangered species and the development of the island as an educational facility. (Rotoroa Island Trust)

marine area. 'Because the island had been closed to the public for a hundred years, by its own act of Parliament, all the lovely mussels and shellfish around the island were untouched. I didn't want to have that destroyed once we opened up the island. We thought it might be nice to spread what we did on land into the water. But we hadn't actually contemplated doing anything in the marine space when we signed the lease, so had not allocated any funding for this purpose.'

Now, about 6000 people visit the island each year, around half by private boat and half by ferry. There could be more, but there are problems with the lack of a regular ferry service. This makes it difficult for people without their own boats to access the island, except over the summer peak when the ferries run daily. As Barrie notes, 'our school educational programme for the year was booked up in the first week of the first term. The ferries don't sail in winter and they only sail daily from Christmas to Waitangi Day. After that it's only four times a week. We would like to increase the schools programme, but we've got to be able to get the kids there and back.' The island is turning into something very special. As Barrie concludes, 'People who go there just say it's such a restful place. There are nice beaches, good walks, a little bit of art and a bit of history. It will be really something in another 20 years' time.' John Gow,

one of the initiators of the project, reflected: 'It's a win-win for everybody. The first 100 years were about the Salvation Army, the second 100 years are about the salvation of a legacy — which is gifting access of this magnificent island to New Zealand, 365 days a year.'[43]

Restoration of islands of the Hauraki Gulf has been a stunning success. Pests have been removed, indigenous forests replanted and endangered species of birds and reptiles reintroduced. Most are being managed as open sanctuaries, where members of the public can freely visit and enjoy the special attributes of each island. Several are being linked with public educational programmes and cultural tourism experiences.

Rotoroa Island is now open to the public for the first time in over a century and is well on the way to being fully restored. There are plans to introduce up to 20 indigenous bird and reptile species to the island and this work is being linked with a school education programme.

There are some problems with transportation to overcome, but the islands are becoming the catalyst for a transformation in the way that many people relate to the gulf: a move from a focus on resource exploitation to an attitude of respect and care. It is an approach which is much closer to the way Māori have always viewed the gulf, as something which is an integral part of themselves. The greater challenge is to extend the island revolution out into the sea.

New era for the inner Hauraki Gulf islands

On 29 August 2015, Tiritiri Matangi, Rangitoto, Motutapu and Motuihe islands were transferred to a trust representing thirteen iwi (Tūpuna Taonga Trust), in acknowledgement of their deep spiritual connection to the islands. Thirty-one days later the islands were vested back to the Crown, with the trust retaining ownership of the summit of Rangitoto (Ngā Pona-Toru-a-Peretā) and the Islington Bay hall and bach number 80 properties, which are associated with waka moorings. The iwi will have ongoing involvement in the management of the islands and a new conservation management plan for them is to be prepared (Tāmaki Makaurau motu plan).[44]

Story of the Gulf | **Rob Fenwick**

BUSINESSMAN AND ENVIRONMENTALIST, WAIHEKE ISLAND[45]

When he was a boy growing up in Remuera during the 1950s and '60s, Rob Fenwick's father used to take him out most weekends over the summer in a little plywood boat. They explored the inner gulf, including the coasts of Rangitoto and Browns islands. During the summer holidays, the family would rent a bach at Scandretts Bay on the east coast of the Mahurangi Peninsula.

Rob continued his interest in the gulf and, whilst a teenager, he got his scuba-diving ticket and dived on the outer coast of Kawau Island and occasionally at Great Barrier Island. He also crewed on the A-class keeler *Ta'Aroa* for races around the gulf to Te Kouma and to Mansion House Bay.

During the 1980s Rob ended up buying a little piece of Waiheke. 'Prior to that, I had never spent any time on the island itself. In the early 1980s, I saw an advert in *The New Zealand Herald* for a landlocked bay on Waiheke. I had a little fizz boat, so I came out from Maraetai to meet the farmer who was selling this gorsy bay. It was on the end of the peninsula between Awaawaroa and Te Matuku bays, which at that time were known as Big Muddy and Little Muddy bays.

'I was entranced by the seclusion of the property, so I bought it. The property was south facing so didn't get a lot of sun. But it had a stillness about it, with beautiful pōhutukawa growing down to the edge of the rocks. It was fully enclosed and at night you couldn't see another light, apart from a glimpse of the Passage Rock light. It was totally remote. We put a caravan on it and for a number of years would come out and camp, bringing fresh water and everything across in a boat from Maraetai. I gradually became a Waihekean.

'The adjacent block of land was a peninsula between the two tidal inlets, a block of 360 hectares more or less. It was progressively reverting to gorse through neglect. It was owned by a chap who got into difficulty with his mortgage and was forced to sell after the financial crash of October 1987. There weren't a lot of bidders after the crash and I was delighted to become the owner of this amazing piece of land. It was largely in gorse, tobacco plant and rampant kikuyu. The fences were all broken down. It became in many ways a life's project.

'I didn't know it then, but a big quarrying company also wanted to buy it, but had been caught up in some transaction affected by the share-market crash a few months earlier. The company's representative rang me and said, "Do you realise that the peninsula is actually a huge big seam of blue quarry metal? We have plans for it that we would like to talk to you about." They came out and told us, "Wouldn't it be nice if the peninsula, instead of being a bush-clad ridgeline, could be a lake in 30 years' time which we could waterski on." They showed us this outrageous plan of an opencast mine of the size of the Mt Wellington quarry. It would open up the whole property for extraction.

'While I'm sure Auckland's development needed the metal, we got very alarmed and realised that, while we might be able to keep the quarrymen at bay while we were alive, unless we did something about protecting the land, they would eventually prevail.

'Graeme Campbell advised me that such was the value of the metal, the quarrymen could make a case to take it under the Public Works Act, so we would need something stronger than a QEII [Queen Elizabeth the Second] covenant. In his view we should use a section 77 Reserves Act covenant which would require an act of Parliament to reverse. This became a complex mission to achieve, as we wanted to protect the whole peninsula, not just the bits with ecological significance. We wrote a comprehensive management plan that enabled the property to be farmed, and potentially allowed for an oyster farm to operate on its shores, but the whole area would come under a covenant. This really confused the Department of Conservation and the council — the idea that productive land could sit inside an ecological covenant. But the upshot of it all was that the whole peninsula was eventually covenanted under section 77.

'The first thing that we did was to look at the land and agree that we would not farm most of it. Out of 360 hectares, it seemed to us that there might be 40 that would be pasture. One of the considerations was evidence that the land had been part of a productive pre-European landscape, with a big community of people living in this bay before any Europeans arrived. Some of the biggest kūmara pits in Auckland are visible along the ridgeline. The balance of the land, around

Top & right: Rob Fenwick has covenanted his entire property at Te Matuku Bay, Waiheke Island, and has let much of it revert to native bush (as shown on the right). The recovery has been dramatic over a 30-year period.

300 hectares, was already starting to revert, with gorse predominant, and we decided it should be left in the hope that, in 100 years, it would be forest again. We got rid of a big mob of wild cattle marauding through the land and a flock of goats destroying the bush.

'There's been a dramatic recovery in indigenous vegetation. It happened far more quickly, and more dramatically from a landscape point of view, than we had imagined. When we got rid of the cattle, under the good remnant stands in the gullies the understorey of nikau and hardwood podocarps just soared up and it was wonderful to watch. Over the past 30 years we haven't done much planting, just a few hundred pōhutukawa, and we welcome the school children from Waiheke Primary who are part of the Trees for Survival programme.

'Most of the revegetation has been natural. Gorse is a marvellous nursery plant and, if you have the patience to let it happen, it will.'

In 2002, the property became part of the Hauraki Gulf Marine Park, the first piece of privately owned land to do so. Rob also gifted a piece of land to Auckland Council as a public walkway, so that the public could walk from Awaawaroa Bay to Te Matuku Bay.

'The islands have been transformed during my lifetime. I can remember visiting them and seeing rats scurrying around on the foreshore, wallabies on Motutapu and possums absolutely destroying the pōhutukawa forest on Rangitoto. Now a group of us on Waiheke are thinking it might be possible to have a campaign for a rat-free Waiheke. It's an aspirational goal. We have the miracle of no possums on the island and, even if we got the rat population down to 10 per cent, that would be a fabulous vision for Waiheke — and also potentially for Great Barrier Island.

'The ticking time bomb is actually the marine environment. There's the pressure of recreational fishing and nitrate loadings from what's happening on the farmland, particularly in the firth. We've got to find a way to ensure that the competing interests — a thriving marine ecosystem, the provision for recreational fishing and enjoyment, and a level of farming activity being allowed around the gulf — all work in harmony. That integrated approach to a jewel like the Hauraki Gulf shouldn't be beyond us all.'

Chapter 16
Restoring the sea

Efforts to protect and restore the Hauraki Gulf marine area started in 1960 and drove new thinking about marine protection. The approach was subsequently adopted throughout the rest of the country and in many other parts of the world. A total of six marine reserves have now been created in the gulf. Five are located on the mainland coast: near Leigh, Hāhei, Tāwharanui, Long Bay and Pollen Island (near Point Chevalier/ Te Atatū in Auckland). One other is situated on Waiheke Island. Collectively, they cover only a small part of the gulf's total marine area, around 0.3 per cent, but they are an important start and something which can be built on.

Cape Rodney-Ōkakari Point Marine Reserve

New Zealand was probably the first nation in the world to develop legislation that would provide for the spatial protection of the marine environment, and the idea arose in the context of the Hauraki Gulf. After a marine laboratory was established on the coast facing Goat Island

After a marine laboratory was established on the coast opposite Goat Island (Te Hāwere-a-Maki) in 1962, scientists soon realised that their ability to undertake scientific experiments would be severely constrained if they were unable to protect their 'subjects' from harvest. This spawned the idea of establishing a reserve in the sea.

Initially, some divers opposed the idea of creating a marine reserve at Goat Island, as they were used to being able to harvest seafood there. But the benefits of marine protection soon became apparent, with stocks of crayfish rapidly rebounding followed by those of snapper (shown here) and other fish. (Tony and Jenny Enderby)

(Te Hāwere-a-Maki) near Leigh in 1962, scientists soon realised that their ability to undertake scientific experiments would be severely constrained if they were unable to protect their 'subjects' from being harvested.

It was Professor Valentine Chapman, Chairman of the University of Auckland's Leigh Laboratory Committee, who, in 1965, came up with what was a novel idea for the time. As Bill Ballantine, the first director of the marine laboratory, recalls: 'Professor Chapman said, "We must get a marine reserve" and the rest of us looked blank. He said, "You know, a place where experimental apparatus is protected and fish are not eaten." We thought that was a good idea.'[1]

Chapman wrote to the Marine Department to suggest that a 'no-take' marine reserve should be established in front of the marine laboratory. He argued that this would enable the area to be restored to its natural state, thus improving the effectiveness of scientific study there.[2] He received an unhelpful response from the departmental officials, who indicated that there were no legal mechanisms available to enable such a measure and, in any event, it wasn't a priority.

'They basically told him to get lost. But Chapman was undoubtedly an activist and you couldn't tell him to get lost. He just ramped the thing up. For several years he wrote to the department every month. His motto was, "If you take on bureaucrats, you need to use their weapon". Their weapon was paper. So, if you wanted to challenge bureaucracy, you needed to create a file and, if you wanted to win, you needed to create a big file. So he created a big file.'[3] Chapman got both the Marine Sciences Association and the New Zealand Underwater Association to support him. He held public meetings and addressed school groups.

'In the end, the department had to invent legislation. Our basic argument was simple. The government is the government and its responsibilities don't stop at the high-water mark. If there is no legislation to make it possible, then there should be, and get on with it.'[4] Finally in 1971, after six years of lobbying, the Marine Department released a draft bill and the Marine Reserves Act was subsequently passed.

The University of Auckland then made an application for the establishment of a 520-hectare marine reserve in front of their marine laboratory. The first application was rejected by the Marine Department and another submitted in 1973. The proposed boundaries were set between the two headlands standing on either side of the marine laboratory: Cape Rodney and Ōkakari Point. Establishing an appropriate seaward boundary was less clear-cut. As Bill Ballantine recalls, 'There was virtually no precedent at the

The Cape Rodney-Ōkakari Point marine reserve is now hugely popular with members of the public, with hundreds of thousands of people visiting each year. This has created economic opportunities for local business, including the glass-bottom boat shown here, and has pumped millions of dollars into the local economy. (Tanya Peart)

time and research scientists, including me, were obsessed with rocky reefs. Flat sandy bottoms didn't seem very real, which is quite wrong, but that's how it was then. The other consideration was that, at that time, trawling was not allowed within 0.5 nautical miles of land. That translates to 800 metres and that's where we set the seaward boundary. There was no scientific justification for it, it was just a piece of political pragmatism. We couldn't complain later that we were so restricted, as that's all we'd asked for.'[5]

Even so, there were still numerous objections to the proposal. Some of these were specific, but others reflected a blanket opposition to any protection within the sea. 'It was widely stated that we were threatening people's livelihoods, trampling on their traditions and generally acting as enemies of the people. I find this really interesting now, because the number of visitors to the marine reserve is huge. So if that is being the enemy of the people, I would gladly do it again.'[6]

As Ballantine wrote in 1991: 'It seems that many New Zealanders, from all kinds of background, feel that high water mark is a kind of last frontier beyond which one is free from regulations and restraints. They feel that the sea is the one place where you can do what you like and don't even have to feel guilty. This idea is often subconscious (and in any case a myth) but is all the more powerful because of these points. Anyone proposing even a sensible and properly structured programme for an area of sea is seen as destroying this treasured ideal, and real anger may develop. The fact

that many who hold such views are quite aware that the arguments in favour of some regulation are sound, and in the public interest, may just make matters worse. The proposers of the regulations then become the bearers of bad news as well as the violators of personal freedom, and no argument is too trivial or too bad to use against them.'[7]

Despite the opposition, the Minister of Marine finally accepted the application and the reserve was gazetted in November 1975, making the Cape Rodney-Ōkakari Point Marine Reserve the first to be established in New Zealand and possibly in the world.

Diver Tony Enderby was one of those who were initially against the reserve. 'When Goat Island became a marine reserve, I was a member of the Dolphin Underwater Club and we opposed the proposal. This was because everyone would come up here and collect seafood. But it only took us about a year to see the changes. We realised that we were onto something really good, as we were suddenly seeing snapper and crayfish in numbers not evident anywhere else in the gulf along the mainland coast. By around the late

1970s, I was hooked on the idea of marine reserves being a totally valuable tool.'[8]

Being close to the marine laboratory, the impacts of the reserve on marine life were able to be closely monitored by scientists. The first species to show a marked recovery was crayfish. Four years after the reserve was created, their numbers had increased five-fold. As the numbers within the protected area increased, so did the catches of crayfish outside the seaward boundary of the reserve, as the animals migrated past the narrow protective boundaries. Although this meant that fewer crayfish were protected, it did maintain the livelihood of crayfishermen in the area, who had initially opposed the reserve, but soon found that their catches were maintained.[9]

It was less clear how soon fish populations rebounded, as counting fish proved difficult. Due to the practice of feeding fish in the reserve for some years, the fish tended to be attracted to divers, thereby skewing the counts. Data indicated that red moki soon tripled in numbers within the reserve. But it took some years for snapper to increase in abundance, although individual fish were larger than those in adjacent fished areas. Over time, the numbers and range of fish increased.[10]

One of the most marked changes in the marine reserve was the recovery of the kelp forests and a reduction in the area of urchin barrens. By 2006, the area of kelp forest had more than doubled.[11] More recent monitoring in 2011 has shown that butterfish, red moki, snapper, John dory, banded wrasse, blue cod and silver drummer are all present within the reserve in higher numbers than outside it. Snapper abundance was four times greater within the reserve and overall species diversity was higher. There are also indications that snapper larvae produced in the reserve are making a strong contribution to surrounding fished stocks.[12]

An economic impact analysis undertaken in 2008 identified an estimated 375,000 people visit the reserve annually and $18.6 million a year is contributed to the local economy. This was compared to the cost to the Department of Conservation of managing the reserve of around $70,000 per year.[13] The reserve supports a number of local tourism enterprises, and the University of Auckland has recently opened the Goat Island Marine Discovery Centre to the visiting public. This provides a touch tank, interactive displays and a wealth of information on the marine environment.

But perhaps the most significant contribution of the marine reserve was to show that it was possible, that closing an area off to fishing was achievable and that it enabled fish and crayfish numbers to rebound and reef systems to repair themselves. It also served to demonstrate the strong public interest in visiting such areas, where plentiful marine life could be experienced at first-hand.

Tāwharanui Marine Park

The success of the Cape Rodney-Ōkakari Point Marine Reserve inspired the Auckland Regional Authority to consider creating a similar protected area along the coastline adjacent to its newly acquired regional park on the Tāwharanui Peninsula. But instead of using the new Marine Reserves Act, the authority opted to apply regulations under fisheries and harbour legislation and to call the new area a marine 'park' rather than a reserve. The new Tāwharanui Marine Park, of around 400 hectares, was opened in 1981. The marine-park model proved popular, possibly because it provided more flexibility than marine reserves, and other marine parks followed around the country.

As marine ecologist Dr Roger Grace recalls, 'The parks department at the Auckland Regional Authority decided to create a marine park on the northern side of the Tāwharanui Regional Park. The initial intention was to allow recreational fishing, but one guy there, planner Walter Willis, was adamant that the area should be a sanctuary for fish and that no fishing should be allowed. At that time, I thought allowing some recreational fishing would be fine. But Willis stuck to his guns and insisted it be a "no fishing" zone. So we ended up with a park where 3 kilometres of coastline was protected from fishing under special fisheries regulations.'[14]

Dr Grace has been involved in monitoring the marine park at Tāwharanui, as well as one to the north of Whangārei at Mimiwhangata, and this enabled him to identify the impacts of different management regimes. 'In the mid-1970s I got involved in the Mimiwhangata marine park proposal. In 1970 to '71, Bill Ballantine, Wade Doak and I mapped the underwater habitats. This was the first biologically orientated marine mapping in New Zealand. At that time we didn't know what kina barrens were. Some areas of rocky reef had kelp and others didn't and we didn't know why.

'Then in 1976 New Zealand Breweries, who owned the land on the Mimiwhangata peninsula, decided that the way forward was to create a marine park, so we started to

monitor fish and crayfish there. Then the following year I was approached by the Auckland Regional Authority which was keen to do a similar monitoring regime at Tāwharanui, with a view to creating a marine park. So we've had a monitoring programme going since the mid-1970s and it's one of the longest in the country on shallow reefs. It's also been good to have parallel programmes running, particularly given the subsequent developments re marine protection.

'A marine park was put in place at Mimiwhangata in 1984 under special fisheries regulations. There were some restrictions on recreational fishing. You could only use one hook, no sinkers and no nets. There was only a limited list of species you could take. The intention was to kick out commercial fishing as well, but they got a grandfather clause, so they continued fishing until 1994, after which it was banned. So it's had a partial protection regime going, with no commercial fishing since 1994 but recreational fishing continuing. Tāwharanui went down a different track with all fishing banned from the start.

'What proceeded from there on proved to be a very valuable experiment, where we could compare total no-take with partial protection which eliminated commercial fishing, and both of those scenarios with open fishing areas outside

A marine park was created along the north side of the Tāwharanui peninsula, adjacent to the regional park, in 1981. Thirty years later it was changed to marine reserve status. The area attracts large numbers of visitors for swimming, snorkelling, surfing and walking.

the protected areas. Those three main scenarios have been the major thrust of my research in that area. We now have a very valuable long-term data set showing the differences. The only thing that worked from a marine conservation point of view was 'no-take'. At Mimiwhangata there was continual decline, not as fast as with open slather fishing, but it continued to get worse. There is now virtually no difference between inside and outside the park. In the park there are kina barrens everywhere, no fish and no crayfish.

'With Tāwharanui, the results have been spectacular. There has been a gradual build-up of fish and crayfish and the habitat has recovered from kina barrens to rich kelp forest. The same sort of thing happened at the Leigh marine reserve. In 2010 there were 1000 legal-size crayfish per hectare of reef and virtually none outside the protected area.'

Despite the success of the marine-park regime at Tāwharanui, during the late 1990s the Auckland Regional

Council decided to change the status of the area to a marine reserve. There had been a dramatic increase in the numbers of crayfish, but it was a different story for red moki. 'Although in 1996 red moki numbers were three times more common inside the marine park than outside, there has been a general decline in red moki numbers inside the marine park and a lack of large fish, despite nearly 20 years of protection. Since red moki are highly territorial, this suggests that the impacts of fishing pressure or other external changes have not enabled the population to increase.'[15] It was thought that illegal fishing was to blame for the low fish numbers and that a marine reserve with simplified boundaries would be easier to enforce and provide a clearer signal to the public that fishing was prohibited.

In addition, the council argued that a marine reserve would better complement the 'mainland island' that the council had created on the adjacent regional park, through the removal of predators and the construction of a predator-proof fence. 'The change in status from marine park to marine reserve will complement this management regime by creating an area of minimal intervention both above and below mean high water springs. The Tāwharanui Peninsula will become one of the few areas in New Zealand where both the mainland and the adjacent marine area are managed in as close to a "pre-human" situation as is possible.'[16]

Councillor Mike Lee first proposed the idea of changing the marine area's status in 1994 and it took seventeen long years to come to fruition. The new marine reserve was formally opened on 28 August 2011 with a pōwhiri [welcome] hosted by Ngāti Manuhiri.[17] It is the smallest of the six marine reserves in the Hauraki Gulf.

Whanganui Ā Hei (Cathedral Cove) Marine Reserve

The third protected area to be created in the Hauraki Gulf, and the second marine reserve, covers 840 hectares of coastal waters near Hāhei. The Whanganui Ā Hei (Cathedral Cove) Marine Reserve opened in 1992. It remains the only marine reserve along the coast of the Coromandel Peninsula and is hugely popular with local and international tourists, with over 200,000 people visiting each year.[18]

The idea of creating a marine reserve on the Coromandel Peninsula was conceived in the Waikato conservancy of the Department of Conservation in the late 1980s. Departmental staff could see the loss of natural values in the marine areas close to where people lived. Species such as crayfish were fast disappearing and there were some bad fishing practices, for example abandoning set nets in bad weather and catching large hauls of kahawai for use as garden fertiliser. An assessment was undertaken of potential sites and, by 1991, attention had focused on Cathedral Cove near Hāhei. It was a location that was accessible, had some facilities, and already attracted international and local visitors. In addition there was some local support for the proposition.[19]

The proposal split the Hāhei community. As former Department of Conservation Coromandel Area Manager John Gaukrodger recalls, 'There were those staunchly opposed and quite vigorous in their opposition and those that were quieter in their support, but still quite enthusiastic about the idea. The public meetings that were held over a period of time were seriously challenging. The crayfishermen came onside reasonably quickly, when they appreciated that they could drop their pots just outside the marine reserve boundary. Most of the opposition came from recreational fishers. They didn't like the idea that their way of life would change and that we had come along to impose on their freedom.[20]

'One thing that was critical to the success of establishing the marine reserve in the end was the support of Peter Tiki Johnson from Ngāti Hei. As we became seriously embroiled in the battle, his staunch support for the marine reserve pulled us through. People were concerned about what they felt they were giving up, but Peter always came back to the point that, "If we don't do something, there will be nothing anyway."[21]

The initial survey of potential boundaries indicated that the whole of Hāhei beach might be included in the reserve, from the Te Pare historic reserve in the south through to the northern end of the beach. But this did not eventuate. As the controversy around the reserve proposal escalated, Department of Conservation officials decided to remove the part of the reserve which fronted Hāhei beach. This was a pragmatic decision, designed to reduce opposition, when it seemed all might be lost. 'The person most put out by that decision was Peter Johnson. He was most upset. But, in the end, we made the call in order to save the proposal.'[22] The department managed to push the reduced proposal through and the reserve was finally gazetted in 1993.

Monitoring data shows that marine life within the reserve has rebounded and that there has been a significant increase in crayfish numbers, which contrasts with the low numbers outside the reserve, although crayfish numbers have been reducing since 2009. More recently Cyclone Pam, which hit the east coast in March 2015, has reduced the abundance of some species within the reserve.[23]

Ngāti Hei kaumātua Joe Davis has been closely involved with the reserve. 'Ngāti Hei supported the marine reserve here, although it was something that was controversial within our whānau. We picked a place that could be easily reached and, with the agreement of the adjacent landowners, it was established. We became involved in the running of the reserve and have four permanent seats on the marine reserve committee. We depended largely on funding and support from the Department of Conservation and still do. But we feel that the reserve is under-resourced and under-managed. It's not the iconic marine reserve we would like it to be. The mana of the reserve needs more support.'

The Te Whanganui Ā Hei-Cathedral Cove marine reserve is hugely popular with local and international tourists, with over 200,000 visiting each year.

Long Bay-Ōkura Marine Reserve

A third marine reserve in the Hauraki Gulf was established at Long Bay, on Auckland's North Shore, in 1995. This was the first urban marine reserve and it is the largest marine reserve in the gulf, covering around 980 hectares. Its impetus came directly from an initiative of local resident Dr David Gray who in 1990, and later with the help of some educationalists and yachtsmen in the area, established a marine education centre (which came to be known as MERC) at the southern end of Long Bay. The Marine Education and Recreation Centre Trust Board Inc. was registered in 1979 to develop the education centre

Story of the Gulf | **Dr David Gray**

RETIRED MEDICAL DOCTOR, AUCKLAND[24]

After working in Indonesia for some years as a surgeon, David returned to Auckland in 1971 and settled in Torbay, becoming a local GP. At the end of his medical training, David had visited Aitutaki in the Cook Islands and had been 'blown away by the skills of the islanders in sailing canoes. When I came back from overseas in the 1970s, I participated in the Auckland Anniversary Regatta and it amazed me that there were no Pacific Islanders or Māori partaking in water sports, when I knew it was part of their ethos.[25]

'At that time, there was a lot of settlement in South Auckland and the urbanisation of both Māori and other Polynesians was not going well. I felt that the sea, and their natural affinity with it, would help them to develop a self-identity and maybe lift their horizons from the gangs, poker machines and infighting that were going on in these suburbs. I felt strongly that the sea was everyone's heritage, but somehow it had become that of the elite.'

After settling in Torbay, David had become involved in the local yachting scene, introducing his six young daughters to the sport. 'From my activities at the yacht club I could see that there was a bit of tension in Torbay between the yachties and the beachies — the swimming people — with the beach being crowded out by yachts and trailers. I was also scared that some kids would be killed as they ran excitedly across the road to launch their boats into the water.

'I made investigations and discovered that there was a plot of land at the end of Long Bay which was a reserve contribution intended for community use. At that time the site was littered with building debris, scraps of machinery and the foundations of early buildings. I could see its potential, not as a place for an exclusive yacht club, but for the use of the general public. I drew up plans for a marae-type set-up, with the definite idea of making it a welcoming place for all.

'Then some local school teachers became interested in the idea, as well as the commodore of the local yacht club, and we shared our thoughts. Not long after this, the patron of the yacht club (Don St Clair Brown) found himself on a flight to Wellington with the Takapuna mayor and the topic was again discussed. I later attended a meeting of the Takapuna City Council, accompanied by Don St Clair Brown and John Orams, and we presented the idea to the councillors. They also liked the idea and indicated that they would be willing to support us. It was a big moment.'[26]

Before further steps were taken, the trust undertook a 'needs' survey of some 242 schools and other potential user groups in the Auckland Region. 'The survey revealed some uncomfortable facts that continue to be relevant today: 88 per cent of schools lacked facilities for developing marine skills; 74 per cent lacked the finance to pursue them; and 69 per cent lacked a suitable location. An average of 23 per cent of children (up to 50 per cent of junior classes) from south and west Auckland had never been to the beach!'[27]

'It took twelve years to raise enough money. We had a mission. I had faith that this was God's call to me to get this project going and to make it non-exclusive. In the last hectic effort to reach our goal, the chairman Peter Maxwell set himself the task of writing 700 appeal letters to business houses with follow-up personal phone calls. The results were outstanding.' Finally, in 1990, the Marine Education and Recreation Centre opened.

In 1998, Sir Peter Blake, who had grown up sailing on the North Shore, agreed to become co-patron of the centre. 'Once Sir Peter changed his act from "screaming around" to "looking around", we persuaded local resident Mark Orams (who had been on *Steinlager 2* with Peter) to approach him on behalf of MERC. I think Peter had the same epiphany that I had experienced. I used to love racing yachts and then, in the end, I thought: 'What the heck? I'm just going around these buoys in circles. So I then spent much more time exploring. Peter came and visited MERC with his son James and said he would be very happy to be a patron. After Peter's death, Mark Orams approached Pippa Blake and she happily agreed to allow the centre to adopt his name as part of MERC, which then became officially known as the 'Sir Peter Blake Marine Education and Recreation Centre'.

The centre has now been going for over 25 years. During that time an estimated quarter of a million children have visited. David Gray explains, 'It's viable, it gets no government funding and we've kept the motivation perfectly clear at

Top: The Sir Peter Blake Marine Education and Recreation Centre at Long Bay has provided marine-related activities for over a quarter of a million children.

Left: Dr David Gray was the driving force behind the establishment of the Sir Peter Blake Marine Education and Recreation Centre (MERC) at Long Bay in 1990. He is shown here (on the right) with Dr Ross Garrett who was one of the main instigators behind the establishment of the Long Bay-Ōkura marine reserve.

the board level. Yes, it gets wealthy Pākehā children, but it also gets at least 10–15 per cent from decile one schools. It is available to any school, anywhere.' The centre can accommodate up to 85 children overnight and 120 during the day. Groups of children stay in the dormitories and learn to sail, canoe and snorkel. Other activities include bushwalking, mountain biking, paddle boarding, river crossing and reef swimming. The centre is becoming so popular that the staff cannot keep up with the demand and they are booked up to two years in advance during the popular summer period. 'Our anxiety is that we are not fulfilling the need. The need is far

too great. So we are looking for a second site.'

David's search has taken him to south Auckland. 'Auckland Council purchased land on the coast near Clevedon at Waitawa and opened a regional park there in 2015. It is close to south Auckland where the greatest need is. This marine and education centre will be slightly different from MERC in that there will be more waka ama [outrigger canoes], te reo speakers, etc. The council has approved the establishment of the centre but we have not yet got the money to set it up. The site is there, north-facing, an ex-bunker. It is about the same-sized site as MERC in Long Bay. All we need is about $4 million and we're away.

'Meantime, Sir Peter Blake MERC, apart from its routine activities, is trying to interest the public into looking at the gulf in a different way. People need to understand what is out there and get enthused about all these wonderful animals — the miracle of a scallop with a hundred eyes, the sponges and the worms, the wandering anemones and the nudibranches. If we can interest and excite people, then they are likely to learn about the creatures of the Hauraki Gulf and care for them.'

The Long Bay-Ōkura marine reserve was the first established in an urban area. Although there is more marine life within the reserve than outside of it, there has been a recent decline in species richness within the reserve, likely caused by sediment from the developing catchment.

interested in sailing themselves and had the financial ability to buy their kids a boat. But clearly a lot of people in Auckland were not in that position. Many children's parents knew nothing about sailing and possibly had no means to buy a yacht. So we thought that an institution like MERC could bring children to an appreciation of sailing and the marine environment in general, the enjoyment of it and the dangers involved in it. We could teach them about both. That was the original idea.'[29]

As well as being involved in marine education, Dr Ross Garrett developed a strong interest in marine reserves. 'I read Bill Ballantine's book and thought that it was a great idea and that we should have 10 per cent of the coastline as marine reserves. We have national parks on land in New Zealand and people accept them. We also have ordinary parks like Albert Park in Auckland. People go there, but they don't chop the trees down or pinch the flowers. So why should we not have the same thing underwater around the coastline, where people accept that there are places where you don't take anything — you don't take the fish or the shellfish and you don't remove the seaweed, just as in a park. I wasn't initially thinking about Long Bay itself.'

Ross published a series of articles on marine reserves in the in-house MERC newsletter, the *Wavebreaker*, the first being published in August 1990. In November of the same year, the MERC board passed a resolution that Ross should work with MERC's Director, John Maxted, to establish a marine reserve. At a similar time to Ross's developing interest in marine reserves, John had become concerned about the indiscriminate plunder of marine life at Long Bay. As David Gray later wrote, John 'recorded seeing 20 sacks of kina, many bags of cat's eyes, buckets full of tuatua — some juveniles — being carted away. Even the tiny periwinkles were being scraped off the rocks — presumably for soups!'[30]

Ross explains, 'John came to the conclusion that maybe we should stop this, as there will be nothing for people to see when snorkelling. We then organised a public meeting in June 1992. A lot of people came to the meeting and there was general agreement that some kind of protection of marine life at Long Bay was a good idea. Nobody at that time really knew what a marine reserve was and how it worked.[31]

'John Maxted said he couldn't do it, as he was involved in MERC, and that we should have a separate committee which should work towards getting marine protection. So a committee, eventually called the East Coast Bays Coastal Protection Society, was formed. I was one of the members.

project. Dr Ross Garrett was part of the trust board from its inception. Ross had been a keen yachtsman, sailing on the waters of the Hauraki Gulf from an early age. He eventually established a career as a nuclear physicist based at the University of Auckland. When he married and started a family, he settled in Torbay. Neighbour David Gray asked Ross to become involved in the marine education project and he agreed, eventually chairing the trust board.

Ross explained his motivation for getting involved. 'By this time my children had grown up and had learnt to sail. I realised what it had done for them and also realised that a lot of kids never got the opportunity to go sailing. So I saw MERC as a set-up which would introduce people to sailing who otherwise wouldn't have the opportunity.'[28]

'What was obvious to me was that the children who got to go sailing at yacht clubs all had parents who were

The Motu Mānawa-Pollen Island marine reserve mainly protects mangrove and salt-marsh areas of significance to wading birds. There had been earlier proposals to turn the area into a port or an airport.

Another was Dick Matthews, who had just retired from being a professor of molecular biology at the University of Auckland. He had a bach at Long Bay, which his parents had built. He said he wanted to be involved, as he could remember what it was like in the 1920s. He was the powerhouse behind the project; he really pushed things. We had meetings, once a week at first, and things happened very fast. In the end we got our marine reserve within three years of the committee being formed.' The reserve was created on 17 November 1995.

'There was a lot of opposition. Fishermen opposed it but, in the end, the people who were for it [201 submissions in support] greatly outnumbered the submissions against [13]. It came at a time when the Goat Island marine reserve had become a popular place for people to go to and lots of people realised what a marine reserve could do, because it worked so successfully up there. There was nothing extra special about Long Bay. It was simply representative of the average beach in the Hauraki Gulf and, therefore, it should be kept in its pristine state as a representative area.

'Unfortunately Dick Matthews died just a few months before it was okayed. After that, I became chairman and our mission was to work to maintain it as a marine reserve and make sure it didn't get polluted by development and so forth. Unfortunately, that was not altogether successful. Development of the catchment did proceed and, despite strenuous effort on behalf of developers and the impacts being supposedly mitigated, a lot of siltation crept down. The amount of marine life one sees now is nothing like what one

saw at Goat Island marine reserve soon after it was formed, although it is certainly better than it was. Children from MERC see baby snapper around the rocks and quite a bit of other stuff there.'

Things were looking good by 2002, seven years after the reserve was established, when eleven times as many snapper were found within the reserve when compared with the surrounding area. In addition, the snapper inside the reserve were on average larger. But a survey undertaken in 2009 found a large decline in species richness within the reserve.

Ross explains, 'The Hauraki Gulf is such a unique and beautiful area. There are not many similar such areas around the world. It would be nice to have it kept as near to a pristine state as possible, in spite of development and population increases in the area which you know have to happen. Surely it is possible to balance the two somehow.'

Motu Mānawa-Pollen Island Marine Reserve

This, the Hauraki Gulf's fifth fully protected area, is in a very different type of locality. Motu Mānawa (mangrove island) is located in the upper Waitematā Harbour, near the head of the Whau River and close to the Point Chevalier and Te Atatū peninsulas. It consists of a low bank with salt meadows, salt-marsh flats and an extensive area of mangroves. It is the most intact salt-marsh area remaining in the Waitematā Harbour. The island is home to a small endemic moth that hasn't been found elsewhere and a population of the regionally threatened fern birds.[32]

The surrounding marine area contains extensive beds of small cockles and nut shells and there are large shell banks. It provides an important habitat for wading birds, such as the white-faced heron, pūkeko, spotless crake and endangered banded rail.[33]

The island was renamed Pollen Island after Dr Daniel Pollen, who purchased the land in 1855 and established the Pollen Brickworks in the area. The island was subsequently acquired by the Auckland Harbour Board. During the 1960s, the area was identified as a potential location for a future port and there was also a proposal to establish an airport there. But neither of these grand plans came to fruition.

The high ecological values of the area drew the interest of the Royal New Zealand Forest and Bird Society, which proposed a 500-hectare marine reserve surrounding the island. This was established in 1995. Access to the marine reserve is difficult, due to the north-west motorway cutting off most of the landward side. Some people visit by kayak or boat, but landing is not encouraged due to the sensitive nature of the salt-marsh environment. Unlike the other marine reserves in the Hauraki Gulf, where abundant fish are the main draw, the primary attraction at Motu Mānawa is the birdlife.

Te Matuku Marine Reserve

The sixth and last fully protected marine area to be created in the Hauraki Gulf is located off the south coast of Waiheke Island at Te Matuku Bay. The reserve, which was also proposed by Forest and Bird, covers around 690 hectares of marine area, including most of the bay and an extension out into the Waiheke Channel. It is located adjacent to land managed for conservation purposes by the Department of Conservation, Forest and Bird and sympathetic landowners, and this protects much of the catchment. This means that the entire ecological succession, running through highland bush, lowland bush, stream habitat, freshwater wetlands, salt marshes, mangrove forests, tidal flats, shallow estuary and deep channel waters, is now protected.

Notable features of the reserve include colonies of spiny tubeworms, which used to be abundant in places, such as Meola Reef in the upper Waitematā Harbour, but have since disappeared from these areas. Also, out in the deep channel are patches of shelly seabed that are inhabited by sponges, anemones and soft corals. These attract juvenile snapper and trevally.[34] In total, 97 shellfish, 33 crustaceans, 21 polychaete worms and 10 echinoderm species have been found in the reserve.[35] The shell spit is one of the prime visual features of the reserve that can be viewed from the road, but its roosting and breeding support for waders, especially godwits and dotterels, has greater ecological significance.[36]

Waiheke resident Leith Duncan was involved in the marine reserve proposal. 'In 1989, Waiheke was preparing to write its first district plan under the Resource Management Act. At that time the marine reserve at Leigh was in the news and the public asked the question: "Do we want marine reserves on Waiheke?" Forest and Bird put out a discussion document which suggested three possible locations. The first was off Oneroa, the second was off the north-east corner of the island, including Gannet Rock, and the third was at Te Matuku Bay.[37]

'The good people of Oneroa and the recreational fishermen said no to Oneroa, as "It's too important to our holidays and going fishing there is part of what we do, so no thanks. Besides, if it ever became as popular as Leigh, our infrastructure, public toilets and roads are already overloaded, so that's no good." The commercial fishermen said: "Not off the north-east corner, as that's too important economically." Everybody, except for the bach owners at Pearl Bay, said: "Put it in Te Matuku Bay." The marine reserve was duly gazetted on 4 July 2005.

One of the unusual features of this reserve is that it surrounds an oyster farm. This was due to the oyster farm being in place prior to the marine reserve proposal. Businessman Rob Fenwick became involved in oyster farming in Te Matuku Bay after he bought property on the western arm of the bay in 1987. 'When we bought this property, slap bang in the middle of the bay we looked out over this derelict old rack-and-rail oyster farm. It was really a wreck. I approached the Ministry of Fisheries to have it removed, because we couldn't find the owners. I later discovered that it was one of the earlier leases in the gulf, lease number 9, which would have been granted during the 1970s. It was designed for rock oysters, being in the shallow intertidal zone. That, coupled with the fact that it was a

The Te Matuku marine reserve, created in 2005, protects a sequence of habitats from intertidal mangrove and salt marsh out to deep channel waters. Unusually, it has an oyster farm embedded within it.

rack-and-rail system, served to encourage sedimentation, making it even shallower. As the industry moved towards the faster-growing and more saleable Pacific oyster, the farm was in the wrong place as it was too shallow. It couldn't grow decent oysters, so the owners lost interest.

'The ministry told me that, as it was privately owned, they couldn't fix it up and it was my problem to deal with the owner. I finally tracked the fellow down and bought the lease from him. At the same time, we were campaigning for a marine reserve in the bay. We sponsored a science project investigating the mangrove forest with WWF and the University of Auckland. We wanted to get rid of the rack-and-rail system which can create sedimentation in tidal bays and we'd heard oyster farmers in South Australia had developed the idea of farming oysters from single seeds in suspended baskets.

'Changing the farm to baskets was quite capital intensive, and the process is labour intensive, but the oysters grow faster and are significantly better quality. We removed the old tanalised racks and rails and set up a completely different system that involved a lot of new infrastructure. Specially made plastic baskets, which are suspended from cables, now run across the lease. The rack-and-rail system has a dramatic impact on sedimentation, not only the silt that is trapped in the artificial groin created by the rails, but also the detritus of dead oysters falling off the racks. This doesn't occur when the oysters are contained in baskets. We bring the oysters in several times during the grow-out, grade and wash them, and then put them out again until harvest size. They grow more quickly, they're a more manageable shape and they're much easier to shuck. Auckland restaurants love the idea of our being able to supply live oysters harvested the day they're shucked for twelve months of the year.

'We were among the first in New Zealand to adopt baskets, and I suspect we are the only oyster farm in the world inside a no-take zone.'[38]

While some local groups were focusing on creating fully protected reserves in the sea to enable fish and other marine life in the Hauraki Gulf to recover, there was a much bigger project coming to fruition. The vacuum left by the disestablishment of the Hauraki Gulf Maritime Park Board in 1990 prompted the establishment of a much broader-based marine park and a wider grouping of people to oversee the future management of the Hauraki Gulf.

Hauraki Gulf Marine Park

During the 1980s, a former member of the Hauraki Gulf Maritime Park Board, Allan Brewster, lobbied for the establishment of a marine park in the inner gulf, where commercial fishing would be excluded. This failed to get political traction, but in 1990 the National Party's spokesperson on conservation announced an intention to promote a complete marine park for the gulf.[39] This was followed by various other initiatives, but it was not until 1998 that the Hauraki Gulf Marine Park Bill was introduced to Parliament. It was finally passed into law in February 2000.

The Hauraki Gulf Marine Park, established under this new legislation, took a very different approach to the earlier maritime park concept. Instead of focusing largely on the islands, the new marine park included the seabed and seawater as well as reserves and conservation land. It also provided for the incorporation of privately owned land into the park. The boundaries of the new marine park were narrower than the maritime one, following the maritime jurisdiction of the Auckland and Waikato regional councils. For example, the Poor Knights Islands were no longer included.

The legislation laid out a set of clear purposes for the marine park. These included recognising and protecting its international and national significance; recognising the special relationship of tangata whenua with the park; and sustaining its life-supporting capacity. Unlike other marine parks, however, no restrictions were explicitly placed on any activity within the gulf.

The new legislation also established the Hauraki Gulf Forum, a new entity to oversee the management of the Hauraki Gulf and its catchments. Instead of having direct management responsibilities, the forum was conceived as an integrating body, to bring together the myriad of agencies that now played a role in the gulf. So its members largely consisted of central and local government representatives. In addition, six tangata whenua representatives were appointed by the Minister of Conservation, thereby recognising the strong cultural linkages between numerous Māori tribal groupings and the gulf.

One of the significant functions of the forum was to prepare a state of the environment report on the Hauraki Gulf every three years. It was the forum's 2011 report which effectively brought to public notice the dire state that the gulf was in. In its coverage of the release of the report in September 2011, *The New Zealand Herald* used the headline 'Hauraki Gulf: toxic paradise?' Reporter Isaac Davison went on to observe, 'Dwindling fish stocks, metal pollution and unsafe swimming — the Hauraki Gulf jewel has lost its lustre, according to the most comprehensive report into its health. The *State of our Gulf* report found nearly all environmental indicators either worsening or remaining at already-poor levels of health.'[40]

One of the ground-breaking features of the report was that it compared the current situation with what the Hauraki Gulf would have been like pre-European settlement. This was to overcome the 'sliding baseline' phenomenon that occurs when people compare what they see today with what they remember during their lifetimes and, as generations move on, the current situation becomes the new norm or baseline.

Purposes of the Hauraki Gulf Marine Park

The purposes of the Hauraki Gulf Marine Park are:

(a) to recognise and protect in perpetuity the international and national significance of the land and the natural and historic resources within the Park;

(b) to protect in perpetuity and for the benefit, use, and enjoyment of the people and communities of the gulf and New Zealand the natural and historic resources of the Park including scenery, ecological systems, or natural features that are so beautiful, unique, or scientifically important to be of national significance, for their intrinsic worth;

(c) to recognise and have particular regard to the historic, traditional, cultural, and spiritual relationship of tangata whenua with the Hauraki Gulf, its islands and coastal areas, and the natural and historic resources of the Park;

(d) to sustain the life-supporting capacity of the soil, air, water, and ecosystems of the gulf in the Park.[41]

Story of the Gulf | **Tim Higham**

HAURAKI GULF FORUM MANAGER, AUCKLAND [42]

Tim Higham grew up in central Taranaki, with little access to the coast, but: 'I remember as a primary school student writing to the Hauraki Gulf Maritime Park Board and receiving a collection of maps and brochures about different islands in the gulf. It captured my imagination at the time. It seemed like an amazing geographical place.'

When Tim left school, he undertook a botany degree and later studied journalism. He worked in publicity for the New Zealand Antarctic and United Nations environment programmes. 'I travelled all around the world looking at environmental-type issues and contributing to communication about them.'

In 2007, Tim came back to New Zealand with his family 'for a bit of a break from that, having bought a place on Great Barrier Island. He started at the Hauraki Gulf Forum in 2007. 'The Hauraki Gulf Marine Park Act provided an opportunity to have conversations about the way we could work together and manage it better. It also enabled us to celebrate the very special qualities of the place. The act didn't seek to duplicate the management responsibilities of agencies, such as the Department of Conservation for the islands, the councils for catchment regulation and the Ministry for Primary Industries for fishing. But it did say that, when you make decisions, you should have in mind the broader requirement of recognising the specialness of the place and the need to integrate and enhance.

'I think the most significant piece of work we've been able to do over that time is the state of the environment assessments, because they've been able to provide a holistic picture of what is really going on. We've been able to step back and say, "Where's the gulf at now, compared to where it's been historically, and what's the overall pattern? Is it getting better or are the pressures we're putting on it making things worse?" In 2011 the answer we gave was, "We're running the place down off a low historical base." That really set the platform for everything from then on. Most people have now come around to accepting that it's an accurate picture of the situation and we need to do better.

'When I look around the gulf now, I see many things happening that are genuine attempts to change that trajectory. One of the most significant milestones, in that growing community of positive actors, is the acceptance of the shipping industry that they can work (with some small exceptions) to a 10-knot speed limit to reduce the risk to Bryde's whales. We've seen the same thing happen with fishing and seabird capture. These represent strong commitments to operating in a way that doesn't impact on iconic species. I think this is the new normal.

'When you look into the future, you can see how every sector could rethink how it produces wealth. As part of their business model, they could do it in a way that's within the carrying capacity of the gulf's resources and even adds to their abundance and health. I don't have any doubt that consumers would respond hugely to businesses that operated in that way. You can start to see how that would play out: farmers getting premium prices for producing meat and milk in nitrogen-constrained environments; fishers getting premium prices for precision-caught fish from stocks that are maintained at higher abundance; and marine farmers recognising their by-product can also contribute to the restoration of the mussel reefs that we've lost.

'The act has created a place where we can have conversations that encourage broader thinking and a deeper response. The Hauraki Gulf Forum needs to continue to occupy that space: to be the table around which we can investigate the bigger picture, encourage integration, innovation and action.'

As a child, Tim Higham was intrigued with the Hauraki Gulf Maritime Park. In 2007, after living on Great Barrier Island for a year, he took on the role of the Hauraki Gulf Forum's inaugural executive officer. (Courtesy of Tim Higham)

Overall findings of the *State of our Gulf* 2011 report

'This report highlights the incredible transformation the gulf has undergone over two human lifespans. That transformation is continuing in the sea and around the coast, with most environmental indicators either showing negative trends or remaining at levels which are indicative of poor environmental condition. It is inevitable that further loss of the gulf's natural assets will occur unless bold, sustained and innovative steps are taken to better manage the utilisation of its resources and halt progressive environmental degradation. The regulatory tools appear to be available to do this, but to date they have either not been implemented or the manner of implementation has not been effective. The challenge facing today's managers and kaitiaki (guardians) who seek to achieve the Hauraki Gulf Forum's vision for the gulf is to find solutions to the progressive decline in the gulf's resources and ecosystem to protect opportunities for future generations.'[43]

The report was not all doom and gloom. As well as describing the current dire situation, it set out a vision for a new management response. This included developing a flourishing 'green-blue' network of restored island sanctuaries and protected regenerating marine areas, enhancing fisheries and keeping sediment and contaminants on the land. These responses were to be underpinned by a strengthened kaitiaki role for Māori and an improving knowledge base.[44]

The report helped inspire two ambitious projects.

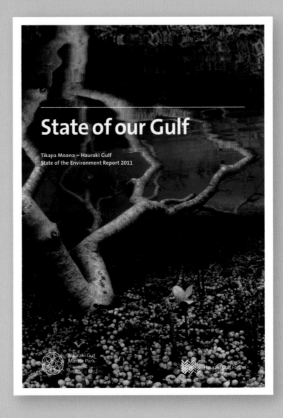

The first was an initiative to restore the gulf's mussel beds. The second was a project to develop a marine spatial plan, through a stakeholder-led collaborative process, in order to develop a pathway for action to turn the current situation around.

John Tregidga (far left) has been chair of the Hauraki Gulf Forum since 2008. This image from the forum's 2015 seminar shows Anne Holdaway presenting the Holdaway prize to Rod and Sue Neureuter for their work on the Noises Islands. On the far right is Richelle Kahui-McConnell who was also awarded a prize at this event for her work at Ōkahu Bay. (Courtesy of Tim Higham)

On release of the report, Hauraki Gulf Forum Chair John Tregidga noted that 'New Zealand needed to move away from an economy based on exploitation. The idea that Auckland had to balance environmental concerns with economic concerns was flawed. If ecosystems were returned to a healthy state, it would improve the outlook for tourism, recreational and commercial fisheries and farming.'[45]

Revive our gulf

In 2011, a group was formed to pursue the idea of restoring the green-lipped mussel beds which once covered the inner Hauraki Gulf. The impetus was the description, in the 2011 *State of our Gulf* report, of the extensive loss of mussel beds between 1920 and the 1960s. Restoring the mussel beds would recreate important juvenile fish habitat and increase the collective ability of shellfish to cleanse the seawater. A single mussel can filter up to 350 litres of water daily. It was thought that, when the mussel beds were intact, they could filter all the seawater in the Firth of Thames in a day, a process that would now take years.[46]

This innovative idea involved placing live mussels on the muddy sea floor to see if they would, in the first instance, survive and, in the longer term, reproduce so that rafts of mussels would develop and expand over time. This had never been done before and no one knew if the mussels would persist.

John Laurence was one of those who agreed to become involved in the project. John brought with him considerable experience in managing community-based initiatives through his involvement in the Motuihe Island restoration project. He was appointed interim chairman of what became the Mussel Reef Restoration Trust.

Trust members met monthly at the Outboard Boating Club premises and developed a simple strategic plan that defined the mission and objectives of the initiative. As John outlines: 'The mission is simply to restore and protect historic mussel reefs in the Hauraki Gulf and associated habitat; to work with iwi and community groups to provide them with education and support to create mussel reefs in their own areas; to advocate for a reduction in sediments coming into the gulf; and to inspire other groups to be involved in the restoration of the gulf generally, by showing we could do it.

'We started off agreeing to put down some mussels and to undertake scientific experiments to see the results. We wanted to find out if they would survive, grow and be predated on. We also wanted to see if they would attract spat, small fishes and marine life generally. In December 2013 we obtained some mussels from NIML [North Island Mussels Limited] and we put down 7 tonnes. The mussels had been harvested after a heavy rain event and this triggered a 'no sell' for these mussels. The company said that, if we paid the cost of collecting and freighting them, they were ours. In an overnight decision, we agreed to pay the costs from the $10,000 that OBC [Outboard Boating Club] had given towards the mussel project. We were also fortunate to have other private donors, although they gifted lesser amounts. Later on, the Hauraki Gulf Forum gave us $10,000 and the Auckland Council Community Fund $4000.'

The trust had difficulty sourcing more mussels, as the export demand for them was high and the mussel farms and processors couldn't even supply export orders. 'Then in September 2014, NIML approached us and said they had some surplus undersized mussels that didn't meet market requirements. If we paid for the harvest and freight we could have them for free. So we obtained 63 tonnes of mussels and NIML placed them in selected areas off the western end of Waiheke Island. The mussels are now doing extremely well in areas not heavily covered in sediment. They seem to be growing and attracting marine life, such as starfish, spotties and snapper.

'Recently a mussel farmer gave us another 4 tonnes of mussels. We have an agreement with a third mussel farmer willing to put mussels in a Coromandel location. We have an understanding with yet another mussel farmer prepared to provide mussels for the western Waiheke area. We are also negotiating with mussel processors to utilise their undersized mussels which are currently dumped in landfills.'

As well as depositing live mussels, the group started to explore other ways of creating habitat suitable for mussels to settle naturally. As John explains, 'We are looking into utilising mussel shell as a substrate for attracting mussel spat. We are also looking into the growing of red seaweeds to attract the spat. It's all to do with their life cycle. Millions of spat are released by the adult mussels and they float around in the sea for a couple of weeks before attaching to very fine filamentous things, such as red seaweeds. After being attached to that fine material for a while, they break adrift and then attach to hard surfaces, such as existing mussels or rocks. As much of the gulf is covered in sediment, we plan to help the spat by providing shell and filamentous material for them to attach to. That is our goal for the next year or two.'

The Mussel Reef Restoration Trust has sourced live mussels from North Island Mussels Limited and deposited them on the seabed near Waiheke Island. They appear to be surviving and are attracting a range of predator species including the starfish shown here. (Revive Our Gulf)

Sea Change — Tai Timu Tai Pari

The call, in the 2011 *State of our Gulf* report, for a step change in the way the gulf was managed also sparked interest in marine spatial planning, a new approach that was being applied to marine areas overseas. Such planning sought to consider the entire marine area as a system and to examine all activities and stressors simultaneously. This enabled the key strategic drivers of ecological decline to be identified and addressed, as well as the spatial conflicts between activities.

The Hauraki Gulf Forum was the entity that took up the cudgels in terms of exploring the new approach and promoting its application in the Hauraki Gulf to the various agencies. The Environmental Defence Society was also supportive of the concept, particularly the adoption of a collaborative approach for the preparation of the marine spatial plan. Such an approach required the agencies to take a back seat. The plan was to be prepared by a stakeholder working group comprised of representatives of the various iwi and hapū groups associated with the Hauraki Gulf, along with stakeholder representatives — commercial fishers, recreational fishers, marine farmers, agriculturalists, community members and environmentalists. All these parties would work together to find solutions on which they could all agree.

It took some time for the agencies to come on board, but eventually they did, and in December 2013 the stakeholder working group met to initiate work towards the preparation of the plan. The group has been given the task 'to develop a spatial plan that will achieve a Hauraki Gulf that is vibrant with life and healthy mauri, is increasingly productive and supports thriving communities'.[47] The group is focused on identifying ways to turn around, within the next generation, the degradation that has happened over the last century or so. It is committed to achieving this through adopting a holistic approach to solutions that is based on mātauranga Māori as well as western science.

If it is to provide a pathway to reverse the downward trajectory of the gulf, the plan will need to include some big moves that make significant changes to the way people interact with the gulf, as we move into the future.

A good start has been made on restoring the marine area of the Hauraki Gulf, but there is still much more to be done. Reversing the damage of the last century or so will not be easy. It will take a compelling vision, strong leadership and a clear plan of action.

Ōkahu catchment ecological restoration plan

In Ōkahu Bay, Ngāti Whātua Ōrākei has been applying traditional principles, based on mātauranga Māori, to address contemporary challenges. The key concept underlying the approach is mauri: 'the binding force that holds together the physical and spiritual components of a thing or being. This encapsulates ecological, cultural, social and economic integrity. Mauri can be enhanced (mauri piki) or diminished (mauri heke).'[48]

In preparing the Ōkahu catchment ecological restoration plan, the hapū consulted widely amongst their people and developed a vision of 'waters fit to swim in at all times, with thriving marine ecosystems that provide sustainable kaimoana resources to a Ngāti Whātua Ōrākei community, who have a strong daily presence in and on the bay as users and kaitiaki'.[49]

In order to achieve this vision and to enhance the mauri of the bay, the iwi is involved in a range of activities, including replanting indigenous trees within the catchment and creating mussel beds within the bay, to help cleanse the water. Another important project is daylighting the tidal stream that once ran through the Ōkahu domain but is now piped. Moana Tamaariki-Pohe recalls, 'The biggest indicator of change for us is the stream. Dad saw it flowing at its fullest in his time and I still remember seeing it in my time. We used to sit at the end of the bay near the stream and go straight out to pick up kaimoana. I would like to see the creek restored as a place for kids to wash sand off their feet before heading home. It needs to have good flow and movement.'[50]

A key component of the programme, which is being led by Richelle Kahui-McConnell, is building capacity and relationships. Richelle works with families, schoolchildren, scientists and council staff to bring together resources and knowledge for the betterment of the area. As she observes, 'It's not just the abundance of kaimoana that is the measure of success, it's the abundance of knowledge and the hours spent out there.

'Some Ngāti Whātua tamariki (children) walked out into the water for the first time when they did the kaimoana survey. Normally they don't even walk past the sand. That's an indicator of disconnect. But things are changing. When we did the first kaimoana survey, it was me and my undergraduate friends. But during the last survey we had aunties, uncles, grandfathers, babies and a total of 120 tamariki involved. Now Uncle Bob walks up to me and says, "How's our mussels?"

'We are committed to the preservation of this place. It's not ours, that's not what makes it important: it's knowing that it will survive and thrive. People say it's the water that separates us, but no, it's what connects us, it's what binds us together.'[51]

The kaimoana survey in Ōkahu Bay has enabled Ngāti Whātua tamariki (children) to reconnect with the marine area. This image shows children from Ōrākei School, St Joseph's School and St Thomas' School participating in the 8th annual kaimoana survey of Ōkahu Bay. (Richelle Kahui-McConnell)

Epilogue

The Hauraki Gulf has supported a multitude of people during the 700 or more years of settlement around its shores.

The gulf's prolific marine life has supplied sustenance and livelihoods and its beautiful coastline has provided places for rest, recreation and reflection. Its sheltered waters have hosted a vast armada of vessels: waka, tall ships, coastal traders, scows, steamships, launches and graceful yachts — and it has shaped who we are.

Local Māori cultural traditions are inextricably interwoven with the sea. For the Hauraki Gulf's first people, the sea is a living relation, a spiritual entity and an integral part of who they are. It was the bounty of the gulf, along with the adjacent rich volcanic soils, that supported the largest Māori population in the country.

Early European settlement was largely shaped by the gulf. Hobson finally chose the shores of the Waitematā for the location of Auckland, by reason of the availability of a deep sheltered harbour. Farming settlements were located close to water access, up the many rivers and estuaries draining into the gulf.

The Hauraki Gulf was an early centre for boatbuilding and innovative yacht design, supported by easy water access and rich supplies of kauri. It honed some of the world's best sailors. It was where the nation's inshore commercial fishing industry first developed and it still hosts one of the country's largest ports. The gulf has enriched a multitude of people's lives, providing a wealth of opportunities for picnicking, swimming, surfing, underwater diving, recreational fishing, cruising, shell collecting and simply mucking about.

We, in turn, have shaped the Hauraki Gulf. But this has not always been in a positive way. Our impact has been progressive and unrelenting. Today, the gulf is in worse health than it has ever been before.

No one factor is to blame. It is the accumulation of multiple pressures, resulting from the actions of many different people, over a long period of time. In many cases, people were unaware of the wider impacts of their activities. In others, they simply didn't care. But now we do know, we have reason to care and it's time to take action. Everybody needs to play a part.

In the sea, commercial fishermen need to use fishing equipment that avoids damaging the seabed, so it can recover. Recreational fishermen need to target highly productive species and only in areas where they are rapidly replenished. Sensitive reef areas, sustaining long-lived resident species, need to be left alone.

On the shore, Hauraki Plains farmers need to reduce the amount of nitrogen leaching off their properties. All landowners, including farmers, foresters and developers, need to ensure that soil doesn't wash off their land and enter waterways. There are many proven ways of achieving this, including regenerating healthy indigenous forest on steep erodible land, providing for generous riparian setbacks along rivers and streams, and reinstating natural systems, such as wetlands and flood plains, that catch sediment before it reaches the sea.

But most importantly, we need to give the Hauraki Gulf the space to rejuvenate itself. It can't be necessary to fish every last corner: every bay, every reef, every channel.

The gulf is large and there is ample room to create places that we leave alone, that we allow to replenish and restore themselves. These would be the sanctuaries of the gulf, places where we allow marine life to reassert itself. They would be our investment in our future.

If we do pull together to turn the situation around, then our children and grandchildren will be able to tell similar stories to those their parents and grandparents have told: of fishing off the wharf near where they live and easily catching a feed; of seeing snapper with their backs out of the water feeding on the rich mussel beds; of wading out at low tide and harvesting fresh pipi and cockles; and of watching schools of thousands and thousands of fish swim past.

They could talk of the flocks of gulls screaming as they circle around the massive boil-ups of fish; of the majestic humpback whales as they linger in the gulf to feed on the rich plankton blooms; of the enormous pods of playful dolphins that undulate as they pass. They could describe the fascinating shells they found on the beach and the wondrous creatures that they discovered under the water.

That is the future that we can give them — or that we can take away. It's our choice.

Notes

Chapter 1

1 Irwin G, 2008, 67
2 Irwin G, 2008, 76; Finney B, 2008, 119
3 Field M, 2013, 'Kumara origin points to pan-Pacific voyage', *Fairfax News*, 23 January
4 Furey L, 2015, pers. comm.
5 Irwin G, 2008, 89; Troup C, 2012, 'Bird migration — New Zealand's migratory birds', *Te Ara — The Encyclopedia of New Zealand*, updated 13-Jul-12 URL: http://www.TeAra.govt.nz/en/bird-migration/page-3
6 Taonui R, 1994, 318 & 321
7 Irwin G, 2008, 80 & 89
8 Irwin G, 2008, 80
9 Tūroa T, 2000, 81
10 Tūroa T, 2000, 185
11 Murphy R J et al., 2001, 354–355; Zeldis J R et al., 2004, 543
12 Taonui R, 1994, 266
13 Tūroa T, 2000, 47–48
14 Murdoch G, 1996, 5; Tūroa T, 2000, 166
15 Davis J, 2015, pers. comm.
16 Tūroa T, 2000, 144
17 Tūroa T, 2000, 49, 124 &164; Rāwiri Taonui, 'Canoe traditions — Te Arawa and Tainui', *Te Ara — The Encyclopedia of New Zealand*, updated 22-Sep-12 URL: http://www.TeAra.govt.nz/en/canoe-traditions/page-5
18 Tūroa T, 2000, 49, 121, 124, 164 & 182; Rāwiri Taonui, 'Canoe traditions — Te Arawa and Tainui', *Te Ara — The Encyclopedia of New Zealand*, updated 22-Sep-12 URL: http://www.TeAra.govt.nz/en/canoe-traditions/page-5; Evans J, 2009
19 Monin P, 2001, 11
20 Tūroa T, 2000, 144; Evans J, 2009
21 Tūroa T, 2000, 156
22 Hogg A G et al., 2003, 121
23 Furey L et al., 2008, 50
24 Sewell B, 1984, 181
25 Taonui R, 2008, 26
26 Tūroa T, 2000, 84
27 Furey L, 2014, pers. comm.
28 Duff R, 1977, 250
29 Davidson J, 1979, 189
30 Berentson Q, 2012, 223–227
31 Anderson A, 1989, 151
32 Biggs B, 2006, 37
33 Smith I, 2005, 9
34 Smith I W G, 2011, 19
35 Lowe D J et al., 2000, 863; Furey L, 1997, 20
36 Watson B N, 2004, 25
37 Smith I W G, 1989
38 Lindsay H, C Wild and S Byers, 2009, 12 & 16
39 Davidson J, 1982, 36
40 Shane P et al., 2013, 174–183
41 Coster J and W Spring-Rice, 1984, 17
42 Coster J and W Spring-Rice, 1984, 17
43 Smith I W G, 2011

44 Davidson J, 1979, 189
45 Beamish L, 2105, pers. comm.
46 Fay M, 2015, pers. comm.
47 Phillipps R et al., 2014, 8–11
48 Mizen P, 1997, 23
49 Mizen P, 1997, 63
50 Mizen P, 1997, 109
51 Monin P, 1996, 29
52 Mizen P, 1998
53 Mizen P, 1998, 175

Chapter 2

1 Hiroa T, 1926, 597
2 Waitangi Tribunal, 1988; Best E, 1986, 9
3 Waitangi Tribunal, 1988; Best E, 1986, 9
4 Waitangi Tribunal, 1988; Best E, 1986, 9
5 Best E, 1986, 5
6 Tūroa T, 2000, 198
7 Waitangi Tribunal, 1988
8 Waitangi Tribunal, 1988
9 Tūroa T, 2000, 190
10 Hauraki Maori Trust Board, 1999, 76
11 Leach F and J Davidson, 2000
12 Best E, 1986, 70 & 77
13 Furey L, 1999, 331
14 Hauraki Maori Trust Board, 1999, 80
15 Hauraki Maori Trust Board, 1999, 74
16 Polack J S, 1974, 28
17 Watson N, 1969
18 Anon, 1867, 'Native intelligence', *The Oamaru Times and Waitaki Reporter*, 14 May, 8
19 Murdoch G J, 1996, 6
20 Campbell M, S Bickler and R Clough, 2003, 125
21 Hauraki Maori Trust Board, 1999, 75
22 Tūroa T, 2000, 161
23 Paulin C D, 2007, 30
24 Paulin C D, 2007, 27
25 Paulin C D, 2007, 28
26 Best E, 1986, 36–37
27 Boileau J, 1980
28 Davidson J, 1979, 187
29 Paulin C D, 2007, 27; Best E, 1986, 38
30 Hiroa T, 1926, 216
31 Best E, 1986, 44; Paulin C D, 2007, 35
32 Furey L, 1996, 7–11
33 Furey L, 1996, 18–21
34 Furey L, 1996, 4
35 Hiroa T, 1926, 598
36 Hiroa T, 1926, 598
37 Best E, 1986, 10
38 Reproduced in Mizen p, 1998, 22
39 Furey L, 2015, pers. comm.
40 Tūroa T, 2000, 88
41 Tūroa T, 2000, 193
42 Furey L, 1996, 74
43 Waitangi Tribunal, 2011, 6
44 Hauraki Maori Trust Board, 1999, 43
45 Hauraki Maori District Council Planning Group, 1987, 15
46 Hauraki Maori Trust Board, 1999, 44
47 Best E, 1986, 12
48 Monin P, 2001, 13
49 Waitangi Tribunal, 2011, 105

50 Waitangi Tribunal, 2011, 106
51 Tamaariki T, 2015, pers. comm.

Chapter 3

1 Reed A H & A W (eds.), 1951, 55
2 Tūroa T, 2000, 145; Reed A H & A W (eds.), 1951, 55
3 Beaglehole J C (ed.), 1962, 424
4 Salmond A, 2003, 32–33
5 Salmond A, 2003, 31–32
6 Salmond A, 2003, 112; Mundle R, 2013, 162
7 Beaglehole J C (ed.), 1962, 425
8 Reed A H & A W (eds.), 1951, 57; Beaglehole J C (ed.), 1962, 427
9 Beaglehole J C (ed.), 1962, 427
10 Beaglehole J C (ed.), 1962, 434
11 Reed A H & A W (eds.), 1951, 58; Beaglehole J C (ed.), 1962, 428
12 Keir B, 2010, 35
13 Reed A H & A W (eds.), 1951, 59–60
14 Reed A H & A W (eds.), 1951, 66
15 Reed A H & A W (eds.), 1951, 67
16 Reed A H & A W (eds.), 1951, 63–64, 66
17 Beaglehole J C (ed.), 1962, 433
18 White J, 1888
19 White J, 1888
20 White J, 1888
21 Ballara A, 2012, 'Te Horeta', *Dictionary of New Zealand Biography, Te Ara — The Encyclopedia of New Zealand*, updated 30-Oct-2012 URL: http://www.TeAra.govt.nz/en/biographies/1t34/te-horeta
22 Reed A H & A W (eds.), 1951, 68
23 Reed A H & A W (eds.), 1951, 69
24 Perhaps referring to the diversion of the Waikato River from the Hauraki Plains during the Taupō eruptions and replacement with the Waihou and Piako rivers, see Tūroa T, 2000, 195
25 Phillips C, 2000, 83
26 Phillips C, 2000, 81
27 Reed A H & A W (eds.), 1951, 73
28 Reed A H & A W (eds.), 1951, 71 & 73
29 Reed A H & A W (eds.), 1951, 72
30 Reed A W, 2010, 350
31 Furey L, 1996, 13–14
32 McNab R (ed.), 1914
33 Furey L, 1996, 14
34 Elder J R (ed.), 1932, 253
35 Elder J R (ed.), 1932, 254
36 Elder J R (ed.), 1932, 255
37 Elder J R (ed.), 1932, 256–257
38 Elder J R (ed.), 1932, 270
39 Elder J R (ed.), 1932, 270
40 Simpson M J A, 2014, 'Dumont d'Urville, Jules Sébastien César', *Dictionary of New Zealand Biography, Te Ara — The Encyclopedia of New Zealand*, updated 10-Mar-2014 URL: http://www.teara.govt.nz/en/biographies/1d19/dumont-durville-jules-sebastien-cesar
41 Elder J R (ed.), 1932, 279
42 Davidson J W, 1975, 105
43 Percy Smith S (ed.), 1909, 414

44 Percy Smith S (ed.), 1909, 414
45 Percy Smith S (ed.), 1909, 419
46 Wright O (ed.), 1950, 152
47 Wright O (ed.), 1950, 152
48 Wright O (ed.), 1950, 155
49 Wright O (ed.), 1950, 163
50 Wright O (ed.), 1950, 164
51 Wright O (ed.), 1950, 167
52 Davis J, 2015, pers. comm.

Chapter 4

1   Rutherford J, 1940, 57; Stone R C J, 2001, 215
2   Stone R C J, 2001, 174–179
3   Rewiti P, 1904, 'The natives and the Governor', *The New Zealand Herald*, 23 July, 1
4   Rewiti P, 1904, 'The natives and the Governor', *The New Zealand Herald*, 23 July, 1; Stone R C J, 2001, 185; Taonui R, 'Ngāti Whātua — Ngāti Whātua and the Treaty of Waitangi', *Te Ara — The Encyclopedia of New Zealand*, www.TeAra.govt.nz/en/music/3863/titahis-chant
5   Pihema A, R Kerei and S Oliver, 2015, 'Te Kawau, Apihai', *Dictionary of New Zealand Biography, Te Ara — The Encyclopedia of New Zealand*, URL: www.TeAra.govt.nz/en/biographies/1t42/te-kawau-apihai
6   Simpson K A, 2013, 'Hobson, William', *Dictionary of New Zealand Biography, Te Ara — The Encyclopedia of New Zealand*, updated 22-Oct-2013 URL: http://www.TeAra.govt.nz/en/biographies/1h29/hobson-william
7   Simpson K A, 2013, 'Hobson, William', *Dictionary of New Zealand Biography, Te Ara — The Encyclopedia of New Zealand*, updated 22-Oct-2013 URL: http://www.TeAra.govt.nz/en/biographies/1h29/hobson-william
8   Simpson K A, 2013, 'Hobson, William', *Dictionary of New Zealand Biography, Te Ara — The Encyclopedia of New Zealand*, updated 22-Oct-2013 URL: http://www.TeAra.govt.nz/en/biographies/1h29/hobson-william
9   Stone R C J, 2001, 185–186 & 216
10 Rutherford J, 1940, 58
11 Rutherford J, 1940, 63
12 Stone R C J, 2001, 220–221
13 Rutherford J, 1940, 158
14 Rutherford J, 1940, 126–127
15 Rutherford J, 1940, 130
16 Rutherford J, 1940, 131
17 Rutherford J, 1940, 132
18 Rutherford J, 1940, 137–138
19 Rutherford J, 1940, 138–139
20 Rutherford J, 1940, 145
21 Rutherford J, 1940, 162
22 Rutherford J, 1940, 164–168
23 Rough D, 1896, 'The Early Days of Auckland', *The New Zealand Herald*, 11–25 January
24 Rough D, 1896, 'The Early Days of Auckland', *The New Zealand Herald*, 11–25 January

25 Rutherford J, 1940, 182
26 Rutherford J, 1940, 183
27 Swainson W, 1853, 11–12
28 Rough D, 1896, 'The Early Days of Auckland', *The New Zealand Herald*, 11–25 January
29 Stone R C J, 2001, 253
30 Rutherford J, 1940, 192
31 Rutherford J, 1940, 192
32 Rutherford J, 1940, 192; Rough D, 1896, 'The Early Days of Auckland', *The New Zealand Herald*, 11–25 January
33 Rough D, 1896, 'The Early Days of Auckland', *The New Zealand Herald*, 11–25 January
34 Rutherford J, 1940, 194
35 Rutherford J, 1940, 194
36 Stone R C J, 2001, 298
37 Bush G W A, 1971, 22
38 Swainson W, 1853, 71
39 Petrie H, 2006
40 Martin M A, 1970, 6–7
41 Petrie H, 2006

Chapter 5

1   Jones L, 2011, 88
2   Barr J, 1926, 46
3   Auckland Regional Council, 2010, 7
4   Diggle L, E Diggle and K Gordon, 2007, 170
5   Diggle L, E Diggle and K Gordon, 2007, 184
6   Hawkins C, 1960, 123
7   Waitangi Tribunal, 2011, 25
8   Waitangi Tribunal, 2011, 26
9   Jones L, 2011, 93
10 Bickler S, B Baquie and R Clough, 2004
11 Jones L, 2011, 96
12 Crampton C, 1991
13 Lee M, 2014, pers. comm.
14 Bush G W A, 1971, 50 & 63
15 Anon, 1870, 'The Ligar Canal', The Daily Southern Cross, 6 January, 3
16 Bush G W A, 1971, 118
17 Bush G W A, 1971, 120
18 Hounsell W K, 1935, 264–266
19 Fitzmaurice J, 2011, 78
20 Bush G, 1980, 18
21 Bush G, 1980, 19
22 Bush G, 1980, 27
23 Bush G, 1980, 39
24 Bush G, 1980, 39–40
25 Bush G, 1980, 58
26 Bush G, 1980, 89
27 Bush G, 1980, 91–92
28 Bush G, 1980, 99
29 Bush G, 1980, 98
30 Bush G, 1980, 107
31 Bush G, 1980, 116
32 Bush G, 1980, 122
33 Bush G, 1980, 126–133
34 Waitangi Tribunal, 1987, 89–90
35 Waitangi Tribunal, 1987, 90
36 Waitangi Tribunal, 1987, 103 & 106; Clarke C, R Kahui-McConnell and E Afoa, 2014, 3
37 Tamaariki T, 2015, pers. comm.
38 Fitzmaurice J, 2011, 71
39 Edgar J, 2014, 'Robinson, Dove-Myer',

Dictionary of New Zealand Biography, Te Ara — The Encyclopedia of New Zealand, URL: www.TeAra.govt.nz/en/biographies/5r19/robinson-dove-myer
40 Petitioner Mr E F Cornman quotes in Anon, 1964, 'A proposed site for dump irks residents', *North Shore Times*, 11 March
41 Anon, 1964, 'A place to dump rubbish', *North Shore Times*, 11 March
42 Auckland Regional Authority, 1974, 10 & 17
43 Raj P, 2009, 57
44 Raj P, 2009, 124
45 Hill A, 1971, 'All piled up and no place to go', *The New Zealand Herald*, 9 January
46 Ashby T, 1975, 47
47 Ashby T, 1975, 113
48 La Roche A, 2011
49 Ferigo N and N Haywood, 2006, 33
50 Archives NA, C357 848 M1 504 Record 4/228 Takapuna and Milford beaches — removal of sand
51 Day D, 1989, 50
52 Day D, 1989, 50
53 Day D, 1989, 50 & 53
54 Ashby T, 1975, 116
55 Ashby T, 1975, 114
56 La Roche A, 1991, 171
57 Julian H, 1999, 21
58 Applied Geology Associates, 1982

Chapter 6

1   Halkett J and E V Sale, 1986, 52
2   Riddle J, 1996, 54–55
3   Halkett J and E V Sale, 1986, 1 & 7
4   Riddle J, 1996, 58
5   Riddle J, 1996, 86
6   Riddle J, 1996, 90–96
7   Riddle J, 1996, 71
8   Riddle J, 1996, 71
9   Riddle J, 1996, 72
10 Monin P, 2001, 92–93; Adams P, 2012, 'Webster, William', *Dictionary of New Zealand Biography, Te Ara — The Encyclopedia of New Zealand*, URL: http://www.TeAra.govt.nz/en/biographies/1w9/webster-william
11 Campbell J L, 1965, 22
12 Bennett F, 1986, 25–28
13 Bennett F, 1986, 65
14 Young B, 2012
15 Hayward B W, 1978, 3
16 Hayward B W, 1978, 3
17 Cory-Wright P, 1988, 45
18 Morcom T, 2015, pers. comm.
19 Conservator of Forests, 1969, 'Forests of the Coromandel Peninsula', *Ohinemuri Regional History Journal*, 12, October
20 Bennett F, 1986, 75
21 Luff H J, 2003, 64–65
22 Luff H J, 2003, 65; Sewell B, 2004, 32
23 Sewell B, 2004, 32
24 Mowbray J, 1931 'Mt Hobson's scroll of fame', *The New Zealand Observer*, 18 July
25 Burrill B, 2015, pers. comm.
26 Green M and J Zeldis, 2015, 19
27 Mead S and A Moores, 2004, 22–29
28 Lowe M L, M A Morrison and R B Taylor, 2015

29 Morrison M A et al., 2009, 3–4
30 Luff H J, 2003, 66
31 Phillips C, 2000, 20
32 Phillips C, 2000, 119–120
33 Monin P, 2001, 72
34 Rufus E T, 1974, 36
35 Elderton G E (ed), 1966, 'Turua — the saw mills — kahikatea or white pine', *Ohinemuri Regional History Journal*, 6, URL: http://www.ohinemuri.org.nz/journal/06/turua_saw_mills.htm
36 Salmon J, 1963, 251
37 Watton G, 1995, 10
38 Watton G, 1995, 10
39 Watton G, 1995, 12
40 Watton G, 1995, 13
41 Waitangi Tribunal, 2006, 806
42 McDonald E A, 1929, 50–62
43 McDonald E A, 1929
44 Waitangi Tribunal, 2006, 858
45 Townshend G, 2015, pers. comm.
46 Watton G, 1995, 14 & 18
47 Watton G, 1995, 20
48 Watton G, 1995, 26–28
49 Watton G, 1995, 41
50 Watton G, 1995, 61
51 Vant B, 2011, iii
52 Watton G, 1995, 77
53 Townshend G, 2015, pers. comm.

Chapter 7

1   Monin P, 1996, 9
2   Haddon A C and J Hornell, 1975, 200–215
3   Jones L, 2011, 89
4   Rough D, 1896, 'Early Days of Auckland', *The New Zealand Herald,* 11–25 January
5   Compain T, 2015, pers. comm.
6   Ross J O'C, 1969, 159
7   Ross J O'C, 1969, 167
8   Admiralty Hydrographic Office, 1856, A2
9   Ross J O'C, 1975, 29–31
10 Rimmer A, 2004, 32–33
11 Maritime New Zealand, 'Mokohinau Islands lighthouse', URL: http://www.maritimenz.govt.nz/Commercial/Shipping-safety/Aids-to-navigation/Lighthouses-of-NZ/Mokohinau-Islands-lighthouse.asp
12 Monin P, 2001, 153
13 Admiralty Hydrographic Office, 1856, 17
14 Monin P, 1992, 97
15 Taylor P, 1975, 42–45
16 Maritime New Zealand, 'Cuvier Island lighthouse', URL: http://www.maritimenz.govt.nz/Commercial/Shipping-safety/Aids-to-navigation/Lighthouses-of-NZ/Cuvier-island-lighthouse.asp
17 Churchman G B, 1989, 68 & 113
18 Walter R, 2015, pers. comm.
19 Monin P, 1992, 46
20 Hawkins C, 1960, 38; Diggle L, 2009, 29
21 Petrie H, 2006
22 Monin P, 1992, 103; Hawkins C, 1960, 73 & 187
23 Hawkins C, 1960, 88
24 Hawkins C, 1960, 77–78; Diggle L, E Diggle and K Gordon, 2007, 56
25 Laxon W A, 2012, 'Niccol, Henry', *Dictionary of New Zealand Biography, Te Ara — The Encyclopedia of New Zealand*, updated 30-Oct-2012, URL: http://www.TeAra.govt.nz/en/biographies/1n13/niccol-henry
26 Laxon W A, 2012, 'Niccol, Henry', *Dictionary of New Zealand Biography, Te Ara — The Encyclopedia of New Zealand*, updated 30-Oct-2012, URL: http://www.TeAra.govt.nz/en/biographies/1n13/niccol-henry
27 Monin P, 1992, 149–150
28 Monin P, 2001, 125
29 Locker R H, 2001, 130
30 Armitage D, 2010, 15–25
31 Admiralty Hydrographic Office, 1856, 67
32 Anon, 1848, *The New Zealander,* 2 December, 2
33 Locker R H, 2001, 121; Ross J O'C, 1969, 146
34 Ashby T, 1975, 26
35 Diggle L, E Diggle and K Gordon, 2007, 348
36 Diggle L, E Diggle and K Gordon, 2007, 395
37 Stewart W W, 1972, 9–11
38 Hansen H J, 2009
39 Walsh T, 1932, 8–9
40 Walsh T, 1932, 12–13
41 Coster J and W Spring-Rice, 1984, 11–12; Department of Conservation, 2010, 12
42 Carter C R, 1866, 154–155
43 Carter C R, 1866, 155
44 Walsh T, 1932, 17
45 Stewart W W, 1972, 49–50
46 Hudson G, 2015, pers. comm.
47 Furniss C, 1977, 39
48 Edwards B, 1991, unpublished recollections
49 Diggle L, E Diggle and K Gordon, 2007, 28
50 Ngāti Manuhiri and the Crown, 2011, Deed of settlement of historical claims, 21 May
51 Anon, 1930, 'Hulk comes to life: Hasty escape from Rewa', *Evening Post*, CX(11), 12 July, 11; Tennyson A J D, E K Cameron and G A Taylor, 1997, 31–34
52 Wray J, 2014, 40
53 Holmes M, 2014, pers. comm.
54 Holmes M, 2014, pers. comm.
55 Diggle L, E Diggle and K Gordon, 2007, 28; Diggle L, 2009, 54
56 Diggle L, E Diggle and K Gordon, 2007, 286–287; Dodd A, 2007a, 5
57 Brassey R, 2013, Unidentified [Compass Rose]? shipwreck, Hauraki Gulf, unpublished paper
58 Brassey R, 2013, Unidentified [Compass Rose]? shipwreck, Hauraki Gulf, unpublished paper
59 Owen W, 1990, 17

Chapter 8

1   McLaughlan G, 2008, 67–68
2   Kidd H, R Elliot and D Pardon, 1999, 14
3   Eaddy P A, 1939, 18
4   Eaddy P A, 1939, 20
5   Eaddy P A, 1939, 25
6   Titchener P, 1978, 12–13
7   Elliot R and H Kidd, 2001, 9
8   Elliot R and H Kidd, 2001, 11; Holmes N, 1971, 35
9   Titchener P, 1978, 13–14
10 Kidd H, 2015, pers. comm.
11 Wilkins I, 2010, 236
12 Kidd H, R Elliot and D Pardon, 1999, 21
13 Wilkins I, 2010, 236
14 Wilkins I, 2010, 240–242
15 Wilkins I, 2010, 244–247
16 Elliot R and H Kidd, 2001, 42–44
17 Elliot R and H Kidd, 2001, 22–23; Wilkins I, 2010, 98–111
18 Kidd H, 2105, pers. comm.; Royal New Zealand Yacht Squadron, 2006, 'Club history', URL: http://www.rnzys.org.nz/RNZYS/RNZYS/tabid/68/Default.aspx
19 Kidd H and R Elliot, 2001, 1
20 Marler B, 2014, pers. comm.
21 Kidd H and R Elliot, 2001, 2–3
22 Kidd H and R Elliot, 2001, 7–10
23 Kidd H and Elliot R, 2003, 1 & 12
24 Kidd H, R Elliot and D Pardon, 1999, 106 & 143
25 Kidd H, R Elliot and D Pardon, 1999, 100
26 Kidd H and R Elliot, 2004, 11
27 Kidd H and R Elliot, 2004, 11
28 Kidd H, R Elliot and D Pardon, 1999, 81–82
29 Kidd H and R Elliot, 2001, 7–10
30 Kidd H and R Elliot, 2001, 11 & 31
31 Anderson G, 1999, 33
32 Anderson G, 1999, 35; Kidd H, R Elliot and D Pardon, 1999, 125
33 Elliot R, 1994, 33–35
34 Gorter S and A Tercel, 2006, 15–16, 97–98
35 Gorter S and A Tercel, 2006, 116–120
36 Gorter S and A Tercel, 2006, 120–128
37 Gorter S and A Tercel, 2006, 133–134
38 Gorter S and A Tercel, 2006, 149
39 Wilkins I, 2010, 343–354
40 Corkin J, 2013, 'Brooke, John Balmain', *Dictionary of New Zealand Biography, Te Ara — The Encyclopedia of New Zealand*, www.TeAra.govt.nz/en/biographies/5b42/brooke-john-balmain
41 Kidd H, R Elliot and D Pardon, 1999, 125; Tubbs C, 1995, 11
42 Kidd H, R Elliot and D Pardon, 1999, 212; Corkin J, 2013, 'Brooke, John Balmain', *Dictionary of New Zealand Biography, Te Ara — The Encyclopedia of New Zealand*, www.TeAra.govt.nz/en/biographies/5b42/brooke-john-balmain
43 Corkin J, 2013, 'Brooke, John Balmain', *Dictionary of New Zealand Biography, Te Ara — The Encyclopedia of New Zealand*, www.TeAra.govt.nz/en/biographies/5b42/brooke-john-balmain
44 Kidd H (ed.), 2005, 65
45 Kidd H, R Elliot and D Pardon, 1999, 142
46 Kidd H, R Elliot and D Pardon, 1999, 180
47 Kidd H, R Elliot and D Pardon, 1999, 195; Becht R, 1995, 105–120
48 Street J, 2015, pers. comm.
49 Wilkins I, 2010, 34

Chapter 9

1 Cottrell N, 1986, 16; Stewart W W, 1972, 37
2 Anon, 1911, 'Premier picnic', *The New Zealand Herald*, 18 January, 8
3 Anon, 1893, 'With the Oddfellows at Motutapu', *Observer*, 11 March, 12
4 Motutapu Restoration Trust, undated, 'Early settlers — the Reid brothers', URL: http://www.motutapu.org.nz/index.php/heritage/european-settlement/58-early-settlers-the-reid-brothers
5 Yoffe S E, 2000, 19
6 Yoffe S E, 2000, 19–20; Woolnough A, 1984, 17–18
7 Woolnough A, 1984, 20; Yoffe S E, 2000, 20
8 Yoffe S E, 2000, 31; Woolnough A, 1984, 20
9 Woolnough A, 1984, 54
10 Woolnough A, 1984, 20; Yoffe S E, 2000, 20
11 Yoffe S E, 2000, 20
12 Yoffe S E, 2000, 20–21
13 Yoffe S E, 2000, 33, 34, 47, 48
14 Woolnough A, 1984, 30
15 Woolnough A, 1984, 44
16 Yoffe S E, 2000, 22–23
17 Conning I, 2015, pers. comm.
18 Tamaariki-Pohe M, 2015, pers. comm.
19 Henry A, 2015, pers. comm.
20 Rickard V A, 1983, 3–4
21 Clough R, 1991, 45; Ministry of Works and Development, 1976, 1
22 Dodds A, 2015, pers. comm.
23 Clough R, 1991, 45; Ministry of Works and Development, 1976, 2
24 Nathan S, 2013, 'Mining and underground resources — Metals known but not mined', *Te Ara — The Encyclopedia of New Zealand*, www.TeAra.govt.nz/en/photograph/9242/copper-smelter-kawau-island
25 Department of Conservation, undated, 'Mansion house', URL: http://www.doc.govt.nz/conservation/historic/by-region/auckland/hauraki-gulf-islands/kawau-island-historic-reserve/mansion-house/
26 Holmes M, 2014, pers. comm.
27 Grey A E, 1983, 'Stockyard Bay', *Kawau Island News*, 9 August, 22
28 Palmer B, 1983, 'Again to catch up with Bunty Palmer down memory lane', *Kawau Island News*, 9 August, 4
29 Wilson N C, 1980, 53
30 Wilson N C, 1980, 55–56
31 Holmes M, 2014, pers. comm.
32 Wright A, 2012, 16
33 Kawau Island Residents and Ratepayers Association, undated, 'Mansion house and Kawau Island history', URL: www.kawauisland.org.nz/history-of-kawau-island
34 Kawau Island Residents and Ratepayers Association, undated, 'Mansion house and Kawau Island history', URL: http://www.kawauisland.org.nz/history-of-kawau-island
35 Kawau Island Residents and Ratepayers Association, undated, 'Mansion house and Kawau Island history', URL: http://www.kawauisland.org.nz/history-of-kawau-island
36 Waitangi Tribunal, 2006, 113
37 Titchener P, 1981, 4
38 The Salvation Army, undated, 'Island restreats for inebriates', URL: http://www.salvationarmy.org.nz/our-community/bcm/archives-heritage/photo-week/island-retreats-for-inebriates
39 Anon, 1909, 'Life at Pakatoa Island: Told by an ex-inmate: some interesting suggestions', *Wairarapa Daily Times*, 5 May, 4
40 The Salvation Army, undated, 'Island restreats for inebriates', URL: http://www.salvationarmy.org.nz/our-community/bcm/archives-heritage/photo-week/island-retreats-for-inebriates
41 Kerridge Odeon Tourist Services Limited, 1965
42 Gibson A, 2015, 'Your own island for only $30m', *The New Zealand Herald*, 2 June
43 Coster J and W Spring-Rice, 1984, 10
44 Whyle I, 1993, 27
45 Whyle I, 1993, 28
46 Monin P, 1996, 'Governor's island was home to Maori displaced by war order', *The New Zealand Herald*, 28 December, A7
47 Armstrong D, 2015, pers. comm.
48 Hudson G, 2105, pers. comm.; Armstrong D, 2015, pers. comm.
49 Whyle I, 1993, 27–29
50 Rakino Ratepayers Association, undated, 'About Rakino Island', URL: http://www.rra.nz/rakino/
51 Spencer C, 1988, 'Cowes Bay's early days when guests would walk the plank', *Gulf News*, 19 August, 32
52 Monin P, 1992, 177
53 Day D, 1989, 132–133
54 Day D, 1989, 133
55 Day D, 1989, 134–136; Monin P, 1992, 176
56 Boulgaris Realty, undated, 'A coastal paradise unto itself: 306 Cowes Bay Road, Waiheke Island', URL: http://www.boulgarisrealty.com/listings/brcbe/
57 Day D, 1989, 158
58 Day D, 1989, 165
59 Anon, 1983, 'Great days on Waiheke: Dances and ferry services', *Gulf News*, 23 September, 36
60 Anon, 1984, 'Early days on Waiheke: Banana crate baches', *Gulf News*, 27 January, 60
61 Anon, 1993, 'Family sells bach after 66 years', *Gulf News*, 19 March, 18
62 Anon, 1981, 'Rocky Bay identity: Early Waiheke memories', *Gulf News*, 13 March, 32; Anon, 1978, 'No interest/no rates: Recollections of Surfdale", *Gulf News*, 17 February, 16; Anon, 1984, 'Early days on Waiheke: Banana crate baches', *Gulf News*, 27 January, 59
63 Ingham G, 1964, 11
64 Garrett R, 2014, pers. comm.
65 Auckland Council, 2014, *Waiheke Local Board Profile — Initial results from the 2013 Census*
66 Neureuter S, 2015, pers. comm.
67 Summary of land registration provided by Rod Neureuter

Chapter 10

1 Quoted in Sayers R (ed.), 1973, 88
2 Anon, 1923, 'Huge sharks in harbour', *The New Zealand Herald*, 13 November, 21
3 Anon, 1912, 'Chased by a shark', *Wanganui Chronicle*, 20 March, 5
4 Quoted in Daley C, 2003, 130
5 Sayers R (ed.), 1973, 88
6 Sayers R (ed.), 1973, 90
7 Sayers R (ed.), 1973, 91
8 Jackson I, 2006, 66 & 138; Harvey R, 2010, 97
9 Jackson I, 2006, 139
10 Williamson L, 2000, 53–54
11 Williamson L, 2000, 61–62
12 Williamson L, 2000, 35–36
13 Parkes W, 2015, pers. comm.
14 Williamson L, 2000, 99
15 Williamson L, 2000, 64 & 68
16 Wray J, 1939, 49–83
17 Tino Rawa Trust, undated, 'Ngataki', URL: http://www.tinorawatrust.co.nz/TinoRawa_Trust/Ngataki.html
18 Auckland Regional Authority, 1970, 20
19 Manukau Yacht and Motor Boat Club, undated, '... In the beginning', URL: http://www.mymbc.org.nz/?page=history#mymbc
20 Hartley R T, 1968, 80
21 Wright A, 2012, 60–63
22 Wright A, 2012, 65
23 Wright A, 2012, 69
24 Wright A, 2012, 100
25 Holmes N, 1971, 84
26 Manukau Yacht and Motor Boat Club, undated, '... In the beginning', URL: http://www.mymbc.org.nz/?page=history#mymbc
27 Wright A, 2012, 104
28 Mercury Bay Museum display
29 Grey Z, 1982, 100
30 Grey Z, 1982, 101
31 Ladd F, 1971, 159
32 Ladd F, 1971, 221
33 Grey Z, 1982, 101
34 Grey Z, 1982, 103
35 Grey Z, 1982, 105
36 Grey Z, 1982, 108
37 Simpson R, 2014, pers. comm.
38 Grey Z, 1982, 128–129
39 Simpson R, 2014, pers. comm.
40 Illingworth N, 1983, 135–138
41 Simpson R, 2003, Speech at opening of new social and administration centre for the Mercury Bay Game Fishing Club
42 Greenstreet S, 1983, 230–231
43 Sutherland T, 1963, 54–55
44 Sutherland T, 1963, 54–57
45 Whitmore B, 2011, 162–163
46 Whitmore B, 2011, 163
47 Blackwell C, 2016, pers. comm.
48 Giacon J, 1983, 1–2

49 Giacon J, 1983, 3
50 Giacon J, 1983, 4
51 New Zealand Underwater Association Inc, 2003, 18
52 New Zealand Underwater Association Inc, 2003, 18
53 New Zealand Underwater Association Inc, 2003, 18–19
54 New Zealand Underwater Association Inc, 2003, 16, 20–21
55 Grace R, 2014, pers. comm.
56 Grace R, 2014, pers. comm.
57 Grace R, 2014, pers. comm.
58 Mizen P, 1998, 51 & 53
59 Mizen P, 1998, 52
60 Moran D, 2014, pers. comm.
61 Shields D, 2014, pers. comm.

Chapter 11
1 Titchener P, 1981, 5
2 Titchener P, 1981, 1
3 Titchener P, 1981, 2
4 Titchener P, 1981, 2
5 Titchener P, 1981, 4
6 Titchener P, 1981, 4
7 Titchener P, 1981, 4
8 Paul L J, 1977, 16
9 Kidd H and R Elliot, 2001, 5
10 Anon, 1898, *The New Zealand Herald*, 20 August, 3
11 Anon, 1898, *The New Zealand Herald*, 20 August, 3
12 Titchener P, 1981, 7
13 Anon, 1899, 'The fishing industry', *Thames Star*, 1 September, 4
14 De Groot S J, 1894, 178
15 Report of the Secretary, Marine Department, *Appendix to the Journals of the House of Representatives*, 1898, H-15, 3
16 Ayson L F, 1908, 2
17 Ayson L F, 1908, 2
18 Ayson L F, 1908, 6
19 Ayson L F, 1908, 6
20 Ayson L F, 1908, 7
21 Anon, 1901, 'The fishing industry', *The New Zealand Herald*, 27 July, 3
22 Anon, 1901, 'The fishing industry', *The New Zealand Herald*, 27 July, 3
23 Anon, 1901, 'Our fisheries', *Auckland Star*, 11 December, 5
24 Anon, 1901, 'Trawling in the Hauraki Gulf', *The New Zealand Herald*, 14 December, 6
25 Anon, 1901, 'Trawling in the Hauraki Gulf', *The New Zealand Herald*, 11 December, 7
26 Anon, 1901, 'Our fisheries', *Auckland Star*, 11 December, 5
27 Anon, 1901, 'Trawling in the Hauraki Gulf', *The New Zealand Herald*, 11 December, 7
28 Report of the Secretary, Marine Department, *Appendix to the Journals of the House of Representatives*, 1903, H-15, 3
29 Titchener P, 1981, 8; Paul L J, 1977, 19
30 Anon, 1902, 'Condensed correspondence', *Auckland Star*, 21 June, 3
31 Anon, 1903, 'Extensive catches of fish', *West Coast Times*, 19 September, 3

32 Anon, 1905, 'Large hauls of fish', *Colonist*, 10 October, 1905
33 Ayson L F, 1908, 5 & 11–12
34 Anon, 1912, 'Scarcity of fish', *The New Zealand Herald*, 10 September, 8
35 Ayson L F, 1913, 2
36 Martin R, 2015, pers. comm.
37 Anon, 1907, 'Sharks in Hauraki Gulf', *The New Zealand Herald*, 21 August, 6
38 Report of the Secretary, Marine Department, *Appendix to the Journals of the House of Representatives*, 1907, H-15, 5
39 Ayson L F, 1913, 6
40 Anon, 1918, 'Utilising the shark: A Matakana industry: Oil and fertiliser', *Northern Advocate*, 8 February, 1; Sanspit Residents and Ratepayers Association, 1998, 13
41 Anon, 1918, 'Utilising the shark: A Matakana industry: Oil and fertiliser', *Northern Advocate*, 8 February, 1; Sandspit Resident and Ratepayers Association, 1998, 13
42 Strongman M, 2015, pers. comm.
43 MacDiarmid A and M Pinkerton, 2014, 'A long view — the impacts of humans on New Zealand marine ecosystems since first settlement', presentation to Sea Change — Tai Timu Tai Pari, April
44 Anon, 1916, 'With the trawlers', *Auckland Star*, 13 September, 8
45 Makarios E, 1997, 16
46 Torkington B, 2007, pers. comm.
47 Anon, 1915, 'Fish trade', *Northern Advocate*, 14 October, 2
48 Pridham E, 2015, pers. comm.
49 Anon, 1915, 'Fish trade', *Northern Advocate*, 14 October, 2
50 Anon, 1916, 'With the trawlers', *Auckland Star*, 13 September, 8
51 Anon, 1916, 'With the trawlers', *Auckland Star*, 13 September, 8
52 Anon, 1916, 'With the trawlers', *Auckland Star*, 13 September, 8
53 Anon, 1916, 'With the trawlers', *Auckland Star*, 13 September, 8
54 Johnson D, 2004, 110
55 Johnson D, 2004, 110–111
56 Anon, 1925, 'Seining in the Gulf: Fish supply threatened. Damage to feeding grounds.', *Auckland Star*, 22 September, 5
57 Anon, 1927, 'Fish in the Hauraki Gulf', *Auckland Star*, 18 January, 6
58 Johnson D, 2004, 113
59 Strongman M, 2015, pers. comm.
60 Strongman M, 2015, pers. comm.
61 Torkington B, 2007, pers. comm.
62 Clow P, 2015, pers. comm.

Chapter 12
1 Paul L J, 1977, 30
2 Owen W, 1990, 19–20
3 Owen W, 1990, 21
4 Owen W, 1990, 23 & 28
5 Owen W, 1990, 30–31
6 Ladd F, 1971, 112–113
7 Ladd F, 1971, 113

8 Ladd F, 1971, 114–115
9 Peart L, 2015, pers. comm.
10 Torkington B, 2015, pers. comm.
11 Seafood New Zealand, undated, 'Live rock lobster earns big export dollars', URL: http://www.seafoodnewzealand.org.nz/publications/seafood-new-zealand-magazine/seafood-articles/item/live-rock-lobster-earns-big-export-dollars/
12 Torkington B, 2015, pers. comm.
13 MacDiarmid A B, D Freeman and S Kelly, 2013, 325
14 Whitmore B, 2010, recorded interview, courtesy of Don Armitage
15 Kellian D, 2014, pers. comm.
16 Whitmore B, 2010, recorded interview, courtesy of Don Armitage
17 Luff H J, 2003, 56–57
18 Whitmore B, 2010, recorded interview, courtesy of Don Armitage
19 Luff H J, 2003, 57
20 Luff H J, 2003, 57–58; Litherland T, 2016, pers. comm.; Litherland C, 2016, pers. comm.
21 Duncan L S W, 2011, 163
22 Auckland Council Library files
23 Paul L J, 2012, 11–12
24 Strongman M, 2015, pers. comm.
25 Paul L J, 2012, 9–10
26 Paul L J, 2012, 15
27 Chisholm D, 2005, 13
28 Paul L J, 2012, 15
29 Kellian D, 2014, pers. comm.
30 Paul L J, 1977, 31–33
31 Torkington B, 2015, pers. comm.
32 Johnson D, 2004, 222–226
33 Simpson R, 2015, pers. comm.
34 Johnson D, 2004, 302–305
35 Clark D, 2014, pers. comm.
36 Johnson D, 2004, 338
37 Dollimore J, 2015, pers. comm.
38 Dollimore J, 2014, pers. comm.
39 Dollimore J, 2014 pers. comm.; Johnson D, 2004, 341
40 Kellian D, 2014, pers. comm.
41 Torkington B, 2015, pers. comm.
42 Torkington B, 2015, pers. comm.
43 Clow P, 2014, pers. comm.
44 Martin R, 2014, pers. comm.
45 Duncan L S W, 2011, 215
46 Duncan L S W, 2011, 125–126
47 Clow A, 2014, pers. comm.
48 Clow P, 2014, pers. comm.
49 Clow P, 2014, pers. comm.
50 Luff H J, 2003, 58; Andrews R, 2014, 10
51 Kellian D, 2015, pers. comm.
52 Duncan L S W, 2011, 151 & 182
53 Pulford D, 2015, pers. comm.
54 Duncan L S W, 2011, 270
55 Torkington B, 2015, pers. comm.
56 Moore D, 2014, pers. comm.

Chapter 13
1 Dawbin W H, 1955, 162
2 Hutching G, 2012, 'Whales — Humpback whale', *Te Ara — The Encyclopedia of New Zealand*, www.TeAra.govt.nz/en/whales/page-4

3   Burnett D G, 2012, 628–629
4   Mizen P, 1998, 32–33; Prickett N, 2002, 125–126
5   Prickett N, 2002, 126
6   Dawbin W H, 1955, 162
7   Prickett N, 2002, 130
8   Luff H J, 2003, 179–180
9   Heberley H, 2011, 79–80
10 Heberley H, 2011, 81–82; Prickett N, 2002, 130
11 Constantine R, 2012, pers. comm.
12 Behrens S and R Constantine, 2008, 3–4
13 Gaskin D E, 1972, 78
14 Baker A, 2011, pers. comm.
15 Baker A N and B Madon, 2007, 6–16
16 Baker A, 2011, pers. comm.
17 Enderby T, 2015, pers. comm.
18 Department of Conservation, 2014, 'Necropsy confirms Bryde's whale killed by ship strike', Media release, URL: http://www.doc.govt.nz/news/media-releases/2014/necropsy-confirms-brydes-whale-killed-by-ship-strike/
19 Anon, 1964, 'For dolphins', *Auckland Star*, 6 August
20 Anon, 1964, 'Young dolphin chooses freedom — baths escape', *Auckland Scrapbook*, Auckland Council Library, May, 164
21 Anon, 1964, 'Playmates cheer dolphin', *Auckland Scrapbook*, Auckland Council Library, May, 151
22 Anon, 1964, 'End of dolphin pool idea', *Auckland Scrapbook*, Auckland Council Library, May, 180
23 Dwyer S L et al., 2014, 109
24 Berghan J et al., 2008, 465
25 Massey University of New Zealand, 2015, Spatial mapping reveals importance of Hauraki Gulf waters', URL: http://www.massey.ac.nz/massey/about-massey/news/article.cfm?mnarticle=spatial-mapping-reveals-importance-of-hauraki-gulf-waters-08-04-2015
26 Constantine R, 2015, pers. comm.
27 Simpson R, 2015, pers. comm.
28 Letter from W M MacQuarrie, Fisheries Management Division, to Auckland Regional Fisheries Officer, Ministry of Agriculture and Fisheries, 1 Apr. 1976
29 Neumann D, A Leitenberger and M B Orams, 2002, 597
30 Stockin K, 2008, 103
31 Baker A N, 1990, 101
32 Visser I, 2005, 28–29
33 Visser I, 2005, 40
34 Howard K, 'Kaikoura's orca fuel growing obsession', *The Press*, 3 Dec. 1996
35 Department of Conservation, undated, 'Pilot whales', URL: http://www.doc.govt.nz/nature/native-animals/marine-mammals/dolphins/pilot-whales/
36 Great Barrier Island History Research Group Inc, 2011, 69–70
37 Williscroft M, 2014, 202–203
38 Williscroft M, 2014, 203
39 Department of Conservation Marine Mammal Strandings Database, 2015
40 Gaskin C P, 2015, pers. comm.
41 Taylor G, 2000 and Taylor G A, 2000

42 Gaskin C P and M J Rayner, 2013, 11
43 Sandager F, 1889, 292–293
44 Sandager F, 1889, 286–287
45 Richard Y and E R Abraham, 2013, 23–25; Abraham E R, K N Berkenbusch and Y Richard, 2010, 3
46 Rayner M, 2014, presentation to Stakeholder Working Group, Sea Change — Tai Timu Tai Pari
47 Rayner M, 2014, presentation to Stakeholder Working Group, Sea Change — Tai Timu Tai Pari
48 Chambers S, 2000, 3
49 Chambers S, 2000, 4
50 Chambers S, 2000, 8–13
51 Chambers S, 2000, 14–20
52 Woodley K, 2015, pers. comm.
53 Woodley K, 2015, pers. comm.
54 Woodley K, 2015, pers. comm.
55 Woodley K, 2015, pers. comm.
56 Woodley K, 2015, pers. comm.

Chapter 14

1   Thomson G M, 1892, 202
2   Thomson G M, 1892, 205
3   Cassie R M, 1956, 707–710
4   Cassie R M, 1956, 710–711
5   NIWA, 2011, 'Stay at home snapper', URL: http://www.niwa.co.nz/news/stay-home-snapper
6   Parsons D M et al., 2015, H-I
7   Paul L J, 1974, 569
8   Paul L J, 1976, 42–43
9   Zeldis J R and R I C C Francis, 1998, 528
10 Francis M P, 1994, 215
11 Paul L J, 1967, 458
12 Colman J A, 1972, 238; Godfriaux B L, 1974, 497
13 Lohrer D et al., 2008, 2
14 Crossland J, 1981, 8 and 11
15 Parsons D M et al., 2014, 256
16 Ministry for Primary Industries, 2013, 30
17 Morton J, 2000, 'Powell, Arthur William Baden', *Dictionary of New Zealand Biography, Te Ara — The Encyclopedia of New Zealand*, http://www.teara.govt.nz/en/biographies/5p36/powell-arthur-william-baden
18 Powell A W B, 1937, 356–357
19 Hayward B W et al., 1999, 22; Hayward B W et al., 1997, 15
20 Hayward C M and B W Hayward, 1999, 137
21 Morley M, 2014, pers. comm.
22 Morley M S, B W Hayward and A White, 2001, 4 & 14
23 King N, M Miller and S de Mora, 1989, 287 & 293; Stewart C et al., 1992, 204; de Mora S J, C Stewart and D Phillips, 1995, 50; Smith P J and M McVeagh, 1991, 409
24 Sea Change — Tai Timu Tai Pari, 2014, 6–7; Hauraki Gulf Forum, 2014, 90–91
25 Powell A W B, 1937, 398
26 Morrison M, 2014, pers. comm.
27 NIWA, 2011, 'NIWA creates designer homes for fish', URL: http://www.niwa.co.nz/news/niwa-creates-designer-homes-fish
28 Cranfield H J et al., 1998, Table 1

29 Johnson D, 2004, 448–449
30 Cranfield H J et al., 1998, Table 1; Lohrer D et al., 2008, 16
31 Auckland Council, 2014, '2014 Marine report card Central Waitematā reporting area', URL: http://stateofauckland.aucklandcouncil.govt.nz/marine-report-card/central-waitemata-harbour-reporting-area-2014/
32 Thrush S F et al., 1995, 142–146
33 Thrush S F, 2014, pers. comm.
34 Thrush S F et al., 1998, 868
35 Thrush S F et al., 1998, 866
36 See Thrush S F and P K Dayton, 2002, 449 which concludes that trawling and dredging threatens both structural and functional biodiversity.
37 Kingett P D and J H Choat, 1981, 289
38 Thrush S F et al., 2002, 277–278
39 See Cummings V J et al., 1998, 227–240; Ellis J et al., 2002, 147–174
40 Morrison M, 2014, pers. comm.
41 Morrison M et al., 2008, 18–19
42 Morrison M et al., 2008, 21
43 Morton J, 2000, 'Chapman, Valentine Jackson', *Dictionary of New Zealand Biography, Te Ara — The Encyclopedia of New Zealand*, http://www.teara.govt.nz/en/biographies/5c19/chapman-valentine-jackson; Gordon D P and B Ballantine, 2013, 280
44 Leleu K et al., 2012, 197; see also Babcock R C et al., 1999, 125–134; Shears N T and R C Babcock, 2003, 1–16 and Shears N T, R C Babcock and A K Salomon, 2008, 1860–1873
45 Ballantine B, 2015, pers. comm.
46 Parsons D M et al., 2014, 263–264
47 Gordon D P and B Ballantine, 2013, 279
48 Gordon D P and B Ballantine, 2013, 280
49 Kingsford M J, 2013, 297
50 Gordon D P and B Ballantine, 2013, 281
51 Kingsford M J, 2013, 304
52 Greig M J, 1990, 149
53 Zeldis J R et al., 2004, 543–544
54 Zeldis J R et al., 2004, 559
55 Green M and J Zeldis, 2015, 40–41
56 Green M and J Zeldis, 2015, 49
57 Green M and J Zeldis, 2015, 27
58 Vant B, 2011, 26
59 Green M and J Zeldis, 2015, 58
60 Zeldis J R, 2015, pers. comm.
61 Green M and J Zeldis, 2015, 65

Chapter 15

1   Hamilton W M, 1961, 21
2   Deed of settlement of historical claims, 21 May 2011
3   Monin P, 1996, 79–81; Dodd A and A McKenzie, 2010, 86; Hamilton W M, 1961, 26; Deed of settlement of historical claims, Ngāti Manuhiri and the Crown, 21 May 2011
4   Monin P, 1996, 81–82; Deed of settlement of historical claims, Ngāti Manuhiri and the Crown, 21 May 2011
5   Department of Conservation, undated, 'Nature and conservation', URL: http://www.doc.govt.nz/parks-and-recreation/

places-to-go/auckland/places/little-barrier-island-nature-reserve-hauturu-o-toi/nature-and-conservation/
6 O'Brien J D, 1971, 9
7 Hauraki Gulf Maritime Park Act 1967
8 Hauraki Gulf Maritime Park Board, 1968, 'Hauraki Gulf Maritime Park: Areas which have been formally added to the Hauraki Gulf Maritime Park as at 14 November 1968', unpublished paper, Hauraki Gulf Maritime Park Board, Auckland
9 Hauraki Gulf Maritime Park Board, 1971, 3
10 Rimmer A, 2004, 24 — There are other translations — 'wind blowing about'; 'the sanctified heaven of fragrant breezes'; 'the gathering place of the winds on the northeast horizon where the kumara grow'
11 Rimmer A, 2004, 22
12 Dodd A, 2008, 11
13 Rimmer A, 2004, 21
14 Hohneck M, 2015, pers. comm.
15 Rimmer A, 2004, 28
16 Armstrong D, 1999, 'Tiritiri Matangi Island restoration programme', at http://www.massey.ac.nz/~darmstro/tiri.htm (accessed 19 August 2008)
17 Rimmer A, 2004, 84
18 Dodd A, 2007, 254
19 Fletcher C, 2015, pers. comm.
20 Coster J and W Spring-Rice, 1984, 12–14
21 Motutapu Restoration Trust, undated, 'Motutapu Farm Ltd: The first and only pest free farm in the world!', URL: http://www.motutapu.org.nz/index.php/about-us/the-farm/the-farm
22 Kiwis for Kiwi, undated, 'Motutapu Restoration Trust', URL: https://www.kiwisforkiwi.org/what-we-do/who-are-kiwis-for-kiwi/community-efforts/auckland/motutapu-restoration-trust/
23 Dodd A and M Turner, 2008, 189
24 Dodd A and M Turner, 2008, 192; Brassey R, 1992, 2
25 Dodd A and M Turner, 2008, 190–191
26 Dodd A, 2006, 5–6
27 Dodd A and M Turner, 2008, 192
28 Slark E, 2015, pers. comm.
29 Dodd A and M Turner, 2008, 192
30 Butler D, T Lindsay and J Hunt, 2014, 47
31 Butler D, T Lindsay and J Hunt, 2014, 47
32 Laurence J, 2015, pers. comm.
33 Laurence J, 2015, pers. comm.

34 Laurence J, 2014, pers. comm.
35 Rotoroa Island Museum display
36 Tūroa T, 2000, 143
37 Rotoroa Island Museum display
38 Eichblatt S, 2011, 'John Gow: The salvation of Rotoroa Island', http://idealog.co.nz/venture/2011/02/salvation-island
39 Brown B, 2015, pers. comm.
40 Brown B, 2015, pers. comm.
41 Brown B, 2015, pers. comm.
42 Hance, J, 2015, 'Conservationists turn tiny New Zealand island into bold wildlife experiment', The Guardian, 21 April
43 Eichblatt S, 2011, 'John Gow: The salvation of Rotoroa Island', http://idealog.co.nz/venture/2011/02/salvation-island
44 Ngā Mana Whenua o Tāmaki Makaurau Collective Redress Act 2014
45 Fenwick R, 2015, pers. comm.

Chapter 16

1 Ballantine B, 2015, pers. comm.
2 Ballantine B, 1991, 22
3 Ballantine B, 2015, pers. comm.
4 Ballantine B, 2015, pers. comm.
5 Ballantine B, 2015, pers. comm.
6 Ballantine B, 2015, pers. comm.
7 Ballantine B, 1991, 23
8 Enderby T, 2015, pers. comm.
9 Babcock R C, 2013, 362
10 Babcock R C, 2013, 362
11 Babcock R C, 2013, 365; Leleu K et al., 2012, 197
12 Haggitt T, 2011, iii; Le Port A, J C Montgomery and A E Croucher
13 Hunt L, 2008, 2
14 Grace R, 2014, pers. comm.
15 Auckland Regional Council, 2003, 3
16 Auckland Regional Council, 2003, 3
17 Mike Lee, 2011, 'A long time coming — after 17 years of battling Tawharanui Marine Reserve formally opened', URL: http://www.mikelee.co.nz/2011/10/a-long-time-coming-after-17-years-of-battling-tawharanui-marine-reserve-formally-opened/
18 Hunt J, 2014, 148
19 Gaukrodger J, 2015, pers. comm.
20 Gaukrodger J, 2015, pers. comm.
21 Gaukrodger J, 2015, pers. comm.
22 Gaukrodger J, 2015, pers. comm.
23 Haggitt T, 2015, 3

24 Gray D, 2014, pers. comm.
25 Gray D, 2014, pers. comm.
26 Gray D, 2008, 138
27 Gray D, 2008, 138
28 Garrett R, 2014, pers. comm.
29 Garrett R, 2014, pers. comm.
30 Gray D, 2008, 139
31 Garrett R, 2014, pers. comm.
32 Nick Smith, 1999, 'Pollen Island to become scientific reserve', Press release, URL: http://beehive.govt.nz/release/pollen-island-become-scientific-reserve
33 Department of Conservation, 2005, 'Motu moana (Pollen Island) marine reserve', pamphlet, URL: http://www.doc.govt.nz/Documents/conservation/marine-and-coastal/marine-protected-areas/motu-manawa-marine-reserve-brochure.pdf
34 Department of Conservation, undated, 'Te Matuku marine reserve', URL: http://www.doc.govt.nz/parks-and-recreation/places-to-go/auckland/places/te-matuku-marine-reserve/; http://www.doc.govt.nz/parks-and-recreation/places-to-go/auckland/places/te-matuku-marine-reserve/monitoring/
35 Hayward B W et al., 1997, 67
36 Duncan L, 2015, pers. comm.
37 Duncan L, 2015, pers. comm.
38 Fenwick R, 2015, pers. comm.
39 Waitangi Tribunal, 2001, 8
40 Davison I, 2011, 'Hauraki Gulf: toxic paradise?', The New Zealand Herald, 11 August
41 Hauraki Gulf Marine Park Act 2000, section 33
42 Highham T, 2015, pers. comm.
43 Hauraki Gulf Forum, 2011, 13
44 Hauraki Gulf Forum, 2011, 145
45 Davison I, 2011, 'Hauraki Gulf: toxic paradise?', The New Zealand Herald, 11 August
46 Revive Our Gulf, undated, 'Filtering machines', URL: http://reviveourgulf.org.nz/#filtering_machines
47 Sea Change — Tai Timu Tai Pari, 2013, 1–2
48 Clarke C, R Kahui-McConnell and E Afoa, 2014, 5
49 Hauraki Gulf Forum, 2014, 96
50 Tamaariki-Pohe M, 2015, pers. comm.
51 Kahui-McConnell R, 2015, pers. comm.

References

Abraham E R, Berkenbusch K N and Y Richard, 2010, *The capture of seabirds and marine mammals in New Zealand non-commercial fisheries*, Ministry of Fisheries, Wellington

Admiralty Hydrographic Office, 1856, *The New Zealand pilot*, J D Potter, London

Anderson A, 1989, *Prodigous birds: Moas and moa-hunting in prehistoric New Zealand*, Cambridge University Press, Cambridge

Anderson G, 1999, *Fast light boats: A century of kiwi innovation*, Te Papa Press, Wellington

Andrews R, 2014, 'Longfin and the fish factory — 1960s and 70s', in Great Barrier Island History Research Group, *True tales of Great Barrier Island*, Great Barrier Island History Research Group, Claris

Applied Geology Associates, 1982, *Coastal sand and shingle resources of Auckland and Northland*, Applied Geology Associates, Auckland

Armitage D, 2010, *Captain John Gillies*, Great Barrier Island History Research Group, Claris

Ashby T, 1975, *Phantom fleet: The scows and scowman of Auckland*, A H and A W Reed Limited, Wellington

Auckland Regional Authority, 1970, *Report on recreational boating in the Auckland metropolitan area,* Auckland Regional Authority, Auckland

Auckland Regional Authority, 1974, *Report on refuse disposal for metropolitan Auckland*, Auckland Regional Authority, Auckland

Auckland Regional Council, 2003, *Proposal to change the status of the Tāwharanui Marine Park to a marine reserve: Discussion document*, Auckland Regional Council, Auckland

Auckland Regional Council, 2010, *A brief history of Auckland's urban form*, Auckland Regional Council, Auckland

Ayson L F, 1908, 'Report on experimental trawling', *Appendix to the Journals of the House of Representatives*, 1908, H-15B

Ayson L F, 1913, 'A report on New Zealand's fisheries — Their present condition and future development', *Appendix to the Journals of the House of Representatives*, 1913, H-15B

Babcock R C, 2013, 'Leigh marine laboratory contributions to marine conservation', *New Zealand Journal of Marine and Freshwater Research*, 47(3), 360–373

Babcock R C, S Kelly, N T Shears, J W Walker and T J Willis, 1999, 'Changes in community structure in temperate marine reserves', *Marine Ecology Progress Series*, 189, 125–134

Baker A N, 1990, *Whales and dolphins of New Zealand and Australia: An identification guide*, Victoria University Press, Wellington

Baker A N and B Madon, 2007, 'Bryde's whales (Balaenoptera cf. brydei Olsen 1913) in the Hauraki Gulf and northeastern New Zealand waters', *Science for Conservation 272*, Department of Conservation, Wellington

Ballantine B, 1991, *Marine Reserves for New Zealand*, University of Auckland, Auckland

Barr J, 1926, *The ports of Auckland New Zealand: A history of the discovery and development of the Waitematā and Manukau harbours*, The Unity Press Limited, Auckland

Beaglehole J C (ed.), 1962, *The Endeavour Journal of Joseph Banks 1768–1771*, Angus and Robertson, London

Becht R, 1995, *Champions under sail*, Hodder Moa Beckett Publisher, Auckland

Behrens S and R Constantine, 2008, 'Large whale and vessel collisions in northern New Zealand', paper presented to the Scientific Committee of the International Whaling Commission, Santiago, Chile, SC/60/BC9

Bennett F, 1986, *Tairua: A history of the Tairua-Hikuai-Pauanui District*, Arrow Press, Morrinsville

Berentson Q, 2012, *Moa: The life and death of New Zealand's legendary bird*, Craig Potton Publishing, Nelson

Berghan J, K D Algie, K A Stockin, N Wiseman, R Constantine, G Tezanos-Pinto and F Mourão, 2008, 'A preliminary photo-identification study of bottlenose dolphin (*Tursiops truncatus*) in the Hauraki Gulf, New Zealand', *New Zealand Journal of Marine and Freshwater Research,* 2008, 42, 465–472

Best E, 1986, *Fishing methods and devices of the Māori*, Government Printer, Wellington

Bickler S, B Baquie and R Clough, 2004, 'Excavations at Britomart, Auckland', *Archaeology in New Zealand*, 47(2), 136–152

Biggs B, 2006, *Kimihia te mea ngaro: Seek that which is lost*, MacMillan Brown Lectures 1992, The Polynesian Society, Auckland

Boileau J, 1980, 'The artefact assemblage from the Ōpito Beach midden, N40/3, Coromandel Peninsula', *Records of the Auckland Institute and Museum*, 17, 65–95

Brassey R, 1992, *Motuihe: Assessment of historical and archaeological significance*, unpublished draft, Department of Conservation, Auckland

Burnett D G, 2012, *The sounding of the whale: Science and cetaceans in the twentieth century*, University of Chicago Press, Chicago

Bush G W A, 1971, *Decently and in order*, Collins Bros & Co Limited, Auckland

Bush G, 1980, *Moving against the tide: The Brown's Island drainage controversy*, The Dunmore Press, Palmerston North

Butler D, T Lindsay and J Hunt, 2014, *Paradise saved*, Random House, Auckland

Campbell J L, 1965, *Poenamo*, Whitcombe and Tombs Limited, Auckland

Campbell M, S Bickler and R Clough, 2003, 'The archaeology of Ōmaha sandspit, Northland, New Zealand', *New Zealand Journal of Archaeology*, 25, 121–157

Carter C R, 1866, *Life and recollections of a New Zealand colonist*, Vol 2, R Madley, London

Cassie R M, 1956, 'Early development of the snapper, *Chrysophrys auratus* Forster', *Transactions of the Royal Society of New Zealand*, 83 (4), 705–713

Chambers S, 2000, *The Story of the Miranda Naturalist's Trust 1973–2000*, Miranda Naturalist's Trust, Pokeno

Chisholm D, 2005, *The mussel poachers of Ōrere Point and other paoching stories*, Hazard Press, Christchurch

Churchman G B, 1989, *New Zealand lighthouses*, G P Books, Wellington

Clarke C, R Kahui-McConnell and E Afoa, 2014, 'Setting objectives through whanau engagement and the restoration of mauri', Paper presented to the 2014 Stormwater Conference

Clough R, 1991, 'The archaeology of the historic copper industry on Kawau Island 1843–55, 1899–1901', *Australian Historical Archaeology*, 9, 45–48

Colman J A, 1972, 'Food of snapper, Chrysophrys auratus (Forster), in the Hauraki Gulf, New Zealand', *New Zealand Journal of Marine and Freshwater Research*, 6(3), 221–239

Cory-Wright P, 1988, *Jewel by the sea: Memories of Tairua and the Coromandel*, Moana Press, Tauranga

Coster J and W Spring-Rice, 1984, *History, archaeology and site management on Motutapu and Rangitoto*, Department of Lands and Survey, Auckland

Cottrell N, 1986, *A history and bibliography of Motutapu and Rangitoto Islands*, Department of Lands and Survey, Auckland

Crampton C, 1991, *Disposal of material dredged from the Waitematā Harbour*, report for the Department of Conservation

Cranfield H J, D P Gordon, R C Willan, B A Marshall, C N Battershill, M P Francis, W A Nelson, C J Glasby and G B Read, 1998, *Adventive marine species in New Zealand*, National Institute of Water and Atmospheric Research, Wellington

Crossland J, 1981, *The biology of the New Zealand snapper*, Fisheries Research Division Occasional Publication No. 23, Ministry of Agriculture and Fisheries, Wellington

Cummings V J, S F Thrush, J E Hewitt and S J Turner, 1998, 'The influence of the pinnid bivalve *Atrina zelandica* (gray) on benthic macroinvertebrate communities in soft-sediment habitats', *Journal of Experimental Marine Biology and Ecology*, 228(2), 227–240

Daley C, 2003, *Leisure and pleasure: Reshaping and revealing the New Zealand body 1900–1960*, Auckland University Press, Auckland

Davidson J, 1979, 'Archaic middens of the Coromandel region: A review', in A Anderson (ed.), *Birds of a feather: Osteological and archaeological papers from the South Pacific in honour of R. J. Scarlett*, New Zealand Archaeological Association, Auckland

Davidson J, 1982, 'Auckland' in N Prickett (ed.), *The first thousand years: Regional perspectives in New Zealand archaeology*, The Dunmore Press, Auckland

Davidson J W, 1975, *Peter Dillon of Vanikoro: Chevalier of the south seas*, Oxford University Press, Melbourne

Dawbin W H, 1955, 'The migrations of humpback whales which pass the New Zealand coast', *Transactions of the Royal Society of New Zealand*, 84(1), 147–196

Day D, 1989, *Waiheke pioneers*, Waiheke Historical Society, Ostend

De Groot S J, 1984, 'The impact of bottom trawling on benthic fauna of the North Sea', *Ocean Management*, 9, 177–190

Department of Conservation, 2010, *Islands of the Hauraki Gulf Marine Park*, Department of Conservation, Auckland

Diggle L, 2009, *Shipwrecks of New Zealand*, Lynton Diggle, Auckland

Diggle L, E Diggle and K Gordon, 2007, *New Zealand shipwrecks: Over 200 years of disasters at sea*, Hodder Moa Beckett Publisher, Auckland

Dodd A, 2006, *Motuihe quarantine station (1870–1930) HMNZS Tamaki (1941–1963)*, Department of Conservation, Auckland

Dodd A, 2007, 'Management of the Motutapu archaeological landscape', *Archaeology in New Zealand*, 50(4), 253–274

Dodd A, 2007a, *S.S. Wairarapa graves, 1894 Heritage Assessment*, Department of Conservation, Auckland

Dodd A, 2008, *Tiritiri Matangi archaeological and historic landscape*, Department of Conservation, Auckland

Dodd A and A McKenzie, 2010, 'Hauturu/Little Barrier Archaeological landscape,' *Archaeology in New Zealand*, 53(2), 84–100

Dodd A and M Turner, 2008, 'Motuihe archaeological landscape and recent investigations', *Archaeology in New Zealand* 51(3), 188–205

De Feu M, 2008, *Kawakawa bay: The story of a seaside community*, Valid Press, Auckland

De Mora S J, C Stewart and D Phillips, 1995, 'Sources and rate of degradation of Tri(*n*-butyl) tin in marine sediments near Auckland, New Zealand', *Marine Pollution Bulletin*, 30(1), 50–57

Duff R, 1977, *The moa-hunter period of Māori culture*, Government Printer, Wellington

Duncan L S W, 2011, *The social implications of rights-based fisheries management in New Zealand for some Hauraki Gulf fishermen and their communities*, PhD thesis, University of Waikato

Dwyer S L, G Tezanos-Pinto, I N Visser, M D M Pawley, A M Meissner, J Berghan and K A Stockin, 2014, 'Overlooking a potential hotspot at Great Barrier Island for the nationally endangered bottlenose dolphin of New Zealand', *Endangered Species Research*, 25, 97–114

Eaddy P A, 1939, *'Neath swaying spars*, Whitcombe and Tombs Limited, Christchurch

Elder J R (ed.), 1932, *The letters and journals of Samuel Marsden 1765–1838*, Coulls Somerville Wilkie Limited, Dunedin

Elliot R, 1994, *Emmy: Seventy years of M-Class yachting*, Vintage Viewpoint, Auckland

Elliot R and H Kidd, 2001, *The Logans: New Zealand's greatest boatbuilding family*, David Ling Publishing, Auckland

Ellis J, V Cummings, J Hewitt, S Thrush and A Norkko, 2002, 'Determining effects of suspended sediment on condition of a suspension feeding bivalve (*Atrina zelandica*): Results of a survey, a laboratory experiment and a field transplant experiment', *Journal of Experimental Marine Biology and Ecology*, 267(2), 147–174

Evans J, 2009, *Ngā waka o neherā: The first voyaging canoes*, Libro International, Auckland

Ferigo N and N Haywood, 2006, *The magic of Maraetai* (2nd ed), Maraetai Beach School, Maraetai

Fitzmaurice J, 2011, 'Auckland wastewater', in La Roche J (ed.), *Evolving Auckland: The city's engineering heritage*, Wily Publications, Christchurch

Francis M P, 1994, 'Growth of juvenile snapper, Pagrus auratus', *New Zealand Journal of Marine and Freshwater Research*, 28, 201–218

Furey L, 1996, *Oruarangi: The archaeology and material culture of a Hauraki pā*, Bulletin of the Auckland Institute and Museum 17

Furey L, 1997, *Archaeology in the Hauraki region: A summary*, Hauraki Maori Trust Board, Paeroa

Furey L, 1999, 'Archaeological excavation of T10/993 at Matarangi', *Archaeology in New Zealand*, 42(4) 314–336

Furey L, F Petchey, B Sewell and R Green, 2008, 'New observations on the stratigraphy and radiocarbon dates at the Cross Creek site, Ōpito, Coromandel Peninsula', *Archaeology in New Zealand*, 51(1) 46–64

Furniss C, 1977, *Servants of the north: Adventures on the coastal trade with the Northern Steam Ship Company*, A H and A W Reed, Wellington

Gaskin C P and M J Rayner, 2013, *Seabirds of the Hauraki Gulf: Natural history, research and conservation*, Hauraki Gulf Forum, Auckland

Gaskin, D E, 1972, *Whales, dolphins and seals*, Heinemann Educational Books, Auckland

Giacon J, 1983, 'The first fish', in T Orman, *Gone fishing: A New Zealand saltwater anthology*, A H and A W Reed, Wellington

Godfriaux B L, 1974, 'Food of snapper in western Bay of Plenty, New Zealand', *New Zealand Journal of Marine and Freshwater Research*, 8(3), 473–504

Gordon D P and B Ballantine, 2013, 'Contribution of the Leigh Marine Laboratory to knowledge of marine species diversity', *New Zealand Journal of Marine and Freshwater Research*, 47(3), 277–293

Gorter S and A Tercel, 2006, *Ranger: The making of a New Zealand yachting legend*, New Holland, Auckland

Gray D, 2008, 'Sir Peter Blake Marine Education and Recreation Centre' in M Gray and J Sturm, *. . . and then came the bridge: A history of Long Bay and Torbay*, Torbay Historical Society, Auckland

Great Barrier Island History Research Group Incorporated, 2011, *True tales of Great Barrier Island*, Great Barrier Island History

Research Group Incorporated, Claris

Green M and J Zeldis, 2015, *Firth of Thames water quality and ecosystem health: a synthesis*, NIWA, Hamilton

Greenstreet S, 1983, 'Gentlemen, move over', in T Orman (ed.), *Gone fishing: A New Zealand saltwater anthology*, A H and A W Reed, Wellington

Grey Z, 1982, *Angler's eldorado: Zane Grey in New Zealand*, Heinemann Reed, Auckland

Grieg M J, 1990, 'Circulation in the Hauraki Gulf, New Zealand', *New Zealand Journal of Marine and Freshwater Research*, 24, 141–150

Haddon A C and J Hornell, 1975, *Canoes of oceania*, Bishop Museum Press, Honolulu

Haggitt T, 2011, *Cape Rodney to Ōkakari Point marine reserve and Tāwharanui marine park reef fish monitoring: UVC survey Autumn 2011*, Coastal and Aquatic Systems Limited, Leigh

Haggitt T, 2015, *Te Whanganui-a-Hei marine reserve benthic and lobster monitoring programme*, prepared for the Department of Conservation, eCoast Limited, Leigh

Halkett J and E V Sale, 1986, *The world of kauri*, Reed Methuen, Auckland

Hamilton W M, 1961, *Little Barrier Island (Hauturu)*, 2nd edition, New Zealand Department of Scientific and Industrial Research, Wellington

Hansen H J, 2009, *The Jane Gifford . . . back from the brink*, Jim Hansen (self-published), Auckland

Hartley R T, 1968, *Boat Building with Hartley*, Boughtwood Printing House, Auckland

Harvey R, 2010, *Between the flags: 100 years of surf life saving in New Zealand*, Surf Life Saving New Zealand, Wellington

Hauraki Gulf Forum, 2011, *State of our Gulf: Tīkapa Moana — Hauraki Gulf state of the environment report 2011*, Hauraki Gulf Forum, Auckland

Hauraki Gulf Forum, 2014, *State of our Gulf 2014: Hauraki Gulf — Tīkapa Moana/ Te Moananui a Toi state of the environment report 2014*, Hauraki Gulf Forum, Auckland

Hauraki Gulf Maritime Park Board, 1971, *Annual Report for year ended 31 March 1971*, Hauraki Gulf Maritime Park Board, Auckland

Hauraki Māori District Council Planning Group, 1987, *Hauraki Whaanui*, Hauraki Māori District Council, Paeroa

Hauraki Māori Trust Board, 1999, *Hauraki customary indicators report*, Ministry for the Environment, Wellington

Hawkins C, 1960, *Out of Auckland*, Pelorus Press Limited, Auckland

Hayward B W, 1978, *Kauaeranga kauri*, Lodestar Press, Auckland

Hayward B W, M S Morley, A Brett Stephenson, W M Blom, H R Grenfell, R Prasad, D Rogan, F Thonpson, J Cheetham and M Webb, 1999, *Intertidal and subtidal biota and habitats of the central Waitematā Harbour: Accompanying notes*, Auckland Regional Council, Auckland

Hayward B W, A B Stephenson, M S Morley, N Smith, F Thompson, W Blom, G Stace, J I Riley, R Prasad and C Reid, 1997, 'Intertidal biota of Te Matuku Bay, Waiheke Island, Auckland', *Tane*, 36, 67–84

Hayward B W, A B Stephenson, M Morley, J L Riley and H R Grenfell, 1977, 'Faunal changes in Waitematā Harbour sediments, 1930s–1990s, *Journal of The Royal Society of New Zealand*, 27(1), 1–20

Hayward C M and B W Hayward, 1999, 'Human impact on Ōrakei Basin, Auckland', *Tane*, 37, 137–152

Heberley H, 2011, 'Whaling at Great Barrier', in Great Barrier Island History Research Group Incorporated, *True Tales of Great Barrier Island*, Great Barrier Island History Research Group Incorporated, Claris

Hiroa, Te Rangi, 1926, 'The Māori craft of netting', *Transactions and Proceedings of the Auckland Institute*, 597–646

Hogg A G, T F G Higham, D J Lowe, J G Palmer, P J Reimer and R M Newnham, 2003, 'A wiggle-match date for Polynesian settlement of New Zealand', *Antiquity*, 77(295), 116–125

Holmes N, 1971, *Century of sail: Official history of the Royal New Zealand Yacht Squadron*, Whitcombe and Tombs Limited, Christchurch

Hounsell W K, 1935, 'Hydrographical observations in Auckland Harbour', *Transactions of the Auckland Institute*, March, 257–271

Hunt J, 2014, *Our big blue backyard: New Zealand's oceans and marine reserves*, Random House, Auckland

Hunt L, 2008, *Economic impact analysis of the Cape Rodney Ōkakari Point (Leigh) marine reserve in Rodney District*, Department of Conservation, Auckland

Illingworth N, 1983, 'The fish that made Whitianga', in T Orman, *Gone fishing: A New Zealand saltwater anthology*, A H and A W Reed, Wellington

Ingham G, 1964, *1000 years on Waiheke and who's who on the island*, Gordon Ingham, Auckland

Irwin G, 2008, 'Voyaging and settlement', in K R Howe (ed.), *Vaka moana: Voyages of the ancestors*, David Bateman, Auckland

Jackson I, 2006, *Sand between my toes: The story of surf lifesaving in New Zealand*, Penguin Books, Auckland

Johnson D, 2004, *Hooked: The story of the New Zealand fishing industry*, Hazard Press, Christchurch

Jones L, 2011, 'Development of Auckland Ports', in J La Roche (ed.), *Evolving Auckland: The city's engineering heritage*, Wily Publications, Christchurch

Julian H, 1999, *Sea in my blood*, Harry Julian, Auckland

Keir B, 2010, 'Captain Cook's longitude determinations and the transit of Mercury — common assumptions questioned', *Journal of the Royal Society of New Zealand*, 40(2), 27–38

Kerridge Odean Tourist Services Limited, 1965, *Pakatoa Island tourist and holiday resort*, Clark & Matheson, Auckland

Kidd H (ed.), 2005, *Devonport Yacht Club: A centennial history*, Devonport Yacht Club, Auckland

Kidd H and R Elliot, 2001, *Ponsonby Cruising Club: The first hundred years*, Ponsonby Cruising Club, Auckland

Kidd H and R Elliot, 2003, *Lee rail: A centennial history of the Richmond Yacht Club 1902–2003*, Richmond Yacht Club, Auckland

Kidd H and R Elliot, 2004, *Vintage New Zealand launches: A Winkelmann portfolio*, David Ling, Auckland

Kidd H, R Elliot and D Pardon, 1999, *Southern breeze: A history of yachting in New Zealand*, Penguin Books, Auckland

King N, M Miller and S de Mora, 1989, 'Tributyl tin levels for sea water, sediment, and selected marine species in coastal Northland and Auckland, New Zealand', *New Zealand Journal of Marine and Freshwater Research*, 23(2), 287–294

Kingett P D and J H Choat, 1981, 'Analysis of density and distribution patterns in *Chrysophrys auratus* (Pisces: Sparidae) within a reef environment: An experimental approach', *Marine Ecology Progress Series*, 5, 283–290

Kingsford M J, 2013, 'Paradigms for planktonic assemblages: 50 years of contributions from the Leigh Marine Laboratory, Northland, New Zealand', *New Zealand Journal of Marine and Freshwater Research*, 47(3), 294–312

La Roche A, 2011, *Grey's folly: A history of Howick, Pakuranga, Bucklands-Eastern Beaches, East Tamaki, Whitford, Beachlands and Maraetai*, Tui Vale Productions, Auckland

La Roche A, 1991, *The history of Howick and Pakuranga*, The Howick & Districts Historical Society, Auckland

Ladd F, 1971, *A shower of spray and we're away*, A H & A W Reed, Wellington

Le Port A, J C Montgomery and A E Croucher, 2014, 'Biophysical modelling of a snapper *Pagrus auratus* larval dispersal from a temperate MPA', *Marine Ecology Progress Series, 515, 203–215*

Leach B F and J M Davidson, 2000, 'Pre-European catches of snapper (*Pagrus auratus*) in northern New Zealand', *Journal of Archaeological Science, 27, 509–522*

Lee M, 2010, *Statement of evidence of Michael Edward Lee*, Application from Pine Harbour Marina Limited to dredge sediment from the marina approach channel and entrance and to discharge and dump this sediment, via a thin-layer disposal technique, in the Beachlands-Howick (Whitford) embayment

Leleu K, B Remy-Zephir, R Grace and M J Costello, 2012, 'Mapping habitats in a marine reserve showed how a 30-year trophic cascade altered ecosystem structure', *Biological Conservation*, 155, 193–201

Lindsay H, C Wild and S Byers, 2009, *Auckland protection strategy*, Nature Heritage Fund, Wellington

Locker R H, 2011, *Jade river: A history of the Mahurangi*, Friends of the Mahurangi Incorporated, Warkworth

Lohrer D, M Townsend, M Morrison and J Hewitt, 2008, *Change in the benthic assemblages of the Waitematā Harbour: Invasion risk as a function of community structure*, Ministry of Agriculture and Forestry, Wellington

Lowe D J, R M Newnham, B G McFadgen and T F G Higham, 2000, 'Tephras and New Zealand archaeology', *Journal of Archaeological Science*, 27, 859–870

Lowe M L, M A Morrison and R B Taylor, 2015, 'Harmful effects of sediment-induced turbidity on juvenile fish in estuaries', *Marine Ecology Progress Series*, 539, 241–254

Luff H J, 2003, *Tales from Great Barrier Island*, David Ling, Auckland

MacDiarmid A B, D Freeman and S Kelly, 2013, 'Rock lobster biology and ecology: Contributions to understanding through the Leigh Marine Laboratory 1962–2012', *New Zealand Journal of Marine and Freshwater Research*, 47(3), 313–333

Makarios E, 1997, *Nets, lines and pots: A history of New Zealand fishing vessels*, Volume 2, IPL Books, Wellington

Martin M A, 1970, *Our Maoris*, Wilson and Horton, Auckland

McDonald E A, 1929, *Western Hauraki Plains: Its history*, Ken Rae, Plimmerton

McLaughlin G, 2008, *The life and times of Auckland*, Penguin Books, Auckland

McNab R (ed.), 1914, 'Extracts from the journal of Lieut.-Governor King, of Norfolk Island, 1791–96', *Historical Records of New Zealand*, Vol 11, John Mackay, Wellington

Mead S and A Moores, 2004, *Estuary sedimentation: A review of estuarine sedimentation in the Waikato Region*, Environment Waikato, Hamilton

Ministry for Primary Industries, 2013, *Review of sustainability and other management controls for snapper 1 (SNA 1)*, Ministry for Primary Industries, Wellington

Ministry of Works and Development, 1976, *Historic buildings on Kawau Island*, A report on the Kawau Domain buildings of the Hauraki Gulf Maritime Park Board, Department of Lands and Sruvey, Auckland

Mizen P, 1997, *Great Mercury Island Ahuahu: The Māori story concerning Mercury Island Te Kōrero Māori mo Ahuahu*, Pat Mizen, Whitianga

Mizen P, 1998, *Great Mercury Island Ahuahu: The Pakeha story concerning Mercury Island Te Kōrero Pakeha mo Ahuahu*, Pat Mizen, Whitianga

Monin P, 1992, *Waiheke Island: A history*, The Dunmore Press, Palmerston North

Monin P, 1996, *The islands lying between Slipper Island in the south-east, Great Barrier Island in the north and Tiritiri-Matangi in the north-west*, Report commissioned by the Waitangi Tribunal for the claim Wai 406, Waitangi Tribunal, Wellington

Monin P, 2001, *Hauraki contested 1769–1875*, Bridget Williams Books, Wellington

Morley M S, B W Hayward and A White, 2001, 'Changes to the intertidal biota 1950s–2000 at Howick Beach, Auckland', *Poirieria*, 27 April, 4–19

Morrison M A, M L Lowe, D M Parsons, N Y Usmar and I M McLeod, 2009, *A review of the land-based effects on coastal fisheries and supporting biodiversity in New Zealand*, Ministry of Fisheries, Wellington

Morrison M, U Shankar, D Parsons, G Carbines and B Hartill, 2008, 'Snapper's-eye view of the inner Hauraki Gulf', *Water & Atmosphere*, 16(2), 18–21

Mundle R, 2013, *Cook*, HarperCollins Publishers, Sydney

Murdoch G J, 1996, *A history of the human occupation of the Whakakaiwhara block*, Auckland Regional Council, Auckland

Murphy R J, M H Pinkerton, K M Richardson, J M Bradford-Grieve and P W Boyd, 2001, 'Phytoplankton distributions around New Zealand derived from SeaWiFS remotely sensed ocean colour data', *New Zealand Journal of Marine and Freshwater Research*, 35, 343–362

Neumann D R, A Leitenberger and M B Orams, 2002, 'Photo-identification of short-beaked common dolphins (*Delphinus delphis*) in north-east New Zealand: A photo-catalogue of recognisable individuals', *New Zealand Journal of Marine and Freshwater Research*, 36(3), 593–604

New Zealand Underwater Association Incorporated, 2003, *50 years of New Zealand underwater*, New Zealand Underwater Association, Auckland

O'Brien J D, 1971, 'Preservation of our national seashores', *Proceedings of the New Zealand Ecological Society*, 18, 8–12

Owen W, 1990, *Hauraki Gulf: A fishing and cruising guide*, David Bateman, Auckland

Parsons D M, M Cryer, M P Francis, B Hartill, E G Jones, A Le Port, M Lowe, J McKenzie, M Morrison, L J Paul, C Radford, P M Ross, C J Sim-Smith, K T Spong, T Trinski, N Usmar, C Walsh and J Zeldis, 2014, 'Snapper (*Chrysophrys auratus*): a review of life history and key vulnerabilities in New Zealand', *New Zealand Journal of Marine and Freshwater Research*, 48(2), 256–283

Parsons D M, M A Morrison, B M Gillanders, K D Clements, S J Bury, R Bian and K T Spong, 2015, 'Variation in morphology and life-history strategy of an exploited sparid fish', *Marine and Freshwater Research*, published online 28 September

Paul L J, 1967, 'An evaluation of tagging experiments on the New Zealand snapper, *Chrysophrys auratus* (Forster), during the period 1952 to 1963', *New Zealand Journal of Marine and Freshwater Research* 1, 455–463

Paul L J, 1974, 'Hauraki Gulf snapper fishery, 1972 and 1973: Some evidence for a declining catch-rate', *New Zealand Journal of Marine and Freshwater Research*, 8(4), 569–587

Paul L J, 1976, 'A study on age, growth, and population structure of the snapper, *Chrysophrys auratus* (Forster), in the Hauraki Gulf, New Zealand', *Fisheries Research Bulletin*, 13, Ministry of Agriculture and Fisheries, Wellington

Paul L J, 1977, "The commercial fishery for snapper, *Chrysophrys auratus* (Forster), in the Auckland region, New Zealand, from 1900 to 1971', *Fisheries Research Bulletin*, 15

Paul L J, 2012, *A history of the Firth of Thames dredge fishery for mussels: use and abuse of a coastal resource*, New Zealand Aquatic Environment and Biodiversity Report 94, Ministry of Agriculture and Fisheries, Wellington

Paulin C D, 2007, 'Perspectives of Māori fishing history and techniques: Ngā āhua me ngā pūrākau me ngā hangarau ika o te Māori', *Tuhinga*, 18, 11–47

Percy Smith S (ed.), 1909, *Captain Dumont D'Urville's visit to Whangarei, Waitemata, and the Thames in 1827*, Read before the Auckland Institute, 22 November 1909

Petrie H, 2006, *Chiefs of industry: Māori tribal enterprise in early colonial New Zealand*, Auckland University Press, Auckland

Phillips C, 2000, *Waihou journeys: The archaeology of 400 years of Māori settlement*, Auckland University Press, Auckland

Phillipps R, A Jorgensen, L Furey, S Holdaway, T Ladefoged and R Wallace, 2014, *Interim report on archaeological investigations Ahuahu Great Mercury Island, November 2012–February 2014*, University of Auckland and Auckland War Memorial Museum, Auckland

Polack J S, 1974, *New Zealand: Being a narrative of travels and adventures during a residence in that country between the years 1831 and 1837*, Vol 2, Richard Bentley, London

Powell A W B, 1937, 'Animal communities of the sea-bottom in Auckland and Manukau harbours', *Transactions and Proceedings of the Royal Society*, 66(4), 354–401

Prickett N, 2002, *The archaeology of New Zealand shore whaling*, Department of Conservation, Wellington

Raj P, 2009, *Pt Chevalier memories 1930s–1950s*, Point Chevalier Historical Society Incorporated, Auckland

Reed A H & A W (eds.), 1951, *Captain Cook in New Zealand*, A H & A W Reed, Wellington

Reed A W, 2010, *Place names of New Zealand*, Penguin Books, Auckland

Richard Y and E R Abraham, 2013, *Risk of commercial fisheries to New Zealand seabird populations*, Ministry for Primary Industries, Wellington

Rickard V A, 1983, *Kawau Island historic and prehistoric archaeological survey*, Department of Lands and Survey, Auckland

Riddle J, 1996, *Saltspray and sawdust*, Gumtown Publishers, Whitianga

Rimmer A, 2004, *Tiritiri Matangi: A model of conservation*, Tandem Press, Auckland

Ross J O'C, 1969, *This stern coast: The story of the charting of the New Zealand coast*, A H and A W Reed, Wellington

Rufus E T, 1974, *Hauraki Plains story*, Thames Valley News Limited, Paeroa

Rutherford J, 1940, *The founding of New Zealand: The journals of Felton Mathew, First Surveyor-General of New Zealand, and his wife, 1840–1847*, A H and A W Reed, Dunedin

Salmon J, 1963, *A history of goldmining in New Zealand*, Government Printer, Wellington

Salmond A, 2003, *The trial of the cannibal dog*, Penguin Books, London

Sandager F, 1889, 'Observations on the Mokohinau Islands and the birds which visit them', *Transactions of the New Zealand Institute*, 22, 286–294

Sayers R (ed.), 1973, *Takapuna: A historical portfolio commemorating 60 years of municipal government 1913–1973*, Takapuna City Council, Auckland

Sea Change — Tai Timu Tai Pari, 2013, *Stakeholder working group terms of reference*, Sea Change — Tai Timu Tai Pari, Auckland

Sea Change — Tai Timu Tai Pari, 2014, *Water quality and catchments: Synthesis of initial information and issues*, Waikato Regional Council, Hamilton

Sewell B, 1984, *The Cross Creek site (N40/260) Coromandel Peninsula: A study of an archaeological investigation in spatial analysis and continuity in the New Zealand archaic*, MA in Anthropology thesis, Auckland University, Auckland

Sewell B, 1999, *The history and archaeology of the coppermine at Miners Head, Great Barrier Island*, Auckland Conservancy Historic Resource Series No. 16, Department of Conservation, Auckland

Sewell B, 2004, 'Human settlement and sites', in D Armitage (ed.), *Great Barrier Island*, Canterbury University Press, Christchurch

Shane P, M Gehrels, A Zawalna-Geer, P Augustinus, J Lindsay and I Chaillou, 2013, 'Longevity of a small shield volcano revealed by crypto-tephra studies (Rangitoto volcano, New Zealand): Change in eruptive behaviour of a basaltic field', *Journal of Volcanology and Geothermal Research*, 257, 174–183

Shears N T and R C Babcock, 2003, 'Continuing trophic cascade effects after 25 years of no-take marine reserve protection', *Marine Ecology Progress Series*, 246, 1–16

Shears N T, R C Babcock and A K Salomon, 2008, 'Context-dependent effects of fishing: Variation in trophic cascades across environmental gradients,' *Ecological Applications*, 18(8), 1860–1873

Smith I W G, 1989, 'Māori Impact on the marine megafauna: Pre-European distributions of New Zealand sea mammals, in D G Sutton, *Saying so doesn't make it so*, New Zealand Archaeological Association, Auckland

Smith I W G, 2005, 'Retreat and resilience: Fur seals and human settlement in New Zealand', in G C Monks (ed.), *The exploitation and cultural importance of sea mammals*, Oxbow Books, Oxford

Smith I W G, 2011, 'Estimating the magnitude of pre-European Māori marine harvest in two New Zealand study areas', *New Zealand Aquatic Environment and Biodiversity Report*, No. 82

Smith P J and M McVeagh, 1991, 'Widespread organotin pollution in New Zealand coastsal waters as indicated by imposex in dogwhelks', *Marine Pollution Bulletin*, 22(8), 409–413

Stewart C, S J de Mora, M R L Jones and M C Miller, 1992, 'Imposex in New Zealand Neogastropods', *Marine Pollution Bulletin*, 24(4), 204–209

Stewart W W, 1972, *Steam on the Waitematā*, A H and A W Reed, Wellington

Stockin K A, 2008, *The New Zealand common dolphin (Delphinus sp.): Identity, ecology and conservation*, PhD thesis, Massey University, Auckland

Stone R C J, 2001, *From Tāmaki-Makau-Rau to Auckland*, Auckland University Press, Auckland

Sutherland T, 1963, *Maui and me: A search for a fisherman's El Dorado*, A H and A W Reed, Wellington

Swainson W, 1853, *Auckland: The capital of New Zealand and the country adjacent*, Smith, Elder & Co., London

Taonui R, 1994, *Te haerenga waka: Polynesian origins, migrations, and navigation*, MA (Hons) thesis, University of Auckland

Taylor G A, 2000, *Action plan for seabird conservation in New Zealand, Part A: Threatened Seabirds*, Department of Conservation, Wellington

Taylor G A, 2000, *Action plan for seabird conservation in New Zealand, Part B: Non-threatened Seabirds*, Department of Conservation, Wellington

Taylor P, 1975, *As darker grows the night*, Hodder and Stoughton, Auckland

Tennyson A J D, E K Cameron and G A Taylor, 1997, 'Fauna, flora and history of Moturekareka, Motutara and Kohatutara islands, Hauraki Gulf', *Tane*, 36, 27–56

Thomson G M, 1892, 'Notes on sea-fishes', *Transactions and Proceedings of the New Zealand Institute*, 24, 202–215

Thrush S F and P K Dayton, 2002, 'Disturbance to marine benthic habitats by trawling and dredging: Implications for marine biodiversity', *Annual Review Ecological Systems*, 33, 449–473

Thrush S F, J E Hewitt, V J Cummings and P K Dayton, 1995, 'The impact of habitat disturbance by scallop dredging on marine benthic communities: what can be predicted from the results of experiments?', *Marine Ecology Progress Series*, 129, 141–150

Thrush S F, J E Hewitt, V J Cummings, P K Dayton, M Cryer, S J

Turner, G A Funnell, R G Budd, C J Milburn and M R Wilkinson, 1998, 'Disturbance of the marine benthic habitat by commercial fishing: Impacts at the scale of the fishery', *Ecological Applications*, 8(3), 866–879

Thrush S F, D Schultz, J E Hewitt and D Talley, 2002, 'Habitat structure in soft-sediment environments and abundance of juvenile snapper *Pagrus auratus*', *Marine Ecology Progress Series*, 245, 273–280

Titchener P, 1978, *Little ships of New Zealand*, A H & A W Reed, Wellington

Titchener P, 1981, *The story of Sanford Ltd: The first hundred years*, Sanford Limited, Auckland

Tubbs C, 1995, *North Shore century of boating*, Devonport Yacht Club, Auckland

Tūroa T, 2000, *Te takoto o te whenua o Hauraki: Hauraki landmarks*, Reed Books, Auckland

Vant B, 2011, *Water quality of the Hauraki rivers and southern Firth of Thames, 2000–09*, Waikato Regional Council, Hamilton

Visser I N, 2005, *Swimming with orca: My life with New Zealand killer whales*, Penguin Books, Auckland

Waitangi Tribunal, 1987, *Ōrakei report: Report of the Waitangi Tribunal on the Ōrakei claim (Wai-9)*, Waitangi Tribunal, Wellington

Waitangi Tribunal, 1988, *Wai 22 — report of the Waitangi Tribunal on the Muriwhenua fishing claim*, Waitangi Tribunal, Wellington

Waitangi Tribunal, 2001, *Hauraki Gulf Marine Park Act report*, Waitangi Tribunal, Wellington

Waitangi Tribunal, 2006, *The Hauraki report Vol 1*, Waitangi Tribunal, Wellington

Waitangi Tribunal, 2006, *The Hauraki report Vol 2*, Waitangi Tribunal, Wellington

Waitangi Tribunal, 2011, *Waitangi Tribunal, Ko Aotearoa tēnei: a report into claims concerning New Zealand law and policy affecting Māori culture and identity. Te Taumata tuatahi*, Legislation Direct, Wellington

Walsh T, 1932, *From wherry to steam ferry on the Waitemata*, Walsh Printing, Auckland

Watson B N, 2004, *Site R10/497: Understanding the evidence of an undefended site on Motutapu Island, New Zealand*, MA thesis, University of Auckland

Watson N, 1969, 'Tribal trouble', *Ohinemuri Regional History Journal*, No. 11

Watton G, 1995, *Taming the Waihou: The story of the Waihou Valley catchment flood protection and erosion control scheme*, Waikato Regional Council, Hamilton

White J, 1888, *The ancient history of the Māori, his mythology and traditions: Tai-Nui* (Vol 5), Government Printer, Wellington

Whitmore B, 2011, 'Fishing in the Tryphena area in the 1950s and 60s', in Great Barrier Island History Research Group Incorporated (ed.), *True tales of Great Barrier Island*, Great Barrier Island History Research Group Incorporated, Claris

Whyle I, 1993, *Rakino Island*, Rakino Ratepayers Association Incorporated, Auckland

Wilkins I, 2010, *Classic: The revival of classic boating in New Zealand*, Random House, Auckland

Williamson L, 2000, *Gone surfing: The golden years of surfing in New Zealand, 1950–1970*, Penguin Books, Auckland

Williscroft M, 2014, 'Pilot stranding at Tryphena, 1984', in Armitage D, *More true tales of Great Barrier Island*, Great Barrier Island History Research Group Incorporated, Claris

Wilson N C, 1980, *Memories of Mansion House*, Richards Publishing, Auckland

Woolnough A, 1984, *Rangitoto: The story of the island and its people*, Angela Woolnough, Auckland

Wray J, 1939, *South Sea vagabonds*, Collins Publishing Group, London

Wright A, 2012, *Wrighty*, Alan Wright, Auckland

Wright O (ed.), 1950, *New Zealand 1826–1827 from the French of Dumont D'Urville*, Wingfield Press, Wellington

Yoffe S E, 2000, *Holiday communities on Rangitoto Island New Zealand*, University of Auckland, Auckland

Young B, 2012, 'Sawmilling at Thames and Coromandel', *The Treasury Journal*, Vol 5

Zeldis J R and R I C C Francis, 1998, 'A daily egg production method estimate of snapper biomass in Hauraki Gulf, New Zealand', *ICES Journal of Marine Science,* 55, 522–534

Zeldis J R, R A Walters, M J N Greig and K Image, 2004, 'Circulation over the northeastern New Zealand continental slope, shelf and adjacent Hauraki Gulf, during spring and summer', *Continental Shelf Research*, 24, 543–561

Index

Page numbers in **bold** indicate images.

Acheron, HMS 125, 127
afforestation 106
Aiguilles Is. 59
Aldermen Is. 47, **51**, 209: diving 209; name origin 47
Alma G (motor launch) 198
Alwyn G (scow) 135
anchovy (kokowhāwhā) 22
Andreason, Andy and Jack 232
Anna Watson (barque) 73, 74
antifouling 287
Anzac Avenue 76
Applied Geology Associates study 99
Arabic volute 287, **287**
Arataki (naval tug) 272
Arch Logan Memorial Trophy 155
Ariki (yacht) 149, 155, 156
Armstrong, Doug **178**, 178–79; tugboat **179**
Arran Bay 180
Ashby, Peter 256
Ashby, Ted 98: *Phantom Fleet* 98
Ashby, Troy **257**
Astrolabe (ship) 58, **58**, 59–61
Auckland **66–67**, 77, **138**: boat races, first 75; as capital 67–68; establishment 66–79; establishing settlement 73–76; Felton Mathew's site investigations 70–72; immigrants 78–79; first European building 75, **75**; first land sale 77; first settlers 73–74; first town plan 76–77, **77**; flag raising 73, **73**, 75; growth 78–79; 80–99; Hobson's arrival/visits to Waitemata 67–70, 72–73; Māori trading 78; naming 73; Ngāti Whātua invitation 68–69; port **64–65**, 72, **79**, **138**, **139**; reclamation 84, 95; sand/shingle quarrying 96–99; sewerage 87, 90–95; speculators 77; surveying 72, 76–77; waste disposal 95–96
Auckland and Suburban Drainage League 91
Auckland Anniversary Regatta **144–45**, 145, **146**, 147–48, 216, 308, 334
Auckland City Council 94, 109, 177, 191: Gulf Islands Committee 109
Auckland Council 291, 334: environmental report cards 291
Auckland District Manchester Unity of Oddfellows 163
Auckland Fishing Club 220
Auckland Harbour Board 83–84, 86, 90, 338
Auckland Harbour Bridge 157
Auckland Harbour: Hamer's plan for 85; McGregor's plan for **85**
Auckland Lady Anglers Club 202
Auckland Metropolitan Drainage Board 92
Auckland Regional Authority 94, 177, 330, 331

Auckland Regional Council 88, 109, 331–32
Auckland Star 88, 228, 232
Auckland Underwater Club 205
Auckland War Memorial Museum 32, 40, 306
Auckland Whale and Dolphin Safari 268
Auckland Yacht and Motor Boat Association 152, 157
Auckland, Lord 73
Avalon (motor launch) 198
Awaawaroa Bay 324, 325
Awana Beach **302–303**
Ayson, L F 226, 232

Bagnall Brothers 112
Bailey and Logan 146–47
Bailey and Lowe 149
Bailey, Charles 147
Bailey, Charles Junior 147, 149
Bailey, Walter 149
Baird, Karen 274
Baker, Dr Alan 268
Ballantine, Dr Bill **296**, 296–97, 328, 330, 336
Balsillie, W A 262
Banks, Joseph 47, 48, 52
barnacles 287
Baroona (steam trawler) 140, 223, 228
Bastion Point 125
Bastion Reefs 60
Beamish, Laurie **30**, 30–31
Bean Rock **120–21**, 283–84; lighthouse **120–21**
Bean Rocks 124–25
Beatie, James Forbes 170
Beddoes, George 147
Bell, Reginald 40
Best, Elsdon 42
Billy Goat Point **311**
birds, *see* birdwatching, seabirds; shore birds
birdwatching 274–75, **275**
Blackpool **183**
Blackwell, Charlie 204
Blake, Pippa 334
Blake, Sir Peter 334
Blows, Vic 156–57
boat/yacht racing *see* racing
boatbuilding 13, 129–34, 195–96: early 129–34; Great Barrier Is. **132**; and Māori 132, 133–34; and racing 147–57; scows 134–36, 137; steamers 136, 138–39, 141
Bouzaid, Chris 157
Bouzaid, Leo 157
Braddock, Rick 314
Bream Bay 53–54
Brewster, Allan 340
Britomart excavation **86**

Britomart, HMS (brig) 74, 123, 125
Brooke, Jack (John) 150, 157
Brown, Barrie 320–322, **322**, 323
Brown, Bob 155
Brown, Phil 266
Brown, William 77, 315
Browne, Gordon 101, 103
Browns Is. (Motu-Korea) 42, 77, 86, 88, 92, 143, **188–89**: and dredgings 86, 88; fish traps 42; sewerage scheme **92**
Buchanan, J 32
Buffalo Beach 101–102
Buffalo, HMS 141, 143
Burgess Is. 128, 130, 274–75, 278: lighthouse/keepers 128 **128**, 130
Burrill, Bill 108–109, **109**
Burrill, Max **108**
Butlers Is. 315
butterfish 330

Campbell, Graeme 312, 313, 324
Campbell, John Logan 77, 103, 315: *Poenamo* 103
Campbells Bay (Waipapa) 97, **99**: sand extraction 97
canoes, *see* waka
Cape Colville 52
Cape Rodney-Ōkakari Point Marine Reserve **326–27**, 327–29, **329**, 330, 337: fish stocks 330
Cassie, R Morrison 284
Cathedral Cove 332, **333**
Chadban, Ernie 198
Chamberlin family 96
Chaney, Bert **200**, 202
Chaney, Neil 234
Chapman, Valentine 295, 328
Chappell, Rob 266
charting gulf 123–27
Cheeseman, Thomas 306
Cheltenham Beach **191**
Cherubs (yachts) 155
Chilly Bin II (boat) **201**
Citizens and Ratepayers 93
Clark, Bill **200**
Clark, Dave 234, 247, **247**
Clarke A C 84–85
Classic Yacht Charitable Trust 158
Clean Harbour League 91
Clevedon 141
Clow, Adam 235, 253, **253**
Clow, Alf 234, **239**
Clow, Ian **239**
Clow, Phil 110, 234, **234**, 235, **235**, 249, 253
cockle (tuangi) 30–31, 36–38, 44: beds 36–38; Māori gathering 30–31

cod, blue **208**, 330
Collins, Tudor 102
Colville Bay 38
Colville Harbour 42: fish traps 42
Commercial Bay 74, 75, **75**, 76, 77, **79**:
      reclamation 83, **84**, **87**
Compain, Tipa 126, **126**
Conning, Bunny 169
Conning, Des **169**
Conning, Isobel 168–69, **169**
conservation 304–25, 326–45
Constantine, Rochelle 266–67, **267**
Cook, Ian 151
Cook, Capt. James 47–54: chart **54**;
      Endeavour voyage 47–54; and kahikatea
      forests 53–54; and Ngāti Hei 62;
      observing transit of Mercury 47–49;
      portrait **48**, potato gifts 51; shellfish
      gathering 49; visit to gulf 47–54; voyage
      to NZ 48
Cook's turban shell 39
Cooks Beach 49, **50**, 105, **105**
coral beds 228: destruction 228
Coral V (motor vessel) **257**
Cormack, William 26
Coromandel Harbour (Wai-au/Wai-aua)
      41–42, **56**, **103**
Coromandel HMS 52, 55
Coromandel Peninsula 101–106: afforestation
      106; deforestation 104; kauri extraction
      101–106; map 102; marine reserve
      332–33; Mill Creek 101; No Gum 102;
      Onuroa Valley 101; origin of place name
      56; river damage 104, 107; sedimentation
      110
Coromandel Ranges 55
Cory-Wright, Phyllis 104
Coubray, Keith 205
Countess (trawler) 228
Cowes Bay (Pikau) 180, **181**, 182
Coxs Creek (Opou) 74, 90, 156, 290
Craig J J 185
Craig, Dr John 309
crake, spotless 338
crayfish 11, 12–13, 31, 62, 206, 207 **208**, 209,
      238–40; **239**, 331, 332: commercial fishing
      41, 238–39, **239**
Crooks, Myra 167
Cross Creek 25, **25**
cruising, home-built 194–98
cuckoo, long-tailed (koekoeā) 21
Custom House Street (Customs Street) **82**,
      83: quay 83; sea wall 86
Cuvier Is. (Repanga) 24, **24**, 88, 129:
      lighthouse 129, 283–84

D'Urville, Dumont 58, **58**, 129, 185: *Astrolabe*
      (ship) **58**; chart of Waitematā **57**, 61; and
      place names 61; visit to gulf 59–61
Daldy, Capt. William 84
Dale, Roy 202
Dalmatians: and fishing 233

Daphne (steamship) 174
Darroch, David (Davey) 134–35, 137
Darroch, George 134
Davidson, Rodney 192
Davis, Joe 62, 63, **63**, 333
Davison, Isaac 340
Dawson, Steve 272
deforestation 104, 110: sedimentation effects
      110
Delamain, John 203
Dell, Capt. Edgar 54, 55
Dennes, George 155
Department of Conservation (DOC) 8, 32,
      86, 109, 165, 170, 174, 178, 266, 268, 297,
      305, 312, 313, 316, 318, 320, 324, 330,
      332–33, 338
Devonport 60, 133, 147, 149: boatbuilding
      147, 149; : shipbuilding 133
Devonport Borough Council 95, 189–90
Devonport Ferry Company 191
Devonport Wharf 138
Devonport Yacht Club 156
Dickensen, Alf 205, 206, **206**
Dillon, Capt. Peter 59
discovery, Polynesian 19–22
diving 205–11, **208**, **209**
Doak, Wade 330
dogfish (kapetā) **37**
Dollimore, Jim 248, **248**
dolphins: bottlenose 268, 269, **269**, 270;
      common (aihe) 22, 270, **270**, 271
Dorrette (ship) 315
dory, John 211, 218, 228, 232, 247, 330
Dosinia lambata 287
Doto (steam trawler) 218
Downie, Captain James 52, 55–57: chart of
      Hauraki Gulf **55**
Dreamtime (yacht) **197**
dredgings disposal 86–89: sites 86
Dromgool 180
Dromgoole, Leo 140
drummer, silver 330
Drunken Bay 133
Drury, Commander Byron 124, 127
Duchess (steamship) 184
Duchess of Argyle (ship), 78, **79**
ducks 71
Duke of Wellington (ship) 132
Dumping Options Advisory Group 89
Duncan, Leith 338
Dwyer, Sarah 269–70

Eaddy, P A 145, 146
East Coast Bays Coastal Protection Society
      336
ecotourism 261, **265**, 268, 274–75
Edwards, Bob 141
eels 36, 42
elephant seal 27
Elliot, Robin 148: *Southern Breeze* 148
Emu (steamship) 138, 139
Emu Point 168

Endeavour, HMS: **46–47**, **48**, voyage 47–54,
      62
Enderby, Tony 86–87, 268, 329–30
environment, and science 282–301: early fish
      records 283–84; fisheries habitat 292–95;
      fishing gear impacts 291–93, **293**; invasive
      species 290–91; horse mussel beds 293,
      293, 295; Leigh Marine Laboratory
      296–97, **297**; plankton 298–301; pollution
      286, 287, 290; rocky reefs 295–98; seabed
      communities 286–91; seagrass beds
      290, **290**; sea urchins 295, **295**; seawater
      circulation 298–301; shellfish 286–91;
      snapper research 284–86
Environmental Defence Society 86, 344
Etude et Enterprises 93
Eunice (schooner) 135
exploration: of gulf, early 22–24; to NZ 19–22

Fabricius, Darrin 257, **257**
Fairburn, William 315
Fairy (steamship) 141
Fancy (ship) 54, 55
Farmer, Andrew 174
farming 106, 113–16: marginal lands policy
      106
Farr, Bruce 157
Fay, Sir Michael 32–33, **33**
Fencible outposts 83
Fenwick, Rob, 324–25, **325**, 338
ferries 136, 138, 139, **139**, 140, 141, 163–65:
      Fullers 140
Ferry Landing 101
Firth of Thames 37, 55–56, 299–301, **301**,
      343: and Hauraki Plains 299–301; oxygen
      depletion 299, 300, 301; pH levels 200,
      plankton 299; sedimentation 110, 116;
      shark fishery 37; water quality 299–301
fish abundance 130, 131, 174, 186, 199–201,
      203–204, 216–18
fish depletion 8, 11, 12, 84, 179, 186, 201,
      206–207, 237, 239, 242, 244
fish habitats 292–95
fishing equipment 34–42, 216–18
fishing fleet, early 216–18
fishing practices, early Māori 11, 34–42:
      bait 35; hooks and lines 34–35, 38–39,
      38, **39**; fish-hooks **38**, 38–39; lines 39;
      lunar calendar (maramataka) 36; lures
      22, **34**, 38, **39**, 40; nets and traps 40–42;
      Oruarangi pā artefacts 40; seine nets
      42; and place names 35; sinkers 39; sites
      36–37; te ika tuatahi (first fish caught) 35;
      traps, stone (poraka) 42; women's role 35
fishing practices, modern 8–9, 236–57:
      seabird-protective 8–9
fishing, big game 198–202, **200**, **201**
fishing, commercial 236–57: box netting 246,
      248; crayfish 238–39; early commercial
      212–13, **214–15**, **216**, **222**; 214–35: and
      Dalmatians 233; Danish seining **212–13**,
      225, 232, **233**, 233–35, **235**, 246; early

fishing fleet 216–18; equipment 216–18; experimental trawling 218–19; fish abundance 218; gear impacts 291–93, **293**; Great Barrier Is. 238–43; green-lipped mussels 244–45; iki jime 248–51, **251**, 252; Japan market 242–43, 246, 248–52; live exports 243; longlining 223–25, 246, 253, 255–57; mullet boats 217; pair trawling 246, 247; quota–management system 252–54; shark fishing 226, **226**, 227, **227**; snapper 243–57; steam trawling 218–19, **223**, **229**; trawling 218–19, 220, **220**, 221–25, 228–31, 246; trawling inquiry 219–22

fishing, recreational 202, **202**, 203, **204**, 205, **207**, 230: charter 202–205; Coromandel **204**; increase in 230–31; off wharfs 204–205, **205**

Fitzroy, Governor Robert 132

Flagstaff 125, 138

Flat Rock lighthouse 129

flax industry 11–12

Fletcher, Christine **312**, 312–13

Fletchers Bay 288

Flora (scow) 135, **135**

Florence Kennedy (motor launch) 202, **203**

flounder (pātiki) 36, 42, 44, 45

Foam (mullet boat) **154**, 216

Forest and Bird Society, Royal NZ 338

Fort Britomart 75

Fort Street 83

Frances (yacht) 158

Francis, Dr Chris 285–86

Francis, Dr Malcolm 286, 294

Freemans Bay 101, 136: timber mills 101

French, Frank 224

Fullers Group 140, 318

Furey, Dr Louise 26, **26**

fur seal, NZ (kekeno) 27, 28, **28**

Galatea Bay 36

Gallagher, Joseph 220

Gannet (scow) **146**

Gannet Rock (Tīkapa) 23

gannet, Australasian 22

Gardiner, Mike 194

Gardiner's Gap **167**

Garrett, Dr Ross 184, 335, 336

Gaskin, Chris 274, **274**

Gaskin, David 264, 268: *Whales, Dolphins & Seals* 264

Gaukrodger, John 332

Gemini (steam launch) 141

Giacon, John 204

Gibbons, Terry 316

Gillies, John 134

Gladwell, Hugh 137

Glen Rosa (ferry) 88

Gloriana (yacht) 158

Gluepot Tavern 152

Goat Is. (Te Hāwere-a-Maki) **326–27**, 327–28, **328**

Goat Island Bay 292

Goat Island Marine Discovery Centre 330

godwits, bar–tailed 278–79, **279**, 338

Going, Sid 270

gold 81, 83, 112–13: discovery 52; rushes 81, 83; stamper batteries 112–13; sludge waste 112–13; Thames 104; Waihi 112–13

Goodwin, Tony 95

Gore Street Jetty 86

Government Store 74, 75, **75**

Governor Wynyard (steamship) **135**, 136

Gow, John 320, 322–23

Grace, Dr Roger 86, 206, 330

Grafton Bridge 98

Graham, John 315

Graham, Robert 163

Granger, John 99

Gray, Dr David 333–36

Great Barrier Is. (Aotea) 10, 11, 21, 22, 39, 102, 106–11, 134, 143, 197, 211, **302–303**: boatbuilding 134; fishing 203, 207, 238–43, **252**, 254; fish-processing plant **241**; kauri 102, 110, 134; map 107; shipwreck 143, **141**; surfing 194; timber mills 102, 106–111; tramways 111

Great Mercury Island (Ahuahu) 21, 26, **26**, 32–33, 41, 198–99, 200; archaeology, 32, 41; Archaeological Project 32; big game fishing 198–99, 200; crayfishing 41; early pop. 32; kūmara 32; Pari Nui te Rā 32; pest eradication 33; settlement 33

Green, Arthur 227

Green, Charles 49

Green, David **226**

Green, Dr Mal 299

Greenpeace 88

Grey, Arthur 174

Grey, Sir George 172, 174, 177

Grey, Zane 13, 198–200, **200**

Guard, Ivan 231

Gull Point (Toroa) 60, **60–61**

Gullery, Tom 262

gulls: black-backed 186; red-billed 130, 186, 278

gurnard, red 42, 207, 225

habitat degradation 286, 291–95, 298

Haddon, Laly 308

Hāhei 291, 332

Half Moon Bay marina 86

Hamer W H 84, 85

Hammond, Toss (Bill) 40

Hanna, Craig 256

Hansen, Charles 194

hāpuku 207, 215, **236–37**: depletion 249

Harataonga Beach **18–19**, 238, **240**

Harris, Snow **142**, 143

Harrison, Ronnie 316

Hartley, Richard 195, 196, 198: Hartley 16s 195, 196, 198, **198**

Hauraki Gulf (Tīkapa Moana): chart **55**

Hauraki Gulf Forum 8–9, 11, 109, 340–44:

environment report 8–9; Holdaway Awards 9; Revive our Gulf project 9; Sea Change Tai Timu Tai Pari marine spatial plan 9, 342, 344; *State of our Gulf* report (2011) 8, 11, 340, 342–44

Hauraki Gulf Marine Park (Tīkapa Moana Te Moananui ā Toi) 8–9, 15, 88, 307, 309, 314, 316, 325, 340–41: map 15; seminar 9

Hauraki Gulf Marine Park Act 8, 9, 341

Hauraki Gulf Maritime Park Board 8, 32, 174, 339

Hauraki Plains 111–17, 299–301: drainage 111, 114, **114**, **115**; farming 113–17; fish 111; flax industry **111**, 111–12; flooding 113, 116; and Māori 111, 115; map 111; meaning of 25; nutrient run-off 299–301; rivers 111, 115–16; sedimentation 116; timber extraction 112–13

Hauraki Plains Catchment Board 116

Hauraki Sawmill Company 112

Hawke, Bob 44

Hawkins, Clifford 83

Hawley, John 318

Hayward, Dr Bruce 287, 288, 289

Heale, Theophilus 172

Heberley, Charlie 262, 264

Hei 23, 62

Hen and Chicken Is. 211

Henry, Alison 110, 170, 312

Herald HMS 67, 69, 70, 123–25, 135–36

Herald Is. 143

Herald's Is. 124

Herne Bay 72, 149, 152

heron, white–faced 338

herrings 42

Hickey, Mike **257**

Hicks, Zachary 49

Higham, Tim 341, **341**

Highet, Harry 153

Hikutaia Stream 53

Hill, Alan 96

Hobbs Beach **2–3**

Hobson Bay (Waitaramoa) 74

Hobson Square 76

Hobson, Capt. William 12, 67–74, **69**, 78, 123: and advantages of Auckland 74; arrival 67–68; background 69; and Ngāti Whātua o Tāmaki 68, 69, 73–74; visits to Waitemata 69–70, 72–73

Hobsonville 72

Hodge, Charlie 99

Hohneck, Mook 308–309, **309**

Holdaway Awards 9

Holdaway, Anne **342**

Holdaway, Jim 9, 312

Holmes Bros 139

Holmes, Marjorie 173, **173**: *The Life and Times of Kawau Island* 173

Home Bay 163, **164**: wharf 313

Hook, Alf 98

Hook, Jimmy 98

Hook, John 98

Hooks Bay (Te Patu) 96, 98: sand extraction 96, 98
Horn (rock) 125
Horobin, Alan 270
Horotiu Stream 75, 90, 124, 134
Horton, Charles 149
Hot Water Beach 248
Hoturoa 24
Hounsell, W K 91
Hovell, Selwyn (Sonny) Te Moananui 40
Howick Beach 83, 289, **289**
Hudson, Douglas 140
Hudson, George 140, **140**, 180
Humphrey (steam trawler) **229**, 232
Hunter (ship) 55
Hunter, Stu 266
Huruhi Harbour **41**
Hydes Beach: sand extraction 99

Ida (scow) 215
Ikatere (research vessel) 284
immigration, 78–79
inanga 36
Infidel (yacht) 156
Insley Guesthouse 182
Insley, Henry 182
invasive species 290–91
Irene (scow) 306
Islington Bay (Ōruawharu) **133**, **160–61**, 165-67, **167**, 168, **168**, 169, 197

J J Craig Ltd 98
Jane Gifford (immigrant ship) 78, **79**, 132, 134
Jane Gifford (scow) **118–19**, 137, **137**
Jane Gifford Restoration Trust 137
JBL Limited 246
Jeffs, Jim and Kevin 246
Jessie Logan (yacht) 147, 148, **148**
Johnson, David 246
Johnson, Dr John 72
Johnson, Peter Tiki 332
Jones, Walter 148
Judges Bay (Taurarua) 78, **78**

kahawai 22, 36, 39, 42, 199, 201, 204, 207, 246: lures (pā kahawai) 39, **39**
kahikatea 53–56, 112: forests 53–54; on Hauraki Plains 112; spars 54–56
Kahui-McConnell, Richelle **342**, 344
Kahumatamoemoe 24
Kaiarāra Stream 107
Kaiaua 41
kaimoana (*see* seafood)
Kaiparaoa, Te Kiri 308
kaitiakitanga (stewardship and care) 8, 13, 43, 342
kākāpō 29
Karaka Bay 70, **70**, 93
Katene, Poaneki **257**
Kauaeranga Valley 105, **105**, **106**: afforestation 106; kauri 104-106
Kauri (scow) **136**

kauri 51, 55–59, 70, 83, 132, 134: boatbuilding 147; and deforestation 104; driving dams 100, 104, **106**, 107; extraction 101–104, **105**, 106–11; gum 102; Mercury Bay mill 101; river damage 104, 107; ships' spars 55–59, 83, 101; timber 101–10; timber mills 101–111; Whangaparapara Harbour mill **110**; Whitianga mill **102**
Kauri Timber Company 106, 110
Kawakawa Bay **97**, 99: sand extraction 99
Kawau Bay 37, 59, 292
Kawau Company 170
Kawau Is. 10, 141, 170, **171**, **172**, 173–74: copper mining 170 **171**, 172; day trippers 174; map 171; recreation 170–74; steamship service 141
Kawerau Avenue 95
Kellian, Dave 243, 246, 248, **249**, 250, 277
Kellian, Ross 238, 240–41
Kelly Tarlton's Underwater World 90, 209
kelp forests 330, 331
Kennedy Bay 262
Kerepehi Flaxmilling Company 111
Kestrel (ship) 140
Kiariki (yacht) 150
Kidd, Harold 148
kingfish (warehenga) 22, 204, 205–206, 207, 209, **209**, 210, **210**, **211**
Kirk, Thomas 306
Kitty Vane (launch) 270
kiwi, brown 315, 321
kiwi, little spotted 29
knot, red 278, 279
Kōheruhahi Point, 35 **36**
Kohimarama 99
Kohimarama Yacht Club 157
Kōtuiti Tuarua (Kōtuiti II) (waka taua) **122**, 126, **126**
Kreft, Ferdinand 138
kūmara 21, 25, 30, ao32, 51, 306, 315, 324
Kupe 21, 22

La Reta (motor launch) 202, 204
La Vega (trawler) **247**
Labour Party 93
Ladd, Fred 199, **199**, 203, 238, 241
Ladd, Mabel 199, **199**
Lady Jocelyn (motor launch) 202, 238
Lake Erie (scow) 134
Lands and Survey Department 314
Lane, Allan 278
Laurence, John 316, 318–19, **319**, 343
leadsman 123–24
leatherjacket **208**
Lee, Greg 150–51
Lee, Mike 88–89, **88**, **89**, 332
Lees, Ted 312, **312**
LegaSea 206
Leigh 8, 209, 230, 328
Leigh Fisheries 246, 250, 252, 254, 255
Leigh Harbour **250**, 254, **255**, 256–57
Leigh Marine Laboratory 286, 295–97, **297**, 298

Lena (scow) 233
lifesaving 192, **192**
Ligar canal **87**, 90
Ligar, Charles 90
Liggins, Dr Jim 40
lighters (boats) 84
lighthouses **120–21**, 127, **127**, 128, **128**, 129–34, 283–84: Bean Rock **120–21**, 283–84; Burgess Is. 128, **128**, 130; Cuvier 129, 283–84; Flat Rock 129; Mokohinau 283–84; Rangitoto Channel 129, **146**; Tiritiri Matangi 127, **127**, 128, **128**, 130–31, **131**, 283–84
Limeworks 98–99
Lipton Cup 154
Lipton, Sir Thomas 154
Litherland, Tony and Carol 242, **242**, 243
Little Barrier Is./Te-Hauturu-o-Toi 8, 22, 53, 211, 275, 276, **304–305**; and Māori 306, 318; map 306, nature reserve 305–307; pest eradication 306
Loch, Jock 166–67
Logan Bros. 149
Logan, Arch 149, 155, 156
Logan, Robert 146, 147, **147**, 148–49, 157
Long Bay 98, **194**
Long Bay-Ōkura Marine Reserve 333–35, **335**, **336**, 336–37
longlining 223, 224–25, 277–78
lure, Māori fishing 22, **34**, 39: kahawai **39**; Marquesan pearl 22, **34**; trolling 40

Mack, Bill 184
Mackerel, horse (kōheru) 36 49, 246
Madon, Dr Bénédicte 268
Mahurangi 37: shark fishing grounds 37
Mahurangi Harbour 134, 293, 294
Mahurangi, Friends of the 146
Maketū 23, 42
Malcolm, Mike 151
Man O' War Bay 129, **129**, 180
Manchester Unity of Oddfellows Premier Picnic 164, **164**
Mangaiti 113
mangroves (mānawa) 110, 338
Mansion House **172**, 307
Mansion House Bay (Momona Bay) **1**, 10, 171, **172**, 174, 197
Manukau Harbour 24, 28, 30, 61, 72, 74, 92, 93, 137: portage to 30, 72, 93
Māori: adzes 28; customary rights 42–43; early agriculture 28–29; early fishing 11, 34–45; and environment 8, 11, 13, 43, 283, 342; and European sailing craft 133–34; food gathering/sources 26–31; forest resources 27–28; introduced animals/plants 25; gods 25; kaitiakitanga 8, 13, 43, 342; land loss 115; lunar calendar (maramataka) 36; middens 26, 28, 32, 38, 39, 42; mātauranga 42, 43, 345; peach trade 133–34, 145; place names map of gulf **14**; seabird harvest 276;

shark fisheries 37; and shellfish 36, 38; whanaungatanga (kinship) 43
Maraetai Beach 30, 96–97: sand extraction 96–7
Maria Is. (Ruapuke) 8, 186
marinas 86–87
Marine Department 96, 97, 283, 328
marine mammals 27–28
marine reserves 13, 260–61, 282–83; 327–40
Marine Sciences Association 328
marine spatial plan 342
Maritime Museum, NZ 158
Marler, Bruce 150–51, **151**: family 151
marlin, black 200, 201, 202
Marsden, Samuel 55–57, 59: in Waitematā 57
Martin, Mary Ann 78
Martin, Ronnie 224–25, **225**, 252
Marutūahu 23
Mason, William 73
Matarangi Spit 36
Matarere (yacht) 155
Matatoki River 52, 54
mātauranga Māori (culture/knowledge) 42, 43, 345
Matheson Bay (Te Kohuroa) 205
Mathew, Felton 67, 70–71, 73–77, 125
Mathew, Sarah 70, 71, 75, 76
Matiatia 184
Matthews, Dick 337
Maukin (brig) 132–33
mauri 42, 345
Mawhiti (yacht) 155
Maxted, John 336
Maxwell, Peter 334
Maxwell, Thomas 31, 129, 132, 177, 311
Mayor Island 47
McCallums Is. (Pākihi Is.) 224
McCarthy, Bill 158
McDonald, Elsie 114
McGregor J 84, 85
McIntosh, Charles 175, 320
McKenzie Bay 165
McKenzie, Captain George 165–66
M-Class yachts 155
McNab, Hon. R 232
Meader, Bert 256
Mechanics Bay 76, **76**, 78, 90
Menzies, Robert 134
Meola Reef 95–96, 338: landfill **95**, 95–96
Mercury Bay (Te Whanganui-o-Hei) 47, 49, 51, 101, 198–200: fishing 198–200
Mercury Bay Game Fishing Club 201, 202
Mercury Bay Swordfish and Mako Club 198
Mercury Bay Timber Company 102
Mercury Islands 210–11: *see* Great Mercury Is.; Red Mercury Is.
Mercury, observing transit of 47, 48, 49
Merton, Don 186
Micronesian/Polynesian origins 19, 20–21: map 20
middens: 26, 28, 32, 38, 39, 41
Mieklejohn, Septimus 134

Milford Beach 97, 191, **191**, 192: sand extraction 97
Milford Girls' Lifesaving Club 191–92
Millar, Hon. John 226
Minnehaha Bay 44
Minnie Casey (steam trawler) 218, 220–21
Miranda Lime Works 99
Miranda Naturalists' Trust 278, 279
Miranda-Pūkorokoro 278–81: Shorebird Centre 280, **280**
Mission Bay 289
Mitchell, Dr Neil 309
Mizen, Edward 32
Mizen, Pat 32, 33, 207, 262
Moa (brig) 133
moa 26–27, 32, 38, 39: bones **27**; fish-hooks **38**, 39
Moehau 21
Moehau (launch) 272
Moir, Dr James 219, 220
moki, red **208**, 330, 332
Mokohinau Is. 128, 130, 211, 215, **275**, 276: fishing 215; fish species 284; lighthouse 283–84
Mokoia (Panmure) 57, 59, 72
Molloy, Janice 277
Mon Desir Hotel 190
Mona (mullet boat) 224
Monin, Paul 32, 122, 134, 180, 182
Moore, Alan 272
Moore, Dave 256–57, **257**
Moran, Dave 209, **209**
Morcom, Toby 105, **105**
Morley, Margaret 288, **288**, 289
Morrison, Dr Mark 285, 290, 292, 294, **294**, 295
Morton, John 295, 296, 298
Morton, Rob 88
Motions Creek landfill **95**
motor/oil launches 153, **153**
Motu Mānawa-Pollen Island Marine Reserve 337, **337**, 338: birdlife 338
Motuihe Is. 13, 30, 61, 197, **315**, **317**, **319**: and Māori 315; pest eradication 320; replanting 316, 317, 318, 320; quarantine station 315–16; restoration 13, 315–20
Motuihe Island Restoration Trust 316, 318
Motuketekete Is. 172
Motukorea Is. 61
Moturekareka Is. **142**, 142–43, 194
Motutapu Is. 8, 13, 27–28, **29**, 30, 31, 163, 164, **164**, 165, **311**, **313**, **314**: excursions to 138; and Māori 311; map 165; pest eradication 8, 314, 315; recreation 163, 164, **164**, 165, 168; replanting 313, 314; restoration 8, 13, 311–315; settlement 27–28; species restoration 313; Sunde site 27–28
Motutapu Restoration Trust 314
Mount Eden (Maungawhau) 75
Mount Hobson (Hirakimata) 21, 107, 111
Mount Moehau (Te Moengahauo-Tamatekapua) 23

Mount Victoria 60
Mount Wellington (Maungarei) 72
Mowbray, John 107
mullet 27, 36, 42; yellow-eyed (aua) 41–42
mullet boats 154, **154**, 217, **219**
Murrays Bay Boating Club 157
Mussel Reef Restoration Trust 343
mussel: Asian date 291, **291**
mussel, green-lipped 218, **245**, **344**: commercial harvesting 244–45; map of beds 245; restoration 9, 342–44
mussel, horse 9, 13, 31, 36, 44: beds 36, 225, 228, 233, 293, **293**, 295, 298: loss of 228, 233

Nagel Cove **132**, 134, 242
Narrow Neck Beach 95
National Institute of Water and Atmospheric Research (NIWA) 285
natural resources/treasures 260–81
navigation, Polynesian 21
Nelson Fisheries 246
Netherton 117
nets/netting: box 246, 248, **248**; Danish seining 130, **212–13**, **225**, 232, **233**, 233–35, **235**; drag/scoop 42; seine (taharoa) 40–41, 42, 49; set netting 130
Neumann, Dr Dirk 271
Neureuter, Rod **186**, **342**
Neureuter, Sue **185**, **342**: family 185–87
New Zealand Company 69, 74
New Zealand Herald: poster series 9
New Zealand Pilot 127, 129, 134
New Zealand Underwater Association 328
New Zealand Wars 83
Newmarket Fishing Club 219–20
Ngā Pōito-o-Te Kupenga-o-Toi-te-huatahi 22
Ngā Puhi 56, 62, 68
Ngāi Tai 27, 30–31, 37, 132, 311, 315, 318, 320: gardens 30, kaimoana 31; and Kawau Is. 170; and Noises Is. 185; and Pakatoa Is. 175; and Rākino Is. 177; trading 30; Treaty settlement 31; Te Haerenga tourism venture 31
Ngapuhi (barge) 109
Ngataki (yacht) 194–95, **195**
Ngataringa Bay 95
Ngatea 117
Ngāti Hako 307
Ngāti Hei 24, 32, 47, 51, 62–63, 101, 104, 307, 332–33: and James Cook 62; and kaimoana 62; timber rights 104
Ngāti Huarere 24, 28
Ngāti Karaua 32
Ngāti Manuhiri 215, 305–309, 332: and islands/restoration 306–309; and Little Barrier Is./Te-Hauturu-o-Toi 305–307; Treaty settlements 308–309
Ngāti Manuhiri Settlement Trust 305, 307
Ngāti Maru 23, 70, 180: and Waiheke Is. 180
Ngāti Paoa 23, 37, 56, 68, 70, 126, 133, 307,

311, 315, 318, 320: and Rākino Is. 177; and Rangitoto Is. 165; and Pakatoa Is. 175; and Waiheke Is. 180; waka taua **122, 126**

Ngāti Rehua 143

Ngāti Rongo 23, 132

Ngāti Tamaterā 23, 42, 77

Ngāti Wai 170, 306: and Kawau Is. 170

Ngāti Whanaunga 23, 32, 40, 49, 52, 103, 307

Ngāti Whātua o Tāmaki 68, 69, 73–74, 77: and British settlement 68, 69, 73–74, 78; and Ōkahu Bay village 94; sale of Auckland 73–75, 76; and sewerage 94; waka races 75

Ngāti Whātua Ōrākei 12, 44–45, 84, 94, 170, 345

Ngatira (yacht) **149**

Ngātoro-i-rangi 23, 24

Ngeungeu 31, 132

Ngeungeu Te Irirangi Zister, Rachel 30, 31

Nias, Captain 123

Niccol and Sharp 132–35

Niccol, Henry 132–35, 147

Ninnis, Captain James 170

Noble, Reg 167

Noises Is. 86, 88, **89**, 163: dredgings disposal site 86, 88; recreation 185–87

Norah Niven (steam trawler) 222

North Cove (Kawau Is.) **173**

North Island Mussels Ltd (NIML) 343

North Shore Ferries 140

North, Basil 203

Northern Steam Ship Company 182

Norton, Tom 262

nudibranch, clown **208**

O'Brien, Darcy 33, 307

Observation Point 125

octopus 44

Official Bay 76, **76, 79**, 81, 190

Ohinau Is. 62

Ōhinemuri River **112**, 113, 116: pollution 113

Ōkahu Bay 44, **45**, 68, 69, 94, **94**: ecological restoration plan 344; kaimoana survey **345**; sewer 94, **94**

Ōkiwi Station 108–109

Ōkupu Bay 238, **241**

Ōkura River 230

Ōmaha 134, 135, 137, 294

Ōmaha Spit 36, 38, 99: sand extraction 99

Omatere (mullet boat) **154**

Onehunga 83

Oneroa Bay Regional Park 98

Oneroa Beach 184, 288, 289

Onetangi Beach 182

Ōpito Bay 25, 26, 39, 291

Ōrākei 60, 68, **122, 224**: hui 68

Ōrākei Basin 287

Orams, John and Mark 334

orca 271, 272, **272**

Ōrere Beach 98

Ōrewa marineland 270

Ormerod, Barry 184

Oruarangi 52, 111

Ostend 182

ostrich foot **289**

Ōtāhuhu 83, 136

Ōtama Beach 293

Ōtata Is. **163, 185**, 185–87, **187**, 245, **245**: mussels 245; pest eradication 186; weed control 186

Ōtuataua stonefields 28

Outboard Boating Club 316, 317, 318, 343

Owen, Bill 143, 238, 240, 241

Owhanake Bay 96

Oyster 51, 71: Bluff 51; farming 339, native rock 291; Pacific 291, **291**

oystercatcher, South Island pied 27, 279

P Class yachts 153, 155

Paeroa **113**, 141: flooding 113, **113**

Pakatoa Is. 10, **175, 176**, 216; map 175; recreation 174–76

Pakatoa Island Tourist and Holiday Resort 176

Pakihi Is. 35: fishing camp **35**

Palm Beach 182

Palmer, Bunty 174

Pandora (ship) 127

Paneiraira 24

Panmure 83

Panmure Basin 71, **71**, 72

Papakura Stream 30

Pari Nui Te Rā 32

Parkes, Wayne 193, **193**

Parkinson, Sydney 47, 51

Parnell 149

parore 207

Parr, James 91

Parris, Innes 182

Parsons, Dr Darren 285, 286

pāua (abalone) 39, 44, 62, 318

Paul, Larry 284–85

peach boats 145

Peart family, 11, **12**

Peart, Lindsay 197, **197**, 239

penguin, little blue 131

Percy Vos Charitable Trust 158

Peregrine (steamship) **139**

petrel, black 8, **258–59**, 276; grey-faced 33, 276; Pycroft's 276

Piako River 24, 36, 71, 111, 115, 116, 299: flax industry **111**; pollution 116

picnicking 164, **164**, 165, 182

pilchard (mohimohi) 22

Pine Harbour marina 86, 87, 88: and dredgings 86, 87, 88, 89

Pinkerton, Dr Max 227

pipi 36, 38, 44: beds, 36, 38

Pipiroa 38

Piritahi marae **43**

plankton 22, 298–301

Platina (ship) 74

plover, shore 315

Plowman, Annette and Neal 320

pōhutukawa 21–22, 72–73

Point Britomart (Te Rerenga-ora-iti) **73**, 74, 75, **79, 82**, 83, 84, 86, 125

Point Chevalier Beach 71, 99

Point Rodney 53

Point Stanley 76

Polack, J S 37

Pollard, Len 96

Pollen Is. 338

Pollen, Dr Daniel 338

pollution 90–95, 95–96, 110, 112, 116, 204–205, 286, 340: antifouling 287, 290; heavy metals 290; rivers 112, 116; sedimentation 110, 298; sewage 90–95; solid waste 95–96

Polynesian arrival, date of 25–26

Ponsonby 72, 149, 152

Ponsonby Cruising Club 153, 154, 155

Ponsonby motor launch regatta **153**

Ponsonby Regatta Committee 152, 154

Pōnui Is. 96, 199, 224, 244, 245: single extraction 96

Poole, C H 232

Pooley, William 166

Port Charles 51

Port Jackson **7–8, 101**

port, Auckland: development 81–87: dredgings disposal 86–89; Hamer's plan 84, 85; impact on Ngāti Whātua Ōrākei 84; lighters 84; McGregor's plan 84, **85**; waterfront **80–81, 82**

portage: Waitematā–Manukau 30, 72, 93

Ports of Auckland Limited 86

Powell, Arthur 286–87, 290: *New Zealand Mollusca* 286; *The Shellfish of New Zealand* 286

Pridham, Ed 230–31, **231**

pūkeko 338

Pulford, Doug 254

Pūrangi River 49, **50**, 51, 105, 110: sediment 110

Pūriri Bay 203

Putiki Bay 182

Queen Street 76, 83, 84, 90, 132, **217, 219**: Lower **87**, sewage 84; wharf **82–83**, 83

Quickcat (ship) 140

quota-management system 252–54, 256

R & A Logan 149

racing (boat/yacht) 75, 144–59: Auckland Anniversary Regatta 145, **144–45**, 146, **146**, 147–48; Bailey and Logan 146–47; first race 75; international designers 157; *Jessie Logan* 148, **148**; Mahurangi regatta 146; motor/oil launches 153, **153**; mullet boats 154, **154**; P Class yachts 153, 155; peach boats 145; post-WWII 156–57; *Ranger* 155–56, **156**; sailing dinghies 153, 155, 157; scows 146, **146**; waka taua **144**,

145; yacht clubs 149, 151–53, 156–57; yacht design 147–49; Z Class yachts (Zeddies) 155, **155**
rāhui (harvest closure) 31, 42, 309
rail, banded 338
Rainbow (yacht) 157
Rainbow II (yacht) 157
Rākino Is. 109, 140, 177–80, 216, 217, **217**: bach **178, 179, 180**; fishing 216, 217; Māori Garden Bay 177, **180**; map 177; Ocean View settlement **180**; pest eradication 178–79; recreation 177–80; subdivision 177
Rakino Island Smoked Snapper 216, 217
Rākino Residents and Ratepayers Association 109
Ramsey, John 176
Rangaunu Harbour **290**
Ranger (cutter) 70–73, 78
Ranger (yacht) 155–56, **156**
Rangi-hua 61
Rangitoto Channel lighthouse **45**, 129, **146**
Rangitoto Is. 8, 29, **29**, 30, 31, 44, 77, 86, 143, **160–61**, 165–66, **167**, 168–70: baches 165–70; eruption 27, 29; Felton Mathew visit 71; fishing camp **16–17**; and local place names; map 166; pest eradication 8, 170; pōhutukawa forest 170; recreation 12, 165–70; restoration 8, 13, 170
Rangitoto Island Conservation Trust 170
Rangitoto Island Domain Board 165, 168
Rangitoto Recreation Club 165–69
Rangitoto Wharf 165–67
Rattlesnake, HMS 69
Rawhiti (yacht) 150, 151, **151**
reclamation 83, 84, 86, 95, 99: and Ngāti Whātua Ōrākei 84
recreation: on sea 12, **188–89**; 188–211: big game fishing 198–202, **200, 201**; cruising, home-built 194–98; diving 205–11; fishing **202**, 202–205; lifesaving 191–92, **192**; spearfishing 205–11; sunbathing 191, **191**; surfing 192–94, **194**; swimming 189–92, **190**
Red Mercury Island 207, **207**
rediscovery and exploration 46–63: Cook's arrival 47–54; D'Urville visit 59–61
reefs, rocky 295–98
Reg's Beach 167
Reid brothers 163, 165
Reidy, Denis 96
reserves/sanctuaries 304–25
resources, land-based 100–17: Coromandel Peninsula 101–106; flax industry 111–12; Great Barrier Is. 106–11; gold mining 112–13; Hauraki Plains 111–17; kauri extraction 101–11; land clearance 110
restoration 8, 13, 99, 304–25, 326–45: sand 99; sea 8, 326–45; *see also* island entries
Revive our Gulf project 9
Rewa (barque) **142**, 194, 195
Richmond Cruising Club 152, **152**

Richwhite, David 32, 33
Rickard, Dr Maxwell 177
Rippon, Geoffrey 108
Rita (yacht) 147
Riu-ki-uta 24
Riverhead 71
Roa (motor vessel) 244, **245**
Robinson, Sir Dove-Meyer 88, 91–93, **93**, 95
Rocky Bay (Ōmiha) 182
Rodney, Admiral Sir George Bridges 53
Ronomor (motor launch) 202
Rose, George 182
Rotoroa Is. 10, 13, 176, **321, 322, 323**: and Māori 320; pest eradication 321; replanting 320–21; restoration 13, 320–23; and Salvation Army 320–21; species restoration 321
Rotoroa Island Trust 320, 322
Rotten Row 143
Rough Point (Te Onewa) 125
Rough, Captain David 72, **72**, 75, 76, 124–25, 127
Royal Admiral (ship) 55
Royal New Zealand Yacht Squadron 149
Rua-mahua (islands) 47
Ruthe, William 320
Ruthes Is. 320

saddleback 315, 321
sailing dinghies 153, 155, 157: designs 157
salt-marsh 338
Salvation Army 175–76, 320–21
San Kawhia (trawler) 230, **231**
sand replenishment 99
sand/shingle quarrying 96–99: Campbells Bay 99; Kawakawa Bay **97**; scows 98; shingle merchants 96; Waiheke Is. 98
Sandager, Andras 276
Sandspit 138, 226
Sandy Bay (Ō-kahu-tai) 23, 248
Sanford, Albert 147, 175, 177, 217, 218, 220, 221, 223, 228, 232
Sanford, Albert junior 220–21
Sanford, Ann 177, 217
Sanford Ltd 216, 217, **217**, 218, **221**, 223, 228, 232, 246, 247, 254
Sarah Maxwell (schooner) 132
Sarah's Gully 26
scallops 30–31, 234, 292, 294: beds 131, 294; degradation 131; dredges 292; Māori gathering 30–31
Scandrett Beach 8
Scott, Sir Peter 310
scows 98, 134–36, **146**
seabed communities 286–91
seabirds 8–9, 274–81: conservation plan 274–75; and longlines 277–78
Sea Change Tai Timu Tai Pari marine spatial plan 9
sea elephant 27
sea slugs 294
seafood/kaimoana, Māori 13, 29, 30–31,

34–45: fishing equipment 34–35, 38–42; harvesting approach 34–35; management 42–43; matauranga Māori 43; seasonal fishing calendar 36, 38; seasonal fishing sites 36; traditional shark fishery 37; *see also* fish/fishing/shellfish and species entries
seagrass (*Zostera*) 13, 21: beds 13, 290, **290**, 295, 298; loss of beds 290
Seagull (scow) **146**
sea lion 27
Sealords 234
seawater circulation 298–301
Seccombe, Richard 104
sedimentation 110, 116, 298
seine nets (taharoa) 40–41, 42, 49
seine, Danish **212–13**, **225**, 232, **233**, 233–35, **235**, 292
Sentinel/Watchman Is. (Te Kākāwhakaara) 72, 73, 224
settlement, European 55, 66–117
settlement, Māori 11, 12, 25–33: archaeological evidence 25–27; dating 25; earliest 25–27; impacts 29; Rangitoto eruption 29; Sunde site 27, **29**
sewerage 87, 90–95: Browns Is. scheme 91, 92, **92**, 93; and poliomyelitis 92; gulf discharge 1930s 91; Māngere oxidation ponds 92–95; and Ngāti Whātua Ōrākei 94; Ōrākei outfall/works 91, 92, 94; and Sir Dove-Meyer Robinson 91–93, 95; and Waitematā Harbour 87, 90–95
shag: 27, 29: NZ king 29; spotted 186
shark 22, 36, 37, 45, 226, 248: attacks 190; dogfish (pioke) 37; drying process **37**; fisheries/fishing 226, **226**, 227, **227**; hooks for 39; mako 199, 200, 201; school shark (tupere) 37; population 227; traditional fishery 37
Sharp, Archibald 132
Shearer Rock 125
Shearwater: Buller's 276, **276**, 278; flesh-footed **277**
shell extraction 98–99: Miranda 99
shellfish 12, 21, 27, 29, 36, 38, 286–91: beds, 36, 38; and pollution 94; spawning 36; *see also* kaimoana; species entries
Shenandoah (motor launch) 202
Shields, Darren **210**, 210–11
Shoal Bay 138, 143, 155
shorebirds, migratory 278–81
Sibson, Richard 278
Simmons family 168
Simpson, Richard 200, 201, **201**, 270
Simpsons Beach (Wharekaho) 51
Sir Peter Blake Marine Education and Recreation Centre (MERC) 333–35, **335**, 336: *Wavebreaker* newsletter 336
Slark, Elaine and family 316, **316**
Slark, Tony 316
Slimbridge Wetlands Project 310
Sloanes Beach 152, **152**
smelt, common 36

Smith, Dr Ian 29
Smokehouse Bay 10
snails, mud (titiko) 38
snapper (tāmure) 21, 27, 35, 42, 204, **212–13**,
    218, 220, **225**, 228, 233, **235, 241**, 255,
    260–61, 282–83, 284–86, 299, 330:
    commercial fishing 237, 243, 244–57;
    depletion 286; diet 286; iki jime market
    248–52; juvenile **284**, 298, 300, 338; life
    history 286; monoculture 294; movements
    in gulf 285; overfishing 218; research
    220–21, 284–86, 295; and seabed 295,
    298; tagging 285, **285**, 286
Solander, Dr Daniel 49, 52
Somerfield, Judy **169**
Sorensen, Hanne 88
Southern Seabird Solutions 277
spar ships 54–59, 101, 129
spearfishing 205, **206**, 206–11
Spence, Captain George 134
Spencer, John 156
Spirit of Adventure (ship) 157
sponges 298, **208**: beds 298
sprats 42
St Clair Brown, Don 334
St Georges Bay 190
St Heliers Bay 98, 99
St Patrick (ship) 59
Stanley Bay Wharf 290
Stanley, Captain Owen 123, 125: charts of
    Waitematā **123, 124**
starfish 287, **344**: brittle 287
State of our Gulf report (2011) 8, 11, 340,
    342–44
steamships 136, 138–39, 141, **172, 180**
Stembridge, Steve 268
Stephenson, H 222
Stewart, W W 139: *Steam on the Waitemata*
    139
stichbird (hihi) 306
stingrays 294
Stirlingshire (barque) 134
Stockin, Dr Karen 271
Stockyards Bay ('Watering Bay') 174
Stokes Point 127, 136, 138
Stokes, Captain John Lort 124, 125, 127
Stone, C J 104
Stone, Robert 104, 136
Store Bay (Oneoneroa) 74, **75**
storm petrel, NZ 8, 275, **275**: white-faced 186
Street, John 158, **158**
Strongman, Merv 227, **227**, 244
Subritzky Shipping Line 137
Subritzky, Bert 108, 272
Subritzky, Les, 205
sunbathing 191, **191**
Surfdale (Huruhi Bay/Te Huruhi) 180, 182,
    183, 184, **184**
surfing 192–94, **194**
surveys, marine 123–25: Navy 125, 127
Sutherland, Temple: 202–203: *Maui and Me*
    202

Swainson, William 78
swimming 189–92, **190**: costumes 190–91
Symonds, Captain William Cornwallis 73, 75

Ta'Aroa (yacht) 324
Tahuna 24
Tainui waka: exploration by 23, 24
Tairua 104, 106: forestry 106
Tairua Harbour 110: mangroves 110
Tairua State Forest 106
Tait, Herbie 99
takahē 313, 315, 321
Takanini, Īhaka 177
Takaparawha Point 90, **90**, 94, **94**
Takapuna Beach 189–90, **190**, 192–3
Takapuna Boating Club 155
Takapuna Borough Council 192
Takapuna City Council 334
Takapuna Class yachts155
Tamaariki, Tamaiti 44–45, **45**, 94
Tamaariki-Pohe, Moana 170, 345
Tamahui (waka taua) 145
Tāmaki isthmus (Auckland) 28, early
    settlement 28–29; forest clearance 28;
    name 28; volcanic landscape 28
Tāmaki River 71, 72, 91, 122, 136, 137
Tāmaki Strait 30, 60, 70, 218: benefits of 69,
    70; early exploration 60; seagrass beds 218
Tāmaki, Te Reweti 69, 74
Tama-te-kapua 23, **24**, 62
Tangaroa 35, 45
tapu 42
tarakihi 207, 211
Tara's Rock 31
Tara-te-irirangi 30, 31
Tarlton, Kelly 209
Tauhia, Te Hēmara 132
Tāwharanui Marine Park 89, 330–31, **331**,
    332: fish stocks 331
Tāwharanui Peninsula 99
Tawhiti 61
Tawhitokino Regional Park 98
Taylor (first recorded European settler) 55
Taylor, Graeme 274
Taylor, Peter 128
Te Arawa waka: exploration by 23–24
Te Aroha 113, 141
Te Atatū 338
Te Hinaki 57
Te Hoe-o-Tainui 24
Te Horeta 103
Te Horetā te Taniwha 52, **52**, 56
Te Huruhi 133–34
Te Irirangi, Tara 132
Te Kawau, Āpihai **56**, 57, 68, **68**
Te Kawerau-a-Maki 306, 307
Te Kiri, Rahui 306, 308
Te Mātā, 38
Te Mataku 32, **33**
Te Matuku Bay 324–25, **325**, 338
Te Matuku Marine Reserve 338–39, **339**:
    oyster farming 339

Te Rangui 59
Te Reweti, Wiremu **68**
Te Riringa, Tenetahi 215, 306
Te Wai-ō-Hua 27, 28
Te Whatarangi 68
Te Wherowhero 145
Te Whitianga-o-Kupe 21
teal, brown (pāteke) 315
Te-Moana-Nui-o-Toi-te-huatahi 23
Tercel, Lou 155–56
tern: NZ fairy 276; white-fronted 186
Thames 113: wharf **222**
Thistle (schooner) 132
Thomas Currell (steam trawler) 232
Thompson, Peter 137
Thornbury, Jim 209
Thrush, Dr Simon 291, 292, **292**, 293
Tikapa Moana 23
timber industry *see* kahikatea; kauri
Tino Rawa Trust 195
Tiri (scow) 197, 230
Tiritiri Matangi Is: **2–3**, 8, 13, 127–31, 145,
    206, 283–84, 307–10, **310**, 311: diving
    206; lighthouse 127, **127**, 128, **128**,
    130–31, **131**, 283–84; and Māori 307;
    open sanctuary 307–11; pest eradication
    311; replanting 310–11; restoration 8, 13,
    131, 145
Titai 68
Toi-te-huatahi 22
Torkington, Barry 206, 233, 239, 246, 248,
    249, 250
Toroa (yacht) 147
Torpedo Bay 138
Tourist Air Travel 199, 238
Townshend, Gray 115, 117, **117**
Townshend, Marie 117, **117**
tramways 111
transportation in gulf 12, 120–43:
    boatbuilding (early) 129–34; charting
    123–27; coastal traders 123; early
    European vessels 123; ferries 139, **139**;
    lighthouses **120–21**, 127, **127**, **128**,
    129–34; Māori 121–23; scows 134–35,
    135, 136, **136**; shipwrecks **141**, 141–43;
    steamers 136–38, **138**, **139**, 139–41;
    surveys of Waitematā 123–25
trawling 218–19, 220, **220**, 221–25, 228–31:
    experimental 218–19; inquiry 219–22;
    pair 246, 247; steam 218–19, **223**, **229**
Treaty of Waitangi 8, 52: and fisheries 84;
    signing 8, 67, 68, 69, 70, 72
Tregidga, John **9**, 11, **342**, 343
trevally 199, 204, 246, 338: depletion 242
tributyltin (TBT) 287, 290
trig station (Devonport) 127
Tryphena 240: wharf **252**
tuatua 29
tubeworms, spiny 338
Tuhaere, Paora 122
Tuhi 56
Tūhoromatakakā 23

Tuitahi Is. 54
Tukituki Bay 35
tuna 201, 248: yellow-fin 201
Tupaia 48, 49, 52
Tūpuna Taonga Trust 323
Tūroa, Taimoana 41
Turua 112, 117

Umupuia 30–31: marae **31**
Una (scow) 135
United Independents 93
United People's Organisation 177
University of Auckland 32, 76, 328, 339
urchin, heart 287
urchin, sea (kina) 31, 62, 295, **295**, 330, 331:
    'barrens' 295, 330, 331
Ureia 24

Vela Fishing Ltd 233
Vela, Filip 233
Viaduct Basin **254**
Victoria (yacht) 157
Victoria Cruising Club 152
Victory (steamship) 216
Viskovich, Alan and Gus 224
Visser, Dr Ingrid 271, **271**
von Luckner, Count Felix 316
Vulcan Lane 132

Wai-au 57
Waiheke Is. (Te Motu-arai-roa) 23, 30,
    70, 72, 76, 180–84, 324–25, **325**: bach
    sections **183**; Blackpool **183**; diving 205;
    fishing 220, 254; kauri timber 132; map
    181; New Year Regatta 180, **181**; pest
    control 325; recreation 180–84; replanting
    325; restoration 324–25; shingle 96;
    subdivisions 182, 183, **183**, 184; Surfdale
    183, **184**
Waihou River 23, 36, 40, 42, 52, 54, 55,
    111, 113, 115, 116, 117, 141, 299, **301**:
    pollution 113, 116; run-off 299, 301; seine
    netting 42
Waikato River 96
Waikino 112, **112**
Waimangō 35
Wainhouse, Capt. Frederick 185
Wairarapa, SS, shipwreck **141**, 143
Wairoa River 30, 141
Waitangi (yacht) **149**, 158, **159**
Waitangi Tribunal 42
Waitawa Wharf **205**
Waitawheta Stream 112
Waitemata (steamer) 139
Waitemata City Council 97
Waitematā Harbour **57**, 70–72, 76, 94: charts
    123, 124; exploration 70–72; pollution;
    reclamation 76; shellfish beds 71, 94; *see*
    also general entries
Waitemata Steam Ferry Company 139

Waiti (scow) **97**
Waiti 115
waka (canoes) 12, 121, **122**, 123, 126, 144,
    145: figurehead (tauihu) 122; *Kōtuiti*
    Tuarua (Kōtuiti II) **122**, 126, **126**; ocean-
    going double-hulled 19, **20**, 21; portages
    30, 72, 93, 122; *Tamahui* 145; waka ama
    (outrigger canoes) 335; waka taua 121,
    122, **122**, **144**, 145; waka tētē 121–23;
    Wharepunga 145
Wakatere (steamship) 182
Wakatere Canoe Club/Boating Club 157
Wallace, Judge Augusta 89
Walter, Barbara **130**, 130–31
Walter, Ray **130**, 130–31
Warkworth 137
waste disposal 95–96
Watchman/Sentinel Is. (Te Kākāwhakaara)
    72, 73, 224
waterfront **80–81**, **82**; *see* port
Watkins, H H 91, **92**
Webster, William 52, 103
Westhaven marina 86
wētā, giant (wētā punga) 306
Whakakaiwhara Point 37
whaleboats 133–34
Whalers Bay 198
Whalers Cove 262
whales: Bryde's 8, 22, **22–23**, 23, 128–29, 264,
    265, **265**, 266, 267, **267**, 268; humpback
    261–62, **263**, 264; pilot 272, 273, **273**; sei
    262; ship strike 266–67, 341; *Songs of the*
    Humpback Whale 262; strandings 272–73;
    whale watching **263**, **265**, 268
whanaungatanga (kinship) 43
Whangamatā: surfing 192, 193, 194
Whangamatā Surf Life Saving Club 192
Whanganui Ā Hei (Cathedral Cove) Marine
    Reserve 332–33, **333**
Whanganui Is. 103
Whanganui-o-Toi 22
Whangaparāoa Peninsula 59, 205, 307
Whangaparapara Harbour 107, **242**, 262, **262**:
    timber mill 107, whaling 262, **262**, **264**,
    265
Whangapoua: afforestation 106
Whangapoua Estuary 108, 294
Whāngateau Harbour 134, 308, 309
Wharekaho 62–63
Wharengo, Rawiri 111–12
Wharepunga (waka taua) 145
Whare-taewa 51
wharves: 81, 82–84
Whau River 71, 337
Whitaker, Frederick 172
whitebait 36
whitehead 315, 321, **322**
Whitehouse, Steve 271, 272
Whites Beach 32
Whitianga Harbour 49, 51, **102**

Whitianga River 101, 110: sediment 110
Whitianga Waterways **63**
Whitmore, Bob 203, 240, 241, **241**, 242,
    253–54
Whitmore, Peter 316
Whyle, Ivan 177
Wilcken, Jonathan 321
Williams, Rev. Henry 67, **67**, 70, 75
Williams, Tommy 233
Willis, Walter 330
Williscroft, Martin 272, 273
Wilson family **313**
Wilson, Capt. William 55
Wilson, Fred 155
Wilson, Nora 174
Wilson, Willie 155
Windsor Reserve 125, 127: trig station **125**
Wood, Capt. James 141, 143
Wood, Michael 316
Woodley, Keith 280, **280**, 281
Woolnough, Angela 133
World Wide Fund for Nature (WWF) 277,
    310, 314, 316, 339
wrasse, banded 330
Wray, Johnny 194–95, **195**: *South Sea*
    Vagabonds 194
Wreck Bay 143
Wright, Alan 174, 196: Variant design **196**
wrybill 278, **281**
Wynyard Quarter 81
Wynyard Wharf 81
Wynyard, Lt-Col. Robert 81

yachts: Cherubs 155; classic 158–59; clubs
    149, 151–53, 156–57; design 147–49,
    156–57, 195–96; Hartley 16s 195–96,
    196; M–Class 155; mullet boats 154;
    P Class 153, 155; post-WWII 156–57;
    sailing dinghies 153, 155, 157; Takapuna
    Class 155; Variant design 196, **196**;
    Z Class (Zeddies) 155, **155**; *see also*
    boatbuilding; racing
Ye Olde Pirate Shippe 191, **191**, 192
Young Nicks Head (Te Ūpotio-o-te-kurī-a-
    Pāoa) 48

Z Class yachts (Zeddies) 155, **155**
Zane Grey (motor launch) 198
Zeldis, Dr John 285–86, 299, **300**, 300–301

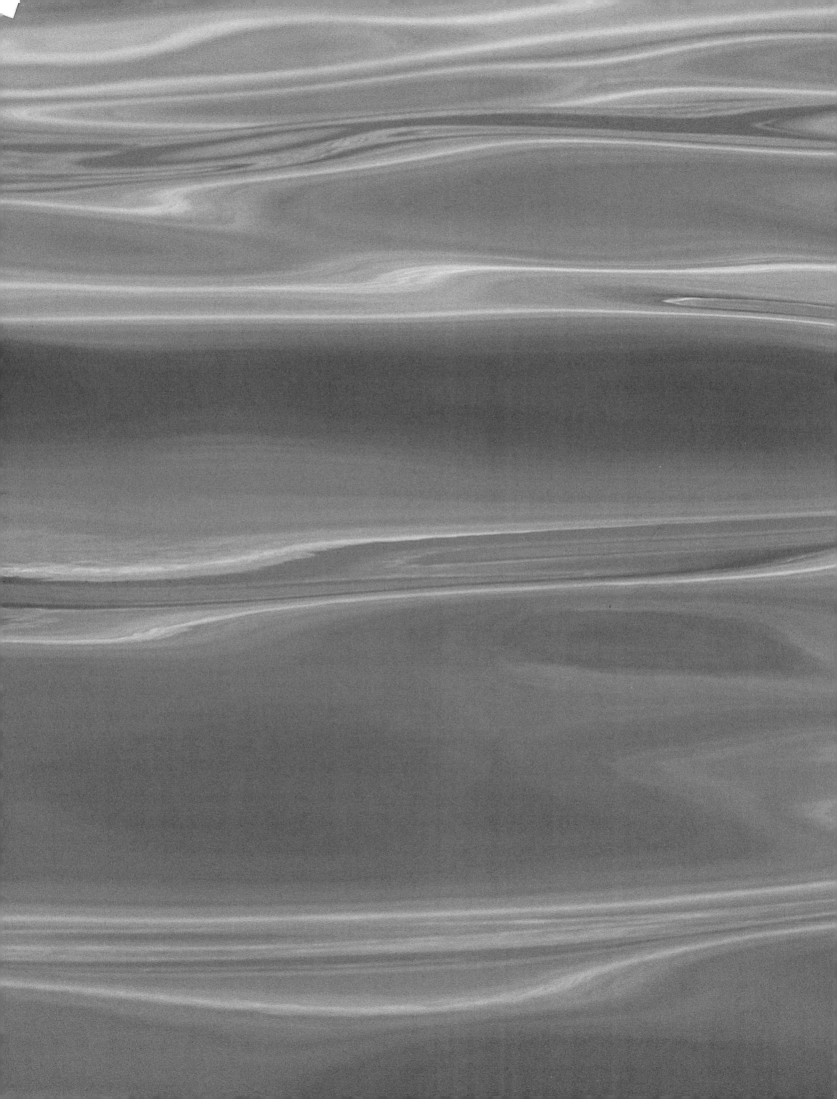